MICHAEL BILTON is [...] y
Times Magazine and an award [...] n
maker. His ITV film about the Yorkshire Ripper case was
nominated for a British Academy Award. He won an Emmy
for his documentary on the My Lai massacre, and his book,
Four Hours in My Lai, was a bestseller that won plaudits all
over the world.

From the reviews

'There is unlikely to be a more comprehensive or carefully
researched account of the case. To read *Wicked Beyond Belief*
is to have a sense of being physically present at the day-to-day
investigation, experiencing the frustrations, the stress and the
public outrage at its lack of success as the years passed and
murder followed murder.'   P.D. JAMES, *Mail on Sunday*

'Bilton knows more about the Ripper case than anyone living
... as a study of a bungled police investigation, it is devastating.'   BLAKE MORRISON, *Guardian*

'The author is admirably fair in declining to attribute blame
for this tragic muddle, while still allowing mistakes to show
clearly ... The book vividly depicts the lives of policemen
under pressure as well as the squalor of prostitution for a fiver
in the rubble ... a fine achievement in supplying the historical
record with a clear and serious account of five years' panic
and despair wrought at the hands of an addictive killer.'

                              BRIAN MASTERS, *Evening Standard*

'After 22 years, the wall of silence finally crumbles, and the
truth emerges, calmly, quietly, within these pages ... The fact

that much of this book will come as a surprise even to some of the senior figures involved tells us all we need to know.'

Manchester Evening News

'The definitive version of what Sutcliffe did and why the police failed to catch him ... There are two revelations in the book – the first of the secret report into West Yorkshire Police's handling of the case that has never before been published, and the second of a crucial piece of evidence that the Old Bailey never knew about, and which could have proved that Sutcliffe's claim to be mentally ill was a lie. Bilton is an experienced journalist and fine writer ... a gripping and probing account of the Yorkshire Ripper's reign of terror.'

ANDREW VINE, Yorkshire Post

'This vital, admirable book ... should be standard issue for all would-be detectives – as the way not to prosecute a murder inquiry.'

Birmingham Post

'I thought I knew all about the Yorkshire Ripper inquiry – until I read Wicked Beyond Belief. This book should be compulsory reading for all young detectives.'

TONY MULLETT, former Director General of the
National Criminal Intelligence Service

WICKED BEYOND BELIEF

The Hunt for the Yorkshire Ripper

MICHAEL BILTON

HarperCollins*Publishers*

HarperCollins*Publishers*
77–85 Fulham Palace Road,
Hammersmith, London W6 8JB

www.harpercollins.co.uk

This paperback edition 2003
1 3 5 7 9 8 6 4 2

First published in Great Britain by
HarperCollins*Publishers* 2003

Copyright © Michael Bilton 2003

The Author asserts the moral right to
be identified as the author of this work

A catalogue record for this book is
available from the British Library

ISBN 0 00 716963 9

Set in Minion by
Rowland Phototypesetting Ltd,
Bury St Edmunds, Suffolk

Printed in Great Britain by
Clays Ltd, St Ives plc

For my Father

CONTENTS

LIST OF ILLUSTRATIONS

George Oldfield, Dick Holland, Jack Ridgway. *Photo: Reproduced by kind permission of the Telegraph and Argus, Bradford*
Police 'mug' shots and photofit images of Peter Sutcliffe. *Photo: West Yorkshire Police*

Jim Hobson in the Yorkshire Ripper incident room at Leeds. *Photo: MEN Syndication*

George Oldfield presents a leaving present to John Domaille. *Photo: West Yorkshire Police*

'Help us stop the Ripper' roadside hoarding. *Photo: Ross Parry/ Yorkshire Post*

'Task Force' officers, September 1979. *Photo: Reproduced by kind permission of the Telegraph and Argus, Bradford*

Professor David Gee with Dr Michael Green and Jim Hobson. *Photo: Reproduced by kind permission of the Telegraph and Argus, Bradford*

Retired detectives Trevor Lapish, Andrew Laptew, Dick Holland. *Photo: Lysander/RFA*

Marcella Claxton and Maureen Long. *Photo: Lysander/RFA*

Megan Winterburn and Sue Neave. *Photo: Lysander/RFA*

Stanley Ellis and Jack Windsor Lewis. *Photo: Lysander/RFA*

Officers search for clues at the scene of Jacqueline Hill's murder. *Photo: Ross Parry/Yorkshire Post*

Alma Road, Headingley. *Photo: West Yorkshire Police*

William Whitelaw visits Leeds. *Photo: Reproduced by kind permission of the Telegraph and Argus, Bradford*

Jacqueline Hill's funeral. *Photo: Ross Parry/Yorkshire Post*

Desmond O'Boyle escorts the Yorkshire Ripper into court. *Photo: Ross Parry/Yorkshire Post*

The crowd outside the court. *Photo: Reproduced by kind permission of the Telegraph and Argus, Bradford*

Lawrence Byford and his Review Team.

Peter Sutcliffe's home in Heaton, Bradford. *Photo: Reproduced by kind permission of the Telegraph and Argus, Bradford*

ACKNOWLEDGEMENTS

This work was conceived and the research begun before I made a documentary film called *MANHUNT: The Search for the Yorkshire Ripper* for the ITV Network in 1999. Early efforts on both projects overlapped and many people gave me help, support and encouragement. I would like to thank the following:

Ray Smith, Times Newspapers Library; Jane Chambers, Yorkshire Television film library; Alan Ormerod, Manchester Evening News Library; David Hartshorne, Yorkshire Post Library; the *MANHUNT* team: Gwyneth Hughes, Jane Bower, Alan Wilson, Graham Robinson, Rick Aplin and Ray Fitzwalter; Mrs Margaret Oldfield, widow of George Oldfield, who very kindly provided family and biographical background about her late husband; the Hoban family: Margaret, Richard and Vincent; Jack Ridgway and Grange Catlow, retired senior detectives from Manchester CID, who came for lunch at Midgley and stayed well past teatime; Sir Lawrence Byford, both for his valuable insights and his hospitality at Yorkshire Cricket Club; Sir Andrew and Lady Sloan, for thoughtful reflection and generous invitations to their home; Sir David Phillips, arguably the most forward thinking and intellectually stimulating police officer in Britain today; Sir Robert Andrew, the

retired senior Whitehall mandarin and former head of the
Police Department at the Home Office; Maureen Long,
Marcella Claxton and Theresa Sykes for their courage in telling
their stories to Jane Bower; John Domaille; Mike and Jenny
Green for their love and support over many years; Andrew
and Sheila Laptew and their three wonderful daughters; Megan
Winterburn and Sue Neave, who told great stories and were
terrific company; Trevor Lapish; Stanley Ellis; Jack Windsor
Lewis; David and Wendy Zackrisson for their valued friend-
ship; Sue Nicholson, Keith Mount and John Dobson of North-
umbria police; Michael Burdiss and Robert Hydes of South
Yorkshire police; Mrs Joan Ring and Joanne Platts; Helen Elliot
and John Mason of West Yorkshire police; Tony Whittle,
Desmond Finbarr O'Boyle and George Smith, all former West
Yorkshire officers; David Barclay of the National Crime Faculty
at Bramshill; Maureen Banham, Simon Steward, Mike Goddard
and Ian Sturrock of the Midland Bank; John Hitchen; Russell
Stockdale; Howard Rogers for the loan of his monograph about
HMS *Albatross*, the ship George Oldfield sailed in at D-Day;
Phil Brown, Mike Hardwick and Alan Gebbie in York; Carol
Jones; Angela Sissons; and Agnes and Jack Fletcher.

Special appreciation is due to those most intimately involved
in this book. Judith Macmillan proofread chapters as they
were written, raised lots of important questions and made very
helpful comments. Robin Morgan has been a colleague and
close personal friend for more than two decades since we
worked in the newsroom of the *Sunday Times* together under
Harold Evans's editorship, and later on the *INSIGHT* team.
He encouraged, cajoled, then finally shoved me into getting
this book written. He read the manuscript and brought his
finely honed editor's eye to bear. My agent, Ali Gunn of Curtis
Brown, and Val Hudson, who commissioned the book at

HarperCollins, were incredibly generous with their professional and personal support over the last few years. There were difficult times when I thought I might not be able to finish this book and it was their direct encouragement which kept me going. When author and publisher are on the same wavelength, bookwriting becomes far more enjoyable and at HarperCollins I was fortunate to have at my side Richard Johnson, whose experience and wisdom have been invaluable. Peter Ford edited the completed manuscript with great skill and sensitivity.

Professor Stuart Kind and his wife Evelyn welcomed me into their home on countless occasions. Professor Kind's legacy to forensic science and the world of law enforcement generally is brilliantly documented in his major work, *The Scientific Investigation of Crime*, which I had beside me as I was writing. His personal legacy to me was the many, many hours of his time in retirement spent discussing his work, my work and the world in general. It was impossible to pass even five minutes with him without gaining some wise and stimulating insight. He read my early drafts of chapters and returned them with helpful comments, correcting my errors of fact as well as my idiosyncratic grammar and spelling. He died in April 2003 and was a great and gifted teacher. I very much valued our special relationship.

My friendship with Dick Holland has lasted since the late 1970s. He was at the heart of the Ripper investigation for four long years and in many respects this book is his story because it could never have been written without him. We have discussed every aspect of the subject endlessly. He has patiently explained very fine points of detail in order that I should understand the life of a detective from the 1960s to the 1980s. We have argued and at times I have criticized his judgements. He in return has pointed out the error of my ways. It is a different police service today from the one he joined in Huddersfield borough in the 1950s. Now it is very advanced in terms of information technology. How different from twenty-five years ago. In the late 1970s in the steep hills and valleys of West Yorkshire it was hard enough for them just to get their radios to work properly! I have never known Dick Holland shirk personal responsibility for the things that went wrong with the Ripper investigation and I believe him 100 per cent when he says these were honest mistakes. He has a habit of being truthful even when the truth reflects against himself. I have never ceased to be amazed that he should place such great trust in me to tell the story of the investigation. My promise to him was that I would do it in a fair and honest way, setting out the good as well as the bad. He and his colleagues did their best, but they have to live with the consequences of their actions and their failure to catch the Yorkshire Ripper sooner. As his colleague Jack Ridgway said when I pointed to the brilliance of some of his detective work: 'But we didn't get him, did we, Michael?'

Dick Holland was built like a giant. On many occasions in his thirty-year police career he was called upon to play the 'hard cop', especially when dealing with dangerous and violent criminals. In the last several years of her life, Dick nursed his invalid wife, Sylvia, at their home with a love and devotion that totally belies his image as a tough crime buster. He now devotes his time to an academic understanding of horticulture, and one day, as he conducts me on yet another tour of his extraordinary garden, I might remember some of the Latin names of plants he throws into the conversation. I count it a privilege to have known him. Any errors in this book are mine and mine alone.

Finally, I send my heartfelt thanks to my precious and wonderful children, Thomas, John and Catherine. There may be better fathers, but none who loves his children more.

DRAMATIS PERSONAE

BOREHAM, LESLIE: High Court judge who presided over the trial of Peter Sutcliffe at the Old Bailey in May 1981.

BOYLE, JOHN: Detective inspector Ripper squad, January 1981. Interrogated Peter Sutcliffe after his arrest.

BYFORD, LAWRENCE: Her Majesty's Inspector of Constabulary, responsible for the West Yorkshire police area. Conducted review of what went wrong with the Ripper investigation. Reported to Home Secretary in December 1981.

CATLOW, GRANGE: Detective superintendent Manchester CID. Jack Ridgway's deputy.

CRAIG, DONALD: Assistant chief constable (crime) West Yorkshire 1975/76 before he retired.

DOMAILLE, JOHN: Detective chief superintendent, senior investigating officer (SIO) on murder of Patricia Atkinson in Bradford, 1977. Head of Special Homicide Investigation Team (Ripper squad) April 1978–March 1979.

ELLIS, STANLEY: Dialect expert and senior lecturer at University of Leeds. Advised police on 'Geordie' tape.

EMMENT, LESLIE: Deputy chief constable, Thames Valley police. Member of Byford advisory/review team.

FINLAY, ALF: Detective superintendent, SIO for Jacqueline Hill murder in Leeds, November 1980.

GEE, DAVID: Professor of forensic pathology at Leeds University and Home Office consultant pathologist. Conducted post-mortems on Ripper victims.

GERTY, DAVID: Assistant chief constable, West Midlands police. Member of Byford advisory/review team.

GILRAIN, PETER: Detective chief superintendent, SIO for Barbara Leach murder in Bradford, September 1979.

GREGORY, RONALD: Chief constable of West Yorkshire.

HARVEY, RONALD: Commander, New Scotland Yard. Special adviser on crime to Home Office. Member of Byford advisory/review team.

HAVERS, SIR MICHAEL: QC, MP. Attorney General. Led prosecution at Sutcliffe's trial.

HOBAN, DENNIS: Detective chief superintendent and head of Leeds CID. SIO for first two Ripper murders, Wilma McCann and Emily Jackson, in 1975/76. Died March 1978.

HOBSON, JIM: Detective chief superintendent. Dennis Hoban's deputy in Leeds. SIO on inquiry into Irene Richardson's murder. Put in overall charge of the investigation in late November 1980, six weeks before Peter Sutcliffe was arrested.

HOLLAND, DICK: Detective superintendent. Pivotal figure in the Yorkshire Ripper investigation. Drafted in after the murder of Jane MacDonald in 1977 and remained until the killer was arrested.

HYDES, ROBERT: Probationer police constable in Sheffield, South Yorkshire. Arrested Peter Sutcliffe, 2 January 1981.

KIND, STUART: Professor of forensic science, head of Home Office Central Research Establishment at Aldermaston, 1980. Member of Byford advisory/ review team.

LAPISH, TREVOR: Detective chief superintendent, SIO on Yvonne Pearson murder in Bradford, January 1978.

LAPTEW, ANDREW: Detective constable on Ripper squad, July 1979, when he interviewed Peter Sutcliffe and named him as a strong suspect.

LEWIS, JACK WINDSOR: Linguistic expert and lecturer at University of Leeds who advised police on tape and letters.

MILNE, HUGO: Psychiatrist who examined Peter Sutcliffe and gave evidence for the defence at his trial.

O'BOYLE, 'DES' FINBARR: Detective sergeant, Ripper squad, January 1981. Interrogated Peter Sutcliffe after his arrest.

OLDFIELD, GEORGE: Assistant chief constable (crime) West Yorkshire police. Ran the Yorkshire Ripper investigation 1977–80.

OGNALL, HARRY: QC. Senior member of the prosecution team at Sutcliffe's trial.

OUTTERIDGE, RON: Forensic scientist. Spent two months with Russell Stockdale advising Ripper squad in 1979.

RIDGWAY, JACK: Detective chief superintendent. SIO on murders of Jean Jordan and Vera Millward in Manchester in 1977/78. Ran five-pound note inquiry.

RING, ROBERT: Police sergeant in Sheffield, South Yorkshire. Arrested Peter Sutcliffe, 2 January 1981.

SLOAN, ANDREW: National Coordinator of Regional Crime Squads in 1980. Member of Byford advisory/review team.

SMITH, PETER: Detective sergeant, Ripper squad, January 1981. Interrogated Peter Sutcliffe after his arrest and took his confession.

STOCKDALE, RUSSELL: Forensic scientist on several Ripper murders. Spent two months with Ron Outteridge advising Ripper squad in 1979.

SUMMERSKILL, SHIRLEY: MP and former Home Office minister who vetoed a public inquiry into the Black Panther case in 1976 and argued that the police had learned lessons from any errors made.

SUTCLIFFE, SONIA: Peter Sutcliffe's wife. They married in 1974 and divorced some time after his arrest.

THATCHER, MARGARET: Prime Minister in 1980 at the time of the killing of the Yorkshire Ripper's final victim in November 1980. Ordered William Whitelaw to beef up the Ripper investigation.

WHITELAW, WILLIAM: Home Secretary, 1979/80.

ZACKRISSON, DAVID: Detective inspector in Northumbria police. Wrote report in 1979 warning the 'Geordie' tape was an elaborate hoax.

CHRONOLOGY

1969

30 SEPTEMBER: Bradford, West Yorkshire. Peter Sutcliffe arrested in the red-light area and charged with going equipped for theft 'with a hammer'.

1975

5 JULY: Keighley, West Yorkshire. Anna Rogulskyj attacked. Senior investigating officer (SIO): Detective Superintendent P. J. Perry.

15 AUGUST: Halifax, West Yorkshire. Olive Smelt attacked. SIO: Detective Chief Inspector Dick Holland.

28 AUGUST: Silsden, near Keighley. Tracey Browne attacked. SIO: Detective Superintendent Jim Hobson. Unacknowledged Ripper attack.

30 OCTOBER: Leeds, West Yorkshire. Wilma McCann murdered a hundred yards from her home. SIO: Detective Chief Superintendent Dennis Hoban.

20 NOVEMBER: Preston, Lancashire. Joan Harrison murdered. SIO: Detective Chief Superintendent Wilf Brooks, Lancashire CID.

1976

20 JANUARY: Leeds. Emily Jackson murdered. SIO: Detective Chief Superintendent Dennis Hoban.

9 MAY: Leeds. Marcella Claxton attacked at Roundhay Park.

SIO: Detective Chief Superintendent Jim Hobson. Unacknowledged Ripper attack.

1977

5 FEBRUARY: Leeds. Irene Richardson murdered in Roundhay Park. SIO: Detective Chief Superintendent Jim Hobson.

23 APRIL: Bradford. Patricia Atkinson murdered in her flat. SIO: Detective Chief Superintendent John Domaille.

26 JUNE: Leeds. Jayne MacDonald murdered. SIO: Assistant Chief Constable (ACC) (Crime) George Oldfield.

10 JULY: Bradford. Maureen Long attacked. SIO: ACC (Crime) George Oldfield.

1 OCTOBER: Manchester. Jean Jordan murdered. SIO: Detective Chief Superintendent Jack Ridgway, Manchester CID.

14 DECEMBER: Leeds. Marilyn Moore attacked. SIO: Detective Chief Superintendent Jim Hobson.

1978

21 JANUARY: Bradford. Yvonne Pearson murdered. SIO: Detective Chief Superintendent Trevor Lapish.

31 JANUARY: Huddersfield, West Yorkshire. Helen Rytka murdered. SIO: ACC (Crime) George Oldfield.

25 APRIL: Special Homicide Investigation Team (Ripper squad) set up at Millgarth police station, Leeds, under Detective Chief Superintendent John Domaille, with Detective Superintendent Jack Slater as his deputy, plus ten other detectives.

16 MAY: Manchester. Vera Millward murdered. SIO: Detective Chief Superintendent Jack Ridgway.

1979

MARCH: Detective Superintendent Dick Holland takes over Ripper squad at Millgarth; also in charge of the centralized incident room.

4 APRIL: Halifax. Josephine Whitaker murdered. SIO: ACC (Crime) George Oldfield.

2 SEPTEMBER: Bradford. Barbara Leach murdered. SIO: Detective Chief Superintendent Peter Gilrain.

21 NOVEMBER: Commander Jim Neville of Scotland Yard arrives in Leeds to conduct review of Ripper case. Stays two months and reports to the chief constable of West Yorkshire, Ronald Gregory.

1980

21 AUGUST: Leeds. Marguerite Walls murdered at Farsley. SIO: Detective Chief Superintendent Jim Hobson. Unacknowledged Ripper killing.

24 SEPTEMBER: Leeds. Uphadya Bandara attacked at Headingley. SIO: Detective Superintendent Tom Newton. Unacknowledged Ripper attack.

5 NOVEMBER: Huddersfield. Teresa Sykes attacked. SIO: Detective Superintendent Tony Hickey. Unacknowledged Ripper attack.

17 NOVEMBER: Leeds. Jacqueline Hill murdered. SIO: Detective Superintendent Alf Finlay.

25 NOVEMBER: ACC (Crime) George Oldfield sidelined as head of the Ripper inquiry. Jim Hobson takes over with temporary rank of ACC.

26 NOVEMBER: External advisory team appointed by Her Majesty's Inspector of Constabulary, Mr Lawrence Byford. Reports to the chief constable before Christmas.

1981

2 JANUARY: Peter Sutcliffe arrested in a car with a prostitute in Sheffield, South Yorkshire.

5 JANUARY: Peter Sutcliffe charged with murder of Jacqueline Hill.

22 MAY: Peter Sutcliffe found guilty of thirteen murders. Sentenced to life imprisonment.

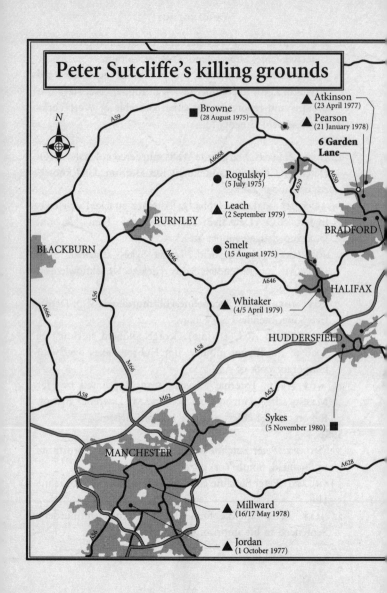

Peter Sutcliffe's killing grounds

N

Browne
(28 August 1975)

Atkinson
(23 April 1977)

Pearson
(21 January 1978)

6 Garden
Lane

Rogulskyj
(5 July 1975)

Leach
(2 September 1979)

BURNLEY

BRADFORD

BLACKBURN

Smelt
(15 August 1975)

HALIFAX

Whitaker
(4/5 April 1979)

HUDDERSFIELD

Sykes
(5 November 1980)

MANCHESTER

Millward
(16/17 May 1978)

Jordan
(1 October 1977)

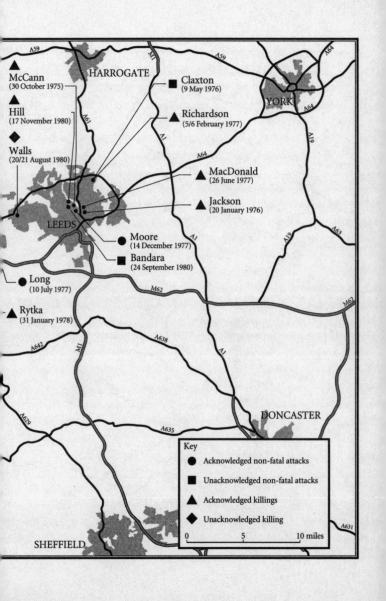

McCann
(30 October 1975)

Hill
(17 November 1980)

Walls
(20/21 August 1980)

HARROGATE

Claxton
(9 May 1976)

YORK

Richardson
(5/6 February 1977)

MacDonald
(26 June 1977)

Jackson
(20 January 1976)

LEEDS

Moore
(14 December 1977)

Bandara
(24 September 1980)

Long
(10 July 1977)

Rytka
(31 January 1978)

DONCASTER

SHEFFIELD

Key

● Acknowledged non-fatal attacks

■ Unacknowledged non-fatal attacks

▲ Acknowledged killings

◆ Unacknowledged killing

0   5   10 miles

PREFACE

Poor Wilma. A strong-willed, feisty woman, she was determined to live life on her terms. It was either her way or no way. A driver picked her up. She agreed, late one night in October 1975, to a risky proposition from a total stranger: sex-for-a-fiver. It was how she made a living. And now? She was dead, the first publicly acknowledged victim of the Yorkshire Ripper.

Her body, shrouded by a low-hanging mist at the edge of a football field, was found early next morning. The damp and miserably cold vapour clung as grimly and insistently to the frail corpse lying on the grassy bank as it did to the rest of the city of Leeds that autumn. The fog was almost a symbol of the terror and fear to come. It seemed to hang constantly over the North of England for a considerable time, like some mysterious impenetrable miasma. And it never lifted for five long years. It enveloped and chilled the lives of millions who lived there, men and women, young and old. But mostly women.

In August 1976, MPs in the House of Commons voiced deep concerns about a recently concluded police investigation that had turned into a fiasco with tragic results. There was little glory for the detectives who had led the hunt for the notorious 'Black Panther', a man called Donald Neilson from

Bradford – a vicious cold-blooded criminal wanted for the murders of three sub-postmistresses and the kidnapping and murder of heiress Leslie Whittle. As with the Yorkshire Ripper case, there was an all-important hoax tape recording that threw detectives off the trail of the real killer. Like the Ripper case, the hunt involved several police forces. Like the Ripper case, there was a great deal of resistance to calling for help from outside; and when the end came it was two bobbies in a patrol car who made the arrest, not realizing they had caught a vicious killer. Finally, as with the Ripper case, when it was over there was a need for scapegoats. The officer in charge suffered the humiliation of being shifted sideways – out of CID and into uniform.

Some MPs demanded an inquiry into the whole conduct of the Black Panther investigation. The Labour government refused. Home Office minister, Dr Shirley Summerskill, stood at the dispatch box in Parliament and said that the case 'has been discussed by chief officers of police collectively and I am quite sure they are fully aware of the need to learn any lessons which may be learned from such an investigation ... the fact that a particular investigation is a matter for discussion by chief officers of police is a reflection of our system of policing in this country. The local control of police forces is an essential element of that system. Chief constables in this country, unlike some continental countries, do not come under the direction of a Minister of the Interior, in the enforcement of the law. The responsibility of deciding how an offence should be investigated is for them and them alone.'

What was absolutely clear five years later in 1981, when the Ripper case was concluded, was that the police had completely failed to learn the lessons of the Black Panther investigation – least of all Britain's chief constables, and via them the police service as a whole. Government ministers, senior officials at the Home Office and the law officers saw little merit in an agonizing debate into the Yorkshire Ripper investigation. MPs' demands were turned down, there would be no public inquiry. But there was a major shock in store for the criminal justice establishment when the case of Regina *versus* Sutcliffe opened at the Old Bailey in London.

The Crown, in the shape of the Attorney-General, Sir Michael Havers, had pushed for a suspiciously speedy hearing by accepting a guilty plea to manslaughter from the accused, Peter Sutcliffe, on the grounds of diminished responsibility. It all seemed done and dusted. The court proceedings would probably be over within half a day because both defence and prosecution were happy. However, they had not reckoned on the reaction of the judge. To his very great credit, Mr Justice Boreham refused what was in essence a plea bargain. Instead he ordered a full and open trial by jury to determine whether Sutcliffe was mad or bad. The jury members would hear the evidence and decide for themselves whether Sutcliffe was guilty or not guilty of murdering thirteen women and attempting to murder seven more; or was guilty of manslaughter because he did not know what he was doing. Justice demanded that this very grave matter should not be swept under the carpet.

The Yorkshire Ripper case raised many crucial questions. Once Peter Sutcliffe was convicted of murder, those questions still needed answers. There were crucial issues about the inability of the police service to solve very serious crimes, issues which should have been openly debated. But the public at large, the media, the taxpayers of West Yorkshire, Members of Parliament, even seasoned high-ranking detectives closely involved in homicide investigations, were never able to obtain answers to those important questions, the chief of which were:

Why did it take so long to catch this terrible serial killer? Had the police been up to the task? Who should be held accountable for mistakes that were made?

Time moves on. What was impossible then – openness, and frankness about the failings of an important public service – could twenty years later suddenly become possible. In contrast with the fallout over the Stephen Lawrence murder in London, which after some years of pressure resulted in a full and transparently open inquiry, public disquiet over the Yorkshire Ripper investigation was never satisfied. There was no open inquiry. Behind closed doors many serious questions were posed and answers obtained, and revolutionary changes were recommended about the way the police investigate serious crime. But openness, transparency and the acknowledgement that the public had a perfect right to know what had been done in their name were nowhere to be seen. Sutcliffe's official toll was thirteen dead and seven attempted murders. We now know he attacked many more women and that many opportunities to apprehend him were tragically missed.

In January 1982, seven months after Sutcliffe was given twenty terms of life imprisonment, the then Home Secretary, William Whitelaw, appeared before Parliament to announce the results of an internal Home Office inquiry by one of Britain's most senior and respected policemen, Mr Lawrence Byford, who had investigated what went wrong with the Yorkshire Ripper case. Intriguingly, among those MPs pressing to make the Byford Report public was the Labour MP and former Home Office minister, Dr Shirley Summerskill, one of whose Halifax constituents died at the hands of the Yorkshire Ripper. This was the very same Shirley Summerskill who had refused an open investigation into the way the Black Panther was handled. The Home Office in the early 1980s was not, however, about to break new ground in the interests of openness, transparency and accountability. Whitelaw refused to publish the Byford Report. Instead, a brief four-page summary of its main conclusions and recommendations was placed in the House of Commons library. This summary only scratched the surface of the crucial facts garnered during a six-month inquiry by an eminent team of senior British police officers and the country's leading forensic scientist. In the Report itself, unvarnished and unpalatable truths were laid out in a 159-page closely typed document containing much extraordinary detail. Such was the confidentiality surrounding the Report that it was printed privately outside London and not by Her Majesty's Stationery Office. No senior civil servant, not even the Permanent Secretary to the Home Office, was allowed to view a copy until Mr Byford had delivered it personally to William Whitelaw.

As one of Her Majesty's Inspectors of Constabulary, Byford knew that in preparing the Report he and his inquiry team had a grave duty to perform, not merely for the benefit of the police service but for the country as a whole. He and his team did not shirk their responsibility. The changes in the way police tackle serious crimes brought about as a result of the Byford Report, particularly in searches for serial killers, were truly ground breaking for the police service, so much so that a cynic might say that had there been no Yorkshire Ripper the police would have needed to invent him in order that dramatic change could be forced upon them.

So, why this book, and why now? As a staff writer for the *Sunday Times* based in Yorkshire from 1979 to 1982, I had a personal involvement in the twentieth century's most sensational murder hunt. The *Sunday Times* was able to reveal crucial facts about the case: that government computers were being used to screen potential suspects; that Sutcliffe had been named as a prime suspect in the case eighteen months before he was arrested; and that the Ripper Squad had the face of the killer already in their files, detectives having missed a crucial photofit from an attack by Sutcliffe that was never regarded as a Ripper crime. The victim here had provided an astonishingly accurate description of the man who tried to murder her.

I became closely acquainted with some of the detectives, pathologists, forensic scientists and outside advisers most closely involved in the Ripper case. Over the years, many of the figures principally involved spoke to me off the record about their work on the Ripper Inquiry and how it personally had affected them. More than twenty years on, some still felt victimized, others believed their actions and motives were totally misunderstood. All were reluctant to talk openly. Some still will only talk privately. Twenty years on, several finally agreed to go on the record and tell what really happened.

Yet, even today, the Byford Report remains an official secret, so much so that many of Britain's most senior policemen, charged with responsibility for the investigation of homicides, have still not been allowed to read and learn the truth about the Ripper case, particularly what went wrong, and more importantly, the rationale behind the very valuable lessons that needed to be learned.

By a piece of good fortune, I eventually got to read the Byford Report. Finally the true story fell into place. Many mistakes were certainly made. But the Ripper detectives also did some amazing work and came agonizingly close to catching the killer on several occasions. Many of those closely involved with the most important criminal investigation in British history agree with me that the complete story deserves to be told so that the British public, and more crucially, future generations of men and women working in the field of law enforcement can learn its lessons. Equally important, I did not want the detectives who tried to apprehend the Yorkshire Ripper to be seen as one-dimensional figures. I have endeavoured to put flesh and bone on some of them so they can be seen for what they were: ordinary people trying to do a difficult job. Some were clearly better than others, but I have no intention of pillorying anyone for mistakes made. As a writer, you cannot examine how an institution works and forget the very people who make up that institution. When the institution fails, you need to look at the whole institution, and in the case of the police service it starts with ordinary policemen and women on the beat and progresses upwards through a hierarchy, beyond the chief officers, to the Inspectorate of Constabulary, the Home Office civil servants in the Police Department, and then the ministers in charge, ending with the Home Secretary. Details about what went on inside the Home Office during the Ripper inquiry will not be available for some time to come, so the overall picture remains incomplete. That is no reason for sitting on one's thumbs. What most people want to know is this: What went wrong? Why did it take so long to catch Peter Sutcliffe? This book tries to answer those questions.

You have to live in the North of England to comprehend how such a terrible series of crimes terrified a major part of the British Isles. Other preventable tragedies which cause grave public concern, ferry disasters, aircraft and train accidents, all seem to get a public hearing as to what went wrong. Why should the Ripper case have been any different? The answer is obvious. It was to save a vital British institution, the police service, from humiliation. Moreover, the supervising government authority for the police, the Home Office and its political masters in Parliament, both Labour and Conservative, would have been embarrassed too. Publication of the Byford Report would have led to serious questions being raised and answers demanded. It could have risked a loss of public confidence in the police. No government likes washing its dirty linen in public, but mature democracies are supposed to be able to deal with politically awkward problems and be the better for them.

The contents of this book will be hauntingly painful to the families of Peter Sutcliffe's victims and make difficult reading. Some of the truth about the investigation seems truly shocking, even twenty years later and allowing for the benefit of hindsight. As with other notorious murder cases, when the subject of the Yorkshire Ripper is mentioned it brings dreadful memories flooding back for those most intimately involved. They, more than anyone, deserve to know what really happened during that awful period when Peter Sutcliffe roamed the North of England creating real terror. They also need to know that some good came out of that terrible era and that lessons were learned.

The public also deserves to understand that the police officers trying to find this utterly ruthless killer were decent and honest men. In the chaos that gripped the investigation there were some brilliant detectives. All were totally committed, but tragically some, just like the police service for which they worked, were way out of their depth. The British police have an extraordinary record in solving homicides. But in such a complex and protracted inquiry as this one, the West Yorkshire Ripper Squad was overwhelmed. They proved the truth of G. K. Chesterton's reflection that 'society is at the mercy of a murderer without a motive'. Many of those police officers paid a high price – ruined careers, ruined health, ruined marriages – and in a few cases the stress led to premature death.

I was never remotely interested in the killer himself. What could he tell me that I didn't already know – that he was a sick and perverted murderer? It would have been a worthless exercise to ask him serious questions and expect believable or valuable answers. The revelations in this book about the Yorkshire Ripper's twisted sexual motivation for his attacks reinforced my initial instincts.

I was more interested in the detectives who tried to catch him, intrigued by them as people and the service for which they worked. I have tried to put the reader in their shoes as they attended a murder scene or an autopsy or a press conference. The police service remains one of our pivotal institutions, for it serves to safeguard much of what we take for granted. There can be no freedom without a system of laws. We need dedicated men and women to enforce those laws. The police force deserves more credit than it receives for the way it copes with the accelerating pace of change within modern society. It has learned to adapt more in the last twenty-five years than at any time in its history. Crime has been on the increase steadily for the last hundred years and people are right to be concerned, especially about street crime, which is often drug related. But let us get it in proportion. The overwhelming majority of British people generally walk unhindered on the streets and sleep safely in their beds at night.

More than twenty years after attending the Yorkshire Ripper trial in Court No. 1 at the Old Bailey in May 1981, I resolutely maintain the view that, apart from the infamous hoaxer, there was only one monstrous villain in the Yorkshire Ripper case. It was, and is, the pathetic and twisted individual whom I saw give evidence in his own, highly implausible, defence of the indefensible: Peter Sutcliffe. He was and remains wicked beyond belief.

MICHAEL BILTON, *October 2002*

Preface to the paperback edition

Serialization of *Wicked Beyond Belief* in the *Sunday Times* and the book's subsequent publication unleashed a torrent of media coverage. This in turn gave rise to the stunning news that a crucial piece of evidence strongly suggesting that Peter Sutcliffe may have feigned mental illness in order to avoid spending the rest of his natural life in a maximum security prison was not used at trial and still exists in the hands of the West Yorkshire Police.

These developments warrant detailed explanation to bring readers fully up-to-date, and are referred to in the new Endpiece written for this paperback edition. I would like to acknowledge the assistance of various people who helped me in my research while preparing the Endpiece for this book: David Bruce, crime correspondent of the *Yorkshire Evening Post*; Diane Simpson; Jeremy Armstrong of the *Daily Mirror*; Charles Collier-Wright of the legal department of Trinity-Mirror Newspapers; Alastair Brett of the legal department of Times Newspapers; David Mone, and Brian Caton, general secretary of the Prison Officers' Association.

MICHAEL BILTON, *May 2003*

1

Contact and Exchange

Exactly twenty-nine minutes after the body of Wilma McCann was found, the telephone rang beside Hoban's bed. It was at 8.10 a.m. Early-morning calls were nothing new for the head of Leeds CID. He had been sound asleep for nearly an hour, having crawled between the sheets next to his wife, Betty, not long before dawn. He had been up since 1 a.m. at a murder scene in another part of the city for most of the night. A phone call now was the last thing he needed. The control room at Wakefield was on the line. 'A murder, sir,' the operator said. 'A woman, at the Prince Philip playing fields, Scott Hall Road, Chapeltown. Found by the milkman, sir. The local police surgeon is at the scene already and Mr Craig is on his way.' Craig! The assistant chief constable in charge of crime was turning out. That settled it – Hoban couldn't take his time, he wanted to be there before him.

Betty was already downstairs making a cup of tea. She knew what to expect. No point in making him breakfast. He'd be up and off. He'd wash and shave, take his insulin, get dressed. Then he'd be gone. She knew it would be midnight before she saw him again. 'There's another murder, young woman this time in Chapeltown,' he said downstairs in the hallway, kissing her on the cheek and saying goodbye at the same time. 'Dennis . . .' she hardly had time to say 'take care' before he was

1

gone. Through the front-room window she saw him reverse his blue Daimler on to the road and drive off. For the umpteenth hundred time in thirty years of marriage, Betty was left alone while her husband went chasing criminals.

A freelance photographer arrived at the playing field before Hoban. The scenes of crime team had not yet put up a tarpaulin screen to shield the body from prying eyes. A uniformed officer prevented the freelance going any further. A 500 mm telephoto lens was clipped on to his Nikon camera. Looking through the eyepiece, he could clearly see one hundred yards away the body of a woman on its back, trousers above her ankles. Just then several figures moved into the framed image from left and right. Two uniform constables from the area traffic car were dragging a crude canvas screen closer towards the woman. And just then, moving slowly into frame from the right, the scenes of crime photographer arrived with his large plate camera already clamped on to its tripod. The freelance had only seconds to take the shot before the body was obscured. His shutter clicked and almost immediately the camera's motor-drive whirred and wound on. A pathetically sad image of a murder victim in the morning mist was captured for all time on 35 mm film.

More newsmen turned up. Film crews from the local television stations; reporters from the *Evening Post*. There was some relief for the waiting journalists when Hoban arrived, clearly identifiable in his light-coloured raincoat, belted at the waist, his brimmed hat hiding his receding hairline. There was an almost symbiotic relationship between them and the local CID chief, and so a formal ritual was played out. They would wait patiently, perhaps go door-knocking to see if any local neighbours knew what happened. He'd do what he had to do, then help them. Those in search of a story and pictures needed the goodwill of the man in charge. They had to be patient and not take liberties, not impinge on the investigation. To solve this murder, any murder, Hoban knew he needed information from the public. The media were a valuable resource, so he'd personally make sure they got the story in time for the first edition of the *Post* and the first news summary on the local TV stations at midday.

Formal greetings with his colleagues were just that. Formal. It was cold. There was low-lying fog. The men around him stamped their feet, arms folded against their chests, trying to keep warm. Some had been waiting at the crime scene for nearly an hour since the woman was found at 7.41 a.m. by the passing milkman. The date was 30 October 1975, the eve of Halloween and only days to go to Fireworks Night. It was that time of year when local kids had been making effigies of Guy Fawkes, standing on street corners, asking 'Penny for the Guy'. The local milkman was making the early-morning round with his ten-year-old brother. Mist hanging over the area made it difficult to see properly as Alan Routledge drove his electric-powered milk van into the rectangular tarmac car park of the Prince Philip Centre. He got out to deliver a crate of milk and there, on a steep banking on the far side of the car park, near the rear of the caretaker's house and the sports field clubhouse, spotted what he at first thought was a bundle of rags or perhaps a children's 'Guy'. Out of curiosity the brothers edged closer. It was the body of a woman. Routledge ushered his sibling away and ran for a phone. He told the police operator he had found a woman with her throat cut.

The uniformed officers laid down a series of duckboards across the grassy area to the murder scene. Hoban moved forward, treading carefully on the slatted wood. Devlin, the police surgeon, greeted him. The woman lay on her back, at a slightly oblique angle across the slope, the head pointing uphill and the feet directed towards the edge of the car park. Her reddish-coloured handbag lay beside her, its leather strap still looped around her left hand. Her white flared slacks had been pulled down below her knees; both her pink blouse and her blue bolero-style jacket had been ripped apart. Her bra, a flimsy pink-coloured thing, had been pulled up to expose her breasts. Blood from stab wounds had leaked over to the right side of her body. The blood had dried. More blood from a stab wound on the left side of her chest trickled down to the edge of her pants, obviously, thought Hoban, because her feet were pointing downhill. Her auburn hair had been back-combed into a beehive style high above her head, but now much of it was spread out on the grass. She had worn a pair of shoes with an inch-thick sole and a four-inch heel. Her knickers were in the normal position covering her genitalia. They bore a large, colour printed jokey motif, part of which Hoban could easily read without bending down: 'Famous meeting places'. A small button lay behind her head and some coins were in the nearby grass. The wounds were divided into several areas: a stab wound to the throat; two stab wounds below the right breast; three stab wounds below the left breast and a series of nine stab wounds around the umbilicus.

By the time the local Home Office pathologist arrived at 9.25 a.m. Hoban knew the dead woman's name and the fact that she lived barely a hundred yards away. The back entrance to her council house in Scott Hall Avenue opened out on to the playing field. Neighbours told officers making house to house inquiries how Wilma McCann lived with four young children, separated from her husband. Two of the children had gone looking for their mother at first light when she failed to return home, after having left the eldest, Sonje, aged nine, in charge. Sonje and her brother went to wait at the nearby bus stop to see if their mother had caught an early-morning bus home. They were standing there freezing when a neighbour found them with their school coats over their pyjamas.

Nothing surprised Hoban any more, he'd seen all this before. Desperate women. Children neglected. Leeds City council officials had already been alerted that the four McCann children would almost certainly need foster care. No one knew at first where their father lived. Initially, because Wilma was found so close to her home, Hoban considered that this might be a domestic incident that got out of hand. Perhaps the former husband was involved. Then he heard that Wilma frequently went out at night to the local pubs and clubs to 'have a good time' – and she got paid for it. Like many single mothers on the breadline, she slept with men for money. She came and went via the back entrance to hide the fact that she left the children alone for several hours and frequently returned late at night. For this she had paid the terrible price. Although she had no convictions for prostitution, Hoban knew the fact that she was a good-time girl would be a major complication.

Standing there that morning, he hoped and expected they could solve this case quickly. The victim would surely have some relationship to the killer – a motive would be established and with luck and a fair wind they would have their man. The other senior man to arrive at the McCann murder scene was the forensic pathologist, David Gee, who knew Hoban well and admired his professionalism as a top detective. Each had earned the respect of the other. They had already spent most of the night together at the scene of another murder elsewhere in the city and Gee also had only just dropped off into a very deep sleep when the phone call came through alerting him to this latest case. Not unreasonably, he regarded it as a bit of a nuisance. He had made good speed, considering he had to drive in to Leeds from Knaresborough, twenty miles away, during the morning rush hour. Hoban filled him in on all he knew so far. Gee – notebook in one hand, biro in the other – stood as he always did, listening intently. For a few minutes he looked at and around the body. Eventually he drew a diagram and wrote a few cryptic remarks. For a murder involving multiple stab wounds it was what he would have expected. There was heavy soiling of the skin at the front and right side of the neck because of the stab wound on the throat. Blood was staining the grass beside the victim's head. The blood trickling from the chest and abdomen had also soiled the right side of the victim's blouse. Other spots of dried blood could be seen on the front of both her thighs, on the upper surface of her slacks and the upper surface of her right hand.

Gee's very first thoughts were that the blood seepages running vertically downwards from the stab wounds in all directions suggested she had been stabbed to death where she lay. One blood trickle ran into the top of her knickers and then along it. When the panties were removed, he could see the trickle did not run down inside, probably indicating that no sexual intercourse had taken place either just before or just after the stabbing. Some blood soiled her long and tangled hair, but this was maybe due to blood escaping from the wound to her neck.

Once the body had been photographed, Ron Outtridge, the forensic scientist from the Home Office laboratory at Harrogate, moved closer and began taking Sellotape impressions from the exposed portions, hoping to find tiny fibres, perhaps from the killer's clothing. Gee took swabs from various orifices – vagina, anus, mouth. Then he began measuring the temperature of the body at roughly half-hourly intervals. In an hour, between 10.30 and 11.30 a.m., Wilma's corpse grew colder by two degrees, falling to 71.5°F. However, once the sun came up, the external temperature began to rise. By a simple calculation Gee determined that death happened around midnight, according to the hourly rate at which the body dropped in temperature. A gentle south-westerly breeze eventually blew the fog away and by 11.40 the temperature was 59°F, quite warm for an autumn day. The sky, however, remained overcast and there were a few spots of rain. For protection, the body was partly covered by a plastic sheet raised above the corpse on a metal frame so as not to contaminate any clues. By this time there was slight rigor mortis. Outtridge then removed the slacks, shoes and handbag. Plastic bags were placed over the head and hands and the body was gently wrapped in a much larger plastic sheet for the short journey by windowless van to the local mortuary. There the rest of the clothing was removed and handed over to Outtridge. A fingerprint specialist examined the body for prints on the surface of the skin.

The team, including Hoban and Outtridge, gathered again for the formal post-mortem at 2 p.m. It was a long and exacting process which took four hours. Most officers hate post-mortems. 'It is not only the sight but the smell of the body and the disinfectants,' recalls one senior detective who had been involved on countless murder inquiries. 'The smell would cling to your clothing and when I got home I would strip, put clothes in the washer and my suit on the line. I would then have a shower but I would also lose my sex drive for several days. I think a lot of policemen are affected in this way.'

After the formalities of measuring and weighing the body, Gee quickly made an important discovery. Because Wilma had been lying on her back when found, there had been no examination of the rear of her head. On the examination table, her head propped up on a wooden block, he quickly located two lacerations of the scalp that had been concealed by her long hair. One was a vertical and slightly curved laceration, two inches in length, its margins relatively clean cut and shelving towards the right. This wound penetrated the full thickness of the scalp and through it a deep fracture in the skull could be clearly observed. Two inches to the left was another head injury, not so severe. Gee pointed out the two wounds, and later this portion of Wilma's skull was shaved so they could be photographed prior to her brain being removed and studied.

Gee then began minutely examining the fifteen stab wounds to the body, trying to follow the track of each beneath the surface of the skin. It was a difficult task. The majority of wounds to her abdomen were very close together. It proved impossible to show the direction of each individual track of each individual wound. He had greater success in tracking the wounds to the neck and chest. Here, patiently, slowly, was a scientist methodically at work trying to learn what kind of weapon or weapons had been used to kill Wilma; and to determine more precisely how she actually died.

Gee's final conclusion was that death occurred within minutes of the victim being struck on the head, then stabbed. He believed the weapon involved in the stabbing was more than three inches long and a quarter of an inch broad. She'd been hit on the head with a blunt object with a restricted striking surface. It could have been a hammer, but at this stage Gee favoured something like an adjustable spanner. There was nothing special about the stab wounds. The victim had been struck from the left side. Death had occurred probably early on the morning of 30 October.

*   *   *

Back in his office later that night Hoban began absorbing the information flowing in. House to house inquiries by the Task Force began to give a more detailed and increasingly depressing picture of Wilma's lifestyle. Her former husband had been traced. Her parents were contacted in Scotland. Criminal records showed she had four convictions for drunkenness, theft and disorderly conduct. The local vice squad believed she was a known prostitute, though she had never been cautioned.

Wilma had been born and brought up near Inverness, one of eleven children. Her father was a farm worker. She had been christened Willemena Mary Newlands. According to her mother, she had been a good speller as a child, full of life but inclined to go her own way. Mrs Betsy Newlands said she had brought up all eleven children strictly. Wilma had to be in bed by 10 p.m. every night and when her father discovered her wearing make-up he took it from her and buried it in the garden. She could quickly become emotional, and when she did everyone would know about it. From leaving the local technical school she went to work at the Gleneagles Hotel near Perth. She had been pregnant with her daughter, Sonje, before she was out of her teens.

After Sonje was born, Wilma met a joiner, Gerald Christopher McCann from Londonderry, Northern Ireland. They married on 7 October 1968. A few years later they moved to the Leeds area, where five of Wilma's brothers lived. She and Gerry had three children of their own in fairly quick succession – a son and two daughters. But by February 1974 the marriage was over. Wilma couldn't settle, she hadn't the self-discipline to adapt to either marriage or motherhood. She liked her nights out. And she liked other men. Gerry left and soon took up with another woman and had a child by her. He continued to see his kids after school and bought them birthday presents.

Wilma did not ask for money from National Assistance but earned it her way – when she went out in the evening. Gerry McCann wanted a divorce on the grounds of his wife's adultery and Wilma was happy to give it to him. Court proceedings were imminent.

From early on after Wilma and Gerry separated, nine-year-old Sonje seemed to be doing most of the caring for her half-brother and half-sisters at the house. In fact Wilma came to rely increasingly on the little girl, who was expected to grow up quickly and take on board responsibilities for her siblings way before her time. As a mother, Wilma was hopeless. She had degenerated into a terrible drunken state. The house, when police searched it, was filthy. She was sexually promiscuous and irresponsible and Gerry, a caring father, had become increasingly concerned that, since their separation, Wilma was neglecting the children's welfare and leaving them alone for long periods in the evenings.

Hoban knew inner-city Leeds intimately. He had worked there for thirty years, he knew the streets, he knew the back alleyways, the pubs and clubs. He met his vast network of informants there – the criminal classes who gave him tipoffs that made him probably the best-informed detective in the city. He knew the wide boys, the spivs, the con men, the burglars, the pick-pockets, the whores, the fences. He also knew the serious criminals, the ones who thought nothing of taking a shotgun on an armed raid on a bank or post office. He had, over the years, locked up hundreds of criminals and earned himself a fierce reputation. Newspapers referred to him as 'Crime Buster', or more particularly as the 'Crime Buster in the sheepskin coat' – a fitting reference to Hoban's liking for sartorial elegance in the city responsible for making the made-to-measure suits that clothed half the male population of England through chain stores like Hepworth and Montague Burton.

Hoban's extraordinary gift for solving crime and his energy and dedication had marked him out from the beginning of his police career. Commendations from magistrates and judges at the assize courts and quarter sessions came thick and fast. There was an inevitability about him rising to the top. He could move easily among those who skated the line between what was legal and what was not. He would drift into a pub or nightclub and soon there would be an exchange of glances as he clocked one of his snouts, some thief, vagabond or ne'er-do-well with information to sell. Thirty seconds apart, they would make for the gentlemen's lavatory where a ten-shilling note was exchanged for a piece of paper or a discreetly whispered conversation.

Hoban was not a great drinker. His diabetes put paid to that. But he enjoyed social occasions and he loved the status his job gave him. He thrived on working his way up from humble origins to the top, to being a Citizen of the Year in Leeds. And he luxuriated in his work as a police officer. It wasn't a job, it was a way of life. It was like a drug. He knew it. Betty knew it. His two sons knew it. And murder was his greatest professional challenge. Finding the person or persons who had snuffed out the life of some undeserving man or woman from among the half million souls who lived in the city of Leeds – that took some doing. And Hoban was very good at it. He had been involved in almost forty murders and solved them all.

The day Wilma's body was discovered and the hunt for her killer launched, Hoban returned to Betty at midnight, his mind troubled by the fact that Wilma McCann, because she persistently had sex for money, might not have known the man who killed her. In these situations the search for an individual who killed with frenzied violence was a top priority because they were such a danger. The early stages of a murder inquiry took precedence over almost everything. The following morning he was due to undergo firearms training on a local range. Before Hoban drifted off to sleep he had to remind himself he must contact someone and cancel the appointment.

For the next week, apart from Sunday, Hoban worked until midnight every day. On the Sunday he went in an hour later, working only a twelve-hour day, so he was home that night shortly after ten o'clock. Wednesday he took off and spent the day with Betty. He tried to be home by 10 p.m. if he could, but frequently it was impossible. Occasionally other crucial duties as the head of the city's Criminal Investigation Department demanded his time which took him away from the murder inquiry, such as briefing the assistant chief constable, Donald Craig, or a conference with prosecution counsel in connection with other cases destined for trial. But Hoban, once these appointments were out of the way, kept himself and his officers hard at it. He made frequent appeals through the press and on local radio for people to come forward with information. He needed eyewitnesses who had seen Wilma, possibly with her killer.

As each detail came in, it was filed in the index system at the murder incident room. This in turn generated more inquiries: men friends, especially previous lovers, to be traced, interviewed and eliminated; vehicle sightings to be checked; follow-up interviews arising from house-to-house inquiries to be actioned, carried out, checked and then more follow-up actions sanctioned. A more detailed picture of Wilma's movements on the night she died began to emerge slowly. She had left home at about 7.30, telling Sonje that the younger kids were not to get out of bed. She was 'going to town again' and would be back later. From 8.30 to 10.30 p.m. she had been in various city centre pubs. About 11.30 she was on her own at the Room at the Top nightclub, in the North Street/Sheepscar area of the city. The last positive sighting of her was about 1 a.m. when two officers in a patrol car spotted her in Meanwood Road. Other witnesses had seen her trying to hitch a lift by jumping out in front of cars, causing them to stop. She was roaring drunk. The laboratory report, while it showed no trace of semen in her body, did confirm she had consumed a hefty amount of alcohol, between twelve and fourteen measures of spirit. Reports came in of a lorry driver who had stopped near where Wilma was seen weaving her way down the road. Initially, there was some confusion, because another lorry was also seen to pull up and an eyewitness saw Wilma engaged in conversation with the driver.

An early search of her home produced an address book and so began the task of locating a large number of Wilma's clients, though Hoban discreetly told the press they were searching for past 'boyfriends'. He appealed for any not yet contacted to come forward. To label a victim a prostitute in this situation was unhelpful. Experience showed the public were somehow not surprised at what happened to call girls. Photographs and stories in the press about Wilma's orphaned children were intended to create sympathy.

A week after Wilma was killed, Hoban had late-night roadblocks set up on the route she had taken when she left the Room at the Top. As a result, the lorry driver who stopped to talk to her revealed he didn't pick her up in response to her plea for a lift home. She was totally drunk and clutching a white plastic container in which she was carrying curry and chips. He was heading for the M62 motorway, across the

Pennines to Lancashire. A day or so later a car driver came forward to say he had seen Wilma getting into a 'K' registered, red or orange fastback saloon, looking similar to a Hillman Avenger. The driver was said to be coloured, possibly West Indian or African, aged about thirty-five, with a full face 'and thin droopy moustache'. He was wearing a donkey jacket.

Six weeks after the murder, Hoban's investigation was clearly floundering. All the normal checks had revealed nothing. The witness pointing them in the direction of the red or orange hatchback also mentioned an articulated lorry, which he said had been parked nearby. Despite inquiries at 483 haulage companies the police drew a blank. A total of twenty-nine former 'boyfriends' were interviewed and eliminated. They were still searching for the driver of the fastback car to come forward.

From December 1975 and into the New Year Hoban resumed more of his duties as the head of Leeds CID. There were important functions to attend – dinners held by the Law Society and the Junior Chamber of Commerce. He had court appearances in Birkenhead as a result of a famous incident at Headingley when a protest group dug up part of the cricket pitch and poured oil over the wicket, causing the Test match against Australia to be abandoned. The protesters were an unlikely group, trying to right an injustice in the case of George Davis, a London criminal they claimed had been wrongly imprisoned for a bank robbery. It was a high-profile case and Hoban was intimately involved.

He made his obligatory appearance at the chief constable's pre-Christmas cocktail party for senior officers at the force headquarters in Wakefield. The chief, Ronald Gregory, had reason to be pleased with the way things were going in his administration. Two years previously the West Yorkshire Police Force had merged with the big city forces in Leeds and Bradford to create the West Yorkshire Metropolitan Police, one of the larger forces in the country, stretching across a wide area of the North of England. Gregory knew there would be tensions in bringing together the county coppers with the city forces. Leeds and Bradford had had autonomy previously, each with their own budget, chief constable and head of CID. Gregory hadn't wanted too much disruption and hadn't insisted on major changes in personnel. The cocktail party, at lunchtime on 22 December, was another getting-to-know-you session.

Hoban knew many of the senior detectives in the newly combined force. Before becoming the senior detective in Leeds, he had been deputy coordinator of No. 3 Regional Crime Squad, which covered a wide area of Northern England. As a detective superintendent he had close contact with his counterparts in the major towns and cities in the West Riding. The senior men were expected to get along with each other and make the amalgamation work. But the easy-going jollity of the cocktail party was in part an illusion. It still rankled the senior Leeds officers that the West Riding men were in the driving seat. As city detectives they were used to dealing with tough gangs and sophisticated crime. They believed the county boys lacked the hard experience needed to deal with ruthless criminals. 'Donkey Wallopers', they called them. However, on this occasion the chat was friendly. Most knew Hoban had an unsolved murder, but this was nothing new in their line of work. His reputation stood him in good stead. He was viewed as 'a hard and occasionally ruthless man' – 'a decent bloke' – 'a fucking great detective'.

Renewed inquiries among prostitutes in the Chapeltown area over Christmas and the New Year of 1976 produced information about a fifty-year-old Irishman, known to drive a clapped-out Land-Rover, who frequented the area. It was a total red herring. Neither the Irishman, nor the driver of the vehicle thought to be an orange/red fastback car, was ever traced. (In retrospect, it seems highly likely that the driver of the fastback car was Peter Sutcliffe, who at the time drove a lime green K registered Ford Capri. It was some years before the Ripper squad learned that street lighting at night could often give witnesses a confusing picture of the colour of vehicles they were trying to describe. Sutcliffe had a swarthy appearance, which at night and at a distance could have led to him being confused for a light-coloured West Indian. And, of course, he had a droopy moustache.)

By the middle of January 1976 the McCann murder squad, numbering 137 officers, had worked 53,000 hours. Five thousand houses had been called at, these inquiries having generated most of the 3,300 separate index card references in the incident room. These in turn had spawned 2,880 separate actions or follow-ups. Five hundred and thirty-eight statements were taken. There were other clues which were never resolved. The vaginal swabs taken by the pathologist found no trace of semen, but there was a positive semen reaction on the back of Wilma's trousers and pants. Forensic scientists at the Harrogate laboratory were unable to produce a blood group, most likely because the person who deposited this sample did not secrete his blood cells in his bodily fluids. (Possibly Sutcliffe masturbated over Wilma after he attacked her.) Keeping details of the injuries secret from the media, Hoban announced at one point that the killer seemed to have 'very personal feelings towards Wilma'. He was clearly speculating elliptically that the frenzied nature of the attack and the physical presence of some sexual motive, i.e. the semen, perhaps made this a personal assault.

In Wilma's home the scenes-of-crime officers amassed a large number of fingerprints. A fragment of fingerprint on a door jamb was never eliminated. A purse missing from her handbag was never found. To help jog the memory of potential witnesses, a woman police officer dressed up in Wilma's clothes and a photograph of Wilma's face was superimposed. Two thousand posters were distributed to shops and other businesses, but little hard information was produced. There was little to distinguish this case from many other unsolved murders. According to Professor Gee: 'We simply had an unsolved murder in which the only slightly unusual feature was the use of two weapons to cause the injuries.'

Eight weeks and five days after Wilma McCann was murdered, Dennis Hoban was once more summoned from home before breakfast to the scene of the homicide of a woman. Soon, because of the nature of the injuries and the circumstances in which she died, he became firmly convinced that the man who murdered McCann had killed again. Newspapers began talking about a Jack-the-Ripper style killer on the loose.

There had been a false alarm only a few weeks previously at a ghastly murder scene which Hoban attended in Leeds after a 'photographic model' and her young child had been stabbed to death. The dead mother also turned out to be a prostitute and Hoban briefly suspected a link. However, this double homicide was almost immediately detected by a combination of good luck and alert thinking by one of Hoban's former protégés on the No. 3 Regional Crime Squad. A mentally deranged seventeen-year-old youth called Mark Rowntree was quickly arrested by Detective Chief Inspector Dick Holland, stationed at Bradford CID. When the burly rugby-playing detective investigated the killing of a young man, aged sixteen, in nearby Keighley, he came away with a confession from Rowntree that included two other homicides he hadn't even known had happened. The deaths of the woman and her son in Leeds were barely a few days old and Hoban, who hated bureaucratic paperwork at the best of times, had delayed circulating full details to surrounding divisions. Rowntree confessed to Holland his guilt in a one-man killing spree which included the sixteen-year-old youth, the prostitute and her son, and an eighty-five-year-old widow. He was eventually sent to Broadmoor.

Now, on Wednesday, 21 January 1976, in response to a control room telephone message, Hoban donned a warm, dark brown car coat and his familiar hat and made his way to a derelict area destined for redevelopment. Part of the Manor Street Industrial Estate off Roundhay Road included a row of boarded-up, dilapidated, red-brick buildings, scheduled for demolition. A uniformed inspector took him to an alley between two derelict houses adjacent to a cobblestoned cul-de-sac, Enfield Terrace. The passageway had been roofed over at some point, but the roofing had caught fire and been destroyed. Now the only parts remaining were charred timbers and the passageway was open to the sky. The front of the passage was open but the back was completely filled by masses of rubbish, burnt wood, scrap metal and junked office and factory furniture. The inspector told Hoban that at 8 a.m. a man on his way to work parked his car at the far end of the cul-de-sac almost opposite the passageway. When he got out of the driver's door, he glanced to the right and saw a pair of legs lying among the rubble about fifteen feet inside the alley. At first he thought it was a shop-window dummy, then realized it was the body of a woman.

Treading carefully, Hoban noticed there were clear drag marks of disturbed earth from the front of the road, along the passageway, to where the body lay on its back. There were also small areas of dried blood on the surface of the cobbles and concrete on the ground. There is never a pleasant place to be brutally murdered, but this was a terrible location in which to die. The first police officer at the scene had earlier noted a boot impression in the roadway, near the entrance to the passageway, and pointed it out to Hoban.

A gale was blowing as the police surgeon, who had been waiting patiently for Hoban to arrive, pulled back a plastic sheet partly covering the body of a middle-aged woman. It had protected the corpse from the wind and rain. The body lay sprawled on its back just outside a doorway, a striped dress pulled up above the waist. The woman's fawn-coloured imitation leather handbag lay several feet from her head, its flap open. Its contents showed her name was probably Emily Jackson, and that she lived near Morley, a town in the west of Leeds. The brown-haired woman had hazel-coloured eyes and nicotine-stained fingers on both hands, more pronounced on the right than the left. She wore a wedding ring.

Mrs Jackson still had on her red, blue and green checked overcoat and was sprawled on the right of the passage, just in front of the piles of rubbish, with the left arm by her side and the left leg stretched out straight. The right arm was directed out at right angles from the body, and the right leg was bent upwards and outwards, flexed at the knee and hip. The lower limbs were clad in tights, which were laddered and bore a large hole six inches above the knee. She also wore black panties, which were in position, though the left side of the upper edge of the tights was slightly displaced downwards, exposing the knickers. The feet were bare. One cheap-looking white sling-back lay on the ground beside the right foot; the other was a short distance away, closer to the right-hand wall. There was a muddy footprint on her thigh similar to the one in the soil at the entrance to the alley. The front of the body was soiled by dirt in various areas, especially the front and outer sides of the thighs. The face was heavily soiled with mud and blood, and there was bloodstaining on the front of the dress, on the right arm and right hand. The ground beneath and above the head was soiled by small pools and trickles of coagulated blood.

Professor Gee arrived at 9.30 a.m. to be followed soon after by Outtridge from the Home Office laboratory at Harrogate. Examining the spot where the woman lay, the pathologist bent down. The exposed part of the body felt cold to Gee's touch. Hoban then took him to the front of the passageway, to the cobbled roadway, opposite a flat-roofed modern factory building, the premises of Hollingworth & Moss, bookbinders. Two duckboards had been placed either side of a large piece of hardboard that shielded some vital evidence from the elements. When the hardboard was lifted Hoban and Gee saw a pool of red-stained rainwater – diluted blood. The woman had been struck, probably at this spot, then dragged up the passageway. A chill wind blew strongly and there were intermittent squalls of cold rain. Gee and Hoban quickly agreed that preserving any evidence in these conditions was going to be difficult – particularly contact trace-evidence, which might have been passed from the killer to the victim in the shape of minute fibres of clothing. Gee was reluctant to record the body's temperature, since this would have involved displacing the victim's clothing. Instead he instructed that the body be enveloped in large plastic sheets and taken to the public mortuary for a more intensive examination.

Task force officers had begun an inch-by-inch fingertip search among the cobblestones along Elmfield Terrace. Ten officers in overalls, some wearing gloves, got down on their hands and knees in the wind and rain and painstakingly grubbed their way along the street. Among them was a twenty-four-year-old Bradford constable, Andrew Laptew. He had joined the Bradford force after sailing the seven seas as a trainee Merchant Navy officer. After experiencing the delights of South America, the Far East and Australia, he made a determined bid to become a police officer. Joining the Task Force had been an exciting moment, since its members regarded themselves as part of an élite unit. 'Fingertip searches were back-breaking work because that is what we did – felt with our fingertips to see if we could find any clues,' he remembered twenty-five years later. They found nothing to help the investigation.

The formal post-mortem began at 11.15 a.m. Until then, no attempt had been made to look more closely at the body, especially at the back. The victim was forty-one years old and slightly overweight, which made her look several years older. She was five feet six inches tall. Donald Craig, the assistant chief constable, stood close to Hoban watching while the normal forensic procedures in a homicide autopsy were applied. Craig was an experienced murder investigator, who had solved all seventy-three murders on his patch during a three-year spell as the West Riding CID chief during the early 1970s. It made him a bit of a legend and people either loved or loathed him. He was tough, uncompromising and, some even said, a bit of a bully at times. He had few social graces and rarely apologized for anything. The West Riding man and the Leeds City man respected one another. You couldn't take away Craig's track record, and he had attended dozens of autopsies, so he knew what to look out for. His father, too, had been a policeman.

For nearly eighty years, since the late nineteenth century, the mechanics of identifying and preserving evidence at crime scenes encompassed a process that combined logic with rigorous scientific method. Minute specks of material could prove vital, and in eighty years the technology had changed dramatically. Forensic techniques now encompassed the use of highly expensive electron microscopes and mass photo spectrometers.

The very process of photographing and measuring evidence, particularly in cases of murder, had been perfected initially in France in the 1890s by the clerk to the premier bureau of the Paris Préfecture of Police, Alphonse Bertillon. He had photographed the bodies of victims and their relationship to significant items of evidence at the crime scene, including footprints, stains, tool marks, points of entry among other details. Even today one of the cornerstones of forensic science remains the 'exchange principle' first developed by one of Bertillon's students, Edmond Locard: 'If there is contact between two items, there will be an exchange.' When anyone comes into contact with an object or someone else, a cross-transfer of physical evidence occurs. They will leave evidence of that contact and they will take some evidence with them. The job of the forensic scientist is to locate this material to help ultimately identify the criminal and achieve a conviction in a court of law. 'The criminologist,' Locard maintained, 're-creates the criminal from the traces the latter leaves behind, just as the archaeologist reconstructs prehistoric beings from his finds.'

The process was necessarily painstaking, time consuming and expensive. What Gee, Hoban and their close colleagues hoped to achieve during the next seven and a quarter hours in the Leeds city mortuary was to lay the vital groundwork to help them find *and* convict the murderer. The application of scientific rigour was not the only process at work. A further ingredient was also required: an attitude of mind or, in more familiar terms, 'a hunch', born out of years of experience. Hunches were not mere guesswork. Even at this stage, Dennis Hoban was already speculating out loud privately to Gee that the murderer of McCann was likely to be 'a long-distance lorry driver'. This intuitive judgement by the senior detective was based on several factors: the possibility that the killer carried tools in his vehicle; the failure to trace the likely killer from among McCann's boyfriends, with whom she sometimes had sex for money; and the fact that many lorry drivers travelled through Chapeltown from the A1 to the M62 motorway.

As with the McCann autopsy, the process of garnering evidence was protracted. Outtridge examined the clothing, taping the material, looking for fibres or other contact traces; the fingerprint specialist looked for possible evidence that the skin had been touched. Swabs were taken in the search for semen; samples of hair were removed from the scalp, the pubic region and eyebrows. The outer clothing showed no sign of having been penetrated by stabbing. Two areas of dirt soiling on the woman's tights were closely examined. They measured roughly three inches by four, on the inner and outer right thigh, and appeared several inches above the right knee. These were the marks resembling the sole of a boot, similar to the footprint found in sandy soil close to the murder scene. A plaster cast of this ridged impression at the scene had already been made by the time the post-mortem started. The area of the boot impression on the tights was carefully cut out before the rest of the clothing was removed from the body, which rested on the autopsy table. Along with all the other samples, these were later taken back to the Harrogate laboratory by Outtridge for microscopic examination.

As the clothing began to be removed, it swiftly became apparent that the woman's bra had been lifted above her breasts and there was a huge number of stab marks to the trunk and back, some so close together as to give the impression of the holes in a pepper pot. They were very small, about one eighth of an inch in diameter, some round, some oval and a few very definitely cruciform in shape, leaving a strange impression on the skin, as if caused by an 'X'-shaped instrument. Gee thought the wounds 'very odd' and subsequently contacted a series of eminent colleagues around the country to see if they could throw light on what had caused them.

Those who had previously attended the post-mortem on Wilma McCann immediately realized the significance of the injuries. It was clear her clothing had been raised to inflict the injuries and then put back in position. Moreover, when Professor Gee examined the head, two significant lacerations were found, one on top of the head, the other at the back. In the first the full thickness of the scalp was penetrated and in the depths of the wound a depressed fracture of the skull was visible. In the second, at the back of the head, a depressed fracture was found beneath the wound. Gee concluded both injuries had been administered with a flat round instrument with a restricted striking surface, like a hammer. A number of bruises and abrasions to the face and throat made it obvious she had been dragged on her face along the ground. When Gee probed deeper, minutely trying to trace the track of a particular wound, he found the blow had passed through the sternum and there reproduced the cruciform shape in the bone. There was also evidence that the neck had been compressed and the victim had been menstruating slightly.

On the body itself Gee counted a total of fifty-two separate stab wounds – in five separate groups – two at the back and three at the front. On the back thirty of the stab wounds were concentrated in an area roughly six inches by eight – hence the impression of a pepper pot. Twelve stab wounds were counted in the abdomen. The killer had turned Emily Jackson over and repeated his frenzied attack. There were so many stab wounds to the trunk situated close together that it was impossible to assign individual tracks to most of them. Since tracks of wounds passed both from the front and from the back of the body into the interior, and many passed into soft tissue, it was impossible for Gee to ascertain the length of any of the tracks with any precision. He thought the weapon might be between two and four inches long. Several people, observing the professor's precise handiwork in trying to track the wounds, commented that a Phillips cross-head screwdriver was the most likely cause.

At the end Gee finally gave Hoban his scenario by which the woman had met her death. There were blows to the head, dragging to the site where her corpse was found, raising of the clothes, stabbing, turning over and more stabs, in the course of which the assailant trod on her thigh, then the clothing was pulled down. She hadn't been drinking. Later analysis by the laboratory at Harrogate found semen on a vaginal swab, but it was thought this was from sexual activity prior to the attack. Gee, the scientist who preferred not to deal in speculation, could not say exactly what kind of stabbing instrument had been used – but among the strong possibilities was indeed a Phillips screwdriver. Neither was he totally sure this was the work of McCann's killer. There were clear similarities, but he could not rule out coincidence. Hoban, on the other hand, felt more certain he was dealing with the same killer for two murders, a suspicion strengthened when he started to hear details of the lifestyle the woman had led.

The murdered woman's husband, Sydney Jackson, had a difficult story to tell the officers who interviewed him. He realized he was under suspicion himself, for the circumstances of his marriage were slightly out of the ordinary, even for Leeds. His story came out in dribs and drabs over the course of many hours of questioning. As he told it, and as Hoban initially understood it, she was insatiable and had had many affairs. He turned a blind eye to her activities, which included having sex with many boyfriends because her sexual appetite was such that he could not satisfy it.

Later that afternoon Hoban gave another television interview in the murder incident room at the newly opened Millgarth Street police station in Leeds city centre. Looking extraordinarily dapper for a senior detective, in his Aquascutum suit, red shirt and floral tie, he relayed some of the few facts at his disposal, putting the best possible gloss on the woman's private life. 'She was a woman who liked to go to public houses,' he declared matter of factly. 'She liked to go to bingo. She led a life of her own, really. We are anxious to contact any friends, lady friends or men friends, who may have seen her last night. She probably went to the Gaiety public house, which is a very popular pub in the area. We know the van she was in finished up on the Gaiety car park this morning ... She had severe head injuries. There are other injuries I don't wish to elaborate on at this time.'

Sydney Jackson at first kept from police the fact that since Christmas his wife had been trying to solve their financial and income tax problems by working as a prostitute. Then, under an intensive interrogation which ended shortly before midnight the day his wife's body was discovered, he finally admitted that he often accompanied her when she went out looking for 'business'. No one in the local community where they lived had a clue. The truth was that Emily and Sydney's marriage was a marriage in name only: they stayed together for their children's sake. Each, it appeared, went their own way, except that Sydney not only knew of his wife's secret life, he drove her to her work. He had gone with her in their van, which his wife drove, to the Gaiety pub, a mile from Chapeltown, on Roundhay Road. It was a large, modern open-plan building that became a popular local drinking haunt, particularly for West Indians. The pub was surrounded on three sides by back-to-back rows of small Victorian terraced houses. Strippers danced at lunchtimes and prostitutes regularly gathered there at all hours looking for punters. Sydney had gone into the pub for a drink. Emily went immediately to work. Sydney stayed inside, listening to Caribbean music being thumped out on the juke box until about 10.30 p.m. He then emerged to find his wife had not kept their rendezvous. They had arranged she would drive him home. Assuming she was with one of her men friends, he instead caught a taxi back to Morley and only discovered what had happened when police called at their house in the morning.

His wife had been born Emily Wood in 1933, one of five brothers and three sisters, who lived with their parents in Hemsworth, a mining village. The entire family later moved to Brancepath Place, Leeds. She and Sydney married on 2 January 1953, when she was nineteen and he twenty-one, and during the early part of their marriage lived at various addresses in the Leeds area. Six years later she left him to live with another man. In 1961 they resumed their relationship and eventually set up house in Northcote Crescent, Morley, and became partners in a roofing business which they ran from home. They had three sons and a daughter, but tragedy struck in 1970 when their fourteen-year-old son, Derek, was killed in a fall from a first-floor window.

Emily was a hard-working, energetic woman, quite attractive in her own way. Neighbours remembered her as someone who was always busy. Because Sydney didn't like to drive, Emily picked up the roofing supplies in their battered blue Commer

27

van. She ferried the men who worked for them from job to job, took the kids to and from school. She also did the paperwork for their business. The day she died one of the neighbours recalled how Emily was supposed to be picking her ten-year-old son up from school. 'When I got back my husband was waiting for me at the bus stop,' said the neighbour, who lived just along the road from the Jackson family. 'I thought something was wrong. And when we got home the boy was sat with a policeman in their house . . . they [Sydney and Emily] often used to go out but we thought they were going to the bingo in Leeds, we never realized what she was doing.'

After the death of their son, which Sydney said Emily never recovered from, they began to live from day to day. 'We decided life was too short, we would live for today and not bother about the future. Sometimes she would go out alone, and I would meet up with her for a drink later on. But I do know that she never went in pubs on her own. She's been in the Gaiety five times at the most, and always with me. We got on together as well as most. We both believed in having a good time – after all, why stop in every night? We believed in having fun while we could.'

Sydney remained strong and reasonably composed for the sake of his children after the murder, but went through a difficult time as he realized he was under suspicion for killing his wife. The day after Emily's body was found the door-stepping journalists were rewarded when Sydney opened his heart to them. Sitting in the lounge of his semi-detached house, holding his head in his hands as he wept, he told them: 'I know what people are saying – but I didn't do it. There's nothing I want to say to the man who did it, there's nothing I can say, but if he's done it once, he'll do it again. I just pray they catch him.'

The information about Emily's secret life was clearly an awkward embarrassment. Emily's married sister refused to believe the things being said about her: 'It's time someone denied what is being said about Emily going into clubs and so on. She just wasn't that kind of person.' Unfortunately for Emily's relatives, the press had quickly been let in on the details of her secret life. Hoban had no choice but to admit she had been soliciting about the time she was killed. Moreover, he could not ignore the obvious link with the McCann murder. He believed he had a duty to warn women who earned money by selling sex that they were in mortal danger. 'While this man is at large no prostitute is safe,' he declared.

Sydney Jackson made frequent visits to the police station to answer questions, insisting he had not killed his wife in revenge for her becoming a prostitute. Eventually Dennis Hoban went to reassure him that they knew he was innocent. He pledged that his detectives would find the man who killed his wife.

The police had taken away the Commer van containing Sydney's tools and equipment for his business, so he couldn't work or earn money. The vehicle had stood, with the ladder on the roof rack, at the Gaiety car park when Emily was murdered. For a while police thought it might have been moved. They were told Emily went touting for business in the van, sometimes taking customers in the back for sex. One look in the rear of the vehicle told them this was an unlikely passion-wagon the night she died. The materials for the roofing business filled up the inside. It was filthy and reeked of bitumen. There was a huge vat for heating tar, gas bottles, cans of paraffin, rolls of roofing felt, half-empty bags of cement, buckets containing trowels and other paraphernalia. Forensic experts gave it a thorough inspection. It was a well-used and abused vehicle, with the front bumper almost hanging off and several dents in the rear nearside panels. Four fingerprints were found that could not be eliminated. They also never determined who left a fingerprint on a lemonade bottle in the van, or another on a sweepstake ticket found in Emily's handbag.

Two days into the murder hunt Hoban appealed for women who worked the streets in the area to come forward. He announced that Emily used her van to solicit clients. 'Sometimes she would leave the van in the Gaiety car park and go with clients in their own cars, when they would drive to some secluded place for sex. It was probably on one of these excursions that she met her killer.' Newspapers quickly linked the murder of Jackson with that of McCann: 'RIPPER HUNTED IN CALL-GIRL MURDERS' announced the *Sun* on 23 January.

A month later a witness came forward to say she had actually seen Emily around 7 p.m. getting into a Land-Rover. Police had begun questioning all convicted and known prostitutes in the area. One, a nineteen-year-old streetwalker, had been casually chatting to Emily moments before she got in the vehicle. A description of the driver, a man with a bushy beard, was widely circulated and an artists' impression issued to the media. All Land-Rovers registered in West Yorkshire were checked, with negative results. Some time later a man answering this description, the owner of a Land-Rover registered in Essex, was interviewed and cleared. He had been temporarily staying in Leeds and admitted consorting with prostitutes. However, he denied that on the night in question he had been out looking to pay for sex with a woman. He had a cast-iron alibi. Some detectives believe he may well have picked up Jackson, and even had sex with her, but denied it emphatically because he had been driving while disqualified. There were searches for other vehicles. Sydney told police Emily had spoken of one of her clients as being 'funny' – they failed to locate him or the

Moskovitch estate car he drove. Another witness saw a dark blue 'L' registered Transit van near the murder scene around 3.30 a.m. A list of 329 vehicles registered in Leeds was drawn up and 278 owners were eliminated from the investigation. The remaining fifty-one were never traced. It proved another frustrating investigation.

No attempt was made to trace the boots the killer wore. Hoban thought too many workmen in the city used this type of footwear to waste time on this particular line of inquiry. It did suggest the killer was not an office worker, but was perhaps involved in manual work. He sent an urgent telex to police stations in West Yorkshire asking that anyone brought into custody wearing similar boots, who might have a vehicle containing tools, such as a workman's van, be held for questioning. He also wanted local criminal intelligence cells in collators' offices to begin examining records for the names of people convicted of series attacks on prostitutes.

Hardware shops were visited to positively identify the kind of weapon used. Hoban was convinced a cross-head screwdriver was the answer; but Gee, when he carried out a variety of tests using different tools, could not reproduce the same kind of wound. When he tried to produce wounds with a Phillips screwdriver, he found that although the flanges of the tip would indeed produce a cruciform wound, as soon as you drove the weapon in with any degree of force, the rounded shaft destroyed the pattern and left simply a round hole. He began searching for a weapon with flanges all the way up its length. 'The explanation of course had to be that some of the wounds were not driven home with sufficient force to extend right up the shaft of the weapon, but there were fifty-two of them and it was difficult to follow the tracks of all,' he said later.

Gee wrote confidentially seeking assistance and suggestions from a number of senior forensic pathologists around Britain and Ireland, including the eminent Professor Keith Simpson. All kinds of possibilities were offered: a carpenter's awl; the implement in a boy scout's knife for taking stones out of horses's hooves; a spud lock key; a roofing hammer; and a reamer. Several pathologists backed the idea of a Phillips screwdriver. 'I am surprised that you had difficulty in getting a Phillips screwdriver through the skin,' replied Professor Keith Mant of Guy's Hospital. 'I have seen fatal stab wounds from such instruments as pokers, and in one case, a boy was stabbed through the heart with a poker during some horseplay with his brother, who had no idea that he had hurt the deceased, especially when he subsequently walked upstairs to his bedroom. He was found dead in bed the next morning – no blood having issued from the wound!'

More media coverage was generated when a police Range Rover, complete with flashing blue light on top, toured the Chapeltown and Roundhay Road area. It contained a large photograph of Emily Jackson and appealed for witnesses who might have seen her on the night of the murder to come forward. Loudspeaker vans toured Leeds, interrupting weekend rugby and football matches. Cinemas and bingo halls suspended proceedings to broadcast appeals from the police. Publicity about two prostitutes having been murdered within three months caused some local women to stop soliciting. Others said they had no choice and accepted the risks: 'There is always a danger when you do this game, but you have got to find a quiet spot, a dark spot,' said one.

Everything told Hoban that Emily Jackson had been picked up in a vehicle while offering herself for sex; she was taken less than half a mile from the Gaiety to Elmfield Terrace, a quiet spot with little street lighting, where she met her terrible end. It was a place to which prostitutes took punters. Some of the girls on the street told him they also had been to precisely that spot. Women gave descriptions of clients, particularly of ones who had been violent. A month after the murder the West Yorkshire Police issued a special notice to all police forces in the country, officially linking the McCann and Jackson murders. They also circulated a description of a Land-Rover driver with the bushy beard. Throughout the next year, a hundred of Hoban's officers worked more than 64,000 hours. Nearly 6,400 index cards were filled in in the incident room, making reference to more than 3,700 house-to-house inquiries and 5,220 separate actions. A total of 830 separate statements were taken and more than 3,500 vehicle inquiries carried out.

'We are quite certain the man we are looking for hates prostitution,' Hoban said. 'I am quite certain this stretches to women of rather loose morals who go into public houses and clubs, who are not necessarily prostitutes, the frenzied attack he has carried out on these women indicates this.'

He knew that a man capable of killing twice probably enjoyed it, which meant he would go on doing it till caught. He was never more serious than when he issued a dark warning to the public via the press: 'I believe the man we are looking for is the type who could kill again. He is a sadistic killer and may well be a sexual pervert.' Emily Jackson had been killed with a ferocity 'that bordered on the maniacal'. 'I cannot stress strongly enough that it is vital we catch this brutal killer before he brings tragedy to another family.'

After several months, to Hoban's obvious distress, his men were getting nowhere. He had tried everything he knew to push the inquiry forward, but the search for the killer was like hunting for a ghost. Every line of inquiry that could be followed was followed. A thousand Land-Rover drivers were checked out. Nothing. Dodgy punters were closely questioned. Nothing. The prostitutes were asked time and again to rack their brains to identify clients who might have been capable of two brutal murders. Countless men were checked as a result. Nothing. An artist's impression was drawn of the man with the bushy beard. Nothing. He wrote to local family doctors asking them to come forward with the names of patients who might be capable of killing prostitutes. He was frustrated yet again. The Patients' Association said such a request would prevent men with violent impulses from seeking medical help. The British Medical Association merely restated that the relationship between doctors and patients was confidential.

Hoban was getting weary and his health was suffering. His diabetes was taking its toll and he began to complain to Betty about a pain in his eye. The strong possibility of the killer striking again continued to bother him. By the time the inquests into both the deaths opened in May 1976, he had little new to say apart from the fact that he was certain the two women had been murdered by the same man. Hoban also knew there was a desperately cruel paradox. If there was to be any hope of apprehending the killer, more clues were needed: fresh clues and lines of inquiry that could only be forthcoming if the killer struck again. Another woman would probably have to die. Hoban could only wait.

2

The Diabetic Detective

Dennis Hoban liked what he knew and his entire life was spent living in the north-west quadrant of Leeds. It was his town, he knew its people, and via the medium of local television and newspapers they knew him. It was the city's prosperity which had drawn his family there. Both his father and grandfather were Irish immigrants from Cork. His father had been first a lorry driver, then a sales rep for a haulage firm. Dennis was born in 1926, the year of the General Strike.

When Hoban became a fully fledged detective in 1952, Leeds was an overcrowded town bursting at the seams, with masses of substandard housing fit only for demolition. Some 90,000 homes needed demolishing, 56,000 of them squalid back-to-backs built a hundred years earlier eighty to ninety to the acre. Post-war housing estates were planned and built across the city, but the council house waiting list stretched out for twenty years. It made Hoban and Betty determined to own their own home.

Their first son was born while they were living next to Dennis's parents in Stanningley, a working-class district well to the west of the city centre. Then they moved to nearby Bramley, where Betty's widowed mother came to join them. In the late 1960s the couple bought a brand-new Wimpey home with a large garden on the Kirkstall–Headingley borders, even though Hoban was the world's worst and least interested

35

gardener. Neither could he turn his hand to DIY in the home, though he loved cars. Shortly after they married he had bought the chassis of a Morris 8 which stood on the drive of their home. Hoban rebuilt it with a wooden frame and aluminium sheeting, but his real hobby was being a policeman. Whatever cars the family possessed were frequently used in his job, often taking part in high-speed car chases.

While his close-knit family endured his obsession with work, all his working life Hoban coped with two ailments, diabetes and asthma. The regime of daily insulin injections was bothersome. Lazy about using his hypodermic syringe, he had no routine for taking insulin. Consequently there were plenty of times when he felt 'squiggly', the word he used for being hypoglycaemic. Then he knew he had to eat something sweet, usually a few cakes from the kitchen pantry. He would administer the insulin in a very haphazard way, never at specific times. Then it would be jab – straight into his thigh. 'He didn't look after himself,' his son Richard reflected. 'He didn't live in a world where he could look after himself. He never ate well because he was at his best when he was in pubs and clubs and smoky dives getting information from his snouts.'

The family evening meal was often a snatched affair. He would arrive home, wash, shave, eat, watch the Yorkshire TV soap opera *Emmerdale Farm*, and then be off back to work. He rarely smoked. It would have exacerbated his asthma, already made worse in his early years by the fact that Leeds was one of the most polluted places in the North of England. Soot and smoke from the mills and factories were blown over the town by the prevailing south-westerly winds. For several generations those who could afford it had moved to the cleaner areas of Leeds in the Northern Heights, and ultimately Hoban and Betty joined them.

They had only just moved round the corner to a new and slightly bigger semi-detached house in 1976 when, a few weeks after the inquest verdicts on Wilma McCann and Emily Jackson, they learned he was on the move professionally. As part of a wider reshuffle among the senior management, he was being transferred to the West Yorkshire force headquarters at Wakefield, fifteen miles away. He was to be deputy to the new CID chief of the amalgamated force. A West Riding man, George Oldfield, was being promoted to assistant chief constable (crime). Within a few months Hoban had moved offices to the brand-new divisional police headquarters in Bradford, still as Oldfield's deputy, but this time in charge of the CID for the entire Western area of the force.

Two and a half years after the amalgamation between West Yorkshire Police and the Leeds and Bradford city forces, the chief constable, Ronald Gregory, had decided to make crucial changes among the senior management. Moving senior personnel around would provide a better balance between the city and county forces. West Riding men transferred into the Leeds and Bradford divisions – some of the senior city boys had to bite the bullet and move to towns like Pontefract, Huddersfield and Halifax. A new culture was being created and these moves were not always popular. Enmities and petty rivalries abounded. Bradford police viewed Leeds detectives as 'flash bastards'. 'More gold than a Leeds detective,' was a popular saying among the Bradford CID, a reference to their Leeds colleagues' penchant for wearing gold wrist identity bracelets and rings bearing a gold sovereign. Leeds and Bradford officers called their West Riding colleagues 'Donkey Wallopers' or 'The Gurkhas' – because they took no prisoners, a reference not to West Riding detectives 'finishing off the enemy', but a belief by the city men that the county boys hardly ever got to make an arrest.

These important structural changes in the way Yorkshire and the rest of the country was policed had been a long time coming. The amalgamations, creating one big West Yorkshire force covering half a million acres and a population of more than 2 million, had been delayed for more than half a century. Bringing about cost efficiencies and rational organization to law enforcement had been a drawn-out, tortuous process. For almost a hundred years very little had altered in the way the various police forces of Britain were controlled.

By this time the West Riding of Yorkshire no longer existed officially. At the stroke of a pen in 1974 a massive local government reorganization approved by Parliament did away with a nomenclature that had defined an entire region of Northern England for hundreds of years. The East, West and North Ridings of Yorkshire – titles originating from the Anglo-Saxon word *thriding*, meaning 'a third' – became mere counties, bits and pieces of their local geography seemingly thrown into the air by civil servants and politicians in London, only to land as new structures called Humberside, North Yorkshire, South Yorkshire and West Yorkshire.

Hoban's home town of Leeds had managed to weather the storms of economic upheaval over the years better than most. In the immediate post-war years, it remained a giant among the great manufacturing towns. In 1952 it was at the centre of the world's clothing industry. Montague Burton was the world's largest multiple tailor, with 600 outlets. Burton's was only one of several large clothing factories in Leeds, all of which subsequently closed. In the words of Denis Healey, a local MP: 'It went on making three-piece suits long after people stopped wearing waistcoats, and failed to adapt to the growing taste for casual wear.'

Leeds was a key part of England's central industrial belt,

whose origins, wealth and history had been essentially determined by two pieces of natural good fortune. First was the topography of the landscape across Yorkshire from the Pennines going eastwards – rough moorland and fells capable of little but sustaining sheep farming. It had done this for centuries. In addition there was the availability of vast quantities of water. Via becks and streams flowing off the fells and moors, water from the heavens poured into an abundance of river systems passing through the West Riding in its search for the sea. The rivers not only provided power for the wool and textile mills; their pure soft water also cleaned the wool. Later canals were built east and west of Leeds and waterways made navigable, allowing the wool, its finished products and other manufactures to be transported to both coasts. As the engines of the industrial revolution turned faster, so the population of Yorkshire's towns and cities multiplied. It doubled and doubled again.

By 1840 Leeds was an industrial and commercial centre with a population of 150,000 and still expanding. Fifty years on and the official census of 1891 recorded Leeds' population as 395,000. Many were immigrants or their descendants. They had come flooding in initially in the early 1800s from the rural areas of England, but also from deprived parts of Scotland and then Ireland, following the potato famine. Later in the 1880s they were joined by Jews escaping the pogroms in Poland and the province of Knovo in Russia. The only word in English many Jewish immigrants knew was 'Leeds'. In an effort to escape compulsory military conscription or religious persecution, they had headed for the place which for them signified a modern term for El Dorado.

Dominating the city centre was the magnificent edifice of the town hall, built to demonstrate the achievements of a city bursting with pride at its commercial and industrial dynamism. But where the urban poor were concerned, Leeds, like many other overcrowded British cities, had little to celebrate. In 1858 a sizeable number of the town's then 15,000 Irish immigrants, who lived in some of the worst housing, were said to have been among the cheering crowds of more than 100,000 who waved flags and shouted greetings to Queen Victoria as she arrived to perform the opening ceremony for the new town hall. The streets were lined with palm trees and triumphal arches and some 18,000 people sang the National Anthem. Looking down on the scene, the town hall's massive clock tower, rising 225 feet above the new building, was the finishing touch, symbolizing Leeds at its grandest. Yet unseen by the sovereign were the depressing conditions in which many of her subjects existed.

Leeds truly was a perfect example of what Disraeli termed the 'Two Nations'. It was a town with a physical divide. While great swathes were dirty, soot-ridden, cramped and crowded, other areas, in the Northern Heights, provided cleaner air and fashionable housing for the middle classes. The wealthy escaped the dirt and soot while the tens of thousands of the urban poor who provided the raw manpower for the factories and workshops were herded into overcrowded, insanitary dwellings. Drinking houses and brothels abounded. There were thirteen brothels within a hundred yards of where one unsuspecting churchman had his rooms. He noted that, 'The proceedings of these miserable creatures who tenanted them were so openly disgusting that I was obliged to call in the rule of law to abate the nuisance.' Forty-six beerhouses were closed down by police on the grounds that they were frequented by thieves, prostitutes and 'persons of bad character'. Prostitutes were easily distinguished from factory girls in beerhouses by their tawdry finery and the bareness of their necks, though the costume and headdresses of the factory girls were not dissimilar. In many establishments there was a convenience upstairs for vice. Lord Shaftesbury described parts of Leeds as 'a modern equivalent of Sodom'.

In accordance with the wishes of the town's middle classes, prostitution in Leeds in the 1850s was controlled by the police rather than banned. They classified and kept a register of the proprietors and inmates of the town's eighty-five brothels and lodging houses. This 'has tended materially to check disorder and to aid the police in detecting crime and bring offenders to justice', said the chief constable at the time. 'Any attempt at the removal of these places would answer no good, for the sons and daughters of vice would find a resting place elsewhere and most like would get into respectable neighbourhoods where their proximity would be deeply deplored.'

Had Queen Victoria taken a full guided tour, she would have gone to the rear of the new town hall, which was used as court and bridewell. Below ground she would have entered a different world, one of thievery, violence and drunkenness. Known as the Central Charge Office, the bridewell held prisoners arrested within the town who awaited an appearance in court. The original cells, situated under the front steps, each contained a wooden bench and shackle rings for wrist and ankle; stone-flagged floors, whitewashed walls and gas lighting. A cell held up to four prisoners, each entitled to half a loaf of bread, a pint of ale and sufficient straw for bedding. Right through to the late 1970s, the central bridewell remained a forbidding place. Hoban even gave his young sons a guided tour of the 'dungeons'. The eighteen cells had no natural light, ventilation or exercise facilities. Conditions in the bridewell, which failed to clear legal certification, had long been criticized, and just at the point of Hoban's move to Wakefield the Home Office cut an improvement programme to save money.

Leeds had formed its own police force in 1836, paid for out of local rates and overseen by a watch committee made up of local burgers. Like many other newly formed police forces, they were also responsible for fire-fighting. Money for equipment, clothing and everything else came from local funding. The wealthy and local taxes paid for peace and law and order. The preservation of peace and good order were the central priorities laid down by the members of the watch committees. Neighbouring Bradford, slower off the mark in setting up its own police force, did so in 1848. Its headquarters were in a building which housed the city's fire engines. Police out-stations in both cities were linked to headquarters by morse-code telegraph until the 1890s, when they were replaced by telephones and police call boxes.

Before 1968 the West Riding of Yorkshire was served by nine separate forces. In addition to Leeds and Bradford, the city of Wakefield and the boroughs of Dewsbury, Halifax, Huddersfield, Barnsley and Doncaster each had their own local force. Most were small organizations. The surrounding local government county area had a force based at Wakefield called the West Riding Constabulary. In 1956 it had 354 men in its ranks. Covering a vast geographical area, it was way ahead of other forces in recognizing the importance of keeping intelligence on criminals and was one of the first in the country to establish a criminal intelligence bulletin, the *West Riding Police Reports*. This confidential publication, printed on the West Riding's own printing press at the force headquarters, circulated details of crimes and wanted villains between forces.

A 1920 Report by a Parliamentary Committee praised the West Riding's lead in drawing up a list of classes of criminals by their *modus operandi*. The force's chief constable stressed the importance of creating a *central* clearing house of intelligence information: 'Its full advantage cannot be developed unless the reports are complete and in the proper form.' The system was mostly used in the North of England, and not by all forces even then. The First World War interrupted a plan to introduce a similar scheme in the Midlands and the South of England. The Parliamentary Committee was enthusiastic about the West Riding clearing house and believed it to be a big advance not only in detecting crime but also in the systematization of the detective method. 'The greatest advantage should be taken of it,' they said, and recommended the Home Office and Scottish Office to develop it further and extend it across the whole of Britain.

Twenty-first century computers can store limitless amounts of information and be programmed to draw links between seemingly unconnected facts in an intelligent way. Police forces around the world, like every other institution and business, are now utterly dependent on them. But in Hoban's time there were no computers in which local intelligence could be stored. He and his detectives in a murder incident room relied on a card index system, with its complex classifications.

The Parliamentary Committee investigating the police service in 1919–20 was given a simple example where police officers knew how a particular criminal worked, but had no way of passing on the information. There was a burglar in Liverpool who regularly defecated in a corner in every house he broke into. This was known to detectives in the city but not outside Liverpool. How could they inform other forces and how could they communicate the information? 'There is any amount of knowledge which is not available beyond the actual man who possesses it, or the actual police force which records it,' a witness told the committee. 'It is difficult to classify that sort of thing. Every police officer had this knowledge fifteen or sixteen years ago, and we tried to card it in Liverpool but we were up against another difficulty. We had many of these cards describing the methods followed by the particular criminal described on the card, but we had no system by which we could index them. So except for the personal memory of the man who prepared the cards, and he had a very good memory, the thing was valueless and we would not get out an index.'

The person who in 1909 solved this problem for Britain's police was the then chief constable of the West Riding, Major-General L. W. Atcherley. He got the cooperation of all neighbouring county and borough forces and established a clearing house for information at his Wakefield HQ. In this way intelligence reports about the routes used by travelling thieves and swindlers were analysed. It was well known that thieves travelled to other towns to commit crimes and had long been doing so. In April 1853 three pickpockets from Leeds were arrested among a large crowd come to witness an execution at York Castle, along with numerous other petty thieves who had travelled from as far afield as Manchester and Yarmouth.

By a careful comparison of a *modus operandi* and a personal description of the criminal, a long list of undetected crimes committed by the same man in different police authorities could be cleared up. Different ways of committing crimes like larceny were broken down and filed separately. A handbook let an individual officer understand and use the system with little delay. He was taught the clues to look for. 'Four years' experience in the West Riding with its twenty-two divisions has proved the utility of this system and although the number of cases of reported crime in the county police area has increased by a third, the percentage of undetected crime is very low, and much less in proportion to what it used to be in former years,' a report revealed immediately prior to the First World War.

The 'peculiarity of method', according to the 1920 Parliamentary Report, gave the policemen their clues to solving crime. 'The leading feature of the Wakefield system which is proving its value against the modern travelling thief and swindler, is the investigation of crime through its methods. In the past, knowledge of this sort has remained far too much in the possession of this or that policeman or this or that police force ... the clearing house is the machinery for the detection of crime.' This prescient observation came to have real force more than sixty years later during the Yorkshire Ripper investigation. The keeping of records, and how and where they were administered, was a key feature unrecognized during the prolonged murder hunt, and it had the most tragic results.

Of all the great institutions in Britain, the police service has been among the slowest to bring about radical reform. The prime reason has been the jealously guarded principle that police forces should be subject to control by local communities through watch committees. The argument raged for more than a hundred years. Bradford and Leeds successfully stayed out of the great amalgamation in 1968, only to be absorbed into the West Yorkshire force six years later. Historically, British police forces have been fiercely independent, even leading to arguments over whether the 'office of constable' was one subject to local or central control under the British constitution. Towns and boroughs fought to achieve the right to choose their own chief constable rather than have one imposed on them by government. Legislation to bring about reform was seen as interfering with their independent control over the organization and expenditure of the police force in their area.

When amalgamations were proposed, they often met with fierce resistance – not least in Yorkshire. The city of York mounted vigorous opposition to legislation which would have amalgamated forces in the 1850s, provided money from the Treasury for efficient forces, and set up a system of inspections. York also opposed Palmerston's Police Bill, fearing 'the police would become a standing army entrusted with powers unheard of in the darkest ages of tyranny'. The *York Herald* proclaimed: 'To surrender up the control of the police to the executive government would be an act of folly which every lover of constitutional liberty ought to do all in his power to prevent.' County magistrates and local watch committees would become mere puppets: 'Local control of policing which allowed local communities to decide which form of policing best suited them would disappear.'

In 1920 Parliament heard arguments pleading for police forces to be banded together if they were to become more efficient. Forty-eight police forces had less than twenty-five men in their ranks and forty forces had less than fifty officers. The boroughs of Louth and Tiverton consisted of a chief constable, two sergeants and eight constables; total strength: eleven men. Bigger forces meant better administration, training and the chance for individual officers to gain wider experience.

Amalgamations were still high on the agenda when the Royal Commission on the Police reported in 1962. So was the question of the educational standards of men being recruited into the police service. The 1920 Parliamentary Committee had found the system lacking in this respect; so did the Report of the Royal Commission. 'We have come across no recent instance of a university graduate entering the service, only about 1 per cent of recruits have two or more GCE A levels, a further 10 per cent have five subjects or more at O level and an additional 20 per cent have one to four O levels.' The report strongly criticized the police service for failing to recruit anything like its proper share of able, well-educated young men. The commissioners' principal concern was being able to attract sufficient recruits who would make good chief constables fifteen or twenty years hence. This without question remained a problem for the British police force for generations. 'They preferred to educate the recruited rather than recruit the educated,' said one senior detective, closely involved in the Yorkshire Ripper case, who had himself given up a university place to get married and join the police force.

Absence of a grammar school or university education had not proved a barrier to men like Hoban, who had left school aged fourteen with no qualifications, joined the Leeds City Police aged twenty-one, and in 1960 become the force's youngest detective inspector. He achieved promotion on grounds of merit and consistent hard work. The police force in Leeds which Dennis Hoban joined in 1947 after wartime service in the Royal Navy aboard motor torpedo boats had hardly changed in technological terms since Edwardian times. They still carried whistles to draw attention. It was only in 1930 that the city police got its own motor patrol section and even then it consisted of one motor car, one three-wheeled vehicle, two motorcycle combinations and a solo motorcycle. For years bicycles provided the extra mobility for the forces of law and order in their everyday fight against crime.

Leeds got its first police boxes containing a telephone in 1931, and these were the mainstay of communication with officers on the beat until the 1950s, when they were replaced by telephones in pillars. Communication between police stations and headquarters was by wireless. In 1955, by which time Hoban was a fully fledged plain-clothes detective, thirty-three police cars in the city were fitted with radios, but it was to be another ten years before individual personal radio sets were issued to officers. In the mid-1950s, Leeds had had plain-clothes detectives for a hundred years, but specialization within the town's CID did not emerge until the 1960s, with the setting up of crime squads, a drug squad in 1967 and a stolen vehicles squad in 1970. Hoban, in the early 1960s, took part in an experimental project involving undercover detectives working over a wide area and drawn from several major cities, towns and county forces. They targeted major criminals, using covert surveillance to gather intelligence, often over weeks and months at a time. It was the forerunner of the Regional Crime Squads.

Many smaller towns had their own chief constables – but less than 300 officers. Unlike Hoban's family, plenty of police officers were tied tenants, living in police houses, including some of the senior officers. There were considerable restrictions in terms of promotion. Some smaller towns, like Dewsbury and Wakefield, had to advertise externally to obtain suitably qualified senior officers above the rank of inspector. The efficiency of the police was a key phrase during the post Second World War period, when important questions about the future were being discussed. Efficiency wasn't simply a value-for-money term, it also called in question the ability of the police to tackle modern problems, and especially modern criminals, who were far more mobile, being prepared to live in one area of the country and commit crime in another. By the time Parliament voted for large-scale amalgamations in the early 1960s, they were long overdue. Rising crime rates were a national problem.

Once amalgamations had taken place, the actual moulding of large new forces from smaller ones carried sizeable headaches in terms of management. Some towns had given their constables special rights. For example, in Huddersfield Borough a constable could not be moved from his home without his consent. Many a police officer, either buying his own home or firmly settled with a young family in a police house, refused to be uprooted and sent to the other side of the county. West Riding officers were used to being moved, but those in the towns and cities were familiar with their back yard and had got used to it. There were other privileges. Huddersfield being a textile town, officers had uniforms made of specially woven cloth, dyed and finished in police indigo blue – top quality worsted – a reflection of the predominance of wool merchants on the local watch committee. Pride dictated that their officers be dressed in the best cloth – and the uniforms were tailor made. 'Then we went into the West Riding,' said one who went on to become a senior detective, 'and it was like the army, they got the nearest bloody size. There were only two sizes – too big and too small.'

The Leeds City Force of Hoban and his colleagues, with a strength of 1,300 men, was already bigger than some of the newly amalgamated county forces like Cumbria, Wiltshire, Suffolk and Dorset. Plenty of policemen and politicians in Leeds and nearby Bradford wanted the two cities to combine into one large metropolitan force instead of being lumped together with the rest of West Yorkshire. The ever-expanding Leeds–Bradford conurbation is such that the two are for all practical purposes virtually joined together, separated only by a small tract of land; even the local regional airport is called Leeds–Bradford, though each city retains its separate identity.

Hoban's move to the Wakefield HQ, and later to Bradford

as No. 2 in the force Criminal Investigation Department, was greeted with some dismay by his close colleagues, who believed he should have got the top job. Privately they blamed inter-force politics. The chief constable was West Riding; his deputy came from Leeds. The retiring assistant chief constable (crime), Donald Craig, was a West Riding man. So was George Oldfield, who had been deputy ACC (crime) and was now being moved up a rank. When Oldfield was named it raised hackles, not least because he had upset a good number of Leeds detectives during the 1960s when he carried out an investigation into alleged police corruption in the city. To put it mildly, Oldfield had trampled over a lot of city officers to get to the truth. Hoban wasn't involved, but it may not have been internal politics alone which affected his future career prospects.

Hoban was seen as an officer possibly destined for pro-motion. Indeed, he himself seriously considered applying for an ACC position. His energy and enormous operational experience as the deputy coordinator of the Regional Crime Squad, and subsequently as head of Leeds CID, had marked him out as the kind of senior man who might benefit personally from the amalgamation. West Yorkshire Metropolitan Police was now a force of 5,000 officers, making it one of the biggest in the country in terms of manpower. There was plenty of opportunity for good men to succeed. But Hoban was going to have to wait before being moved further up the promotion ladder. He needed greater management experience. Where paperwork – the bureaucracy of running a large team of officers – was concerned, his boredom threshold was very low. He frequently passed the buck to junior colleagues, sometimes dumping an in-tray of documentation on them with the words: 'Sort that lot out – I'll be back later.'

Brilliant detective he may have been; skilled at administration he wasn't. Virtually his entire career had been at the sharp end of detective work: feeling collars, making arrests, locking up criminals, and in the process earning twenty-nine commendations from judges, magistrates and senior officers. For this he had been awarded the Queen's Police Medal (QPM) in 1974, a mark of great merit in the police service. 'It's for what you have done, rather than what you are going to do,' said one of Hoban's contemporaries.

Few of Hoban's senior detective colleagues around the country at that time had received the QPM, and in 1975 another honour came his way – an award for gallantry, the Queen's Commendation for Brave Conduct. Alerted by a blackmailer's phone call that a bomb had been planted in the Leeds city branch of Woolworths, Hoban went immediately to the scene. The blackmailer had demanded £50,000 for revealing the whereabouts of the explosive device in the packed store. Staff and shoppers were quickly evacuated and a suspicious holdall was discovered in the toilets, placed on top of the cistern. Inside were explosives and a timing device. A fire brigade hosepipe was placed inside the room and Hoban proceeded to stand on top of the toilet seat and reach with one hand into the bag and hold the device while detaching two wires with the other. Hoban thought there was about twenty minutes left before the device went off, and he knew the bomb disposal squad could not reach Leeds from Catterick in time. He disconnected the wires from the battery before the army arrived, so defusing the device.

It was a typical piece of reckless heroism, for which he was named Leeds' first Citizen of the Year by the Junior Chamber of Commerce. But it gave Betty nightmares. She had been on at him to retire as soon as he completed his thirty years' service. Betty grew resentful, which added to the constant stress she felt about the way Dennis had put his job first throughout the whole of their married life. He never took off the time due to him and frequently worked a fourteen-hour day or longer. She would often say: 'Please don't go in today' – but some inner compulsion clearly made him put his job first. On the few occasions when they did get the chance to go out together, there would be a telephone call and Betty would be left high and dry. They could never plan a proper holiday. And when they did go as a family to Scarborough with their two sons, after three days away from the job, Dennis needed to get on the phone. According to his son, Richard, many years later: 'It was as if he was suffering withdrawal symptoms.' 'If we got to Christmas Day and we got as far as Christmas dinner, he would have to go to the office for a couple of hours.'

Hoban loved his family, and the feeling was mutual, but always, always in the eyes of his wife and two boys, the job came first. Richard Hoban remembers being carried in his father's arms at the age of three on a family shopping trip in an arcade in Leeds when they witnessed a jewel robbery. 'I was slung into the arms of my mother and off he went, hurtling after this jewellery thief and caught him. It was the last we saw of him for several hours.'

At home, Richard, his brother David and their mother would become Hoban's telephone answering service, which included taking messages from informants. 'We would be "Leeds 66815" – the number is etched on my memory. The snouts would say: "Is that Richard? Tell your dad something's going to happen, tell him to get in touch with me and it will cost him ten bob or a couple of quid or whatever." Occasionally you'd get someone ringing up who'd crossed my Dad's path at some time and they'd tell me what they were going to do to me or David or my mother.' As well as the household's phone being used in the fight against crime, the family blue and white Triumph Herald was used to chase criminals. Once Hoban crashed it into a bridge trying to stop someone escaping his clutches.

He loved being where the action was: nabbing villains, being involved in car chases, arresting criminals at an armed bank robbery. Even at the rank of detective superintendent, as the deputy coordinator of the regional crime squad a decade earlier, he made sure he was at the sharp end, posing under-cover as a taxi driver complete with cap when a notorious gang was under surveillance. The gang had him drive from Leeds to Grimsby via a nightclub in Doncaster. He had to decline an invitation to go into the nightclub, because the moment the gang got out of the vehicle it was commandeered by a group of drunken sailors who wanted to be taken back to Grimsby. He then returned and collected the gang when they had finished drinking. Later the undercover squad of detectives, secretly guarding Hoban, were treated by him to a night out on the proceeds of the fare for the long trip, paid by the gang. He wasn't exaggerating when he told a journalist: 'It's more than just a job – coppering is a way of life, a hobby, everything – I wouldn't swap it for anything.'

While Hoban's abilities as a detective were considerable, his critics could point to his relatively narrow experience in terms of large-scale policing. As one of the biggest constabularies in the country, the new West Yorkshire force would provide plenty of opportunity for qualified men to move up the pro-motion ladder. All things being equal, Hoban should have been one of those. But his detractors, all of whom came from the old West Yorkshire force, believed his driven personality was a major barrier to him obtaining higher rank. Some accused him of self-aggrandisement, always pushing himself forward –

anxious to have his photograph taken for the *Yorkshire Post* or the northern editions of the national press; or keen to offer himself for interviews on television. From Hoban's viewpoint, communicating with the public was a big part of the job. He was well known throughout Leeds as the city's top detective, and he used this image to speak directly to the man or woman in the street, in the hope that they might come forward with some vital clue. A few very senior but quite impartial colleagues saw his administrative weakness as a major flaw.

Some senior West Riding detectives had worked closely with both Hoban on the regional crime squad based at Brotherton House in Leeds and the new ACC (crime) George Oldfield, the senior detective in the West Riding force. They viewed Oldfield, a former wartime Royal Navy petty officer, as the better team player. 'Dennis was a seat of his pants operator, always a bit fly and capable of going off at tangents. He had a single objective – to catch criminals, and at that he was brilliant. But a modern police force needs people with a broader perspective.'

This professional criticism of Dennis Hoban was a reflection of the different cultures of policing in the bigger towns and cities. It also reflected different methods of tackling serious crime. The West Riding's operational procedures for solving murders were radically different from those in operation within Leeds before the 1974 amalgamation. The old West Riding force had a paper-led system which was time consuming in the short term but in the long term garnered evidence in statement form from witnesses which would in a protracted inquiry prove crucial in mounting a successful prosecution. Prior to amalgamation, most provincial borough and county force murder inquiries involved bringing in a senior detective from Scotland Yard, because historically the Metropolitan

Police was the only force in the country with wide experience of dealing with homicides. County forces tended to adopt the Metropolitan Police way of doing things. The bigger cities, like Leeds, Bradford and Manchester, had the manpower and experience to run murder inquiries without help from the Yard. Each had its own system for tackling murders. The Manchester force took very few statements in a major crime investigation until they were needed for court proceedings. In Leeds, Hoban operated a similar system. Like a general on the battlefield, he was in charge of strategy. He relied on his middle managers to keep him briefed on those lines of inquiry most likely to yield results. He never immersed himself in detail until it was absolutely essential, and as a consequence rarely needed to read reams of paperwork.

Most murders in Britain are solved quickly because there is some domestic involvement such as the victim being known to the killer. In Leeds, Hoban could throw a hundred officers into a murder inquiry and blitz the local area in terms of finding crucial evidence. Over time in Leeds, this method proved very efficient because it found the link between the victim and the killer. Hoban solved nearly all the fifty murders he had tackled, but by the time he was moved to force headquarters at Wakefield, the killer of McCann and Jackson still totally eluded him. He realized that the man who killed these two women had struck at random. They had simply been unlucky victims. In terms of solving murders, finding killers without a personal motive was a nightmare for everyone – the public as well as the police.

One senior officer from outside Yorkshire reckoned that Hoban was the best detective he ever met: 'He had that great amalgamation of all those qualities that it takes. He had an ability to pick, which is very important. He had an ability to listen to you even though he might not agree with you. He made you feel comfortable in his presence. He had all the qualities you require in a man who is trying to do that job. He has confidence in his team, to let his team deal with the dross and to say to him: "Here you are, boss – this is the one you should look at." Not for him to be in the sea of what is going on but to be looking at the one aspect really likely to produce a result. He had the ability to pick people round him who were really good and that is a great quality in any senior policeman: "Can you pick the people who've got qualities you haven't got that can support you well?"

'Dennis Hoban was a very pragmatic, hands-on murder investigator. A lot of people say he overplayed the PR, but I personally don't believe that. Crime detection is about the senior detective being good at PR. There are all those members of the public out there who can help you, yet you have only a few men to make inquiries, so that mobilization of the public is very important, and Dennis did it.'

In Hoban's view, public support was at its most crucial in murder inquiries. As a detective, he had too often seen the results of the sudden impulse to kill. As a father, he was absolutely strict with his own sons and he despaired of the way young people were surrounded by violence, seeing it almost as an illness of society: 'The trouble is that youngsters today see violence all around them, every day. It's becoming the norm. They see a man getting hit over the head with an iron bar on a television programme, and the man shakes his head and walks away. But it's not like that in real life. What can and does happen is that the man probably ends up with a steel plate in his head, brain damage, deafness or blindness. He loses his job and his family can break up. I have come across many a criminal who, when faced with the reality of his crime, has had a change of heart. The criminal should be made to pay for his crime. I am a believer in the deterrent effect of hanging, I believe it works.'

Each year Leeds saw, on average, ten homicides, most of them solved because of some link between killer and victim which Hoban's team managed to uncover. The difficulty came when no such link was found. Most colleagues who knew Hoban well felt he had an extraordinary knack for solving murders and getting the best out of his men, often working on hunches which proved amazingly accurate. He rarely pulled rank, because he didn't need to, and he displayed remarkable qualities of leadership because he earned the respect of his troops as both man and detective. His key ability was to weigh up the suspect psychologically, a knack which proved him right time and time again. These hunches were the result of years of experience, observation and a deep understanding of people. He always gave credit to the team who worked for him, leading from the front, showing a sense of humour and often pushing himself for forty-eight hours at a stretch, particularly with serious crimes like murders, where he knew you had to crack it early while people's memories were still fresh.

A perfect example of his approach came in the early 1970s when he masterminded a murder inquiry and threw every resource he had at the problem for thirty-three days. Within a few minutes of the body of Mrs Phyllis Jackson, a fifty-year-old mother of two, being found brutally murdered at her home in Dewsbury Road, Leeds, a master plan for homicide investigations was put into operation. A vehicle equipped with a radio went to the murder scene to act as a control point and a hundred detectives were drafted in immediately. There was evidence she had been raped.

The answer would most probably lie close to the victim and

her lifestyle – find the motive, then find the link to the killer. A murder incident room was opened at the police HQ in Westgate. One vital clue emerged from the post-mortem. Mrs Jackson had been strangled, then stabbed with a knife which probably had a serrated edge. A massive search began that included bringing in the army with mine detectors, which made for great photographs and local television news footage that Hoban knew would keep the murder in the public eye. Corporation workmen searched the drains, and every conceivable place where a fleeing killer might have hidden the murder weapon was searched. Much of this was standard in an unsolved homicide, but the procedure was galvanized by Hoban's sense of urgency, enthusiasm and inspiration.

Experience had shown him the killer was most likely a local man. The victim lived in a new housing scheme within a development area, but with no local facilities to attract people from outside – no cinema, shops or places of entertainment. Anyone present in the area was most likely to be there because they were acquainted with someone locally rather than having stumbled on the place by accident. When the search for the weapon proved fruitless, Hoban tried another tack. A survey of every home in the vicinity was carried out. Every day detectives went to local houses armed with a questionnaire to establish exactly where every man in each household had been at the time of the murder and to see if anyone had noticed anything suspicious.

By such painstaking methods are murders traditionally solved. Reports filtered in about other attacks on women in the city, and while each was carefully probed, none could be linked to the murder of Phyllis Jackson either by method or motive. Fear among women in the city became palpable. There was a run on people buying door locks and safety chains, and stocks at hardware shops ran out in some areas. Special lifeline buzzers were distributed to the elderly so they could summon help if frightened. Some two hundred calls a day were coming in to the incident room offering information, and each call was followed up by detectives working long hours. At that time police officers were very poorly paid, so a chance of overtime was rarely turned down. Murders frequently made the difference for a young detective between having or not having a week's holiday with his kids at Bridlington, Scarborough or Filey.

Every house within a half-mile radius of the murder scene was visited – without a breakthrough. So Hoban extended the search area by another half-mile. A twenty-year-old illiterate Irish labourer living with his wife in a corporation flat in Hunslet filled in a questionnaire that attracted attention. This former altar boy from County Wicklow, one of twenty-two children, learned many passages from the bible by heart, but he was a womanizer. He had been working on a sewer scheme near the murder scene and claimed that on the afternoon of the murder he saw a man running down Dewsbury Road. He identified the individual involved. But when the other man was checked, his alibi for the time of the murder was perfect – witnesses confirmed his presence in Leicester.

The Irish labourer had recently been released for larceny in Dublin and Hoban's men were ordered to keep him under close observation day and night so he shouldn't escape the net tightening round him. Finally, as is so often the case, forensic scientists provided the proof. Despite the fact that the man had washed his bloodstained clothing at his kitchen sink, the Home Office laboratory in Harrogate found thirteen fibres on trousers belonging to the suspect exactly matching those from clothing the victim was wearing when she was killed. Moreover, two hairs, similar in colour and appearance to those of the Irishman, were found on the dead woman.

Another protected inquiry masterminded by Hoban began on 2 April 1974, the day after Leeds City was amalgamated with the West Yorkshire force. Lily Blenkarn, an eighty-year-old shopkeeper known to everyone as 'Old Annie', had been brutally killed in a burglary that went wrong. She was severely beaten and suffered horrendous injuries, including a broken jaw and broken ribs. One fingerprint was found on a toffee tin and another on a bolt on the rear door of the premises, a sweet and tobacco shop in a terraced street. Hoban was convinced they belonged to the killer and organized a mass fingerprinting of all males in the area. They were invited to come to two local police checkpoints to provide their fingerprints.

It was the first major operation for the newly amalgamated force and it involved 150 detectives and the task force, a hand-picked team of mobile reserves trained to work in major incidents. Some 24,000 people were interviewed in house-to-house inquiries, but some sixty men were unaccounted for. Some on the list had travelled abroad to Canada, Australia, Iceland and Hong Kong. Through Interpol they were traced and eliminated. The mass fingerprinting attracted huge media attention, including TV crews from America.

The killer turned out to be a cold, calm, sallow youth aged seventeen. He had persuaded a friend to give fingerprints in his place, allowing him to slip through the net. The one who impersonated him was the same who had given him an alibi early on in the inquiry. None of this came to light until the murderer gatecrashed a local party. When an argument ensued, he threw a brick through a window. Under arrest, his fingerprints were taken, and after a routine examination by the murder squad fingerprint experts they realized they had their

THE DIABETIC DETECTIVE

man and someone must have impersonated the killer and given his fingerprints twice. Hoban said it taught him a valuable lesson. Never take anything for granted. 'Should mass finger-printing be required again – people would be fingerprinted in their own front room.' It had been too easy for a killer deter-mined to cover his tracks to collude with someone else to cover up his crime. Hoban's inquiry had been thrown completely off the trail for a while.

Dennis Hoban's bid to find the killer of Wilma McCann and Emily Jackson was an ambition that completely eluded him. He felt utterly frustrated, but he had other concerns. The huge volume of crime on his patch never stopped growing. Other women were randomly murdered in similar style and for a while he briefly flirted with the idea that the same man might have struck again. Then his handiwork was ruled out. The file on the McCann and Jackson murders remained open, but resources eventually had to be switched elsewhere. There was a horrible but unremitting truth he had to reconcile him-self to: unless the killer struck again the chances of catching him were slim. So long as the murderer kept his head down, the investigation would go nowhere. Another poor unfortu-nate soul was probably going to die before this man could be put away.

3

'A Man with a Beard'

In 1963, a seventeen-year-old youth called Peter Sutcliffe appeared before local magistrates accused by Keighley Police of driving unaccompanied while being a provisional licence holder and for failing to display L-plates. There was a similar traffic conviction against him in May the following year at Bradford City Magistrates Court. They were the first of his eleven motoring convictions and an innocuous introduction to the judicial process. But a year later came a more serious encounter. Peter Sutcliffe's first criminal conviction.

On 17 May 1965 he was fined £5 with £2 7s. 6d. costs at the Bingley West Riding Magistrates Court for attempting to steal from an unattended motor vehicle. The brown-eyed labourer, with black curly hair and (at that time) a fresh, clean-shaven complexion, had been caught 'bang-to-rights' trying to break into cars. It had happened on a quiet Sunday night the previous March, in Old Main Street, Bingley, beside the river Aire, not far from his home on the other side of the Leeds and Liverpool Canal at Cornwall Road, in the Gilstead area of Bingley. He and another youth, Eric Robinson, had been seen trying the door handles of a locked car that had property left on the rear seat. They were disturbed by two people who saw the pair then try the door handles of other cars parked near by. Police were called and a Constable

Thornley quickly arrested the youth who would, ten years later, start a series of murderous attacks that became notorious in the annals of crime.

This conviction generated two separate official records: the first at the West Riding Regional Criminal Record Office at Wakefield, the second at the Central Criminal Record Office at New Scotland Yard in London. Each record detailed Sutcliffe's name, age, date of birth, address, description and information about the offence. More motoring convictions followed in 1965 and 1966, but these were never filed at the criminal record offices.

The next recorded criminal violation by Peter Sutcliffe was during the early hours of 30 September 1969, in the Manningham area of Bradford, close to the city's red-light district. He was seen late at night sitting in a motor vehicle deliberately trying to be unobtrusive, with the engine running quietly and the lights switched off. When a police officer called Bland approached the vehicle, Sutcliffe immediately drove off at high speed. A search was carried out and the officer later found the car unattended a short distance away. When nearby gardens were searched, Sutcliffe was caught and arrested. *In his possession was a hammer.*

Questioned by police, he could not provide a satisfactory explanation for having the hammer, but denied criminal intent. He was charged only with the banal offence of going equipped to steal rather than being in possession of an offensive weapon. We now know from Peter Sutcliffe's own words that he fully intended attacking a woman that night, but the police had no inkling of this. Two weeks later he pleaded not guilty at Bradford City Magistrates' Court, but the case against him was found proved by the bench and he was fined £25, to be paid at £2 per week. The West Riding CRO based at Wakefield and the Bradford City Police, which had its own separate criminal records office, both listed this offence in their files as 'Going equipped for stealing', whereas their counterparts in the Central CRO at New Scotland Yard in London made crucial reference to: 'Equipped for stealing (*hammer*)' and listed under the heading 'Method' the words: 'In possession of housebreaking implement by night, *namely a hammer* [my italics]'. The Bradford criminal record office carried a passport-size head and shoulders photograph of the offender, whereas the West Riding CRO had three pictures of Sutcliffe in his file – one full length, one head and shoulders facing the camera, a third in profile. All three clearly showed Sutcliffe had dark curly hair, a dark-coloured beard and moustache.

For his next court appearance several years later, Sutcliffe presented the dapper and somewhat discordant colourful image for which he had become infamous within his circle of friends and family. He wore black trousers, brown platform shoes, a leather jacket with a multicoloured shirt and a red tie. By now he was married to the daughter of Czech émigrés and living with his parents-in-law at Tanton Cresent, Clayton, Bradford. He and a friend, Michael Barker, had stolen five second-hand car tyres worth 50 pence each from Sutcliffe's employer, the Common Road Tyre Company, where he worked as a driver. Sutcliffe had been employed as one of the firm's tyre fitters. On 15 October 1975, the company reported him to the police, claiming he had stolen tyres from them. When arrested and questioned Sutcliffe immediately admitted the offence and opened up the boot of his car to reveal his booty. By the time he appeared at Dewsbury Magistrates Court on 9 February 1976 to admit a charge of simple theft, Sutcliffe was already a double murderer. But there was nothing to connect him with those crimes. He was fined £25.

The name of Peter William Sutcliffe would not, in fact,

feature among the complex index card system in the murder incident room of the West Yorkshire Police 'Ripper Squad' until November 1977. Even then he was the subject of only a routine inquiry. But the fact remains that by the summer of 1976 the 'face' of the man who had killed twice and would go on to murder another eleven women was buried in a filing system. With the benefit of hindsight we now know he was a serial killer, but successful murder investigations are not about hindsight. They are about foresight, hunches, risks, intuition, leadership, good communication and, of course, a series of standard operating procedures which involve the time-consuming task of knocking on doors, asking questions and comparing the answers with other information in police files.

Yet the 'face' of the Ripper, and clues to what he looked like, were lying hidden in the police files of investigations into unsolved, unprovoked assaults on women and a fourteen-year-old schoolgirl at various locations across West Yorkshire during the preceding three and a half years. The victims had been attacked in similar ways by assailants bearing roughly the same description. Tragically for the women Sutcliffe subsequently killed or attempted to kill, for their families and for the children made motherless over the succeeding years, most of these horrendous assaults were never linked as part of any series. More crucially, police ignored the descriptions provided by survivors who had given near-perfect illustrations and helped to prepare photofits of a dark-haired man with a moustache and beard who looked uncannily like Sutcliffe. But in 1976 there was nothing to point to him as being more than a petty thief. When the photofits are seen together today – alongside a police mugshot of Peter Sutcliffe taken in September 1969 – it all looks so blindingly obvious.

*   *   *

It was nearly teatime in Wakefield one day in October 1998. An attractive woman approaching middle age, but whose striking good looks and long dark hair made her appear years younger, answered a knock at her front door. She spoke a few words with a researcher from a documentary film-making company who had called at her home unannounced. Within seconds she was in a state of shock and a feeling of coldness started to overwhelm her. Suddenly she had a flashback at the mention of a terrifying incident that had happened to her twenty-five years beforehand. In the intervening years she had spoken about it to very few people, pushing the subject to the back of her mind. The woman had since married, had two teenage children, and wished to maintain her anonymity. She invited the researcher into her neat, well-kept home. Ushering her into the lounge, she said in her quiet Scots accent: 'I was sure I had been attacked by the Yorkshire Ripper, but nobody had ever confirmed the fact.'

She was nineteen years old in 1972, working as a clerk-typist in a local firm. It was December, two days before New Year's Eve. 'I remember it like it was yesterday,' she went on. She was living on her own in a house in Westgate, at the bottom end of Wakefield. It was a 'queer' foggy night. She had been to 'Dolly Grey's' for a drink, but left quite early, about 10.30 p.m., and begun walking down Westgate towards home. As she neared the train station she realized she was being followed. She looked back at the man, noticing his staring eyes, dark longish hair, and beard. She clearly remembers thinking he was up to no good.

With her heart thumping, she carried on walking, thinking carefully about which route to take when she got near home. She planned carefully in her mind which way to get to her house, because there was a beck running at the front of where she lived and she feared the man might throw her in. A few houses near by belonged to prison officers at Wakefield's maximum security gaol, and she hoped against hope they might not have gone to bed.

Walking past a pub called The Swan with Two Necks, she toyed with the idea of going into one of the bars as people would still be on drinking-up time and she might know them and feel safe in their company. Then she had second thoughts, fearing they might wonder what on earth she was imagining. So she kept walking, still very anxious, and stuck to the middle of the pavement, trying to walk quickly past the ginnels – dark passageways that ran between some of the terraced houses.

She had just reached the row of houses where she lived when she was grabbed from behind. Immediately she screamed loudly and her attacker urgently put his hands over her mouth, telling her: 'Shurrup, shurrup,' a couple of times. She still remembered this vividly because his accent sounded local. As a Scot living in Yorkshire, she noticed immediately. She screamed out again and this time he hit her on the back of the head with his fist and pushed her into a low wall, where she received a graze to her face – her only real injury. One of the prison officers opened his bedroom window to see what was happening, and then swiftly came running downstairs to help, chasing after the attacker, but losing him.

The police came and the victim gave a statement. She was told to go to the local police station the following day, to help provide a photofit description. Next morning her sister accompanied her, but while she was there, she said, she felt as if she was the one under suspicion and thought the police did not take her seriously. She was very glad the prison officer could confirm her story. Before she went to the police station she had looked at a photograph of the pop singer 'Cat' Stevens

– because the attacker looked so similar. He had been a man in his mid-twenties of medium build and about five feet ten inches tall, with long dark hair, dark eyebrows, a beard and moustache, and a similar tuft of beard between chin and mouth. Years later, when the Yorkshire Ripper was apprehended and photographs of Peter Sutcliffe appeared in the newspapers and on television, she said out loud to her family: 'I'm sure that's the man who attacked me . . .' But after she made her initial complaint she never heard from the police again.

Almost two years later a twenty-eight-year-old student was attacked twenty-five miles away in Bradford. On 11 November 1974 Gloria Wood was approached as she walked across a school playing field some time between 7.30 and 8 p.m. A man offered to carry her bags and then attacked her about the head, causing severe injuries and a depressed fracture of the skull that left a crescent-shaped wound. The weapon was thought to be a claw hammer. According to the victim, the man had worn a dark suit and looked smartly dressed. She couldn't provide a photofit, but described him as being in his early thirties, 5 feet 8 inches tall and of medium build. He had dark curly hair to the neck, a short curly beard to the hairline. She was unable to remember how he spoke.

The summer of 1975 was long and hot. The sun continued to blaze down all day from clear blue skies for weeks on end. Clothes dried quickly on washing lines, reservoirs emptied, drought warnings were issued, the harvest was safely gathered in and half the country had hay fever. On the edge of the Pennines in West Yorkshire, a mile from the village of Silsden and its early eighteenth-century parish church of St James, lived the Browne family. Upper Hayhills Farm stood nearly 700 feet above sea level. It was there that Mrs Nora Browne bred dogs. She and her husband, Anthony, had four daughters, including fourteen-year-old twins, Tracey and Mandy. Like most parents they laid down house rules and expected their children to abide by them.

One August evening, with only a week or so to go before they returned to school, the twins went visiting friends in the village. Since it was still the school holiday, they were told to be home by 10.30 on what was a balmy, clear and moonlit night. Tracey had hung on too long saying goodbye to her pals while her sister went ahead up Bradley Road, knowing their dad would 'go mad' if they were late. As it was a clear summer's night in a remote rural area, their parents were not unduly concerned that Mandy arrived home first, minus her sister. The girls had walked up and down this country lane on their own dozens of times.

Tracey meanwhile was struggling, her young frame tottering uphill in platform-soled sandals. Her feet ached and as she sat down on a large stone beside the road to take off her sandals and rub them she noticed a stranger, in his late twenties or early thirties, also walking up the lane. He stopped briefly to look at her, standing only a few feet away as he drew level. Then he walked on. She wasn't afraid and assumed the man was living near by. Her only worry was to get home to avoid her father getting angry with her. The man was clearly dawdling since Tracey soon caught him up again.

'There's nothing doing in Silsden, is there?' he said.

'Not really,' she replied, walking beside him.

He then asked how far she had to go, and she answered casually: 'About a mile.' When he asked, she told him her name. He said his was 'Tony Jennis'. Tracey had a friend called Tony Jennison with whom she had spent a lot of time during the holidays playing at a local park. She believed this must be a coincidence, but kept the thought to herself. He then asked if she had a boyfriend and she said she had and that he lived in the village.

They continued walking in silence for a while, so Tracey got a good look at the man, who kept blowing his nose, as if affected by the high pollen count. His knitted V-neck cardigan with two pockets at the front was worn over a light blue open-necked shirt. He had dark Afro-style crinkly hair and beard. He wore flared, dark brown trousers with slit pockets at the front, and brown suede shoes. Suddenly, in his quiet, high-pitched voice, he said: 'My pal normally gives me a lift home but he's in the nick for drink driving.' That term 'the nick' stuck in her mind. The man seemed to be dropping back to tie his shoelace or blow his nose. He said he had a summer cold. Otherwise, he never took his hands out of his pockets. Tracey still had no reason to feel fear. Indeed, at times she stopped and waited for the man to catch her up. Finally they reached the gateway to the family farm and he hung back yet again. The pretty schoolgirl was about to turn towards the farmhouse. As well-brought-up kids do in the countryside, she intended to part on pleasant terms by thanking the stranger for his company. Instead she came under ferocious attack. Suddenly he rained down blows on her head and face. In his hand he held something heavy.

At that time a popular hero among young girls the world over was a handsome American tennis star who featured in the finals at Wimbledon. His name was Jimmy Connors and when he power-served to an opponent, he did something he became famous for. He let out an extraordinary grunt, '*eeeu-uuuugggghhhhhh*', as he unleashed an excess of forceful energy through arm and shoulder and simultaneously exhaled air from his lungs. Tracey Browne remembered how, with each blow to her head, the man trying to kill her made a similar grunting noise.

'Please don't, please don't,' she cried as the first blow drove her to her knees beside the tarmacked road. Her immediate thought was that this was the notorious 'Black Panther' – an as yet unapprehended multiple killer being hunted by police for the kidnapping and murder of the heiress Leslie Whittle. She even shouted out the name, 'Black Panther', several times in the hope someone would hear her. To no avail. By now, lying at the roadside, she was in a dreadful state, blinded by both the shock of the attack and blood from her head filling her eyes.

Ultimately a car coming up the lane with its headlights on saved her life. The attacker put an arm under her legs, another round her waist. Scooping Tracey up, he tipped her like a sack of potatoes over a barbed-wire fence and into a field. Then he ran off. She heard his footsteps as he made good his escape. As she lay in the grassy field, she felt numbed by the force of the blows. Staggering around the field, she became disorientated, fearing the man might return and attack again. Covered in blood, she staggered towards a farm worker's caravan, pleading for help. An elderly man took her in, then helped her to her parents' farmhouse. She almost fell through the door, her mother gasping at the dreadful sight confronting her: 'When she came through the door her jumper was squelching with blood.' At first she thought someone had thrown a pot of paint over her daughter. But then her family saw a severe wound that appeared to leave a hole in the top of her head.

Tracey was rushed to Chapel Allerton Hospital in Leeds for emergency neurosurgery. She had a fractured skull. Doctors removed a sliver of bone from her brain. She remained in hospital for a week, and later recalled the moment the bandages were removed. Nurses gave her a mirror and told her to take her time. When she looked at herself she saw the truly shocking extent of the injuries to her face. Her eyes were blackened and she had extensive bruising. 'I never expected it to be so bad,' she said much later. She stayed off school for six weeks and wore a wig over her shaven head. For the next two years she had brain scans, and drugs to prevent seizures.

The victim had survived the assault and was able to give an excellent description of her attacker. It therefore seems extraordinary that Sutcliffe remained at large. The accuracy of Tracey Browne's description and photofit was confirmed by another witness who provided police with details, and a photofit, of a dark-haired man with a beard and moustache seen in the neighbourhood. But while Tracey's photofit description of her attacker appeared briefly in the local press, the one provided by the other witness was never shown publicly. In some ways, it was even more accurate. The man had been seen standing near a 'white' Ford car, and Sutcliffe was at that time apparently the owner of a lime green Ford Capri. While searching the area, police found a distinctive 'hippy'-style bracelet with wooden beads, and a paper handkerchief, which the attacker was thought to have used to blow his nose on.

Taking charge of the case was Detective Superintendent Jim Hobson, who had spent almost all of his career in the Leeds City force as a detective, working frequently with Dennis Hoban from the days when they were constables in uniform. Indeed, he was godfather to Hoban's son, Richard. At first it was suspected that Tracey's head had been smashed with a large stick. Later, after a more thorough forensic analysis, a claw hammer was thought to have been used. Through the local press, Superintendent Hobson appealed for anyone who had been in Silsden between 10.15 and 11.15 on the night of the attack to come forward. He was fairly confident, because of the lateness of the hour, that the attacker was a local man. But one particular thing puzzled the police. The man had told Tracey he was living at 'Holroyd House'. They wanted the help of the public in finding Holroyd House.

Since 'Holroyd' is a common enough West Yorkshire surname, dating back to the early fourteenth century, it could be expected that there are any number of places called Holroyd House. In fact, there were very few. Almost certainly the nearest was a 200-year-old house at Micklethwaite, on the outskirts of Bingley, the town which had been Sutcliffe's home until he married and moved in with his parents-in-law at Clayton, near Bradford. Holroyd House stood adjacent to Holroyd Mill, built in 1812, which for generations had manufactured fustian, a coarse twilled cotton fabric with a nap, like velveteen. Jim Hobson's early instincts were right: the attacker of Tracey Browne was probably a local man.

Two weeks after the attack, Tracey, wearing a wig and accompanied by a woman detective, made a tour of pubs and discos in the Silsden and Streeton area of Keighley, looking for the man who had tried to kill her. The search proved fruitless. (It appears that Sutcliffe immediately left with his new wife, Sonia, for a holiday visit to Prague with his parents-in-law to visit relatives, stopping off in Rome on the way.)

In recent weeks there had in fact been two other assaults on West Yorkshire women who suffered severe injuries which left crescent-shaped wounds to their skulls, but neither of these was linked with Tracey Browne's attempted murder. The first was on a thirty-seven-year-old woman, Anna Rogulskyj, in an alleyway in Keighley. Five weeks previously she had been attacked from behind with a hammer and left on the ground suffering head injuries and a number of superficial slash wounds across her body. And on Friday, 15 August 1975, an office cleaner, living at Boothtown, Halifax, received two depressed fractures of the skull, one on the midline at the top of the head, the second at the back. Mrs Olive Smelt, aged forty-five, said she had before the assault been talking to a man aged about thirty, slightly built, dark haired *and with a beard or some hair growth on his face.* She did not think there was anything unusual about his accent, which again indicated that he was probably a 'local' man. One other feature of the attack became clearly visible when Mrs Smelt was examined in hospital. There were two abrasions on her back. One, twelve inches long, ran upwards from the small of her back; the other, four inches long, ran backwards on the right side.

Dr Michael Green, a Home Office pathologist based at St James's University Hospital in Leeds who examined both women's injuries, came to a startling conclusion: 'It might be interesting to look again at the case of Mrs Rogulskyj, who was assaulted on 5 July, and compare the photograph of a wound on the abdomen with a wound on the back of Mrs Smelt,' he wrote in his report to the police. Unfortunately, it would take two years for the attacks on Rogulskyj and Smelt to be linked to the murder series by the Ripper Squad.

Yet further assaults, by virtue of their *modus operandi* very similar to those already described, were also excluded from any series. An eighteen-year-old shop assistant was followed down the side of a field at 6.30 p.m. at Queensbury, Bradford, early in 1976. Her assailant then lunged at her from the rear, causing serious head injuries. He was twenty-five to thirty years old, of slim build, between five feet nine or ten inches tall, and with dark hair and moustache, dressed in dark jeans and a green jacket. Seven and a half months later, in August 1976 at Lister Hills in Bradford, a twenty-nine-year-old housewife was set upon during the early hours. Unable to provide any description of the person who assaulted her, she had stab-like wounds to her abdomen and injuries to her head.

In neither of these assaults was a photofit available. But a savage attack on an intellectually challenged West Indian woman in Leeds in the early summer of 1976 produced a description and photofit that perfectly matched the one provided in the Tracey Browne case at Keighley ten months previously. Yet these attempted murders were never linked, primarily because detectives in the Leeds case believed the victim misled them.

Marcella Claxton was a twenty-year-old native of the Caribbean island of St Kitts, who had come to Britain with her mother at the age of ten. She had had a hard upbringing at the hands of her father, and bore the physical and emotional scars to prove it. Educationally she was officially graded as subnormal, with an IQ of 50. However, this doesn't square with the opinions of those who know her well and say it gives a misleading impression. While Marcella had always had a problem expressing herself, she eventually became a good mother to her children.

In 1976 she was unemployed and living in Chapeltown, the run-down quarter of Leeds that had once been a favourite residence of the city's prosperous, and not so wealthy, Jewish community. They lived in large late-Victorian and Edwardian terraced houses, originally the homes of respectable working and middle classes, many of which were later subdivided into flats. It became the second largest Jewish community outside London. Some 12,000 of the city's 20,000 Jewish population lived in Chapeltown until the 1930s, when the majority began moving out to the newer, more desirable suburbs of Moortown, Roundhay and Alwoodley, leaving behind them, as J. B. Priestley put it in the 1950s, 'traces of that restless glitter which is the gift of the Jew'. In their wake came other immigrants – Latvians and a sizeable community of Poles who opted to stay in Britain after the war, who established their own Polish Catholic Church in Chapeltown, and then West Indians and Asians. By the 1970s, however, the area was termed by the media 'a Mecca of Vice' or 'a red light suburb'. The sizeable influx of immigrants from the Caribbean led the York-shire *Evening Post* in 1973 to describe it as 'The Colony Within'. Chapeltown was 'the melting pot for immigrants from many lands, for many years'.

Marcella was a single mother of two children (in foster care) and expecting a third. She was three months' pregnant. She was poor, and the police believed, wrongly, that she was a prostitute. Marcella insists she was not a prostitute. On a Satur-day evening in early May 1976 she went out late at night to drink in a West Indian club. At around five in the morning she left her friends, rather the worse for wear. As she walked back home along Spencer Place she saw a white-coloured car cruising the area. Eventually the driver stopped to ask if she was 'doing business'. She says she said 'No', but the driver got out, took her by the hand, led her to his car and said he was going to take her to Roundhay Park for sex. At the park the driver asked her to take off her clothes. He gave her five pounds. She told him she wanted to urinate and went to hide among the bushes until, believing the man had gone, she returned ten minutes later to retrieve her shoes. At this point she received a number of vicious blows on the head. Knocked to the ground, she pretended to be unconscious. The attack stopped and the man drove off. Marcella claimed in a later interview that he had masturbated in front of her before walking back to his car. He told her: 'Don't phone the police.'

With her head bleeding profusely, she took off her knickers

and held them up to stem the flow. Realizing she was in bad shape, she began half-crawling and half-walking towards the edge of the park. She managed to reach a telephone box beside the road one hundred yards away and made a 999 call. The ambulance took ages to arrive. Slumped in a huddled position, waiting anxiously in the telephone box, she saw through the glass window the driver of the white car touring around as if looking for her. Finally he stopped some way off and walked across to the place where he had launched his attack. Unable to find Marcella, he drove off. 'He come back to see if I were dead,' she said years later. 'He didn't see me, so he kept on driving.'

At Leeds General Infirmary doctors discovered eight severe lacerations to her scalp, each about an inch long, needing a total of fifty-two stitches. Discharged after six days, it was then Marcella's second nightmare began. She feared the man would come back for her because she could identify him. She had provided police with a description of a smartly dressed *white* man with dark hair, a beard and moustache. Amazingly the police did not believe her and said repeatedly when questioning her that the person responsible had been a black man. 'I said no black man would have done this to me.' She lost the child she was carrying and began to suffer dreadful headaches and the occasional blackout. The trauma remains to this day, twenty-five years later. 'It is like my brain is bursting and hitting the inside of my head, sometimes all day,' she said.

Not long after coming out of hospital Marcella had the shock of her life when she was out for a drink at the Gaiety pub. The man who had assaulted her walked in, took a look round, then went out again. She told friends that he was the person police were looking for, and they rushed outside, but he had gone.

An internal West Yorkshire inquiry some time later reported: 'Although she had been struck about the head with an unknown instrument there were factors which were dissimilar to previous "Ripper" attacks. Most significant was the absence of stabbing to the body and there was the motive of taking the money and running away ... officers were aware of the dangers of including details of an incident which was not part of the series because it would mislead the investigation as a whole.'

In 1978, at a hearing before the Criminal Injuries Compensation Board, West Yorkshire Police claimed Marcella had misled them during their inquiries, giving a picture of her attacker that was 'hopelessly inaccurate' because her memory was impaired. Her application was rejected.

4

Tracks in the Grass

In the 1870s, seven hundred acres of rolling fields, woodland and two large lakes provided a much-needed gigantic lung for the city of Leeds. It allowed the overcrowded population the chance to breathe clean air, free of soot, grime and chimney smoke. Roundhay Park was personally purchased by the then Lord Mayor, a wealthy clothing manufacturer called John Barran, who intended it as 'an ideal playground for the people of this city'. At the end of the nineteenth century it was observed of the park: 'Although it is four miles from the centre of the city it is quickly reached by means of a capital service of electric cars. Once within its gates, the pleasure-seeker or the holiday-maker may quickly persuade himself that Leeds is far away.' For more than a hundred years it has provided a magnificent prospect for the city people to wander amid a wildlife setting containing whooper swans, Canada geese, great-crested grebes and herons. The crocuses remain abundant in spring, followed by daffodils, bluebells and orchids. Even today keen-eyed inner-city children from Leeds' bleak urban landscape are often taken to Roundhay Park to spot roe-deer, foxes, rabbits and grey squirrels.

By night, though, it becomes a different kind of habitat, a venue for courting couples and lovers seeking seclusion for amorous recreation. Prostitutes in the 1970s brought their cli-

ents here, so it would have been nothing unusual late on a
Saturday evening in 1977 for the residents living in the great
Victorian mansions along Park and West Avenues, which over-
look this part of the park, to see a car pull off the road and
stop, and for the headlights to be switched off. Opposite
these grand homes with names like 'Woodlands' and 'The
Clockhouse' stands Soldier's Field, nowadays a recreation area
for organized sport, so-called because the army used it as a
training ground in the 1890s.

Standing amid a number of beech trees on the periphery of
this vast expanse of playing fields was a large flat-roofed pavilion, built of York stone and used as changing rooms by
visiting amateur football teams. Sunday morning, 6 February
1977, was bitterly cold with a clear sky. The beech trees stood
denuded of leaves, and cast across the ground long shadows
in an unexpected burst of warmth and light from a winter sun
that hung low in the temporarily cloudless sky behind the
houses in West Avenue. Lying on muddy ground in the pavilion's shade, and hidden from the road, was a body, discovered
by a man out jogging at 7.50 that morning. John Bolton, a
forty-seven-year-old accountant, lived a stone's throw from
the park. Most mornings he got in a run before breakfast and
it was on one of these that he spotted the corpse. At first he
wasn't sure what it was. Then, as he got closer, he could see
it was a woman lying on her side. Her face, turned downwards
towards the grass, was concealed by her shoulder-length brown
hair. 'I brushed the hair to one side,' he said, 'and then I saw
the blood on her neck. Her eyes were glazed and staring. She
was obviously dead and I ran to one of the houses to call the
police.'

Dennis Hoban, as deputy ACC (crime), attended the scene
with his longtime friend and colleague Jim Hobson, now detec-

tive chief superintendent in charge of the Eastern Area CID. This was Hobson's patch and he was senior investigating officer. Hoban wore his traditional suit and a Burberry trench coat, but had abandoned his usual trilby or peaked cap, leaving his balding pate that morning devoid of headgear and exposed to the balmy rays of the sun, which after a long winter was something akin to a tonic. Hoban wasn't treading on anyone's toes. He saw it as a courtesy to Hobson more than anything else, or so at least he would have convinced himself. Living only a few minutes' drive away, Hoban could not possibly have passed up the opportunity to visit a crucial crime scene like this, particularly with the murders of McCann and Jackson unsolved for a year and fresh in his mind. The most superficial examination had made it clear to everyone that this young woman had suffered severe head injuries. However, it was not until Professor Gee arrived at the scene that the full horror became apparent.

Gee arrived at 10 a.m., followed fifteen minutes later by Edward Mitchell, a forensic scientist from the laboratory at Harrogate. By then the standard murder investigation procedures had swung into action. The crime scene was taped off, duckboards laid on the muddy ground, the twenty-strong uniformed task force alerted to conduct a fingertip search; and a black plastic screen about thirty-five feet long was placed in front of the body to veil it from prying eyes. In the distance, officers in uniform began alerting the football teams arriving to play their fixtures that the matches would have to be cancelled while the pitches were minutely examined for clues. When Gee first saw the body it lay on the grass with the face directed towards the left shoulder. The upper part was clad in a long brown, machine-knit woollen cardigan with a zip fastener; the lower part, from the waist downwards, was covered by a short brown imitation suede coat with fur trimming. The feet protruded beyond the end of the coat and there was a sock on the left foot but the right foot was bare. Blood soiled her head, hair and cardigan as well as her neck. Leaves beside the body also had a little blood on them. Beside the body was a tampon. Later laboratory analysis confirmed she was having a period at the time she was killed. The tampon was lightly covered in blood, showing she was nearing the end of her monthly cycle. On the other side of the body, nearer to the pavilion, a trail of blood ran between the body and a handbag lying on leaves nearly four feet off. The flap of the handbag was open and a cosmetics bag and a lipstick were next to it. Beneath the handbag was a mortice key and a 1p coin.

Tyre tracks from a vehicle could clearly be seen between the body and the back of the pavilion in an area of muddy ground clear of trees. The tracks led from the roadway, along the back of the pavilion, and stopped close to the body. Mitchell began to examine the surrounding area, collecting his array of samples and taping the woman's face. Adhesive tape was stretched across areas of bare skin on her arms, legs and back to pick up fibres, possibly from the killer's clothing. These fibres would be examined under powerful microscopes and compared with the woman's clothing. Anything 'foreign' would be possible confirmation of Locard's theory of contact and exchange.

After the body had been photographed *in situ*, the coat covering the lower part of the body was removed to reveal some bizarre details. Originally the woman had worn two pairs of pants, one pair over her tights, as well as a pair of long light-coloured socks over the tights, presumably to make her footwear more comfortable. Now the woman's long brown leather boots, with three-inch block heels and two-inch soles, lay along the backs of her legs. As she lay dead on the ground, they had been deliberately placed on her legs, stretching from her thighs down to her calves. When the boots were lifted off, the left leg only was found to have a rolled-down pair of tights bunched up around her left knee. Rolled up into the tights was a pair of red pants and the missing sock from her right foot. There were also fragments of leaves and ground debris tucked into the top of the tights. The woman's other pants, a small brown nylon pair, were in position over her backside and covering her genitalia.

Once the cardigan was pulled upwards towards the woman's head, her yellow skirt was found bunched up around her waist, together with a blue underslip. She also wore a yellow jacket beneath which her yellow bra was still fastened. After her temperature was recorded and the body photographed once more, she was turned on her back on to a large white plastic sheet. Her hands were crossed over the lower part of the body, the left wrist overlaying the right. Around her right wrist were four metal bangles. There was a seventeen-jewelled fake-gold watch with a narrow expanding strap on the left wrist, its glass partly obscured by droplets of water inside. It was no longer working and the hands were stopped at the 8.50 position. Time had literally run out for her.

Now Gee, Hoban, Hobson and the others could see there was a large wound at the front of the throat, with soiling of the surrounding skin and the front of the jacket, which was fastened with one button. Beneath her hands in the lower part of the abdomen was a truly shocking wound. A large slashing cut on the left side of the stomach had sliced through the abdominal wall. A number of coils of intestine protruded and these were slightly soiled with blood, matted with leaves and pieces of twig. Still more photographs were taken before the body was wrapped in the plastic sheet, ready to be taken to the mortuary for Gee to carry out a more detailed six-hour examination.

Hobson's team had meanwhile been examining the contents of the woman's handbag to see if they could identify her. As the senior investigating officer he quickly needed to know as much about her as possible. The handbag yielded a vital clue: a name and address in Roundhay. From this it transpired that the dead woman was called Irene Richardson; that she had applied for a job as a nanny with a family in Roundhay a week or two previously. The person who advertised for the nanny was then able to provide Irene's home address, a miserable rooming house in Cowper Street, Chapeltown. Apart from a packet of cigarettes and a box of matches, a few bus tickets and a Yale and mortice key, Irene Richardson's entire wealth lay in her purse – all 35½ pence of it.

Everyone agreed that what was learned from inquiries over the next few weeks about the lost soul who was Irene Richardson amounted to an immensely sad story. She had been twenty-eight years old, penniless, and fending for herself in very straitened circumstances. Born into a large family called Osborne in the Possilpark area of Glasgow, she had six sisters and three brothers. Their mother was a Roman Catholic and they had a Church of Scotland father. The children were brought up as Protestants. It was said to be a poor, large, but loving family. At primary school Irene was a normal child, though somewhat shy and sensitive. She enjoyed music and loved to laugh. But at Springburn Secondary School she turned into something of a rebel, smoking and playing truant. At some point the entire Osborne clan had settled at various places in England: a brother in Corby, Northamptonshire; a sister at Canvey Island in Essex. Another sister, Helen, worked in the hotel and catering industry in Blackpool, then married a York-shireman and later set up home in Sheffield. In 1965, at the age of seventeen, Irene Osborne ran off to London and for the next five years or so completely cut herself off from her family. When her father died, they were unable to contact her and she missed his funeral. Before her teens were out she had two children. Her daughter Lorraine's father was a man called John Henry Wade. Police believed that Alan, the second child, might have been fathered by someone else, a friend of Irene's called 'Dennis', who was never found. Irene could hardly cope by herself, let alone with two small children. Baby Lorraine was fostered out aged eighteen months in 1968 to a dealer in repro-duction antiques and his wife, George and Mary Dwyer, from Croydon. They then adopted her when she was four. Irene's son Alan was also fostered out.

Subsequently she moved to Blackpool, where her sister Helen was then working. There she met her future husband, George Richardson, a barman turned plasterer, in November 1970, and married him in June the following year. They set up home in Blackpool and had two daughters. Until the summer of 1975 Irene was working at the local Pontins Holiday Camp. Their daughter, also named Irene, was two years old and Irene was expecting another baby, Amanda. She almost certainly suffered from severe postnatal depression, for very soon after the baby was born she suddenly left Blackpool for London without say-ing where she was going. Mr Richardson reported her missing to the police, but she made contact a few months later. As a result, George Richardson travelled to London and located his wife in South Kensington, working in a hotel. They set up home in Kensington briefly, in an attempt to patch up their marriage. It did not last long. In April 1976 Irene left again without leaving a forwarding address. George Richardson did not see her alive again and their children, too, were subsequently fostered.

In London Irene Richardson met and cohabited with a six-foot ex-seaman, Steven Bray, who had absconded from Leicester Prison and was now working as a chef. Irene kept secret from him the fact that she was still married to George Richardson. Bray and Irene arrived in Leeds in October 1976 and moved between various boarding houses in the Chapeltown area. He was employed as a doorman at Tiffany's Club and Irene began using the name Bray and worked at various hotels in the city as a chambermaid and also as a cleaner at a YMCA hostel, the Residential Boys' Club in nearby Chapel Allerton. Incredibly she and Bray had organized to get married at Leeds Register Office on 22 January 1977, but neither turned up. Some time later Bray left for London, and then caught a ferry to Ireland, where he remained for several weeks.

Ten days before her death, Irene failed to turn up for work at the YMCA hostel. She had asked the warden for an advance on her wages because she had a large bill to pay. Mrs Nellie Morrison was only able to give her £1. They didn't see Irene for a few days and then she came to collect her shoes and overalls and apologized for her behaviour, saying she had to get away from a man she had been living with. A week before she was murdered, a man suddenly arrived at the YMCA and collected the wages due to her. But she never saw the money. Hobson learned that in the last ten days of her life she had been wandering the streets practically destitute.

A woman in the rooming house in Cowper Street told detectives that Irene and Bray had twice rented an attic room in the house, and shortly before her death the landlord had let her occupy a ground-floor room rent free for a few days. Rent for a room was normally between £5 and £8 a week. Severely depressed and down on her luck, Irene had been hanging around street corners in Chapeltown. She had been living rough on the streets for about two weeks and spent several nights sleeping in a public lavatory. A few friends allowed her to take the occasional bath in their flat. The room in Cowper Street should have been a life-saver for Irene, who was urgently trying to get a job. She didn't drink a great deal and only went out at weekends.

On the Saturday night of 5 February Irene spent some time getting ready, trying to dress tidily and applying a considerable amount of make-up, especially around the eyes. At about 11.15 she told her friend Pam Barker, who also had a room in the Cowper Street property, that she was going to Tiffany's dance hall in the Merrion Centre in Leeds to find Steven Bray. She then briefly visited a house in Sholebrook Avenue and talked to a friend, Mrs Walsh. They parted company at 11.30. Some time before midnight she got into a stranger's car, apparently willing to have sex with him for money.

The next time George Richardson saw Irene was at the Leeds City Mortuary. The police arranged for a car to bring him from Blackpool to identify her. It was a sight which was to haunt him for years to come. He was convinced Irene had never been a prostitute. 'She was sick. She just couldn't settle down,' he said. Her funeral in Blackpool the following week, he said, would end two years of a living hell. But George Richardson's life in subsequent years went from bad to worse. He became an alcoholic.

Following the post-mortem Hobson had a clearer idea of what had happened to Irene. For a few days at least she had been prepared to resort to prostitution to get money. He knew from forensic lab results that she had had sex with someone in the twenty-four hours before her death. Swabs from her vagina showed the presence of semen. On the inside of her coat an area of seminal staining was also found, from an 'O' blood-type secretor, a male who secreted blood cells into his saliva or semen. There were similar seminal stains on her tights and knickers, but in neither case was sperm found in the semen. The man who previously had intercourse with Irene was definitely aspermous.

It seemed certain she had been picked up in Chapeltown shortly before being killed. Later it was learned that at 11.35 p.m. on the Saturday night another woman had been propositioned on several occasions in Nassau Place, Chapeltown, by a man in a white car. Could the same man have picked up Irene and taken her to Soldier's Field? She had got out of the car intending to have sex with the driver, but first had to discreetly remove the tampon she was wearing. As she crouched down the killer struck her a massive blow to the head, followed by two more. It was self-evident that if Irene was crouching or kneeling in the split second before she was killed, a hammer raised above the murderer's head as he stood over her would have been brought crashing down with a greater velocity than if she had been standing. The only saving grace was that Irene would have known nothing about it. The blow would have stunned her and instant unconsciousness would have followed.

'This was an almost circular, punched-out depressed fracture,' Professor Gee wrote in his autopsy report, 'with the central disc of the bone driven deeply into the underlying brain.' He made another chilling discovery: 'The bevelling up of one edge of the fracture of the skull clearly showed where the hammer had got stuck by the force of the blow into the skull and had to be levered out to get it clear of the bone.' The nature of the hole indicated it had almost the precise dimensions of a hammer head. Gee thought the woman had then been dragged from the position of the tyre tracks to the spot where she was found and further injured. The murderer had slashed at her throat, causing a gaping wound exposing the larynx. In a frenzy he then tore a wound nearly seven inches long down the left side of the abdomen, which caused her intestines to tumble out, and two more stab wounds to the stomach followed. The weapons used were probably a hammer with a flat circular striking surface and a very sharp knife of some kind. For Gee the importance of this case lay in it being able to confirm they were dealing with a multiple killer. He preferred to deal in certainties rather than speculation. It was essential not to make a mistake because it could confuse the whole investigation. Now he felt sure he knew. 'Here was a clear pattern,' he said later, though it took some time for everyone to agree.

Hobson still wasn't certain in his own mind that all three murders were linked, but this didn't prevent speculation in the media. The fact that two other women had been slaughtered in similar circumstances in Leeds, coupled with the grisly detail of Richardson's throat injury, prompted one tabloid the next morning to splash its story. 'JACK THE RIPPER MURDER HORROR': 'A girl was found brutally hacked to death in a sports field yesterday. And it started a hunt for a Jack the Ripper killer.' The *Sun* partially regurgitated the sensational headline it used a year previously, following Emily Jackson's death: 'RIPPER HUNTED IN CALL GIRL MURDERS'. This third death was clearly major front-page news. With a madman slaying prostitutes on the loose, Britain had not seen anything like this since the Thames nude murders in London during the mid-1960s. However, it would be another year before the term 'Yorkshire Ripper' became common currency.

Sensing the urgency of the situation, Ronald Gregory, the chief constable, was among those who turned up at the murder scene before the body was moved. When suspicions were eventually confirmed that the killing was the work of the man who had also slain McCann and Jackson, Gregory knew he had a maniacal killer in his force area, equal, in his mind, to the worst work of the notorious multiple murderers, Haigh and Christie, a few decades earlier. Gregory's foreboding was well justified. The search for the 'Ripper' would become the most notorious criminal investigation in British history, and far more complex than either the infamous Haigh or Christie cases. For in February 1977 West Yorkshire police had an *on-going* murder hunt on their hands, a series of crimes to be solved, whereas the Haigh and Christie cases presented no great mystery for investigators, even though they produced sensational trials and equally sensational headlines. The killers were under arrest before police knew they had multiple deaths on their hands. Haigh admitted straight away he was a serial murderer and became infamous as the 'Acid in the Bath' killer. There was no police hunt for him as such. Christie had killed eight women over a period of ten years, including his own wife, but none of them were linked to a series for the bodies were not found till very late in the day. Indeed, they were discovered by accident. Christie walled up his victims or buried them in the back yard or under floorboards at 10 Rillington Place in London, where he lived. They later gave off a rather unpleasant smell. Four days after the discovery of various skeletons he was arrested and immediately confessed. Both Haigh and Christie had their defence pleas of not guilty of murder by reason of insanity rejected by a jury at the Old Bailey and both were hanged.

Convinced the man who killed Richardson had to be bloodstained, Jim Hobson telexed a warning to all West Yorkshire divisions and surrounding forces to keep an eye out for anyone coming into custody with bloodstained clothing. He also wanted urgent inquiries made at local dry cleaners. One hundred officers then began house-to-house inquiries. Among those soon interviewed was one of Britain's top television stars, Jimmy Savile, who lived in West Avenue, opposite the murder scene. He wasn't at home at the crucial time, but when a neighbour gave him the news he was badly shaken and kept repeating: 'This is terrible. It is a ghastly thing to happen practically in your own front garden.' In the following weeks numerous men were hauled in and questioned closely; several items of potential suspect's clothing were examined at the Harrogate laboratory, along with various pairs of shoes and a bloodstained raincoat retrieved from a dry cleaners in the centre of Leeds. Tools, hammers and knives were also handed over for scientific analysis. A fragmentary fingerprint found on a bus ticket near the scene could not be eliminated. Prostitutes in Leeds were asked to come forward if they had been ill-treated by their clients. Courting couples using Roundhay Park over the weekend were asked to report anything suspicious. None of these initiatives led anywhere. Hobson appealed directly to women not to accept lifts from strangers. The last thing he needed was another murder before they had exhausted all lines of inquiry from the current one.

Four days after Irene died, he sought the cooperation of the public in finding Marcella Claxton, who nine months previously had been attacked in virtually the same spot at Soldier's Field. Now she had moved home and police couldn't find her. The local press claimed it as 'a carbon copy' attack and reported that Marcella could hold vital clues to the killer's identity. Hobson told reporters that there were striking similarities. Both women had been viciously attacked with a blunt instrument from the rear; both had clearly been picked up in Chapeltown for sex and taken to Roundhay Park, a favourite place for prostitutes to take their clients.

Hobson said of Marcella: 'She could help us with vital clues to the identity. It is essential that we interview this woman in view of the recent murder. There may be some connection between the attack on her and the murder of Mrs Richardson.' An eminent biographer once declared that although hindsight is often the last refuge of the instant historian, scorning hindsight is always the first escort of the evasive politician. He might also have said policeman. With the benefit of hindsight and twenty-five years on, Hobson's prophetic comment seems like irony heaped upon irony. There was indeed a connection between the two events, but it was overlooked. Marcella Claxton had repeatedly told police that the man who attacked her had been driving a *white* car; so was the man who tried repeatedly to pick up a woman in Nassau Place, Chapeltown, not long before Irene Richardson was walking in the same area, probably half an hour before she was murdered. Even more damning, Marcella had helped prepare a photofit, but again its value to the investigation was never realized.

Later that day, Marcella spoke to detectives and repeated her description of the man in a white car who attacked her. But next morning at a press conference Hobson briefed the media saying Marcella had given them a description, '*but this is not necessarily the description of the murderer* [my italics]'. It was a comment hardly likely to inspire confidence. The public was told he was aged twenty-five to thirty-five, five feet nine inches tall, medium build, with dark wavy hair, who at the time of the assault was wearing a dark suit with a multicoloured shirt and tie. He was well spoken and drove a white car which was fairly new. Anyone recognizing this description was asked to contact the police immediately. Tragically, the detail police left out from Marcella Claxton's description was that the man had *a beard and a moustache*. Nor did they issue to the press the photofit Marcella prepared on 10 May 1976, the day after she was attacked. It had been published in *Police Reports*, a confidential internal police publication sent to northern police forces, and in a separate police circular a week later. However, the public was never given the opportunity of seeing the actual photofit (which bore a stunning likeness to Sutcliffe). True, Marcella had problems selecting the components for the photofit, but when it was finished *she* was satisfied it was a good likeness of the man who tried to kill her. But Hobson was not convinced, and was moreover doubly concerned that the public could be misled if given the wrong information. The simple truth was that the West Yorkshire police did not believe what Marcella Claxton was telling them.

Ever cautious, Hobson repeated his warning to the 'good time girls' of Chapeltown to be wary of accepting lifts in cars: 'From our observations taken over the last week it seems that women are still getting into cars in the area. I would again warn them of the dangers.'

Over the next few months, Leeds police mounted a crackdown on prostitutes in the Chapeltown area, arresting and issuing cautions to more than a hundred women. Hobson's policy was to get sex workers out of the vice area, a policy which appeared to be working. 'We have clamped down to try to get prostitutes off the streets,' he said. 'It is as much for their safety as anything else. We are making every effort to prevent another murder.' If they insisted on plying their trade, he believed they should let one of their friends know where they were going, or take the car number. Then another tactic was tried. Special squads of police operating in the Chapeltown area noted the registration numbers of cars belonging to men cruising around looking for sex. A similar stratagem had been applied by the Metropolitan Police in London more than ten years previously during the hunt for the Thames nude prostitute murderer. In a proactive effort to apprehend the London killer, all the 'pick-up' places in Bayswater, Shepherd's Bush and Notting Hill had been kept under observation. 'A system of "flagging" was introduced whereby the same car in an area more than once became suspect, and if it appeared three times the driver was questioned.' The operation was not a success.

Under some pressure from the media Hobson was extraordinarily open with information. The press knew the latest victim had head injuries, that her throat was cut and she had wounds to her stomach; they knew files from previous cases were being reviewed and a special watch was being kept on people driving through the Chapeltown red-light area. Hobson also informed the media of a possible connection with the murder of a prostitute in Preston, Lancashire. The Leeds *Evening Post* was able to inform readers on 8 February 1977, two days after Richardson's body was found: 'Police are comparing notes from the files of three brutal murders committed in the last 16 months – two in Leeds and one in Lancashire. In each case a prostitute was the victim.'

The next day the local Leeds evening newspaper gave more information: 'Mr Hobson said Chief Supt. Brook from Lancashire who is leading investigations into the murder of a prostitute – Joan Harrison – who was found battered to death in Preston in November 1975, was travelling from Blackpool to Leeds today to liaise with Leeds detectives.' Wilf Brooks, the head of Lancashire CID, had his meeting with Hobson, then left a file on the Harrison case for the Leeds CID chief to examine, 'because of the striking similarities', according to the *Evening Post* on the 10th.

The similarities were indeed striking: twenty-six-year-old Joan Harrison had no convictions for prostitution but had been cohabiting with several men. She had once been a houseproud mother, devoted to her children, but then her life appears to have descended into chaos. She was prepared to have sex to fund her chronic alcoholism and addiction to cough mixtures containing small doses of morphine, often getting through as many as eight bottles a day. She suffered severe head injuries when she was killed in a garage in Berwick Road, Preston, less than a month after Wilma McCann was murdered. Her body was found lying face down, covered by her coat. Her clothing appeared to have been displaced in a similar way to the West Yorkshire killings. She had been wearing two bras, both unfastened. The inner one had been pulled up over her breasts, leaving the outer one in position. The left leg was outside her pants and tights, with the trousers replaced on both legs and partly pulled up. Finally, and most intriguingly, her left boot had been placed tightly between her legs with the zip opened. But there were also several differences. Robbery was thought to be a motive. Her handbag and some of her possessions were missing, and several injuries were thought to be due to kicking or stamping to the head and body. There were no stab wounds and it was thought she had had sex immediately before she was killed. Brooks himself was not convinced of a link between the killings, neither was Hobson. The Lancashire CID chief was more intent on finding the man who had normal and anal intercourse with Joan Harrison. Semen traces were identified as being from a blood group B secretor and police began a mass screening of local men in the Preston area.

In Leeds, Jim Hobson believed he had a more positive line

to follow, the most important clue found in the three Leeds murders so far, and something the police could get to grips with: the tyre tracks left behind in muddy ground at the scene, almost certainly by the killer's car. Scenes of crime officers quickly took plaster casts and calculations were made by the Harrogate laboratory. This herculean task of finding the car that left the tyre tracks began as a matter of urgency the very day Irene Richardson's body was found. It became known as 'the tracking inquiry', because the initial goal was to ascertain the make of vehicle involved by measuring the track width of the vehicle from the distance between the tyre marks left at the scene. Only a certain number of cars would match that particular measurement. If the experts could narrow it down there was a good chance they might isolate the make of the killer's car, and hopefully find it and, more crucially, the murderer.

As principal scientific officer at Harrogate, Ron Outtridge quickly contacted the murder incident room at Millgarth Street, the brand-new purpose-built police headquarters in Leeds which had been open less than a year. He had narrowed down the track width after a careful analysis of the plaster casts and photographs taken at the crime scene. The inner width was forty-six inches, the outer width fifty-four and a quarter inches. But there was one complication. It was impossible to tell whether the tracks had been made by the front axle or the rear axle. This doubled the number of vehicles involved. Outtridge had isolated the makes of tyres from the 250 different types of tyre available to motorists, but couldn't determine whether the car had been driven straight on to the grass beside the pavilion or reversed in. All four were cross-ply tyres – one a Pneumant brand, manufactured in East Germany, worn down to 2 mm of tread, with an Esso E110 on the other side of the same axle; and there were two India Autoways tyres, both well worn, on the other axle. Each tyre had certain characteristics peculiar to its make, whether it was winter type, normal road use, remould, cross-ply or radial. In terms of mathematical probabilities, the chances of reproducing this *exact* combination of tyres were nearly 159 million to one. Another set of tyre tracks at the scene was eliminated. They were found to belong to a Leeds Corporation parks department trailer used to deliver chemicals to the pavilion three days before the murder.

By 5.15 p.m. on the day following the discovery of the body, Outtridge, with the help of the Home Office Central Research Establishment, had produced a list of a hundred different makes of vehicle which could fit the various combinations of these measurements. They were telexed to the Millgarth Incident Room as a matter of urgency. The twentieth vehicle on the schedule of makes was a Ford Corsair, which had a front track width of four feet two and a half inches. (Peter Sutcliffe was at the time driving a white Ford Corsair, which he had purchased second-hand shortly before he attacked Marcella Claxton.)

Jim Hobson wanted to move the inquiry forward quickly and instructed night duty officers throughout the Chapeltown Division to examine all parked vehicles during normal routine patrols. Every time a car was examined the officer took the registration number and tyre details, and a card was filled in showing that car had been eliminated from the inquiry. Other checks were carried out in scrapyards, vehicle breakers and auctioneers, and also of vehicles regarded as abandoned and due to be written off and crushed under the Civil Amenities Act. Tens of thousands of cars were checked in this way, but after six weeks the exercise was abandoned.

Hobson's team had consulted an expert in the tyre industry,

R. J. Grogan of Dunlop Ltd, who confirmed that the vehicle concerned was probably one of twenty-one makes and fifty-one models. His more rigorous and specialized analysis allowed the original list of a hundred models to be cut in half. The tyres fitted to one axle could have been of a diameter of twelve inches, thirteen inches or fourteen inches, while the other pair were of a type only manufactured in thirteen and fifteen inches. The science of determining which kind of vehicle was involved in a crime by analysing the combination of tyre tracks left at a scene was not perfect. A series of complex mathematical probabilities was involved. It was sometimes possible to determine the wheel base when a vehicle had sunk into soft ground when parked, or been reversed and driven off again. It might also be possible to measure the turning circle if the vehicle had been turned on its tightest lock, and again this could narrow down the car involved. However, it was unsafe to rely totally on measurements from front wheel tracks alone, as opposed to the rear wheel tracks, because of wear in the steering joints. A quarter of a century on, the situation is even more refined and tyre tracks can be as good as a fingerprint, according to one eminent forensic scientist: 'The marks left by tyres when they are examined contain far more evidential value than would, say, a wound relating to the weapon that produced it. If you get a car with [a particular] track width and the turning circle and if that particular tyre is a Firestone, and there is a cut in it there – it's virtually as good as a fingerprint.'

In a bold move Hobson got approval to carry out a mass screening of all vehicles of these models within the West Yorkshire police area and in the Harrogate division of the North Yorkshire police. It was a massive task and particularly arduous for the inquiry team involved, whose morale and motivation became seriously affected as time went on. Manual searches were carried out at vehicle licensing offices and a search was made of computer records by the Police National Computer (PNC) unit. Hobson learned that 53,000 vehicles would need to be examined. Then there was another problem. The Police National Computer was a relatively new resource, first introduced in 1974. Today it employs twenty-first century technology and there is a second-generation PNC which deals with 200,000 queries a day from British police forces. A vast array of information has been loaded into the system, which includes 42.5 million vehicles registered in the United Kingdom and their owners; stolen property; criminal records; missing and wanted people and disqualified drivers; and people subject to court orders.

But in 1977 the PNC was still in its relative infancy, and programmers were continuing to input the data to build the vast index of vehicles and their owners. A great deal of 'back record conversion' had yet to be done, transferring the records of the Driver and Vehicle Licensing Centre in Swansea on to the Police National Computer. Some information was held in the PNC, but to be sure they would not miss anything Hobson's team also had to check manually with the local Leeds Vehicle Licensing Office. Sutcliffe's white-coloured Ford Corsair – KWT 721D – *was* among the 53,000 vehicles, but would Hobson's team be able to get to it?

A long list of vehicle owners was compiled. The cards which had earlier been completed during the special night duty check in Chapeltown were cross-checked to eliminate those already examined. What in effect was happening was a mass elimination exercise on the basis of gradually purging vehicle registration numbers until what you had left was the car you were searching for. Hobson rightly gambled that, since all three murders so far had involved the Leeds red-light area, it was reasonable to begin looking in West Yorkshire first. But there was a danger that the vehicle might have been scrapped, or the tyres changed, especially if the suspect became aware that police were making inquiries about tyres. For several years the tracking inquiry remained a highly secret part of the investigation.

The next stage was to develop an index card system for all the remaining vehicles to be checked by personal home visits by police officers. However, the index cards used were filed in registration number order, and then carried the owners' names. Tragically, no index cards were made out for names of *owners* as a reference system in itself. Had an index such as this been operated within the murder incident room at Millgarth Street, then the name of Peter William Sutcliffe would have been referenced in connection with the tracking inquiry. Any officer looking up his name in connection with some other aspect of the Ripper investigation would immediately have seen that he owned a car which could have been used in the murder of Irene Richardson.

Even more tragically, circumstances conspired against Hobson and his team. They were simply overtaken by events – another murder and a very serious attack in which a victim survived. Demand for manpower in the investigation became totally overloaded. The incident room was operating a manual, paper-led system. There was nothing in the police armoury at the time to help them sift through the masses of information they were accumulating, let alone the mountains of paperwork yet to come as the bodies of Sutcliffe's victims increased, along with the fears and anxieties of tens of thousands of women in Yorkshire and the North of England after the discovery of yet another woman found murdered at the hands of the Ripper.

The double tragedy was that Hobson's team had broken the

back of the tracking inquiry when a halt was ordered because further murderous attacks on local women demanded his manpower be shifted elsewhere. The drain on resources had been immense. Of the 53,000 vehicle owners in West Yorkshire whose cars may have left the tyre tracks on Soldier's Field, only 20,000 car owners remained to be seen. Sutcliffe's white Ford Corsair was among those on the list waiting to be checked.

5

Impressions in Blood

Just four words made the hair on the back of John Domaille's neck stand on end. 'Boss, we've got one,' the voice at the other end said with an air of breathless desperation.

Domaille, the new head of Bradford CID just two months into the job, had answered the call that Sunday night in late April 1977 after returning from a teatime stroll. He was planning a relaxing night in front of the television when a detective chief inspector telephoned with the news that a thirty-three-year-old prostitute had been found dead in her flat in the red-light district.

'I knew what he meant,' Domaille recalled. 'It meant we had one of these so-called Ripper murders in Bradford. I said "Okay, I'll come over" and I went immediately.' The DCI gave him a few more details. Her name was Patricia Atkinson. The woman had been convicted of soliciting two years previously. She had been found by her boyfriend at a block of flats in Oak Avenue, off Manningham Lane.

Detective Chief Superintendent Domaille, then a month short of his forty-third birthday, sped off in his car at about 8 p.m., and did not return home until the crack of dawn the following morning. He took the M62 across country towards Bradford, before turning off on the motorway spur, past a large number of factories and distribution centres located among a myriad of newly built industrial units. Then it was down into the city centre and on towards Manningham. His head was buzzing. He wondered who the pathologist would be. Who would forensics send? He wanted the best he could get. The new lab at Wetherby needed to send someone down immediately.

'There's so much going through your head when you get a call like that,' he said. 'What mortuary am I going to move this to? What time is the PM going to be, when am I going to see the press, which DCI will I have, which detective superintendent? What am I going to tell the boss? What am I going to tell the chief constable?'

The second he saw her he knew she was a Ripper victim. The DCI had indicated as much. Looking at her, he could see why. There had been a massive attack to the head; it was almost smashed in. The clothing was disarranged and there were curious stab wounds and cuts to the body. The signature was the attack to the abdomen. He had seen this before at the scenes of previous Ripper killings which he had attended as the senior officer with overall charge of media and community relations for West Yorkshire Police. Keeping the media onside then was an absolute priority. Now that he was the senior investigating officer, the man in overall charge, it would be no different. He and Dennis Hoban thought alike in that regard.

Going through his mind was the management of the crime scene and what followed. Domaille thrived on this kind of pressure, especially in his dealings with the media. Aware of the need to get it right, he thought of the first two murders and Hoban's control of the crime scene. That had been total management. It had always seemed to work for Hoban in Leeds until the Ripper appeared. Now in Bradford, Domaille was working with a totally new set-up. If he didn't get all the bits and pieces on the chess board very quickly, he realized, he would face criticism later. In his own mind he was determined to give the media all he could, even if it conflicted with George Oldfield's instincts. The ACC (crime) was obsessive about not giving the press too much. He warned Domaille about not keeping enough back to use when he got someone in who was a serious suspect for a killing. Domaille could see the sense of this, but preferred to deal with a prime suspect when the time came. Of course you needed something held back from the press and television which only the murderer could tell you. You had to sort out the genuine article from the cranks who came in to confess to crimes they didn't commit – but you had to catch your killer first.

'I've always been very keen on telling the media what I've got because I believe in the people out there, there's thousands of them. You've got all those eyes and ears working for you and they bring stuff to you. I didn't have the snouts but I'd got the people. You don't actually detect it by yourself. You detect it because of all the bits people tell you. This was the first [Ripper killing] in Bradford whereas previously he had been in Leeds. He'd gone outside his area. I wasn't surprised because Bradford also had a sizeable prostitute area. I thought: "This person is not very far away" because it doesn't take long to drive from Leeds to Bradford.'

The apartment block Atkinson lived in was seedy. Before he entered the door into the victim's flat Domaille saw an old mattress from a double bed propped against a wall in the corridor outside. Someone had abandoned it there instead of arranging for it to be taken away. 'Tina' Atkinson, as she was commonly known, had rented a self-contained bed-sitting room with a separate bathroom and kitchenette, both of which were in a deplorable condition, with no sign of any effort to clean them. Domaille's immediate thought was that the flat was used for one thing only: sex. The main room contained a bed, pushed into a corner up against the wall; there was also a two-seater sofa, a dressing table and a couple of dining room chairs. A flower-patterned curtain ran in sections right across the only wall with a window. On a three-drawer dressing table with a large mirror stood an empty vase and two ornamental glass gondoliers.

Two dresses, one a sort of shift with a separate belt, hung on coat hangers suspended from the top of the large double wardrobe, one from the side, one from the door. A third dress, which had also hung on a coat hanger, had been thrown on to the sofa, a simple two-seater affair with wooden arms. Two pairs of pants with black frilled tops lay crumpled on a sofa cushion. A few feet away was a three-bar electric fire, the kind which gave a glow of imitation coal. It was plugged in by a short cable to a socket on the wall. Above the socket, the wall was bare except for a map – an RAC road map of Yorkshire.

To Domaille's eye the main room seemed reasonably clean. On a sideboard stood a pair of sling-back shoes with platform soles and a plastic tray. On the table, which had a partly check-patterned tablecloth, was a leather handbag, a large ashtray, a box of Scotties tissues and a can of Harmony hair spray, plus a bottle of cheap scent and a tube of hand cream. There was a towel thrown over the back of a chair. On the floor just in front of the table was a large denim shoulder bag. And beside that was a pool of blood. The victim was on the bed, with blankets and a flower-patterned duvet covering her, face down with her head turned away from the door to face the wall. She wore a black brassière, the left shoulder strap visible under the bedding. A pair of Scholl wooden sandals lay just under the edge of the bed. There were spots of blood on the front of the left sandal.

The room was getting crowded with people doing their work. The scenes of crime photographer took several shots of the sandals from different angles, including the soles, to see if there were any traces of blood. Beside the electric fire was a single blue thick-soled lady's shoe. Domaille briefly pondered whether she had been wearing the sandals when she was killed, or had she just slipped them off and kicked them under the bed? Where was the other blue shoe? He looked down. The floor was covered in a threadbare carpet which looked as if it hadn't been cleaned for a long time. The photographer bent down to frame a shot of a spent match and a filter-tip cigarette stub.

The woman had probably bled to death on the bed. Her dark hair was soaked in blood, as were the sheets and pillow, which was covered in a striped pillowcase. Her arms were spread out down her side. She had been wearing bell-bottomed jeans. When the bedclothes were pulled back by Professor Gee, the jeans were shown to have been tugged below her knees. Her white cotton pants had been pulled down to expose her buttocks. Her T-shirt had been hitched up and her bra unfastened. There was clear bruising on her right leg above the knee. Her tights had been pulled way down to her ankles and she was wearing one shoe – a blue sling-back denim shoe with a platform sole. This answered Domaille's question as to whether she had been wearing the wooden sandals. Then someone pointed out what looked like a shoe print in blood on one of the sheets.

Gee's attention was drawn to the large bloodstain in front of the wooden chair beside the bed, but he could also see spots of blood on the front of the chair legs. He was then shown a short dark leather jacket which was heavily bloodstained in the middle of the floor adjacent to the wardrobe. Pulling back the bedclothes had also revealed the body twisted at the lower part of the trunk so that the abdomen was almost at right angles to the bed. The body was clad in a patterned jumper pulled upwards towards the shoulders. On the edges of the bed, lying on the undersheet in front of the knees, was a mortice lock key. Underneath the right knee was another key – a Yale. It was nearly 10.30 p.m. before Gee began the process of measuring the body temperature at half-hour stages. An hour later the bedclothes were completely removed from the body and handed to an exhibits officer.

By the time the forensic scientist from the new Wetherby laboratory arrived, the bed-sitting room was crowded with activity. The place reeked of alcohol. Fingerprints were being taken. The photographer's camera flashed intermittently, and several people in suits stood around chatting. Russell Stockdale had the furthest of anyone to travel to the scene of the murder – from Rufforth, near York. He was new to West Yorkshire, only just posted to Wetherby from the laboratory at Newcastle. Having been on call this Sunday night, he was the one who had to turn out. He hadn't been involved with West Yorkshiremen before, so it came as some surprise to find the SIO, John Domaille, turned out to have a soft Devonian accent. With the exception of Professor Gee, all the others in the room were clearly Yorkshiremen. On the drive over, Stockdale was conscious he hadn't yet had the opportunity to strike up a rapport with the police from Bradford and Leeds. He was going to meet a new investigating team. Stockdale knew from experience that there was a process of trust and confidence to be built before either side could get the best from each other.

Domaille gave Stockdale the impression of being very young for the senior rank he held, but it soon became apparent that he was extremely confident and more than up to the job. The usual formalities to break the ice with the newcomer were exchanged. Stockdale had long ago decided that professionals in such circumstances be accorded the status they deserved. If you adopted the role of the shrinking violet, you would be treated like a shrinking violet. It was the way of the world.

He strongly believed the forensic scientist had an important role to play at the crime scene. That did not mean he could march in in an arrogant way, because it was very much a joint operation, especially between the pathologist and the forensic scientist. Much of his learning had been on the job training. Stockdale had been a grave-digger on leaving grammar school in Battersea, South London, and was then commissioned in the RAF. He resigned his commission twelve months later and went off to London University. Having graduated as a zoologist he applied for a job at the Newcastle lab in response to a newspaper advertisement. The then director, Stuart Kind, later told him why he appointed him: 'You were such an odd bugger, rather like myself, that's why I gave you the job.'

In the bed-sitting room Stockdale discussed with Peter Swann, the fingerprint man, the sequence in which they would do their work. It was crucial they did it as a team, so as not to damage what the other was trying to achieve. 'Preserving the crime scene is critical,' Stockdale says of this kind of work. 'You can preserve a crime scene by not walking into it, but at some stage you have got to go in there and decide on an operational procedure which is going to work and be followed. Everyone else who has an input to make has to know what everyone else is doing.' He recalled something he particularly learned from later watching David Gee at work. The Leeds University professor, regarded as a gentleman among gentlemen by whose who knew him well, was standing in a muddy field somewhere looking at a fresh corpse and scribbling in a notebook. He said to Stockdale out of the corner of his mouth: 'What I am doing now – the police think I am very busy working, but actually I am giving myself time to think.'

'This was a tremendous piece of advice,' Stockdale reflected. 'I thought about standing there with him on that occasion over the coming years, and what David said encapsulated the whole experience. You have to make time for yourself to think. You can't, if you allow yourself to be rushed by people saying: "Come on, get on with it, we have got to get the body moved." Why? Where is it going? It isn't going anywhere because I haven't finished yet.'

On this call-out to Bradford, Stockdale wasn't aware he was going to a Ripper murder. He had only just arrived down from Newcastle and did not know that three other prostitutes had been murdered in nearby Leeds. Examining the blood distribution patterns in the room, he kept reminding himself not to impede Peter Swann and his team looking for fingerprints. 'It is well established with all the forces I have worked for, that if the investigation officer's fingerprints are found, then it costs them a round of drinks in the bar. You tend to go around the crime scene with your hands in your pockets. It is very easy to unconsciously pick something up or touch it, which you really ought not to do. I wasn't going to break the habits of my career so far.'

Stockdale became conscious of comments passing between other members of the team. 'Is it him, then?' 'Do you think it's another one?' The questioning was addressed to no one in particular, like a murmur rising almost to a groundswell. Finally he turned to Peter Swann and asked: 'Is it who? What's going on?'

Swann explained. 'We've got a serial killer – he's being called The Ripper.'

'Bloody hell, just my luck to pick up one of these,' Stockdale exclaimed. It was the first time he had heard the words 'The Ripper'.

Stockdale examined the woman's clothing carefully. He believed that after they were pulled down, the jeans and possibly the tights as well had been pulled up again partially. Neither the tights nor the zip fastener of the jeans was damaged in the operation and it was evident that some care had been exercised by the killer. The surface of the body was smeared with blood and gave the appearance of having been manoeuvred by the killer, who must have had wet blood on his hands. Looking around the room generally, he could see there had been no violent struggle or any attempt to ransack the place. He concluded that the sequence of events had been as follows:

1. Atkinson was struck on the head from behind as she entered the room.
2. She fell to the floor bleeding and lay where she fell for some minutes.
3. The killer moved the unconscious body to the bedside where probably her leather coat was removed before being dumped in the corner of the room. The jeans could have been undone at this stage and pulled down, together with her underclothes, and this caused the loss of the left shoe. Bloodstaining on the carpet, the handbag, and the smearing on the leg of the bedside chair, showed probably that another blow to the skull had been struck and that the head had moved about on the floor.
4. The killer, with wet bloody hands, manoeuvred the body on to the unmade bed, probably by clambering on to the bed and dragging the body, rather than by lifting it. In

doing so a bloody footwear impression was left on the bottom sheet between the body and the wall.

5. The bloodstream distribution on the bed indicated further blows to the head and a great deal of blood being lost as a result of the wounds sustained. He also believed the stabbing injuries to the abdomen were probably sustained on the bed.

6. The killer then began a process of 'tidying up', during which the jeans were partially pushed or drawn on to the legs. The bedding was then piled on top of the body and straightened out sufficiently to cover it almost completely, leaving the injuries and the greater part of the bloodstaining hidden from view.

Shortly before midnight all the work that could be done by Domaille's team, Gee and Stockdale was complete, and the body was placed on a large plastic sheet and put into a coffin shell before being taken to the Bradford city mortuary. There Tina's ex-husband, Ramen Mitra, identified her body in the presence of Professor Gee and the coroner's officer. At 1.30 a.m. on the Sunday morning Gee began his post-mortem. It continued until 5 a.m. The usual crowd of officers was present, including a young constable called Alexander, who was, as the first officer at the scene of the murder, also required to attend the post-mortem.

During the autopsy Gee discovered four major depressed fractures of the skull caused by it being struck with a blunt instrument which left crescent-shaped wounds. There were also wounds to the trunk in the form of abrasions to the middle of the back and another group of grazes and stab wounds over the lower abdomen, linked by an irregular linear abrasion across the left side of the chest. He believed that some kind of large-size hammer was involved. Domaille noticed several stabbing wounds just above the pubic region. The killer obviously had some kind of serious sexual hang-up. These and some of the other stab wounds caused Professor Gee particular problems. He thought some object with a blade half an inch wide might have been used – perhaps a screwdriver or chisel.

What he was looking at confirmed what they had seen in the three other murders – a clear and established pattern: similar kinds of head injuries; similar movement of the clothing; the absence of sexual intercourse; and multiple stab wounds produced by a variety of different instruments. 'So far we had two different knives, one screwdriver, and, I now thought, some rectangular-shaped, rather blunt object, like, say, a cold chisel,' he said later. 'In fact, in this I was wrong. I had by now got the clear impression that what happened each time was that the victim was knocked down purely to make them immobile, possibly with the same hammer, then the clothing was disarranged and the stab wounds inflicted with a different weapon each time, because that act provided the necessary satisfaction [for the killer]. One of the big problems I found in an extended series was trying to keep distinct the themes of the patterns of pathology on the one hand and the nature of the actual weapons on the other. But certainly in this case my conception of a hammer on one hand and a blunt chisel on the other prevented me from putting the two together – into one weapon.' He only ascertained the truth much later.

For Gee, as a forensic pathologist, it was crucial to determine how the death was caused. He examined the pattern of injuries, the position of the body, the nature of the wounds, and endeavoured to reconstruct a form in which the injuries could have been sustained. This meant developing, sooner or later, some idea of what actually happened – the order of events. It also meant developing preconceived ideas about the situation, but this could be dangerous, though he saw no way to avoid it. Sometimes it led to mistakes. In his own mind he saw a clear and logical sequence of events for all four cases in the series so far.

'I was quite wrong,' Gee said. 'It turned out that this particular girl [Atkinson] was indeed struck with a hammer, but the penetrating injuries were caused by the claws of the claw hammer, which was used on this occasion.' He should have realized this, he said, by noticing that there was a small second abrasion alongside the main one on the side of the body and from the general pattern of marks on the abdomen. 'I am sure I was misled on this occasion because of having developed this preconceived idea of two weapons being used – a hammer *and* a stabbing instrument of some kind.'

A thorough search of the flat produced a diary among Atkinson's meagre possessions. It contained the names of some fifty men, a good many of whom were probably clients. Two days after the body was found Domaille briefed the local news media about the latest killing.

This was a brutal murder, a very brutal murder. The man we are looking for could be a maniac. The leads that we are following are that there are a number of people in the area that I know knew this lady. I have her diary. This lists a lot of people, names a lot of people, and I would like to see all those people, I shall be making inquiries to trace them. I shall treat as a matter of complete confidentiality any information that comes to me. Anyone can ask to see me personally and I think it might be helpful to some people if they came forward to see me, rather than me making inquiries about some of the facts that I know.

Domaille's team of ninety officers had begun working hard to learn more about the murdered woman. It emerged that Patricia Tina Atkinson's family had lived in the Thorpe Edge district of Bradford and she had two brothers. In 1960, when she was sixteen years old, she met her husband, Ramen Mitra, a Pakistani, at a dance hall in the town. She was working as a burler and mender at a mill in Greengates, Bradford. Perhaps it was an omen that they married on All Fools Day – 1 April 1961. They then lived for a short time with her parents before moving to their own home at Girlington, an area of Bradford next to Manningham. During this period both of Tina's parents died. She and Ramen, known to most people as 'Ray', had three daughters during subsequent years and went on to live mainly in the area of Thorpe Edge where Tina had grown up.

In her mid-twenties she was attractive – slim and with long dark brown hair – and she liked a good time. She knew she looked alluring to men whatever she wore. Dressed in tight jeans and a blouse tied at the waist, as she was the night she died, she appeared quite vivacious. Tina – the mother of three and married so young – felt she hadn't yet done any real living. She enjoyed men's attention and couldn't stop herself being unfaithful; the couple separated on a number of occasions, but then got back together for the children's sake. Finally she left home. In 1975 she had been convicted for prostitution and her husband divorced her on 25 September 1976. He was awarded custody of the children. For a while at least Tina gave up the sex industry. She had met a man called Robert Henderson. They became lovers, but it was a strange, desultory relationship made worse by the fact that she was an alcoholic, and an uncontrollable alcoholic at that. More than that, she got into debt from accumulated fines. A short time before she was killed she went 'back on the game' to improve her finances.

Ten days before she was murdered, Tina rented a small flat in a purpose-built 1960s block in Oak Avenue, Manningham, close to the red-light area of Lumb Lane. The block of apartments, which had a flat bitumen and felt roof, was run down and in poor condition. Surrounded by large Edwardian houses, themselves converted into separate flats and maisonettes, the flats were built on sloping ground, two storeys high at the front and three at the back. Atkinson's was on the ground floor at the back of the premises. To reach it from the Oak Avenue entrance you had to go downstairs.

The Friday night before she died, her boyfriend slept with her. They had sex when the effect of the previous night's alcohol was beginning to wear off – at about four o'clock on the Saturday morning. On the Saturday night, 23 April 1977, Tina went out determined to have a good time visiting her regular drinking haunts, including the Carlisle Hotel. She had been drinking for most of the day. When the stripper who had been booked for the pub failed to turn up, Tina did an impromptu turn, climbing on to the stage. She knew she was good looking, but she was in no condition to entertain the Saturday-night crowd. Tina was totally out of control and things got rowdy. Instead of stripping down to her bra and pants, Tina took all her clothes off. An argument with the manager ensued and by 10.15 Tina was out of the door and on her way to the International Club in Lumb Lane. The last time she was seen it was by another street girl at about 11.10. Tina was weaving and staggering her way down Church Street towards St Mary's Road, completely drunk, having consumed the equivalent of twenty measures of spirits.

The next day Robert Henderson became concerned for his girlfriend's whereabouts and at about 6.30 on the Sunday evening decided to call at her flat. Failing to raise a response for his urgent knocking on the door, he forced his way in and made the appalling discovery of Tina's body on the bed. She was obviously dead. He rushed to the caretaker's and urged him to call the police.

During the inquiry, Domaille made time to meet with Tina's ex-husband and children. 'She had led him a terrible life,' he said. 'He was a Pakistani, an insignificant, ordinary fellow who did his best for her, did everything he could to help her. He wasn't that hard up, reasonably well off money wise, but she was a bad girl.

'I thought about why she may have gone that way, I thought about it a lot. She was in the Manningham environment where the girls get together and the girls talk. I've met and talked with a lot of prostitutes. They are people who have a great understanding of people in the main, a lot of them are mixed up and are to be pitied. Many girls do it because they have been driven towards it. Every now and then you meet one who is going to make her way out of it and they actually do.' Yorkshire police officers can be as hard as nails when discussing women who take to the streets. Others working on the Yorkshire Ripper case over the years came to share Domaille's view of most prostitutes as more sinned against than sinning. 'Murder is murder,' said one. 'Even prostitutes are somebody's daughter, somebody's sister, maybe somebody's wife and somebody's mother.'

The impressions of the boot print in blood found at the bottom of the bed sheet was later thought to have come from a Dunlop 'Warwick' wellington boot. However, since the bed sheet was crumpled it was difficult to determine the exact size, but a match with the boot impression found at the scene of Jackson's murder was thought possible. The flat was full of fingerprints which then had to be gradually eliminated. The previous occupants were traced and had their fingerprints and palm prints taken for elimination purposes, but no matches were found. One set of prints belonged to a man who had returned to live in Africa, who was then traced and eliminated. A total of nine fingerprints were discovered which could not be eliminated. Domaille's team began overhauling all the 'live' inquiries that were still continuing from the three previous murders. Nothing emerged that assisted their effort, with one exception, and that proved a red herring.

Tina Atkinson was a frequent user of taxis – even for the shortest of journeys. Every known taxi driver in Bradford, some 1,200 of them, was interviewed by Domaille's murder squad, along with all convicted and known prostitutes in the city. It was during this phase of the operation that the inquiry went off on a false trail. Questioning taxi drivers revealed nothing of value. But a woman called Barbara Kathryn Miller came forward to reveal she had been attacked in Bradford *two years previously*. The thirty-six-year-old professional stripper was known by police to be an active prostitute in Wolverhampton, Derby and Manningham. She knew Atkinson well and was anxious to help all she could. She told of a man with a beard who picked her up in a pub in Lumb Lane. He drove a Land-Rover with a hard top and a long wheelbase. She could even remember the colour: blue with a dirty cream top. It was in a dirty condition, with a six-inch tear in the black vinyl of the passenger seat and a white square petrol can and sacking behind the driver's seat. He drove her to a quarry in the Bolton Woods area of Bradford for sex. She believed it happened on either a Wednesday or Friday night at about 9.30 in March 1975. The punter told her to get out of the vehicle, and when she refused, he dragged her out and assaulted her, punching her stomach, chest and face. Then he threw her against the vehicle, banging the back of her head. The man fled after the woman began fighting back.

Putting the experience down as a professional hazard, she failed to tell the police. But now, in answer to the appeal from Domaille for prostitutes who had dealt with violent clients to come forward, she provided detectives with a description of her attacker which in some respects matched the description of the man who tried to kill Claxton and Tracey Browne, but in other crucial areas was wide of the mark. The woman said he was thirty-five to forty years old, five feet eight inches tall, of stocky build with untidy ginger hair, a full ginger beard and moustache, but with the beard cut short under the chin. He had blue eyes, a possible Irish accent with a slight Birmingham dialect, a scar on his left hand, and a blue and red tattoo. The photofit she gave police again bore a good likeness to similar descriptions from other women. However, it was the attacker's use of a Land-Rover to which police paid most attention. A description of a similar man had been provided by witnesses in an earlier murder. Emily Jackson was said to have been spotted getting into a Land-Rover at about seven o'clock on the night she was killed, at the junction of Roundhay Road and Gathorne Terrace. He too was described as late forties with ginger beard and a scar on his left hand. Nearly 1,250 Land-Rovers registered in West Yorkshire were eliminated, leaving 159 untraced.

During the next three months the ninety officers investigating Atkinson's murder made 2,300 house-to-house inquiries and 1,924 vehicle checks; completed 3,915 separate actions and took 2,161 statements. All to no avail.

Several years later Domaille ended his police career as an assistant chief constable in the West Yorkshire force. He then had a spell working for the Security Service, MI5. Now long into retirement and living in his native West Country in a town on the edge of Dartmoor, he *still* feels frustration and passion in equal measures about the Atkinson inquiry: 'The only thing wrong with the inquiry was the bloody leader of the investigation – me – didn't catch the man! What can I tell you? I tried and my team bloody tried.'

Four brutal murders and still no conceivable sign of the police catching the man responsible. News of the police investigation was now national headlines, covered extensively in the press and on radio and television. Sunday newspapers dispatched feature writers to Leeds to prepare in-depth stories. The London Weekend Television channel sent its 'Weekend World' team to the North to report on what it saw as a compelling story deserving in-depth analysis.

The pressure to solve these homicides was now firmly on George Oldfield and his men. It was the worst kind of pro-fessional nightmare for a senior detective. A sadistic maniac was randomly choosing vulnerable women as his prey and then cal-lously slaughtering them. There was no motive as such, only the inner compulsions of a sick and twisted mind wielding a murder weapon. The only connection between the victims was that they were all women down on their luck with absolutely no relation-ship to the murderer. He appeared to have a burning inner desire to kill loose women. So far the Ripper had made fourteen chil-dren motherless, one of the few elements of the media coverage which registered in any emotional sense with the general public. That the victims were all prostitutes seemed to count against them in the public mind. While there could be sympathy for the children they left behind, their mothers received very little simply because of their active role in the oldest profession.

It was even harder for the various murder squads dealing with the separate homicides to persuade the victims' various clients to come forward so they could be eliminated. Most men naturally feared exposure as clients of streetwalkers. A knock on the door and awkward questions from a police officer inquiring why a particular individual was in the red-light area on a given night would be understandably unwelcome in either the marital home or the workplace. The fact that the victims were selling sex ensured there was no sense of urgency among the public in seeing the killer apprehended. While the compassionate might sympathize with women forced to go on the streets, others with sterner views saw it as a sordid activity and had little empathy. The law-abiding citizens of Leeds and Bradford might have eagerly come forward with potential evidence if an elderly woman or schoolgirl had been murdered. But in the case of the Ripper victims they hung back. Senior investigating officers had to think of ways of keeping the story in the public eye in the hope of jogging a potential witness's memory. In the red-light areas prostitutes frequented in Leeds and Bradford, actual witnesses seemed few and far between.

Yet again the local police exhausted all the tried and tested methods of solving murders. Yet again there were precious few clues. The only positive evidence was the tyre tracks found in Roundhay Park during the Richardson slaying. The team eliminating all the vehicles in West Yorkshire that could have left such tyre marks continued their foot-slogging work. Thousands and thousands of vehicles were being screened. But such huge and painstaking inquiries brought no returns and it was never easy trying to maintain morale among those given the day-to-day tasks of relentless door knocking.

Each detective taking part in this kind of inquiry has to live with the knowledge that a single false move, a question forgotten, a momentary loss of concentration, might eliminate the killer, passing over the real culprit and rendering the whole exercise futile. Such an error would leave the inquiry team working in vain, without knowing their quarry had already escaped the net. For the conscientious officer wanting to do everything he can to catch a killer, the strain of possibly making such a mistake must be enormous.

The easiest vehicles to screen in the tyre inquiry were done quickly. People who had not moved home and had kept their vehicle since the time of the Richardson murder could be seen and eliminated reasonably swiftly. It was thought unlikely that an owner would have changed all four tyres. The remaining unseen vehicles proved gradually more and more difficult to eliminate. The vehicle may have been sold, scrapped or abandoned. Each generated new lines of inquiry for the beleaguered force. Where someone said they no longer had the car, its current whereabouts had to be checked. There was also a critical need to keep the reason for the tyre operation top secret in case the killer realized the vehicle he owned might trap him. The tyres might be changed and dumped, or the vehicle crushed and turned into a three-foot cube of metal. Hobson's 'tracking' inquiry moved past the half-way stage and before midsummer 1977 more than 30,000 vehicles had been seen. For the Leeds murder squad under Hobson's command, it seemed the best chance they had of catching the killer – providing he still had his car with him.

The process of recording who had been seen in relation to the Richardson tyre inquiry involved indexing vehicle makes and registration numbers on special cards, but with no separate name index of vehicle owners who had cars with tyres which could have matched those left at the Richardson crime scene. Although Peter Sutcliffe was the owner of one of the vehicles on Hobson's vast list of over 50,000 potential suspects, his name as yet figured nowhere within the incident room card index system – though a record of the vehicle he owned had yet to be eliminated from the tyre inquiry. If Sutcliffe's name should arise in connection with some other aspect of the inquiry, no one would be able to tell he had been on the list of potential suspects for the Richardson murder. There were still separate incident rooms for each of the four murders. With no computers available to handle the ever-expanding number of inquiries or the information they produced, the various incident rooms relied on the paper-led system: the keeping of various indexes relating to different aspects of the inquiry and the taking of statements – lots of them. It all took time and manpower.

In any area of Britain the number of police officers and their supervisors is a scarce resource. Precisely how much manpower was needed to devote to a 'tracking' inquiry that covered the whole geographical area of West Yorkshire as well as Harrogate in North Yorkshire was highly questionable. The normal pace of life in the region continued unabated, which meant other crimes also had to be tackled. Prostitute victims or not, the existence of a multiple murderer operating in the Leeds and Bradford area raised the stakes for a force CID already burdened with an average twenty-six murders to investigate every year, along with armed robberies, rapes, and sexual assaults as well as routine burglaries and vehicle crimes. Altogether in 1977 West Yorkshire Police had 128,000 crimes reported, including 5,000 crimes of violence. Roughly half these crimes were being solved.

Responsibility for not simply doing something, but being *seen* to do something rested ultimately with Oldfield's boss:

the chief constable, Ronald Gregory. As chief, he had total autonomy to run the operational side of the force as he thought fit. In legal terms, he alone had 'direction and control' of his force. As long as he carried out this task 'efficiently' within the terms of the 1964 Police Act, no one could tell him what to do. By tradition and by statute chief constables are independent office holders, a key feature of British democracy. A local police authority or watch committee could oversee the work of the police, but they couldn't tell the chief constable what to do. The task of overseeing the efficiency of police forces rested with the Inspectors of Constabulary, who reported back to the Home Secretary. For generations in Britain this general rule for the well-ordered preservation of the public good had been observed: no one wanted politicians telling police officers who they could or couldn't arrest. In 1968, Lord Denning, Master of the Rolls, made the legal position of chief constables clear: 'No Minister of the Crown can tell him that he must or must not keep observation on this place or that; or that he must not prosecute this man or that one. Nor can any Police Authority tell him so. The responsibility of law enforcement lies on him. He is answerable to the law alone.'

However, a massive investigation by one police force into four unsolved murders by the same person had its price. Manpower was stretched, and with it came a rising bill for police overtime. With the costs mounting, Gregory consulted with his local police authority and so ensured that the necessary financial resources to solve the killings were found from within the West Yorkshire Police budget. But it was also clear that something more had to be done for the public to continue to have confidence in their local police service.

De facto, the buck in 1977 stopped at George Oldfield's first-floor office as assistant chief constable in charge of crime at the Wakefield HQ. For a year he had followed the normal procedure of handing day-to-day responsibility for each individual murder inquiry to the various senior investigating officers. In 1977, as the number of incidents involving the Ripper increased dramatically, there were sensational headlines and public disquiet. How Oldfield dealt with the pressures of the case became the source of considerable controversy over the years. That his response was to overwork himself, drink too heavily and habitually smoke his Craven A cigarettes, was undeniable. The mode of life led eventually to him having two heart attacks.

Later the spotlight would fall on Oldfield's judgement calls. His management of twentieth-century Britain's most important criminal investigation became the subject of unique official scrutiny. After a five-year killing spree by the Yorkshire Ripper, the failure to capture him became a national scandal and a group of Britain's most senior detectives descended on West Yorkshire police. Their orders from the very top of the Home Office were to 'Sort out what is going wrong'. This unprecedented move came after an outraged Margaret Thatcher herself told the Home Secretary that she was inclined to take personal charge of the Ripper inquiry.

But no one could accuse George Oldfield of being either lazy, uncommitted or a fool. He was typical of many who held similar jobs up and down Britain. He knew about crime, serious crime, and he was a good thief taker. Taking over as ACC (crime) from Donald Craig meant he had a lot to live up to. His predecessor had investigated seventy-three murders and solved every one. It had been Oldfield's ambition, according to his wife, to become head of CID, and now he was in the hot seat. He had learned the art of mastering internal politics. Indeed, he could never have risen to assistant chief constable had he not understood the value of discretion or been in the habit of making enemies among the force hierarchy. There was, however, a persistent rumour among the higher echelons of the force's CID that, when offered the job of ACC (crime), he had been warned he had to cut down on his drinking.

Professionally he was an enthusiastically hard worker who took his job very seriously and demanded an equally determined effort from subordinates. Though undoubtedly a leader at local level, he lacked the sophisticated knowledge and intellectually rigorous mind necessary to employ innovative procedures to break the deadlock confronting him. Normally a soft-spoken man, in the latter years of his career he could be mistaken for a country farmer. Rough shooting was his favourite pastime. He presented a bucolic appearance typical among those brought up in rural areas who have improved their station in life. He wore on occasions country tweeds, and his round face and cheeks bore the ruddy features of someone who liked the outdoor life and knew a good quality whisky when he drank it. However easygoing he was at home, his outbursts of temper at work were legendary, though not necessarily understood. He was essentially a private man, rarely speaking about his family, preferring to keep home and professional life separate. When riled by something or someone at work his anger could turn to fury in an instant. He could swear like a trooper, yet he was never one to hold grudges. Once an admonishment was delivered, so far as he was concerned it was over and dealt with, though those who worked for him frequently remembered it for years.

'He could go bloody mad when he was angry,' a close colleague and admirer remembered. 'He would use abusive language and then it was all forgotten. You had had your bollocking. The next job you did for him, you were just as likely to get a pat on the back. Some of the other senior officers bore you malice; if you had dropped a clanger it was with you for life, but it wasn't so with him.'

Oldfield ran a tight ship. He wanted to know about serious crime when it happened within the force area. A divisional detective chief inspector was expected to let Oldfield have information quickly, rather than keep him in the dark. 'We had to ring in, he never objected to being told about something at three in the morning,' said the same officer, who worked closely with Oldfield over many years. 'He was quite happy, once he got to know you and how you worked, to leave a serious job that happened during the night to you. But you had to contact him before 8.55 the following morning. This was so he had the story when he was asked by the chief constable about it and when the headquarters press conference took place. If ever something came up at either of those two meetings, which he had every morning, without him having been told, you got the mother and father of a bollocking. If it happened a few times, you didn't keep your job.'

He was born Godfrey Alexander Oldfield in 1924 and grew up in that area of eastern Yorkshire where the terrain of flat, featureless pastureland is strikingly similar to Holland and the Low Countries. He lived in his early years with his brothers, who were twins, amid the farming community on the far eastern fringes of what was then the West Riding at Monk Fryston, a small village tucked away out on its own a few miles from Castleford. His grandfather was the local blacksmith. Like many villages in those days it still had a working windmill where flour was produced. The surrounding farmland hardly rose more than twenty feet above sea level all the way to the Yorkshire Wolds.

Oldfield's father worked for the LNER (the London and North Eastern Railway). When he was eleven the family moved several miles across the Vale of York to Cawood, where his father became local station master. It was another closely knit rural community, more a small town than a village, but it had its own branch line to the inland port of Selby five miles away. The line halted at Cawood, which had grown in importance historically because of its proximity to the River Ouse, in whose flood plain it lay. Its swing bridge provided the last crossing point on the navigable River Ouse before the ancient City of York ten miles away. Several other rivers fed the Ouse on its journey via the Humber to the North Sea forty miles distant. Formerly Cawood was one of the chief residences of the Archbishop of York, who had a fortified palace-cum-castle built there, and frequently the royal court moved there from Windsor. It was the place where Cardinal Wolsey was arrested and charged with high treason.

The move coincided with Oldfield attending one of Yorkshire's top boys' grammar schools, Archbishop Holgate's in York, where he became known as 'George'. Indeed, he insisted on the name being used because of his intense dislike of being called Godfrey. The family never used it. At home, and to his future wife, Margaret, who also lived in Cawood, he was always called 'Goff'.

After leaving grammar school he worked briefly at Naburn Station, just outside York, on the LNER route from London to Edinburgh. His first exposure to iron discipline came as a young naval seaman during the Second World War after he joined the Royal Navy, aged eighteen, in 1942. He hardly ever talked to his family of his war service, either after he got home in 1946 or in later years. He came from that generation of stoical men made brittle by the experience of war who preferred to keep to themselves the awful truth of what they had personally witnessed rather than burden those closest to them.

As a twenty-year-old seaman he saw enemy action aboard HMS *Albatross*, a much-overhauled former Australian seaplane carrier. In May 1944, she set sail from Devonport and headed up the English Channel in a convoy towards the Goodwin Sands. In darkness, at four o'clock in the morning on the 23rd, she ran aground. 'We were high and dry,' Phil Mortimer, then a nineteen-year-old telegraphist from Poole, remembers. 'It was dark and I think we lost our way. We had to wait for the tide to turn. We came under attack from German shore batteries at Cap Gris Nez. You could see them flashing as they fired, and then the shells landed, splashing in the water around us. It was pretty nerve wracking.'

Two weeks later, the 6,000-ton vessel was positioned off SWORD beach during the D-Day landings on the Normandy coast around Ouistreham. The *Albatross* had been converted specially for the invasion of France into a repair ship for landing craft. Its cranes could hoist the flat-bottomed boats out of the water so engineers could work on them. She was armed with anti-aircraft and machine guns.

Twice in late June she was hit by shellfire from German coastal batteries, which penetrated the upper deck, though the damage was superficial. Eventually she came under torpedo attack on 11 August, off Courselles, and suffered sixty-nine dead and many seriously injured, at about 6.30 in the morning. The torpedo struck in the forward mess-deck on the port side. Phil Mortimer recalls how the *Albatross* immediately keeled over to one side. There was a general power failure and the lights went out. In shallow water the surviving crew members managed to shore up the damage. She made her way heavily down in the water to the safety of Portsmouth Harbour, listing badly and towed stern-first by a Dutch tug, with an escort from the minesweeper HMS *Acacia*. On this difficult journey some twenty of those killed were lashed in their hammocks and buried at sea. Those crew members who were able were mustered aft to witness the skipper reading the prayer to the dead.

In dry dock in the minesweeping section of the naval base the water was pumped out of the *Albatross*. Another fifty dead lay below decks, most still in their hammocks. Members of HMS *Acacia*'s crew were among those detailed to go below and retrieve the bodies. They included a nineteen-year-old steward/cook from Blackpool, Frank Roberts. 'Retrieving the trapped bodies was a really gruesome task,' he remembered. 'We were given a mask and a tot of rum and told to get on with it. Some of the dead we found stuck in the portholes as they tried to escape. There was a hole in the side of the ship the size of a bus. We wrapped up those still in their hammocks and brought them out. It was very traumatic and of course we had no such thing as counselling in those days.' The bodies were then transferred to a landing craft and buried at sea off Chichester. Immediately afterwards George Oldfield was sent home on sick leave to Yorkshire, where he remained for six months with a stress-related illness.

In 1946, after demob from the Navy as a petty officer, he arrived back in Cawood as one of thousands of reasonably educated young men throughout Britain wondering what to do with the rest of their lives. The local village policeman recommended a career in the police, and Oldfield joined the West Riding force the following year. It would, he assured his family, provide him with a good steady job and a pension. It was time to get on with life and forget the awful carnage he had witnessed.

Oldfield was to become living proof that it was possible in Britain gradually to rise from humble origins via a meritocratic police service to hold an important position within the local community. Like Dennis Hoban in Leeds, he spent virtually all his career in the CID gradually rising through the ranks. Unlike Hoban, his postings were far and wide, from one end of the West Riding to the other. Harrogate for one job, Barnsley for another. By 1962 he was a detective chief inspector at Dewsbury. Two years later, he returned briefly to uniform at Keighley before being transferred to the CID staff at the Wakefield headquarters as a detective superintendent and deputy head of CID for the whole of the West Riding. In 1971 he went back into uniform as a chief superintendent for two years. Then, in 1973, he returned to West Yorkshire CID as its head, taking the place of Donald Craig, who had become an assistant chief constable. When the major amalgamation with Leeds and Bradford took place in 1974, Donald Craig held the top job in overall charge of CID. Oldfield was his deputy.

Generally he got on well with his senior colleagues. However, he did have longstanding problems with some senior detectives from the Leeds and Bradford force after amalgamation. Some of the city detectives had no time for Oldfield, nor did he for them. A great deal of the mutual distrust had its origins in an official inquiry Oldfield conducted during the mid-1960s into corruption among some city detectives in Leeds. Called in to investigate as a senior officer from outside Leeds, he was utterly ruthless during this inquiry, often undertaking forceful interrogations in an effort to get to the truth. He had the homes of suspected officers put under intense surveillance, then had their homes searched, and thus put pressure on them through their families.

'The allegations involved taking backhanders from villains, taking things from people. We are talking about detectives,' said one officer, familiar with the inquiry at the time. 'Some of the Leeds lads on the Crime Squad were interviewed and they thought they had had a hard time, that they were treated like villains.' In short, Oldfield did as he was supposed to do: his investigation was run on the lines of an inquiry into criminal behaviour. But the result was an abiding resentment amongst some officers that he had damaged officers' careers unjustifiably.

Much of Oldfield's effort during the corruption inquiry had centred on Brotherton House in Leeds, the City Police HQ and also the home of the local Regional Crime Squad in which some of the suspected officers had served. During the Christmas festivities that year, Oldfield was invited by the local RCS boss to their annual dinner. 'He [the RCS boss] made a tactical bloomer,' said one of those present. 'It was a stupid thing to do because you do not invite someone who is conducting an outside inquiry of that sort to a Christmas dinner. George also made a bloomer in that he came to the dinner . . . when he came in we all walked out and went to another bar to have a drink. We had arranged that if he turned up, we'd leave as a protest. We left him with the boss.'

The same detective, who was seconded to the RCS, felt no personal animosity to Oldfield. Later he came to realize what Oldfield was up against when he returned to his home force and was subsequently himself asked to conduct an inquiry into a corrupt Leeds officer. 'It concerned several thousand pounds worth of missing metal and an investigation that went bad,' he said. 'This officer tipped off the thieves. He didn't take money for it, he was crafty enough to have gone on a foreign holiday with his wife and kids, paid for by the criminals.'

Oldfield was by nature a private man and remained very much an enigma. He virtually cultivated the image. Few of his colleagues got really close to him over the years. He and his wife Margaret, his longstanding friend from Cawood, had married in 1954. He was thirty, she twenty-six. Tragedy came seven years later when their six-year-old first born, Judith, developed leukaemia. The doctors told Oldfield that their little girl had just six months to live. Unable to give Margaret such heart-breaking news, he told his wife their daughter would live for another year. In the end she did survive another twelve months. It was a heart-aching period in both their lives. His wife saw Oldfield develop a nervous affliction as a result of the child's death: a twitch in his shoulder, which never left him.

At work he showed the obsessive behaviour traits familiar in many senior detectives: long hours, a devotion to detail and the ability to sit through the night poring over reports, aided by cigarettes and whisky. But his home life provided an important kind of relief from the stresses and rigours of crime and criminals. He was devoted to his wife, who came from farming stock, and their three other children, two boys and another girl. The youngest, Christopher, was born when Oldfield was forty-one. They put the money aside to have them educated privately in Wakefield and all three offspring took up professional careers in, respectively, the law, accountancy and dentistry.

For a good many years the Oldfield family had to move with his job. They lived in a variety of police houses across the West Riding, in Dewsbury, Keighley and Wakefield. In 1968 they bought their first home, a bungalow high up at Grange Moor on the fringes of Huddersfield, 750 feet above sea level. From there it was a relatively quick journey down to the M62 or M1 motorways, which gave him easy access to most places within the force area. His journey to his office at Wakefield was straightforward: down the A642 and through Horbury into the city.

At home when the children were young he played with them and shared their interests as best he could. In truth the family did not see a good deal of him, but one almost sacrosanct occasion was lunch on Sunday, when the Oldfields ate *en famille*. Most weeks Oldfield checked the fish in the ornamental pond in his front garden, and at weekends he would poke about in his vegetable patch where he grew some of the family's produce. At the outbreak of the Ripper killings he had just started work on building a greenhouse behind his garage. 'He loved getting out of suits and into his old clothes to go out into the garden,' his wife reflected. He also amused himself with old blacksmith's and tinsmith's tools, getting the rust off and restoring them to their original condition so he could display them in the home.

Margaret was a keen cook, and like many women from farming families she was good with the pastry and baking. When a police colleague occasionally visited the bungalow, she would bring out the results of her home baking with coffee on a tray, then discreetly take her leave so as to allow the men to discuss police business. Margaret Oldfield saw her role as keeping things normal at home. 'If anything came up on television we would just laugh it off. We tried to keep quiet about the things he was involved in, so that he didn't have to talk about it at home.'

His abiding sense of justice and personal knowledge of the fragility of childhood demonstrated itself in one of his inquiries as a detective chief inspector earlier in his career. He was brought in, again as an outside officer, to investigate criminal allegations of sexual assault against two young girls by a uniformed police officer. He particularly asked for a detective sergeant called Dick Holland to act as his bagman during the delicate inquiry. Holland had three daughters of his own. After some while spent gathering evidence, Oldfield determined that the officer was guilty, but they would have grave difficulty mounting a successful prosecution. He told Holland: 'If we take this to court these girls will not stand up in court in giving evidence against a police sergeant and they will break down. It might ruin their lives.' Oldfield had had a long talk with the girls' parents. He wanted to ensure that the police service was not stuck with an officer who had been acquitted on a technicality of a serious offence against young girls. 'What we want to do is get rid of this bastard. The girls have suffered enough. If they break down in court and he is reinstated, what are we left with?'

'His whole attitude was that the police service had to get rid of this bad egg, but he was not having anything adverse happen to these little girls,' Holland recalled. 'Another investigator may have done it by the book and it would have gone all the way to court.'

While Oldfield was deliberately reticent at home about the crimes he was investigating, it was impossible for his wife not to see how he could be deeply affected by his work, especially when tragedy struck families with children. One night in 1974 the phone rang at 1.30 a.m. It was at the height of a series of IRA terrorist outrages in England. He answered the call and then put the phone down, telling Margaret: 'They've blown up a bus.' He got dressed and headed for the nearby M62, where a bomb had exploded on a coach carrying army personnel and their families back to Catterick Camp in North Yorkshire. He then led the major inquiry into the murders of a dozen people. Among the dead were two small children. He had witnessed for himself the horrendous aftermath of the bombing. Body parts were spread all over the carriageway. The carnage sickened him.

During murder inquiries, Oldfield always tried to spend as little time as possible at the post-mortem, perhaps as a result of what he had seen aboard HMS *Albatross* as a young man. He couldn't bring himself to spend too long at the autopsies on the coach bombing victims, telling a close colleague that the mortuary resembled 'a butcher's shop'. Dick Holland, by now promoted to detective chief inspector, remembered: 'He didn't like post-mortems. He didn't shirk his duty, but he did have the minimum contact with the bodies. He was a bloody good commander and gave the right orders [at the scene of the outrage], things like that came naturally to him. The sight of the children blown apart affected him like it affected all of us.'

Oldfield was to describe the coach bombing as the most horrifying scene of mass murder in his experience. It confirmed his view that terrorists deserved capital punishment. 'I had the misfortune to see the terrible injuries inflicted on the victims . . . As long as I live I will never forget the grievous injuries suffered by those two children.'

After the first news of the coach bombing, his family didn't see George Oldfield for several days. A week or so later he appeared to have developed a phobia about alarm clocks. 'He told me to get rid of the clock in our bedroom,' said Mrs Oldfield. 'I know that incident affected him because he simply couldn't rest, couldn't sleep properly if he heard the ticking noise of the clock. He couldn't stand the sound of the ticking.'

6

A Fresh Start

Several weeks before the midsummer of 1977 a key decision had been made by George Oldfield. If there was another murder in the Ripper series, then he would take command as senior investigating officer and continue with his role of ACC (crime), doing the two jobs back-to-back. He didn't have long to wait. On Sunday morning, 26 June, nine weeks after the death of Patricia Atkinson, a woman's body was found on waste ground in Chapeltown, Leeds. The discovery was made by two young children. The fact of the body being found in an area frequented by prostitutes was enough to justify a call to Oldfield. He immediately told the control room at force headquarters to contact Dick Holland at home. By now a detective superintendent, Holland was deputy head of CID for the Western Area, operating out of Bradford. Preparing to don an SIO's hat, he wanted a senior detective at his side who knew how the old West Yorkshire force investigated murders.

'He knew me and the way I worked, and he knew I would work the West Yorkshire system,' says Holland. 'This wasn't going to be my murder – it was Oldfield's, but George would be able to keep nipping off to do his job at headquarters and leave me there, knowing his will would be carried out. He regarded me as an extension of himself. If he had left Hobson in charge, it would have been done Hobson's way.' Holland was Oldfield's protégé – they were West Riding men and there was mutual respect and trust. Holland, then a divorcee, would become one of the few officers invited to Oldfield's home. The two thought alike. In Holland's view they were 'a bit like bookends'. A close colleague once told Holland the only difference between him and Oldfield was that, 'George's answer to stress and problems is a bottle of whisky. Yours is to go out and buy a steak or a meal.' Holland – a giant of a man who turned out rain and shine for the force rugby team – was a non-smoking, non-drinking foodaholic. 'I knew how to switch off and I enjoy the company of women. George was set in his ways. You weren't going to change George,' he said.

He drove to Leeds at high speed down the motorway, to find Oldfield had just beaten him to the murder scene. Oldfield came to greet him, then directed him to a patch of derelict land in front of a children's adventure playground in Reginald Street, next to a dilapidated factory building scheduled for demolition. It was overlooked by two streets. Three-storey Edwardian terraced houses in Reginald Terrace faced the playground on one side; the rear gardens and outhouses of a row of large semi-detached houses looked across on to the crime scene on the other side of Reginald Street. The playground itself resembled a Wild West stockade, its boundary fencing made of timbered railway sleepers driven several feet into the ground, with sawn lengths of barked timber secured at the top to a height of about seven feet. The equipment in the children's play area was made from large timbers, including telegraph poles. One half of what had been a pair of hinged timbered gates at the entrance into the stockade remained shut. The other gate was missing.

A mobile police command with a tall radio mast had been positioned in Reginald Street, complete with its own power generator. Roads had been cordoned off and detectives with clipboards were already knocking on doors. Milling around were members of the Leeds murder squad, who had received an early 'shout' of possibly another Ripper killing. They did not know Oldfield had decided on a change of tactics. Neither, apparently, did Jim Hobson, who as head of the city's CID was present and expecting to lead another murder inquiry. He was trying to drive along his Ripper investigation, anxiously following the progress of the tyre inquiry and organizing a small proactive undercover operation in the Chapeltown area using a few women police officers as decoys. His team were starting to gear up for a major investigation when Oldfield announced he was taking charge and bringing in his own team of supervisors.

Oldfield wanted a fresh start, using the West Yorkshire murder investigation system drawn up by his predecessor, Donald Craig. Holland's most important task would be to indoctrinate the Leeds murder incident room team into using the West Yorkshire system of keeping records. It meant more statements would be taken. The Leeds system relied not on paper but on activity, with paperwork kept to a minimum. Oldfield wanted much more detail, especially in terms of descriptions of people seen around the crime scene at relevant times.

Holland explained the reason: 'If somebody says, "I was saying goodnight to my girlfriend outside No. 14 Reginald Terrace when I saw a man come past in a navy blue blazer with brass buttons, pale blue shirt and dark blue trousers," you want to be able to consult the index system in the incident room to find out who fits that description and see who has been identified and make sure this person has been properly eliminated.' The Leeds system was excellent at dealing with murders committed by local people. Most were quickly solved because detectives were not bogged down by paperwork; they could put manpower to better use. But if the inquiry became protracted, Oldfield believed, a more thorough system of record keeping based on detailed statements was essential, especially if they were going to mount a successful prosecution. And that was the ultimate goal: to get the guilty man into court and put away.

Inside the playground area was a single-storey, white-painted clubhouse covered in graffiti. A scenes-of-crime photographer stood on the felt-covered flat roof taking pictures, looking down at the corpse on the ground behind the wooden fence, and at the general area of waste ground towards Reginald Street already marked out in white tape. The senior detectives had to wait until the photographer completed his work on the roof before going to see the body. Near the corpse lay an old spring mattress, dumped alongside a pile of rubbish, including a rolled-up length of disused carpet. One of the woman's shoes, which bore an impossibly long high heel, lay beside her foot.

Because a local pub was a regular haunt of prostitutes, the automatic assumption was that the victim was a street walker. Oldfield and Holland strolled over a tarmac path crossing the waste land, which contained a considerable amount of rubbish. Oldfield pointed out a woman's imitation leather handbag lying beside the path, a few feet from Reginald Street. Adjacent to it was a piece of rough paper which appeared heavily blood-stained.

The sandy soil leading to the playground entrance was bone dry. A clear trail, consisting of a line of spots and splashes of blood, together with furrows in the soil that looked like drag marks, led down the gentle slope from Reginald Street towards the gateway. Inside the playground on the right side, close to the boundary brick wall of the derelict factory and lying parallel with the timber fencing, was the body of the young woman. From the street she was completely hidden. She lay face down with her head six feet from the brick wall. The legs were stretched out straight and the feet were crossed, the left over the right; the left arm was bent up with the hand beneath her head, the right arm stretched out beside the body. There were large quantities of rubbish and refuse, old tin cans, broken bottles and other material around the corpse.

The body was clad in a grey jacket which had been partly pulled upwards to the shoulders exposing bare skin in her lower back. Her blue and white checked skirt was rumpled towards the upper part of her thighs. One of her high-heeled pale yellow 'clog' shoes was still in place; her black tights had a hole visible in the left heel. On closer inspection, the detectives could see blood soiling her head and left hand as well as her jacket and skirt. Vertical trickles of blood ran downwards from the back of the chest across the sides of her body.

By now Professor Gee had arrived. He walked across the wooden duck-boarding into the playground to join the group of officers behind the fence. A fingerprint officer and forensic scientist were making a superficial examination of the body. Green bottle flies buzzed around the victim who they could now see was a young woman, probably in her teens. As the photographer took his pictures flies appeared on her jacket and hair. After a while Gee himself lifted the skirt to expose her underwear. A pale blue underskirt had been raised slightly upwards. Her tights were in the normal position and beneath them she wore a black pair of pants and an external sanitary pad. Peter Swann, the fingerprint expert, wanted some of the woman's clothing sent away for special examination. The jacket had obviously been pulled up towards the victim's head by the killer. To prevent contamination, plastic bags were placed over her shoes and hands. The body was then gently raised, the belt of her skirt and the zip fastener at the side were loosened so the skirt could be removed. Her jacket, held by one button across the front of her chest, was also undone and removed, revealing a blue and white sun top bunched up in the upper part of the back. Beneath it was a single stab wound.

Indications confirmed she had been dragged along the ground. Debris was caught in the centre of the straps at the back of the sun top. A piece of paper was discovered in the folds of the left side of the skirt in front of the abdomen. When the body was turned over and placed on a plastic sheet they saw blood soiling the young woman's face. She looked very young and wore no bra. Her sun top was displaced, exposing the nipple of her left breast. In the front of the central upper region of her abdomen was a large wound and embedded in it was part of the broken top of a bottle with a screw top. Gee pointed out two irregular wounds to the scalp. After mortuary officials took the body away, two more pools of blood were found – one where the abdomen had lain, the other close to the head.

During a four-hour post-mortem that afternoon Gee found three semi-circular lacerated wounds to the scalp typical of other Ripper killings, along with depressed fractures to the skull. In the chest area, in addition to the large wound containing the bottle top, was a series of long scratches and cuts. A large stab wound in her back had penetrated various organs, including heart, kidneys and lungs. Gee thought a thin-bladed weapon, not less than six and a half inches long, had been thrust through the two openings on the front and back of the body. Multiple thrusts, perhaps as many as twenty, had been made in and out of the same wound, causing it to become much enlarged. The broken bottle top probably entered the chest as the victim was turned over on the ground. She had first been hit on the back of the head at the edge of the waste ground and fallen. She was then struck again on the head and, while still alive, dragged by hands under the armpits from the point where her handbag was found, down the slope and into the playground area.

The body initially lay on its back when the stab wounds at the front were inflicted. Then it was turned on its face and further stab wounds made to the back. Gee knew for sure she was not yet dead when some of these stab wounds were made because he found a large quantity of blood in each chest cavity. The killer had removed the knife from the back wound and then wiped each side of the blade on the skin on the woman's back. Death had occurred some time between midnight and 3 a.m.

Soon after arriving at the crime scene, Jim Hobson had someone search the handbag found on the waste and her identity was quickly established. She was Jayne Michelle Mac-Donald, a sixteen-year-old who lived near by in Scott Hall Avenue. Wilma McCann, the Ripper's first victim, had been a close neighbour in the same road, just six doors away. It seemed probable that Jayne MacDonald was mistaken for a prostitute when she was killed taking a short cut home across the waste ground, probably only a hundred yards from safety. She had gone with a girlfriend to a city centre bar, the Hofbrauhaus, at eight o'clock on the Saturday night, and left in the company of a young man aged about eighteen, with broad shoulders and a slim waist.

Jayne was a singularly pretty teenager with shoulder-length light brown hair; a good-looking girl, according to her friends, always smiling and truly the apple of her father Wilfred's eye. He collapsed when police told him Jayne had been murdered, and subsequently developed nervous asthma and chronic bron-chitis and never returned to his job with British Rail. He spent days on end staring at a photo of his daughter and patiently carving a wooden cross from the ladder of her old bunk bed. It came to mark Jayne's last resting place. He couldn't forget what he had seen in the mortuary when he went to identify her body. According to his wife, Irene, all he would say was that there was blood over Jayne's beautiful hair.

Jayne had left a local high school a few months previously at Easter to work in the shoe department at Grandways super-market in Roundhay Road. It sounds like a cliché to say she was a happy-go-lucky teenager, but in her case it was true. She loved life, indeed had everything to live for, and liked to spend her money on clothes and going out dancing or roller skating. Hers was a close-knit community, the kind where neighbours and friends did favours for one another and whose children were in and out of each other's homes. One such family were the Bransbergs, who had a telephone, unlike the MacDonalds. Normally, if Jayne was planning to stay over at a girlfriend's house, she would call the Bransbergs and they would tell her parents. Wilf MacDonald and Irene were a loving and devoted couple who kept a close eye on all their children, four girls and a son. Recently Jayne had broken off a relationship with a boyfriend, believing he was getting 'too serious'. In their eyes, she was a bonny girl with a trim figure for her age, who simply drew the boys. They liked to believe their daughter was 'innocent', which in 1977 meant they thought she had not yet lost her virginity. In fact she had been having regular inter-course with her two previous boyfriends.

Jack Bransberg worked for British Rail with Jayne's father. She had called to see him and his wife before going into town on Saturday night. She was going dancing at the Astoria

Ballroom, then on to another discotheque. When, later that night, Jayne didn't phone to say she would be late, both her parents and the Bransbergs assumed she had had a little too much to drink, stayed with a friend and forgot to telephone. Wilf MacDonald was furious Jayne had not called, more concerned about her thoughtlessness than anything else. After the death of Wilma McCann, all local parents had been alarmed the killer might strike again. But that was twenty-one months before and the fear was starting to wear off. Nevertheless Jayne had several times promised her mother she would never walk home alone in the dark.

As with all the relatives of the Ripper's victims so far, the tragedy had a devastating effect on the family, the more so perhaps because this was a sixteen-year-old, carefree girl about to begin life when she was snatched away in such a brutal fashion. 'He has killed my Jayne,' cried a tearful Mrs MacDonald. 'She was a virgin. A clean-living girl. How many more?'

Her husband was still under sedation, too shocked to be interviewed. The family doctor said the entire family was in a terrible state: 'The husband is very bad and I have had to give him a sedative injection this morning because he has been in a state of complete collapse. This has been added to because of the fact that he had to go down and identify his daughter and see the terrible injuries she had suffered. This is an awful lot for any man to put up with. The murder itself is something which is a terrible thing to have to accept but to have to go down and identify the body and see the full extent of this is just making it even worse.'

Neighbours and friends of the MacDonalds rallied round to give them support, with several helping around the house. Others vented their feelings in a different way. The day after the murder white painted graffiti appeared on a nearby wall: 'SCOTT HALL SAYS HANG THE RIPPER!'

Piecing together the last few hours of Jayne's life took detectives several days of foot slogging. Oldfield wanted a minute breakdown of where she went after leaving the city centre. A detailed surveyor's street map of the area, showing every house, was blown up and placed on a wall of the incident room on the top floor of Millgarth Police Station. He wanted to flag everyone who had been in the area at the relevant time in the hope someone must have seen the killer and possibly his car.

The Hofbrauhaus in the Merion Centre in Leeds was a *Bierkeller* and one of the city's earliest themed pubs. It advertised German beer for only 32p a pint, and although trade could be slow early in the week, come Thursday, Friday and Saturday the place hotted up and the ale began to flow. Chief attraction was an 'Oompah Band', a fake German band dressed in leather shorts and Tyrolean hats which played songs like 'The Happy Wanderer' and waltzes associated with the Black Forest and Austria. Despite being under legal drinking age, Jayne had no trouble gaining entry. She met a local lad, Mark Jones, whose fair hair was brushed back off his face and who wore a dark velvet jacket, a light coloured shirt and dark flared trousers. There was a clear mutual attraction. She had not drunk any alcohol in the crowded bar, preferring soft drinks on what was already a warm night. When the Hofbrauhaus closed at 10.30 they left to walk into the city centre with his friends. Eventually the others drifted off until he and Jayne were left alone. They stopped for a bag of chips in the city centre, and then realized Jayne had missed her last bus. It was about midnight. They started walking up the York Road towards Chapeltown, Mark promising that his sister, who lived near by, would drive her home. When they reached his sister's house, he saw her car wasn't there, and they continued walking towards St James's Hospital. They went into the garden of the nurses' home and lay there on the ground for forty-five minutes, having a kiss and a cuddle. Jones later told detectives that Jayne was still having a period. She had promised him they would have sex together if he met her during the week.

The young couple later set off walking towards Harehills, but when they reached Becket Street they parted company. It was now 1.30 a.m. Mark himself had to go to his home on a nearby council estate. Jayne didn't seem at all bothered. Close by was Greenways, the supermarket where she worked. If she couldn't hail a taxi, she was used to walking home. So they bade each other farewell and promised to renew their assignation the following Wednesday. She walked off along Becket Street towards Harehills Road. Several people saw her walking along in her ridiculously high 'clog' shoes, including two AA patrolmen in their vehicle parked near St James's Hospital. At about 1.40 she was seen in Bayswater Mount, walking in the direction of Roundhay Road. She was last seen about five minutes' walk from the murder scene at 1.45 a.m. walking through Chapeltown. A woman living in Reginald Terrace said that around 2 a.m. she had heard a banging and scuffling from the adventure playground, followed by the voice of what sounded like a Scotsman mouthing obscenities.

The murder squad's attempts to detail individual people's movements along a few residential streets at 2 a.m. in the morning might seem reasonably straightforward, given the expectation that most people would be tucked up in bed asleep. But not in Chapeltown on a Saturday night. It was a veritable hive of activity. This was a strong immigrant area. There were people here from Eastern Europe, working-class Jews who could not afford to reside in the northern hills around Leeds.

There were families from the New Commonwealth, particularly West Indians, many of whom attended illegal drinking clubs, where the sacred brown 'weed' was rolled into six-inch joints for mutual recreation and spiritual enlightenment. Oldfield later estimated some two hundred people were out and about in the immediate vicinity of the route Jayne walked once she left Mark Jones. Of these, some fifty were thought to be in or around the Reginald Street/Reginald Terrace area at the crucial time. Oldfield was desperate to identify and eliminate any of these people. Forty revellers were drinking in a West Indian club and left to attend a party in nearby Sholebroke Avenue.

A free-phone telephone service was set up in the incident room in the hope that someone might just have seen Jayne or the killer. But this was a time preceding the inner-city riots of the 1980s by only a few years. There was a recession, with rising unemployment, government cutbacks and little funding for the inner cities or urban renewal. There were tensions between police and some in the immigrant communities, particularly the younger element. They tended to avoid each other if possible, so it was not surprising if witnesses from among this section of the community were not flooding forward to help in the Ripper investigation.

On the blown-up wall map in the incident room were two hundred taggings of people and vehicles from 1 until 4 a.m. Some were individuals, some groups. Each was represented by a flag. Some were positive sightings where police had identified or interviewed a particular person. But there were also blanks. Oldfield was anxious to fill them in: 'My problem is in identifying those people. Once I can identify them and eliminate them I am hoping I shall be left with one or two or three, or a handful of individuals, who have not come forward and have a reason for not coming forward. The trouble I am having is that we are getting cooperation from certain members of the public who are feeding this information of having seen people there, but some sections of the public, for reasons best known to themselves, are reluctant to come forward and admit they were in that area on this particular night. They are the ones who represent the blank spaces I cannot fill. It is frustrating . . . I am not interested why they were there. The only individual I am concerned about who was in that area at that time is the killer. Anyone else I want him to come forward so I can eliminate him, and find that killer.' Oldfield told the local TV news: 'I believe the man we are looking for has a good knowledge of the Leeds area but he does not necessarily live in Leeds.'

Oldfield began to get more and more desperate in his appeals for help. They had a paucity of evidence. The finger-tip search of the area around the playground revealed absolutely zero. In Jayne's handbag there were some bus tickets on which the forensic lab found fingerprints that could not be identified. A cigarette packet discovered near the body bore fingerprints which were never eliminated. The Ripper had appeared and disappeared like a phantom, and this in itself added to the gossip-driven mythology surrounding both his identity and the supposed 'ritual' slaying of his victims.

Oldfield's greatest fear was that the killer would strike again – and soon. 'There is no doubt in my mind that he will strike again. The big questions are when, where and who is going to be his next victim.' He was convinced there were many people living in the immediate area who had not come forward. He made several urgent public appeals for witnesses before there was another murder, asking local church and community leaders for assistance. The murder squad also began re-examining old files of attacks on women.

Oldfield believed the killer had definitely taken four of his previous victims in his car after picking them up for sex. He was positive other women who probably were not prostitutes may have been propositioned or offered a lift and had turned the killer away. He hoped the man's face peering out of the car window would still be fresh in their minds. 'We believe the man we want must have tried it more than once and been turned down.' One case they focused on closely was a serious assault on a thirty-four-year-old woman in an alleyway in Keighley two years previously in July 1975. Mrs Anna Rogulski had been assaulted and left badly injured. Oldfield told journalists she had been struck over the head with a blunt instrument and had injuries to her body similar to those of the Ripper's victims. Sadly they failed to listen to Marcella Claxton from Chapeltown, who was convinced it was the Ripper who attacked her. The day after Jayne was killed, she told a reporter she was sure the man who bludgeoned her was also responsible for the girl's murder.

A ten-year-old boy and a housewife, both living in Chapeltown, contacted the incident room. The woman had started noting down the registration numbers of kerb crawlers after being pestered by a man in a car. The boy had been collecting car numbers – hundreds of them. Officers were detailed to check the owners. Oldfield, by now very much the public face of the police investigation, asked residents to jot down the registration number of any vehicle acting suspiciously or kerb crawling and ring the police. 'They will not be wasting our time,' he said. Nothing more clearly reflected the desperate situation he was in as senior investigating officer.

Finally Oldfield made a firm decision to bring the documentation for all five murders under one roof. The paperwork for the four previous killings was integrated into a major incident room on the top floor at Millgarth. A few doors down from the purpose-built incident room, Oldfield shared an office with Dick Holland and another superintendent, Jack Slater. They were working an average thirteen hours a day, arriving at 9.15 a.m. in time for a ten o'clock briefing at which they updated officers conducting house-to-house inquiries. Top priority was trying to maintain their morale. They left to go home between 10 p.m. and midnight. At that stage Holland and Slater were reviewing the paperwork, dispensing actions to the troops on the ground, checking follow-ups. They filtered the stuff Oldfield ought to see, and the paperwork began to pile up. Occasionally his other job at the Wakefield HQ held up his work on the Ripper inquiry. Suddenly he would announce: 'I'm stopping tonight.' He would make sure he had half a bottle of decent whisky on hand, taking frequent sips until he had cleared the backlog. Then he would go and bed down in the section house of the police station, where a number of single constables had rooms, so he would be ready and available for work first thing the next morning.

Holland directed that a detective inspector or detective chief inspector trained in the West Yorkshire murder system should work on every shift in the incident room. Their job was to check incoming statements. The Leeds staff hadn't taken kindly to the changes Holland made. 'Their reaction was hostile to start with,' he said. 'They were moaning and trying to get away. At that stage I actually worked in the incident room seeing that everything that went there was done in the West Yorkshire style. Now that had never been done in Leeds until then.'

The house-to-house inquiries were widened until the occupants of 679 homes in twenty-nine streets were seen and interviewed. Many houses were in multiple occupation. Nearly 3,700 statements were taken. Checks were made on all men taken into police custody for offences of violence, particularly if they involved women. Oldfield also organized a seminar with twenty-five psychiatrists from Yorkshire in an unsuccessful effort to get assistance from mental hospitals about patients who might be suspects.

Prostitutes were questioned in detail about regular clients even as the Leeds police began clamping down on soliciting in Chapeltown. On the one hand, they wanted the women's cooperation; on the other, they were trying to put them out of business. At the same time Jim Hobson was mounting a covert operation of static observations, with officers recording registration numbers of vehicles trying to pick up women in the red-light district. Lists of registrations numbers could then be examined after any future murder and the drivers traced and interviewed. Over the next few months, 152 women were arrested and reported for soliciting, and sixty-eight more cautioned.

It was a measure of Oldfield's frustration and desperation that he virtually begged people to support the police effort: 'The public have the power to decide what sort of society they want. If they want murder and violence then they will keep quiet. If they want a law-abiding society in which their womenfolk can move freely without fear of attack from the likes of the individual we are hunting, then they must give us their help.'

A month after the murder the trail had gone cold, but the Home Secretary, Merlyn Rees, MP for a Leeds constituency, seemed to have full confidence in the West Yorkshire force. He paid a visit to the incident room in Leeds and was asked how concerned he was that 'The Ripper' had been at large so long. 'I am no more concerned than the chief constable,' he replied. 'Often piecing evidence together, considering it, analysing it, does take time unless someone is there with a camera when the murder is committed.'

Considering that five women had been killed by the same hand within a small geographical area, this answer appeared somewhat flippant. But as the law stood, the Home Secretary could have said little else. He simply could not interfere. His own Home Office colleague, Dr Shirley Summerskill, had made the position clear during a debate on the Black Panther case twelve months previously. Britain's criminal justice system relied on the operational autonomy of the police.

The press at this stage was describing 'The Ripper' as Yorkshire's most wanted killer. No policeman pointed out to the Home Secretary during his visit that this was a national problem rather than a little local difficulty. Neither did they reveal they hadn't a hope of catching the man – unless he tried to kill again. In such a hopeless situation there were few words of comfort that Oldfield or his colleagues could find for the MacDonald family when they buried Jayne. Those who have never suffered bereavement in such circumstances can have no comprehension of the feelings of the families. Wilf MacDonald later described in a television interview the moment he learned of his daughter's death:

> The police came in and said 'Are you the father of Jane MacDonald', I said 'Yes'. I said 'I'll kill her when she comes home because she didn't phone last night'. They said you may not have to . . . and that's as much as I knew . . . if she had died of you know illness or accident but when it happens like it did, mutilation and everything, I went to identify her and . . . I just collapsed there and then. He has murdered the whole family you can almost say.

Oldfield's surviving daughter was about the same age as Jayne, and a pupil at Wakefield Girls' High School, hoping to go on to university to study dentistry. His heart went out to Wilf MacDonald, and soon after her murder he made a private visit to the family to pledge he would not rest until the man who killed Jayne was caught. In October 1979, Wilf MacDonald too was dead, aged sixty. He was buried in a grave next to his beloved daughter. His family emphatically believed he never recovered from Jayne's murder and died of a broken heart.

In the months following the death of Jayne MacDonald, Oldfield's nightmare scenario, that the killer would go on attacking women again and again, came true. Two weeks after he struck down Jayne, Mrs Maureen Long became his latest victim. She survived the attack but at a terrible cost. Twenty-five years later, in her sixties, she still suffers as a result of the head injuries she received. In conversation she is very nervous, clasping her hands to stop them shaking. She cannot watch anything on television that involves violence. She has bouts of depression and anger.

In July 1977, Maureen was forty-two, the mother of several children and separated from her husband. She hadn't had an easy life by any means. At various times she had been in trouble with the police. She enjoyed the company of men but was certainly no prostitute. She lived with another man in Farsley on the borders of Leeds and Bradford. According to a police report, although she and her husband were separated, they continued to have a friendly relationship and she still held a good measure of affection for him. On Saturday night, 9 July, they met up in a Bradford pub and she drank four pints of lager in his company. When the pub was closing, around 11.10 p.m., she headed alone in her long black dress for the Mecca Ballroom in Manningham Lane. She was a woman who loved dressing up in her finest and going out for the evening, especially to a night out dancing. Maureen was a regular at the Mecca and well known to many of the staff. The music played, she danced with several men and continued drinking. Her last clear memory was of going to the cloakroom at about 2 a.m. on the Sunday morning. Outside a 'hot dog' salesman preparing to close up his pitch for the night saw her leave the Mecca heading for the city centre.

Her recall of subsequent events is hazy. Police believe that, infused with alcohol and in a befuddled state, she may have been going to see her husband, who lived in Reynell Street. Later, at around 3.15 a.m., a security guard, Frank Whitaker, who worked at the Tanks & Drums Ltd factory abutting on Bowling Back Lane, heard his dog bark. He went to the main entrance and looked up the lane. An engine revved up and he saw a car without lights initially drive off at high speed out of Mount Street. He was certain it was a white Ford Cortina Mark II with a black roof. He thought there might have been something heavy in the boot.

Next morning, at around 8.30, the residents of a gypsy caravan site off Bowling Back Lane heard shouts for help coming from near by. Police were called and on a patch of rubbish-strewn open land they found Maureen Long in a deeply distressed condition.

'All I remember was trying to pick myself up,' she said. 'I kept falling and then I wondered what was wrong with me, and I kept falling back and as I were trying to pull myself up, falling back again. Then I was screaming and I heard this dog barking, and someone say: "Oh, you're all right," and that's all I remember. When you get hit over the back of the head you can't remember things. If I hadn't had beer that night I'd have died of hypothermia.'

The person who attacked her obviously left her for dead.

Her clothing was displaced. Her bra had been pulled down to her waist, her tights and pants pulled to her knees. Suffering very severe head injuries, she was rushed by ambulance to Bradford Royal Infirmary, where doctors saved her life. There was a large depressed fracture of the skull, and five stab wounds to the front and side of her trunk and left shoulder. She also had three fractured ribs. Her head injuries were so severe that she required specialist neurosurgery at the Leeds General Infirmary. Professor Gee examined Maureen in hospital at Bradford a few hours after she was admitted. Accompanied by Oldfield and Holland, he stood beside her bed in a cubicle in the casualty department. Her head had been partially shaved by the neurosurgical senior registrar, revealing the severe lacerations to her skull. A police surgeon took various swabs from intimate areas, searching for potential forensic evidence. One of the stab wounds had penetrated her liver, though she had not suffered from gross bleeding. Gee thought her lucky to be alive.

She spent nine weeks in hospital before being discharged but continued as an out-patient for many years because of fits as a result of her head injuries. Maureen couldn't provide the police with much help. She had woken up in the intensive care ward of the local hospital. That Maureen's memory was poor did not surprise Holland. He had recently worked on a stabbing case in Bradford where a (non-Ripper) victim's memory was impaired because of loss of blood and consequently loss of oxygen to the brain. 'They got her brain functioning again perfectly, she hadn't brain damage, but everything that was stored on her "disk", if you like, to use a computer analogy, prior to the stabbing had gone forever.'

Holland's belief that extensive head injuries made a surviving victim's memory unreliable was understandable though tragically mistaken. Yet he eagerly grasped at one clue provided by Maureen Long. She described the man who gave her a lift as being a fair-haired white male, aged about thirty-five, thickset, over six feet tall, and having what could have been a *white car* . . .

The Ripper squad had already targeted taxi drivers in Leeds and Bradford as potential prime suspects. Many prostitutes, including Tina Atkinson, used taxis. More than 600 cab drivers were interviewed. A taxi driver called Terry Hawkshaw, whose physical appearance was similar to the description provided by Long, was top of their list. He lived with his sixty-seven-year-old mother in an old terraced house at Drighlington, between Leeds and Bradford. He was thirty-six, six feet tall, weighed fifteen or sixteen stone and had rather long fair hair brushed back, a fresh complexion and a round, almost babyish face – a bit saggy and flabby, as was his whole build. He dressed casually, but not scruffily – a typical taxi driver who did his own repairs. He also drove a white car.

Hawkshaw was one of fifteen men at that stage regarded as strong suspects, whose alibis were to be thoroughly checked for the night Jayne MacDonald was killed. Some were flagged to be kept under observation and taken in for questioning the moment another Ripper incident occurred. Hawkshaw, now dead, had been seen in his taxi near the Mecca Ballroom on the crucial night. He came under close scrutiny because he was a taxi driver who drove a white Ford Cortina with a black vinyl roof and made a living ferrying prostitutes and their clients. 'He allowed them to have it off in the back of his taxi,' Holland revealed. Oldfield suspected Hawkshaw got sexual thrills out of watching the prostitutes at work on the back seat. A search of his accounts revealed taxi receipts proving that he had the opportunity to have carried out several of the Ripper attacks – he was in close proximity to the red-light area at the material times.

There was not enough evidence to hold him in a police cell, so Oldfield arranged for him to help the police with their inquiries without arresting him. He was virtually kidnapped and held incommunicado. Oldfield took him in as a prime suspect despite the fact that legally the police were not allowed to hold him at a police station. So he was kept for over thirty-six hours at the Detective Training School at Bishopgarth in Wakefield, which has a thirteen-storey accommodation block just across the road from the force headquarters. No student courses were being held and the flats on the top floor were empty.

This was not the first time this had happened. Suspects in other serious cases had previously been questioned at the Detective Training School when there was a danger of leaks to the media. Oldfield was anxious also that other police officers were kept in the dark about the fact that they were questioning a 'prisoner' who was not a prisoner. It was a high-risk strategy and could have landed some of West Yorkshire's most senior detectives in hot water had it backfired. Hawkshaw's civil rights were clearly denied in the belief they had a strong suspect for five murders. Nowadays, he could probably have sued for wrongful imprisonment; the officers involved would have been disciplined, the Police Complaints' Authority involved, questions asked in Parliament, with the media becoming self-righteous and the civil rights lobby having a field day. Today, without question, someone's head would have rolled, probably several. That it was done at all was a measure of the sheer desperation the Ripper's reign of terror had caused among the senior detectives. The cost of the inquiry so far was approaching £1 million.

'He was not arrested, and I'm playing with words here,' Holland admitted. 'There was a detective who slept at his door to make sure he went nowhere, but he was not arrested. It was a long way down, thirteen storeys, if he'd gone out of the window. We took him there because there wasn't enough evidence for putting him in one of the cells. We found a way of holding him, without "holding him". In the euphemism of the day, he was "assisting police with inquiries". He knew where he was going. I would have defended it to his lawyer by saying he was just being interviewed. The legal test then was that if he had chosen to go, if he had said, "I'm leaving", would you have stopped him? I would have said, "No." He agreed to come, so he couldn't have made a complaint that we had kidnapped him. We did not give him the impression he was under arrest. We didn't read any caution, but the law was different then. You only had to caution when you had some real evidence, but we felt we had strong grounds for suspicion. We had all day on him verifying his story, verifying what he was doing, forensically checking his car. He really fitted the bill as described by Long, and had the car described by the night watchman, so we hadn't dreamed his name up. He had also visited the pubs and clubs frequented by Richardson and Jackson. He also had two hammers which were checked – so circumstantially he was a strong candidate. Forensic later gave us a negative report [on the hammers].

'He didn't get rough treatment. We'd been going all day and well into the night. This is typical George. Hawkshaw was quite open. He was talking to us and he was saying, "Yes, I do run prostitutes. I get paid, they pay a bit more than the standard fare if they use my taxi. I might help prostitutes, but I am not a murderer." That was his line and he was quite frank and he was softly spoken. He might have had a kinky

ABOVE AND BELOW: Interior of Patricia Atkinson's flat in Bradford where she took her clients for prostitution.

A miserable place to die. The railway embankment
beside Garrards woodyard in Huddersfield where
Helen Rytka was murdered in January 1978.

ABOVE: The scene of crime at Helen Rytka's murder. Peter Sutcliffe covered her body before making his escape.

BELOW: At the incident room in Huddersfield, January 1978, Helen Rytka's twin sister, Rita, assists George Oldfield, heading the Yorkshire Ripper murders.

ABOVE: Jayne MacDonald's body was hidden behind the timber wall of this children's playground a hundred yards from her home in Chapeltown, Leeds, in June 1977.

LEFT: A beautiful girl. Jayne MacDonald, at 16, the youngest murder victim of the Yorkshire Ripper.

streak and I think he was a soft touch for the prostitutes. But he made a bit more money.'

Information provided by Hawkshaw was checked with the files. Oldfield, convinced that he'd got his man, cross-questioned him for hours on end. For Hawkshaw, the whole experience was terrifying: 'It was a nightmare,' he said. 'When George Oldfield sits behind his desk and tells you he thinks you are the Ripper, blimey, it turns your stomach over. They told me: "Come and sit here. Terence, this fellow wants catching. He is not bad, it's just his mind." The police nearly convinced me I was out of my head. They said someone with a split personality could be like the killer. He could be normal in the day and all of a sudden his mind goes click and he kills someone.'

After a considerable time – by now it was 3.45 in the morning – Oldfield decided: 'It's crunch time.' Holland was unsure whether Hawkshaw was out of the frame. Looking at his watch, Oldfield decided to defer a decision which wasn't going his way. He thought they should snatch some sleep in the empty training school study/bedrooms. 'We will start again at nine o'clock,' he said. 'Tell you what, we'll have an extra half-hour, we'll start at 9.30!' He had laid on breakfast and an early call.

'Now that was the sort of boss he was,' said Holland. 'He thought he'd given us the earth because he'd given us an extra half-hour and paid for our breakfast. He hadn't paid himself, he'd authorized the force to pay for our breakfast. So we got a free cooked meal and an extra half-hour in fucking bed! We had worked all day until a quarter to four in the morning.'

After thorough searches of his taxi and his mother's home, in the end Hawkshaw was allowed to return home: 'We had no evidence, forensic had turned up absolutely nothing; because it wasn't him, they'd done their job. Forensic can be a two-edged sword to the investigator, but it's a good thing from the point of view of the innocent person. It revealed absolutely nothing to connect him [with the attacks] and we would have expected something. The hammers he had were not of the same dimension and weight we were looking for. We needed time to have those things examined. We had him for the best part of forty-eight hours when the point came when we had to say: "Thank you, Mr Hawkshaw," and let him go. Then we fixed up a team of detectives to shadow him discreetly night and day. That was done chiefly with crime squad cars supplemented by murder squad detectives. There were twelve men a day on this. Eventually he realized he was being followed. We checked with his books and records of taxi runs and he was in the right area to have the opportunity to have committed eight of the attacks.

'I don't think we did anything illegal. In order to do our job, we were deliberately sailing as near to the wind as we could. We were just on the side of legality. We planned to interrogate him and keep him away [from any potential leak of information]. You've got to appreciate, it would have been all over the media if we had a suspect in for the Ripper.' The surveillance on Hawkshaw lasted for some considerable time until he was completely exonerated and alibied for one of the Ripper murders.

John Domaille decided he could not afford to wait for the Ripper to strike again in order to move the inquiry forward. He decided as a new tactic to enlist the help of the latest victim herself. So, several months after the attack, Maureen Long cooperated with the Ripper Squad in mounting an undercover operation to see if she could recognize the Ripper and help them arrest him. For three weeks running she went out on Thursday, Friday and Saturday nights in Bradford, accompanied by a woman detective sergeant, Megan Winterburn. To the uninitiated they were two women out on the town together, and Winterburn, then in her thirties, found Maureen affable and pleasant. 'She didn't deserve what happened to her,' she said. 'She was very fortunate to have survived the injuries she had. Maureen made no bones about saying she was a Ripper victim and liked to show off her scars.'

To prepare for this undercover assignment in the pubs and nightclubs of Bradford, Megan Winterburn had ceased washing her hair, letting it go lank. She found a seedy outfit, including a rather old Afghan coat. 'Mr Domaille said that if I dressed up as I normally do to go out, I'd stand out like a sore thumb,' she said. 'I had the most smelly Afghan coat, a raw suede coat with this horrible fur round the collar and embroidered sections on the front, and fur round the bottom. I went a little bit over the top with the make-up and tried to blend in with the rest of the clientele.'

During a night out she let Maureen do her own thing. Another detective accompanied them, keeping in the background but maintaining close watch as they drank and danced at West Yorkshire police expense. The pair built up a good rapport. On a few occasions Megan watched her new friend get loaded. She once asked her whether she always got this drunk when she went out. 'No,' replied Maureen, 'it's just that it makes me feel safe.'

Megan Winterburn, a married detective on plain-clothes undercover duty, handbag slung over her shoulder, was getting an education into the seedier side of life. She visited pubs she would otherwise have avoided and she had never been a night club person. To her Maureen appeared somewhat naïve and lived in an insular world, doing the same things, week in, week out. Going out drinking was part of her social world. But

Megan didn't find any of it the least bit offensive. She had been brought up in the mining village of South Kirkby. Her father was a miner who after he was injured became a steward of a club. Policing was what she had always wanted to do and after a couple of years as a shorthand-typist after leaving school at seventeen, she joined the West Riding force. 'Maureen was quite funny and entertaining when she had a drink,' said Megan. 'She knew everybody in every pub we went into and everyone knew Maureen. It opened my eyes to the sort of person Maureen mixed with. They were the salt of the earth. Everyone was concerned about her. The people she knew didn't think any the less of her because she had been a victim. They didn't shun her. She was mortified that [some] people were saying she was a prostitute, which wasn't true. You had this very naïve and pleasant lady who was leading a normal life, with an active social life, labelled by the press as a prostitute. To have to explain this to your family, who were still coming to terms with you being attacked, must have been horrendous to her and her family.'

On one occasion they were on the Mecca dance floor. Suddenly Maureen stood stock still and stared at a man across the room. 'I said, "What's the matter?" She shook her head and said, "Nothing." I said, "Yes there is, what is it?" She said, "It's him over there." I'll never forget him. He didn't have a gap in his teeth and it wasn't Sutcliffe, but he did have a lot of jet-black curly hair. Obviously her subconscious had said: "The hair." ' The man was checked out and eliminated quickly.

Another time the pair were pub crawling in Manningham Lane, close to where the prostitutes hung out. A young colleague of Winterburn's, in the dark about the operation, came into the pub. 'I recognized him and he was looking at me and I was looking away, trying to make him not look at me. Eventually he plucked up courage and walked over to me and said: "What are you doing here, Sarge, dressed like that?" I remember taking the lad out to the toilet to have an appropriate word. I pinned him against the wall and told him to leave. It was serious and I couldn't afford to let my guard slip.'

The undercover operation with Maureen Long, though it showed commendable courage on her part, went nowhere. She failed to recognize her would-be killer. The rest of the murder squad had plenty of other avenues to explore. The bosses knew proactive policing was working, for the clampdown against prostitutes and the covert operations in Chapeltown were clearly having an effect, the most important being that they appeared to have driven the Ripper back to strike again in Bradford.

Oldfield immediately stepped up the covert observations recording the registration numbers of vehicles in the red-light areas, extending them from Chapeltown to Manningham in Bradford. The attack on Long was treated as attempted murder. A major effort was mounted to find everyone who had been at the Mecca Ballroom on the Saturday night. Thousands were interviewed during the inquiry. It led nowhere. The information provided by the security guard was critical. In response a search was launched for Mark II Ford Cortina owners in West Yorkshire. Three thousand owners were interviewed and no positive evidence obtained.

More crucially, Jim Hobson's 'tracking' inquiry was, over his profound objections, brought to an abrupt halt because the Mark II Ford Cortina was not on the list of vehicles which could have left the tyre marks at the Richardson murder scene. (As we now know, the Ford Cortina inquiry was a complete red herring. The security guard *had* seen Peter Sutcliffe's car leaving the scene of Long's attack, except he was driving a white Ford Corsair – which was on Hobson's list of 'tracking' inquiry vehicles waiting to be eliminated.) But Oldfield was faced with a massive problem – lack of manpower. Eliminating 30,000 vehicles had been a colossal task, and Oldfield felt the remaining 20,000 vehicles would take forever to check. Experience had shown that, as you got nearer the end of such an inquiry, progress on eliminating one vehicle took far longer than the straightforward checks at the beginning. As an inquiry continued, the man hours that went into it got higher and higher in relation to the finished product, while the actual productivity of the investigating team got lower and lower. All the difficult vehicle checks were those that had dragged on and were left to the end. They were cars that had been sold to gypsies six times under false names, had gone through car auctions, had changed owners, had been stolen, written off or not correctly recorded on the fledgling PNC.

Oldfield thus found himself in a complete bind. He had major murder inquiries involving a maniac on the loose going on in Leeds and Bradford, and the tyre inquiry seemed never ending, with no assurance of success. 'We were desperate for men,' Holland said. 'If you were warm and breathing you were on the bloody Ripper case. We had checked roughly 30,000 vehicles and eliminated those, but there were in fact 22,000 to go . . . Sutcliffe's vehicle was in there and unfortunately it was missed.'

Hobson took the cancellation of the tracking inquiry very badly. In the incident room for the Long investigation at Bradford police headquarters, a few senior officers, including Holland, Oldfield and Hobson, were standing in a corner late one afternoon when Oldfield broke the news as a *fait accompli*. Hobson had seen the tyre inquiry as the one good chance to find the killer. They had a positive clue from a murder scene and his inquiry ought to run its course. Now they were suddenly looking for a Ford Cortina. Oldfield believed the Ripper had changed cars. There was a good chance the one which made the tyre tracks in Roundhay Park had been destroyed. Hobson was furious, visibly angry and muttering under his breath. But the decision had been made. The Leeds murder squad believed Oldfield was being deliberately partisan because of his known disagreements with the senior city detectives. It was a fracture in relationships that never really healed.

The Ripper by now had murdered five women: McCann, Jackson, Richardson and MacDonald in Leeds; and Atkinson in Bradford. The police believed he had attacked Long, intending to kill her, and were now casting an eye over several other serious assaults on women. In reality there were eight other women that Sutcliffe had almost certainly attacked in the West Yorkshire area, though the squad had ruled most of them out as Ripper attacks because they could not rule them in *for certain*. Indeed, they were gripped almost by a phobia of putting an attack into the Ripper series, for fear it would turn out *not* to be his handiwork and might contaminate the investigation with erroneous evidence. Moreover, if the Ripper was caught and prosecuted for one murder he did *not* commit, he could escape justice. Thus Tracey Browne and Marcella Claxton along with several other victims were never included in the series, though there was an extraordinary similarity in the photofit descriptions they had given, which now lay unnoticed in police files. Day by day the cost of the investigation was assuming mountainous proportions: 300 officers had worked 343,000 man hours; 175,000 people had been questioned, 12,500 statements taken and 101,000 vehicles checked. The attempt to find the man with a ginger beard said to have been seen by witnesses in the MacDonald and Jackson inquiries was stepped up. Police had 117 tips of men who bore such a description. They traced fifty-six such men and eliminated them; the rest were never found because there was no real clue to their identity. Already inside the mountain of paper were the clues and the evidence that could have identified the Yorkshire Ripper.

7

Punter's Money

In the mid-1970s the backbone technology of British industry, its businesses and institutions, was still a Victorian invention: the typewriter and shorthand note. Computers were as yet the hugely expensive private tools of government, vast number crunchers gobbling up and spewing out punchcards. They occupied whole floors to do the work a child's toy can perform today, but the world was still only on the verge of the revolution.

Within a year or two advertisements began to appear in colour supplements offering home computers to be built by hand, whose programming language needed to be learned before simple mathematic problems could be solved and tic-tac-toe games played. Pocket calculators, costing the equivalent of a working man's weekly wage, were finding their way on to the market. But the white heat of silicon technology was still ten years from our desk tops. The Home Office, the government department primarily responsible for the security and policing of Britain, wanted to be at the forefront of this revolution. The computer, when it arrived, would be a vital tool in the battle against crime, reducing the burden on manpower and budgets and speeding up detection. But the use of computers and the application software would have to be tailor-made to the task, specifically designed to handle, sort, cross-check and deliver information.

In August 1976, the House of Commons learned that the Police Scientific Development Branch at the Home Office was studying the use of computers to assist the investigation of major crimes like murder. Computers, according to the Home Office minister, Dr Shirley Summerskill, would organize the collection of information and the identification of key elements in murder inquiries. Parliament was debating criticism of the police handling of the Black Panther inquiry when Dr Summerskill reiterated a key principle of British justice affecting any criminal inquiry – that overall command in an investigation rested ultimately with the chief constable: 'It is for him to decide when to call for assistance and help and what to call for.' So if a chief constable wanted a computer, he had to ask for one. For the overburdened West Yorkshire Police in the summer of 1977 it seemed like a lifeline – or at least a straw to clutch at.

Ronald Gregory therefore set up a working party at his headquarters in Wakefield to look at ways of using computers in the Ripper inquiry. The force's new Computer Project Unit in turn approached the Home Office to see how close its scientists were to achieving the goal of a computerized incident room which could actually handle a complex murder investigation. They had been working on the problem for three years. After several meetings, the West Yorkshireman learned that more development work was needed by government scientists and the Police Research Services Unit before they could hand over a computer they were certain was reliable. The only experimental working police computer in the country was in Staffordshire, in the Midlands. The working group and Gregory paid a visit, but the project was still in its infancy and the budget for the experiment was prohibitive, already running at more than £1 million.

Breakthroughs were being made in pushing back the frontiers of computerized systems, but in August 1977, when the West Yorkshire force needed one as a matter of desperate urgency, no machine was available. The writing of programs of such complexity was in its infancy. Moreover, three of the most senior Home Office scientists had just departed from the project, leaving only a junior colleague to work on the necessary research.

Then West Yorkshire Police were given the chance to use spare capacity on the mainframe computer at the Atomic Energy Authority Establishment at Harwell in Berkshire. It was a rare opportunity. Even the suggestion of such an offer was a clear indication that at least someone in Whitehall recognized the importance of catching the 'Ripper' and the difficulties the police in West Yorkshire were facing. Whether the senior officials in the Police Department of the Home Office appreciated that the murder investigation was not just a little 'local difficulty' facing their friends in the north is open to question.

It wasn't the first time a branch of the Home Office, faced with a major investigation, had received help from atomic scientists with access to the country's best computer technology. In the early 1960s, the Security Service (MI5) approached the Atomic Weapons Research Establishment at Aldermaston, which at the time had the biggest computer facility in Britain. MI5, in conjunction with the code breakers at GCHQ, were trying to decipher intercepted Soviet Union espionage messages intended for Eastern bloc agents in Britain. The traffic was known by the code name 'VENONA'. The AWRE began a top-secret project, with its computer running code-cracking programs for six hours every night for two months.

To help catch a serial killer, the AEAE at Harwell was now willing to allow its mainframe computer to be accessed via telephone lines by the Ripper squad directly from West Yorkshire, with additional information on cassette tapes being sent physically to Harwell by courier. There were huge problems with this imaginative plan. To back-convert existing records held at Millgarth would taken thirteen man years of effort, costing a nominal figure of £25,000, which the Home Office was prepared to fund. But West Yorkshire would have to stump up £3,000 a week to run the system. Finally, Ronald Gregory decided, on the grounds of budget and the experimental nature of the project, to turn the offer down. At this stage the experiment would have involved using equipment not yet proven at the operational level. Gregory was later backed by the hierarchy of the police service for making a brave decision to stick with the manual system of managing information within the incident room. Though the volume of material grew larger every day, it was at least a tried and tested method. The problem was there had been nothing like the Ripper case before.

Gregory authorized his working party to contact the private sector to see whether the nominal index in the incident room could be computerized. IBM suggested a mainframe computer called STAIRS. The quote was in excess of half a million pounds. Again back-record conversion would be a mammoth task. A number of the biggest multinational computer firms and local government agencies in Britain were also approached, but could not come up with a viable scheme to automate the incident room. As the amount of information in the system grew, the problem of back-record conversion became the biggest obstacle to computerization. At that stage no one had designed a full-text retrieval system that could solve the incident room problems. Another worry by some senior officers was that serious money would be wasted if the murderer should be apprehended quickly.

Home Office officials knew the urgency of the West Yorkshire problem, which became worse as the years went by and the toll of yet more Ripper victims began to rise. Yet development of a police incident room computer system was never a priority, and it took several more years before one was available. An increasing number of attacks by the Ripper meant greater information-overload both for the incident room and the men and women having to manage it. The more the documentation piled up, the less likely the chance grew of back-converting it into a computerized system. The West Yorkshiremen seemed to be chasing their tails. And their problems were about to be compounded by the very next, and sixth, Ripper murder, across the Pennines, in Manchester, England's second largest city. Here he murdered another prostitute on 1 October 1977 – a twenty-year-old mother of two children, Jean Jordan. Then he hid her body under bushes, where it lay undiscovered for over a week. The killer's decision to strike in a completely different town reflected a pattern of sorts. When the heat was on in Leeds, with Hobson's undercover teams keeping watch on Chapeltown's red-light area, he moved to Bradford and found a victim in Manningham. With the pressure on in both Leeds and Bradford, he visited Moss Side, the red-light district of Manchester.

Positioned in the north-west of the country, some two hundred miles from London, Manchester spreads itself over sixty square miles. With local government reorganization in 1974, it had become Greater Manchester, absorbing a number of local towns like Salford. Within five miles of the city centre lived a million people; within ten miles, two and a half million. Manchester dwarfed the Leeds–Bradford conurbation and was the hub of many industries – not least as the northern head-quarters of the national newspapers, who all had offices and printing plants there. It was also home to one of Britain's great liberal institutions, the *Manchester Guardian*. In the nineteenth century, as in Leeds and Bradford, the manufacture of textiles was a dominant industry, the humid air apparently assisting in the production of cotton products.

In the 1950s and 1960s redevelopment schemes swept away the old and the derelict to produce a modernized city centre. A new road on stilts was built, the Mancunian Way, designed to ease traffic congestion. Piccadilly, a large square in the heart of the city, became a central shopping area, dominated on one side by a towering modern hotel designed to appeal to a fast-moving, international clientele. Around the periphery of the city were arterial road links – the M6 and M62 motorways – taking traffic north and south, east and west. In no time at all, a driver could speed from Bradford and Leeds, over the Pennines and into the heart of Manchester. From there to Moss Side took ten minutes by car. Just like Chapeltown in Leeds, and Bradford's Manningham, Manchester's red-light district was a formerly prosperous area fallen on hard times where large terraced houses had long been converted into flats. Together with Hulme, where Jean Jordan lived in a run-down council block, it was, and remains today, among the poorest areas in the country. In twenty-first century Britain, Moss Side and Hulme score first and fifth on the government's most recent index of urban deprivation. A high concentration of ethnic minorities form a third of the local population. Lone parent households abound and the area has had high levels of unemployment, poverty and social exclusion for years. Sixty per cent of households receive social security and a third of local people are long-term unemployed. Fifty-four per cent of local youngsters leave school without qualifications, and only 3.7 per cent of them manage to get five GCSE passes at grades A–C.

Nine days after Jean Jordan was murdered, her body lay on an old allotment site off Princess Road in the suburb of Chorlton, near Manchester's Southern Cemetery, two miles from where she had lived. It was found at lunchtime on 10 October. Adjacent to Princess Road was an iron gateway opening on to a track, bordered on both sides by trees. The track led into an area of disused allotments, measuring roughly a hundred yards square. The murder scene was between the cemetery and a new area of ground recently provided for allotment holders by Manchester Corporation. The new allotments had been fenced off from the disused land, which then became quickly overgrown. It was well known as a place where prostitutes took clients for sex. Those among the Greater Manchester Police murder squad who saw the body claim it as one of the most horrific crime scenes they have ever witnessed. And for twenty-three-year-old Bruce Jones, the unfortunate local dairy worker who called the police, the sight left him with nightmares for years to come. He held an allotment on the adjoining land and had merely been looking for disused house bricks with a friend.

The man who would investigate Jordan's murder was forty-four-year-old Jack Ridgway, the detective chief superintendent in charge of Central Manchester. He had been in the job a month, having been recently promoted following several years as head of the force Serious Crimes Squad. While he was having lunch with his deputy, Detective Superintendent Grange Catlow, the call came through that a corpse had been found near the Southern Cemetery. His first task was to view the body and call out the Home Office pathologist, Dr Reuben

Woodcock, a consultant to the Bolton Group of Hospitals and lecturer in forensic medicine at Manchester University.

Ridgway was at the crime scene a good ninety minutes before Reuben Woodcock arrived. A uniformed constable was already there, along with a local CID officer from Chorlton-cum-Hardy police station. It took Ridgway only seconds to realize they had a really savage murder on their hands. 'Jesus – what a bloody mess,' he said to his deputy. He had been involved in umpteen murder investigations during his twenty-three-year career with Manchester police, and he had long since learned to bring a high degree of emotional distancing to the job of murder investigator. Objectivity was essential and he tried to engender it in members of his team, but this was an indelible experience. 'It was a really bad body,' he recalled. 'I had never seen anything like it before. It was in an advanced stage of decomposition. The weather was quite warm and it had laid there over a week and it was heaving. It was clear she had been murdered. Half her guts were hanging out.'

The body lay in grass near a wooden hut, next to a cinder track. It was completely naked, the head twisted to the left, the trunk and legs in a semi-prone position with the arms spread apart. A coil of intestine was wrapped around the waist. The head was blackened due both to injuries received and changes brought about by putrefaction. The rest of the body was clean and white. The skin on the trunk and the upper legs showed numerous yellowish areas caused by physical damage and degeneration. There were clear wounds to the abdomen and scalp, and small pieces of paint on the skin matched that on an old door found near by. There was a large area of bloodstaining under the bushes.

Soon at the scene was Manchester's fingerprint expert, Detective Chief Inspector Tony Fletcher. His immediate thought was that someone had robbed a grave at the nearby cemetery, then mutilated the corpse. In the long grass near by he found scattered randomly items of women's clothing – pants, bra, tights, boots, cardigan, coat, skirt and jumper. 'Most of the top clothing was badly bloodstained and crawling with fully developed maggots. Under the privet hedge which separated the allotment from the pathway there was a depression which was absolutely teeming with maggots. Leaning next to the adjacent shed was a wooden interior house door.'

Ridgway realized fairly quickly that the corpse must have been recently moved. The body had at one stage been underneath the bush out of sight. Anybody walking along the path wouldn't go looking under the bush and it could have escaped notice. 'But lying where it was when we saw it, there is no way it could have escaped notice. It stuck out like a sore thumb. You looked at the body and you thought: "I know this is a fairly isolated place but there is no way this body has lain in this position a week." The state of decomposition told you it had to have been there a long time. So I thought it couldn't have lain in this position without it having been discovered. However, at that stage it didn't occur to me that the killer had gone back to move it.'

Now a full-scale murder hunt kicked into action. A suite of offices on the third floor at Longsight Police Station in Stockport Road, Manchester, was permanently on standby as a murder incident room. It was fully equipped with the kit needed for a major inquiry. The four-storey Edwardian building was very big, having started life as St Joseph's Approved School, where young tearaways, seventy years before, were sent to be weaned from a life of crime. The police station's cleaner's cupboards were located in rooms that years earlier had been used as punishment cells. Some of the rooms were huge, and had been partitioned with chipboard and wooden panelling to make them smaller and more useful as offices and workrooms for the police force. Ridgway had a hard core of officers he wanted to man the incident room. They had done it many times before and knew the ropes.

A brief story about the murder appeared that night in the *Manchester Evening News*. It prompted a man living in nearby Hulme, Alan Royle, to walk into his local police station. He said his 'wife' had been missing for a week. His initial thought had been that she had taken herself off on one of her jaunts to Scotland. He identified items of clothing found at the murder scene as belonging to Jean Jordan. He was advised by DCI Fletcher not to view the body. An identification was very quickly made with the briefest glimpses of the face in the mortuary by Jean's friend, Anna Holt, who sometimes worked the streets with her. Dental records later confirmed the identification.

No one on Ridgway's murder squad was surprised by the story which soon unfolded. Alan Royle and Jean had met some four years earlier, in October 1973, when Jordan, then aged sixteen, ran away from her parents' home in Motherwell, near Glasgow, and headed south. Royle was then a twenty-one-year-old chef who, travelling home from work, spotted her wandering about alone on Manchester's main Victoria Station. After buying her a cup of tea and something to eat, he took her under his wing and they started living together. But Jean and Alan had a strained and turbulent relationship and grew tired of each other, going their separate ways while still living together. Royle later told police they drifted apart when Jean started going out with her 'girlfriends'. It was a familiar tale. They had no money and she turned to prostitution to feed her children, working the streets of Moss Side and Cheetham

Hill for a couple of years. Sometimes, especially in the winter, she and Anna Holt used the same flat where they took men for business. It was rented by a mutual friend.

Previously the couple had lived in a small flat in the suburb of Wythenshawe. They were anxious to find somewhere bigger, to give the children more room to play in, and had been in their council flat in Hulme only a matter of weeks. Royle said that occasionally Jean would take off for several days at a time, hitch-hiking to Glasgow and leaving him to care for the two children, Alan, aged three, and James, aged twelve months. Jean had once actually left him and gone to live with relatives, but later returned. She was an attractive woman – slim with a pretty face, about five feet six inches tall, with long auburn hair. On her pitch in Moss Side she was known to the other working girls as 'Scotch Jean'. In the summertime she, like the other street girls, took men to the quiet patch of land near the Southern Cemetery, once part of the original Manchester Airport. But according to Anna Holt, Jean was growing tired of selling herself for sex and was trying to settle down. She had twice been arrested and cautioned for soliciting by the vice squad. 'Jean was not really cut out for it,' she said. 'She was guilty about her kids.' Neighbours described her as 'quiet', 'shy' and 'timid'.

On Friday, 1 October, at 9.30 in the evening, Jordan left her children in the care of a babysitter, saying she was going to get a breath of air and buy cigarettes from the local off-licence. Royle, who had no job, was already out. When he returned from having a drink she had gone. 'When she didn't come back on Saturday morning I wasn't too alarmed,' he said. 'I thought she had taken one of her trips to Scotland again. I didn't think to tell police because she had done it so often before. It wasn't until I read the description in the paper that I began to worry.'

DCI Tony Fletcher and a fingerprint specialist then proceeded to search the family home for a print to match ones taken from the dead body. A five-hour search of all the likely places yielded nothing. Finally, at around midnight, he instructed all remaining items to be collected in tea chests and taken to the fingerprint bureau. A team of six specialists began work next morning at 8.30. Within five minutes a left thumb print matching Jean Jordan's was found on a lemonade bottle removed from under the kitchen sink. None of the other articles removed from Jordan's flat yielded a trace of her fingerprints. Why? Because Alan Royle did all the cooking and most of the household chores.

Royle told detectives that Jean Jordan had a fake leather handbag which appeared to be missing. Police flooded the area with printed notices about the murder, specifically mentioning the dark-brown vinyl handbag, which had two carrying handles and a shoulder strap made of the same material. It was believed to contain about £15 in cash, a few cosmetics and some yellow tissue paper. Every person who used the allotment site was interviewed and a fingertip search of the disused allotment site failed to find the handbag.

The post-mortem was carried out by Reuben Woodcock at the brand-new, purpose-built central police mortuary in Rachel Street, Manchester, Jack Ridgway at his side. They had worked closely together many times and an easy-going familiarity resulted. The police officer always found the pathologist thorough, not to say painstaking, and quite approachable. He would discuss his findings with Ridgway, and more importantly from the detective's viewpoint thoughtfully listened to what he had to say. 'Some tend to be a little remote,' Ridgway reflected. 'They are the pathologist and not particularly interested in what your views are, whether they may or may not be valid. I always found Mr Woodcock was quite prepared to listen to your views, and if they didn't coincide with his findings, he would explain why it couldn't be right medically.'

Woodcock began to itemize the injuries – first to the head. There were eleven in all, some causing depressed fractures of the skull, some fairly superficial, others in a cluster of wounds each about one inch in diameter and all with fractures of the skull beneath. The woman had been hit with enough force in the mouth to loosen the middle four teeth in her upper jaw and there were tooth fragments in her mouth. He had little doubt that a heavy weapon with a rounded end, such as a hammer, had been used.

Moving to the shoulder, neck and trunk, he found a series of nineteen massive injuries, dark brown in colour, on her arms and upper chest. He believed they were also caused by blows from a hammer. Further down were more savage wounds – incisions to the front of the trunk. Other slashing wounds were found on her right thigh. As he examined the body, Woodcock felt sure the wounds were made in a series of slashes from the left shoulder to the right knee. He noted in his report: 'Eighteen wounds were seen on the abdomen and chest and six on the right thigh. The largest wound on the abdomen was seven inches long and the intestine protruded through it.' There was a neighbouring large wound through which gut protruded. It had been made with such ferocity that the intestine had been cut, the wound extending deep into the abdomen and into the front of the backbone. He could see fly eggs present but no maggots in this wound. 'This indicates that the wound had not been exposed to flies as long a time as the head,' he wrote. More wounds were on the left side of the trunk.

It all added up to an extraordinary conclusion: the evidence in the stomach wounds of fly eggs not yet become maggots meant they had been caused very recently and most certainly after the woman was killed. The head injuries alone had caused her death, he believed. Convinced the body had been attacked with a sharp instrument like a knife some time after death, Woodcock's report concluded: 'There were indications suggesting that the body had been clothed for some days after death and then stripped a day or so before the body was found. The age of the maggots indicated that death had occurred nine or ten days before being found.' Samples of the maggots were sent off to Manchester University in an effort to determine the exact timing from fly eggs being laid to becoming maggots.

The pathologist, who was some years older than Ridgway, had made some startling discoveries. Massive injuries to both head and stomach immediately reminded Ridgway of a special conference of senior detectives from Northern England a few months previously in Wakefield, at which George Oldfield gave a presentation with slides on the injuries found in the five Ripper murders so far. Ridgway sent a senior colleague back to his office to find the special West Yorkshire Police intelligence report covering the Ripper murders, and once reminded of the fact felt certain he had a Ripper killing on his hands.

There was, however, one additional gruesome fact which Woodcock deliberately omitted from his report at Ridgway's request. There had been a crude attempt to sever the woman's head. Clear marks in two separate places showed that a saw had been used in an effort to decapitate the woman. Ridgway wanted this information kept top secret. Over the next few years very few people were privy to it. It was, Ridgway believed, one of those facts which only the person who had tried to cut the head off would know. If any head bangers came forward to claim false ownership of Jordan's murder, the fact that they could not disclose this evidence meant he would be able to eliminate them quickly.

It all added up to a pretty extraordinary story. A woman had been murdered with considerable ferocity, with injuries to her head, shoulders, neck and upper trunk. The wounds were probably caused by a hammer. She had then been hidden in a depression in the ground under the privet hedge beside the shed in the disused allotment before being covered with a wooden door. Eight days later her body had been deliberately moved into the open, stripped, her clothing strewn over the long grass and another series of savage injuries inflicted. She had not just been murdered, she had been defiled in grotesque fashion. Ridgway called George Oldfield's office in Leeds and arranged to see him the following day.

The two men were neither friends nor acquaintances. They had met briefly previously. West Yorkshire detectives had worked closely with their Manchester counterparts on the M62 coach bombing investigation, but there was little regular contact. Arriving in Leeds the next day, Ridgway gave Oldfield a verbal report and his reasons for believing this to be a Ripper murder. He had no photographs from the lab – nor a written report from the pathologist. These would take some time to arrive at his desk.

'I told him we had a Ripper murder,' Ridgway remembered twenty-four years later. 'His reaction is that he doesn't want to know.' Ridgway's impression was that the West Yorkshire force had cornered the market on Ripper murders and didn't want anyone else getting in on the act. 'This was the feeling I got, not in those words, but it was the impression he presented. An expression of interest but no more. The first sour note – and it was only minor – came later. George said: "I think we should keep this thing quiet for the time being." He knew I had not told the press it was a Ripper murder and he said it would be beneficial for all if we kept this under our hat. In fairness they had a lot more Ripper murders and I did not want to rock the boat. I was prepared to go along with it and see how it panned out.

'Then I was driving back to Manchester over the Pennines and had the radio on. An announcement came on that West Yorkshire police had said the murder in Manchester is one of the Ripper series! I was so incensed. We knew the world and his wife would arrive on our doorstep once the announcement was made that Manchester had a Ripper murder. It was something we could have done without for a little while. What made me angry was that we had made an agreement, I had gone along with his request that we keep things quiet for a while. I could have made it public myself. I never had it out with him later. What could I have done?'

Ridgway hedged with the press over whether he was really dealing with a Ripper murder, merely saying there were only 'similarities' with the West Yorkshire killings. He refused to confirm she had been a prostitute: 'There is nothing to suggest it,' he said. 'It could be that while she was walking some motorist stopped and offered her a lift and that she expected she might be able to get a ride up to Scotland. She has hitch-hiked on occasions before.' Oldfield had previously only ever referred in the most guarded terms to the injuries inflicted on Ripper victims. Ridgway was equally cautious. The reporters were always anxious for more details, but the CID chief was having none of it. In some senses Jordan's murder bore the hallmarks of a Ripper killing, he told them, in other ways they were different. There had been no sexual assault, although the passage of time might have dissipated evidence of a sex attack. The CID chief had never had a cosy relationship with the media at the best of times. He provided them with the minimum information necessary to get the job done. 'I just have never been a media person,' he says. 'I used them because I had to. I would play ball with them because I wanted something out of them.'

But soon Ridgway would be launching a media offensive. The cause of this turnabout was a crucial discovery made five days after Jordan's body was uncovered. During the fingertip search of the disused allotment, every effort had been made to find the all-important handbag, but the team of uniformed officers halted their search at the wire fence between the new and disused allotments. On the morning of Saturday, 15 October, a man called Cox found the handbag – *on the other side of the wire fence.* It was exactly 189 feet or 60 yards from where the body was discovered – more than half a football pitch away. Ridgway drove quickly to the scene. The handbag was green, not dark brown. (It transpired that Royle was colour blind.) It had a zip fastener and a wrap-over strap which fastened with a clasp on the side. There were two external pockets. Ridgway examined these and in one of them found a concealed compartment. He felt inside and pulled out a folded-up brand-new five-pound note and a used one-pound note. 'Punter's fiver,' he exclaimed to no one in particular.

Suddenly, in Ridgway's mind, some of the most bewildering features seemed to fit. The handbag had clearly been searched by the killer, then apparently hurled away over the wire fence. He had returned to the scene more than a week after the murder to try and recover the five-pound note, which he realized might incriminate him. This would explain the stripping of the body and strewing Jordan's clothes all over the place. If he thought the five-pound note was hidden on the body or in her clothing, he probably hurled the clothing about in frustration at not finding anything. It went some way also to explaining the additional wounds inflicted on the corpse – again, in anger most probably. He went berserk when he couldn't find the money he had given her, kicked and slashed at her body and perhaps tried to remove the head to cover up the fact it was a Ripper killing.

Back in his office next to the control room, Ridgway knew he had to find who had issued the five-pound note. He felt certain Jordan's last client had given it to her – the man who murdered her. She had last been seen around 9.40 the night she was murdered. No semen had been found in or on the body, so it was unlikely she had had another punter that evening. No, in Ridgway's mind, the man who gave her the fiver also killed her. But finding exactly where the note originated from would not be easy. In an earlier case in Manchester where a prostitute had been murdered, three one-pound notes had been found on her. Tracing their origin, detectives succeeded in finding and convicting the man who killed her. Ridgway was certain this note too was probably from a payroll. Standard wages were such in 1977 that ten-pound notes were less likely to be given to employees in their pay packets. The crisp note appeared brand new. Fletcher's fingerprint specialists used every trick they knew to yield evidence – but without success. But they had a banknote serial number: AW 51 121565. The next task was to phone the Bank of England in London, who, it turned out, also had a branch in Leeds. The bank agreed to provide the information quickly. Ridgway arranged for the Metropolitan Police to assign an officer to collect it from the bank's premises in Threadneedle Street in the City of London. It was to be addressed to Ridgway personally at Baildon Police Station. The officer was to take it personally to King's Cross Station and hand it to a guard on a train going to Bradford. The officer was then to ring Ridgway and tell him what time the train would arrive. Ridgway in turn designated an officer to meet the train and collect the envelope.

The man duly met the train, only the package wasn't on it and the guard knew nothing about it. At some point the train had split in half – one part went to Huddersfield, the rest on to Bradford. The package was waiting at Huddersfield and a motor-bike rider went to collect it from there.

Jordan's five-pound note had been part of a delivery of new notes from the Bank of England printing works, sent to its Leeds branch on 27 September, just four days before the murder. This was extraordinary news. The chances of a brand-new note finding its way so quickly from West Yorkshire into the handbag of a prostitute in Manchester, on the other side of the Pennines, must be remote indeed. The likelihood was that it had been paid out as payroll by a local firm. They quickly followed the trail of the note. It was one in a parcel of new notes numbered F87947, which totalled £25,000. This had been released to the Midland Bank in nearby Park Road, Leeds, together with three others, totalling £100,000 in all. They had been collected by a bullion van from the Midland Bank for delivery on a very specific run to a number of branches in the Leeds and Bradford area. Each parcel of £25,000 was made up of ten bundles in heat-sealed polythene packs, each containing £2,500, with each bundle being made up of five smaller packets, each containing £500.

The trail was complicated by the fact that the original parcel containing Jordan's five-pound note had been joined on the bullion van with other parcels of brand-new notes, plus used five-pound notes from the Midland Bank's own vaults. Thus there was on the bullion van a total of £127,500 to be distributed in Leeds, Headingley, Otley, Guisely, Manningham, Bingley and Shipley. Some banks needed £25,000, which meant they were given a complete self-contained parcel. Others wanted smaller amounts. This involved breaking open a parcel and handing over only part of the contents. With records from the Midland Bank, and a powerful piece of deductive logic, Ridgway's team began to narrow down where the contents of parcel F87947 had gone. Some £2,500 had been paid into the Midland Bank at Bingley, along with £7,500 from a different parcel, totalling £10,000 in all. This left £22,500 in parcel F87947. Of that amount, £17,500 was handed over to the Midland's Shipley branch, leaving £5,000, which was then distributed to the bank at Manningham. All the money was scheduled for paying out at the end of the week.

Ridgway again met with Oldfield and worked out a plan of action. Leaving a skeleton team at the Longsight incident room, a team of thirty officers from Manchester would travel across the Pennines on the M62 each day, making enquiries at firms in the Shipley area, since that is where the bulk of the money from the parcel F87947 was distributed. They set up an incident room in a small police station in Baildon, on the northern fringes of Bradford. Oldfield offered thirty West Yorkshire detectives to assist the Manchester inquiry.

On 26 October, the *Yorkshire Post* reported a sudden influx of Manchester officers into West Yorkshire in connection with the Jean Jordan murder: 'NAKED GIRL KILLER HUNT SWITCHES TO WEST YORKSHIRE', ran its headline. Oldfield and Ridgway tried playing their cards close to their chest, worried the killer might dispose of evidence. Initially they declined to say what the line of inquiry was about. They were, Ridgway said, keeping an open mind on whether there was a link with the Ripper murders. They would be visiting factories in Bingley, Shipley and other areas of Bradford. Oldfield was more emphatic: there was no link with the Ripper killings.

The following day the Leeds *Evening Post* was reporting details of the five-pound note in Jean Jordan's handbag. Ridgway had come clean. 'We are looking for a very strange man,' he said. There was a distinct possibility that the man who gave Jordan the note, probably in payment for sex, was also the killer. The lead they had was so vital they would interview every single person they needed to, even if it took a month. They would visit every factory in the area if necessary, and interview every employee.

The newspaper revealed: 'She has died from head injuries but she also had stomach injuries. Forensic evidence suggested the stomach wounds were inflicted after [the] body had been stripped, eight days after her murder.' At a press conference Ridgway said what was in his mind: 'I believe the killer was annoyed or disappointed when Jean Jordan's body wasn't found immediately. At some time, probably during the hours of darkness, he went back to the body to make sure it was found.'

Next day, Ridgway revealed the number of the five-pound note. It was one of sixty-nine consecutively numbered brandnew notes. With Christmas coming he hoped local people might be saving for the festive season. 'We have been quite surprised at the number of people who still have notes given to them in their pay packets nearly a month ago. So, I am appealing to the thrifty Yorkshire people to have a look in their purses, wallets or savings tins for the notes in this vital series. I would even go as far as asking wives to look through their husband's wallets to see if they find one of these notes.' If they could narrow down which firm issued the note to an employee, they would be much closer to catching the killer.

Officers had already visited factories in Baildon and Shipley. During a three-day period, 28–30 September, thirty-four firms had drawn money from the Midland Bank at Shipley. In addition, a large number of private customers had received five-pound notes over the counter. Thousands of fivers had also been paid to the Bradford and Bingley Building Society in Shipley, and they in turn had paid out money to nearly 200 clients. In breaking down the trail of the five-pound note, Ridgway had the assistance of the Midland Bank staff at Shipley.

At the age of thirty-three, Mrs Maureen Banham had done two key things since leaving Ilkley Grammar School. She had had a full-time job with the Midland Bank, left to have her children after she married and returned later part time to the Shipley branch in October 1975, when her two daughters were ten and twelve. She went in on regular days, and always occupied the same cashier's point.

Shipley was a sub-branch of the firm's Manningham bank. Only half a dozen people worked there and it was very much a centre of the community. Maureen Banham and the rest of the staff got to know their customers pretty well, including the people sent from local firms and retailers each week to collect cash to be paid in the weekly wage packets. Some of them had been doing the same thing for several years. The firms would say how much they needed and in what denominations. In the true tradition of banking which still prevailed before there was a computer on every desktop, each transaction was written down – in a blue till book. One side was for people paying in, the other for people taking money out. Customers would come in with a cheque to cash, it would be stamped, the money paid out and an entry made in the till book. On the back they put a trap stamp: this showed the denominations paid out for the cheque. Says Mrs Banham, married at the time to a lorry driver and living in Baildon: 'We knew exactly how much we had given them and in which denomination.'

But finding who had that particular five-pound note wouldn't be easy. There were three counters in operation in the Shipley branch on a busy payout day. The newly delivered money was kept in the bank safe along with money paid in the day previously, and remnants of previous batches yet to be paid out. To keep a check on how much was being paid out from the safe, they had a cash sheet and a reserve sheet. Each morning an amount of cash would be removed from the safe to commence the day's business. It was handed to counter number one, which redistributed it to counters two and three as the day progressed. If they ran out of money, more was taken from the safe and the same process started over again. Good fortune had it that when the notes were taken from the safe the amount was recorded, and since the money in the delivery was mostly new notes, the numbers would run in sequence. Because they knew each other's writing, they could see which of the bank's tellers had handled which batches of notes.

It was almost a month after the five-pound note was distributed that the police arrived and asked for assistance in their murder inquiry. 'They wanted us to try and determine which batch of notes the five-pound note had come from and who the batch had gone to,' said Mrs Banham. 'It was a process of elimination. We went through all the paperwork trying to work out who we had given the note to. We knew we had given the note to a customer, but I wasn't sure he was necessarily the killer. He could have gone over the road and given it to a newsagent. We had to get the cheques and the vouchers out and go through everything carefully. Three or four policemen were with us, working after bank hours. We finished our normal job and accounted for all the money during that day's business, making sure everything balanced. When that process was completed, we could turn our attention to the police investigation.'

Another bank worker was Simon Steward, aged twenty-nine, who had been with the Midland since leaving school at sixteen. He and his wife were both bank staff and had been married four years. He commuted from his home in Burnstall by bus. Mr Steward was in charge of the cash in the bank and had four other cashiers under him. Today the whole business is recorded by computer. In 1977 it was he who ordered money from the Midland Bank bullion van. Money taken from the safe was recorded in the 'To and From Safe' cash book, which tabulated into columns – one-pound notes, fives and tens – so they knew the stock of the day they had drawn out. Then there would be a balance of what was left in the safe. At the end of the day, in the late afternoon, the money left in the cashier's tills would be gathered in and put back in the safe. The figures would be added up and everything, with luck, would balance.

On a wall in Baildon police station Ridgway had prepared a huge wallchart on which to plot individual five-pound notes as they were located, trying to determine when they had been paid out and to which firm or person. In this way they could eliminate some firms if their batch of five-pound notes was in a sequence so far removed from the number of Jordan's five-pound note that it was certain the money could not have been paid to their company. But it was slow progress filling the chart in. When money was taken out or put into the Shipley branch safe, cashiers did not write down the serial numbers, only how much was taken out or put back. Also, cashiers had idiosyncrasies in the way they paid money out. Some paid out old five-pound notes first before touching new notes. Others retained new notes for their regular customers, who sometimes demanded them, holding back old notes for people who were not regular clients.

To assist Ridgway's team, Simon Steward prepared a cash analysis of each till on a large piece of ruled paper measuring three feet by two. He had broken his arm in an accident and was brought to work each day at Baildon police station in a police car. He was brilliant at his job. On the one side was credits, on the other debits. Each cashier had a cash book for the day, so there was cash paid in on one side and cheques paid in on the other. In preparing the cash analysis, they recorded how the amount was paid out in twenties, tens, fives, single pound notes, ten-shilling notes, right down to individual pennies. Steward had been taught the process on a special cashier's course. In the old days, if they were a pound wrong in working out the balance for the day, they did a complete cash analysis. It was necessary, according to company rules, to show where you had gone wrong. 'It was a sort of slap on the hand,' he said. 'A pound was a lot of money in the 1970s, and also you won't make that mistake again because it's going to take you so long to do the cash analysis. It evokes self-discipline in the staff.'

His branch manager, Ian Sturrock, had been away on a banking course and arrived back at Shipley to find the police carrying out a major murder investigation. A native of Consett in north-east England, this was his first managerial appointment. He had joined the bank fourteen years before after three years with the TSB. 'The police were very confident they were going to capture the killer because of the five-pound note,' he said. 'They thought it would take them to his door and were almost planning the drinks party and getting ready to invite us.'

It wasn't that easy. Filling in Ridgway's wallchart at the tiny

Baildon police station was a time-consuming process. Tracking the flow of money in and out of a bank was like hunting a needle in a haystack. Occasionally a bus driver might arrive in Shipley, stopping close to the bank to bring in a huge amount of loose change, wanting fivers in exchange. The transaction might not be recorded in precise detail. Another cashier might suddenly have a run on cash and turn to a colleague and say: 'Hey, can you let me have some cash quickly because I've run out.' Individual cashiers had particular ways of distributing notes.

Ridgway had also expected that, in a bundle of £500, the new notes would run consecutively from 1 to 499. 'That is not the case,' he revealed. 'That was the premise we had been working on up to that point, but when we received the breakdown from the Bank of England, there were several numbers missing. It may very well be that a bundle of notes starts at '1', but instead of finishing at 499 to account for 500 notes, finishes at something like 627. The reason is because of spoils. There could be dozens of reasons why a note was not acceptable to be put into circulation. But they had to be perfect and any that were faulty were removed and of course that meant the sequence went completely to pot. It put us on the back foot straight away. We had been working on the assumption that there would be a sequential run through all the notes.

'The cashiers at the Shipley branch were amazing. They could recall whom they paid, how much, and who they paid old money to. There was a local bookmaker very close to the bank, and he was often paying money in and taking money out. On one of the crucial days he had withdrawn a large number of five-pound notes. But the cashier was able to tell us that the bookmaker would only take old fivers. He never took the new notes because of the danger that, when he was paying out to his customers, some of the notes might stick together.'

There was some luck on their side. Occasionally someone might have been ill in bed for two or three weeks and could not spend their wages because it was still in the safe at work, waiting to be collected. It was possible then to firmly establish that a particular bunch of notes went to a certain firm.

Ridgway remained convinced the Jordan note was key to solving the murder. He thought it highly unlikely that a five-pound note paid into a shop for goods could, in the normal course of business, come into circulation again on the other side of the Pennines within just a matter of days. Equally he thought it unlikely the five-pound note would have been received as part of change from a ten-pound note. A ten-pound note was, in his view, an even rarer animal. These deductions were made by Ridgway sitting in his office in Baildon. He hadn't much else to do, other than toss around in his mind various permutations of how the money could have got into Jordan's hands. Again and again he came back to the simple conclusion: the punter was the killer.

Ridgway knew his team had a long slog ahead. They were up early, leaving Manchester at 8 a.m. and driving across to Bradford on the M62 every day. They didn't get back till late at night, frequently after 10 p.m. Each morning he briefed them. The journey could be miserable and cold, especially on dark grey autumn mornings, when there was mist or fog on the motorway. Thinking his team needed a bit of a morale boost, the CID chief hit on the perfect idea. One morning, driving to Bradford, he made a break from his normal routine of listening to tapes of classical music and instead tuned into Radio Two and the Terry Wogan show. The Irish DJ was playing a Yorkshire brass band's rendition of the 'Floral Dance', a traditional Cornish tune. Ridgway arranged to get a cassette tape of the music. At the briefing, every single morning, the Manchester and West Yorkshire officers then had to listen to the brass band playing the 'Floral Dance' before they could start work. 'It's a super tune,' Ridgway said. 'It's catchy. It's lively and it gets you going. I played it all day.'

He had utmost faith in his own team and made sure officers worked in pairs – one from Manchester, one from West Yorkshire. 'I was one hundred per cent reliant on the quality of the work done by those men. They were prepared to really graft; if they believed in what they were doing, they would give you one hundred per cent. I gave them all the information I had in my possession, with the single exception of the attempt to remove the head. I was prepared to do that with them on the strict understanding that I was the only person who spoke to the press, because obviously you have to control the information going to the press. It was clearly understood that if I ever discovered a member of the team had been talking, or passing information to any member of the press, they would have been off the inquiry the moment I found out. Detectives are sensible people, I've found after years of experience. I don't think many of them indulge in idle chit-chat among their friends. I don't discuss murder inquiries with my family, and I assumed they didn't either.'

Despite every effort, Ridgway's wallchart didn't point him to the precise firm which received the crucial five-pound note. At one briefing the inquiry teams were given confidential information about the case. The murder weapon was thought to be a hammer; some form of cutting/stabbing instrument was used; the killer had worn size seven wellington or industrial boots. Finally, the murderer's vehicle might be fitted with two India Autoway tyres, though not too much reliance was placed on this because Oldfield believed these tyres may well have been replaced. Oldfield went through the list of injuries inflicted on the West Yorkshire victims. He was still interested in taxi drivers, and particularly Terence Hawkshaw. Inquiry teams were asked to take a particular interest in men who used taxis and paid for a trip with a new five-pound note. Finally, there were two crucial questions Ridgway wanted the men on their list to answer. 'Where were you on the night of Jordan's murder (1 October) and on the night of 9/10 October, when the killer returned to inflict further wounds on the body?'

Ridgway narrowed down the total number of firms he was interested in to thirty-four. They employed between them some 6,000 people, but he was more than prepared for the task. Going through the companies in alphabetical order, his officers quickly arrived at the firm of T. & W. H. Clark (Holdings) Ltd in Hilliam Road, Bradford, a firm of Bradford engineers who had received several thousand pounds of payroll from the Shipley Branch at the relevant time. The detectives needed a complete list of employees, with names and addresses. Before October was out, the inquiry teams began interviewing employees in their homes. Individual firms on the list had been given an alphabetical prefix, and individual employees a number, so they could be identified. T. & W. H. Clark had the prefix 'F' and one of their employees, called Peter Sutcliffe, was given the number '44'. For the purposes of the five-pound note inquiry, his reference was 'F44'.

On 2 November 1977, two detective constables, one from Manchester, the other from West Yorkshire, called at Sutcliffe's home, 6 Garden Lane, Heaton, a narrow, detached house built on a steep embankment. The lorry driver was at home with his wife, a twenty-seven-year-old supply teacher called Sonia. They had married a few years earlier and then lived with her parents, post-war refugees from Czechoslovakia. They had only recently moved into their new home, having paid £16,000 for what Sonia was to call 'my castle, the house of my dreams'. Sonia's mother lent them money towards the deposit.

She had been given the name 'Oksana', which in Czech means 'peace loving' after her birth in a maternity home in Horton Lane, Bradford, three years after her parents arrived in Britain as penniless refugees fleeing communism. Before the outbreak of the Second World War, her father, Bohdan Szurma, had been a physical education teacher who left his native Ukraine to join the staff of a grammar school in Prague. When Russian tanks entered Czechoslovakia, he was sent to a displaced person's camp. There he met and later married a young woman, Maria Mrstikova, from Prague. Their first real home in Britain was a two-up, two-down terrace house in Earl Street, Bradford. Bohdan worked as a machine-minder in a local textile factory. Both their daughters grew up speaking Czech, Ukrainian and English fluently.

When the detectives called at the house, Sutcliffe was unable to produce any of the five-pound notes from his wage packet of 29 September. He said that on 1 October he had been at home with Sonia, and that on 9 October they had held a house-warming party. Both accounts were verified by Sonia. Sutcliffe claimed he had last visited Manchester a year previously while making a delivery for the firm he worked for before he joined Clarks. But while she confirmed what her husband had said, Mrs Sutcliffe failed to mention how after the house-warming party on 9 October, Peter 'had taken some of his relatives home by car and had been gone some time'. Curiously, when the officers came to file their report, they wrote that Sutcliffe did not own a car. They may not have seen a vehicle at the house, but at the time Sutcliffe owned a red

Ford Corsair, bought about five weeks earlier. However, this stage of the inquiry was merely to determine whether or not Mr Sutcliffe, who worked for one of the firms which could have received the Jordan five-pound note, had any money from his wages in his possession. The answer was 'no'.

A second phase of the inquiry involved a separate team of officers from Manchester and West Yorkshire visiting employees to ask more detailed questions about the murders in the Ripper series. Ridgway insisted on different teams of detectives calling for the second visit to each worker, to avoid anyone being questioned developing 'a cosy relationship with one pair of inquiry officers'. No person would be seen twice by the same pair of officers, though it was vital that detectives who carried out the follow-up interview should have access to all the relevant papers gathered earlier. Six days later, on 8 November 1977, Sutcliffe was questioned again. He repeated his alibis for the relevant dates and his wife again confirmed them. Given that the couple had only moved into their new home on 26 September, this seemed a reasonable explanation. Moreover, 'the alibi for 9/10 October was strengthened by Sutcliffe's mother who had been present at the party'. The detectives called on her and she signed a statement confirming she had been at the house-warming party that weekend.

The detectives also discovered that Sutcliffe actually owned a red Ford Corsair, and had earlier owned a white car of the same make, which he had taken to a scrapyard some time previously. They didn't examine the red Corsair or carry out a full search of the home, though they questioned Sutcliffe about his tools and boots, but there was nothing to point the finger of suspicion. In fact the officers took little advantage of the information provided at the detailed briefing on the case. Had they examined the red Ford Corsair they would have certainly found it had two tyres that could have left tread marks similar to those at the Richardson murder. This might have prompted them to probe further and question the alibi regarding the house-warming party. Their instructions demanded that the house, garage and cars be searched. But, equally, Oldfield had not stressed the importance of the tyre marks left at the Richardson scene because he was convinced the killer was driving a Ford Cortina when he attacked Long. No specific instruction was given to record the makes of tyres on vehicles owned by people interviewed. Neither were the officers briefed that they should look for a hacksaw – which had been used to try to sever Jordan's head. Ridgway still felt it was vital to keep this back from them. But it was possible, had all officers been instructed to collect every hacksaw they found in interviewees' toolboxes or garages, they could have been sent for forensic analysis. It would have been a gigantic task, but this was an extraordinary investigation. A golden opportunity to catch the Ripper thus slipped by.

No trace of the sixty-nine five-pound notes with consecutive numbers was ever found by Ridgway's team, and a few months later the inquiry was wound down. There were simply too many people who could have received the Jordan five-pound note. Nor was it possible at that time to run a computer check trying to match owners on Jim Hobson's list of the 53,000 vehicles that could have left the tyre marks at the Richardson crime scene with the 6,000 employees who might have received the five-pound note. The question was simply never posed. The paperwork developed at the Manchester end of the inquiry was sent to Leeds to be included in the files of the incident room at Millgarth.

The forensic scientists had managed to isolate one or two microscopic clues yielded from the post-mortem. A hair from an Asian male had been found on Jordan's jacket. And a multi-coloured man-made fibre was found on an inside cuff on the coat, coloured red, blue and yellow, and thought to come from either a piece of woman's clothing or a man's tie.

Jack Ridgway was bitterly disappointed that his operation hadn't found the killer. He remained convinced he was on the right lines, but recognized when it was time to call it a day. Ridgway felt they had almost certainly already interviewed the killer and that his name was already in 'the system'.

8

'The Job Is Life; Life Is the Job'

In Leeds, during the aftermath of the MacDonald murder, Oldfield had toured the streets of Chapeltown chatting with the street girls. He felt no personal animus towards them and urged the women to look after themselves, operate in pairs and take the car numbers of one another's clients. It had been a terrible year. He was no nearer fulfilling his promise to Wilf MacDonald to bring his daughter's killer to justice. At Christmas 1977, somewhere in the North of England, a vicious madman with a profound hatred of prostitutes was on the loose. Five women on either side of the Pennines had died as a result of plying their trade. A sixth – sixteen-year-old Jayne – had clearly been mistaken for a streetwalker simply because she had passed through a red-light area late at night on her way home. And so the word went out from police, social workers and probation officers: women selling sex were now in the gravest danger, particularly those who stood in the dark, at night, at street corners, trying to pick up men in cars.

For most of the women involved it was a miserable life: sex for a fiver or less with a total stranger in the back of a car, or lying on the ground in some lonely, seedy spot, frequently surrounded by the detritus of life and sex – especially used condoms. A few, like Tina Atkinson, had found a room with a bed somewhere to take a punter back to. Many women were beaten or abused or both; some had money stolen and dared not report the theft to police. Some had to hand their money over to pimps; still more took their money home to pay the rent and feed their children. Others drowned their sorrows in drink.

A few worked, and like Emily Jackson had the backing and cooperation of a spouse. One husband in the mid-1970s, accused of living off his wife's earnings, supposedly banked £3,000 of unexplained cash during a three-month period. He told the court he earned it 'selling finches to pet shops'. His wife said they wanted to buy a house away from the vice area.

With a serial killer on the loose, and prostitutes in grave danger plying their trade, one answer, according to Mrs Cynthia Stein, chairman of the Bradford branch of the National Housewives Register, would be to legalize brothels. 'I am sure we would not have had a Ripper if brothels had been made legal.' It was a view shared by Ronald Gregory, who said prostitution 'legalized in some way would eliminate a lot of these vicious attacks'. But when a group of prostitutes in Bradford took their clients to a house in Belle Vue, Manningham, rather than have sex in cars, the local vice squad raided the place, claiming it was being used as a brothel.

Even before the Ripper attacks, the attitude of police in the 1970s towards violence against prostitutes was hugely ambivalent. Vice squads in inner cities clamped down on street women, because many crimes of drunkenness and violence took place within red-light areas. Police officers felt it was hard enough keeping the peace and controlling crime at the best of times, without women putting themselves in harm's way by going with men for money and making themselves vulnerable. This sentiment included women whom police regarded as a grade down from those openly prostituting themselves – the ones who occasionally slept with men in exchange for a present or a good time or perhaps even a few pounds. They called them 'women of loose moral fibre'.

In the mid-1950s the great and good of British society had debated the current law on prostitution and homosexuality. A committee in London, under the chairmanship of the vice-chancellor of Reading University, Sir John Wolfenden, deliberated on the moral and legal issues and made a series of supposedly liberal recommendations. Wolfenden's committee claimed it did not want to moralize by interfering in the private lives of British citizens. Its goal was to preserve public order and decency and provide safeguards against the exploitation of women, particularly the vulnerable. London and a number of large towns in the provinces were of principal concern because of the visible and obvious presence of prostitutes in considerable numbers on public streets. It was the very openness of the activity which seemed to appal Wolfenden and his committee. They labelled London the world's capital of vice, pointing to 'the impudence of prostitutes in the streets' and 'the existence of soliciting in daylight' and women who openly flaunted their trade, behaving in embarrassing and shocking ways.

In 1959 Parliament passed the Street Offences Act. Women accused of selling themselves for sex were now officially 'common prostitutes' and it was illegal for them to loiter or solicit in a street or public place for the purpose of their chosen trade. To ensure that 'innocent' women were not arrested, no prosecution could take place until a woman had been officially cautioned for soliciting by police on two separate occasions. Patrolling members of the police vice squads got to know the women in the red-light districts. Cautions were issued, but then the women moved on elsewhere, to another suburb, occasionally to a nearby town, sometimes even to London or one of the other big cities. Manchester in 1977 had its own vice squad, clamping down on street women by issuing cautions, then prosecuting persistent offenders.

Unable to find witnesses who had seen Jean Jordan at her normal pitch the night she died, Detective Chief Superintendent Jack Ridgway thought it was likely the latest Ripper victim had moved on from her usual place in Moss Side for picking up punters after receiving two cautions. Two years before Jordan was murdered, a Working Party on Street Offences reported that the Street Offences Act had been a considerable success in clearing the streets of prostitutes. The numbers of women convicted of loitering plummeted from 19,663 in 1958 to 2,828 in 1960 and 3,466 in 1972. But the law didn't stop the likes of McCann, Jackson, Richardson, Atkinson and Jordan plying their trade. As one writer noted, the nuisance did not go away – it just went somewhere else: 'The middle class shoppers in Manchester were spared the sight of whores in leopard-skin coats and stiletto heels leaning against the windows of Lewis's arcade. Instead the girls went to Moss Side and Whalley Range where the police weren't so thick on the ground and working class and immigrant inhabitants were less vocal in protest.' The problem was not the supply side of the equation – it was the demand. Men in large numbers, young, middle aged and elderly, representative of all classes and professions, continued actively to seek the services of street prostitutes. There were bank managers and solicitors, lorry drivers and labourers. Mass ownership of cars from the 1960s onwards made the situation worse and brought a new phenomenon to some of the most deprived inner-city areas: kerb crawling.

It wasn't illegal to be a prostitute. It was illegal merely to solicit for the purposes of prostitution. Smart women moved their trade indoors. They rented rooms and hired a maid. They advertised in shop windows and telephone boxes and tended to keep their professional activities secret from families and friends while regarding their chosen profession as a legitimate career, almost akin to social work. This was the respectable, even acceptable end of the market. As one observer commented: 'Each prostitute is, for each client, a kind of professional concubine, as Mademoiselle O'Murphy was for Louis XV.' A survey found that most women who moved their activities indoors engaged in prostitution mainly for money after trying other jobs and becoming bored. Friends had introduced them to the work; they tried it for a few weeks and decided to continue. Some were even budding entrepreneurs, dreaming of starting their own businesses or of going to university and having a legitimate career.

But at the lower end of the trade were the streetwalkers, who practised prostitution as a lifelong trade because life had dealt them a difficult hand and few other opportunities were available to them. Some were mentally backward or disordered; others apathetic and generally hopeless in their attitude to life. There was a marked excess of alcohol consumption among the street girls. Many were single mothers, so had to become the breadwinners. A few, like Emily Jackson, enjoyed the work as well as needing the money.

In 1976 early police tactics following the attacks on McCann and Jackson in Leeds had been to gather a list of all known prostitutes operating in the areas where attacks took place. They were then traced and interviewed about violent or 'queer' clients. These men were tracked down and interviewed in an effort to eliminate them. Detectives quickly discovered many prostitutes in Leeds and Bradford were married and earning money during the evenings without their husbands' knowledge.

Several hundred men were interviewed, but the killer was never in the frame. They tried a crackdown by arresting prostitutes in the hope they would get off the local streets – but the women were too desperate for money and moved to ply their trade elsewhere. Women detectives were used in Manningham and Chapeltown as decoys, hoping to trap the Ripper. Shadowing them were detectives with radios. This tactic too was abandoned.

Journalists began speculating on why the killer was attacking prostitutes: 'Police believe the man is probably from West Yorkshire, certainly with a good knowledge of Leeds and Bradford, and has possibly developed a psychological hang-up about prostitutes, either at the hands of one, or possibly because his mother was one.' All this was true. Detectives were mystified why he was attacking prostitutes. But Oldfield was constantly wondering who would be the next victim because, in the absence of any tangible clues, he could only hope the Ripper would make a mistake. Just ten days before Christmas 1977 he got his answer. A twenty-five-year-old mother of two children was rushed to hospital after being viciously attacked in Leeds. She had a conviction for prostitution and her name was Marilyn Moore. Mercifully she survived.

The woman had a son, aged six, and a daughter, aged twelve months, neither of whom lived with their mother. She had left home at fifteen and was married at sixteen. Later she divorced. Since then she had been plying her trade for six years in London, Slough, Bradford and Leeds, but clearly kept the fact secret from her landlord. Moore lodged in an upstairs room at a house owned by fifty-one-year-old Peter Sucvic, in the Harehills area of Leeds. He revealed that she often went with a friend to nightclubs in Bradford and Halifax and on many occasions stayed away a week. Hobson realized this would be when she went travelling, looking for trade outside her normal haunts. The night she was attacked, according to Mr Sucvic, she had been waiting for a friend to call, then said she would go and look for her, promising to return around 11 p.m.

It was Wednesday, 14 December 1977, and Marilyn Moore, working the streets of Chapeltown at about 8 p.m., noticed a man driving a car who seemed obviously looking for a woman. She swiftly walked down several streets to be in a position where she was facing the car on her side of the street so she could pick up a client. When next she saw the car it was parked at the kerb and the man was standing near the driver's door. They agreed a price of five pounds and she sat in the front seat. Before he got into the car he appeared to wave to someone he knew. He then drove off, claiming to know 'a right quiet place'. He chatted casually, saying his name was 'Dave' but he preferred 'David'. Moore asked him who he had been waving to; he said it was his girlfriend who was ill, and claimed to know two prostitutes in Chapeltown called Gloria and Hilary: 'The one with the Jamaican boyfriend.' Since the area was full of West Indians, it was a good guess that local prostitutes might have a boyfriend from the Caribbean. He pulled up a mile and a half away on a piece of spare ground next to a beck, behind Brown's Factory in Buslingthorpe Lane.

Agreeing to sex in the back of the car, Marilyn got out to open the rear passenger door. It was then she was clubbed from behind. She screamed and put her hands up to shield her head. She slid to the ground, trying to hold on to the man's trouser leg as more blows rained down. She slipped into unconsciousness. A dog began barking near by. The attacker returned to his car, reversed quickly and drove off, wheels spinning. A local man called Hayward, who lived in Scott Hall Farm, heard the screams at about 8.45 and went outside with his dogs, but heard nothing more. Marilyn Moore had staggered into Scott Hall Street, an unmade road, and from there into Buslingthorpe Lane. A girl and her teenage boyfriend were standing chatting idly as she approached them, bleeding profusely from under her ginger hair. She begged them to call an ambulance. More people came to her aid before the emergency call was answered.

Soon the ambulance was rushing her to Leeds General Infirmary, where she was immediately seen by a neurological registrar, who decided to operate. Some time past midnight, Professor David Gee went to theatre six in the main theatre block and watched the tail end of the delicate operation to save Marilyn Moore's life. She had a number of lacerations to the head, perhaps eight in all, one of which was caused by heavy force. This blow had depressed the skull into the brain and the neurosurgeon had elevated the skull bone to relieve the pressure. Most of the head injuries had been excised and restitched, but Gee could see two lacerations of the scalp: one at the nape of her neck, semi-lunar in shape, concaving backwards. The depressed fracture had also been an oval shape. A long stitched wound on her left thumb and bruising on her right hand showed where she had tried to protect herself, but the giveaway for Gee was the head injuries, 'very reminiscent of some of the others' – and almost certainly caused by a hammer.

Gee was able to make a superficial examination, while she was being moved from the theatre table to a trolley, prior to being taken back to a hospital ward to recover from the operation. She bore no obvious injuries to her face, nor to her trunk or legs. Marilyn Moore was a very, very lucky woman. Her screams had probably saved her life. It should have been the breakthrough everyone wanted. A Ripper victim had survived and, unlike Maureen Long, whose memory was shot to pieces, Moore was able to provide a positive description of her attacker and the car he drove.

Next day, as Hobson attended the inquest into Jayne Mac-Donald's murder and was telling the coroner how 13,000 people had been interviewed and 4,000 statements taken so far in the Ripper inquiry, two of his officers were questioning a heavily bandaged Marilyn Moore in her hospital bed. Her repaired injuries bore fifty-six stitches and she was very poorly, but she was able to describe her attacker as white, twenty-eight years old, and five foot six or eight inches tall, with a stocky build. He had long dark curling hair, a 'Jason King' moustache, a short full beard. He spoke softly and had brown eyes, bushy eyebrows and a swarthy or suntanned complexion. He was wearing a yellow shirt, blue jeans, a dark coloured zip-up lightweight car coat. It was as good a description from a prospective murder victim as the police were ever going to get.

Jim Hobson next day gave the press details and left them in no doubt that the spot where Moore was attacked was a favourite haunt of prostitutes and their clients. The 'Jason King' description, after a character in a 1970s TV drama series, was well publicized, as was the photofit a couple of days later. Journalists were told the attacker drove a maroon or dark-coloured car and was well acquainted with the back streets of Chapeltown and the Sheepscar area of Leeds. To Hobson it indicated he was regularly in the area. Later Marilyn Moore, a pudgy and overweight woman, described her attacker in more detail: 'He was good looking – and he knew it. He had a drooping moustache and come-to-bed eyes.'

The clues about the driver being called 'Dave' and the names he gave of two local prostitutes led to a large number of inquiries by detectives and the task force. The index in the main incident room was searched for men called 'Dave' or

'David'. There were 1,037 of them already seen and eliminated. All were interviewed again and asked to provide alibis. Two hundred prostitutes were questioned.

A witness called Jimmy Pearson, aged forty, lived in a caravan in an adjoining scrap metal dealer's yard. He and his girlfriend described a 'dull red' car containing two people going into the lane behind Brown's factory at about 8.20 p.m. The engine and lights were switched off. 'I saw figures which looked as though they were going to have a cuddle.' Moore herself described the car as maroon or dark coloured, and recalled that inside were two interior rear-view mirrors. It had had four doors, which meant that six from the long list of vehicles which could have been used at the Richardson murder could be eliminated. At the scene of the attack crime officers had taken plaster casts of tyre tracks. Three of the tyres were of a similar make to those which left tracks at the Richardson murder scene. The track widths seemed identical. But the experts were in disagreement. They could not be certain whether the car had been on full lock when it negotiated a small bush and a pile of rubbish. Finally it was deduced to have been on full lock, which meant a particular measurement of the turning circle. This then reduced the number of possible vehicles to eight.

From the description of the car's interior, officers from the stolen vehicle squad believed Moore had been sitting in a BMC 'Farina' – a range produced by the British Motor Corporation in five separately named styles between 1958 and 1962: the Austin A55 Cambridge Mark II, the MG Magnet Series III, the Morris Oxford Mark V, the Riley 4/68 and the Wolseley 15/60. But there were three other vehicles which could have left the tracks: two Rootes group cars, and one Ford – the Corsair 2000E – made between 1966 and 1970.

Moore, who discharged herself from hospital on Christmas Eve, was asked to sit in different cars to see if it was the one the attacker used. She firmly ruled out a Hillman Minx and a Singer Gazelle, and thought it couldn't have been the Corsair, because the bell-housing was too big. Also, she said she had noticed 'fins' at the rear of the car. (It transpired in 1981 that Peter Sutcliffe had by this time got rid of his white Corsair because it wouldn't pass the MOT. He purchased a second-hand red Corsair 2000E, registration PHE 355G, swapping some of the better tyres from his old vehicle on to his new one. He had also used the spare wheel from the white Corsair. The assumption the Ripper Squad made was that the killer was using the same car. They were struggling in trying to determine the make of car he used.)

A few months later, Dr R. P. Snaith, a senior lecturer in psychiatry at Leeds University, put both Moore and Maureen Long under hypnosis on several occasions to see if they could remember more about their attacker. Long's memory was severely impaired, but in April 1978 the much younger and robust Moore provided a second photofit impression. It was different from the first in that now the suspect had longer hair, though the drooping moustache and beard remained a prominent feature. Under hypnosis she recalled seeing a cardboard box on the dashboard and the letters 'T-R-I . . .' written on it. Unfortunately, shortly after Dr Snaith completed his hypnosis sessions on the Ripper's surviving victims, Marilyn Moore made a frantic telephone call to the Millgarth incident room. She sounded desperate and claimed she had just seen the man who attacked her driving a mini-saloon in Bradford. She gave the registration number and the man was traced. He bore a striking resemblance to the second photofit description, but had a rock-solid alibi and was eliminated from the inquiry.

The press were linking the attack with the previous Ripper murders, but Hobson and Oldfield were having serious doubts about Moore's photofit description. Moore later picked out yet another man in the street and he too was checked and eliminated. It only served to cast more doubt on her description and the validity of the photofits.

For one family, the first photofit resurrected memories of a horrifying night a few years earlier. After it was prominently published locally, the mother of Tracey Browne, savagely attacked near Silsden in August 1975, became concerned enough to take her daughter into Keighley police station. Tracey was convinced the same man had attacked her, and Nora Browne decided the police should know as soon as possible. Tragically, because of doubts about the value of the photofit, a golden opportunity was wasted. A young constable serving behind the desk didn't take the matter seriously enough. They showed him the newspaper and Mrs Browne explained what had happened to her daughter. Tracey was absolutely certain it was the same man. The constable looked at them and said: 'We are all having fun and games today, aren't we?' He gave them a form to fill in. Mrs Browne was furious. Just then a detective happened to be passing and stopped to talk to them both, trying to calm the women down. He took down their details, but they were never followed up.

'They didn't take me seriously,' Tracey Browne said years later. 'I don't know why, maybe it was my age. A lot of people didn't. If I told them I had been attacked by the Ripper they'd just dismiss me, so I didn't broadcast it.' She was left with a permanent three-inch, crescent-shaped dent at the top of her head, and a smaller one at the rear. She also suffered constant nightmares. Many years later, the photofits provided by

Browne and Moore were examined side by side. They looked remarkably similar and bore a stunning likeness to Peter Sutcliffe. Added to the photofits provided by Barbara Miller in Bradford and Marcella Claxton in Leeds, a clear and distinct pattern emerges. As an internal West Yorkshire Police report produced in the early 1980s later commented: 'If her photofit had been compared with those provided by other survivors, the similarity is so striking that it is beyond belief that they would not all have been linked and considerable emphasis given to tracing the bearded man described.'

Following the murder of Jayne MacDonald, the incident room had started a special beard index because a witness had seen someone they thought had a ginger beard. From that time on the beard index referred only to men with ginger beards. Had the criteria been widened to include dark or black beards, it seems highly likely that photofits provided by earlier victims who survived attacks would have surfaced. Officers who subsequently interviewed a suspect with a beard would then have placed that name within the beard index.

'The tragedy is that Moore was seated in the relevant cars that could have made the tyre tracks,' a retired Detective Superintendent Dick Holland reflected twenty-five years later. 'She went for the Morris Oxford and not the Ford Corsair. She was certain it was not that and as a result she got it wrong. But with the photofit, she got that so right, despite her serious head injuries.'

Holland was a permanent fixture on the Ripper Squad for almost four years, at George Oldfield's behest. For the first time in ages in that year of 1977, Holland spent both Christmas and New Year at home in Ellend, on the outskirts of Huddersfield, the town where he had lived all his life. Personally he had little to celebrate during the festive season. His marriage had broken up – not surprising, given the stresses and strains his work imposed. But his wife had taken half their furniture. He neither drank nor smoked, and hadn't the heart to impose himself on any of his friends. Besides, he was a lifelong atheist, preferring the assured certainty of science to what he regarded as the sophistry of those who argued the existence of a Higher Being.

A close colleague, senior to Holland, once calculated that 70 per cent of detectives under his command were either divorced or having marital difficulties. 'Detectives are a peculiar animal,' he said. 'The job that they do is so exciting no one day is the same as any other. People you interview are all totally different. You can go on working and working and working and thoroughly enjoy it. What a lot of detectives don't realize is what it is doing to their home life, to their wives and families. I hoped when the troops went off duty at night they would go home and enjoy their family life. But the adrenaline is still pumping and a lot of them don't go home straight away, they go for a pint and then have another. The detectives were working long, long hours, they were getting tired, they were working days off that they should have spent with their family. Family life suffers, they suffer, they get tired and one can see the drain on physical and mental attitude as the thing goes on. I saw them suffer throughout the Ripper inquiry; the morale got lower and the tiredness got greater.

'The public relate police work very much to what they see on television. They have no conception of the pressure detectives are under, from the lowest detective, the detective constables who are the absolute front rank, going out knocking on doors and asking the questions that matter. Were they up to the job, because they were working long hours and they were tired? Were they capable of recognizing things for what they were? If they were to knock on the door and speak to the man who had committed all these murders, would they recognize it, would they be able to get inside his mind and say, "I'm not happy, come with me," and then go into the depth it deserved? Tired detectives, although they try, are not always capable of doing that. As a senior manager you've got so many inquiries going on, so many murders in this particular series, that the thin blue line is so thin it's got gaps in it. Where do you produce other people from? You've only got a certain number of detectives and uniform staff in the force. It's up to the chief constable to decide whether he needs help from outside, but when you start wanting outside help you are admitting a certain amount of failure, and people don't like to admit that. I think there were senior detectives all over the country sitting back and saying, "Thank God it's in West Yorkshire, and not in my area." '

Holland's marital breakdown mirrored a situation repeated in police forces around Britain. Heavy demands had been placed on all West Yorkshire detectives, both those on the Ripper Inquiry and the remainder, who were left having to carry the burden of an enormous extra workload. Good officers, and especially detectives, were normally deeply committed. The challenge of solving serious crimes, of being part of a team working on a major inquiry, especially a murder, acted like a drug for many. It required dedication in superabundance. The higher up the chain of command you were, the more committed to the work you had to be. So infrequently did they spent time at home that they had more in common and shared more genuinely memorable times with colleagues than with families. How could a senior detective explain to his wife the sheer electric excitement of arresting a four times serial killer, or of cracking the murder of an eleven-year-old Boy Scout with only the fibres from a worn carpet as a clue?

Both these things happened to Holland during the dying months of his marriage.

In truth, Dick Holland lived for the job. It was his life and had been for many years. If he wasn't working on an inquiry, then he was playing cricket or rugby for a local police team. He could be considerate, even kind to subordinates, but he didn't tolerate fools. People liked working for him and he expected his officers to have the same commitment to their work as he did. So it was that Holland was at first blind, and then, as his relationship with his wife Catherine broke down, somewhat indifferent to the effect his work was having on his marriage. She was fed up with being put second. Like countless other women married to dedicated detectives, his wife could not be blamed for believing he cared for the police service more than her. Of course he *loved* her, in the way men do after four children and twenty-plus years of marriage – but he was *passionate* about his work. It provided him with comradeship, intellectual challenges and the tangible rewards of being a successful detective, the most important of which were the admiration and approval of close colleagues whose opinion he valued. Chief among them was his boss: George Oldfield, to whom he was utterly loyal. In Holland's view, loyalty bred loyalty. In times of trouble, police officers stuck together. He never in his career sanctioned corruption and he viewed bent police officers as a curse. But he knew what was expected of him where THE JOB was concerned. Results. Villains had to be locked up, taken off the streets, in order that the tranquillity of local citizens be preserved. Keeping the Queen's Peace meant precisely that – allowing local people to go about their lives unhindered, safe in the knowledge that the police were there to protect them. If Judges' Rules were broken, it was done in true utilitarian fashion and with honest intent.

Holland was born in 1933 in a village called Moldgreen, on the Wakefield Road out of Huddersfield. His was an extended family, with three grandparents and an aunt living in close proximity. His maternal grandfather was a tuner in a mill, keeping the looms going and remaking machine parts when they broke down. Like countless others of his generation, when it was snowing so bad the buses couldn't run, Holland's grandfather would walk eight or nine miles to work. His parents, Edith and Cyril Holland, were one of the few couples in their street not to work in the textile mills. They were in the catering trade. His grandfather had bought Holland's mother a small bakery, and one of his father's jobs was hawking bread and cakes locally from a basket. They had to sell the business in the 1930s depression.

Holland attended Huddersfield College, an academic grammar school, whose prime purpose was gearing its pupils for university, so much so that if boys went into a blue-collar job, their headmaster thought they had failed in life. The school was in an old Victorian castellated building and the masters wore gowns and mortarboards. Proudly displayed on the Honours Board were the names of boys who had won scholarships and exhibitions to Oxford and Cambridge. By the time Holland won a place at the college, his father was in the army and the family were excused the fees of three guineas a term. For someone who hardly moved from his home environment for almost all his life, Holland regards the grammar school as the saviour of bright working-class children who could do better for themselves and move up and out of poverty. One effect of his grammar school education was to make him a lifelong supporter of rugby union, while his family, and most other local schoolboys, were rugby league men, a sport most commonly associated with the hard industrial areas of northern England.

In 1951 Holland should have been on his way to study for a degree in agricultural zoology at Leeds. He gained the higher school certificate and did particularly well in physics, chemistry and biology at A level to gain his place at university. Then, when his girlfriend announced she was expecting a child, his dreams of becoming a veterinary surgeon fell by the wayside. Catherine had been working in his parents' bakery and the fact that she was pregnant was at the time quite scandalous.

'My headmaster was disgusted and my parents weren't right pleased,' he said. Having to get married at eighteen meant he wouldn't be able to take up a university scholarship and instead was called up into the army to do National Service. Impaired hearing denied him the opportunity of being an officer and he quickly became a sergeant in the Ordnance Corps, spending most of his two years' army service at a depot in Bicester, north of Oxford.

In 1953 he returned to Huddersfield. He was married with a baby son, and had just bought a small house on a mortgage. He weighed up the possibility of becoming a civil servant, but then considered a police career. A second child was on the way and the police had a good pension scheme. He was a good prospect: fit, powerfully built, had completed his National Service and run a platoon of men at the age of nineteen. He was virtually able to walk into the Huddersfield borough police, who sent him for training at the local police college at Pannell Ash near Harrogate. His initial weekly pay was less than he had earned in the army, but police officers had various extras – a rent allowance which helped with the mortgage, a boot allowance, even a bicycle allowance. One of his new neighbours was a detective sergeant, and Holland had his heart set on joining the CID. It took him three years to get a permanent place.

By 1968, when Huddersfield was absorbed into the West Yorkshire force along with other boroughs like Wakefield, Halifax and Dewsbury, Holland was a detective sergeant with several years' experience on the regional crime squad under Denis Hoban. Huddersfield was a violent place and the borough police were very tough in their efforts to enforce the law. Little had changed in local police methods since Victorian times. In 1931 Huddersfield police had made a technological breakthrough when they got their first mechanized patrol section – three motor cycles and side-cars – but a dog section had to wait another thirty-five years. In terms of mainstream policing, the local watch committee set the tone. Many of its members were wool men steeped in the textile trade, who ensured that their officers had the finest tailor-made uniforms of worsted cloth dyed indigo blue. They wanted an orderly town and made sure the local chief constable knew it. Hooliganism and violence in Huddersfield were quickly jumped on. It was not unknown for officers to draw batons to sort out local gangs of roughs.

Early on, as a probationer, while walking down a street with his inspector, Holland stepped into the roadside to avoid some youths coming towards him. It earned him a dressing down: 'You walk down this bloody pavement as though you own it, you own the main street of Huddersfield, you're not a bloody trespasser. When you get to an incident you take charge. You do something, it doesn't matter if it's wrong, you show the public that you're doing something and you take charge. You-are-in-charge-of-it. They are going to do what *you* say.'

He was taught that you could only succeed as a detective if you were capable of being 'a bigger bastard than the bigger bastards you had to deal with'. The CID needed real evidence in court to obtain a conviction. Particularly helpful was the return of stolen property and a voluntary statement in which the accused admitted his wrongdoing. To be able to obtain these without being over forceful, the prime requirement for being in the CID was an ability to empathize with criminals, use their language, strike a rapport. Denis Hoban had done it in Leeds with aplomb.

'Sometimes detectives who are a bit thick have an ability to talk to people and come down to speak a thief's language and use a thief's mannerisms. They do extremely well,' Holland said. 'We had three ex-coal miners in Huddersfield CID and none of them got above sergeant rank because they couldn't pass the exam. You don't have to be a real brain box to pass the inspector's exam. None of them did, but they were good detectives. What they learned down the pit was how to deal with people, something never taught in college or detective training school.'

By the time of the second great amalgamation, with Leeds and Bradford in 1974, he was a detective chief inspector, but the road to these lofty heights was full of pitfalls. Two of his children were still youngsters and the pay of police officers remained poor. While still a detective sergeant, Holland had turned down two earlier offers of promotion to detective inspector as it would have meant moving his family across the country and disrupting the children's schooling. Then he was offered promotion back into uniform, but as an inspector who could live in the family home. He spurned the idea, having worked out he would earn less money as a uniformed inspector, and also be forced to buy a car to travel to and from work at Hebdon Bridge. He was able to turn down these offers of promotion and continue to live in his house in Huddersfield because Huddersfield borough police had given its constables the legal right not to be moved from their home without their consent. 'And I wasn't consenting,' he says. 'It was the third move I had turned down.'

Called to force headquarters in Wakefield a few months later, he was 'offered' the job of uniformed inspector in Huddersfield. It meant he wouldn't have to move, but he would have to leave the CID. An assistant chief constable left him in no doubt that this was his last chance: 'Take it or you'll never get another bloody thing and you'll be blacklisted for everything. Don't forget you're senior detective sergeant now, and you can soon become a uniformed sergeant!' A miserable four and a half months of being a uniformed inspector made Holland prepared to accept a demotion if he could get back into the CID. Then things changed. He was told to set up a new task force – a go anywhere, help anyone flying squad of officers, the brain child of the chief constable, Ronald Gregory. 'I had a bloody good relationship with him when I was on the Task Force because I covered the whole county,' said Holland. 'He sent for me several times and treated me very well. We got all the big jobs – murders, serious crimes, emergencies. With murders we did house-to-house inquiries and fingertip searches, and manned the mobile control room vans.'

Six months later he was summoned to see The Chief, promoted to detective chief inspector and moved to Halifax, where he also became an integral member of the head of CID's murder team. Holland had gone from detective sergeant to DCI in ten and a half months. Then, in 1976, at the age of forty-three, with his marriage all but broken down, he was promoted superintendent, and in October that year became deputy head of Bradford area CID.

Yet, curiously, the genial giant, Dick Holland, had no real ambition to be a high flyer with ACC rank, nor did he want transfers to the Inspectorate of Constabulary or the Home

Office or an attachment to Special Branch. He had hung on tenaciously to the family home in the divorce settlement with Catherine because, as a former Huddersfield constable, so long as he lived there he would never be forced to move. In this sense, for a highly intelligent man, he was deeply parochial. He wanted still to be able to go to his local cricket club, where since the age of eleven he was just Dick Holland. 'I was totally accepted there,' he says, speaking of it with the kind of pride only Yorkshiremen can muster and, frankly, only Yorkshiremen can comprehend. 'I couldn't have moved elsewhere and got that sort of life. I needed that. I would work round the clock if I had to, but when I had some time off I wanted to be plain Dick Holland back in my bloody village. I liked what I knew and I knew Yorkshire, Yorkshire folk, Yorkshire crime. I was good at what I did, had some status and these were reasons why I did not want to leave.'

In these few sentences is captured the essence of Dick Holland, and to some extent that of his mentor, George Oldfield. They were men content to be big fish in a little pond, at home in the backwaters and midstream they grew up in, their horizons and methods limited by environment. Holland knew and understood a great deal, absorbing complex facts without effort. He read widely, eschewing fiction. At heart he was a frustrated scientist who enjoyed working with colleagues from the forensic labs or the pathologists at autopsies. From them, because he understood first principles, he absorbed complex scientific knowledge without difficulty. Ronald Gregory had recognized, when asking him to set up the task force, that as a policeman he was courageous, a team player, and had good leadership skills. In harm's way he was brave – as he proved when arresting armed men or a deranged killer who had just murdered two strangers. The grammar school boy, whose intellect was never tested or trained through the rigour of a university education, simply liked what he knew. He was content with the knowledge he had, which was a great deal more than most officers above him. However, he also had his limitations. He had never heard the adage: 'An intelligent man is one who knows. The more intelligent man knows what he knows. But the most intelligent man understands what he doesn't know.'

In the relatively small gene pool that was the West Yorkshire force, the hierarchy at that time was chosen mostly from among their own. From Holland's perspective, he had done well and could with luck expect to do better – perhaps become a detective chief superintendent. He applied to go on a command course at the Police College at Bramshill in Hampshire. Success there would probably have meant going on the senior command course. But it wasn't to be. Part of his final college appraisal said that, with his forthright and occasionally 'abrasive attitude', Holland was unlikely to reach top rank within the police service.

'I think that was fair,' he said, in a self-deprecating manner. 'I've always believed if somebody's a stupid fool then there comes a time when you've got to tell them. The thing that annoyed me about the police college was that it was rather like an officers' mess in the army. They had superb silverware on the oak dining tables but the food was crap. Now I played hell about that. I didn't enjoy it at all. This was a game they were playing and I didn't want to be an ACC badly enough for me to change.

'Political correctness has never been one of my strong points. They were having some kind of problem because gypsies had set up an encampment on the college grounds near the front gate. They were talking about injunctions. I told them how we got rid of gypsies. You'd see the local beat man and make sure their horses were set free each night. Go round every hour and waken the dogs up and set them off barking and they'll soon realize they are not wanted. I said that if they did it on farmland, you give them notice and you tell the farmer he'd going to be out with the muck spreader, and if they are still there at eleven o'clock in the morning, they're going to get a load of shit over them. The others on the course thought it was appalling that a policeman should talk about things like that. They were from all over the country. I quite openly told them.'

Before leaving to travel south on his three-month command course at the Police College, Holland was involved in setting up the top secret intelligence-gathering operation that would come to dominate the Ripper investigation. Following the murder of Jean Jordan, George Oldfield was keen to build on the proactive efforts to catch the killer which Jim Hobson began a year earlier in Leeds. The concept of undercover units monitoring punters cruising Chapeltown in cars to look for prostitutes had considerable merit in Oldfield's view. The Ripper was certainly using a car and it was abundantly clear he switched between red-light areas in his search for victims. The very vulnerability of prostitutes made them an obvious target. Somehow the Ripper was able to find a street walker on her own, with no witnesses about, pick her up and take her off somewhere quiet to attack her. Oldfield, with Ronald Gregory's sanction, decided Hobson's scheme needed reorganizing and expanding. They needed intelligence on the prostitutes and the men they went with, the areas where they worked and the places where they took their clients. Three red-light districts in Leeds, Bradford and Huddersfield were to be kept under covert surveillance by officers, and details of all vehicles passing through the observation points would be noted. 'We reasoned that prior to each murder he must do some touring around to find that person in such a suitable position,' Holland said.

The idea was to gather intelligence on those regularly trying to pick up women for sex, not simply record anyone passing through the area. This meant observation points had to be established at various locations, to ascertain which vehicles were actually 'trawling' or kerb crawling. They were interested in single men on their own, or in the company of known prostitutes. A total of thirty-three observation points were established: fourteen in Chapeltown; twelve in Manningham; seven in Huddersfield. Every evening approximately a hundred officers were engaged in the operation. Initially they wrote down vehicle registration numbers, but it soon became obvious that at certain locations the traffic flow was so high it was difficult to record all details properly. They discovered they were missing as many as 80 per cent of the cars passing through a particular zone. Some officers started experimenting with cassette tape recorders, dictating the numbers instead of writing them down. Soon all officers involved were using pocket tape recorders. The cassette tape was used at one location only, with the date and time a vehicle was seen being recorded. The tape would then be filed for three months. If another attack occurred in a red-light area, the tape for that date would be retrieved and details of all the vehicles spotted that night in that particular area could be obtained.

Terrible as it sounds, the desperate truth was that the Ripper Squad needed the killer to strike again if they were to catch him. 'We were hoping we would have an attack while the observations were on and we would have him recorded touring round in the area, immediately before the woman was picked up and killed,' Holland explained. 'We didn't anticipate any witnesses because, in almost every case, no one had seen the prostitute disappear with the killer. He had been careful, but that told us hypothetically that he had been touring round looking for a pro whom he could get into his car without anyone seeing. He must have therefore toured round to find a woman, probably in more than one area.'

Clearance for the operation had to come from the top. It was a huge commitment for the West Yorkshire Force. For each group of observation points within a zone, they needed reserves, so those on duty could obey a call of nature, have a break or a hot drink. They could radio in and ask for someone to take over briefly. Some of the street walkers quickly realized they were under close observation and told would-be punters they were being 'clocked' by the police, and if they didn't drop them back at the right spot, safe and well, then they'd be in trouble. Usually they waited until they got their money before breaking the news, for the men then tended to lose interest and with it their sexual appetite, and the women could be back at their pitches all the sooner.

The exact spots where teams were positioned had to be precise, so they could view a rear number plate accurately. It was impossible to see front registration plates, because the headlights dazzled. Some street lighting was perfect, other lights made it near impossible to read the number plates perfectly. Most teams worked in couples, not always as a man and a woman pretending to be courting, because it wasn't always possible. Occasionally they might stand in doorways or view from a special observation vehicle. Manningham was Bradford's only red-light area. It involved six streets and twelve observation teams. Two-way streets had to be covered in both directions. It was very labour intensive.

The system was by no means perfect. Some women worked streets just outside the generally defined red-light area; or they worked at different times, some starting and finishing early, before the observation teams arrived on site, others working late on through the night until three or four in the morning. Occasionally officers would witness a crime taking place and be forced to break cover and intervene. One night in Lumb Lane, Bradford, a coloured man blasted a nightclub with a shotgun and had to be arrested. Another team, in Chapeltown, Leeds, witnessed a vicious assault that turned out to be an attempted murder when one West Indian man began hitting another with an iron bar. They pursued and arrested the attacker. They had a duty under the law to intervene, Holland said. 'I can't begin to imagine what would have happened if we had a copper who witnessed an attempted murder and didn't do anything.'

Sometimes there simply wasn't the manpower to mount a full operation every single night. The task force occasionally had to undertake other urgent operations. The observation teams did not record the index number of the vehicle which picked up Marilyn Moore in Chapeltown. And the flaws in the operation were thrown into stark relief when the Ripper next struck. Officers had been redirected to raid an illegal drinking club in Huddersfield when, by luck or design, he murdered another young woman and disappeared into the night.

9

A Miserable Place To Die

At eighteen years old, Helen Rytka had hardly had time to begin being an adult. Through her childhood and teenage years she felt constantly lonely and permanently deprived of a parent's warm embrace. All she ever really wanted was to be loved. Put into care as a tiny tot, along with her siblings, she had been shunted all her life from pillar to post, from one care home to another all over Yorkshire – from Leeds to Bradford to Knaresborough to Dewsbury. Finally she ended up in Huddersfield, where she died at the Ripper's hands. A report prepared by West Yorkshire Police for the Director of Public Prosecutions summed up the story of Helen's bleak existence in these few words: 'She had lived a short and sad life.'

For almost their entire lives, the Rytka children, who included two sets of twins born to a Jamaican mother and a Polish father, had been cared for in Roman Catholic orphanages or by foster parents. Helen, a petite girl with a beautiful face, an Afro hairstyle and a narrow frame, worked as a £20 a week packer in a sweet factory at Heckmondwyke. A few weeks short of their nineteenth birthday, she and her identical twin sister, Rita, were living in a small bedsit in an Edwardian house on the northern fringes of Huddersfield, close to the M62. The house was run down, the paint had peeled and the stonework crumbled. Rita decorated the flat in bright colours to cheer it up. A talented young woman, she had attended art school in Batley, but dropped out a few weeks into the second year of her course. She was strapped for money. For a while she lived in the flat alone, but became increasingly depressed, missing her twin desperately. When Helen agreed to give up her job in the sweet factory and join her, she cheered up greatly. By now Rita was paying her way by prostitution in the town's small red-light district. In late January, just as the weather was turning bitterly cold, Helen agreed with Rita that it was an easy way to make money. She had been working the pavement of Great Northern Street, going off with men in their cars for sex, for only a couple of days when she became the seventh victim of the man the newspapers now began to call 'THE YORKSHIRE RIPPER'.

The twins shared a double bed with a light-blue counterpane. With only a small gas fire to heat the room on the coldest of nights, they would huddle together under the blankets to keep warm. On 31 January 1978, they got up at 1.30 in the afternoon. Breakfast was actually lunch. They made a stew of meat, potatoes, yam, sweet potatoes, black-eyed beans, and some dumplings made from flour and corn meal. Thyme was added for seasoning. The stew boiled on the stove for thirty minutes before they sat down at the only table in the room to eat their main meal of the day. Later, around 5.30 p.m., they had tea and biscuits.

Just after nine o'clock that evening they were out in the cold night air stamping their shoes, trying to improve the circulation in their frozen feet. They were down in the red-light area trying to pick up men in the cars that slowly cruised by them, hoping the drivers were eager for their services. It was a miserable place, more industrial than residential and nothing like Chapeltown or Manningham in terms of size, the number of working girls or the volume of trade. Half a mile from the town centre, there were only a few houses in the street. The women collected close to a men's public toilet in Great Northern Street, opposite the junction with Millhouse Lane. Eighty yards down on the same side of the road was a large unfenced timber yard where a number of them took their clients. To the rear of these premises was a viaduct of dark and mostly deserted railway arches, along which ran passenger trains from Leeds to Manchester. Further down the road was the town's abattoir, the local cattle market and the bus depot.

Two men in plush limousines jointly approached the twins outside the public lavatory. The twins agreed to go off with them. Rita left with one man in his car. Sitting in the front seat, embracing the warmth from the heater, she looked back to see her sister getting into the other vehicle. Helen was the first to be dropped back outside the public lavatory. The time was 9.25 p.m. Five minutes later Rita returned to the same spot, dropped off after doing business for a fiver with one of the chauffeurs. She started looking for her twin but couldn't find her. Later she was picked up by another client in a white sports car and decided to take him back to the bedsit for sex, hoping her sister would turn up later.

When Helen had failed to reappear by Thursday, 2 February, Rita reported her missing to the police, at first keeping quiet about the reason they had been in Great Northern Street. Then she revealed they were both on the game and she had last seen Helen going off with a man in his car. Alarm bells began to ring in the mind of the Huddersfield's CID chief, John Stainthorpe. He initiated an urgent missing person alert for Helen and a hunt began. The following afternoon, a Friday, a police dog handler turned up at Garrards timber yard to begin a search. The main Garrards building was a huge warehouse of corrugated metal with a pitched roof of the same material. Next door was a wholesale carpeting company. The yard was filled with stacks of sawn unplaned timber of different sizes for the building trade. Piled eight or nine feet high, they created a maze-like warren.

Garrards' foreman, Melvyn Clelland, had that morning been telephoned by an inspector from Huddersfield police to say they wanted to search the yard. The parish clock was just striking 2 p.m. when the dog handler arrived. Mr Clelland walked with him round the yard, thinking they were looking for a young boy called Lester Chapman, just reported missing from home.

Near the back of the premises, close to some disused toilets next to a steep railway embankment, the Alsatian police dog began to get excited, pulling on its lead. It had clearly picked up a scent. 'I think this might be it,' said the handler, giving the animal a bit more lead. The dog walked forward ten yards or so and stopped near a stack of timber between a shed and the wooden fence. The dog handler again spoke out loud to the foreman behind him: 'I think that's it.' The officer edged forward and looked closer. Behind the stack of timber was Helen's body, concealed in an inaccessible spot by a sheet of corrugated asbestos and some pieces of wood. She had been deliberately covered over and wedged into an eighteen-inch space between a brick wall and the timber. He could see her legs and the front of the trunk but not the head or arms. A wound was clearly visible in the front of the chest, with some staining of the surrounding skin. Blood had run from the wound towards her belly button and then dropped to the ground.

The dog handler asked the foreman to wait by the timber stack and prevent anyone else coming near. He returned the dog to his van, collected a roll of blue tape and radioed through to the local police control room. They then taped off the area of the crime scene and waited for the cavalry to arrive. Minutes later sirens began to wail and whine through Huddersfield town centre as police vehicles weaved through the afternoon traffic from different directions to converge on the murder scene.

It didn't take long for the word to go round. A girl had gone missing. A prostitute. Her body had been found. 'It looks like another Ripper attack!' Everyone locally knew the woodyard was a place prostitutes took their clients. It was also a haunt of homosexuals. A used condom was found near the crime scene and the yard foreman told the dog handler that only a few days previously a pair of women's black lace panties had been found in the yard with dried blood on them. Some of the lads working there nailed them to one of the packing cases for a laugh, thinking one of the prostitutes who regularly took clients into the yard at night had left them behind. 'You know what young lads are like,' said Mr Clelland. One of them had also found a handbag containing a lighter and kept quiet about it until detectives started questioning him.

Now Melvyn Clelland noticed what he thought was blood on the wall of an asbestos shed, scattered up and down, as though something had been thrown at the wall. There was clothing scattered here and there. 'The lads in the yard were very shocked because they thought the clothes they found were left by prostitutes. They just picked them up, as lads do as a joke, and nailed them up. I think they felt guilty about it then. It was big news, national news, everybody was talking about the murder everywhere you went, in the pubs, on television. They were talking about this chap, the Ripper. It was the first murder in Huddersfield. It came out of the blue to me that there was a chap going about killing women, I didn't know anything about it.'

Soon it was getting dark and a van load of equipment was brought to the yard to enable police to respond to a major night-time incident. A mobile control room was towed into position in a nearby street and floodlights and lamps were lugged over to the crime scene. When Professor David Gee arrived at 6.45 p.m. with a female colleague from his department of forensic medicine at Leeds University, the full West Yorkshire murder team was already turned out in force. Old-field, who had immediately taken charge, was waiting for him. John Domaille, the Southern Area head of CID, was present along with DCI Swann, in charge of the fingerprint and scenes of crime department. Ron Outtridge was also there from the Home Office laboratory at Wetherby. A large piece of polythene sheeting had been hung between the wall and the stack of timber to form a makeshift tent protecting the murder scene from rain which felt like it might turn to snow, it was so cold.

Removing the asbestos sheeting Gee could see Helen's peril-ously thin body with its protruding bony hips lying tilted on its right side. Her head was covered by what seemed to be cloth or tarred paper. She was virtually naked, clad only in dark-coloured socks and a black bra entangled with a black woollen jumper that had been pulled up and over her chin. There were oblong marks on her thigh which left a depression, as if something like a plank of wood had been placed over her. Her arms were stretched above the head. Around the left upper arm was a piece of blue material. Gee noticed a silver cross at the front of her neck, apparently from a necklace, though the chain appeared to be missing. There was a large laceration on the forehead. Feeling behind with gloved hands, Gee discovered another wound at the back of her head. There were also three clear but separate stab wounds to the chest.

They had some difficulty easing the body, feet first, out from the space between the timber and the shed. It was then placed gently on a plastic sheet. The body felt very cold, as if it had lain there some time. It was a bitterly freezing night with a steady downpour but thankfully no wind. Nearly three hours after Gee's arrival, the body was wrapped and taken to the mortuary at Huddersfield Royal Infirmary. Later that night the mortuary assistants, with considerable care, slowly cleaned Helen's face. It was always a desperately painful business preparing a relative or loved one for what happened next. In front of two police officers, Rita Rytka identified her twin sister's body. Now she knew the worst.

Back at the crime scene, with the corpse removed, Gee conducted a quick examination of the immediate area. Some senior officers accompanying him held small portable lamps. Only a tiny amount of blood soiled the debris, pieces of wood, tarred paper and strips of metal that had been beneath the body. But nearer to the back of the main building, behind another stack of timber, he was shown an area of blood soiling the ground, covered with a plastic sheet to protect it. His immediate assumption was that the girl had been killed here or had lain here before being moved to where she was found and covered with the asbestos sheet. He decided to postpone the autopsy until he had made a more thorough examination of the crime scene the following day.

Saturday morning was still cold and miserable, but the chief constable himself turned out. Oldfield briefed him before phoning Dick Holland at home, even though he was not on the call-out roster that weekend. Oldfield simply said: 'I want you on Rytka.' He didn't say 'now'. He didn't have to. Holland knew he meant 'now' and he had to get himself down to the murder room at Huddersfield. In those situations, Oldfield was a man of few words. According to his acolyte, Holland, he simply barked orders to get things going.

Earlier, at dawn, police had raided the home of taxi driver Terence Hawkshaw in Drighlington, on the Bradford to Morley road. Since the earlier intensive interrogation of Hawkshaw on the top floor of the training academy, Oldfield had been obsessively convinced he was a prime suspect. A plan had been hatched for detectives to swoop on Hawkshaw as soon as there was another murder. Officers searched his home and took away various house contents and tools from a wooden garage, including several hammers, later examined at the Wetherby Laboratory by Ron Outtridge. Hawkshaw's white Ford Cortina was taken to Huddersfield's Castlegate police station and the front seats and wheels removed. Nothing of any significance was found.

It was raining very hard as the forensic experts and the task force used the available daylight to comb the woodyard and the railway embankment, placing any material found in plastic bags for microscopic examination. Several feet from where the body had lain, they discovered a thin metal bangle, a gold hinged-stud earring, a button and some coins. All were painstakingly marked and photographed. Helen's sling-back platform-sole shoes were retrieved some distance away, thrown over a dilapidated wooden fence next to the railway embankment. Her dark denim jeans and fake fur jacket were found by the fence on the woodyard side. High up on the viaduct overlooking the scene, a police officer was positioned to keep onlookers away.

After lunch senior officers gathered at the Royal Infirmary for the post-mortem, among them Jack Ridgway from Manchester, alerted by John Domaille the previous night. As the mortuary attendants removed the clothing from around

Helen's neck, they found the tiny silver chain which had held the small silver cross. A minute search and taping of the corpse on the mortuary table revealed different traces of mud and several small hairs on the surface of the body, including what turned out to be a pubic hair in the victim's mouth. The head bore six lacerated wounds, one in the centre of the forehead, three to the right side and two to the back. The tell-tale semicircular fractures of the skull were present in some of the wounds, indicating to Gee a hammer striking with considerable force. The stabbing of the chest had caused wounds to both lungs, the heart, the aorta, the liver and the stomach. Dissecting and tracking the wounds, Gee could see that the knife, which a blade some six or seven inches long, had been thrust through the same two stab openings at least thirteen times, causing injuries to the internal organs.

The absence of significant bloodstaining on the ground where Helen was found, and the presence of deep impressions on the thigh, suggested the body had been lying against a hard object some time after death. 'The body was killed somewhere else and after death remained in another place for some time, already naked,' Gee wrote in his report. 'The body was subsequently moved to the position in which it was later found.' Ron Outtridge believed the body had first been covered with a plastic sheet, and then, after a considerable time, perhaps overnight, been removed to where it was found. Ridgway was able to confirm the same thing had happened in the death of Jean Jordan. The killer had returned to the body, except that in the case of Helen Rytka, instead of deliberately moving it into the open where it would be found, he had dragged it to where it could be concealed.

Now, for the first time, the press gave the murderer a specific name, 'The Yorkshire Ripper', to make him geographically distinct from the London-based Jack the Ripper of the late nineteenth century. The same day the phrase was first used, Oldfield broke new ground and made an appeal direct to Britain at large on BBC radio's *Jimmy Young Show* – a mid-morning light-entertainment programme that mixed popular music and current affairs. It had a huge listening audience and Oldfield hoped to reach out to large numbers of women at home as they went about their domestic chores. He said the Ripper was in his thirties and he believed someone in the Yorkshire area was shielding him, for he could not believe the killer had not aroused at least some suspicion. 'The Ripper is someone's neighbour and he is someone's husband or son,' he told the ageing disc jockey.

The shock of Helen's death hit hard for people who had spent years caring for her and Rita. The twins had been fostered for more than a year by a Roman Catholic civil servant and his wife, who lived in a large house in the up-market area of Dewsbury. With no children of their own, they had answered an appeal from the local diocese, which was anxious to find the sisters a normal home after they had spent great portions of their lives in orphanages. They needed a half-way house to help them adjust eventually to taking responsibility for them-selves. The twins attended a local school and Helen frequently made visits to a nearby hostel for girls run by Catholic nuns. In charge of the hostel was Sister Delorosa, who knew her well. She was, she said, a warm, vivacious and outward-going girl, who was also very ambitious and dreamed of being on the stage. She and Rita talked of forming a girl's pop group – Helen loved to act, her twin was the singer.

The nun could not bring herself to accept that the twins had become prostitutes: 'Their one dream was of becoming famous and they would have gone to any lengths to achieve this and I think this is exactly what has happened. They were both gullible and would have believed anyone who would have held out promises of stardom. I know there has been a lot of talk about the kind of lives these girls were leading, but we know that these girls were not promiscuous. They were young and ambitious and had childish dreams; they could so easily have been persuaded into a way of life that might have promised them an opening into the entertainment business. The heartbreaking thing about this tragedy is that girls like Rita and Helen have to leave our care when they are eighteen and many of them are not ready to face the world on their own.'

Oldfield's appeal for witnesses became desperate. Few had been on the streets that cold winter's night and detectives struggled to find people who actually saw Helen. As always, the punters who picked the girls up were reluctant to come forward. Checks were made to trace a number of vehicles in the vicinity at the crucial time. Among the most vital was a dark-coloured Morris Oxford saloon, series VI – the same make of car which featured in the 'Farina inquiry', begun after the attempt to kill Marilyn Moore in Leeds six weeks earlier. A car of this make had been seen near the public toilets where the girls were standing. Once more Oldfield warned the men cruising the area to come forward to avoid the embarrassment of policemen knocking on their doors at home and asking awkward questions.

The police investigation zeroed in on men using the public lavatory on the night of the murder. It was a haunt for homosexuals, which made the detectives' inquiries even more difficult. In his public appeals, Oldfield stressed he wasn't interested in people's morals – only in whether they had evidence to help him find the killer. Two chauffeurs working for a nationalized industry in South Yorkshire were interviewed after they came forward to volunteer information. They had both taken their bosses separately to a directors' dinner at the George Hotel in Huddersfield on the crucial night. With the overtime money they were earning for night work, they decided to treat themselves and pick up two women for sex. They headed down to Great Northern Street, where they 'hired' the Rytka sisters and told them to wait while they went into the lavatory to relieve themselves. As they stood urinating, a third man came in and occupied the stall between them. He turned to one of them and said: 'They tell me you can find birds down here, girls on the game?'

'Yes,' came the reply, 'but those two outside are booked, they're waiting for us. You'll have to wait your turn until we come back.'

Helen and Rita took the men in separate cars to a quiet corner of the large parking area behind Huddersfield Town football club. As this was a Friday night, it was totally dark and the ideal place for illicit sex. The drivers returned the women to Great Northern Street at different times and then drove back to where their bosses were dining. They said the man who came into the toilets asking about prostitutes had been driving a two-tone Ford Granada. It had been parked outside. With the taxi driver Terence Hawkshaw by now in the clear, Oldfield believed there was a good chance the driver of the Ford Granada could have waited for the twins to return before driving off with Helen and killing her. The task force began making house-to-house inquiries in the immediate vicinity, seeking to find anyone who had seen the Ford Granada or what the driver did after he came out of the public toilet.

They soon came to a house occupied by a mother and her fourteen-year-old daughter – a shapely but highly precocious teenager with an ample bosom. The girl was a juvenile in the eyes of the law but certainly didn't look it. She was interviewed in front of her mother. Some time after nine o'clock on the night of the murder, the girl had gone on an errand to buy cigarettes for her mother from a corner shop run by a Pakistani family, two hundred yards from her home. As she walked back from the shop a car pulled up beside her. The driver wound down the window and asked: 'How much for a short time, love?'

OFFICER: And what did you say?
GIRL: I told him to 'fuck off', didn't I mum?
OFFICER: Can you remember what kind of car it was?
GIRL: Yes, it was a Ford Granada.
OFFICER: Can you remember anything about the car number plate?
GIRL: I wrote it down on the cig packet, didn't I mum?
OFFICER: Have you got the cigarette packet?
GIRL: No, mum burnt it the following day!

The officers urgently pressed the girl's mother on whether she could remember anything about the registration plate. She had spent twenty-four hours with a cigarette packet in her possession looking at the car's number. 'Think,' said the officer. 'Can you remember?'

Wracking her memory and making a joint effort with her daughter, the woman came up with a number. Painstakingly the officers drew it out of her subconscious memory. Having taken statements, the task force men returned urgently to Castlegate police station, where the murder incident room had been set up. It was only a few days after Helen's murder when they fed the number into the terminal of the police national computer. It came back 'no trace'. They flipped the digits round and tried again: out came the registration details – for a two-tone Ford Granada.

Meanwhile, Oldfield has held a press conference, asking for the anonymous driver of the Ford Granada to come forward. It hit the afternoon papers and the local TV news programmes with a splash. The response in the incident room was fairly immediate. A male caller telephoned and the tape recorder attached to the special phone line kicked on. One of the incident room staff answered while another listened on an extension.

'I'm the driver of the Ford Granada you're looking for. I was down there that night but I'm not the murderer. I left when I couldn't find a woman.' The GPO was alerted to intercept the call and by the time the caller had rung off the police knew it was coming from an exchange west of Barnsley. The officer on the phone had tried to keep the man talking and urged him to come into the police station to give a statement in confidence. The caller's final words were: 'Look, I'm not the murderer and I'm not coming to see you. You'll have to fucking find me.' Click . . . the line was disconnected.

Incident room staff now began tracing the owner of the vehicle which was registered to an ICI subsidiary in Hertfordshire on the outskirts of London. They immediately sent colleagues in the Metropolitan Police to the address of the key holder to discover who had been actually driving the car. Back came an address for the firm's northern area sales agent, a man covering the Sheffield area, but based in Penistone – which was west of Barnsley.

Task force officers visited the man's home and arrested him in front of his wife. 'We genuinely thought he was a strong prospect for the Rytka murder, bearing in mind that he had been waiting for a prostitute while the twins were away with the chauffeurs,' says Holland. 'Then he tapped up the teenage girl. He had a lot of explaining to do, but eventually he was able to convince us quite conclusively that he was in a hotel on the date of one of the other murders. I think he had a sight more explaining to do to his wife when he got home.'

Tracing the Ford Granada driver and hauling him in for a probing interview provided a fillip for the incident room staff. Detective Sergeant Megan Winterburn, who six months earlier had gone on the undercover operation with Maureen Long to Bradford's dives and dance halls, was transferred to the Huddersfield incident room to start work as an indexer. At the beginning of a murder investigation information came into the incident room thick and fast. Indexers had little time to sit and think about the true value of the information they were handling. It was a manual indexing system based on a circular drum. Soon the volume of paper they were handling grew rapidly. One single piece of information could generate one action to be dealt with, or ten actions. The public were phoning and writing in, trying to be of help. For each snippet of infor-mation an action form was generated, which went to the indexer, who then underlined what they believed was the rel-evant part to be followed up. It was an important job. Given that relatively junior ranks manned the system, they bore great responsibility to ensure that each piece of paper was indexed correctly. When the indexer had done her job, the various actions went to members of an outside inquiry team via a team leader. Someone may have been walking their dog down Great Northern Street and happened to see a yellow car pass by at a relevant time. The person walking, the fact there was a dog, the fact they had seen a vehicle and it was coloured yellow – all this had to be indexed, then followed up. Who else had seen the woman with the dog? Who else had seen a yellow car? Did they know its make or index number? And so on. A relatively tiny snippet, apparently insignificant, could generate weeks of additional work and keep the snowball rolling, gathering bulk and momentum.

Some time after Rita Rytka returned to the gents lavatory, she went off with a local man in a white sports car. Inquiries revealed that they were followed by a 'peeping Tom', driving a scruffy Ford Transit van, who regularly kept watch on the activities of prostitutes and their clients. The mainstay of his social life was to creep up on a punter's car while he was having sex inside and peer in through a window. Holland's team could only curse their bad luck. Had the sexually challenged van driver chosen not to stalk Rita, but to follow Helen instead, they could have had a vital witness to a murder, or at least the best clue yet as to the kind of car the killer was driving. In the absence of any dramatic breakthrough, the search for the missing Morris Oxford 'Farina' style car, featured in the Marilyn Moore inquiry, was moved into high gear. An urgent appeal was made for the driver to come forward. Because of the possible link with the Richardson and Moore attacks, the checks on 'Farina' type cars were widened when this appeal failed. All similar vehicles owned or used in West Yorkshire were to be tracked down. Most owners were traced and eliminated in thousands of time-consuming interviews with drivers who had their car tyres examined and alibis checked.

Police played down the reasons why they needed to find this particular kind of car. They did not want the killer disposing of his tyres. Likewise, they kept details of the injuries to the victims to themselves, speaking only of head injuries and stab wounds in the broadest terms. In order to avoid copycat attacks, there was no mention of the displacement of clothing by the killer. Indeed, the media was given very little real information. Keen to find another angle on the story, the local ITV news station in Leeds interviewed a local psychiatrist, Dr Stephen Shaw, wanting to know what could have prompted the Ripper's savage deeds.

'I would have thought it would build up over a few days,' replied Shaw. 'He would begin to get the urge, begin to think about it, and he is bright remember, and he would begin to plan it carefully because he knows he has got to avoid the police. For several days he will build up quite meticulously because if he is working he hasn't got to be out all night, and he has got to get cleaned up afterwards because there is a lot of blood about. He has got to plan it very carefully and then after three or four days he will go out and do it.'

Shaw had told Oldfield more or less the same thing. It didn't take a genius to work out that the killer had a screw loose, but as the psychiatrist pointed out, he was also remarkably cunning, or remarkably lucky.

Holland's team began probing why the killer had left it so long between the slayings of Emily Jackson and Irene Richardson – a period of fifty-four weeks. They suspected the murderer might have been in prison and began a check of violent criminals entering and leaving Britain's gaols between the two killings. Records were searched through the Prison Department at the Home Office, but threw up no useful suspect. Again, it meant a considerable effort – and took Oldfield nowhere. Pressure was mounting now on the local police authority who held the purse strings, because 250 officers were working full time on the various murder inquiries. It was a huge strain on financial resources with West Yorkshire receiving no additional funding from the Home Office.

Hoping to push someone into turning informant, the police

authority announced a £10,000 reward for information leading
to the capture and conviction of the Ripper. Six murders by
the same man being investigated by a single force was a unique
situation – the original Jack the Ripper in London's White-
chapel had only murdered five. Home Office civil servants
initially opposed offering a reward in case it prompted people
to provide false or misleading information. There was concern,
too, that innocent people might be embarrassed. After howls
of protest, the Home Secretary, Merlyn Rees, MP for a Leeds
constituency, sanctioned the reward. It was added to money
put up by a local paper and a group of private individuals and
came to total £20,000. Those claiming the money had to phone
a special telephone number and provide a six-figure number
of their choice, plus a code word. If their information led to
the killer's capture, they could thus be identified.

Calls from the public now came thick and fast. Inquiries
took officers all over the country. In London they questioned
a prostitute who had been attacked by a man in late November
or early December the previous year, in a Doncaster multi-
storey car park. The woman had since gone south, where she
felt safer. She remembered the man as being aged thirty-five
to forty; tall and slimly built with dark hair brushed back and
a moustache. She later saw him drive out of a lorry park in
Doncaster and concluded he had left his truck there while he
went searching for women. Other prostitutes in Doncaster were
interviewed and shown a photofit of the man with dark wavy
hair and a moustache. It was published in the local press, but
no one identified him.

A few weeks after Helen's murder, Oldfield seemed convinced it was now only a matter of time till they nailed the
killer. True, he needed to keep his own spirits up as well as
those of his officers. 'I am satisfied that we are closer to him

on this inquiry than we have been on any of the others,' he said optimistically, trying to reassure the general public, which was clearly now in a state of alarm. The known toll so far was seven murders and two attempted killings. For the first time people were coming forward with information and Holland's staff in the incident room had managed to narrow down the time-frame in which Helen must have met her killer. If someone had seen them together, the police would at last be on the verge of cracking the case.

Two walls of the Castlegate police station incident room were covered with blown-up large-scale street maps of Great Northern Street and Garrards woodyard. Each one was devoted to a specific fifteen-minute time period: 9–9.15 p.m.; 9.15–9.30 p.m.; 9.30–9.45 p.m.; 9.45–10 p.m. and so on up until 11 p.m. Tiny blue-coloured tickets indicated the time and presence of a witness or a vehicle. A person or car may yet be unidentified, but its presence was recorded and the detectives needed to trace them as a matter of priority. Holland directed his investigating teams to break down to the last minute the specific times when witnesses might have seen anything. Their responses were then cross-checked and reverified by the incident room staff. This team of twenty male and female officers were now working twelve- to fifteen-hour days consuming countless cups of coffee or tea, taking bites from stale sandwiches at moments of dire hunger, but spurred on by Oldfield's conviction that they were closing in. The crucial time-frame was the short period between Helen being dropped off by one of the chauffeurs and picked up by the killer: perhaps no more than ten minutes at the most; maybe even five. This relentless process of eliminating all possible suspects in the area until you were left with only one vehicle or person who had not been eliminated was the well-tried method by which murders were frequently solved. After six murders in which no one saw anything, Oldfield's optimism was being fuelled by a gut instinct that he was getting closer to his quarry.

People who were in the area of Great Northern Street after 9.45 p.m. were traced and interviewed. Had Helen still been around after that time, Oldfield believed she would have been noticed. Crucially, a man was seen standing at the entrance to the woodyard at around 9.30. He was aged about thirty, well built, five feet eight inches tall, and wore dark clothing. When he failed to come forward after a public appeal, Oldfield considered he might be a prime prospect. However, the homosexuals who also frequented the area and used the woodyard for sexual activity with men met in the public lavatory, a well-known 'cottage', had been reluctant to come forward. The man outside the woodyard might have been looking for 'trade'. Oldfield wasn't bothered about his love life if he was a homosexual, or whether he had gone into the yard to steal timber. He just needed to find him.

Oldfield appealed to the killer directly, trying to prick his conscience by making him think about his own family. Speaking into a camera for a local TV documentary, he said softly, and with an air of calm certainty: 'We are getting nearer and nearer to you and it is only a matter of time before you are caught. In your own interests and in the interests of the relatives and friends of past victims, in the interests of your own relatives and friends, and in the interests of any potential future victims, it is now time for you to come forward and give yourself up. The net is closing. I am anxious that we catch you before you have time to add another death to the appalling catalogue that you already have to your credit.'

The crime chief was clutching at straws, keeping the publicity bandwagon going in the vain hope someone might turn the

Ripper in or a crucial missing link be offered by a reluctant witness. Dick Holland's team of detectives had been fired up by the prospect of cracking a case which had now achieved notoriety. The worldwide media were talking of the hunt for the Yorkshire Ripper, a seven times killer. 'For the first time there were people about and witnesses in the area who were able to give us leads and descriptions and we hoped through them we would trace the murderer,' said Holland. 'They all turned out to be useless. We spent a lot of time following them up, but no one in fact had seen the killer. We traced a lot of people who were punting, going off with prostitutes, but none of them were the murderer or gave any description of the murderer.'

In his heart Oldfield wanted to avoid yet another tragedy. His direct appeal to the killer was a clear sign of his desperation. He spent time talking alone with Rita Rytka, who was not much older than his own daughter. He saw how the violent death of her twin sister had torn Rita apart emotionally. Helen, after all, had followed her sister into prostitution, and he could sympathize with Rita if she felt to blame for the terrible tragedy which followed. Oldfield remembered, too, Wilf MacDonald's anguish and trauma at losing his beloved daughter, Jayne. He was prepared to go any distance, try any tactic, to catch this madman before he killed again.

Yet what Oldfield never countenanced was enlisting the help of his deputy, Dennis Hoban, in grappling with a murder inquiry that was slowly but surely ebbing out of control. As any objective observer would have had to conclude, by this stage Oldfield was never going to solve the Ripper investigation unless he had an amazing piece of luck, and, to be fair, luck eluded him throughout the inquiry. Had he handed the case over to Hoban, the outcome would have been different in terms of the future critical and flawed decisions made by Old-field, where Hoban would have exercised more caution. Hoban would certainly never have become so emotionally involved, nor as territorial. He had had broad experience of working with senior officers from other forces from his time on the Regional Crime Squad. He would not have immersed himself in mountains of paperwork, as Oldfield did, and he could have had the luxury of spending time thinking without also trying to run the entire CID of a huge force like West Yorkshire.

Oldfield was trying to do the two jobs and finding difficulties with both. He should never have been allowed to take over the inquiry in the first place. Allowing him to do it had disastrous consequences. When Jim Hobson's tracking inquiry was half-way complete, Oldfield abandoned it. Yet, as ACC crime, he should have been a court of last resort for Hobson to appeal to. A neutral crime chief would have immediately seen Hobson's tracking inquiry as the best hope of finding the killer since it hinged on positive evidence found at a crime scene and not a wild guess. Oldfield as ACC crime should have assessed the manpower required to see the tracking inquiry through, then lobbied the chief constable for the resources for the job to be completed. To abandon it half completed was totally irrational. Equally, wearing two hats was an impossible position for Old-field. The responsibility for this rested with Ronald Gregory, the chief constable, who should never have allowed it. Putting Oldfield's deputy in overall charge would have been the obvi-ous management decision and an imaginative solution. Instead Oldfield kept Hoban at arm's length from the Ripper investi-gation. They didn't work well together, but ultimately even their non-relationship was overtaken by events.

As Oldfield's No. 2, and head of Western Area CID based in Bradford, Dennis Hoban had had other murders to investigate but never another Ripper killing. His health became a major problem. He was working as hard as ever but knew he couldn't continue at this pace. He had pains in his eyes, almost certainly because of damaged retinal blood vessels, a byproduct of his diabetes. Too frequently Hoban's brain felt 'squiggly' and he knew he was about to undergo an attack of hypoglycaemia. The lifestyle he was leading simply didn't go hand in hand with controlling diabetes safely.

Glucose levels within the body had to be kept within normal range, which meant getting to grips with the delicate balancing act of the right amount of insulin combined with the right diet. Injecting yourself with insulin was a serious business and had to be done correctly if it was to be absorbed by the body properly. Blood glucose is also affected by stress and surges of adrenaline if the patient becomes excited. It was a fact that Hoban didn't particularly care much for being posted to Bradford. He didn't know the town and felt like a fish out of water. In Leeds people had recognized the man in the Aquascutum suit, wearing his trench coat or sheepskin jacket invariably topped off with a Trilby or a peaked cap and a splash of Old Spice aftershave. He missed that status.

In the middle of February 1978 Hoban was still grappling with the particularly vicious murder of a twenty-year-old sales clerk, Carole Wilkinson from Bradford, found beaten over the head with a fifty-six-pound coping stone at nine in the morning four months previously. Her head injuries had been horrific and she was judged clinically dead when, a few days later, her parents had her life support system switched off and a murder inquiry began. The investigation was hampered in the early stages by a false report from local children that they had been attacked by a man wearing a blue anorak. It turned out to be a lie. Time was wasted, valuable men were sidetracked, on a false inquiry that lasted several days. 'It was one of the worst things that could have happened,' Hoban said in an interview with the *Bradford Telegraph and Argus*. 'The trouble with this kind of hoax is that members of the public whom you depend on for information get descriptions and times fixed in their minds, and they stay there long after the whole thing has been dropped. I am sure there are dozens of people who still think we are looking for that man in a blue anorak.'

The date the interview appeared was 14 February 1978, the day after Hoban's first grandson, Paul, was born. He saw him once but never got to hold him. His observations about the dangers of a hoax sidetracking a murder investigation proved a remarkable foretaste of what subsequently happened in the Yorkshire Ripper case. Hoban did not speak again on the subject, or of the murderers who had eluded him, particularly the killer of Wilma McCann and Emily Jackson. On 8 March he was suddenly admitted to the Leeds General Infirmary with a chest infection. During an investigative operation the following day he had a heart attack and lapsed into unconsciousness. His son, Richard, then aged twenty-seven and a schoolteacher, had an emergency phone call at work and dashed to his father's bedside. 'He was in intensive care and then he looked a bit better and I thought "He's going to pull through."' It was not to be. On 15 March 1978 he died at the age of fifty-one.

In people with diabetes, heart attacks, strokes and peripheral damage to blood vessels become more common and can be a leading cause of premature death. He had been ill during both the McCann and Jackson murder inquiries. While probing the McCann killing he temporarily went blind in one eye, and a few months later found himself short of breath. Sometimes it was so severe he was left gasping, unable to breathe. He was diagnosed with heart disease. His best friend, Jim Hobson, who had taken over as head of Leeds CID, said straight away that Hoban had worked himself to death. Only half-jokingly, he told close friends the only way he could get Hoban to a rugby match was to suggest they might grab a few pickpockets while they were there. Later Betty Hoban confessed she felt bitter at how hard Dennis had worked and the stress he endured when there were unsolved murders on his hands: 'He should never have got married, because his job meant so much to him. If he hadn't put so much into his work, he might not have died.'

The funeral was a grand affair, attended by the top brass of the West Yorkshire police, led by the chief constable. The funeral procession went along the Leeds Ring Road to the Rawdon Crematorium. Crowds came out to pay their respects and much of the route was lined by policemen. Considerable numbers of mourners had to stand outside the crematorium and hear the service over a tannoy system. The event was covered on that night's local TV news. Old clients – men arrested by Hoban in his younger days, whose favourite haunt was a café in the city centre – clubbed together to take out an 'In Memoriam' tribute in the *Yorkshire Post*, expressing respect 'for the copper they were proud to be nabbed by . . .'

Two days earlier, the inquest had opened into Helen's death. The coroner issued an urgent appeal for anyone having a suspicion about the killer's identity to come forward. He understood people might have reservations if the suspect was a close friend or relative. 'But unless this person is apprehended, there is the gravest possible likelihood that he will commit another similar offence and we shall have another death on our hands. The person who is feeling mental anguish will have the added burden of another death which they could possibly have avoided. Their anguish and responsibility will be even greater than it is now.'

Mr Philip Gill's words were echoed in the coroner's court by Detective Chief Superintendent John Domaille, who said the police had a hundred officers trying to find Helen's killer. 'It is likely, looking back on the events leading up to this tragedy, that unless this person is apprehended, another death will follow.' These warnings, added to that of Oldfield in the aftermath of Helen Rytka's death, were grave indeed. But they were already too late, and with Dennis Hoban's passing the West Yorkshire police had probably lost their best real chance of quickly apprehending the man who was to terrorize northern England for several more years.

10

Chinese Walls

Easter Sunday in 1978 came much earlier than usual, on 26 March. For most people in Britain two Bank Holidays in quick succession represented a welcome four-day break from Good Friday to Easter Monday. Detective Chief Superintendent Trevor Lapish had put the trials of being the head of the Western Area CID behind him for the weekend. He had only recently taken up the post, based at the brand-new police headquarters in the centre of Bradford, after several years running the Detective Training School in Wakefield. The son of a railway signalman, Lapish was a born educator, so being responsible for teaching a new generation of detectives from all over the country was a job he had thrived on. He then relished returning to the CID and found himself back at the sharp end of crime detection. The pressures turned out to be immense.

Already on his patch in the Bradford area were two recent unsolved but very vicious murders of women. Neither had anything to do with the Ripper case, but the West Yorkshire force remained four hundred officers short of its proper manning levels, and with the ongoing Ripper inquiry there was little slack in the system. There were problems with recruiting and huge pressures on the police budget. Every detective under his command was working flat out, and so were their bosses.

Being one of the top men in the West Yorkshire CID was a position that carried a lot of stress, as the very recent death of his colleague Dennis Hoban had shown. The two men weren't really close friends, but Hoban regularly lectured at the training school.

Thirty-two uniformed and CID officers had formed a guard of honour for Hoban at the crematorium, and six senior detectives were picked to carry the coffin, including Dick Holland. Dennis's wife, Betty, had insisted there should be no sad music or morbid talk. They should remember Dennis as he was, 'full of life, full of fun, full of vitality'. Which was all very well. But Hoban was dead aged fifty-one, leaving a grieving widow, two sons and his first grandchild. For Lapish, at forty-three, it was one of those critical signals which made him silently promise himself he would not work a day longer than the thirty years' service he needed to qualify for a full police pension.

On this Easter Day, Bradford's CID chief had an important duty to perform. He was at home in Ossett with his wife and two sons, preparing himself for the traditional ritual of carving a roast turkey. The family was playing host to his parents. A phone call at about 12.30 put paid to this scene of domestic bliss. An arm had been found sticking out from underneath an abandoned sofa on wasteland in Bradford. His presence was required as a matter of urgency.

By the time Lapish arrived at the plot of rough ground, bordering a short road called Arthington Street which ran at right angles to one of Bradford's main roads, the B6144 at Whetley Hill, his colleagues had already convinced themselves they knew the identity of the victim. A twenty-one-year-old local prostitute, Yvonne Anne Pearson, mother of two young children, had been reported missing since 21 January. A major police search for her yielded nothing. She left her two children in the care of a babysitter, had a drink in a local pub, the Flying Dutchman, then announced she was going off 'to earn some money'. Her disappearance sparked off press speculation that the Ripper had struck again, but police played down the idea. Photos of her appeared on the front pages of national newspapers. Yvonne was a trim-looking woman, and even at five feet five inches tall she weighed only eight stone. She dyed her hair platinum blonde and sported what in the 1970s was called a 'Purdy' haircut, after a character in *The Avengers* series on television.

Already a convicted prostitute with one term of imprisonment behind her when she went missing, Yvonne was on police bail and due at the local magistrates' court in a few days' time on a charge of soliciting. She had been arrested in November 1977 in Manningham. The man she lived with, a Jamaican, Roy Saunders, who was father of her children, aged two years and five months respectively, had recently returned to the Caribbean on a visit to relatives. Yvonne had apparently made arrangements for her children to be cared for in the event of receiving another prison sentence. Friends and neighbours in the back-to-back row of terraced houses where she lived were mystified why she had taken nothing with her. One claimed she hadn't looked well for a while, and that she was not eating, which some saw as proof she was worried about her impending court appearance. 'She would not leave her children, because she idolized them,' said Margaret Kenny, a neighbour. 'If she had been going away she would have taken her bank book and her family allowance book. All she had with her was a small handbag and only the price of two drinks.'

There were rumours she had absconded to London, and a prostitute in London who knew Yvonne came forward and told police she had seen the vice girl working in the capital.

It was assumed she had, after all, fled south to avoid a prison sentence. But not everyone was happy with this explanation. Another neighbour claimed Yvonne wasn't really bothered about the magistrates' hearing. She was only concerned for the children. 'She just wouldn't leave them like that,' she said. 'She had a lot of guts. She faced up to things. She was easygoing and easily offended. She's the sort of person who plans things. She's one of those people who are punctual, that's why it's worrying. If she was going away anywhere she would have taken her stuff with her.'

Nine weeks after her disappearance, the presence of so many police vehicles in Arthington Street caused a small group of local people to gather in front of factory buildings and a garage overlooking the crime scene. Detectives questioned the local youth who had made the 999 call. He had walked past the overturned couch on the wasteland and seen a human arm sticking out. The rough ground, at the end of the road just beyond the garage, was covered in scrubby grass. At the back was a steep bank and closer to Arthington Street was an area where piles of rubbish had been burned by local firms. Jim Hobson took Lapish over to the decaying settee. Standing behind an area already taped off by the task force were the on-call members of the murder team, along with Russell Stock-dale from the Wetherby lab, who was talking with a forensic pathologist called out from Professor Gee's department at St James's Hospital. It was David Gee's weekend off. Lapish, Hobson and several others quietly agreed it was an odds-on certainty the victim would turn out to be the missing woman. And so it later proved.

The pathologist wanted the settee lifted to get a better look at what was underneath. Almost all its covering was missing, revealing the wooden frame and internal springs. The armrests still retained a kind of dark velvet material. Only one of the six castors was still in place. Crouching forward the pathologist, Lapish and Stockdale could see a decomposing head which bore obvious injuries. The right forearm, that had been sticking out from under the two-seater settee, was totally discoloured. A shoe and a piece of wood were on the ground on the left side. Placing this death at the hands of the Yorkshire Ripper required no leap of the imagination as far as Lapish was concerned. The woman had head injuries; she was probably from Manningham, plied her trade there, had numerous convictions for prostitution, a professional who travelled widely, sometimes as far as Leicester, Bristol, Manchester and London. The mere suspicion this was another Ripper victim was enough for Lapish to summon the attendance of David Gee, even on his weekend off. It was crucial to maintain continuity with previous forensic examinations in the series, but several hours elapsed before Gee could be tracked down. He arrived a few minutes before 6 p.m.

Meanwhile, scenes of crime officers wearing yellow waterproofs and wellington boots examined the area around the settee for evidence. The police photographer had already begun to take wide-angle shots to show the area of waste ground, close-ups of the settee with the arm sticking out and the position of the body in relation to the wider area. He snapped carefully away at a platform shoe found about twenty yards away at the top of the ridge, overlooking where the body lay. It matched one under the settee. He then photographed a purse, a pair of tights, and a contraceptive sheath close by. There was a large stone on the ground near the sofa, as well as several others near by. Another officer placed a cone at the point where the shoe was discovered on the banking, so it could be photographed in relation to the settee and the immediate surroundings. Lapish began pondering whether the shoe had been thrown away or whether it had been displaced when the victim was attacked before being dragged to where she was found.

Once the settee was completely turned over, the lower part of the body became visible. From the wrist down the right hand was darkened and discoloured. Underneath the hand was a copy – back page uppermost – of the *Daily Mirror*, dated 21 February 1978, a full month after Yvonne Pearson had been reported missing. The weather was dry but bitingly cold and a strong wind blew Lapish's tousled hair over his forehead and across the bridge of his nose. Wrapped up in a warm sheepskin coat and wearing gloves, he looked down at the corpse and saw the headlines of 'Mirror Sport' staring up at him – something about the England football team. Yet apart from the decomposing arm, hand and head, it seemed almost impossible to believe there was actually a body here. It was covered with sods of earth, springs from the settee, grass, other debris and horsehair stuffing from the inside of the sofa. The left arm was raised above the head, stretching out in rigor mortis. It had been stuck in the springs of the sofa.

Gee's very presence gave the senior detective great reassurance. The 'Prof' reflected a state of total businesslike calm to everyone around him. He and Lapish were old colleagues from years back, and on first-name terms. 'Everything he did, he did by the book and nothing was ever missed,' Lapish enthused years later. 'He was absolutely at the top of his profession. Watching him do a post-mortem was like seeing an artist at work. He got on well with everyone, especially with some of the young police officers who by law had to attend the post-mortem because they were the first officer to see the body. Knowing the ordeal of some of these young coppers watching their first autopsy, he would say to them: "Have you seen one before?" He would then explain what he was going to do and how he would do it. He was a great teacher.'

Over by the settee the material covering part of the head was eased back for Gee to get a closer look at the body. It was badly decomposed. There were several holes in the skull, and a small metal comb had been placed upright between the thighs, which were themselves covered in dried grass and horsehair from the settee. The victim had worn a greenish-yellow jacket with a zigzag design, a black polo-neck jumper and a white bra, all of which were pulled above her chest area. Her pants had been rolled down slightly around her upper thighs, but her legs and feet were bare. Once the body was lifted on to a sheet of black plastic, Gee and Lapish could see there were a pair of dark blue slacks sticking to its undersurface. A small bottle of perfume and a leather handbag were close by. There were also a small number of maggots on the surface of the body, especially around the neck. It was starting to get dark and little more could be done in the failing light. Half an hour after Gee arrived, the body was taken to Bradford public mortuary.

George Oldfield had turned up part-way through the afternoon in a practical frame of mind. 'Sorry, but you can't have any more men,' was the immediate message he brought to Lapish. He would have to manage with what he had in terms of manpower. Oldfield had one hundred men on the Rytka murder over in Huddersfield, a good many of whom normally worked for Lapish. The ACC reckoned that, with the Rytka murder, he had more chance of catching the killer than Lapish had with a two-month-old corpse: 'You'll have to manage with what you can get because Rytka is the one that is going to find who the Ripper is and convict him.'

'George made it plain, right from the word go, that he was going to detect it on the Huddersfield one,' Lapish remembered.

The detectives, the forensic scientists and the two pathologists, after standing around for hours in a chillingly cold wind, headed for the canteen at Bradford's police headquarters and a warm meal before starting the four-and-a-half-hour post-mortem. Despite the horrendous state of the body Lapish wasn't deterred from the idea of food. It promised to be a long night and he needed sustenance. 'One detective I remember simply couldn't cope with seeing bodies,' he said. 'It may seem harsh, but to me they were a piece of meat at that stage, there was absolutely nothing you could do for them except find out everything which would help with the inquiry. You simply could not be emotional about it.'

The post-mortem began shortly after 8 p.m. and finished well past midnight. The body, covered in horsehair, clumps of earth and other debris, had first to be photographed then cleaned. It was only half-way through the autopsy, as Gee dissected the throat, that he found a large oval-shaped ball of horsehair had been thrust back into the victim's mouth, presumably in an effort to keep her quiet before she died. It completely filled the back of the mouth and the upper part of the throat, blocking the larynx by pushing the epiglottis over its upper surface. Lapish took a decision that this information would be held back from the other detectives on the team. Only the killer would know he had stuffed the victim's mouth with horsehair.

A great deal of the work at the post-mortem was technical and painstaking and Lapish, for the umpteenth time in his life, watched Gee at work with such fascination that time flew by. Organs, including the brain, had to be taken out, photographed and weighed. Individual wounds had to be photographed, then rephotographed at various stages of dissection as Gee tried to discover how each one had been made. It was a difficult post-mortem because of the advanced state of decomposition. The talk among the detectives at the autopsy table was that this looked like another Ripper attack, but Gee had profound doubts. The more he studied and probed the body, the greater his uncertainty became. The skull had been smashed with a heavy object into many different parts. He counted seventeen in all. 'So badly damaged was the head,' Gee commented later, 'that in order to reconstruct the actual pattern of the fractures, we had to rebuild the skull around a large ball of modelling clay, so that it could be photographed in roughly the form it must have been at death.' 'These were obviously quite unlike any of the neat depressed fractures we had seen in other cases.' The fractures were such that they gave the appearance of a severe crushing injury to the head, a diagnosis later confirmed by X-rays of the skull.

Clearly missing, though, were the tell-tale signs of the hammer – the crescent-shaped wounds seen in other cases. There were no wounds visible on the trunk or the limbs, or to the vagina or breasts. When he dissected the chest area he found fractured ribs and later various ruptured organs, as if she had been kicked. Death had clearly been due to multiple injuries, but exactly what caused those injuries in pathological terms he found it difficult to say. He deduced from the fact that there was no significant blood soiling of the lower air passages, in spite of the fractures of the skull around the nose and upper jaw, that the ball of fibrous material in the throat was in position obstructing the air passages very soon after the head injuries were sustained.

'The absence of gross bleeding in the abdominal cavity or

around the fracture of the left rib suggests that death occurred soon after these injuries had been sustained,' Gee wrote in his post-mortem report. 'Considerable force would have been necessary to cause the damage to the skull. It is possible for this damage to have been caused by one impact on the head by a heavy object.' For a while he thought the body might have been involved in a motor accident, and then partly stripped in order to mislead as to the real circumstances of death, and afterwards concealed. The absence of injuries to any other principal bones in the body then persuaded him otherwise.

Finally he concluded: 'The most probable circumstances are that the deceased's injuries were caused by a deliberate attack on her . . . apparently causing the head injuries by a blow with some heavy object, causing the injuries to the trunk either by a blow with a similar object or, for instance, by a kick, and pushing into the throat a mass of the material found at the scene. The clothing could have been disturbed either before or after the attack.'

For the time being the Pearson killing was not placed in the Ripper series, and for some years Gee continued to express grave reservations. He told Lapish: 'While I could not say that this woman was not killed by the same person who killed the other women in the series, my findings were so different that I could not with certainty include this case in the series on pathological grounds.'

Being undecided was not a problem for the quietly spoken professor. His ambivalence was professional and scientific. There was no place in his work for speculation when certainty could not be proved. He was a scientist, they were police officers. He understood their desire for certainty. Indeed, he personally liked many of them, especially those who were enthusiastic. Some reminded him of men he met in the army in the 1950s when national service interrupted his time at King's College Hospital Medical School in South London, where he had graduated with considerable distinction as a Jelf Medallist in 1954. This award is given annually by King's College to the most distinguished final-year student. Later, at Guy's Hospital, Gee was a protégé of Professor Keith Simpson. Gee held some junior hospital posts before going into the army. He travelled to the Far East, to the jungles of Malaya, where he served as medical officer with a Gurkha regiment, one byproduct of this time being learning Nepalese. When he later returned to King's, it was as a demonstrator in pathology. Then, in 1959, he took up a post at Leeds University, initially as an assistant lecturer.

Gee earned his 'chair' the hard way, moving up through the posts of lecturer and senior lecturer and becoming head of department in 1972 without getting a higher degree. He once told a colleague who equally had not obtained a PhD that he seemed to have spent a considerable amount of his working life helping others get their higher degrees and never had time to earn one for himself. He would be out at the coalface of forensic pathology on cold winter nights, examining a body in some godforsaken muddy field in the middle of nowhere, while others researched for their doctorates.

Forensic pathologists and scientists who had observed Gee at work commented on his self-discipline. His method of working was not merely routine – it was a ritual. He took the most detailed notes any of them had ever seen, and often his formal reports of autopsies could run to twenty pages or more. His brief spell in the army had taught him the value of discipline and order. There was one way to do it – the proper way. No matter how tired he was, or what the time of day, or how many miles he had just driven, Gee would always carry out his inspections on the ground methodically. His subsequent post-mortems were conducted in exactly the same way. He started with the head. He let the blood drain out, then moved on to the body, and if anything else was found – 'it had to have been put there by someone else'.

Gee, the son of a bank clerk, was brought up in Romsford and had gone to grammar school. Initially he did not consider becoming a forensic pathologist. He had gone up to Leeds for the interview, hoping for a job as a microbiologist at St James's University Hospital. They asked him instead if he would take a six-month contract as a pathologist. Needing the work and the money, he took the temporary post and never left. Over the years, he served on numerous official committees and became a key member of the university establishment and the hierarchy of the forensic pathologists' profession, pre-eminent in his field.

He and his wife, Eileen, set up the family home in North Yorkshire and had three children. He worked in various advisory capacities for both the Home Office and the Ministry of Defence and was a consultant to the Chemical Defence Establishment at Porton Down. His status was very high, and when there was a politically sensitive mystery to be solved, they turned to Gee. Six months after the Pearson case, in September 1978, he was the forensic pathologist called in by the CDE at Porton Down after the strange death of a Bulgarian émigré writer. Georgi Markov had been a major problem for the Bulgarian government with his broadcasts on the BBC World Service. His fate was to be assassinated by an East European intelligence service. Gee helped with the discovery that the killer had used a minute quantity of a highly toxic poison called ricin, said to be more deadly than cobra venom. While walking across Waterloo Bridge Markov had been stabbed in the back of his right thigh by a needle disguised in the ferrule of an umbrella. He died a few days later.

Off-duty, back in his home territory, Gee was not a great socializer, but he would make an effort when required. His main interests were his family, then painting and gardening, and the study of the 'Green Man' in English culture. He was not an emotional person. Indeed, he could appear quite reserved and cool to many who did not know him well. As a young man his early passion in life was revealed by his sizeable collection of jazz records.

A close university colleague summed up why Gee was so admired: 'Niceness, transparent honesty, innocence, guilelessness and lack of aggression sound doubtful attributes for a successful career in university life, yet it was just through these very qualities that David became so highly respected and it was a delight to find that these benign characteristics could more than match deviousness, intrigue and self-seeking ambition. It seemed particularly pleasing that such gentle features were dominant in one whose professional activity was concerned with the harshest facets of human behaviour.'

This was perfectly true. For the quiet and modest professor, sudden and violent death in all its forms was his professional life. Murders provided him with many challenges, and none more so than the Ripper case. Gee viewed himself as an integral member of the investigating team, but he could also distance himself from men like Lapish, Oldfield, Hobson and Holland. His relationship with senior investigating officers was a partnership. His role was to link appropriate cases and reject unrelated ones, no matter how inconvenient. This intellectual neutrality on the part of the pathologist was similar to that of a forensic scientist. For Gee it was an absolute, though, consciously or unconsciously, police officers were capable of pressing for black-and-white answers in ways that at times showed little subtlety. However, the intense pressures on the police officers had little effect on him professionally. There was a Chinese wall between him and the pressures on the police force – the public, the media, the police authority who held the purse strings, and especially the hierarchy of the police service. Gee rarely, if ever, gave interviews.

He could sympathize with the position senior officers found themselves in with the Yorkshire Ripper, because he wanted to help them catch this despicable killer. More than anyone, Gee knew *exactly* what the murderer was doing to these women. He was getting considerable pleasure from these murders, particularly in the way he stabbed them. He was sick and twisted and a considerable threat to women everywhere. But the dangers of putting a particular murder into a series which ought not to be there were considerable, especially if the police apprehended the real killer. If, in court, the accused was able to show he had a perfect alibi for a murder wrongly attributed to the series, the prosecution case would be considerably weakened. Placing murders in or out of a series is fraught with difficulty, but Gee's approach was straightforward. By creating a basic pattern that linked the killings, he could see whether a particular case conformed in all or most of these features.

With the Ripper, the features were the occupation of the victim – indeed the very sex of the victim, and the fact it was a woman. Then there was the presence of injuries to the head caused by hammer blows struck mainly from behind, the presence of stab wounds, the displacing of clothing before stabbing with the bra pulled up but the pants left more or less in position; the situation of the body itself, out of doors; an association with a motor vehicle; the presence of the killer's boot marks; the absence of sexual intercourse with the victim.

Yvonne Pearson's murder was atypical of the series. Some features were similar, but her head injuries were unlike any of the previous neat hammer marks he had seen during earlier autopsies. 'They were massive injuries with a shattering of the skull into many separate fragments like the damage produced by a large rock, and there were no penetrating injuries in the body at all,' he said later. 'I never felt I could honestly say that it was one. The pathological features were so different that I would not include this case in the series, speaking from the medical point of view, though for other reasons the police thought that perhaps she was in the series.'

So, too, did Russell Stockdale, at the forensic laboratory at Wetherby, who had also attended the crime scene and the post-mortem. Aware of the dangers of sending the police inquiry off at a tangent if the wrong murder was included in the series, he believe Pearson was firmly in the series. 'David Gee and I did not see eye to eye on that,' he remembered. 'We had several long discussions back at the laboratory. She had horrendous injuries, her clothing had been displaced and she had been moved. Rytka had been moved, so had Jordan in Manchester.'

Lapish also was sure he had a Ripper victim on his hands, even if the killer had changed his method of attack. Yet for now, as so often with previous victims, the press was told the police were keeping an open mind. As the senior investigating officer Lapish wanted to know as much as possible about Yvonne Pearson: last sightings, all her friends, relatives, associates, the area she worked from, who she knew, where she went drinking, everything it was possible to know about her. Every single inquiry that ensued would be actioned and require a detective or member of the task force to follow it up.

It appeared she had changed her method of working by

going with men in cars after previously taking them back home for sex. She lived not far from where Patricia Atkinson had been murdered in her flat. Searching her home, police found a white-coloured address book edged in gold. Yvonne had clearly been active in her work and Lapish wanted the men she had been with to come forward.

Having come from Wakefield City, where there wasn't a vice problem, he told some of his team about the time when the force was being inspected by Her Majesty's Inspectorate. The inspector asked one of the local officers whether there was any problem with prostitutes. 'We don't have any prostitutes in Wakefield,' came the reply.

'None?' asked the inspecting officer, eyebrows raised.

'No sir, we have no prostitutes, but we've got bags of enthusiastic amateurs.'

Bradford was a major area for women selling sex. It had its own vice squad, who of course had dealings with Yvonne. They interviewed every known prostitute in Bradford, along with many of their clients. Again little relevant information was gathered. One woman claimed to have seen Yvonne getting into a light-coloured mini-van the night she died, and all similar vehicles in Bradford were checked and eliminated. Some of the sex workers in Manningham had decided to move on, and went on the nationwide vice circuit. Others took the inter-city express train to London, looking for business in some of the classier hotels.

In her locality Yvonne's death came as a great shock. Neighbours had high praise for her. 'She was well thought of in the street,' one commented to a local television news programme. 'She only cared about her kids, too much. She didn't care, more or less, what people thought of her. She only went out on the game so she would have enough food and clothes for the children. She didn't do it for anything else anyway. I have tried to persuade her to stop. She did say herself that she were afraid she might be the next one, but she just had to go down to get food for the children.'

The women who worked the streets of Manningham doubted Yvonne's death would make them give up the work. 'She was cautious who she went with,' said one. 'She wouldn't get into any car, just like that.' She suspected the Ripper had killed Yvonne and that he came from Bradford. 'We are going to get a shock when they eventually catch him because we're sure he's going to be somebody we know and have seen around once or twice a week,' she said in a prescient moment.

While her body lay undiscovered, Yvonne's parents in Leeds had been through hell, wondering what had happened to their daughter. Despite speculation that the Ripper had struck again, her father, John Pearson, a warehouse foreman, couldn't believe she was dead. Two weeks after she went missing, he said she had been having domestic problems. A few years earlier, she had been a bit wayward. One of four children, born into a Roman Catholic family, Yvonne had left home at seventeen with the aim of being 'independent'. She had a flat in Leeds but for the next two years she cut off contact with her parents. Then, one day, she turned up out of the blue. It appeared she had been travelling all over England. Her father didn't believe she was a prostitute.

This background knowledge hardly helped Lapish. As with the other Ripper murders, the clues in the case were negligible, and some sent them off on red herrings. The maggots discovered on the corpse by David Gee turned out to be larvae from the trichocerid fly, which normally feeds on cow dung. A Leeds University colleague in the Department of Pure and Applied Zoology studied the specimens closely and consulted an expert at the British Museum in London. It was a full six months before any of the flies pupated and an identification was made. Since there were few cows grazing in the centre of Bradford, it was assumed they must have come from a rural area. For a while detectives began probing farmers and their workmen around the Yorkshire Dales, suspecting the killer might have been a farm worker who carried cow dung on his wellington boots. The inquiry went nowhere. How the flies got on the corpse was never solved.

Russell Stockdale's laboratory tests also proved negative. He found smears of mud on the lower seat of Yvonne's slacks and inside a split seam in the seat. There were more smears of mud on the backs of the trouser legs at the bottoms and near the calves. One of the shoes was also smeared with mud. Stockdale thought this pointed to her being dragged backwards across an area of muddy ground, probably while being supported under the arms. He found no signs of mud staining anywhere else on the trousers, nor on any of the other items of clothing. It was likely there was no struggle and that Yvonne was dragged while unconscious. It was likely the trousers were then undone by the assailant and pulled off, probably by tugging at the right leg.

'From the sequence of events indicated,' he wrote in his report to Lapish, 'the inference is that Pearson's killer derived some benefit from interfering with her clothing after she had been rendered unconscious. The position of the knickers would preclude an attempt having been made at sexual intercourse. I have found nothing else which at this stage is likely to assist your inquiry.'

Lapish was hardly surprised. He didn't expect anything else from a murder two months old when the body was discovered. 'If you're going to be successful on a murder inquiry, the first twelve or twenty-four hours are absolutely vital because you are relying on people remembering things, seeing somebody, seeing a vehicle or whatever, and it coming into the system to be analysed, cross-referenced, and then sending out a team to do an individual inquiry. So, if she has been there for two months, you've no chance at all of reconstructing the whole thing, or getting that sort of information to help you with the inquiry. I don't think there was a single clue that arose from the Pearson murder which helped me build a better picture of who the Ripper was. I never thought as a result of my efforts that I would find this man. The delay was a terrific barrier. You have got someone picking up a prostitute, it could be one of any number of dozens of people on any night in that area. It was the same situation that developed throughout the whole of the inquiry. Someone picks up a victim, they don't know them, had nothing else to do with them. And there is no link at all.'

The discovery of the *Daily Mirror* underneath the body dated a month after Yvonne disappeared told Lapish the killer had yet again returned to his victim, as he had done with both Rytka and Jordan. There was absolutely no way the newspaper could have appeared underneath Yvonne's hand as she lay dead unless it had been put there deliberately.

At a crisis conference of senior CID chiefs at the force headquarters in Wakefield in mid-April, Lapish proposed a bold tactic in the event that another Ripper victim was found. He suggested to his colleagues around the table in the oak-panelled conference room that they ought to transfer a dummy in similar clothing and then keep covert surveillance. It would require cooperation for a total news blackout from the local and national media, but this already happened with kidnapping cases. 'We could have got the heads of the media together and done an embargo. We could have removed the body and replaced it with a dummy and put in cameras and covert surveillance. I thought it was very feasible. If he was going to keep coming back to victims that he had concealed, then I thought it was a very obvious thing to do, to try and catch the man who had been doing these terrible offences.' Oldfield vetoed the idea point blank on the grounds that valuable forensic evidence might be lost that could prove crucial later. He could see only difficulties and no merits in Lapish's argument.

'I was sure this bloke was so full of his own importance and so bloody cocksure that he would go back again if it wasn't discovered and the press hadn't got on to it,' Lapish recalled. 'He was on an ego trip *par excellence*. He was glorying in what he was doing. I can see Mr Oldfield's point of view. Forensic evidence is vital when it comes to getting a conviction in court. But how much better in my mind to catch the perpetrator coming back red handed. You don't really need too much more to convince a jury and get a conviction then. Of course it would have been difficult to explain to relatives of the next victim – sometimes you don't know the identity – but all things being equal I thought we could put a substitute body in place.'

After the conference Ronald Gregory announced that, two and a half years on, the Ripper case had cost his force £1.5 million in overtime payments, transport and other facilities on top of normal operating costs. Scores of police officers were resigning because of the pressures resulting from the case; the crime rate was up 17 per cent and fewer criminals were being caught. The Ripper killings, according to Gregory, had reached epidemic proportions. He believed he would go on killing and before long would switch to non-prostitutes. It was time, he argued, to go on the offensive and develop proactive methods of catching the killer. It was also time to release other officers from the inquiry to concentrate on the fight against the rising crime rate.

He now planned to set up an élite group of twelve detectives whose sole task was to devote themselves to catching the Yorkshire Ripper. Their boss was to be Detective Chief Superintendent John Domaille, who had investigated the Atkinson murder. His colleagues regarded him as a high flyer and almost the chief constable's 'favourite son' because of being specially chosen for the job by Gregory. His squad would have its own offices at Millgarth police station, down the corridor from the Ripper incident room. For a brief period a Formica nameplate was screwed to the door of their office. It said: 'Special Homicide Investigation Team'. Even after someone in the hierarchy had ordered the notice to be changed, so that the word 'Special' was removed, among their colleagues throughout the West Yorkshire force they continued to be referred to as the SHIT squad.

11

The Wrong Track

The domestic demands on John Domaille's time were perhaps less than those on other officers with families. His wife was happily settled in Wakefield and his son and daughters already set on career paths. The eldest, aged twenty-one, was in nurse training at the Leeds General Infirmary, and her sister, a sixth-form pupil at Wakefield Girls High School, wanted to follow suit. His son intended becoming an accountant. Domaille was generally free to immerse himself in his work. The Ripper inquiry was the most important job of his life and he felt the burden of responsibility acutely. Being the father of daughters, he had genuine sympathy for the victims' families' suffering, heightened by his knowledge of the killer's sadism. He couldn't imagine how it would feel to lose one of his girls, only that it would be unbearable. He constantly worried about his daughter living in Leeds, and later told her she had to move out of the flat she shared with other nurses in Chapeltown.

Domaille travelled far and wide, discussing cases with Ridgway in Manchester and Wilf Brooks at Lancashire CID headquarters in Preston. He made frequent trips to the Home Office in London to discuss with the boffins how the Ripper squad could use computers. The investigation was now deluged by paperwork and they desperately needed to improve the flow of information. There were dozens of meetings with colleagues, ranging from round-table conferences with the whole team to one-on-one discussions with individuals assigned a particular aspect of the review inquiry. There were also long meetings with the senior investigating officers in the various Ripper murders and attacks. These were delicate matters. Here was the detective from the West Country, whom his colleagues believed was the chief constable's man, probing the efforts of senior officers with vastly more experience than he had. Domaille, certain they had left no stone unturned in their efforts to catch the killer, was anxious to reassure them. There were just too many stones. The pressure had shifted from individual senior investigating officers and now it was his team which had to achieve results. Domaille knew he had to raise his professional game way beyond anything he had done before in his police career.

His squad had a broad remit to overhaul all reported serious assaults on women and to forage for any common link that might produce a new line of inquiry. An in-depth study of all previous attacks placed the earlier Ripper investigations under the microscope to ensure they had been pursued 'as far as practicable'. In doing so, Ronald Gregory signalled the Ripper murders as his force's highest priority. No previous chief constable had dealt with a case of this magnitude. West Yorkshire was Britain's fifth largest force, covering a huge area of metropolitan England, with a population of 2 million spread over a huge area of rural and urban landscape. It contained major towns and cities as well as vast swathes of farming land and rural landscapes. The Chief had poured resources into catching the killer, yet the man continued to elude them. With each new murder the Ripper seemed to be taunting his best officers, defying them almost to catch him. How was he able to snatch these women and slaughter them with no one seeing anything?

Gregory knew the answer lay in the work his force had done, the murders already investigated. They had missed some vital clue which lay buried in their files and they needed to redouble their efforts to close the gap between them and the killer. His top detectives had been distracted by other important crimes while trying to investigate the Ripper murders. It was not their fault they had to turn their attention to dealing with some other crisis, another murder, a serious rape or an armed robbery. Why should the public of West Yorkshire suffer a crime wave simply because all the police efforts were directed to catching a prostitute murderer? Now the crime detection rate was beginning to plummet and Gregory decided it was time to regroup, to focus one senior officer and detective squad on the Ripper murders rather than individual murder squads investigating the deaths on their patches. The chosen one was John Domaille.

The new strategy of a dedicated team of detectives being set up to hunt the Yorkshire Ripper was quickly picked up by the local media. When Domaille said the officers conducting the Ripper inquiry so far had been 'the most experienced detectives in the country', it was intended to reassure public opinion. Diplomatic he may have been in countering any suggestion of a lack of faith in colleagues' abilities, but it was an overstatement bordering on wishful thinking. They were as good as their experience and training allowed them to be. It was true West Yorkshire's top detectives had solved countless murders in their time, as had dozens of other leading CID men across the country. The high level of detection of individual homicides by the British police was a success story and Domaille had had his fair share of experience in murder inquiries, which gave him confidence in taking on his new job.

He had been with the West Yorkshire force ten years, having

transferred from Exeter, where he had been a detective inspector working on the local regional crime squad. A thoughtful person, sensitive to others' feelings and opinions, he was also ambitious. The police service, which considered itself a meritocracy, warmly embraced individuals like Domaille. Until now he had done everything right. There were no blots on his personal character, he got on well with people and he was a hard worker.

Domaille had been a police cadet in Exeter at fifteen, did his national service in the RAF and after completing police training school went on the beat. Within three years he achieved his goal of becoming a detective. Domaille's family originated from Guernsey, but he was a Devonian through and through. Exeter was a softer and calmer place than Leeds or Bradford. It had 120 police officers and its own chief constable for the best part of a century. Its style of policing was completely different from that in the northern towns, and Domaille's quiet, easygoing charm reflected the place he spent all his early life. In 1969, he had applied to the West Yorkshire force for a detective superintendent's job – and got it. Then, aged thirty-five, he moved his wife and three children from one end of the country to the other, from a relatively quiet West Country cathedral town to Barnsley, an industrial landmark, at that time still in the West Riding and the hub of the coal-mining industry. Immediately rumours began that, because the new chief constable, Ronald Gregory, had previously been boss of Plymouth police, then deputy chief of Devon and Cornwall, he must have handpicked Domaille personally. This was completely untrue. The first time they met was at the interview in Wakefield, though there was a common link of sorts. It came through a man called Proven Sharpe, head of CID for Devon and Cornwall. Domaille worked with him while on the regional crime squad and Proven Sharpe gave him a glowing reference when he applied for the West Yorkshire post.

Domaille took north some new ideas for the CID which had not been tried out in West Yorkshire, especially with regard to administration. In Exeter a major incident room used printed duplicate forms provided by NCR. It meant information had only to be written down once and duplicate copies sent to appropriate people. The West Riding system was paper-heavy, very slow and hadn't caught up with modern methods. On arrival in Yorkshire, Domaille quickly came under the wing of Donald Craig, the West Yorkshire CID boss. There were a couple of murders in which Domaille swiftly arrested the guilty men. His calm demeanour allowed him to bring them in without the need for handcuffs. He had only ever handcuffed two people in his life: 'I believe in saying "You're nicked. You are going down the nick and you will come down with me." I've always treated people, whatever they've done, as human beings and as well as I could possibly treat them.'

Ultimately Domaille was promoted to chief superintendent and put in charge of the force community affairs branch, a job that involved the considerable diplomatic skills he had in abundance. He mixed easily with the media and ethnic communities. The force knew he was an operational detective doing this job and in the eyes of many it gave him considerable credibility. The only senior officer he had slight difficulty with was George Oldfield, who thought Domaille's policy of giving the media as much information as he could was wrong. At each of the early Ripper murders, Domaille had turned out promptly to ensure the press and television and radio reporters were properly briefed. He gained a good inside knowledge of the crimes and working methods of the senior investigating officers, which helped when he took over Bradford CID and investigated the Atkinson murder. Now he had been given a huge job, but from Domaille's viewpoint there was only one drawback: he had to channel his review of the Ripper investigation through George Oldfield, who would have first sight of his report *before* it went to the chief constable.

Surrounding divisions within West Yorkshire and other northern forces were telexed for details of women who had been seriously assaulted or murdered. Team members read the case files, interviewed surviving victims, witnesses and the original investigating officers to decide which offences were rightly part of the series. Across one wall of the squad's offices a large chart displayed details of other attacks similar to the series. Coloured in red were those they felt sure were the work of the Ripper. If there was some doubt, they were coloured black, which meant these cases could not be used for elimination purposes. A suspect could have a firm alibi for one of these offences, but still not be cleared of involvement in the attacks and murders coloured red on the chart.

'We were influenced by the twin form of attack which appeared in these offences,' Domaille said later, 'the blunt instrument to the head and knife or sharp object to the body. Often women who survived attacks suffered severe head injuries. I was aware that officers interviewing these women became very suspect of their ability to recall what had actually happened or who they had seen at the time of their attack. The more often officers saw these women, the more dubious the officers became regarding the validity of what the witness would say.' Domaille placed great store by the instincts of the original investigating officer. They looked at many cases where women had been knocked about the head but decided not to include them in the series. Some were as far away as Bristol and Wales.

He paid an early visit to the Police Scientific Development Branch, who with the Police Research Services Unit made several return trips to West Yorkshire in May 1978. They came up with plans to use the Police National Computer (PNC) to process intelligence from the covert vehicle monitoring operation in the red-light areas. Domaille wanted the entire nominal index system in the incident room put on a computer, but this proved a pipe dream and was turned down. Information held about different people varied to such an extent between individual murders that it would be nigh on impossible to convert it into a coherent database. However, retrieving vehicle index numbers was a much more viable proposition, made easier because the Police National Computer was now networked throughout Britain's police forces and made communications quite easy. The cost, however, was high: £240,000 by the time the Ripper inquiry was finished.

Ten visual display units were installed at the main incident room on the fourth floor of Millgarth police station in Leeds. Home Office experts spent considerable time ironing out teething problems. A special PNC code allowed operating staff to record vehicles seen at all the observation points within the red-light areas. They could also obtain printouts relating to particular inquiries, which was a major breakthrough since nothing like it had been tried before. The Ripper Squad was now truly at the frontier in the investigation of serious crime. But before this system was up and running there was another murder in Manchester which had a critical effect on the inquiry. It took John Domaille across the Pennines to Jack Ridgway's office. Only a few months previously, it was Ridgway who made the journey in the opposite direction, to liaise on the Rytka murder in Huddersfield. This time a much older woman was involved. It was 18 May 1978. Yet another workman making an early-morning start discovered the body of a Ripper victim. His ninth.

Just after eight o'clock a team of six gardeners working for a Rochdale landscaping firm arrived in two vehicles at the small brick-walled compound of the private wing of Manchester's Royal Infirmary. Jim McGuigan saw what he thought was a large doll or tailor's dummy lying on the ground. It was close to a part of the wall which had collapsed and been replaced by a temporary wire fence. Taking a closer look, he saw it was the body of a woman who had been battered about the head. A coat had been placed on top of her from her knee to neck and a piece of paper covered her head. Skid marks in the gravel of the nearby car park made him think the woman had been dumped from a car. A passing nurse came over to look at the woman's corpse huddled beside the wire fencing and a doctor was immediately summoned from the nearby infirmary. He confirmed she was dead. Manchester's murder team turned out in force with Detective Chief Superintendent Jack Ridgway once more in command.

Twenty uniformed officers began an inch-by-inch search of the compound and the car park. Four yards from the body they discovered marks in mud on the ground where a struggle could have taken place, and some tyre tracks. Near by was a pool of blood with hair and brain tissue in it. There were also scrape marks and blood splashes leading to the body, which lay on its right side in a semi-prone position, the feet extended towards the pool of blood. The woman's blue/brown reversible checked coat with a blue collar and cuffs was open. Her tights and slacks were in place but her blue cardigan, floral-patterned yellow sleeveless dress and underslip had been pulled up to expose the abdomen. A blue and white bra still covered her breasts. A pair of blue canvas wedge-heel slingback shoes had been placed neatly beside the body. Taking a closer look, Ridgway had little doubt that this was another Ripper murder. There was a large wound on her stomach through which a coil of intestines protruded and she had severe head wounds covered in blood.

By the time the pathologist, Dr Reuben Woodcock, arrived from Bolton at 12.30 p.m., rigor mortis was fully established. When he tested the body temperature an hour later, it showed death had occurred roughly twelve hours previously. Later that afternoon, Professor Gee and John Domaille watched Dr Woodcock perform his autopsy at the Manchester Central Mortuary. The woman wore a wedding ring on her left hand, and there was an obvious operation scar on her lower abdomen. She had several skull fractures and the brain had been lacerated. She had probably been attacked about the head from the right side. There was a circular fracture and a disc of bone had been displaced into the skull. One chest wound passed between her ribs and penetrated the left lung, the liver and the stomach. Woodcock thought three separate thrusts had been made into the wound with a weapon, without it being withdrawn completely. Another wound in the stomach area, eight inches long, had jagged edges caused by a large number of separate cutting movements. It was this that led the intestines to protrude.

The pathologist concluded that the woman had suffered three blows to the head, probably from a hammer, and that these had caused her death. A wound at the back of the head could have been inflicted first, while she was still standing. From its shape it was a glancing blow. The two other head injuries were caused as she lay on the ground. The stomach and chest wounds were inflicted either near death or after she had died.

A fingerprint check identified the victim as forty-one-year-old Vera Evelyn Millward from Hulme, a convicted prostitute with various aliases. She had two children aged eight and six by her common-law husband, a bearded West Indian from Jamaica called Cy Birkett. The couple had been together eight years. He knew her not as Vera, but as 'Eva'. They lived in a council flat in one of the toughest run-down areas of Manchester. The place where she was found was yet another area where prostitutes took clients. There was never any direct evidence she was still soliciting, but Ridgway learned Vera had been seeing the same man every Tuesday night for five years. He was more a friend than anything else and provided her with food for the children. Each Tuesday evening he would appear in his Mercedes car in the road outside her council flat, flash his car headlights, and she would leave to spend the evening with him. Questioned later by detectives, the man insisted the relationship was not sexual. They were friends and he had taken pity on her. However, on the night she died he had failed to turn up at her flat and later was positively cleared of any involvement in the murder. A former prostitute living in the same council block said that two years earlier she and Vera had been working the Moss Side area together. Her last conviction for prostitution was in 1973.

However, Vera Millward was not a well woman. She was described as both quiet and frail. She walked unsteadily and had a tendency to drag her right foot. Cy Birkett told Ridgway's officers she had a stomach complaint. The night she went missing, she indicated she might go to the infirmary to get some tablets because of bad stomach pains. Ostensibly she was going to the local pub to buy cigarettes, but it was obvious she had been picked up at some point by her killer. Piecing together Vera's family background was not easy. She had been born in Madrid, Spain, before the Second World War and came to England in her teens to work as a domestic help. She had seven children in all. Previously she lived with a man called Yusef Mohammed Sultan, by whom she had five children. Detectives interviewed the three eldest. When the youngest was fifteen, Vera left home and started working the streets of Moss Side. Yusef Sultan died two years later, but by then she was living with Cy Birkett. Going out to buy cigarettes could have been a pretext to go looking for men, to help out with the family budget.

Mr Birkett was convinced Vera had been on her way to the hospital and that her killer had given her a lift. Newspapers reported him saying that when her stomach complaint got really bad, she went to the Royal Infirmary to get painkillers. She had been complaining about the pain before she went out. When she didn't come back after ninety minutes, he went out to look for her briefly, but then returned home as the children were alone in the flat.

'This man has destroyed my life,' Birkett told reporters. 'I went to see her body in the mortuary, it was a terrible shock, it broke my heart. What do I say to my children? She was a very ill woman. She had undergone three major operations in the last couple of years and had only one lung.' He knew she had at one time been a prostitute, but believed she had given it up. 'It was an enormous shock to me to learn the police believe she was working the streets and that is how she met this man. I cannot believe it. If I met this man I would go berserk.'

Vera, possibly the most frail of all the Yorkshire Ripper's victims, may have struggled very briefly with her killer. A man taking his son for emergency treatment to the infirmary prob-ably heard her last dying cries for help. He was a hundred yards or more away some time around 11.15 p.m. when there were piercing screams in the night. 'Help . . . Help . . . Hel . . .' – the final scream was cut off. Then silence. The witness thought it was a patient in the hospital having a nightmare.

On arriving at the car park the Ripper had reversed his vehicle so it pointed towards an exit, allowing him to make good his escape after he enticed Vera Millward out of the car to kill her. By doing so he left a crucial clue pointing to the track width of the vehicle and the type of tyres. The vehicle still had the Esso and 'India Autoway' make of tyres seen in earlier attacks. Plaster casts were made. Soon forensic experts at the Home Office lab at Chorley linked them to those found both at Richardson's murder and the attack on Marilyn Moore. Even so Ridgway declined to confirm Millward's murder as part of the Ripper series being investigated by West Yorkshire police. Manchester, he said, were still keeping an open mind. There were similarities but no 'direct evidence' to connect them. This was untrue. He was protecting evidence from the tyre tracks, which some months later gave the Manchester team an important breakthrough that was then completely wasted. Ridgway's experts showed that the tyre tracks could not have been made by a car in the 'Farina' range.

Two officers, Keith Fletcher and David Booth, had been pestering Ridgway about the tyre inquiry. 'They did excellent work, although early on I thought they were a bit of a pain,' he revealed. 'They kept coming to me and saying they were not happy with West Yorkshire's theory about the "Farina". I told them eventually to pursue their hunch. They could not conclusively say which kind of car it was, but they definitely showed it was not in the Farina range. That got it down to a very small number of vehicles which could have left those tracks. It was a great piece of work.'

The arguments were complex because there were different sets of measurements to be considered. Some were a matter of a fraction of an inch. There was the track width of the vehicle, made by measuring the turning circle of the car and the distances between the front and back wheels. Then there was the actual size of the tyres. West Yorkshire was using data which included vehicles with tyres that could have measured twelve, thirteen, fourteen or fifteen inches in diameter. Keith Fletcher in September 1978 revealed that Esso and the East German manufactured Pneumant tyres which had first appeared at the Richardson murder were not available for the fourteen-inch wheels, the kind fitted to all vehicles in the 'Farina' range. 'To fit both the tracking data and the tyre type in the Richardson, Moore and Millward cases, a BMC "Farina" car would have had to be fitted with rogue wheels,' a confidential report later stated.

In October 1978 Ridgway travelled across the Pennines to Leeds yet again, this time taking with him the results of Manchester's tyre research which pointed to flaws in West Yorkshire's 'Farina' hypothesis. 'I was convinced that George Oldfield was on the wrong track and I told him, but he would not have it at any price,' he said. 'The only concession Oldfield made was to have the tyre evidence re-examined. I told him we were not going to pursue the Farina inquiry. The West Yorkshire team continued to believe the killer had probably been using a "Farina" style of car.' Oldfield had invested heavily in terms of manpower in West Yorkshire's tracking inquiry. Their expert was an inspector called Brian Sidebottom, a tall and supremely fit half-marathon runner. He had charge of West Yorkshire's stolen vehicles squad. Oldfield had every confidence in Sidebottom's ability and approved a plan for all West Yorkshire officers to report every sighting of any 'Farina' car they saw. These were cross-referenced against the 'Farina' master index in the incident room. Vehicles which hadn't been cleared were then thoroughly screened. The tyres were discreetly examined and all men having access to the vehicle checked and eliminated for one of the 'firm' Ripper murder dates. It represented a massive commitment in terms of resources, but Oldfield had little else to go on.

However, Keith Fletcher then provided Ridgway with another devastating piece of evidence. After more research, he noticed that Marilyn Moore had described the interior door handles of her attacker's car. When he applied that description against the list of vehicles West Yorkshire was relying on, it showed that only *two* vehicles fitted the criteria. These were a Ford Cortina Mark I and Ford Corsair models from 1964 onwards. Tragically, it was another missed opportunity, because by this time Ridgway had lost faith in the vehicle aspect of the Moore inquiry. Instead the Manchester detectives drew up a list of vehicles for the Millward killing based on their own evidence: the tyre tracks left in the car park at Manchester Royal Infirmary. Information was collected from the Ripper vehicle index in Leeds, but soon even this operation was aborted. Ridgway decided to halt the operation completely and use his resources elsewhere. Cooperation between the two forces over tyre tracks had not taken place until September 1978 – four months after Millward's murder. Brian Sidebottom in Leeds also did more research and came up with a list of five vehicles, including the Mark I Ford Cortina and the Ford Corsair. It was a golden opportunity for the forces to cooperate and narrow the scope of their inquiries. In the space of nineteen months the tracking inquiry had gradually whittled down the makes of vehicles which could have left the suspect tyre tracks.

The process had started after Irene Richardson was

murdered at Roundhay Park, Leeds, in February 1977. One hundred possible makes of car were reduced to fifty-three, and later to eight and finally, had Manchester's evidence been accepted, down to only two. But with Oldfield's commitment to the red-herring Farina, and because Ridgway now tragically decided to use his resources elsewhere, the tracking inquiry was aborted. Tens of thousands of vehicles had been checked. For Oldfield to have accepted Manchester's findings would have been to admit that almost the entire effort of the previous twenty months had been a complete waste of time and money, and by then the force had already spent £1.5 million on the Ripper inquiry. To understand the processes which led up to this major mistake, it needs to be understood that Oldfield and his team were charting new territory, like the early geographers trying to navigate the source of a great river through a vast wilderness. Such a journey required decisions based on imperfect evidence. At a divide in the river they might take a wrong turn and travel many miles before realizing their mistake. Unconsciously, perhaps Oldfield couldn't face turning round to go back again. The difference between him and the navigators was that they chose to make the journey and volunteered for adventure. Oldfield did not. Often he had to rely on his gut instinct, and sadly at times it let him down.

The Ripper investigation had outgrown West Yorkshire's ability to deal with it, both in terms of physical resources and the skills required to manage an inquiry of such mind-boggling size and complexity. There had never been a case like it before, in which a serial killer struck without mercy and completely at random. The only motive was his sheer enjoyment in having power over the women he murdered. The man was a head case, but a lucky head case. Senior detectives had attempted complex pieces of work, like the initial tyre inquiry, that were then abandoned when manpower pressures arose. But such a vast undertaking as attempting to check the tyres of 53,000 vehicles after Richardson's murder was a noble effort which had a morale-sapping effect on the officers involved. If the senior investigating officers had refined the 'tracking inquiry' data to reduce the total number of vehicles screened, it would have made the job more manageable. The Manchester and West Yorkshire forces had each brought in their own experts rather than hand a complex piece of research and mathematical analysis over to the Forensic Science Service, who had the experience to tackle the job. Even so, Manchester's men got it down to two makes of vehicle, which was both amazing and tragic. One of these, a Ford Corsair, was being driven by the Ripper at the time he murdered six women and assaulted Long and Moore. A clear opportunity to resolve the case in 1978 was thus missed, with awful consequences.

In this desperately long investigation, there would be no prizes for being nearly right. The ultimate penalty for errors made by the police was paid by the women who had a rendez-vous with death. Mistakes quite literally cost lives. The clues were there in the tracking inquiry, but the detectives remained over-influenced by Moore's insistence she had not been in a Ford Corsair. She told detectives the position of the bell-housing covering the Corsair's large gearbox for its V4 engine would have ruled out having sex in the front of the car. Dick Holland, who interviewed Moore, believes she probably got into a 'Farina' type vehicle some time before the Ripper picked her up and, confused after being attacked about the head, simply made a genuine mistake.

Domaille's homicide investigation team completed its major review of attacks on other women, and more crimes were formally attributed to the Ripper for the first time, which meant that documents from these investigations were added to those being accumulated in the incident room. In June 1978, details of all suspected Ripper crimes were published in a confidential Criminal Intelligence 'Special Bulletin', circulated to all British forces. They added an additional murder to the tally, as well as two serious assaults on West Yorkshire women who had survived. The Ripper's official toll of attacks since 1975 by now totalled fourteen – ten homicides and four attempted murders.

Domaille's team had re-examined the case files on the attempt to kill Anna Rogulskyj in Keighley in July 1975; and also Olive Smelt in Halifax five weeks later on 15 August 1975. Neither was a prostitute. David Gee's deputy in the department of forensic medicine at St James's University Hospital in Leeds had examined both surviving victims within a few weeks of each other. Dr Michael Green was a highly experienced forensic pathologist, who later became an eminent professor of forensic medicine at Sheffield University. A grammar school boy from Leeds, Green had had a varied career, including a spell as a flying doctor in Australia.

Auburn-haired Anna Rogulskyj, then aged thirty-four, had only just returned semi-conscious from the operating theatre when he made his examination at Leeds General Infirmary. Her scalp was shaved and heavily bandaged. Three head injuries had left crescent-shaped lacerations with depressed fractures where she was struck with a heavy object. Bruising across her hands and right forearm suggested she tried to defend herself. On her abdomen was a peculiar mark or grazing of some kind, seven inches long, running horizontally below the navel. Above this mark were six or seven small but deeper scratches.

The injured woman had been born Anna Patricia Brosnan in March 1941 at Tralee, in County Kerry, Ireland, one of a large Catholic family, with three brothers and eight sisters. After leaving school at fifteen she moved from Eire to Keighley to live with her eldest sister. She worked as a shop assistant in Woolworths, which was where she met her future husband, who was also employed in the store. Roman Rogulskyj was of Ukrainian extraction, and the pair married in February 1957. They had lived in Keighley but had no children and the marriage ended in divorce in July 1973. A few years later, she took up with a man called Geoffrey Hughes, also living in Keighley. On American Independence Day – Friday, 4 July 1975 – the pair had had an argument and Anna went off on her own into Bradford city centre for a night on the town with some girlfriends. She had been drinking in a pub, and later a nightclub called Bibby's. She left about midnight, by which time she was decidedly merry. Two Jamaicans gave her a lift back to Keighley and dropped her off at her home.

She discovered Geoffrey Hughes had packed up his belongings and gone back to his own house near Keighley town centre. In a maudlin state, Anna put on her favourite record. When it finished she decided to go over to Hughes's home, probably to seek a reconciliation. Shortly before 2 a.m. she tried to wake him up by banging on the front door. The noise was heard by an elderly neighbour. When this failed to bring Hughes downstairs, she picked up one of her shoes in a temper and used it to break a ground-floor window.

At 2.20 a.m. she was found in a nearby alleyway behind the local Ritz cinema, lying on her back, fully clothed with severe head injuries. Part of her clothing had been disturbed. She was only fifty feet from Hughes's house and her handbag was close by with nothing stolen. The blood on her head was beginning to congeal. Taken to the local casualty department, she was quickly transferred to the general infirmary in Leeds for specialized neurosurgery. Anna was desperately lucky to suffer no brain damage and made a good recovery, only to discover three years later that she had been included in the Yorkshire Ripper's list of victims. Since all but one at that stage had been prostitutes, she felt quite rightly she had been slurred with the same label, which she saw as a gross injustice. When her hair grew again it had turned grey. Like all the Ripper's victims, Anna had simply been in the wrong place at the wrong time.

Six weeks later in Halifax, a forty-six-year-old office cleaner, Olive Smelt, was attacked and left for dead. She and her husband Harry, who was four years older, were married in September 1948 and had two daughters and a son. Before their wedding, twenty-one-year-old Olive Tempest lived with her mother and uncle in Boothtown, Halifax. Olive and Harry resided briefly with her mother before moving to the Ovenden area and starting their family.

In the mid-1970s Olive Smelt worked during the evenings from Monday to Friday at three separate firms in Halifax. She regularly went out for a drink in the town centre with her close friend Muriel Falkingham on Friday nights. On 15 August 1975 they had been in the White Horse pub and she left ten minutes before closing time, parting company with Muriel. She went on to the Royal Oak pub and stayed there until almost 11.30 when two friends gave her a lift. They dropped her four hundred yards from her home. She walked down Woodville Road and turned into a narrow lane. It was then that she noticed someone walking on her right-hand side. They spoke briefly. He said: 'Weather's letting us down, isn't it.' Olive walked off down an alleyway, thinking about the fish and chip supper she was supposed to have taken home for her family, worrying that because it was so late the shop might now be closed.

The next thing she remembered was waking up in hospital. Her life had been saved by the surprise intervention of a car driven by a local man, whose headlights picked out her sprawled, bleeding body in the dark. She could have lain there all night and died very quickly from her appalling injuries had the driver not alerted the authorities. Olive Smelt was on the ground face down. Her skirt had been pulled up, exposing her buttocks. Again, her handbag was near by and nothing had been stolen.

At Leeds General Infirmary Michael Green noted two depressed fractures of her skull, one on the top, the other at the back. She had lacerations above her left eyebrow and right eyelid. She also had two curious abrasions in the small of her back – twelve inches and four inches long. Writing to Dick Holland, at that time in charge of Halifax CID, Dr Green noted a possible connection with an earlier case: 'It might be interesting to look again at the case of Mrs Rogulskyj, who was assaulted on 5 July, and compare the photograph of a wound on the abdomen, with a wound on the back of Mrs Smelt.' On his original examination notes, Green drew a small picture of a hammer – but then crossed it out. As with the attack on Anna Rogulskyj, he couldn't make up his mind what had caused the injury to the head.

Poor Olive Smelt recovered through grim determination, mainly because she was anxious to get back to her family, and especially her nine-year-old son, Stephen. Friends and neighbours were kind, one sent her flowers, and she later learned some had been praying for her recovery. However, Olive and her family were left to carry the repercussions and mental scars of this devastating attack for many years. Like Anna Rogulskyj, Olive knew what people were saying about her because she had been a Ripper victim, and it was completely unfair. She had been a warm-hearted woman who loved fun and laughter, but the attack left her at times depressed and angry. Several years after the Ripper attempted to kill her, she gave an interview in which she accepted she was lucky to be alive: 'But sometimes I get so depressed I almost think it would have been better if he had finished me.' Harry came under suspicion. He had been panelling out the kitchen of their home and had plenty of tools available. Olive later became afraid of all men and it placed a great strain on their marriage. Ultimately it was the love of their close family that pulled Olive and Harry through a terrible nightmare she has never been allowed to forget. Even twenty-seven years later, the occasional person recognizes her in the local market. One, unbelievably, even stopped her and asked for an autograph.

Almost a quarter of a century later, John Domaille remembered he had good reasons for including both women in the series. 'It was because of the way they were attacked. Their clothing had been either pushed up or pulled down and they had head injuries, plus they had been slashed with some kind of sharp instrument.'

Domaille says he equally had sound reasons for believing they shouldn't include in the series the attacks on Tracey Browne and Marcella Claxton from several years earlier. 'We were very much influenced by the twin form of attack which appeared in these offences,' he said, 'the blunt instrument to the head and the knife or sharp object to the body.' He was also particularly aware that the survivors had suffered severe head injuries. 'Officers interviewing these women became very suspect of their ability to recall what had actually happened or who they had seen at the time of their attack. The more often officers saw these women, the more dubious [they] became regarding the validity of what [they] would say.' They had examined the case of Tracey Browne and decided a number of factors excluded her. She was a young girl, not a prostitute, walking in a country area when assaulted about the head with a single weapon. She had not been stabbed. The investigating officers thought at the time that a local person was responsible and did not see it as part of a series.

Despite her denials, the police believed wrongly that Claxton had accepted money for sex and then tried to rip the man off. 'Prostitutes often get treated badly by their clients, especially if they take the money and fail to provide sex,' he said. She had a wound on the head, possibly made by a bottle, requiring fifty stitches. She had not been stabbed. Even though the offence occurred near where Richardson had been killed, it was not unusual for prostitutes to frequent this area.

Domaille was not absolutely certain the murder in Preston of Joan Harrison was a Ripper killing, either, but decided to include her in the series as a 'possible', though in time the doubts got fewer and fewer and many officers in West York-shire came to regard Harrison as a definite victim. Earlier, in February 1977, Jim Hobson and Detective Chief Superinten-dent Wilf Brooks from Lancashire CID had consulted about the Preston murder after Irene Richardson had been killed. There were certain similarities, notably the head injuries and the displacement of clothing. Also her left boot had been placed tidily over her legs with the zip opened. But the former machin-ist and shop assistant had not been stabbed, robbery could have been a motive and she had had sex with two men before she was killed. Domaille had long conversations with Wilf Brooks, and his team had thoroughly examined the files of the case, which was still regarded as an unsolved murder by Lancashire CID. Brooks did not think it was a Ripper case and Domaille always remained wary.

Among the forensic clues yielded during the investigation was the fact that Harrison had had sexual intercourse with a man who was a 'B' secretor type blood grouping, someone who secreted blood antibodies into their bodily fluids, like sweat, saliva and semen. She had also clearly been bitten on the left breast. The bite mark surrounded the nipple and measured 1.4 by 1.1 inches. There were also three small grazes on the inner side of the left breast, and three separate grazes, the largest 1.3 inches long, on the pit of her stomach. A forensic odontologist believed the man who bit her had a gap of an eighth of an inch in his teeth, though this information was never released to the public.

Domaille's ten-page report was compiled on 25 August 1978, by which time more than two hundred West Yorkshire officers were permanently engaged on the Ripper inquiry, in addition to another fifty in Manchester. Gregory used the report at a seminar he organized on the Ripper attacks three weeks later at the annual meeting of the Association of Chief Constables in Preston. It was rare for Britain's most senior police officers to engage in a 'live' murder inquiry, but the Ripper case had reached spectacular proportions in terms of victims. Gregory wanted to brief his fellow chief officers in case Ripper attacks occurred in their territory. He confirmed Yvonne Pearson had been part of the series, and now added the name of Joan Harrison.

The official cost of the inquiry was now put at £2 million, but money was not an issue according to Gregory: 'We will be pressing on and on and we will get this man in the end. You don't think in terms of how much money it is costing, or as some people might put it, the fact that all but one of these women [who died] were prostitutes. They were members of society. I can honestly say there is a burning keenness to solve this mystery – and we will.'

12

Going Covert

Two Ripper murders in Manchester convinced Jack Ridgway that the killer was using his car to tour red-light areas in northern England for women who were vulnerable. Despite protracted inquiries, his team had failed to turn up anyone who saw Jean Jordan or Vera Millward with the man who later killed them. The killer operated with deliberate stealth in choosing the women he wanted to murder. Once West Yorkshire had computerized its covert operation in the red-light areas, Ridgway recommended that the Manchester force should participate. He was a firm believer in taking the offensive rather than wait for the Ripper to strike again. Moss Side came under covert watch from thirteen police observation points in July 1978. Two months later, South Yorkshire Police joined in with four points in Sheffield, swiftly followed by Humberside, who set up three covert observations in Hull.

Using throat microphones, the undercover officers, making the night-time observations, dictated car registration numbers of men punting on to cassette tape along with the make and colour of car and whether the driver was alone or in the company of a prostitute. The tapes from all four police forces were couriered nightly by police motor bike to Leeds, where the whole operation was controlled. One hundred uniformed officers from West Yorkshire's police divisions and task force transcribed the tapes and typed data into the Police National Computer. It went on twenty-four hours a day for eighteen months. They quickly discovered staggering numbers of men across the North of England were out at night looking to pay for sex. Details of thousands of vehicles were being inputted from the West Yorkshire area alone *every night*. In the first month, 150,000 vehicles were logged with the PNC. In Manchester, 4,000 cars a night were being sighted and logged. A drastic change of plan occurred. To make the information more manageable, the computer would only print out the registration details of vehicles seen in at least two separate red-light areas.

At the end of the first month, 918 vehicles were identified by the PNC for punting in *two* towns. The drivers of these cars and vans now became suspects to be eliminated, in the same way as men who could have received the five-pound note found in Jean Jordan's handbag were suspects. During the second week the registration number PHE 355G appeared on the printout sent up from Hendon. When cross-checked with the Swansea computer, it was confirmed it belonged to a red Ford Corsair owned by a Peter William Sutcliffe of 6 Garden Lane, Heaton, Bradford. He was scheduled for another interview – his third.

The computerized cross-area sightings operation began on 19 June 1978. Between then and 7 July, Sutcliffe's red Ford Corsair was seen six times in the Bradford red-light district and once in Chapeltown, Leeds. When the computer printed off his car registration number, he became one of countless 'actions' which the incident room staff passed to the inquiry teams. A detective constable called 'A' was tasked to eliminate Sutcliffe from the inquiry by accounting for his movements on one or more of the murder dates. Each officer had a list of key dates suspects should be alibied for. They would examine diaries, passports, holiday booking forms, records of periods in hospital or family anniversaries in order to positively alibi an interviewee. On no account could they let slip that the police were mounting secret observations in prostitute areas, nor were ball-pein hammers to be mentioned.

Detective Constable 'A' had to discover whether the man he was interviewing had been with prostitutes and had a motor vehicle which could have made the tyre tracks at the Richardson, Moore or Millward crime scenes. Although cars in the 'Farina' range were most suspect, if other vehicles which could have made the tracks were found, the make of tyres fitted had to be noted. It was not a difficult task, but it required tact and determination.

'A' knew Sutcliffe had been interviewed twice before, during the five-pound note inquiry, and that he had a 'loose' alibi. He wanted a stronger one for the recent murder of Millward in Manchester in mid-May. What he did not know was that in the month following the sighting of Mr Sutcliffe's Ford Corsair in Leeds on 7 July, he had purchased another car, a black Sunbeam Rapier, which was then spotted a further nine times in the Manningham red-light district.

When 'A' turned up at the Sutcliffe home in Bradford on 13 August 1978, he found a typical domestic scene taking place. Peter and Sonia Sutcliffe were decorating their house. All seemed normal enough. They were like a lot of young couples, putting their spare-time energies into improving their home. Their outward demeanour was one of complete calm at his visit.

Sonia Sutcliffe remained during the early part of the interview. Having recently purchased the house, they were spending all their leisure time, they explained, on alterations and decorations. So much so, they said, that they seldom went out, and when they did it was always together. At first they had difficulty remembering where they were over the weekend of 16 and 17 May. (Mrs Sutcliffe hadn't a clue she was married to a serial killer.) Sonia Sutcliffe told the detective that on 16 May her husband 'would have come home from work and stayed home all evening'.

The couple each made a written statement on the same lines, and while Mrs Sutcliffe was out of the room briefly, her husband denied he used the services of prostitutes. 'A' then asked him some general questions about his car movements, keeping quiet about the fact that he had several times been seen obviously punting. Sutcliffe said he drove through Bradford via the city centre from his workplace to home. But he denied having been in Leeds recently. The officer knew there were errors in the information coming out of the covert monitoring operation and took Sutcliffe's response at face value. However, he didn't check the tyres on Sutcliffe's car, neither did he search the house or garage. From documents he collected from the incident room, he believed the house had been searched earlier. Perhaps influenced by the continuing effort to find the 'Farina' car, 'A' did not believe a Ford Corsair was the car they were looking for.

Since the red-light area in Bradford straddled a number of main access routes into the city, he thought Sutcliffe was telling the truth about passing through Manningham on the way home from work. Yet again, a golden opportunity slipped by. 'A' didn't have with him the actual times Sutcliffe's Ford Corsair was recorded passing through the red-light areas. The computer printout only displayed the time the data was put *into* the Police National Computer, not the actual time the vehicle was *spotted* going past observation points. In fact the earliest time Sutcliffe was sighted was 8 p.m., and the latest

12.30 in the morning. If 'A' had had this information at hand, he would immediately have realized it contradicted the Sutcliffes' story that they hardly went out at night and only together. Neither could 'A' challenge Sutcliffe's denial of having been in Leeds. Orders were that there were to be no confrontations with men who had clearly been seen out looking for prostitutes but denied ever doing so. In addition, no one could be arrested without the express authorization of George Oldfield himself.

Of course, a suspect could always 'voluntarily' accompany an officer to a police station to 'assist with inquiries'. Detectives issued with a special notice a year earlier were given ten points that must be strictly followed *before* a suspect could be arrested. They paid particular attention to the tenth point. A person could not be taken to a police station for questioning until all nine points had been completely covered, and only then if the ACC (crime) approved after the submission of a full report. Fear of sparking marital strife inhibited detectives from using their gut instincts about a potential suspect. Seeking the approval of the ACC before arresting someone was a huge disincentive for a detective; he'd be sticking his neck on George Oldfield's chopping block if he were wrong. A dressing down if you were wrong from your immediate superior was one thing; a bollocking from the man at the top could, in the minds of young detectives, be career threatening. Oldfield's prime concern was being landed with multiple claims for wrongful arrest and the costly litigation that would follow.

Detective Constable 'A' eventually returned the paperwork for this interview to the Millgarth incident room, together with the statements from the Sutcliffes. The file passed through various channels until it ended up on the desk of Dick Holland. He was not happy with the lack of progress 'A' had made.

Ford Corsairs were still on the list of suspect vehicles drawn up by Brian Sidebottom, even though the 'Farina' range was the red-hot favourite. Sutcliffe had owned two Ford Corsairs and Holland instructed that the tyres of both vehicles must be checked. He also wanted details about Sutcliffe's employers and his personal banking arrangements. The Ripper squad was certainly on the right track: the tyres, the banking details and the five-pound note, the sightings and alibis that would not add up. This new action was authorized by the incident room staff on 29 August 1978. However, Sod's Law prevailed. The majority of members on the outside inquiry team were seconded to the 'Farina' inquiry and the search for a Morris Oxford seen near the spot where Helen Rytka was killed. There was a delay of several months before the Sutcliffes were seen again. When Detective Constable 'A' revisited the Sutcliffes' home on 23 November 1978, he had another officer in tow. For both officers this follow-up inquiry appeared a matter of routine. While 'A' went inside the house, his colleague stayed sitting in the car.

Sutcliffe had banked with Barclays, but in 1977 switched to the Halifax Building Society at Bradford. His purchase of the black Sunbeam Rapier had resulted in the sale of the red Ford Corsair. When 'A' visited the new owner of the red Ford, new tyres had been fitted. 'A' had no knowledge of the fact that Sutcliffe worked for T. & W. H. Clark, one of the firms that figured in the five-pound note lead, and duly reported the fact. The file of papers relating to Peter Sutcliffe was then returned by the detective to the incident room. Yet again Peter Sutcliffe was to benefit. For some inexplicable reason his file was misplaced for nearly a year. This crucial breakdown in the administration of the incident room was to have dire consequences for the whole investigation. No one had put the evidence together, but they might have done so if the file had remained alive. Although he was one of thousands of men being questioned throughout West Yorkshire, by this time Sutcliffe should have been firmly in the frame. His car was on the list of possible vehicles used in some of the killings, he could have received the five-pound note given to Jean Jordan and he had been seen punting in the red-light areas of Bradford and Leeds. Moreover, he still had not been positively alibied. The odds on finding someone who fitted all three categories was fairly small and at the very least his name should have been flagged up as a potential suspect. The incident room was dangerously overloaded with paperwork, and Sutcliffe's file had been broken into separate parts. A special record was kept of people regarded as suspects, known as a 'D62' file, which ultimately had 494 names in it. Some of the men on this list were rated so highly as suspects they were placed on round-the-clock watch, or were listed to be interviewed the moment another Ripper murder took place, in order to check their alibis. Peter Sutcliffe should have been on this list. He was not.

The incident room was under heavy pressure from both the cross-area sightings and the 'Farina' operations continuing at the same time. That papers went missing was perhaps inevitable, given the huge workload involved in collating a massive investigation in a paper-led incident room. At the time of the Rytka murder, Sergeant Megan Winterburn had been working on the drugs squad before being transferred across to Huddersfield to work in the incident room after gaining considerable experience on several murders previously. When the paperwork for the Rytka investigation was transferred to the main incident room in Leeds, she went with it. Her experience gives just a small illustration of the complexity and confusion which had come to mire the Ripper squad in paperwork.

Holland asked Megan Winterburn to begin a new index for a secret operation in the red-light areas. 'We started off with one table, an index box, which was like a long wooden shoebox with five dividers in it,' she said, explaining the system. 'We would index each bit of information which came in about a particular car – vehicle make and type; model; colour; registration number alphabetical and registration number numerical. For the first week we were coping quite adequately. All the information fitted into the wooden box. Then within a week or ten days we realized we were going to need more than one box. So we got two boxes, but within another fortnight there were so many men going through these observation points we needed two desks and about a dozen of these boxes, and this was for index cards alone. On top of that, you had trays of action forms. You could cope quite adequately, but quickly there would be a pile of them. Within a month we ended up with four desks and twenty boxes crammed full with registration numbers. This was just a tiny section of the whole inquiry.'

Yet more cumbersome was the red-light observation operation. The tapes were collated at Millgarth early the next morning. At 6 a.m. operators wearing earphones used foot-pedal controlled recording machines especially adapted so they could slow down the speech as the tapes were played back. They transcribed information by hand on to purposely designed forms, which were then passed for typing into the Police National Computer.

In bad weather or poor visibility, the undercover observers had frequent problems obtaining correct vehicle registration details. One of the Millgarth team, Adrienne Parkes, became expert in interpreting the right numbers. Known to everyone as 'Blod' because of her Welsh connections, she developed great dexterity in keying permutations of licence plate details into the PNC which had earlier proved to be non-existent. Parkes noticed a familiar pattern and realized the bolts fixing a number plate to a vehicle often became rusted and in difficult lighting conditions could confuse the observer. 'D' could be mistaken for 'O', 'T' for 'F', and the figure '8' was often confused with '3' or '5'. She was able to bring up the right number on the computer when the details were cross-checked with the Driver and Vehicle Licence Computer at Swansea. The Police National Computer at Hendon and the computer at Swansea were not compatible, so information had to be retrieved from each separately. It was the first time a spare channel on the PNC had been used for a large-scale top-secret intelligence gathering operation.

The whole issue of secrecy was clouded by arguments about civil rights, the protection of computer data and the dangers of government turning into 'Big Brother'. There was enormous political opposition to the government linking police, tax, licensing, banking and other computer networks into one homogenized spy machine. The work of transcribing and inputting the data was mind numbing. Those transcribing swapped places every hour with those inputting data. Periodically officers rotated back to their divisions or the task force for normal policing duties. Domaille planned that, in the event of another murder, drivers who had been in a particular red-light area could be swiftly interviewed. The intelligence gathered would prove they had been there looking for prostitutes. If the last sighting of a victim was in a particular street within an observation area, it would drastically reduce the number of murder squad inquiries and hopefully allow them to get to the killer quickly. A vast intelligence file began to pile up of the vehicle details of all known men regularly visiting prostitute areas in West Yorkshire and Manchester. It was known as 'the punters' index'. But everyone, from the local vice squads to the computer experts from the Home Office, had completely underestimated the huge trade in sex in the North of England. So many vehicle registration numbers were being logged that a change of tactic was hastily made. The punters' index was completely swamped. The PNC was reprogrammed to print out only those vehicles which had been seen in *two* entirely separate red-light areas. This refinement drastically reduced the numbers of vehicles and, as a result, the number of follow-up interviews required. Even so, during the course of the eighteen-month operation, 21,000 males were identified as having been 'punting' in at least two prostitute areas across Northern England.

When a tape was fully transcribed at the fortress-like red-brick police station at Millgarth in Leeds, the transcription sheets were passed to another operator for entry on to the PNC. All these sheets were gathered together and filed on a daily basis and formed a permanent record. Each day a hard copy of the collated data was made in Hendon and rushed up the M1 to Leeds by police motorbike. It arrived at Millgarth in the form of a concertina printout in order of the vehicles being seen in a particular area. They were not in any alphabetic or numeric order, but had to be laboriously sorted manually before being fed in to the Vehicle Licence Computer at Swansea to obtain details of the owner-keeper. To check the details of a particular vehicle, the printout often had to be spread out across the entire floor of the incident room like a roll of toilet paper. Officers crawled on their hands and knees to check a piece of information. When the Ripper squad first began to check these details, they realized almost 40 per cent of the owner-keeper records provided by Swansea were out of date, so even more checks had to be made with the last known owner of the vehicle in an effort to determine who was the current owner. It wasn't long before there was a backlog of interviews with would-be suspects.

From the start of the organized watch on the red-light area in Chapeltown in 1977, officers were instructed that the entire operation must be completely covert, though there is little doubt that over time prostitutes knew they were being watched. None of the men interviewed could be told their vehicle had been positively sighted in a red-light district. More crucially, officers conducting the interviews were instructed they had to be totally discreet with the womenfolk of men known to be using the services of prostitutes. Officers carrying out interviews had been issued with special written instructions.

The information coming out of the cross-area sightings operation staggered the Ripper squad. 'We were utterly amazed at the figures the PNC threw up of men who were punting in prostitute areas and we soon realized that with each one of those we had a potential divorce,' said Dick Holland, in charge of running the incident room with its twenty-seven full-time staff working round the clock. 'Some men were even taking their wife's car to go seeking prostitutes, so she was the first person we had to see to find out who was driving the vehicle. When we were briefing the troops we stressed throughout our favourite phrase: "Softly softly catchee monkey." We did not want them to go barging in and letting out the true use of that car or why we were doing the inquiry.

'The detectives were there to alibi the driver for the Ripper murders, not for driving in the red-light district. We did not want to stir up divorces or domestic problems. We didn't either want police officers who had witnessed such activities in prostitute areas being subpoenaed in divorce hearings. If a person denied having been in a prostitute area for the purposes of punting, we didn't follow that up. We were not really worried about that. We knew he'd been there and that's how his car number appeared. We were only interested in alibiing him for a murder date. That was the object of the exercise, eliminate him for a definite Ripper attack if he had nothing to do with it, or involve him if he was the Ripper.

'If we got someone who was deliberately awkward, then they could be brought down to the police station, but we wanted that keeping to an absolute minimum. In all murder inquiries, particularly in prostitute areas, you require the cooperation of the public. You must not go in and immediately antagonize 22,000 men in West Yorkshire by causing domestic strife.' In the end there was no public fuss and no one had to be arrested. Men being interviewed cooperated more often than not simply to get the detectives out of the house. Scores voluntarily went down to the local police station to avoid being interviewed at home.

By now Constable Andrew Laptew, the merchant seaman officer trainee who had given up a life at sea for a career in the Bradford police, had moved on from the task force to become a detective. He was one of the team carrying out follow-up interviews from the cross-area sightings operation. It called for great sensitivity.

'We had to be very diplomatic and always preferred to get the gentleman of the house away from his wife for obvious reasons,' Laptew confided more than twenty years later. 'We would say to the wife, "Excuse me, do you think I could have a glass of water?" Invariably she would offer to make tea, which meant she would be out in the kitchen for five minutes. We would talk quickly to the husband about his association with prostitutes and then make an appointment to see him either at the police station or where he worked.'

West Yorkshire's strategy was to eliminate from the inquiry the male driver population who used prostitutes until they were left with only one man – the killer. Getting the man being interviewed out of the inquiry appeared to be the main purpose. If they could eliminate him positively for one of the murders, then he was out for all of them. It was a totally non-confrontational approach to detective work.

'It meant you wouldn't have to go and see that person again if he was one hundred per cent alibied,' Laptew went on. 'When there were other murders in the series we could forget about those who had been eliminated and concentrate on those we had not seen before or those that we had seen but who had not been alibied properly. We were always told at the briefings that it could be the next door you knock on, the next phone call you get. So you went to that house with an open mind and you would base any decision or judgement on the information you got at that house. While this man was on the loose the whole atmosphere within the North of England was one of great gloom. We really wanted to capture this man, so we could get back to normal.'

For Megan Winterburn the results of the covert operation were an eye-opener: 'It really hit me how many men were involved with prostitutes. I had never policed areas where they worked and had never come across prostitution until we started the cross-sighting index. After a fortnight there were so many actions coming through I remember thinking: "Surely there cannot be that many men who need to go to a prostitute?" I couldn't believe the numbers of men doing it. I began looking at men and wondering if they went with them. When the statements came in and they'd traced these people and they got the details, you realized what a cross-section of the male community were using prostitutes. Even though I was a police sergeant, I got it in my head it was just sad old men. We were talking rich, young, professional, old, vicars, a bishop, different ethnic groups. I remember thinking these prostitutes must be rich. The money that they were earning . . . it had never crossed my mind before.'

The pressure at times was very intense. 'Information at the beginning of an inquiry comes in thick and fast and as indexers you don't have time to sit and think, "Is this a little bit of information or is it a lot?" All you are aware of at the time is that there is information coming in. When you are indexing by hand on a manual system, twelve sheets of paper in a statement is a lot of information, and when you get to boxes full of paper, it becomes a mountain. We were getting a lot of information in.' When the indexer received a statement or any other document, it had to be gone through slowly, underlining the relevant parts that would need to be indexed and cross-indexed. It was a slow process if done thoroughly. Winterburn had been an office worker with secretarial skills before joining the police. 'We needed to pay attention to detail and make sure that every little scrap of information was actioned-out or indexed.'

One major consequence was the lack of social life. When a Ripper attack occurred, all leave was halted, days off were cancelled, and they were already working twelve or fourteen hours a day. Meg Winterburn became tired, though never to the point of physical exhaustion. 'Your mental agility lessened a bit but you had to sit back and take stock, have a five-minute break, have a cigarette or a drink and then come back and get on with the job because you couldn't afford to make mistakes.'

She was married to a police officer, but rarely saw him because both worked shifts. 'I think single people had it a bit easier, but there is no doubt it caused an awful lot of grief and marriages did break up,' she confided. 'There were people who went under, and it was pitiful, because they were working their best, but the long hours, their domestic problems, not seeing their families – the weaker ones got ground down and were sent back to their divisions. Everyone had their breaking point and there was no counselling available. You either sank or swam and if you didn't swim you sank into oblivion. Even at home you had to be careful because you couldn't talk to anyone about what you had been doing.'

The nucleus of officers working the incident room, including the senior supervisory staff, knew each other well enough to play good-natured practical jokes. One senior officer used to help himself to a cigarette from a packet on someone's desk every time he came into the room. One of the team sabotaged the cigarettes with explosive pellets from a joke shop. The superintendent duly sneaked a cigarette, went to the doorway to light up – and it exploded in his face. He stopped taking cigarettes. Another superintendent, fond of helping himself to the contents of the office sweet tin, found himself sucking on a joke sweet which turned his tongue blue and caused him to foam at the mouth. Unfortunately he was in a senior officer's briefing at the time.

Gallows humour was ever present, a natural release for any profession dealing with stress, injury and death. The local radio station came round and asked if the incident room team had any requests for songs. One joked to a colleague: 'What about "If I had a hammer . . ."' In the end, because she had spent so little time at home, she asked for 'When will I see you again?' to be played. The staff did a sponsored slim to see who had lost the most weight in a week. They put money in a cup every day, but at the end of the week went out and bought a box load of Cadbury Creme Eggs and stuffed themselves silly.

Through the spring, summer and autumn of 1978 the inquiries rolled on relentlessly, the paperwork piled up – even more so when the documents in the Rytka and Pearson investigations were transferred to the central incident room at Millgarth. The Ripper squad visited colleagues at police stations throughout West Yorkshire, giving slide shows to uniformed officers and detectives, stressing the dire need for confidentiality. A special lecture on the Ripper attacks was included in the syllabus at the detective training academy at Wakefield and talks were also given to other police forces and a conference of police surgeons. The main incident room was now working round the clock, manned by Dick Holland's twenty-seven officers. Tens of thousands of index cards tightly filled the long wooden boxes. Filing cabinets were crammed full of papers and statements. Cardboard boxes filled up with the backlog of action forms yet to be passed out to interviewing teams. An audit of the paperwork in the incident room found disturbing evidence that some officers making follow-up inquiries had been cutting corners and fabricating reports on the tasks assigned to them. Heads were set to roll and the deputy chief constable, Austin Hayward, carried out disciplinary hearings. Two officers were suspended and resigned from the force, thirteen appeared before Mr Hayward and were fined and reprimanded. Senior officers outside West Yorkshire later blamed poor morale for the detectives taking short cuts – 'a malpractice prompted by the lack of confidence in the tasks they were undertaking'.

Five separate indices were the key to a veritable mountain of information. A 'Name or Nominal Index' housed details of everyone seen or mentioned during the entire investigation; the 'Vehicle Index' listed all vehicles mentioned or thought to be relevant; the 'Farina Index' held details of all Farina vehicles owned by people living or sighted within West Yorkshire; the PNC 'No Trace' index detailed all vehicles where they could not find the owner. A vehicle might be a 'no trace' because it was not taxed; had false number plates; or the wrong registration details could have been taken or the file misplaced by the Driving and Vehicle Licence Centre at Swansea. Finally, there was the 'Prison Check Index', made up of the names of men serving sentences between the dates of the murders of Jackson and Richardson – a gap of fifty-four weeks. The Home Office gave the Ripper squad details of 1,700 such prisoners.

As Christmas 1978 came and went, the North of England held its breath, wondering whether the Yorkshire Ripper would strike again. John Domaille had now moved from overall charge of the small homicide investigation team to running the detective training school at Wakefield. Everything had gone quiet since Vera Millward's murder across the Pennines in Manchester in May. By February 1979, the official bill for the as yet unsolved murder investigation was £2.5 million; 147,000 cars had been checked; 112,606 people had been interviewed. Police had made 20,951 house-to-house inquiries. They followed up information volunteered from the public 38,314 times. A year had passed since anyone in West Yorkshire had been murdered. To the public at large and the top men leading the manhunt, it seemed Britain's most notorious killer must be lying low. The absence of an attack presented detectives with an awful paradox. Detective Superintendent Holland explained the difficulty about multiple murder investigations during the pre-DNA age: 'If you haven't caught him after a fairly lengthy inquiry into the last one, and he then stops killing, you are unlikely to catch him. If he continues he gets more and more careless, he leaves more and more clues, they build up and hopefully you will get him. It is only by him continuing that you do get him. But unfortunately that would mean another life gone – and that was one of the things we were desperately trying to avoid.'

The truth was the Yorkshire Ripper had not halted his merciless attacks on vulnerable young women. Throughout 1978 and the early months of 1979 he had, in addition to Vera Millward, attacked even more victims, only they were not recognized as such. Worse still, one of the survivors presented the Ripper squad with a perfect opportunity to catch him, but yet again he slipped through the net.

In the space of exactly twelve months from 2 March 1978 to 2 March 1979, at least four women suffered serious assaults, yet none was recognized as part of the Yorkshire Ripper series. In two of the latest cases, survivors gave descriptions of their attacker very similar to those given in earlier assaults, also never included in the series – the nineteen-year-old clerk-typist in Wakefield in 1972; Barbara Miller in Bradford in 1975; Tracey Browne near Keighley in August 1975; and the attempted murder of Marcella Claxton in Leeds in the summer of 1976. The most recent descriptions said the man responsible had dark hair and a beard or mandarin or 'Jason King' moustache. This was incredibly close to those descriptions given by women already ruled in as Ripper victims. Alarm bells should have been ringing loud and clear. Olive Smelt herself, only recently included in the series, had described her assailant as having dark hair and a beard or growth on his face.

At the very least, someone should have suspected that either the Ripper was conducting even more attacks than realized or another individual was out there in West Yorkshire, assaulting women by battering them over the head, and that this man had a beard and a moustache, just as Marilyn Moore, a recognized Ripper victim, had claimed. The criteria for including or excluding women in the series had been drawn too tightly, and in doing so some of the most crucial clues were missed which could have led to the killer's arrest in March 1979. The striking feature of the most recent attacks on women in West Yorkshire was how similar they all were. They were all beaten about the head from the rear and rendered unconscious. If none of these most recent attacks was to be included in the series, then logically it should have occurred to the Ripper squad that they had an even bigger problem on their hands. There was at large a potential serial killer attacking women in addition to the murderer known as the Yorkshire Ripper. There was credible evidence that they were one and the same person, but it was never spotted at the time.

On 2 March 1978, an eighteen-year-old shop assistant, Miss R, was walking along Kingston Road in Leeds late in the evening. Attacked from behind, she was struck about the head and knocked unconscious. She did not see her assailant and could give no description. The following autumn, on 28 November 1978, another eighteen-year-old, an Addressograph operator, Miss F, was in Bradford during the middle of the evening. She was followed along the road by a man who grabbed her by the hair. Miss F struggled, threw a brick at him, and he ran off. She described him as follows: 'Male, thirty years old, slim build, dark straggly hair below the shoulders; a mandarin moustache and a goatee beard.' Detectives helped her produce a photofit.

The next victim was another teenager, aged sixteen, still at school in her home town of Harrogate in North Yorkshire. On 17 February 1979 she was attacked from behind during the early hours of the morning and hit across the head with a blunt instrument. The girl, Miss M, suffered severe head injuries, but since she had not seen her attacker could not help police with a description. Somewhat extraordinarily, the police in North Yorkshire did not regard this as a crime and concluded she had fallen on an icy pavement and injured herself. Professor David Gee, at the behest of North Yorkshire police, went to Leeds General Infirmary on 1 March to conduct an examination of Miss M, then being cared for in Ward 26. She was sitting on the bed, her head enveloped in a large surgical bandage, and Gee could not get a look at her scalp. She appeared quite well and fully conscious. One of her doctors drew Professor Gee a sketch of the lacerations on her head. There was one linear laceration on the left side of the top of the head two and a half inches long and on the right side of the top of the head two inches long. A third curved laceration at the back of the head was about one inch long. The physician indicated that there had been two localized areas of depressed fracture beneath the left side of the head. Gee examined the post-operation X-rays.

Four days later, he was back in Ward 26 of the Leeds General Infirmary, this time to examine a twenty-two-year-old student, Miss B. On 2 March 1979 she had been walking in the grounds of Horsforth College some time during mid-evening. An attacker followed her. She, too, was viciously assaulted from behind and struck three times across the head with a hammer. She described her attacker as male, in his twenties, five feet ten inches tall, of broad build, dark curly hair with a drooping moustache. When Professor Gee examined her, part of her hair had been cut off and within the exposed area of scalp at the back of the head were three very distinct semicircular wounds recently sutured. She had no other injuries and appeared normal. Again X-rays showed an area of depressed fracture under the largest wound. Gee believed she had probably been hit with the circular head of a hammer.

A few minutes later, Gee turned his attention to the adjacent bed, where Miss M was still recovering. Now, with the bandages removed, he could clearly see her shaven scalp and the positions of the three lacerated wounds caused by an object with a localized striking surface. They didn't have the obvious curved shape to suggest the head of a hammer and Gee could not determine exactly how the injuries had been caused. An official report would conclude several years later: 'Although Professor Gee studied the X-ray photographs of Miss M's skull and said that the injuries were not consistent with a hammer attack, she had three clearly visible semicircular injuries to her scalp which even to the layman were not consistent with an accidental fall.'

Miss B provided detectives with what could have been a vital clue. She was positive that before she was attacked she had spotted the man sitting in a dark-coloured Sunbeam Rapier car. At the time West Yorkshire police had ignored the suggestion of Home Office scientific experts that they appoint a senior officer to the Ripper squad with detailed knowledge of computers. They could then have taken greater advantage of the data being inputted on to the PNC. Few officers working on the murder squad understood the codes applied to the different red-light areas on the printout provided by Hendon each day. In fact hardly anyone in the West Yorkshire police had a detailed understanding of the PNC operation and its capabilities for descriptive searches. The computer was never asked, for example, for a printout of all the sightings of vehicles within the 'Farina' range, yet the search for a 'Farina' vehicle was a high priority for Oldfield, convinced one of these might have been used in both the Moore attack and the Rytka murder.

The Home Office experts had ironed out the difficulty of constantly having to search the Swansea computer separately for the names of vehicle owners after obtaining the printout of the registration numbers. It caused a severe bottleneck for a time, but now the owners' names were automatically printed out with the registration numbers. What the program lacked was the ability to search the punters' index by vehicle owners' names. The computer could not answer the question: which car or cars owned by Joe Smith have been sighted?

With more than 10,000 names in the 'punters' index' of men seen in two red-light areas, the PNC program had had to be refined still further to reduce the number of follow-up interviews. Now it printed out only 'triple-area' sightings. A car seen going through the vice area of any three of the six towns being watched would automatically appear on the printout.

Detective Inspector Brian Sidebottom, West Yorkshire's stolen vehicle expert, who analysed the data in the 'tracking inquiry' to discover which car made the tyre marks at various Ripper attacks, decided to try something new. He asked for a printout of all Sunbeam Rapier and Alpine cars which had been put into the punters' index since the cross-area sightings operation commenced. He received a list of 850 registration numbers and owners' names. One of those belonged to Peter Sutcliffe of Heaton, whose Sunbeam Rapier had been sighted on countless occasions going through the red-light areas of Leeds and Bradford. Between 26 June 1978 and 22 November 1978, Sutcliffe's black Sunbeam Rapier was logged in the system passing through Manningham thirty-six times and Chapeltown twice. On 22 February 1979, he had been spotted in Moss Side, Manchester. By this time he had been seen both in Leeds and Bradford on three further occasions. The next day's printout from Hendon flagged him up as a 'triple-area sighting' who would be automatically actioned for an interview. Triple-area sightings were men who made a habit of looking for prostitutes and thus became at least potential if not prime suspects.

On the list of sightings requested by Detective Inspector Sidebottom, twenty-one other Sunbeam Rapiers were printed out as 'cross-area sightings'. But Sutcliffe's was one of only *three* which the coded data listed as triple-area sightings. Unfortunately the officers on the Miss B inquiry were not computer experts and did not realize the importance of the data. They hadn't a clue how to interpret the information. They never realized that, of the 850 Sunbeam Rapiers listed, only *three* had been printed out as triple-area sightings. The Miss B attack had been excluded from the Ripper series on the narrowest possible grounds: her injuries were caused by a hammer of a different size from the one it was believed the Ripper was using.

It would not have taken a rocket scientist to make the breakthrough with the computer printout. Anyone who understood which codes applied to the different red-light areas would have probably been able to analyse the printout within thirty minutes. As an official report later concluded: 'The emergence of Sutcliffe as a prime suspect in the [Miss B] case, if not for the whole series, would have been inevitable.'

Mr Sutcliffe was not scheduled for a follow-up interview until midsummer 1979, because the hunt for the Yorkshire Ripper case took a sudden and violent turn. There was another Ripper murder, this time in Halifax. Every member of the external inquiry teams working from the major incident room at Millgarth, including Andrew Laptew, was sent across to Halifax to work on the latest investigation. No actions were sanctioned from Millgarth for several months. By the time he was next seen, Peter Sutcliffe had changed cars again.

13

'He Comes from Sunderland'

When Halifax people talk of 'The Moor', they refer not to a barren wilderness inhabited only by sheep and grouse, but to one of the biggest parcels of open space locally, a hundred acres of neatly cut grassland. Skircoat Moor was renamed 'Savile Park' after the family that once owned it and had its place in history long before anyone heard of the Yorkshire Ripper. Large meetings of Chartists clamouring for reform of Parliament gathered there in the 1830s. The moor was purchased by Halifax town council from the Savile family in 1866 for the give-away sum of £100, on condition it was never enclosed. Its true worth was said to be nearer £40,000. The only request made by Captain Henry Savile was that the burgers of Halifax should do something about the smoke pollution caused by the town's wool and textile mills.

Halifax stands in the Calder Valley among the steep foothills of the Pennines, several hundred feet above sea level. In the mid-1970s Dick Holland was the town's CID chief, overseeing a more lenient form of law enforcement than had prevailed a few centuries earlier when the 'law of the gibbet' meted out rough punishment for offenders. With a cry of, 'From Hull, Hell and Halifax, good Lord deliver us,' beggars and vagrants tried to avoid the town. Until the mid-seventeenth century in Halifax, theft of a piece of cloth valued at more than thirteen and a half old pennies meant the offender being beheaded at the town's guillotine-type gibbet, whose huge blade swiftly decapitated offenders.

When a teenage clerk was found murdered on Savile Park in early April 1979, such was the terror now felt by people throughout Yorkshire and Lancashire that many believed the gibbet would be too good for the Yorkshire Ripper. Families who had suffered at his hands had mixed responses about the cold-blooded killer. By the time of the death of his latest victim, Josephine Whitaker, a nineteen-year-old clerk at the head office of the Halifax Building Society, Mrs Irene MacDonald in Leeds had lived with her daughter's murder for nearly two years. Mrs MacDonald prayed for Josephine's family: 'If there is a God this monster will be caught and will be stopped from doing these terrible things. I hate the Ripper, whoever he is, for what he did to Jayne and our family. He has wrecked our family one way or another. The way I feel I would find some way of killing him myself if he was caught.'

Some of those intimately involved with Josephine Whitaker had surprisingly different emotions. Immediately after her murder, reporters asked her forty-seven-year-old stepfather for his feelings towards her killer. With incredible dignity and great Christian charity, Mr Haydn Hiley responded: 'I don't hate anyone. I suppose I should be hating someone after what has happened, but it hasn't really sunk in yet. I just hope Josephine's death contributes to apprehending this man. Then it has not all been in vain.' The following weekend at St Jude's Church, where the Whitaker family worshipped, the vicar asked for prayers not just for them but also for the murderer who had caused them much anguish and torment. 'He needs help,' the Rev. Michael Walker told his Palm Sunday congregation. 'He is someone's child, husband or father. Pray not only for

Josephine and her family but for the Ripper and his family. They may be unwittingly protecting him.' A memorial service for Josephine a few weeks later was attended by more than five hundred local people, including the chairman of the Halifax Building Society, who read the lesson. Still in a state of bewilderment about how and why such a horrible deed could happen on their doorstep, the local community mourned not just Josephine but also perhaps for themselves. They, too, were tormented by three and a half years of killing. The Ripper's official toll now stood at eleven.

The Halifax murder sent shockwaves throughout Britain, and most especially across northern England. The fear factor was dramatically raised when George Oldfield urgently warned that no woman was safe out alone at night: 'We have a homicidal maniac at large and I believe he lives in the West Yorkshire area. This man will continue to kill until he is caught. We cannot stress how careful every woman must be. Unless we catch him ... he will go on and on.' When she heard the Ripper had struck again, Tracey Browne, now aged eighteen, had flashbacks to the night when she was attacked and left for dead in August 1975. Her tortured mind kept thinking the man was going to come back for her. She insisted the lights were not switched off at night on the top landing of the family home. Her bedroom door had to be left open and the curtains could not be drawn. She began breaking into cold sweats, a condition that persisted for six months.

Dick Holland addressed a gathering of detectives from across the force area who were drafted in for urgent house-to-house inquiries. The briefing took place in the old Victorian court at Halifax in Harrison Road. As he entered the ornately woodpanelled courtroom, the 150 detectives crowded into the room let out a burst of rapturous applause of welcome for their boss.

'We applauded him,' said Andrew Laptew, one of the young detectives present, 'because he was revered, held in high esteem – it went above mere respect. The only thing I can liken it to was the Roman cavalry returning from defeating the Barbarians and the Roman soldiers banging their shields with their swords. It might sound a corny analogy, but that's how I saw it, like a great leader returning to lead his troops. Mr Holland was a down-to-earth person, a very hard-working man, who never forgot his roots, a man of great charisma, of strong personality, a great orator, an extremely eloquent man and a man you would go the extra mile for.' Holland had quickly arranged for all the main incident room staff in Leeds to be bussed the eighteen miles to Halifax to see the actual spot where Josephine Whitaker was murdered. They needed to appreciate the geography of Savile Park and the surrounding areas, so that when they took phone calls from the public or dealt with documentation they had better local knowledge. Women working in the incident room at Millgarth shared the fear caused by the latest murder. Sue Neave, a twenty-six-year-old indexer, was born and brought up in Halifax and her mother still lived there. After leaving grammar school, she, too, worked at the Halifax Building Society, as a shorthand-typist. She then joined the police as a civilian worker and later became a policewoman. Her clerical skills were employed in the incident rooms on the Atkinson and Rytka murders before she moved full time to Millgarth.

'When Josephine Whitaker was murdered – that's when it hit home to me,' Sue Neave recalled. 'Before that my thoughts about the victims were: "She's a prostitute, she's hanging about, she was certainly living dangerously." When Mr Oldfield described Whitaker and MacDonald as "innocent women" as opposed to the other kind, there was a distinction for me . . .

Before that I just thought, well, he seems to be hanging around prostitutes, I'm OK, but after that one, I thought, no one was safe. It made me very wary of where I went. I used to sit in with my mother. Everybody was the same, you couldn't afford to relax about it. It was a horrible feeling. There had been murders in Bradford, murders in Leeds, and now in Halifax, on my own doorstep. What struck me was the position of it, on the moor, walking across that stretch of grass in the best area of Halifax at that time of night. I would have thought nothing of doing it myself. The horror of what happened. This man just struck anywhere, at anyone. That had a big impact on me and made me more aware of where I could go on my own and where I had to be accompanied . . . That lived with me. I thought: "When is he going to be caught?" That's all I wanted.'

Oldfield and Holland believed undercover police activity in Leeds and Bradford was almost certainly driving the killer to look elsewhere for victims. He had killed in Huddersfield, twice in Manchester. Now Halifax had provided him with prey. The most ghastly fact they had to face was the complete uncertainty of when and where he would strike. It was pure random chance that he happened upon poor Josephine. The more the Ripper squad learned about the circumstances, the more they realized how unlucky she had been. Fate had dealt her a dreadful hand.

From the time she was a month old until she was nearly four, Josephine lived with her mother at the home of her grandparents, Tom and Mary Priestly. She was the daughter of Thelma Whitaker, who had married Trevor Whitaker and later separated from him. Josephine was born a few days before Christmas 1959. Thelma and her husband were divorced in 1961. Thelma returned to live with her parents, and after her divorce lived with another man and had two sons, Michael and

David, but that relationship also ended. Josephine's mother, a forty-four-year-old teacher, later married a local builder, Haydn Hiley, in 1972, and the family continued to live in Ivy Street, Halifax, only a hundred yards or so from Savile Park.

From an early age Jo, as her family called her, had a passion for horses and horse riding. She started work at the building society after leaving school in 1977, and had recently had a promotion and a pay rise. She had had a few boyfriends and was briefly engaged to a lad who lived in Gibbet Street. She was anxious to get married and have children, but according to her ex-fiancé the pair grew apart and broke off the relationship. Josephine also had a part-time job behind the bar at a local hotel. She remained deeply attached to her grandparents. Every Sunday without fail she took tea with them. They watched her grow up, took a keen interest, helped with her schoolwork. They decided Jo would want for nothing as long as they were alive. She was the world to them. They regarded her as the perfect grandchild, kind, thoughtful and considerate.

The journey from Ivy Street to her grandparents' house in Huddersfield Road was about a mile. Josephine knew it blindfolded. She adored the moor, and frequently, when returning home from her grandparents, took a short cut via a narrow road running along the right-hand side. The day she died two things caused her to change her normal routine of staying in for the evening. It was Wednesday, 4 April 1979. Through a mail order catalogue club run by a colleague at work she had purchased a £65 silver watch, a tidy sum at the time. It arrived that day and Josephine was thrilled with it. However, during the early evening at home there was an argument with her mother, possibly because, like a lot of nineteen-year-olds not knowing the real value of money, she had been over-extravagant. It was one of those silly arguments that go on in every family, which seem important at the time and everyone laughs about later. The row concerned Jo's fish tank and the cost of the electricity which powered its filter. Jo got pretty worked up and after ten minutes stormed off to her bedroom, saying that she would get rid of the fish tank. She stayed in her room fretting for an hour. Then she put on her coat and, on impulse, decided to visit her grandparents, probably feeling in need of tea and sympathy. Besides which, she wanted to show them the new watch.

She arrived to find her grandmother was out for the evening at a local church event, so she stayed by the fire with Tom Priestly, who suffered from emphysema, chatting and watching television. The news came on at 9 p.m. The prime minister of Pakistan had just been executed. Josephine told her grandfather no one deserved to die like that, no matter what they had done. No one had the right to kill someone else, even if they were a murderer. 'What about the Yorkshire Ripper?' asked Tom. Josephine said he didn't deserve to be killed either when he was caught. Mary Priestly returned home around 11 p.m. and they briefly chatted before Josephine said she ought to go. It being so late they urged her to sleep over, but Josephine had left her contact-lens box at home in her bedroom. She would have to go home. She left promising to see them as usual on Sunday. The return journey to Ivy Street should have taken no more than twenty minutes.

Early next morning in the half-light, a woman spotted something unusual on the moor. Standing at a bus stop in Free School Lane next to Savile Park at 6.30, the woman, a factory machinist on her way to work, spotted a brown leather shoe with a stacked heel, and further away what she thought was a pile of clothing. Approaching closer, she realized it was the body of a young woman. Not long after police first arrived,

Jo's thirteen-year-old half-brother David left their home to do his newspaper round. Walking across the moor, he saw several police officers and noticed that a body had been covered over. It was then that he recognized one of his sister's brown shoes. In a state of shock, he rushed home to tell his parents, who thought Jo was asleep upstairs having let herself in with her own key the night before, after they had gone to bed. Finding Jo's bedroom empty, and utterly distraught, they called the police.

Yet again Oldfield left instructions for the force control room to contact Dick Holland immediately and tell him to make his way to Halifax. The first police officer at the scene noted drag marks extending from where the body lay to the edge of Savile Park, near Free School Lane. The drag marks ended at the point where Josephine's shoe lay. Near by the officer found bloodstains. There were several clear stab wounds to the back and right side of the trunk as well as obvious head injuries. Her clothing was disarranged. All West Yorkshire officers had been briefed about how Ripper victims had been found, and so from the very first phone call Oldfield knew it was an odds-on certainty his quarry had struck again. He wanted Holland on the case as soon as possible to maintain continuity. Living in the Ellend area of Huddersfield, the detective superintendent would have only a few miles to drive.

Unable to find him at home, the control room put out a radio message for Holland to check in, but his radio had broken. Another officer, hearing the radio message, suggested they contact the security gate of the Phillips Electronics factory at Lightcliffe. Unknown to Holland, some of his colleagues had begun taking a close interest in his private life. For six months he had been seeing a thirty-seven-year-old divorcee, Sylvia Swanson, a volunteer 'Special' constable who worked in an office at the Phillips factory. The senior detective had been spotted in his car several times dropping her off at the factory gates. Gossip had gone round the incident room at Millgarth that the 'boss' had a new girlfriend. They were all pleased for him, especially some of the female staff, who had taken his domestic arrangements under their wing. Aware that he was working fourteen hours a day, a few of them visited a local supermarket and made sure he had fresh milk and eggs for his fridge at home. Plain-speaking Mrs Swanson, a Yorkshire farmer's daughter with two teenage boys, initially only accepted a dinner invitation from the equally plain-talking detective superintendent. From those beginnings a loving relationship blossomed over time. She spent the occasional night at his home and the morning Josephine Whitaker was found he had given Sylvia a lift to work. The control room finally reached him and passed on the ACC's urgent message. One look at the body at the crime scene left Holland in no doubt. Later Oldfield, Ridgway and Trevor Lapish were of the same opinion. It was a Ripper murder, and Easter leave for all 250 officers working on the manhunt would have to be cancelled.

When Gee arrived the body was covered by a blanket with the head visible at one end and feet protruding at the other. Eventually a large plastic tent was erected to protect the body from any precipitation. A long black tarpaulin was in place to screen the crime scene from onlookers. The whole area had been marked out with flagpoles, tapes and traffic cones, showing where the victim had been dragged across the grass. Gee examined the body, jotting in his notebook the position of small stab wounds on the skin and the position in which the body lay. There were blood streaks on her face, both backwards behind the right ear and downwards and forwards across the right upper eyelid and bridge of the nose. Two large wounds to the head were clearly visible and blood had soiled the surrounding hair. The ground was muddy, and Gee looked closely at several clearly visible footprints near by.

At the beginning of a six-and-a-half-hour autopsy at the local Royal Infirmary an attendant removed the brand-new silver watch from Jo's right wrist. Its hands had stopped at 7.20. Her hazel-coloured eyes still bore her soft contact lenses. She had been felled by a single blow to the back of the head. Then Gee discovered a new stabbing weapon had been used. The trunk had twenty-one stab wounds, nine to the front and twelve at the back. They had been caused by an object very sharply pointed which created triangular wounds with rounded corners, and with a definite hilt mark reproduced in mud around the wound; suggesting a round-faced hilt to the weapon, which was fairly long. Gee noticed that around one of the entry wounds was a faint ring of bruising. In some cases, the weapon had penetrated the same wound twice. At the front of the left breast, in the areola immediately above the nipple, he noticed a tiny puncture, barely penetrating through the skin, an eighth of an inch in diameter. She had fractures to the skull associated with being hit with a hammer, but more disturbingly Gee discovered injuries to her genitalia. She appeared to have been stabbed several times through the vagina.

In this, more than any other Ripper murder so far, forensic analysis yielded several important pieces of evidence. Tiny flecks of material from the weapon used were found in some of the wounds. A scanning electron microscope showed traces of a mineral oil and carborundum grinding paste, a kind of emery powder, suggesting the killer had an engineering connection. Prints from an industrial boot in the soft mud on the ground underneath the body and in other areas near by showed the wearer was size seven and that there was wear in the centre of the right sole. Boot prints of a similar size had been found at the scenes of crime for Jackson and Atkinson. It confirmed the theory that the Ripper was a manual worker rather than someone with an office occupation. A trail of these near-perfect footwear impressions was also found going in the opposite direction from that in which the body had been dragged. Measurements between the boot impressions on the left and right feet showed the wearer had run towards the nearby road and then slowed down. The pattern on the composition or moulded sole was fairly common, but the Shoe and Allied Trade Retail Association were consulted over how the right boot came to have a peculiar pattern of wear on the sole. Experts suggested the killer may have operated machinery of some kind, stamping with his foot while using a mechanical digger or press.

'Josephine had been attacked in the middle of a football field,' Dick Holland revealed. 'It was a muddy pitch where the grass had been worn off and there were some superb footprints, so much so that we were able to show a differential wear between the left boot and right boot. The right one had more wear on the sole than the left.' They examined many types of boot with the same sole, issued to the army and air force, and to miners working for the National Coal Board. They tried comparing the soles of boots worn by lorry drivers, but found they didn't match. Close examination of a mark on the breast suggested the victim had been bitten by a man with a gap of an eighth of an inch in his upper front teeth. Harrison, murdered in Preston, also had a bite mark on her breast, caused by someone with a similar gap in their teeth.

In subsequent months, Professor Gee tried to discover what kind of instrument made the peculiar triangular-shaped wounds. He began collecting tradesmen's tools of all kinds from small engineering factories in dozens of towns across Yorkshire, as well as tools used by farmers and in slaughter-houses. The nearest implement to it he could find was an engineer's scraper, commonly available in big industrial cities, for scraping out the bores of piston engines. It was sharp, three-sided and quite often had a flat, wooden-faced handle. When he tried to replicate the wounds, it produced sharp, not rounded corners to triangular wounds. Gee had to anaesthetize a pot-bellied pig in his laboratory because this breed of animal, when its hair was shaven, has the closest match to the texture of human skin. The pig was stabbed while asleep to see if they could reproduce the type of marks left on Josephine Whitaker. Holland and Oldfield also began collecting tools and then took them to an abattoir to test different weapons on the carcasses of various beasts.

In contrast with other Ripper murders, there was a flood of information from the public: a thousand calls within a few days. Exactly a week after the murder police descended on Savile Park and its environs to check the movements of local people. As a result a witness who had been walking his dog near the moor shortly before midnight described a woman, almost certainly Jo, walking in the direction of Savile Park beside a man who had not shaved for four or five days and had stubble on his chin. This was crucial evidence because there was now the distinct possibility Jo spoke with her killer before he attacked her. Another witness came forward and described hearing an unusual noise coming from the moor. He likened it to 'a laugh or wail – the type of noise that makes your hair stand on end'. He looked across the moor to where Jo's body was later found and saw 'a figure or figures'. Thirty seconds later, he said, the noise was repeated. He looked again and a figure was still standing there. Thinking no more about it, the witness went home to bed.

The Ripper squad began searching for a dark-coloured Ford Escort car seen parked alongside the moor around midnight. A Sunbeam Rapier also seen in the vicinity was never traced. Neither was a driver who tried to pick up a woman in the town centre around 9 p.m. She had left work and was on her way to a bus stop to go home when she was propositioned and offered a lift by a man in a Ford Escort. When he saw her reaction he swiftly drove away. She provided details for a photofit which bore a remarkable similarity to the one provided by Marilyn Moore. When she saw this latest photofit, Moore was convinced the Ford Escort driver was the same man who attacked her. The woman in Halifax described him as aged about thirty, with mousy-coloured greasy collar-length hair curled at the ends. His face and jaw were square and he had a drooping 'Jason King' style moustache. However, George Oldfield seemed to downplay the value of this description when he stressed they were only seeking to eliminate the driver from their enquiries: 'Don't jump to the conclusion this is the Ripper,' he told a press conference at the local police station four days after Jo's body was found. He didn't want the public to concentrate on the photofit to the exclusion of any information they might have. There was nothing sinister in the police issuing the photofit of the Ford Escort driver, he said. 'We merely want to contact him to see if he saw anything on the night of the murder and to eliminate him from our inquiries.' (Much later it was discovered Peter Sutcliffe had had access to a Ford Escort car during this period. It belonged to his mother-in-law.)

Suddenly, and very dramatically, the Yorkshire Ripper investigation went off at a complete tangent and the attention of the inquiry turned its focus on a narrow corner of the north-east of England. Little more was said of the Ford Escort driver, and the press was asked to stop publishing photofits in case they confused the public. Instead, detectives started contacting companies in Yorkshire and the north-east, wanting to know of engineering firms whose employees had contact with the Sunderland area on very specific dates: 7 and 8 March 1978; 12 and 13 March 1978; and 22 and 23 March 1979. Equally suddenly, Oldfield provided reporters with the most detailed description of the killer so far: 'White, between thirty and fifty-five years of age, at least average to above average height, an artisan or manual worker, either skilled or semi-skilled, with engineering or mechanical connection, possibly a skilled machine tool fitter, electrical or maintenance engineer. He lives or works in West Yorkshire or in close proximity to that area and in all probability lives alone or with aged parents or a parent and he has some connections with the north-east.' He wanted local engineering firms connected with these industries to check their records to see if they had business with the north-east and whether any of their employees were in that area on the dates given.

On 25 February 1979, six weeks *before* Josephine Whitaker was murdered, the *Daily Mirror* tabloid newspaper in Manchester carried a Yorkshire Ripper case exclusive that was part fact and part speculation. It revealed Oldfield had received a number of letters claiming to be from the killer and signed 'Jack the Ripper'. This much was true. One of the letters had been analysed by a graphologist, who believed it might be from the actual murderer. Oldfield was quoted as saying the graphologist had confirmed 'many of the impressions we have about the man we are looking for'. A year earlier, shortly after the letters arrived, Oldfield had sent a copy to Northumbria police, wanting checks made in Sunderland to see if the hand-writing was that of a local crank. They were unable to help. Oldfield refused to publish the letters or extracts from them. They had been postmarked 'Sunderland'. Sent on white, lined paper, their contents were top secret and very few senior officers were given access to them. No traces of fingerprints were found on the letters or the envelopes they came in.

The two earliest, both undated, arrived in March 1978. The first was directed to Oldfield; the second to the editor of the *Daily Mirror*. The texts, including grammar and punctuation, are taken directly from the original letters. The first read:

Chief Constable George Oldfield
Central Police Station
Leeds
West Yorkshire

Dear Sir,
    I am sorry I cannot give you my name for obvious reasons I am the ripper. Ive been dubbed a maniac by the press but not by you You call me clever and I am. You and your mates havent a clue That photo in the paper gave me fits and that lot about killing myself no chance Ive got things to do, My purpose to rid the streets of them sluts. my one regret his that young lassie Macdonald did not know cause changed routine that nite, Up to number 8 now you say 7 but remember Preston 75, Get about you know, you were right I travel a bit You probably look for me in Sunderland don't bother I am not daft just posted letter there on one of my trips. Not a bad place compared with Chapeltown and Manningham and other places

Warn whores to keep of streets cause I feel it coming on again. Sorry about young lassie.

Yours respectfully
Jack the Ripper

Might write again later I am not sure last one really deserved it. Whores getting younger each time. Old slut next time I hope, Huddersfield never again too small close call last one.

The second letter read:

Chief Editor,
Daily Mirror Publishing Office (STD code 061)
Manchester
Lancs

Dear Sir,
    I have already written Chief Constable, Oldfield 'a man I respect' concerning the recent Ripper murders. I told him and I am telling you to warn them whores I'll strike again and soon when heat cools off. About the Mcdonald lassie I did nt know that she was decent and I am sorry I changed my routine that night, Up to number 8 now You say but remember Preston 75. Easy picken them up dont even have to try, you think theyre learn but they dont Most are young lassies, next time try older one I hope. Police haven't a clue yet and I dont leave any I am very clever and don't think of looking for any fingerprints cause there arent any and dont look for me up in Sunderland cause I

not stupid just passed through the place not bad place
compared with Chapeltown and manningham cant
walk the streets for them whore, Dont forget warn
them I feel it coming on again if I get the chance.
Sorry about lassie I didn't know

Yours respectfully
Jack the Ripper

Might write again after another ones' gone Maybe
Liverpool or even Manchester again, to hot here in
Yorkshire, Bye.
I have given advance warning so its yours and their's
fault.

Oldfield's interest was piqued by the reference to the murder
in Preston in 1975 and it was drawn to the attention of John
Domaille's homicide investigation team. Later, the threat to
kill 'an old slut', perhaps in Manchester or Liverpool, was
seen as possibly a prediction of the murder of Vera Millward.
Oldfield was utterly convinced no one had publicly linked the
murder of Joan Harrison to the Ripper series. However, there
was so little to go on that the letters were put to one side. The
arrival of a third letter before Josephine Whitaker was murdered caused a sensation inside the higher echelons of West
Yorkshire police. Addressed personally to 'Assistant Chief Constable Oldfield, at West Yorkshire CID in Leeds', it ratcheted
up the Ripper inquiry several notches. Dated 23 March 1979,
it was again postmarked 'Sunderland'. It said:

Dear Officer,
   Sorry I havn't written, about a year to be exact but

I havn't been up North for quite a while. I was'nt
kidding last time I wrote saying the whore would be
older this time and maybe I'd strike in Manchester for
a change. You should have took heed. That bit about
her being in hospital, funny the lady mentioned
something about being in the same hospital before I
stopped her whoring ways. The lady wont worry about
hospitals now will she I bet you are wondering how
come I hav'nt been to work for ages, well I would
have been if it hadnt been for your curserred coppers
I had the lady just where I wanted her and was about
to strike when one of your cursen police cars stopped
right outside the land, he must have been a dumn
copper cause he didn't say anything, he didnt know
how close he was to catching me. Tell you the truth I
thought I was collared, the lady said dont worry about
coppers, little did she know that bloody copper saved
her neck. That was last month, so I don't know know
when I will get back on the job but I know it won t
be Chapeltown too bloody hot there maybe Bradfords
Manningham. Might write again if up North.

Jack the Ripper.

PS Did you get letter I sent to Daily Mirror in
Manchester.

This extraordinary turn of events lit a fire under George
Oldfield for several reasons. The writer claimed Vera Millward
had had medical treatment at the hospital where she was murdered. For some unfathomable reason, both Oldfield and his
No. 2 on the Ripper squad, Dick Holland, became convinced

this knowledge could only have been divulged by the dead woman to her killer – ergo the letter writer. It wasn't until some time later that Oldfield learned from Jack Ridgway himself that both he and the dead woman's common-law husband had informed the press in Manchester that Vera Millward had been treated for an illness in a local hospital and had an operation there. Joan Harrison was now deemed by West Yorkshire police to be a Ripper victim, but the writer had claimed the Preston murder as his own work well before this news was made public. Again, both Oldfield and Holland were completely ignorant of certain crucial facts. Newspapers in Leeds had earlier publicized a possible link with the Preston murder at the time when Irene Richardson was killed in Roundhay Park in February 1977, and Wilf Brooks of Lancashire CID had a long discussion with Jim Hobson. Yet apparently no one told Oldfield this two years later. Holland had obtained from Lancashire CID the scenes of crime photographs of the Harrison murder, including the autopsy pictures. Both he and Oldfield believed the head injuries were probably caused by a hammer. The photographs showed the skull injuries were similar to the semicircular lacerations that featured in most Ripper attacks. Yet Wilf Brooks thought she had been hit with a shoe heel. Also, the photos showed one of Harrison's boots placed on top of her legs, just as the Ripper had done with Richardson.

Following Josephine Whitaker's murder, Oldfield had in his possession two devastating new clues which he was certain tied the 'Jack the Ripper' letters to the Harrison murder. The gum on the flap of the envelope containing the third letter had been analysed by Home Office forensic scientists at Wetherby. Traces of saliva showed it had been licked by a man who was blood group B, the same grouping as the man who had sex with Joan Harrison before he killed her. Moreover, the autopsy on Joan

Harrison revealed she had been bitten on the breast by a man with a gap in his front teeth. So had Josephine Whitaker.

Forensic analysis had yielded extraordinary clues. B blood group antibodies were a common feature, but since group B secretors make up only 6 per cent of the population, George Oldfield was certain it was no coincidence. The chances of the letter writer being the same blood group as the man who actually murdered Harrison were too close to be ignored. Oldfield also believed the writer had made a number of predictions, such as prophesying Millward's murder in Manchester. In his third letter the writer indicated he would strike again soon. Twelve days later, Josephine Whitaker was killed. It added up to only one possible conclusion in Oldfield's mind: the letters were from the Yorkshire Ripper himself.

He never seriously considered an elaborate hoax or the possibility that the *Daily Mirror* article, by revealing the Ripper had written directly to Oldfield, had given credence to the police chief's acceptance of the first two letters as *genuine*, so prompting the author to write again. The forensic evidence and the content persuaded Oldfield they were from the killer. By early May 1979 he was claiming they were close to catching the Ripper. He went after the murderer for all he was worth. He put to one side the fact that he was constantly tired, that climbing the stairs at work left him out of breath; that he had a constant hacking dry cough. He was getting by on cough mixture and whisky. His renewed energy came from his belief that after three years he was getting closer to the killer.

The tracking inquiry had got nowhere; the cross-area sightings operation had not yet identified the killer; the five-pound note inquiry had fizzled out. Now, though, for the first time, the Ripper squad had some positive evidence. The task was straightforward: find the letter writer and they would find the bastard they were looking for. Throwing a detective's normal caution aside, Oldfield allowed himself to believe the killer had made an arrogant mistake in sending a letter. The Ripper was taunting him. He had turned it into a personal contest between the hunter and the hunted, between the forces of good and the force of evil. For the first time Oldfield allowed himself a degree of optimism. He had the forensic clues from Whitaker up his sleeve: a bite mark, boot prints and evidence of an engineering connection. The killer had come unstuck because now police had his handwriting. Detectives on the outside inquiry teams were provided with specimen texts based on the content of the letters, which the men they were interviewing were asked to copy out in their own handwriting. These were analysed by forensic experts. Soon, with luck, the Ripper would be apprehended. Moreover, anyone whose handwriting was different could be eliminated from the inquiry.

Northumbria police however were taken somewhat by surprise by Oldfield's sudden assertion that the Yorkshire Ripper had a definite connection with the Sunderland area. No one had consulted them for more than a year. Two Sunderland-based detectives travelled quickly to West Yorkshire to get more information. Detective Superintendent Peter Docherty, the Sunderland CID chief, and Detective Inspector David Zackrisson were briefed on the murders and then the letters. Oldfield stressed that in all probability they were the work of the Ripper, because only he could have had the necessary information they contained. He outlined the circular flow of evidence linking the letters via the B secretor blood grouping to Harrison and back to Whitaker via the bite marks on their breasts, as well as some of the predictions.

Five Sunderland officers were tasked with checking local firms for employees, based in Yorkshire, who were in the north-east when the letters were posted. For each one traced, a hand-writing sample was obtained and sent to Leeds for comparison with the 'Ripper' letters. Eighteen large local firms volunteered information. By early May the Sunderland team had processed nearly two hundred employees, taking alibi statements from a third of them. The inquiry was turning out to be much bigger than Docherty imagined. Checks were made with the North-Eastern Criminal Record Office and the Northumbria vice squad. Dick Holland visited Sunderland and briefed detectives, using graphic colour slides of the grizzly details of the murders. Letters posted within the city were handled and franked at one of two local sorting offices. Each processed alternate collections of mail from the local postal area and it was impossible to isolate where the letters had actually been posted.

Neither Docherty nor Zackrisson was local to Sunderland, a shipbuilding town at that time, standing beside the River Wear. Both were Geordies, born at Hebburn on Tyneside. As a youngster in the war, Docherty had been bombed out of his home. Zackrisson, the younger of the two, had been brought up by his mother and grandfather, an Anglican vicar. His father was a Swedish seaman. Both detectives had different careers marked out for them after leaving school. Docherty became a professional footballer. Zackrisson in the 1960s trained as a fingerprint officer and worked at Scotland Yard in London. Both later joined the Newcastle City police force. When Zackrisson was a sergeant with four children, his pay was so low he and his wife, Wendy, could have claimed supplementary benefit. Pride dictated that his family manage as best they could. On promotion to detective inspector, he was posted to Sunderland in 1977. He continued living with his family in Blyth, commuting thirty miles each way to work.

There was a rivalry of sorts between Sunderland and

Newcastle. Sunderland had been County Durham's largest town, an urbanized area of 220,000 people where more council homes had been built per head of population than any other place in Britain. By the time Zackrisson arrived there, his boss Peter Docherty had a deserved reputation as a good detective with a steely courage, earned during his footballing days. He was not afraid to tackle violent criminals. He was seen as fair and commanded huge respect. His nickname among junior officers was 'Papa Doc'. Softly spoken, Docherty could be volatile when riled. His officers had to prove their worth. He wasn't beyond listening outside an interview room to see how one of his detectives handled the interrogation of an awkward criminal. Likewise Zackrisson knew, as a new detective inspector, that he had to earn the respect of colleagues when he first arrived in Sunderland.

'There were a lot of older police officers and it took some time to win their confidence,' he said. 'There had been a jewellers' burgled and they couldn't get a cough. The thieves had crawled through a derelict property and into the jewellers by opening a window. I said: "Are there any fingerprints?" DIs don't usually get involved in the run-of-the-mill stuff, although in this case there was £3,000 of property taken. "Yes," they said. I saw one of them was a "tented arch" fingerprint, extremely rare. There were three lads downstairs locked up in the cells, and as it turned out two had nothing to do with it. I'd only been at Sunderland a month, so I went down, had a look at their hands and then said to the third lad: "You're the guy who climbed through the window." He huffed and puffed. "Look, that's your fingerprint, your ring finger." He was charged and of course he coughed it. Detectives like to see that you can do the job. Some of them think the higher up you get the less you know about policing.'

Zackrisson learned a lot from Docherty about dealing with people. He remembered how they were called out one Cup Final day to the mysterious deaths of a man and his wife. Two sons in their thirties had had to break into the new council house their parents recently moved into. They found their mother in the kitchen and their father in an upstairs bedroom. The scene was horrifying – a bloodbath upstairs and downstairs. The sons were in a state of shock and believed both parents had been murdered. But neighbours had heard the parents quarrelling and there was no sign of forced entry. Docherty and Zackrisson determined that the father had lost his temper because of problems settling into the new council house. He killed his wife and then, as the pathologist explained to them, died an agonizing death himself. A semicircular series of blood spots showed how he had stabbed at himself in the throat. It took him twenty-four hours to die.

'It was one of the most appalling things that could happen, an awful situation because the sons had lost their mum and dad and were convinced a third party was responsible,' Zackrisson recalled. 'We had done our homework and it was obvious there was no third party, plus forensic evidence tied the two together.' Docherty had turned to his younger colleague and said: 'This is a bloody awful thing. There is only one way we can do this and that is to come straight out with it. Leave it with me.' He put the sons at ease, Zackrisson noted. 'He was a student of human nature. At the correct time and in very measured tones, he said to them: "There is something I've got to tell you and when I say it hurts me to say so, please believe me, it does. All I can say is this is how it occurred. Your mum and dad had a quarrel. Your dad, I'm quite sure he never intended it, lashed out and he's been so overtaken by remorse because he loved your mother, he's killed himself."

'I remember one of the sons couldn't take it in. I sat there thinking Docherty was a guy with real feeling for other people. He took that task of telling the sons on himself. It's bad enough for someone to say your nearest and dearest has died, but to explain what had happened in that house was more difficult.

'Peter Docherty mixed easily and his ethical stance matched mine. He was a stickler when it came to expenses. We are all entitled to expenses. There's a nickname in the police service: "The Destroyer". He is the one always after a sub. What I remember from Peter Docherty is that technically he could go out and buy a pie and claim whatever – £2.50. He wouldn't claim for it. I knew I had to prove my mettle. It's a fairly shallow human being or manager who just opens his arms to anyone and says, "You're one of my guys because we both come from Newcastle City, hail fellow and well met." With Peter Docherty, once he was confident you had the ability, you would want to give him one hundred per cent and he would give one hundred per cent in return. You don't want to let anybody down. He was honest and direct.'

It would be several months before the Sunderland detectives could express their true feelings to their own Northumbria police bosses about the way West Yorkshire were handling the Ripper inquiry. During this time Docherty and Zackrisson felt certain that Oldfield in Leeds must have something else up his sleeve to be going so firm with the Sunderland connection. They were not shown the three letters in their complete form, only sections, so they imagined, like all murder squad detectives, that Oldfield was keeping something back, some rock-solid clue which had convinced him they were about to nail a man who had murdered eleven women and tried to kill four more. They were only pleased they didn't have this madman running around on their patch. But no one was prepared for what happened next.

Early one morning in mid-June 1979, Sergeant Megan Winterburn was at her desk in the Millgarth incident room, in Leeds. Oldfield came in and shouted across to her from the doorway: 'Meg, can you come over here?' She went across to the door where he was standing. Oldfield said: 'I want you in my room now, please.' For Oldfield to say 'please' suggested something was amiss. Usually he would be quite gruff, not even using a junior officer's name. He would simply point at them and say: 'You – now – my office.' But he had actually said 'please' so Winterburn knew something significant had happened. She followed him down the corridor to the room he shared with Dick Holland. Both Jim Hobson and Holland were in the small office, which now seemed rather crowded. A tape recorder stood on top of a desk. The ACC said to her: 'I just want you to listen to this.' 'Mr Oldfield pressed the switch on the top of the tape recorder,' said Winterburn, 'and there was a tape being played, reportedly from the Ripper. The atmosphere in the room was most peculiar.' The voice, in a soft Geordie accent, said:

> I'm Jack. I see you are still having no luck catching
> me. I have the greatest respect for you, George, but
> Lord, you are no nearer to catching me now than four
> years ago when I started. I reckon your boys are
> letting you down, George. Ya can't be much good, can
> ya? The only time they came near catching me was a
> few months back in Chapeltown when I was
> disturbed. Even then it was a uniform copper, not a
> detective.

I warned you in March that I'd strike again, sorry it wasn't Bradford, I did promise you that but I couldn't get there. I'm not sure when I will strike again but it will definitely be some time this year, maybe September or October, even soon if I get the chance. I'm not sure where. Maybe Manchester, I like there, there's plenty of them knocking about. They never learn, do they, George? I bet you've warned them, but they never listen. At the rate I'm going I should be in the book of records, I think it's eleven up to now, isn't it? Well, I'll keep on going for quite a while yet. I can't see myself being nicked just yet. Even if you do get near, I'll probably top myself first.

Well it's been nice chatting to you, George. Yours, Jack the Ripper.

No good looking for fingerprints, you should know by now it's clean as a whistle. See you soon. 'Bye.

Hope you like the catchy tune at the end. Ha. Ha!

Oldfield wanted the tape transcribing but didn't want to give it to one of the civilian typists. He wanted a police officer to produce a transcription. Megan Winterburn went into a separate room on the same floor. Using headphones, she took shorthand notes from the tape and played it back to herself, reading from her shorthand notes.

'There was this tape that had come from the Ripper. I had to play it over and over again to be able to write the shorthand and then to transcribe it,' said Megan Winterburn. 'My first reaction was: "This man knows what happened. It's the Ripper." The more I listened the more sinister it became, it made the hairs stand up on the back of my neck. It was horrible, a real low point for me. I sat there typing it up on an old manual typewriter. I felt sick to the pit of my stomach. Just the thought that it might actually be this man's voice, instead of being elated, made my stomach churn. I realized the significance of the tape, that it would start up a whole new line of inquiry. There would have to be a forensic analysis done on the tape and the envelope it came in, so I knew there was going to be a lot of extra work. I automatically knew that the incident room staff were going to be back to working long hours and that days off would be cancelled.'

The recording had several long gaps – nine silences of three seconds or more, four of which were six seconds long and one of thirteen. The obvious question for Oldfield, Holland and Hobson was whether it was genuine. The handwriting on the plain white envelope seemed similar to the earlier letters. This one was addressed to 'ASST. CHIEF CONSTABLE OLD-FIELD'. A signature 'Jack the Ripper' had been written on the underside flap of the envelope, which bore a ninepenny postage stamp issued for the Christmas season in 1978. There was only part of a postmark, one edge of a franking stamp showing fragmentary lettering. Scientists at the Wetherby laboratory said the lettering was consistent with it having been produced by a Sunderland franking stamp. The gum on the undersurface of the flap contained saliva from a blood group B secretor. This was the clincher for Oldfield. Handwriting experts also confirmed the sender of the tape was the same person as the letter writer.

Holland from the start believed the tape and letters were genuine: 'I must have played it twenty times to analyse all the information the tape contained. I thought the Ripper was taunting us for not having caught him – the actions of a psychopath in that he enjoys the chase and taunting the investigators. The voice was so distinctive we felt sure that we were going to get him.'

The tape itself had no manufacturer's label, but the scientists found faint scratch marks on the outer plastic surface of the cassette which indicated the label had been scraped off. The cassette had a small hole in one edge and on the inside of this hole were more faint scratch marks. 'This hole and the accompanying scratch marks, coupled with the fact that the two halves of the cassette have been stuck together, indicate that at some time the tape cassette has been opened and then reassembled,' the Wetherby lab report noted. A fragment of light-brown human hair and some fibres were found inside the cassette. Later analysis showed the tape had been stopped and started on many occasions. There was even a chance it had been produced on more than one tape recorder. At the end was a tune from a record called 'Thank you for being a friend', recorded by Andrew Gold in 1977. It was clearly aimed at Oldfield.

For Oldfield and the West Yorkshire force this seemed a most extraordinary breakthrough. The only Sunderland connection until now had been the letters posted there. Now Oldfield believed the killer originated from the north-east, and that they actually knew what he sounded like. The crucial question was whether to make the tape public. A conference of the most senior officers involved in the investigation, including those from Manchester, Lancashire and Sunderland, took place on 20 June at Halifax. Oldfield played them the tape with the pauses edited out. Docherty confirmed the voice was clearly from the Sunderland area. The consensus was that they would go public first with the tape, then with the handwriting, in the hope an arrest would quickly follow. They prepared for a huge public response.

In Sunderland, sixty-four additional officers were drafted in. Ten West Yorkshire detectives arrived for a prolonged stay and were put up at a hotel in Roker. More phone lines were installed and a special incident room set up. The all-important press conference at which the voice of the Yorkshire Ripper would be revealed to the world was scheduled for 2 p.m., Tuesday, 26 June 1979. The venue was the detective training school at Bishopgarth in Wakefield, next to the force headquarters. A full twenty-four hours before the press conference, the local evening paper in Leeds blew the story of the tape wide open. Someone at a very high level had deliberately leaked its contents to the paper's crime correspondent. Oldfield, beside himself with anger, blew a fuse. He believed the leak came from a senior Leeds detective and took the matter up with the chief constable. Nothing happened. A great deal of work had been done preparing for the press conference, and some of it now had to be redone. Oldfield had had reservations about playing the full tape, though the chief constable believed the public had to hear it. Both men eagerly anticipated the case being finally solved.

More than fifty journalists turned up after the leaking of the tape caused widespread interest. Television crews and photographers joined the throng at the press conference. The senior officers stood before a battery of film and still cameras. Oldfield, wearing a striped light-grey two-piece, held his spectacles in his hand, fiddling with them as he addressed the audience. He had aged several years within the space of only a few months. He was flanked on one side by Wilf Brookes from Lancashire CID. On the other was Brian Johnson, the far younger ACC (operations) from Northumbria, who had travelled down to Wakefield with Docherty and Zackrisson. Jack Ridgway sat passively at the back, taking stock of the surroundings but saying very little. Dick Holland stood beside him.

There was a brief moment of confusion when the hushed audience got ready to listen to the vital tape through a loud-speaker. Oldfield tried to start the tape recorder but had difficulty finding the on-switch. The senior detective in charge of the biggest manhunt in British criminal history didn't know how to work a tape recorder. Holland leaned forward to do it for him. Sound recordists drew closer to pick up the voice clearly. Cameras continued to flash and motor drives whirred. The audience sat in silence, listening to the voice mocking Oldfield, announcing that he was the Yorkshire Ripper and that he would rather commit suicide than be captured. In the annals of the history of crime it was truly an electric moment. After the brief extract of the song at the end, the tape recorder was stopped. There was a brief pause. Oldfield quietly announced they now had the break they had been looking for. They would keep going until they caught the killer.

REPORTER: This is the break you have been looking for, why do you say that?

OLDFIELD: Before we know we have been looking for *a man*. There are literally millions and we didn't know where he came from. But now that we can localize the area the field is narrowed appreciably as I am sure you must agree.

REPORTER: Are you fairly convinced he comes from Sunderland; is there anything significant about the times they were sent perhaps, the month?

OLDFIELD: I think there could well be some significance in this, it could be perhaps that he went up in March last year or March this year for some anniversary or something like that.

REPORTER: What has been said in the letters, you've talked about the tape, what about the letters?

Amid the misery caused by the Yorkshire Ripper murders, two happy events. In Bradford Det. Con. Andrew Laptew (left) celebrated his marriage to his local bride, Sheila; and in Huddersfield Det. Supt. Dick Holland (below) married the love of his life, Sylvia.

Dear Officer.   March 23rd 79

    Sorry I haven't written, about a year to be
exsalt, but I haven't been up North for quite a while.
I was'nt kidding last time I wrote saying the whore
would be older this time and maybe I'd strike in
Manchester for a change, you should have took heed.
That bit about her being in hospital, funny the
lady mentioned something about being in the same
hospital before I stopped her whoring way. The lady
wont worry about hospitals now will she. I bet
you are wondering how come I haven't been to work
for ages, well I would have been if it had'nt been
for your cursed coppers I had the lady just
where I wanted her and was about to strike
when one of your cursing police cars stopped
right outside the lane, he must have been a
dumb copper cause he did'nt say anything, he
did'nt know how close he was to catching me. Tell
you the truth I thought I was collared, the lady
said don't worry about the coppers, little did she
know that bloody copper saved her neck. That
was last month, so I don't know when I will
get back on the job but I know it wont be
Chapeltown too bloody hot there maybe
Bradford, Manningham. Might write again
if up North.
        Jack the Ripper
P.S Did you get letter I sent to Daily Mirror
in Manchester.

The infamous third 'hoax' letter sent to George Oldfield.

ABOVE: 'The Moor' at Halifax, April 1979, scene of the murder of 19-year-old Josephine Whitaker (inset).

BELOW: George Oldfield in June 1979 plays to a crowded press conference the tape of the Sunderland man claiming to be the Yorkshire Ripper. Beside him are (far right) Det. Ch. Supt. Jack Ridgway of Manchester CID; and Det. Supt. Dick Holland.

The final two pictures (bottom right) in this collection are police 'mug' shots of Peter Sutcliffe, taken after his arrest for 'going equipped for theft' in 1969, and twelve years later in 1981 when he was charged with

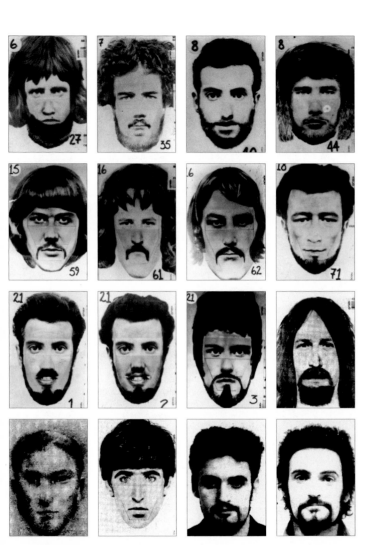

multiple murders. The photofit images are
based on descriptions by witnesses and
survivors of a series of attacks on women
in West Yorkshire from 1972 to 1980.

ABOVE: Det. Ch. Supt. Jim Hobson in the Yorkshire Ripper incident room at Leeds. The bank of index card boxes can be seen behind him.

BELOW: Point of departure, autumn 1978; George Oldfield (centre) presents Det. Ch. Supt. John Domaille with a leaving present on behalf of his Yorkshire Ripper Squad colleagues. Domaille had been appointed head of the Detective Training School in Wakefield.

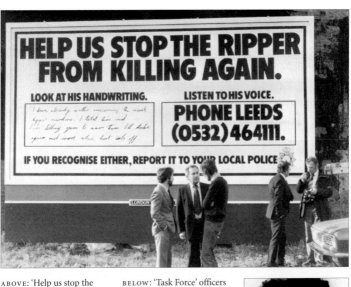

ABOVE: 'Help us stop the Ripper' roadside hoarding – part of a massive advertising campaign launched in the autumn of 1979 by West Yorkshire police.

BELOW: 'Task Force' officers in September 1979 conduct a fingertip search in Bradford, at the location of the murder of university student, Barbara Leach (inset).

Professor David Gee (front) of Leeds University, with his fellow pathologist
Dr Michael Green (left) and Det. Ch. Supt. Jim Hobson.

forces before the Second World War. The calls rapidly multiplied, each one having to be logged and passed up the chain
of command for someone to decide whether the information
was worth acting on. Officers in Yorkshire and Wearside began
touring local pubs, offices, factories and social clubs playing
the tape, hoping someone would come forward to say: 'I know
that voice.' Plenty did, and all of these required follow-up
checks by hard-pressed officers.

The next morning several newspapers noted how the man
on the tape had crudely imitated his nineteenth-century
counterpart in boasting the police would not catch him. The
Yorkshire Post went further, referring to the 'uncanny similarity'
between the taped message and a letter said to have been
written in September 1888 by the original Jack the Ripper to
the Commissioner of Police in London:

Dear Boss,

I keep on hearing the police have caught me, but
they won't fix me just yet.

I have laughed when they look so clever and talk
about being on the right track. The joke about the
leather apron gives me real fits.

I am down on whores and I shan't quit ripping
them till I do get buckled. Grand work the last job
was.

I gave the lady no time to squeal. How can they
catch me now?

I love my work and want to start again. You will
soon hear of me and my funny little games.

Good luck.

Yours truly

Jack the Ripper.

Oldfield also released brief extracts from the letter sent to him in March 1979, hoping someone would recognize the handwriting, perhaps a teacher or fellow employee. Kept from the public were the passages which bore an extraordinary similarity to the phraseology used by the nineteenth-century Ripper. In Sunderland, Detective Inspector David Zackrisson belatedly received copies of all three letters written to Oldfield and the *Daily Mirror*. He quickly sent a detective to the local library to obtain a copy of the original Jack the Ripper letter. The resemblance was obvious. The original Ripper said he was *'down on whores'*; his modern counterpart wrote *'my purpose is to rid the streets of them sluts'*. *'The joke about leather apron gave me real fits,'* said the nineteenth-century writer; *'The photo in the paper gave me fits,'* said the letter posted in Sunderland on 8 March 1978. Jack the Ripper wrote in 1888: *'It's no use for you to look for me in London because I'm not there'*; and in the letter of 13 March 1978, its author mimicked: *'Don't look for me up there in Sunderland 'cause I not stupid, just passing through.'* Finally the 1888 letter proclaimed: *'I want to get to work right away if I get a chance'*; while the voice on the tape recording said: *'I will strike again . . . if I get the chance.'*

These similarities nagged away at Zackrisson as he and Docherty supervised the Sunderland end of the inquiry. The tape was constantly played throughout the local area – in prisons at Durham and Acklington, at local Social Security and probation offices, at banks and DHSS offices; to coal miners in pits on South Tyneside and County Durham; at job centres, mental hospitals, as well as large local factories and offices. More than sixty working men's clubs were visited to see if anyone recognized the voice. Extracts from the letters were reproduced and posters printed: 'DO YOU RECOGNIZE THIS HAND-WRITING?'. A separate team of fifteen officers with special training in recognizing handwriting screened more than 100,000 written applications for local council houses and 7,500 letters from men on probation. Those that were suspect were sent for expert handwriting analysis. Officers from the No. 2 Regional Crime Squad were placed in the main postal sorting offices in Sunderland. Every day they examined envelopes to find any follow-up 'Ripper' letter before it left the city, to determine more accurately where it had been posted. Over the next eighteen months they checked 15 million letters. Oldfield was particularly interested in tracking down people who had borrowed books about Jack the Ripper. He accepted the recent author had been influenced by the 1888 killer's letter, but did not let it dissuade him the voice on the tape was authentic. Libraries in Sunderland checked on borrowers who had taken the books about the original Ripper murders. The central library had a computerized record dating back twelve months, which made the task simple, but other libraries in the area still used the old-fashioned card system, which left no record of who had borrowed the books previously. A few men were seen and eliminated. In what eventually cost the Northumbria force more than £600,000 (at 1980 prices), Sunderland police left no stone unturned in their search for the man who sent the letters and the tape.

In eliminating suspects they took a radically different approach. Docherty and Zackrisson seriously doubted the letter writer was the Yorkshire Ripper and consequently refused to eliminate people from the inquiry on the basis of alibis for the murders. The more certain Oldfield became that the voice on the tape was the killer, the less happy was his more junior colleague in Sunderland. Zackrisson became increasingly perturbed by the writer's lack of originality. If he was so influenced by the original Ripper, he asked himself, what were the possibilities he was equally influenced by what he read in newspapers about the Yorkshire Ripper case? Zackrisson ordered a check of all available local, national and regional newspaper cuttings to see if they could determine how the letter writer got his information.

Within six weeks of the tape being made public, the Sunderland incident room had actioned 2,200 separate tasks following more than 2,000 phone calls from the public. They had committed themselves to a massive effort on behalf of a force a hundred miles away. Disturbingly, though, they were being asked to eliminate suspects in a murder case whose handwriting and voice were different from the letters and tape. Docherty and Zackrisson felt this was a highly dangerous practice. If the killer was not the letter writer, he would get away. Oldfield had pressed his Sunderland colleagues to eliminate people, if possible, without *any* direct approach to a suspect. West Yorkshire officers based in Sunderland were already eliminating suspects on the basis of handwriting obtained from work record sheets which showed the suspect was on a night shift on the night of a particular murder. But it meant the letter writer could easily slip through the net if he wasn't the killer. Officers from Leeds were also eliminating men on the basis of handwriting samples obtained from their employers or government agencies, even though there was no guarantee the handwriting had been definitely written by the suspect. Docherty and Zackrisson well knew some men got their wives or mothers to fill in forms and documents for them. They insisted individual suspects had to be checked personally if the job was to be done thoroughly, otherwise the killer or the letter writer could slip through the net and all their work would be for nothing.

Their boss, Brian Johnson, telephoned Oldfield, wanting

some assurances about the West Yorkshire policy on interrogating suspects. The gist of Oldfield's reply was as follows: 'This is my policy. I do not wish to embarrass or cause distress to innocent people. Only in cases where it is absolutely necessary should individuals named in "actions" be seen.' If they were definite suspects, they could be confronted.

In terms of protocol and inter-force diplomacy, Northumbria police, working on behalf of their colleagues in West Yorkshire, felt obliged to continue with Oldfield's policy. They did so with one subtle difference. Whereas West Yorkshire continued with the line: 'This is the handwriting and voice of the Yorkshire Ripper,' the police in Sunderland were only looking for the letter writer. If he turned out to be the so-called Yorkshire Ripper, then that would be a bonus. By contrast the West Yorkshire approach meant that any suspect with a different accent or writing couldn't possibly be the killer and consequently should be completely eliminated from the inquiry.

14

Bad Feelings

At the end of July 1979, the teams of Ripper squad detectives switched to Halifax earlier to work on the Whitaker murder began clearing the 'actions' piling up in shoeboxes at the centralized incident room in Leeds. Since 23 February an 'action' had been outstanding for a Mr Peter Sutcliffe of Garden Lane, Heaton, to be interviewed because his black Sunbeam Rapier car had been printed out on the 'punter's index' as a 'triple-area sighting' – spotted cruising for prostitutes in the red-light areas of Bradford, Leeds and Manchester. Five months went by before two West Yorkshire detectives turned up at his door. The date was 29 July 1979, the fifth occasion he would be questioned about the Ripper case.

Andrew Laptew, by now aged twenty-nine, believed he was about to make yet another routine call. The investigation seemed to be going on for ever. As a uniformed officer on the Western Area task force, he had worked on all the early murders – grubbing on his hands and knees in all kinds of weather conducting fingertip searches; making house-to-house inquiries; carrying out checks on vehicles and alibis. Laptew and twenty of his colleagues had had their own wellington boots checked because of a footprint found at the Jackson crime scene. The forensic team had to eliminate all police bootprints.

'We were completely dedicated,' Laptew recalled not long after he retired from the police force after thirty years' service. 'When you worked on a murder there was a buzz of excitement. If there was a positive result at the end, it was a real boost. The wonder of the job for us, the magic if you like, was how the murder was detected. You went to work, did your job, and suddenly someone was charged. Then you learned how it had come about. There was a fascination for many of us because it was only by checking and rechecking that inconsistencies emerge and that's the way killers are caught.' Laptew was then still living at home in Bradford with his Italian-born mother, but was engaged to be married in six weeks' time to Sheila Leadbeater, an attractive farmer's daughter from Wyke. She was twenty-one and worked in the typing pool at Bradford police headquarters, which was where they met. Laptew had just joined the CID full time. Like most of his colleagues, aware of just how vulnerable all women were in Yorkshire, he warned Sheila to take special care. 'Yorkshire was a place of fear for all women,' he said, 'because this madman was on the prowl. It was like a gothic cloud was hanging over their heads.'

For the Sutcliffe interview he was teamed with another detective constable, Graham Greenwood, who as a youngster used to work on Sheila's father's farm. The two officers went down to the farm to visit her for lunch before driving off to Garden Lane in Bradford, where Mr and Mrs Sutcliffe lived. Sutcliffe's name had resurfaced because his car had been seen in Manningham thirty-six times, in Leeds twice and once in Manchester. Neither detective knew Sutcliffe had been questioned four times previously by their colleagues, nor that he worked for a firm involved in the five-pound note inquiry. Nor did they know the papers relating to the previous interviews were out of 'the system', either waiting to be filed, being followed up or held pending additional information before going back to the incident room.

Laptew and Greenwood had to obtain information about Sutcliffe's journeys in the red-light areas and his alibis for the murders. What clues they had about the Ripper came from briefings by the higher-ups and a confidential 'Police Reports' intelligence document which described the killer as being white, aged between thirty and forty-five and born in the Sunderland area: 'He is literate and of reasonable intelligence. It is known that in the past he has worn wellington boots and industrial protective or army-type boots, both of which were size seven. There are defects in his upper teeth which are natural, not false, and which can be identified. His blood group is B and he is a known secretor. He is known to have been in possession of a motor vehicle.'

These follow-up inquiries were a grind. The officers felt they had very little autonomy as they searched for a needle in the haystack. They did the work, handed it in, then got on with the next task. If the higher-ups wanted to pursue anything, they were called back for another inquiry. Going into the incident room to gather further information became a chore for someone like Laptew. Among the more junior officers, the workers in the incident room were known as the 'Tufty Club' because they were always the same old faces.

'You went into the incident room and people were buzzing about everywhere trying to sort things out and it was difficult to get their attention. You wanted information but were greeted with sighs and moans and the rest of it. Frankly I felt they should have been more cooperative, more willing to assist us because we were the ones going out to do the job.' Laptew was unaware of the tremendous pressures facing incident room staff. There were changeovers of personnel. Senior officers elsewhere in West Yorkshire frequently seconded to the incident room people they personally regarded as their least motivated officers. Good experienced staff in the incident room were the ones who were ordinarily highly motivated.

The Sutcliffe interview came out of the blue. Laptew and Greenwood happened to be the next in line. The 'action' was taken from its box and that was their job for the day. They knew nothing about the man other than a few details: 'P. W. Sutcliffe, lorry driver, triple-area sighting' – all on one sheet of paper. Laptew had done hundreds of these interviews and this was just one more.

They stopped their unmarked police car outside the Sutcliffes' detached house, which stood on raised ground overlooking Garden Lane. A sloping driveway up the right-hand side led past the kitchen door to a garage. The front of the house had bay windows, upstairs and downstairs. On a nearby playing field Laptew had played rugby as a schoolboy. He remembered having been in the area before as they knocked at the front door. A few moments later Sutcliffe appeared, still adjusting his clothes, as if he had come down from upstairs. It was a Saturday afternoon and he was wearing a golf shirt and trousers. He took them into the front lounge, where everything appeared clean and tidy. There were plastic covers on the furniture, the carpet was well hoovered, there was a place for everything and everything in its place. Soon he was joined by his wife, a neat, thin-looking woman with dark hair. Laptew took notes as both officers asked questions. They had a set routine of things to record, like his full name, date of birth, what he did for a living, who he worked for. This was how they learned Sutcliffe was employed by Clark's – one of the firms that featured in the five-pound note inquiry. Laptew made a mental note.

As he looked at the man, several features slowly began to register in Laptew's mind. His facial appearance was similar to the 'Jason King' photofit provided by Marilyn Moore. There was also a gap in the front teeth. He had a beard trimmed close to the contours of his face, and a very obvious drooping moustache. Laptew felt he was maybe over-reacting. Sutcliffe was a local lad, born in Bingley. He had a softly spoken Bradford accent, its pitch slightly raised. He was no Geordie, that was certain. Then Laptew remembered the ransom demand tape in the Black Panther case. They got that wrong. The wife? She appeared slightly strange, he thought.

The longer the detectives were in the house, the more of an 'odd couple' Sonia and Peter Sutcliffe appeared – she the teacher, he the lorry driver. An odd mix, Laptew felt. 'Peter Sutcliffe was a very quiet man who was very difficult to communicate with,' he said. 'It was like drawing teeth talking to him because he would take so much time over his answers. We were trying to get on to the relevant questions, especially while his wife was out of the room. If he was terrified inside, he never showed it. We were reasonable judges of body language and we can tell whether someone is being evasive because they won't look you in the eye, or they turn away or the old vein in the neck starts throbbing. There was nothing like this there, just a slow deliberation in answering questions.'

They tried a well-worn joke to break the ice: 'Now's the time to get rid of your husband if you want to,' Laptew said to Mrs Sutcliffe. Normally it got a laugh, but from Mrs Sutcliffe? Nothing. From her husband? Nothing. Not even a black look. They appeared oblivious to the attempt at humour. One of the detectives asked for a glass of water and Mrs Sutcliffe went into the kitchen, suggesting she make tea. Laptew used her absence to ask Mr Sutcliffe if he ever went with prostitutes, adding that they could arrange a private interview with him with his wife not present. He denied paying for sex. 'I don't have anything to do with them,' he said firmly. He explained his frequent journeys through Bradford. They realized from the location of his lorry yard that he could have been going to and from work when he was sighted in Manningham, or into the city centre with his wife. (The officers did not have the actual time of day he had been seen in the red-light area.) He said he had taken his wife to a nightclub in Leeds and driven down the Chapeltown Road, but firmly denied the visit to Manchester. Under strict instructions not to divulge the covert surveillance operation, neither Laptew nor Greenwood challenged Sutcliffe, though there could be little doubt about the Manchester sighting. He couldn't account for his movements on the dates when the murders took place, but said that when he did go out it was always with his wife.

When Sonia Sutcliffe returned with a pot of tea, they made a point of asking her husband again whether he visited prostitutes, and then asked for a statement confirming his reply. Mrs Sutcliffe also made a statement, alibiing her husband for several dates. Sutcliffe did not know his blood group but was prepared to offer a sample for analysis. In separate statements the couple mentioned their visit to Leeds but could not recall going to Manchester. The interview had taken almost two hours. The Sutcliffes appeared calm, quietly answering questions without apparent difficulty or embarrassment, but volunteering no additional information. The officers obtained a letter Sutcliffe had written to his wife, to compare his handwriting. They searched his car and the garage, but found nothing to connect him with the crimes. Later they visited Clark's, where Sutcliffe was described as a model worker. His timesheets were obtained with further examples of his handwriting.

Laptew learned Sutcliffe had visited Cole's Cranes in Sunderland, driving his lorry, although from checks he and Greenwood made, he had not been there when the letters and tape were posted. Laptew wrote down a detailed description of the man, his quiet Bradford accent, the colour and style of his hair, details of his beard and moustache and the fact that he took size eight and a half shoes and wore soft crepe-soled boots. By now Sutcliffe had already sold his Sunbeam Rapier and owned a Rover 3.5 saloon. The new owner of the Sunbeam Rapier was traced and the officers examined its tyres and searched it. They found nothing. Laptew had, by that time, become increasingly suspicious of Sutcliffe and made arrangements for the Sunbeam Rapier to be available for forensic examination if his senior officers thought it necessary. 'Unfortunately,' an official report said later, 'no examination of that sort ever took place.'

The detectives were unhappy about the interview. 'I had bad feelings about the man,' Laptew said. 'He had too many uncanny links with what we knew and the thing that struck me more than anything was the striking resemblance to the Marilyn Moore photofit.' Sutcliffe had been alibied by his wife, which was unsatisfactory; he denied having been in Manchester after his vehicle was positively sighted; he had visited Sunderland and travelled throughout the North of England; his size eight and a half shoes were close enough to the footprints found at the Whitaker crime scene; he had a gap in his teeth; and his manner was unbelievably casual for someone supposedly helping an investigation for a serial killer. 'There were too many things that fitted what we knew, what we suspected, and there is always your own particular irrational gut feeling about a person.'

The pair debated arresting Sutcliffe on suspicion, but

decided against it, remembering the instruction two years previously that people being interviewed were not to be hauled in without the approval of the assistant chief constable (crime). Instead they decided to submit a comprehensive report covering their feelings about the man, including their intuitive assessment that there was something not quite right about Sutcliffe.

Laptew did a West Yorkshire CRO check. Sutcliffe had one conviction for the theft of tyres in 1975, and one conviction for going equipped for theft in 1969. There was no mention of the hammer Sutcliffe was carrying at the time he was arrested for the latter offence. The following Monday morning Laptew called by the typing pool at Bradford police headquarters. He wanted Sheila to type his report: 'I had never asked her to type anything for me before. I hand wrote the report and then Sheila typed it up for me. We did it in the office. I signed it, two pages of A4. I didn't keep a copy, I only wish I had. The report, dated 2 August 1979, stated unequivocally: "The reporting officers are not fully satisfied with this man."

'I didn't check whether he had been interviewed at Clark's,' admitted Laptew. 'The incident room was like a bloody fortress and to get in there if you wanted anything . . . it was so user hostile, you would not believe the animosity. I hated the bloody place because you got nothing without making a bloody nuisance of yourself . . . I couldn't get the written statements together because it was sacrosanct territory there. I would nowadays go in and thump the table and insist on the information, but you have the likes of Dick Holland, whom I revered, and they had their approval from him, they were sanctioned by him, a superintendent. I was a DC living in the valleys. Shit rolls downhill and if I offended any of these, who knows?

'The point came when I bypassed my team leader and went

direct to Mr Holland. He didn't read the report at that point, it was left in his in-tray. I said: "I am not happy about this bloke, will you have another look through it?" I outlined what it was about and then I mentioned the Marilyn Moore photofit. The tone of his reply shocked me: "Anybody who mentions photofits to me, they'll draw uniform and do traffic for the rest of their service." I'm talking about a guy who was almost a deity to me. You have got to understand the culture bearing in mind these guys, you held them as gods. He bit my head off. They were privy to everything. I was in the wrong for even daring to go and front him up with this. You don't labour the point with a guy like that. You didn't mess with Dick Holland. Firstly you respect him and secondly he knows best. He knows more than me and I could be wrong. When he blew my head off I thought, "You big ignorant bastard." That's what I thought. I lost respect for him at that point because the incident room heard all of this, there were enough of them in there. I felt: "Well, fuck you to the power of ten." I thought, "I must have got it wrong, it can't be the guy," and I carried on with my normal duties.'

The completed action for the Sutcliffe interview went to Dick Holland, who marked it in green ink: 'File', because Sutcliffe's handwriting did not match that of the Ripper letters. An official Home Office report into the conduct of the Yorkshire Ripper investigation said later there was a possibility that Holland himself may not have seen Laptew's special written report, but the action sheet certainly mentioned its existence. Holland himself certainly did not remember Laptew's report when questioned in depth about it several years later. Neither did he recall that thirteen months earlier he had himself ordered a special examination of the tyres on Sutcliffe's red Ford Corsair. The official report said:

Despite the most probing investigation it has not been possible to trace what happened to Constable Laptew's report after he submitted it. Detective Superintendent Holland is adamant that it was not attached to the papers which he marked 'File' and in spite of the fact that the report is referred to on the completed action, there are grounds for believing that he is accurate in this assertion. Some support for this has been given by Detective Superintendent XXXX who also saw the papers but his recollection is that the Laptew report appeared on his desk separately sometime after Christmas 1979 and that he then brought it to the attention of Detective Superintendent Holland. Superintendent Holland disagrees with XXXX's recollection of events and is adamant that he cannot remember ever having seen the report.

The official report's author, at the time one of the most senior policemen in Britain, added:

I cannot help concluding that one or other of the senior officers involved in these events is now loath to accept responsibility for what in effect was a serious error of judgment . . . The question must be asked whether Det. Supt Holland actually had time to read Det. Con. Laptew's completed action [of the interview] before he wrote 'File' on it, or whether it was one of a huge pile which he recognized had to be disposed of during the day in the knowledge that a similar pile would be waiting for him the following morning. If he had had the time to read it properly, surely he would have asked for Laptew's special report, had it not been attached to the action, and having read it surely he would have felt that the

reservations which Laptew expressed about Sutcliffe were
worth a major probe to resolve.

However, it is now clear that the incident room filing system
had already gone badly wrong because, when Laptew and
Greenwood were told to interview Sutcliffe about the triple-
area sighting, no records were found of the four previous
interviews. When a new separate line of inquiry was about to
begin, a name index card was made out for the person about
to be seen *before* a check was made to see if that person already
had an entry in the central name index. If their name had
previously been recorded on an index card, the new one was
simply stapled to it. It was here that things began to go awry.
No index cards for Sutcliffe were found immediately before
Laptew's interview, even though there had been two separate
lines of inquiry concerning Sutcliffe: the five-pound note
inquiry and the cross-area sighting, as well as two re-interviews.
Somehow the index cards had become separated, or completely
misfiled, or both.

With hindsight, had Laptew and Greenwood taken Sutcliffe
down to a police station to 'help with inquiries' there is every
possibility it would have cracked the case wide open. A
thorough trawl through incident room files would certainly
have followed and this should have brought all the relevant
paperwork concerning Sutcliffe together. Moreover, once his
name had gone round as having been arrested, word would
have quickly reached other officers who had also interviewed
Sutcliffe and a wealth of information should have been
unearthed. The probabilities of Sutcliffe working for one of
the firms that could have received the five-pound note, and
to have had a make of car on 'the tracking inquiry list', coupled
with his denial of having recently been in Moss Side, Man-

chester, should have been enough to elevate him immediately to the D62 file – the list of men who were serious suspects. But Oldfield had laid down an edict and the junior officers did as they were told.

When the police forces in Britain wanted help with recognizing voices on tape they turned to one of Britain's greatest authorities on phonetics, Stanley Ellis, a senior lecturer at the University of Leeds. He started work there in 1952 as research assistant to Professor Harold Orton, who was undertaking his *Survey on English Dialects*. Ellis's father and mother had worked in the textile industry. He was brought up in a suburb of Bradford and went to a grammar school there. After war service in the RAF he returned to his roots in the West Riding and did a degree at Leeds. It was Professor Orton who encouraged him to study regional dialects and Ellis conducted fieldwork for the survey. During early married life, he and his wife and their young child lived in a caravan for five years, travelling throughout the country from Northumberland to Cornwall as Ellis listened to and recorded regional dialects. He would call at remote villages and persuade four or five local people to talk for several hours about their lives, and particularly about the 'old times', so providing him with samples of local language and pronunciation.

Over the years Ellis appeared regularly on radio and television, on which he was known as 'The Dialect Man', making programmes about the diversity of the English language in Britain. First and foremost, though, he was a teacher and someone with great empathy for the ordinary people of Britain. 'When you start talking to folk they are fantastic,' he said with his typical enthusiasm. 'Do you know what really impressed me? I was working in some really backward places in the 1950s, no electricity, no piped water. I remember one man well. I asked him what his job was. A carrot washer. That particular man would have been capable of being a chairman of a county council in our present day. He had all the intelligence. If he had had the educational opportunities that I had, he certainly would not have been a carrot washer. This is what society did to people in those days. I felt that this was what I was observing in society.'

As well as appearing in court on behalf of various police forces, Stanley Ellis also had a secret life. He worked for the Security Service: MI5. From time to time they needed expert help with tracing the origins of a voice on a telephone intercept, or a bug planted in a building owned by a foreign government hostile to the interests of the United Kingdom. Ellis was one of several people during the Cold War who quietly assisted the authorities in the defence of the realm. His thanks for his long service to his country came in the form of a letter from the then director-general of MI5, Stella Rimington, which he had framed. It still hangs today in his study at home.

The Ripper squad sent Ellis a copy of the Geordie tape in the hope that he might pinpoint more accurately where the voice came from. It was obviously from someone on Wearside, but Ellis believed the people who could identify it more accurately were in Sunderland. It was a very distinctive local voice, in his view. He didn't think the man had altered a great deal socially by changing his voice in order to live somewhere else. Ellis already had an archive of Wearside accents. In his own mind, the accent was more north of the River Wear, in an area known locally as 'The Barbary Coast'. At Sunderland police headquarters, Detective Superintendent Docherty arranged for a car to take him on a tour of the area. Ellis took with him two expensive Uher tape recorders, one to play the Ripper tape, the other to record local dialects. They toured the area to the north, calling in at small towns and pit villages, asking locals in pubs and working men's clubs if they could narrow down the dialect on the tape. They edged gradually up river and stopped at two villages, Southwick and Castletown. There, people immediately recognized the voice as one of their own. This was where the tape sender had spent his formative years. Officers from Sunderland soon began making extensive inquiries in the area while Stanley Ellis took off on holiday to Corfu. He was convinced that by the time he returned the identity of the voice on the tape would be known to police. 'I was absolutely certain his family, friends and neighbours would have recognized it at once,' he said.

In his absence, West Yorkshire police received a number of telephone calls purporting to be from the killer. Helping them was Ellis's colleague from the Department of Phonetics at Leeds University, Jack Windsor Lewis. He listened to tapes of the phone calls and decided they were fakes. Asking casually about the letters the police had received, he was astounded to learn they had been examined by a handwriting expert, but had not been analysed for linguistic content. They agreed to let him see copies of the letters, but only if a police officer was present in the room, and check if the letter writer was the same as the person on the tape by analysing the kind of language used. 'I decided they definitely were linked,' Windsor Lewis said. 'There were lots of little details, idiosyncratic and unusual expressions. He even crossed his sevens in the continental style, which is something very unusual for the most part in this country.' Listening to the 'Ripper' tape, Windsor Lewis was also convinced the identity of the person who made it would be quickly known: 'If ever a voice was going to be unhesitatingly attributable to an individual when he was found, this was surely it.

I was certain that a number of people must have recognized him at once and [known] whether he was a murderer or some sick-minded hoaxer.'

Elsewhere in Sunderland, David Zackrisson was a troubled man after attending conferences in West Yorkshire where Oldfield was present. The young detective was slightly overawed to be in the same room as the man in charge of the most important murder investigation in Britain, if not the whole of Europe. Oldfield appeared a genial figure, quite gentle, easygoing, but with a steely determination to get his man. 'There was no doubt at all it was the focus of his being,' Zackrisson said. 'He projected total single-mindedness but not in a manic way.' Holland attended some of the meetings. 'He was a man you initially might see as having more physique than intellect but when you talked to him you realized he had both. Oldfield had a good deal of trust in Dick Holland. He was a faithful servant and sometimes Oldfield turned to him for reassurance. Oldfield was looking to us and thinking, "They are going to crack the case." I thought commonsense would prevail, that there would be a reasoned debate on the flaws which were appearing.'

His team had begun finding references in newspapers to Vera Millward having been in hospital for an operation. One of them turned up a *Daily Mail* article quoting her common-law husband saying precisely that. There were other references to Joan Harrison being discussed as a possible Ripper victim as early as February 1977. The *Daily Mirror* had produced an article showing all the possible links in the Ripper case, including Preston. Moreover, Zackrisson was still bothered by the letter writer's lack of originality in using the 1888 letter as a template for his own scribblings. 'After all, if you are the murderer you know so many intimate details of the murders. That's why the police keep so much back, because only the murderer will know. It would be very very easy if you were the murderer to prove conclusively within half a dozen lines that you're the man, and he did not do that. If I was the killer and I was enjoying taunting the police, I could have brought out so much more. "Have you guessed what weapon I am using?" "Did you notice that I moved the body in Manchester, because you didn't find it?"'

Zackrisson had a chart on his office wall tabling the murders and the dates the letters were sent. The listing for Pearson was for the day her body was discovered. One Sunday morning in August 1979, he was looking attentively at the chart. He suddenly remembered a phrase from one of the early letters: 'Up to number 8 now, you say 7 but remember Preston 75'. At the time the letter was sent, Yvonne Pearson's body still lay hidden beneath a sofa on waste ground in Bradford. It was not found until nearly two weeks after the letter was posted. It dawned on Zackrisson that, if the killer's mathematics were correct, the total number of murders should have been nine if they included the Harrison slaying. The writer clearly hadn't known anything about Pearson. 'The real killer would have adjusted these figures and thrown in the taunt – "you haven't found number 9". On the tape which arrived later, he says "I think it's eleven up to now, isn't it?" By this time Pearson's body had been found and he had now included it in the totals.'

Zackrisson looked several times at the chart, telling himself such an error was impossible, but concluding: 'I've got it wrong.' He laid the copies of the letters on a table and began writing a detailed chronology of events. Leaving his office, he went across the corridor to the incident room and spoke to a detective sergeant, Alan Whitwood: 'Our letter writer may not be all that he says he is because he doesn't seem aware of the

Yvonne Pearson murder at the time he wrote the letters.' They had known each other for years, so Zackrisson didn't mind making a fool of himself, though he was sure he was on firm ground with his assertion. Whitwood had a quiet demeanour, but he would tell anyone they were talking absolute claptrap if he thought it was true. After listening to the argument, he believed Zackrisson had made a compelling case for saying the letters and tape were nothing more than a hoax.

At home that night Zackrisson weighed up his responsibilities. He found himself in a moral dilemma and told his wife that, for the first time in his career, he might have to go public with a piece of information to save lives. He believed the entire Ripper investigation was being led down a blind alley. But what should he do? The idea of going behind Docherty's back and leaking these findings to some journalist went against every instinct. His first loyalty was to the police service, which had ways of doing things, channels of communication meant to remedy things that went wrong. He wanted to avoid a diplomatic row and the humiliation of his colleagues in Leeds, who had been coping with an out-of-control serial killer for nearly four years. He *still* kept thinking that Oldfield must have something up his sleeve to convince himself the man on the tape was the Yorkshire Ripper, but this analysis of the letters finally convinced him otherwise. He would have to do something. One of the most powerful tools in any organization was the written word. Conversations could be conveniently forgotten, but a written report had certain consequences attached to it which could not be ignored either by its writer or its recipients. He would do more research, then write a report for his own bosses.

Soon afterwards, detectives in the Sunderland incident room began slowly to raise doubts about the letters and tape with their West Yorkshire colleagues stationed in the north-east. It usually happened in a quiet, good-natured way, over a drink in the police club bar, so as to get nobody's back up. The Sunderland men were deliberate in not trying to rain on Oldfield's parade. Such talk was never discouraged by Docherty or Zackrisson, because they hoped the message would filter down to Leeds and bring about a thorough re-examination by Oldfield of the so-called 'Geordie' connection.

Sunderland police carried on questioning every male between twenty and sixty-five among the 1,500 homes in the mining village of Castletown. When Castletown inquiries were completed, they planned to move on to neighbouring Hylton Castle, an estate of 3,000 houses; then to the Town End Farm Estate. It was an operation that would keep local officers fully employed for the next eighteen months, a huge commitment in terms of manpower. When the onset of winter arrived, the police caravan parked in the village gave way to more substantial accommodation. A disused police house at Town End Farm Estate was used as a base of operations as birth records were scrutinized for men born north of the River Wear between 1924 and 1954. School records were cross-checked for men born outside the area but who spent their formative years around Castletown and went to school there. It involved checking 176 birth registers containing 88,000 names, and 60 school registers with 55,000 names. Armed with this massive index of names, the police approached the DHSS headquarters in Newcastle, which housed all the computerized records of everyone in the National Insurance scheme, in conditions of great secrecy. Senior civil servants agreed that their computer could be used to provide the addresses of those on the names index. This could determine whether any of the men had moved to Yorkshire, where they would be interviewed by Oldfield's team.

Northumbria police continued to try and eliminate all the men who could not have written the letters and sent the tape, providing they lived north of the River Wear. But not everyone took the investigation seriously. One weekend the BBC was recording the local football team's match against Fulham. On that evening's 'Match of the Day' programme, the London team's supporters could clearly be heard loudly chanting to the tune of 'Guantanamera': 'There's only one Jack the Ripper.' At the police caravan parked for several weeks in the Castle-town village centre next to a bus stop, plenty of people stopped by with suggestions as to the identity of the man on the tape. Everywhere the police went the locals plied them with hospital-ity – tea and cakes. Several said they knew the voice but couldn't put a name on it. Some thought the investigation cast a slur on the tight-knit local community. 'We all have daughters and this man is an animal,' said a local working men's club official. 'Nobody believes he comes from here. If he did we would have turned him in by now.' Already reeling at the thought the Yorkshire Ripper may have come from the village, the locals were about to receive another blow – the imminent closure of the village's only pit after eighty years.

There was a major shock also in Leeds at the sudden hospi-talization of George Oldfield. A cold turned into a severe 'chest infection', but the rumours, later confirmed, were that he had had a heart attack. Jim Hobson took temporary charge of West Yorkshire CID and Dick Holland ran the Ripper squad. Doctors ordered Oldfield to take a complete rest. His health had completely run down. He didn't know how to switch off in what had become a personal quest. It was the first thing he thought about when he woke up. When he visited the bath-room in the middle of the night, he would still find himself thinking about the Ripper case, not the killer himself, but the details of the investigation. Had they done this inquiry or that inquiry properly? Had they missed something? Others, like his colleague Trevor Lapish, found that after a day of dealing with murder and mayhem the perfect antidote was to sit quietly listening to Beethoven's 'Pastoral' Symphony, played on the hi-fi in his front room until he felt he could return to the land of the living and go back and join his family. Oldfield simply fretted in the office, stayed until late at night, refusing to let go, wanting to clear that last piece of paperwork, some unread statement or other, in case he missed anything vital.

Now aged fifty-five, he had been a police officer for thirty-three years and was entitled to a full pension. Close colleagues knew he wouldn't rest while the Ripper remained at large. Holland, undoubtedly the man closest to him, had watched his boss's health gradually deteriorate, particularly after Josephine Whitaker was killed. Oldfield started believing his own rhetoric – that it *was* a personal battle between him and the killer. He was sure the Ripper was trying to reach him personally in the letters and tape and waited for him to make contact again. 'The voice is almost sad,' he reflected just before he went sick. 'He is a man fed up with what he has done, fed up with himself. A man who feels he knows me enough almost to take me into his confidence, confide in me. I am probably an obvious person for him to feel he has something in common with. I feel I know him already. Every time the phone rings, I wonder whether it is him.'

A bug had gone round the office at Halifax and Oldfield was virtually living off Benylin cocktails, aided by cigarettes and his daily diet of whisky. Holland knew he had had a heart attack for sure. He visited Oldfield in hospital after his boss phoned him personally in the incident room, wanting to be updated. If he hadn't gone to the hospital, Oldfield would have become more stressed, worrying about what was happening. 'He became obsessive,' Holland said. 'He was determined that everything we did would be designed to save another girl, and of course he didn't succeed.'

This absence of success haunted Oldfield. He was now probably the most famous detective in Britain, but he was also under tremendous pressure from both the press and his own force. It was the hardest murder case anyone had undertaken. His management of the investigation was being closely scrutinized. He didn't express self-doubt, and the only time Holland saw him depressed was when he had been to force headquarters asking for more resources. He came back from having seen the Chief and the finance officer and said: 'I've had a hard day and I've got fuck all. All I have had to listen to is what demands there are elsewhere.'

He vividly recalled how he and Margaret felt when their own daughter died of leukemia, eleven years previously. She would now have been Jo Whitaker's age. It played on his mind and, sentimental man that he was, he knew how her parents must have grieved. He told Roger Cross on the *Yorkshire Post*: 'Our only concern is to get to this man before he takes another life and I am sure he will try.' It proved a prophetic statement. Only two weeks after Oldfield went into hospital, the Ripper struck again, in the heart of the university quarter of Bradford.

On 3 September 1979, Dick Holland had just begun his first real holiday in years. He hired a caravan intending to tour Scotland with Sylvia and her two sons. They had reached Glenrothes, Fife, on the other side of the Forth Road Bridge, where Sylvia's mother lived, and planned staying a few days before heading up the east coast towards John O'Groats. The moment he heard the news of another Ripper murder in Bradford, Holland was on the telephone. A new senior investigating officer for the latest Ripper murder had been appointed, Detective Chief Superintendent Peter Gilrain, a former Wakefield City man. Holland agreed to return first thing next morning. Sylvia realized he had no choice but knew how disappointed he was at not being able to go fishing with her young sons. He had even upgraded his angling tackle before setting off on holiday. It was never unpacked. She and the boys stayed in the caravan at her mother's house while Holland drove straight to Bradford, still in his holiday clothes, hoping that this time the Ripper had left a clue that would lead to his swift detection.

Barbara Leach, aged twenty, from Kettering near Northampton, had been about to start her third year at Bradford University, studying humanities and economics. Her parents were quiet, hard-working people, who lived simply and encouraged both their children to go to university. Barbara's brother, Graham, had gone to Cambridge. Her mother, Beryl Leach, was a teacher and her father, David, a bank clerk. Barbara had knuckled down to her A levels at the local girls' high school to win her university place, but then she was used to hard work. Before becoming a student she had a Saturday job at the local branch of Boots the Chemist. In the university vacations she grafted away as a casual worker at the local Prime Cut processing plant and at a handbag factory in nearby Desborough. She and her best friend had had a wonderful carefree holiday in Greece that summer and they were planning a trip to Crete the following year. She was a lively young woman who enjoyed horse-riding and dancing and had a close circle of friends in Bradford. She lived with a number of undergraduates from the university in a shared house in Grove Terrace – right in the heart of studentland.

On Saturday, 1 September 1979, she and her friends enjoyed a night out in their local pub, the Manville Arms, just round the corner in Great Horton Road. Barbara had a steak and kidney pie and drank two pints of cider. The landlord was a friendly type and decided to hold a 'late stop' – closing the pub but inviting some of his regulars to stay on after hours. At forty minutes past midnight on Sunday morning the private party began to break up and the students started to drift off home to their lodgings, in Barbara's case a bed-sitting room. It had started to rain, but Barbara fancied a walk rather than accept a lift, and was never seen alive again.

It was not until after teatime on Sunday, when she had still failed to appear, that the alarm was raised and a big police search commenced. A phone call that night was made to her parents' home in Kettering. They were watching *The Onedin Line*, a seafaring drama series on television, when they heard the news that would change their lives for ever. Their daughter was missing from the flat she shared with her five friends and police were searching for her. She had gone for a late-night walk and not returned. Beryl and David Leach immediately feared the worst, knowing full well that the Yorkshire Ripper remained at large. The following day, at 9.15 p.m. on Monday, 3 September, two police officers, one of them a woman, called and broke the sad news that their daughter had been found dead and was a victim of the Yorkshire Ripper. In the past Barbara had talked briefly about the Ripper, but her parents had felt safe in the knowledge that their daughter would always walk with a friend, not on her own. Like every person who had a beloved child murdered, Barbara's parents thought it would never happen to them. 'Barbara always managed to give a good account of herself,' her father told the local paper. 'I remember our son Graham saying once he and Barbara had some kind of minor argument and she had playfully hit him and practically floored him.'

Earlier that Monday, at 3.55 p.m., a police constable walking down a cobbled lane behind the rear of the houses in Ash Grove had come to an open yard behind No. 13, a large stone-built detached house with a tarmac pathway running along the side of the house to the lane at the back. In a crudely built recess housing some dustbins, he saw something concealed beneath a piece of old carpet, which was weighed down by a number of stones. A red boot protruded from one corner and part of someone's head at another. Underneath was Barbara's body, seated in a slumped position, propped against the angle where two stone walls of the recess met. The head was turned downwards and towards the right shoulder. The left arm was directed across the front of the body and the right hand rested on the ground. Both legs were bent at the knees and twisted towards the right. A deliberate effort had been made to hide the woman. Her blouse and bra were bloodstained and had been displaced upwards; the belt and zipper of her jeans had been undone so that the lower part of her abdomen was exposed. She still wore her red calf-length leather boots and her brown canvas bag was next to her body. Nothing appeared to have been taken.

A forensic scientist from the Wetherby lab, arriving before Professor Gee, soon spotted blood on the wall near the girl's head and also on the ground two feet away. There were stab wounds visible on the body. It seemed she had fallen over and lain briefly on her side before being pushed up against the wall and covered with the carpet. No struggle had taken place in this area. The scientist deduced she had been struck elsewhere and dragged down the lane and into the recess.

A task force search of the area included a number of drains

which yielded a screwdriver head, a wallet, a table knife, a Stanley knife and a spanner. Dustbins were examined and a breadknife and a pair of tights were retrieved. All were sent for forensic examination, but none turned out to have any connection with the murder. Because the body was cold and rigor mortis had set in, David Gee had difficulty removing the body from the recess and on to a large black polythene sheet so he could examine it more thoroughly. Blood soiled her brown-coloured hair, and the exposed skin of her chest and abdomen. Now he could see several stab wounds in the front and sides of the abdomen and chest and a lacerated wound to the back of the scalp. The available light had gone and it was now completely dark. When the body was taken to the city mortuary for the post-mortem Gee found the familiar semi-circular laceration. A depressed fracture of the underlying skull was clearly visible. On the trunk he found a number of oval-shaped stab wounds and others triangular shaped. In the tracks of some of these wounds, which had penetrated several vital organs, he discovered some kind of streaky black material which he thought was a kind of grease. Again the stabbing instrument appeared to have been reintroduced through the same wound without being fully removed.

Gee believed she had been hit once on the head with a hammer head just over an inch in diameter. The impact had been in a downwards and forwards direction, so she had obviously been struck from behind. The eight penetrating wounds to the trunk were made by an object with a three-sided blade at least five inches long – similar to the injuries seen in Whitaker six months earlier. Again he felt the instrument had a handle with a flat face. The injuries had to have been inflicted before she was moved to where she was found.

The new senior investigating officer, Peter Gilrain, had

formerly been in charge of the force administration at the Wakefield headquarters. A quietly spoken, thoughtful man, he had an alert brain but his demeanour seemed at times more like that of a bank manager than a murder squad detective. He wasn't emotional, especially in public. Indeed, he was keen to avoid personal publicity. He had a droll sense of humour and rarely lost his temper. He was born in Wakefield and had spent five years heading the city's CID. Although briefed about the generalities of the Ripper case, he had little in-depth knowledge of it. While he concentrated on investigating the Leach murder, Holland took the day-to-day decisions regarding the rest of the investigation. Gilrain conceded the killer was crafty, but he couldn't be invisible, and he remained convinced someone must have seen him either approaching or leaving the area. In subsequent days, forensics managed to turn up a footprint with the same pattern of impressions found at the Whitaker scene. But then, as with all the other Ripper investigations, they began to run into brick walls. The hoped-for breakthrough from the Whitaker murder had not materialized and a considerable number of actions were still outstanding. Witnesses who saw something definite were scarce. One suspect was described as being white, early thirties and of athletic build, with short dark hair and thin dark moustache. He was seen putting some kind of bundle into a green Hillman Avenger estate car parked near the crime scene. They also tried to trace a blue Datsun spotted close by at the material time, but neither vehicle was ever traced. The same footslogging inquiries, house-to-house checks, vehicle checks and taking of statements went on without let-up.

A new and updated confidential police intelligence 'Special Notice', sent to all British police forces, gave details of sixteen Ripper murders and attempted murders. It also included information about the tyre tracks found at three crime scenes, as well as the letters and tape, and firmly stated that suspects could be eliminated from the inquiries if they were not born between 1924 and 1959; were obviously coloured; if their shoe size was 9 or higher; if their blood group was other than B and they had an accent 'dissimilar to a North Eastern (Geordie) accent'. This crucial document, hastily put together by a detective sergeant, was issued without Gilrain having seen it, but on Dick Holland's authority, as temporary head of the Ripper squad.

Among those outside West Yorkshire police there was now a profound sea change in attitude towards the Ripper squad's four-year investigation. The Fleet Street tabloids began a campaign to call in Scotland Yard. An editorial in the *Sun* urged the force to swallow their pride: 'The fact is that they seem no nearer capturing this monster than they were four years ago.' It brought a glib response from a senior detective: 'They haven't caught their own Ripper yet, what makes them think they can catch ours?'

Public faith in West Yorkshire's ability to solve the case began to erode rapidly. Criticisms were widely aired. On a local radio station callers began openly discussing the undercover police operation in Manningham and Chapeltown. They ridiculed the fact it was supposed to be secret and made the reasonable point that, if they knew a covert operation was taking place, it was a sure bet the Ripper did too, which was why he had gone looking for a victim in the university area.

The emotional reaction to this latest murder, both in Bradford and Barbara's home town of Kettering, was one of devastation. Neighbours who had known her all her life openly wept as they spoke of the kind, intelligent girl they knew. The *Northampton Evening Telegraph* put up a £5,000 reward for the capture of the killer, bringing the total money available to anyone wanting to turn bounty hunter to £30,000. In Yorkshire women took to the street, protesting about male violence. Staff and students at the university were beside themselves with sorrow and anger that the Ripper was still at large, menacing a huge swathe of the country. When Peter Gilrain warned that women were not safe to be out in the early hours on their own, it brought three hundred feminists on to the streets of Bradford in protest. They marched on the police headquarters, urging for men instead of women to be given a curfew. Self-defence classes started being taught and some women took to carrying knives to protect themselves. Local firms made special arrangements to transport female workers home at night.

On holiday on the Greek island of Corfu, Stanley Ellis read news of Barbara Leach's death in an English newspaper. Seeing the word 'Ripper' in a headline, he purchased the paper at a newsstand in the lobby of his hotel, fully expecting that the police had found the killer after someone had identified the voice on the tape. Learning of yet another murder sent a shiver down his spine, he says. 'It gave me such an awful jolt. I felt awful, absolutely awful. There was I thinking that he had been caught, and he's done another murder right on my doorstep. This was my home patch, I knew the street where she was murdered. It so depressed me that I began wondering about the possibility of a hoax. I was certain that any number of people would have recognized the voice by now. I think if he had really been a murderer it is more likely that people would have disclosed the fact. I spoke to Jack Windsor Lewis about it when I got home. We were shattered when we found they hadn't located the person. They must have in fact interviewed him and passed him by simply because he had an alibi.'

Both men thought they were alone in their thinking. Neither

knew of the profound doubts about the authenticity of the tape and letters gathering pace in Sunderland. One of the most extraordinary facts about the way West Yorkshire police dealt with the tape was that, before the end of September 1979, four separate written warnings about the possibility of a super-hoaxer had been communicated to senior officers on the Ripper squad. On 14 September 1979, an extraordinary event took place which was never made public. There is convincing evidence that the person who actually sent the letters and tape tried to undo the damage and to warn the police.

It was the day after publication of the confidential police 'Special Notice' authorizing suspects to be eliminated if they did not have a 'Geordie' accent. A desperate-sounding telephone call to the local incident room in Sunderland was answered by a young constable, Keith Mount, who had been seconded to the inquiry in August and had played the tape to the inhabitants of Castletown over and over until he knew it backwards. Verbatim. They had walked round the village armed with a clipboard trying to attract a crowd to whom the tape could be played through a loud hailer. They had stopped at the clubs and pubs hoping someone would identify the voice. After the Castletown operation, PC Mount, who was brought up in Chiswick, West London, was sent over to Sunderland to help with index filing and other paperwork in the incident room. There was an answerphone in the room so people could call in and hear the tape. It played over and over again in the background, until the voice became deeply embedded in Mount's subconscious. Not being from the north-east, he had an acute ear for this individual accent. He would recognize the voice on the tape anywhere.

He and a detective were the only ones present around tea-time when, at 5 p.m., his colleague went to get a sandwich from the canteen. The phone rang on a specially installed number, Sunderland 43146. Picking it up, Mount simultaneously grabbed a pen and a pad ready to take a message. He said: 'Police incident room, Sunderland, can I help you?' He heard an intermittent tone which indicated the call was coming from a payphone: 'Then a voice came on the other end. It was the voice that made the tapes, the voice I'd been listening to for months and months. It made the hair stand up at the back of my neck and I thought, "Shit, this is the person, this is the person we're looking for." I went for the tape recorder, I was trying to talk to him and set up a recording of the telephone call. I got it plugged in eventually. I don't know how many seconds or even what parts of the conversation I lost, certainly the first few exchanges.' The remaining part of the call went as follows:

MOUNT: I can't hear you, it's a bad line.
CALLER: Tell him it's a fake.
MOUNT: What's a fake?
CALLER: The tape recording.
MOUNT: What one is this, the one he's just received?
CALLER: The Ripper tape recording.
MOUNT: How do you know that?
CALLER: Just tell him.
MOUNT: Just tell him?
CALLER: The one in June.
MOUNT: Pardon?
CALLER: The one in June.
MOUNT: Sorry, it's a bad line, you're going to have to repeat it.

At that point the phone call terminated.

'The caller was trying to tell us that the tape was a hoax, that the person who made the tapes obviously wasn't the Ripper,' Mount said. 'He was trying to say, tell them the tape is a hoax. It was like listening to the radio or television, knowing the person very well and then meeting them face to face. You recognize the voice. It was just him, I can't explain anything else, I knew it was him, the person who made the tape, he was trying to tell me the tape was a hoax. There had been a murder recently and he had taken an awful long time to phone up. I am sure to this day that that was the person I spoke to. He was trying to convince me in a very short burst, not chatting. He was trying to say, "the tape is false, tell them the tape is false". I had played the tape to so many people I was brainwashed with that voice, brainwashed with it. I knew it better than my own voice.'

After the phone call, Mount got through to the local telephone exchange to have it traced. This meant not replacing the handset to avoid disconnecting the line at his end. The hope was an engineer at the exchange could manually follow the call back to where it originated. Nevertheless the line was lost and they were unable to see where the call had come from. Zackrisson heard the tape of the phone call first thing next morning and went to consult with senior officers. Those who listened to the tape were completely convinced it was the same voice as that on the tape sent to Oldfield. It was confirmation that their approach of trying to find the tape sender without alibiing him for the murders was the correct one. The 'tell him' on the tape was definitely a reference to Oldfield.

Within twenty-four hours the Sunderland incident room was buzzing with the news. It was the only time Sunderland police ever received a call suggesting the tape was a hoax. Eventually the tape was passed to a Home Office laboratory at Sandridge,

388

where a phonetics expert declared there were significant differences between the Oldfield tape and the phone call to Sunderland. However, there is evidence from many years later when the tape of the phone conversation with Keith Mount was examined by another phonetics expert, Dr Peter French, in York, for analysis. In the intervening period the science of voice printing had technologically moved on apace. In the 1990s, Dr French took over many of the responsibilities of Stanley Ellis after he retired, working for the police and other government agencies. French subsequently told a third party that he had examined both tapes and concluded the voices were the same.

A few days later, with no knowledge whatsoever of the telephone call to the Sunderland incident room, both Stanley Ellis and Jack Windsor Lewis wrote independently to the Ripper squad, expressing reservations about the veracity of the tape and letters. Ellis had been increasingly troubled by the thought that they could be hunting someone for sending the letters and tape who was not the Ripper murderer. Probably the most experienced man in his field in Britain, he remained certain that someone must have already identified the voice on the tape and the man had provided an alibi for the killings. Several years before, Ellis and Windsor Lewis had been brought in by police to identify a voice on a tape recording during the Black Panther investigation. That turned out to be the work of a hoaxer and he was afraid the same had happened again. West Yorkshire police had convinced themselves the Ripper tape and letters contained 'privileged' information and were equally certain they were from the killer. 'It must be at least possible that this is not so,' Ellis wrote. 'Unless we keep before us the possibility, then a great deal of time and effort could be wasted.' His colleague Windsor Lewis also wrote, warning the police to keep an open mind.

Another with grave concerns who committed himself on paper was David Zackrisson. On 25 September 1979 he resolved his moral dilemma about the dangers of a super-hoaxer by writing a nine-page report entitled 'Commentary on the "Ripper" Letters and Tape' for his superiors in Northumbria police. He pointed out the errors in the arithmetic concerning the numbers of killings, the obvious omission of the Pearson murder, and he highlighted the way the writer had mimicked the original Jack the Ripper letter. Finally Zackrisson demonstrated how the letter writer could have gleaned his information from articles in the press and revealed how, at a conference of top detectives at Bradford two weeks previously, Jack Ridgway informed colleagues that he himself had told the press how Millward had received medical treatment in order 'to generate some public sympathy'. Zackrisson firmly believed the writer was a hoaxer, seeking self-publicity. By writing the report he was putting himself on the line. He wanted to be certain Sunderland police did not miss the letter writer because he had larger feet than size nine, or had been in prison when the murders were committed. 'I felt that by taking this unilateral action we would be creating greater objectivity,' he said many years later. 'West Yorkshire had the pressures of the murders. George Oldfield himself was under a terrific amount of pressure. At least I had the luxury to be able to sit back and examine [the letters/tape] for what they were, because after all that was the only connection with Sunderland . . . My intention was simply to say, "Let's be cautious about this." I had the greatest admiration for what the officers in West Yorkshire were doing. They were the ones directly in the firing line, they were the ones who had accumulated huge amounts of information. We were dealing with a random killer and there was no connection between the culprit and the victim. He didn't leave anything at the scene. I was seriously concerned.'

Yet a fourth warning about the dangers of a hoaxer was sent to the Ripper squad on 26 September 1979, the day after Zackrisson wrote his report. The Home Office forensic science laboratory at Wetherby had been analysing the evidence in the Harrison murder. Acknowledging there were some similarities with the Ripper murders, a forensic scientist warned there were aspects of the Harrison killing which were atypical and therefore 'the certainty of Harrison having been murdered by the Ripper is diminished'. The report continued: 'It may therefore be unsafe to place too much reliance on the B grouping result of the semen found, which is itself one of the atypical features ... again the authenticity of the letters and tape as being communications from the murderer must be regarded as doubtful, even though the degree of doubt may be small, for a number of reasons which include the paucity of verifiable information which they contain.'

These doubts clearly bothered Detective Chief Superintendent Gilrain, because a few days later he issued an instruction that elimination of a suspect on accent alone was not good enough and some other factor was required. This change of policy was communicated to senior officers on the Ripper squad, who were actually eliminating suspects. There are grave doubts that it was followed because the public and many junior detectives making inquiries were left believing the Yorkshire Ripper definitely had a Geordie accent. Gilrain's caution, however, was completely overridden by his chief constable's decision to launch a massive publicity drive. Ronald Gregory had concluded the reason the killer had not been arrested was because not enough people had heard the tape or seen his handwriting. He decided the Ripper squad needed the public's help, one of the carrots available being the £30,000 reward.

Over the objections of Gilrain and Holland, Ronald Gregory personally went ahead with a massive publicity campaign organized by a Leeds-based advertising agency. Graham Poulter & Associates had managed to persuade a large number of media organizations – newspapers, radio and television stations – to carry for free advertisements publicizing the tape and the letters. It was the equivalent of a £1 million advertising campaign, huge by any standards at the time, and made even more effective in that the campaign itself made news, filling many additional newspaper column inches and valuable radio airtime. Gilrain and Holland had argued for a delay of three months, to give them time to work on the Leach murder and clear the long-delayed actions from the Whitaker killing.

There was massive pressure on Ronald Gregory to do something. Questions were being raised by politicians, the press was hostile and local people were up in arms about the four-year reign of terror by the Yorkshire Ripper. Gregory's response was a massive public information campaign called 'Project R', which in terms of audience reach was an amazing success. The campaign captured the attention of the whole country. It was impossible to escape the half-page advertisements in 300 newspapers across Britain, repeated on 5,500 billboards throughout the country, and incessant announcements on radio and television.

THE MAN NEXT TO YOU MAY HAVE
KILLED 12 WOMEN

He may be sitting or standing next to you in your pub, club or canteen. Or in a queue. On a bus. He may be working at the next machine, desk or table. But he is in fact a vicious, deranged maniac, whose method of murder and mutilation is so sick that it has turned the stomachs of even the most hardened of police officers. Here's how you can help. **Look closely at the handwriting.** It's the writing of a sadistic killer. And if you think you recognize it from a note, letter, envelope, signature, cheque, anything, report it to your local police. **Listen to the killer's voice.** By phoning Leeds (STD 0532) 464111 you can hear probably the most important clue to the killer's identity. His voice. It won't be a pleasant experience but it could lead to the end of these brutal murders. If you think you recognize the voice, tell the police.

HELP US STOP THE RIPPER FROM KILLING AGAIN
Look at his handwriting. Listen to his voice.

Throughout October, November and December 1979 a mobile exhibition toured West Yorkshire. Two million copies of a four-page newspaper were delivered throughout the North of England – from Berwick-on-Tweed to South Yorkshire. 'The hunt for the "Yorkshire Ripper" is the largest murder investigation ever undertaken in British Police history,' read one of the articles on the back page. 'The workload is enormous but the dedication is awesome.' No team of ad men could have done a better job of publicizing the fact that the Yorkshire Ripper was a 'Geordie', and no blame could attach to the local advertising agency, who went to town with the brief they were given. It was a wonderful opportunity to put their firm on the map with a successful campaign. The effect on the investigation, however, was an unmitigated disaster. The public responded with a massive number of calls from people trying their best to finger the killer, some undoubtedly motivated by the large reward. Thousands of phone calls came in, many of the 'I knew a man before the war at HMS *Ganges*' kind. Box-loads of actions were generated in Leeds, Bradford, Sunderland, Manchester. They totalled more than 5,500, resulting from nearly 19,000 phone calls offering help. Three thousand calls came in on the first day.

While this was happening, the Police National Computer was spewing out ever-increasing numbers of motor vehicles spotted in the red-light districts. Details of vehicles simply kept on climbing. It was another reason for Dick Holland to plead for the publicity campaign to be delayed, but by then the chief constable's plans were too far advanced. The advertisements were placed, the billboards donated. It was too late to turn back. 'I pleaded with the chief not to have the "Project R" press conference,' said Holland. 'I wanted us to catch up with the backlog of work before we went public. I didn't say don't go public. We were getting behind and not gaining so I wanted it held back. The net effect of "Project R" was to overload an already overloaded system. It increased the number of index cards and slowed down the inquiry.'

Swamped with useless low-grade information, the inquiry was now seriously out of control. As an official report later stated, it was 'a situation which ought to have been foreseen by the Chief Constable and his senior officers . . . this additional publicity further brainwashed police and public alike into accepting the validity of the north-east connection'. What had been needed was a senior investigating officer in overall charge who could recognize the problems likely to follow from his decisions and use the skills available within the force to over-come them.

A comparison can for instance be made between the launch of the sponsored publicity campaign on the letters and tape and the launch of a new product by a commercial company. A commercial manager making plans for the launch of a new project would have to be assured that all his wholesale and retail trade outlets were fully stocked to meet the demand for the product before he put his major advertising campaign into effect. Senior officers of the West Yorkshire force did not obtain such assurances about their capacity to meet the likely response before they allowed the £1 million publicity campaign to be mounted.

While they were no better or worse than those in other forces, the senior officers were, the official report stated in a particularly damning phrase, 'not well equipped in management terms to control an inquiry of the size and scale which the Ripper inquiry proved to be ... they lacked the flexibility of mind which was required to identify failures in existing systems and take rapid corrective action.'

Meanwhile the Yorkshire Ripper remained at large, safe in the knowledge the police were looking for someone else. Knowing this, one autumn afternoon in late October 1979 Peter Sutcliffe answered the front door of his home to be confronted for the sixth time by murder squad detectives who had come to interview him.

15

Swamped by Paper

The backlog of incomplete actions was tackled at a trickle. A worse problem was developing within the incident room itself. Documents, statements, completed action forms and index cards relating to Peter William Sutcliffe were all over the place, either missing from 'the system', held pending or incorrectly completed. By now there were *four* separate index cards relating to Sutcliffe in the centralized 'nominal' (or names) index. There were two cards each for Peter William Sutcliffe and William Peter Sutcliffe; each had different dates of birth. An estimated four tons of accumulated paper was placing a considerable physical weight on the incident room floor. On 9 October 1979 an inspector came across an action report completed nearly a year before when Sutcliffe was interviewed for the fourth time. His wife and mother were his only alibis for the Jordan and Millward murders and this was recognized as unsatisfactory. A reinterview was requested.

Eleven more months had thus elapsed before, on 23 October 1979, two West Yorkshire detectives were tasked with a more detailed questioning of Sutcliffe about the recent murders to see if they could finally eliminate him. Some of the outstanding papers relating to earlier interviews with Sutcliffe had found their way back into the incident room filing system, others had disappeared. The two detectives knew Sutcliffe had been questioned twice in 1977 about the five-pound note inquiry. They carried with them the papers from the fourth and fifth interviews. What they had not seen was Andrew Laptew's completed action form, with its crucial accompanying report, which clearly pointed the finger at Sutcliffe as a prime suspect. It was sitting in someone's pending tray waiting for documents to be returned.

When the detectives appeared at their front door it was Sonia Sutcliffe who answered the call with, 'Oh, not again,' adding they had already been questioned three times. Her husband was out and the officers arranged to come back later. When they saw Sutcliffe that evening, he announced he had already provided a sample of his handwriting. He meant the letter to his wife which he handed to Laptew for analysis, but the detectives knew nothing of this. Sutcliffe agreed to provide a new handwriting sample. He was writing down a text dictated by one of the officers when Mrs Sutcliffe said suddenly: 'My husband is not the Ripper.' Trying to get a reaction from Sutcliffe, the detective replied: 'I think he is.' Sutcliffe stopped writing and looked at the officer but showed no reaction. He then continued writing the text.

Since they lacked more positive alibis, the Sutcliffes were warned they might have to be questioned again in the event of another murder. The two detectives, thinking they were looking for a Sunderland man, did not consider Sutcliffe a suspect. They regarded him as 'strange' and were bothered they could not positively eliminate him. Their completed report about the interview noted his continued insistence that he had been at home with his wife in the evenings because, as a long-distance lorry driver, he travelled a lot during the week and wanted to be with his wife at weekends, decorating their home. Strangely, even though he had previously been interviewed, Sutcliffe had made no point of remembering exactly where he was on the nights of previous murders. This niggled the detectives, because people questioned about the murders could subsequently remember exactly where they were when the next Ripper attack happened. They noted Sutcliffe's remark about having provided an earlier handwriting sample, but could find no record of it in the incident room. No one picked this up and three weeks later a senior officer marked the papers to be 'filed' because the handwriting did not match that in the letters and Sutcliffe's was clearly not the voice on the tape.

By now the actions of the hoaxer were having detrimental effects on detectives psychologically. They had ignored what should have been clear warning signals to follow up apparent inconsistencies. Officers doing laborious interviews for a long time had grown weary of the repetitive nature of the work. The Leach killing had taken the Ripper squad no further and morale was on the floor. No one on the squad was standing back and looking at the problem as a whole. Holland and Gilrain and the hundreds of detectives making inquiries were simply chasing their tails, unable to investigate one murder thoroughly before being overtaken by another.

Occasionally there was an injection of some new blood, people with a fresh viewpoint and a totally different way of thinking. It was drastically needed, but whatever good it did is, ultimately, open to doubt. Two forensic scientists seconded to the Bradford police headquarters for several months by the head of the Forensic Science Service, Dr Alan Curry, had been struggling for more than a month to inject some intellectual rigour into the inquiry. Both Russell Stockdale and Ron Outtridge had worked on the earliest Ripper murders. Now they were back with the task of liaison and coordination of scientific services. But they acted more like management consultants, drawing up briefing papers and suggesting new lines of inquiry. What they discovered when they arrived disturbed them. They found a group of men and women swamped by paper although any number of detectives could quote them chapter and verse on each individual murder. As scientists they quickly realized something was missing: 'a dispassionate orderliness of relevant linked information'. Or the ability to step back and look at what they were dealing with.

Stockdale, at the time a principal scientific officer, observed: 'Research ability was not there. The information had reached such proportions that it defied a logical weave running through it. They were bright people, very bright people, and they were good blokes. But there was no file which contained all the forensic science reports or all the autopsy reports. They had masses and masses of paper and there didn't seem to be sufficient interaction between the separate murder incident rooms.' There was no logic running through the filing system.

The scientists would drop in on Peter Gilrain, cocooned in his office surrounded by piles of paper. These had become like a brick wall which subconsciously he could hide behind while he worked himself into the ground. Like Holland, he rarely left for home before eleven at night. So long as Gilrain and Holland and the other senior officers remained hidden behind their paper walls, they did not have to come out and confront the flaws in their own logic. Stockdale and Outtridge pointed out how Gilrain's working methods meant he had no time to stop and think. He would come in early in the morning and follow the same obsessive pattern adopted by Oldfield, Holland and the rest: staying late into the night, including weekends, surrounded by the myriad of documents he felt he had to wade through. Stockdale said bluntly he thought the situation was ridiculous and that, as senior investigating officer, Gilrain needed to step back.

'We used to go in and sit there and say: "Put that down, Peter, push your chair back and let's have a cup of tea." And we would say: "Why are you fucking about with all these pieces of paper?" He said that he had to initial them before they went on to the next stage. We told him to delegate. He said he couldn't. We used to despair that here was the man leading the hunt for the Yorkshire Ripper on a national basis and he was essentially counting beans. It was a personal observation. It was no real business of ours, but Peter was a mate, so we told him what we thought.'

The scientists themselves became frustrated, observing men who had set themselves more to do than could reasonably be managed in a twenty-four-hour day, with no margin for creativity, no margin for emptying the mind and seeing what popped up. It reminded them of the saying that if all time was taken up with administering trivia, where was the intellectual space for the unusual?

There was no centralized file containing all the forensic scientists' reports or autopsy reports. Few detectives on the ground understood what type of weapons they were searching for. Stockdale and Outtridge collated all the information and arranged for sketches of particular implements to be drawn by an artist so detectives had a three-dimensional picture in their minds when they made searches of suspects' homes and garages. Every forensic science laboratory in the country and all police forces were thoroughly briefed on the scientific evidence in the case and what action had to be taken in the event of the Ripper striking outside his current killing zone in the North of England.

The scientists made another startling discovery. The Ripper

squad had not collected together all the descriptions of the killer provided by vital witnesses who possibly saw him. On 1 November 1979 Ron Outtridge drew up a memorandum for the Ripper squad chiefs in Bradford, headed 'The Physical Appearance of the Ripper'. It said:

> There must be in the records several reports of persons who have seen or claim to have seen, persons thought to be the 'Ripper'. However, so far as I am aware, no 'photofit' pictures have been given to the press for publication and nothing in the way of a description has been given to police officers to enable them to recognize likely suspects while performing their multifarious duties in contact with the general public.
>
> RECOMMENDATION
> 1. That all the descriptions given by witnesses over the years be brought together and a study made of them in order to produce a composite picture.
> 2. That key witnesses if there are any be reinterviewed by a different inquiry team to see what further information comes to light. There may be some value in attempting to include the 'white male profile' photofit technique, if this has not already been done.
> 3. That the results of (1) and (2) be evaluated in order to provide police officers with a [illegible] description picture.

There is no evidence that this suggestion was ever followed up.

Stockdale and Outtridge noted that while everyone they met was cordial, they never had any link with the most senior

officers from West Yorkshire police, even though they were
working at Bradford on the personal instructions of the con-
troller of the Forensic Science Service, who was a chief scientific
officer and key adviser to the Home Secretary. Oldfield's temporary replacement, Jim Hobson, never came to see them;
neither did the chief constable or his deputy want to be briefed
by them. 'We were not test-tube washers,' Stockdale reflected
years later. 'We were fairly senior scientists. [Outtridge was
director of the Nottingham Laboratory.] We thought the hierarchy might at least acknowledge our presence by saying hello.
Instead, our contact was Peter Gilrain.' They were not there to
question existing police procedures – they were only supposed
to give guidance about the scientific evidence. They, too, had a
chart on the wall of their office. It stated in stark terms: WHAT
WE KNOW ABOUT THE RIPPER and WHAT WE THINK
WE KNOW ABOUT THE RIPPER. 'There was nothing on
the first column and in the second there were quite a few entries,'
Stockdale added. 'Every now and then the detectives came into
our office, looked at the chart on the wall and would say: "Bloody
hell, you're right." They found it quite sobering.'

If the scientists were constrained in criticizing police procedures, there was one man who could criticize, and did. That
autumn of 1979 Ronald Gregory was under real pressure from
the Home Office, the media and public opinion when the
Home Secretary, William Whitelaw, was due to pay a flying
visit to the incident room. Two days earlier, Gregory went to
New Scotland Yard in London to see Sir David McNee, the
Metropolitan Police Commissioner. As a result McNee agreed
to send two of his top men to Leeds to cast an eye over the
Ripper inquiry. Gregory had always resisted demands by
the press to 'bring in the Yard'. Oldfield, thinking back to the
time before amalgamation when Scotland Yard would send a

superintendent with a bagman to help with a tricky murder, considered it would be a waste of time. Local knowledge was far more important; the days of Fabian, Burt or Guyver coming in and solving a case were over. Besides, his officers had as much skill in solving murders as the London-based detectives.

But now, Gregory had no alternative. The publicity campaign had failed to find the killer and he personally had to be seen to act. Knowing his own men would be deeply unhappy about the involvement of Scotland Yard, he disclosed the impending arrival of the Scotland Yard men to the northern correspondent of the *Sunday Times* several days before he informed his own senior officers. His men were happy to take advice from any quarter, he said. 'Their pride comes second to catching this man.' When Whitelaw turned up at Millgarth, Oldfield took a few hours off from convalescing at home to meet him. The ACC (crime) wasn't going to have the chit-chat with the top brass left to his temporary stand-in, Jim Hobson.

It would be a further six weeks before Oldfield returned to work, by which time much had changed. Peter Gilrain would be placed in overall command of the Ripper investigation and George Oldfield effectively taken off the case. This urgent change was prompted by the month-long visit to the north by Commander Jim Nevill, at fifty-two one of Britain's most experienced detectives and the head of Scotland Yard's anti-terrorist branch. He was accompanied by an experienced murder squad officer, Detective Chief Superintendent Joe Bolton from Croydon. The arrival in Yorkshire of the dapper, silver-haired Nevill merited a photo opportunity for the local news media followed by a press conference. He was met off the high-speed 125 Express from London at Wakefield station by a local police inspector and driver. Nevill came with high credentials. He was capable of great political sensitivity and could easily have passed for a diplomat. He had worked with George Oldfield on the M62 coach bombing and investigated the Georgi Markov assassination in which David Gee assisted. Nevill was accustomed to dealing with the most secretive and sensitive departments of government and had acted as a negotiator with a group of IRA killers at the Balcombe Street siege. He understood the pressures detectives had to cope with when dealing with high-profile cases. Gregory announced he was looking for new ideas, something his men hadn't tried yet.

Nevill and Bolton travelled around the North of England bringing themselves up to speed, asking questions and reading reports. They talked to all the senior officers, and it didn't take Nevill long to spot what was wrong: the man in overall charge of the Ripper inquiry needed to do the job to the exclusion of everything else. Gregory acted immediately and moved to put Gilrain in overall command. But the end result of Nevill's visit was symptomatic of everything that was wrong with the investigation. Bright men spotted the problems, pointed them out, but, for reasons which are not clear, these problems remained. Few, if any, of Nevill's major recommendations were carried through, apart from the decision to appoint Gilrain as full-time senior investigating officer.

Nevill wrote to Gregory early in the New Year to recommend streamlining the major incident room system in an effort to clear outstanding actions and to review the method by which suspects were eliminated. The inquiry had become overburdened by the sheer volume of material. Detectives on the ground needed clearer information from the incident room when questioning suspects, a properly coordinated docket of papers so they had all the information about an individual at their fingertips. The senior investigating officer should be insulated from dealing with dross, not overburdened with paperwork that should have been filtered out and dealt with at a lower level. An intelligence unit should re-evaluate information from previous crimes, and there needed to be more dialogue between forensic scientists and investigating officers. Nevill also warned that other women in West Yorkshire who had been attacked could well also be Ripper victims and have valuable clues. Crucially, he argued, senior officers were having to deal with information that could be handled by junior detectives. 'It was disturbing to find that the officer in charge of the case was having to deal with a vast amount of non-relevant paper, much of which we thought could have been settled at a much lower level of command,' Nevill said in his report. 'The present system imposes an enormous workload on such an officer and we would, therefore, propose that there should be established a filter system at a lower level in order that only relevant statements, actions and letters are personally seen by the investigating officer.'

While he agreed the Sunderland operation should continue, he urged caution, suggesting a review of suspects previously eliminated on the grounds that they were not the letter writer or tape sender. 'While it is agreed that the author of the letters and tape is probably the murderer, it is not a complete certainty,' he wrote. The logical corollary of this warning should have been that suspects cleared because their handwriting was different were to be reinterviewed. Amazingly, it never happened. A secret Home Office inquiry into the conduct of the Ripper case provided a damning indictment of the failure to do anything: 'Unfortunately we have been unable to trace evidence that Commander Nevill's more important recommendations were implemented by the West Yorkshire Police.' It would be a further ten months before decisive action was taken to address the problems of the incident room, and then only after another young woman was killed. Nevill's cautionary warning about the Sunderland connection had little or no effect on the thinking of senior detectives. By now the decision to treat the letters and tape as if they had come from the killer had resulted in disastrous consequences because it wrongly eliminated the real killer from the inquiry. Had the recommendations been implemented, especially those which involved a change in existing priorities, beneficial results could have followed.

The secret official report continued:

> By the time Commander Nevill and others had advised against the positive elimination of suspects by reason of the tape and letters, it would have been a mammoth task to search the records in the overloaded incident room with a view to re-checking all those previously eliminated from the inquiry. It would have been an even greater task for the outside inquiry teams to have followed through, and certainly could not have been done by the resources then available. *It would also have meant admitting publicly, with potential dire consequences, that the earlier decision to use the tape and letters as eliminating sieves had not been justified.* [Author's italics]

The report's author, Mr Lawrence Byford, one of HM Inspectors of Constabulary, gave his opinion as to why Zackrisson's and Nevill's advice was ignored: '*In my view the reluctance to follow the advice proffered by the discerning Detective Inspector Zackrisson of Northumbria, [and] Commander Nevill of New Scotland Yard ... can be attributed to this latter factor more than any other*' [my italics]. In other words, he thought that there was a tremendous resistance to admitting that the inquiry had taken wrong turns.

This reluctance to face the truth can be seen also in an early 'Introductory Report' of the Ripper investigation, *Regina v Sutcliffe*, prepared by West Yorkshire Police in 1981. It stated reassuringly: 'Commander Nevill's comments prior to leaving the enquiry at Christmas 1979, was to the effect that all that could be done had or was being done and there was nothing further that he could do to assist.' Surprisingly, it did not mention the recommendations that Nevill had made in the New Year, after leaving the inquiry. In fact, before he left West Yorkshire for London, Nevill added his voice to several others by even going public in urging caution about the central plank of the Ripper squad's investigation: the voice on the tape. 'It might provide a good lead, but as the Black Panther tape showed nothing can be 100 per cent certain. From the tape recordings left by the Black Panther, experts said the voice had a Black Country accent – Neilson was a Yorkshire man.'

By the time he returned to his office at the Wakefield headquarters early in the New Year, George Oldfield had a depressing series of statistics awaiting him. In the previous four years the Ripper investigation had clocked up 24,693 statements, 152,230 vehicle checks, 194,771 people interviewed and 25,200 house-to-house inquiries. All this, and still they had not got their man. Oldfield himself took a back seat, under strict instructions from his wife, Margaret, and Ronald Gregory not to overdo it. There would be no more late nights poring over piles of statements and no more Benylin and whisky cocktails. 'I don't intend to be his next victim,' he said. But still he wanted to see the man caught before he retired.

Unknown to Oldfield, the best opportunity yet to arrest the Yorkshire Ripper was about to unfold, but it happened at the very time when the investigation was at its most dangerous, depressing and muddled phase, with carelessness piled upon misfortune piled upon incompetence. A startlingly original piece of detective work was conceived and proved extraordinarily successful, only for its success to be promptly wasted and another golden opportunity thrown away. This new operation was set in motion well before Oldfield's return from ill health. Jim Nevill shared Jack Ridgway's conviction that the best chance of catching the killer lay with restarting the five-pound note inquiry. The key was to narrow down the actual firms which could have received the five-pound note from the Midland Bank in Shipley. Nevill had made this a priority in his report.

Since Barbara Leach's murder, Ridgway had been making frequent visits to Leeds and Bradford to attend conferences and meet one-on-one with Peter Gilrain, with whom he got on well. Ridgway was seeking another crack at the five-pound note inquiry and Gilrain was equally enthusiastic but had grave manpower problems. Six thousand people had been interviewed during the first investigation. If Ridgway could reduce this number somehow, then Gilrain would support reopening a combined West Yorkshire/Manchester inquiry.

From the time of Jean Jordan's murder in 1977 Ridgway felt there had been little real cooperation from the Bank of England in London. He believed the bank had dragged its feet instead of helping with a major criminal investigation. After several attempts, he arranged an appointment at the end of October 1979 with a senior Bank of England official. What convinced him to take the Manchester CID chief's plea for help seriously on this occasion is subject to speculation, but Ridgway's boss was James Anderton, a high-profile chief constable not afraid of saying what he thought. Ridgway let it be known that his chief was unhappy with the earlier lack of real help from the Bank of England.

'I more or less hinted that he was very upset and might even go public about their previous refusal to cooperate,' he recalled. 'I think what prompted them to help were a few vague threats and a little nudging in the right direction.' As a result of the meeting, the senior official secured permission for Ridgway to visit the bank's high-security printing works at Loughton in Essex. There he was able to watch the entire operation as bank notes were printed. Each stage of the process was explained to him in minute detail, a privilege granted to few outsiders. What he witnessed helped him to understand why they had been unsuccessful with their earlier inquiry. Moreover, Ridgway was now convinced it gave them a much better chance of discovering where the five-pound note went after it left the Midland Bank at Shipley.

'There was a great roll of paper at one end,' he said of the printing run, 'and it comes out as little bound packets of notes at the other. They showed me how they numbered them, how they recorded those numbers and how there are people who sift through them. They have a great sheet of notes and ladies sit there with a marker pen and mark the ones that are going to be taken out. They are numerically and sequentially numbered and when you see them doing that, you understand how you can get these gaps in the numbered sequence of notes. I even saw one woman draw a line right across the sheet and they scrapped the whole sheet. I couldn't see anything wrong with it. By the time I came out, I was perfectly happy that the original list of numbers they had supplied me with were correct. At one stage I had doubted it, but now I knew it was right.'

The Bank of England had supplied Ridgway with the exact numbers on the notes distributed during the bullion delivery run by its Leeds branch two years previously, which culminated with £25,000 being dropped off at Shipley. Bank officials at the printing works, at last recognizing how crucial it was to find the York-shire Ripper, now made Ridgway an extraordinary offer. Uniquely, they would get their staff to reprint exactly the entire bundle of five-pound notes originally sent to Shipley. These would be processed and packed in exactly the same way before being taken out of the local Midland Bank strongroom and distributed to local firms as payroll. All the numbers of the notes would be printed in sequence on blank sheets of paper, then wrapped in packets in precisely the same way, down to the right number of smaller bundles and packages delivered from the van into the Shipley bank strongroom. Incorporated into the operation would be the exact numbers on the notes discarded from the print run as 'spoils'. These would be removed and replaced by 'perfect' notes before the large sheets were cut into packets of notes, just as had happened twenty-four months earlier.

Ridgway was staggered by the help the bank was now giving. He had only asked casually if they could make him up a bundle of 500 dummy notes. 'We will make you up a bundle of £25,000 in fake notes,' they replied. The big bundle contained ten smaller bundles of £2,500 each, each divided into smaller packets of £500. These were individual white pieces of paper cut to five-pound note size. 'They had gone to the trouble,' Ridgway said, 'of putting the correct number of every single note in that bundle, including the gaps. The large bundle I received was a replica of the one the Bank of England staff put into the van in Leeds.' Ridgway was being given the opportunity to switch careers temporarily and play banker. He would be allowed to enter his own slow-motion time warp, travelling back two years so he could painstakingly re-create the exact way the five-pound notes were distributed by the bank staff at Shipley. And they were going to do it with the help of staff at the Bank of England in the City of London.

On 5 November 1979 Ridgway travelled to London with Tony Stevenson, a detective sergeant from Manchester CID. They were scheduled to meet up in the City with the chief cashier from the Midland Bank at Shipley, Simon Steward, who travelled up from Bradford with his wife, Christine, and the precious cash-analysis books. He carried the time-honoured bank documents in a large, burdensome leather suit-case. He was thirty-two and had been married seven years. Christine, also a cashier for the Midland Bank, had taken the day off to make the excursion to London and go shopping. To other travellers on that early-morning train from the wool capital of the north to the financial and political capital in the south, they would have seemed like a young couple visiting London on holiday, or even on their honeymoon. For a man in his early thirties, Mr Steward presented a youthful, almost boyish, countenance. His face never seemed to age and his physical frame remained constantly trim. He had worked for the Midland Bank in London for several months in the early 1970s when there was a staff shortage one summer. Since then his professional horizons had been confined to a fairly narrow corner of the banking universe north of Bradford. Now, out of the blue, the Dewsbury-born bank worker found himself summoned with his bank records to the most famous financial institution in the world, to spend the day at the 'Old Lady' of Threadneedle Street. It was hard for the Yorkshireman not to compare his workplace at the tiny provincial bank in Shipley shopping precinct with the mighty pile that was the Bank of England, spread across nearly four priceless acres of the Square Mile. Until 1973 the streets outside it had been patrolled over-night by a special bank picket of armed soldiers from the Brigade of Guards, which had vague memories for Ridgway. In the mid-1950s he once mounted the bank picket when serving in the Coldstream Guards: one of a squad of eight guardsmen who marched with sloped arms from Wellington Barracks near Buckingham Palace to the City of London in greatcoats and bearskins.

The high windowless walls of the bank towered above the visitors from the north as they quickly made their entrance. They were met by a commissionaire in pink frock coat and black top hat, who escorted them through the ornate banking hall, resplendent with arches and pillars, vaulted walls and domed ceilings. They were steered in the direction of the 'parlours', as the bank's workrooms are known. Upstairs, they sat in a large panelled room with a number of bank officials around a magnificent mahogany table, its reddish-brown top highly polished. The subject under discussion was how Simon Steward and his colleagues handled five-pound notes. They had first been issued in 1793 and remained the longest-running banknote of any denomination currently in circulation. Bank of England staff are normally involved in more weighty matters of high finance than how an individual fiver could arrive in the pocket of a murdered prostitute and finding who gave it to her. Now here they were with a detective chief superintendent from the murder squad involved with one of the most notorious cases in British criminal history, discussing how to play 'cashiers and customers' with pretend fivers run off from the bank's own printing works.

The day's proceedings began with Ridgway reading from his well-prepared notes, and Simon Steward consulting the cashier's book and the large 'to' and 'from' safe book, measuring twenty-four by twelve inches. They spent many hours discussing the banking exercise Ridgway intended to replay, slowly but surely, over the next month at his first-floor office at Bootle Street, Manchester. For many hours the Bank of England staff cast expert eyes over Simon Steward's cash-analysis sheets and bank records. Ridgway and Stevenson needed to understand fully the process of paying money out, and to have complete faith that the figures and records were reliable. Steward patiently explained how he and his colleagues worked, demonstrating how money was taken out of the strongroom, passed over to fellow cashiers and later placed back in the vault after the Shipley branch closed for the evening. Within the normal daily transactions inside the small provincial branch were many nuances: cashiers running out of money, small transfers of cash between tills when a cashier ran low of fivers; old notes, new notes; money paid in by cheque and cash; money paid out; small withdrawals; large payments in from shops and large payments out in used notes to the local bookmaker. The bank officials looked at Simon Steward's bank records and after many hours concluded Ridgway's audacious re-enactment plan was entirely feasible. The senior detective's intention was to take Steward's cash-analysis sheets back to Manchester and, using the statements and other information gathered during the first five-pound note inquiry, go through and repeat the day-to-day business of the Shipley branch of the Midland Bank after bundle F587947 had been delivered.

For cashier Simon Steward it was a daunting experience. While Christine shopped along Oxford Street, he was helping track down the most notorious murderer in Britain: 'I was in a position where I had been helping to suggest someone as a suspect for a number of murders. I had to put that to the back of my mind. It was something that had to be done, otherwise the exercise wouldn't have succeeded.'

Back in Manchester, it took the two detectives almost a month of exhausting mental labour to complete the exercise. Stevenson was a working detective and Ridgway had a division to run. At about four or five o'clock every workday afternoon, Stevenson would appear at his boss's office. Everyone else was cleared out and the door remained firmly closed. They then spent the next five or six hours, until 10 p.m. or later, going over the figures, paying money out from the bundle of substitute notes. It was a bit like Monopoly. They started the process by going to the 'strongroom' and taking out cash at the beginning of the bank working day. Money would be paid out either to individuals or firms, and notional money paid in. Sometimes old fivers were put in a casher's till and these would be paid out instead of new notes.

From the conference at the Bank of England, Ridgway realized that 'cashiers' at various stages ran out of money and needed more fivers from the bundle in the strongroom. They several times made errors and realized things hadn't worked. Then they needed to calculate where they had gone wrong when a customer had come in to cash a cheque for £10 and been allocated two old five-pound notes. After checking the records again and again, the detectives realized this person must have had two new fivers. Ridgway consulted his chart and police statements for the few people he knew for certain had received particular numbered notes. These were the witnesses who came forward when he made his appeal after Jean Jordan's murder in 1977 for the thrifty folk of Yorkshire to look in their savings tins and under mattresses to see if they retained any fivers from the bundle of notes he was interested in. He knew the date these had gone to the bank, and roughly the time and which cashier gave them the money. He and Stevenson had worked out which firms had received payroll and when. Ridgway kept watch on the 'Jordan' five-pound note, stashed in its new packet within a small bundle of notes inside the 'strongroom' in his office, awaiting the moment of destiny when it ceased to be a mere slip of paper and became a vital clue in the ritualistic murder of a young mother of two children by the Yorkshire Ripper.

Time inside the room clicked on far more slowly than real time as they went painstakingly through the first day's banking proceedings. This in itself took many days. Occasionally the clock stood completely still as they relentlessly checked paperwork to determine whether a customer had been paid in old notes, or who had made withdrawals or deposits and from which cashier's till. Relentlessly the small sheets of paper passed over the counter and between cashiers. When a cashier ran out of money, they had to replenish from Simon Steward in his position as No. 1 cashier. When he ran low, he went to the strongroom for more. Ridgway noted the point at which the 'Jordan' replica note came out of the strongroom and went to one of the cashiers. There it remained for the rest of that first day's banking until put back in the safe at the close of business. Rechecking his research, the detective chief knew which of the larger firms had come into the bank for payroll, who had served them and how much they took. 'We had the information from the cashiers, from the odd notes we had recovered and from Simon Steward's cash analysis,' said Ridgway. 'We knew that a particular cashier had run out of money and thus Simon had to go to the strongroom to pay her some more money. We followed the trail of the money.'

Over days and weeks the fake bundle of fivers in Ridgway's office grew smaller and smaller. On the second day of bank transactions, but nearly two weeks later in Manchester time, the bundle got smaller still, until again Ridgway observed the 'Jordan' note coming out of the 'strongroom' into one of the tills and then being placed back into the vault at the end of the second day's business. The excitement was palpable as they were able to account for more and more money being paid out. Neither man knew what the actual outcome might be, but as an intellectual exercise it was both fascinating and absorbing, like a three-dimensional game of chess. But Ridgway was constantly aware he could fall on his backside. The gamble could have failed through some faulty piece of analysis. The only way they could know they were successful would be if it led them to the killer.

In early December 1979, as they were conducting the third day's trading, they came to the point where the crucial note had gone. It had been paid out and left the bank, Ridgway and Stevenson were certain. Through diligence, patience and brilliant teamwork the numbers of potential people who could have received that five-pound note was whittled down from 5,943 to 240 employees working for eleven firms in the Shipley area. On being given the information, Oldfield asked for one additional name to be added (almost certainly that of his *bête noire*, Terence Hawkshaw), making 241 people who were then rechecked against information held within the main incident room files. Among the eleven firms was T. & W. H. Clark, who had 49 employees. A Mr Peter William Sutcliffe was No. 76 on the list of 241 names. Ridgway couldn't be absolutely sure the Ripper was among them – a woman could have received the note and given it to her husband or lover – but he felt agonizingly close.

Ridgway conferred with his West Yorkshire colleagues and a new operation was mounted, this time from Idle police station, in North Bradford. The Manchester officers found it hilarious that near by was the Idle Working Men's Club. Detectives again worked in pairs made up of one from each force, and started questioning people on the list. All 241 suspects were in the 'system' because of the original five-pound note inquiry. Any additional information accumulated was photo-copied and given to the inquiry teams. Yet it was at this precise point that Ridgway's painstaking work began to fall apart. Only seven of the 241 names had any additional information discovered about them in the incident room system, and Sut-cliffe was not included. Much later it was discovered that he was among eighteen additional people wrongly marked as 'no trace', his cards either missing or misplaced in the nominal index, even though he had by now been questioned six times, including the two five-pound note interviews in 1977.

Even more tragically, among the eighteen 'phantoms' only Sutcliffe had featured as a 'triple-area sighting', a cross-area sighting, and as someone who had a vehicle that featured in the 'tracking' inquiry. If a thorough search had been carried out, this information should have been collated together. It would have leapt out at the Ripper squad. Whoever checked for information on the 241 people on Ridgway's list totally missed finding any additional information about Sutcliffe. Much later, the secret report prepared personally for William Whitelaw, the Home Secretary, condemned whoever carried out this search. Even allowing for an overload of work in the Millgarth incident room, it could not 'excuse the abject failure of an unidentified member of the major incident room staff whose responsibility it was to check the list of 241 people in the nominal index. The failure to identify Sutcliffe and ten other persons on the list of 241 who were subjects of separate lines of inquiry in the investigation, sowed the seeds of further interview failures and basically allowed Sutcliffe to commit two more murders and two further serious assaults.'

On 7 January 1980, the day Oldfield returned to work, Ridgway's strict instructions to officers conducting the inter-views were that no one was to be eliminated on the basis of handwriting or accent. In a half-day briefing, he set out all the information they had about the Ripper's crimes, but not before having a spat with Ronald Gregory. The West Yorkshire chief constable informed the Manchester detective the press would sit in on the briefing. Ridgway said that most assuredly they would not, and if they did, he would not give the briefing. Eventually a mute photocall of Manchester and West Yorkshire officers being 'briefed' was allowed before the press were ushered politely but firmly away.

Ridgway's talk to his team was comprehensive and confidential. He showed slides of the various crime scenes and detailed many aspects of the inquiry. He instructed that houses, garages and vehicles were to be thoroughly searched, and anyone who did not satisfy the detectives could be taken in for a more rigorous interview. People could only be eliminated if they had a verifiable alibi. In the space of a month Peter Sutcliffe was about to be interviewed yet again by Ripper squad officers on three more occasions.

The three interviews were all connected to the new five-pound note inquiry, each conducted by different pairs of officers. At 1.25 p.m. on Sunday, 13 January 1980, just six days after Ridgway's briefing, Detective Sergeant X from Yorkshire and Detective Constable Y from Manchester turned up on the Sutcliffes' doorstep. They had papers relating to the earlier five-pound note inquiry from 1977 but no knowledge of the interviews after Sutcliffe had been spotted in first two, then three red-light areas. Despite it being early afternoon, Sonia Sutcliffe came to the door wearing a nightie and dressing gown. She let the officers into the front lounge and called her husband. It was obvious he had just got out of bed. They asked him about his work and then for an alibi for the most recent murder on

2 September the previous year, when Barbara Leech was killed. He could not give one but said he had provided a sample of his handwriting at an earlier interview. This came as a surprise to the detective sergeant, who mentally decided to check with the incident room. They searched the house and examined Sutcliffe's boots and tools in the adjacent garage. Sutcliffe did not draw attention to himself, but something about the man struck the Yorkshire officer, who was an experienced murder squad investigator. The detective made a telling observation in his notebook: 'a strange runner . . .', he wrote of Sutcliffe. But then strange people were nothing unusual in this investigation.

Back at the incident room the pair made a discovery which should have sent the Ripper squad rocketing back to Garden Lane, Heaton, to arrest Sutcliffe, or at the very least suggest he accompany them back to the police station for an in-depth interrogation. In the nominal index they found three separate cards relating to previous inquiries about Sutcliffe. These showed he had been questioned about the original five-pound note inquiry, on the cross-area sightings when he was driving his red Ford Corsair, and as a triple-area sighting in his black Sunbeam Rapier. A Manchester detective inspector sent across to Idle police station to run the incident room for the five-pound note inquiry was immediately made aware of the discrepancy. On the one hand Sutcliffe had been labelled a 'no trace' in the paperwork check on the 241 suspects, but here were records showing there should be extra paperwork. Detective Inspector Z ordered a further search for the additional paperwork to which the index cards pointed. He got back only those documents referring to the 'cross-area sighting' of Sutcliffe's red Ford Corsair. Out of the system were papers relating to questioning about being seen in three red-light areas, as well as Andrew Laptew's report. The outstanding documents were waiting for work records about Sutcliffe to be returned to his employer, but no reference was made in the index system to papers being absent. It was a fatal omission. Sadly, the detective who regarded Sutcliffe as 'a strange runner' did not bring his feelings to the attention of a senior officer and did not take the opportunity, offered by Ridgway, to bring in anyone they felt unhappy about to the police station for interrogation.

The in-depth analysis of what went wrong with the Ripper inquiry concluded later that the inspector in the incident room at Idle should have pursued the search for papers about Sutcliffe with greater enthusiasm, because he had in his possession a copy of a nominal index card with references to papers which could not be found. 'He must therefore share the responsibility for the failure which allowed Sutcliffe to remain at liberty when he clearly should have been arrested . . . the surprise information that Sutcliffe, who was marked "no trace", had in fact been interviewed on several occasions during the inquiry, should have alerted him to the possibility that the search had not been properly carried out and should be double-checked.'

However, knowing a Ford Corsair might have featured in the Millward murder in Manchester, the inspector drew up an 'action' ordering that Sutcliffe be questioned again about the possible use of prostitutes, whether he had access to a tape recorder, whether he had a pronounced accent and his alibis for the Whitaker and Leach killings. The follow-up interview took place on 30 January 1980 in Leeds, at the Kirkstall Forge Engineering Works, where Sutcliffe was loading his lorry. He said his wife could verify he was at home on the night of the Leach murder. He again explained his journeys through Bradford and Leeds. Examining the papers they carried that referred to Sutcliffe, which showed his home and car had pre-

viously been searched, the two new detectives confined themselves to a search of the driver's cab of his lorry. Yet, their
report claimed, their search of his home and car was negative.
The thirty-minute interview was perfunctory, to say the least.
The senior of the two men, a detective sergeant from Manchester, had more or less psychologically put Sutcliffe out of
the frame for the murders, because his West Yorkshire colleagues were still using the letters and tape as a prime means
of elimination despite strict instructions from Ridgway, only
three weeks earlier, that no one was to be eliminated on these
grounds.

Again the incident room inspector was unhappy with the
action report. He ordered an immediate reinterview to discover
the dates on which Sutcliffe's two Ford Corsair cars were disposed of. If he got rid of them before Millward was killed,
Sutcliffe could probably be eliminated from the inquiry. The
detective inspector personally instructed the next two officers
to question Sutcliffe that he wanted a more in-depth probe of
the cross-area sightings in his red Ford Corsair, and a proper
alibi for the night of the Whitaker murder.

Two detective constables conducted the ninth and final
interview with Peter Sutcliffe on 7 February 1980 at T. & W. H.
Clark's offices. He plausibly explained the visit to Leeds when
he and Sonia went to a club and later met a couple called Paul
and Wendy in a pub at Kirkstall. The Sutcliffes gave them a
lift home to the Roundhay area. He did not know their last
name or what kind of car he was driving, but later Sonia
confirmed meeting the couple and giving them a lift. The
officers checked and discovered police observation points had
indeed been in the area, which they believed explained why
Sutcliffe's vehicle had been spotted in Leeds. Sutcliffe said his
white Ford Corsair had been taken to a firm of car breakers,

but the detectives could trace no record of this when they visited the scrapyard and studied the incoming scrap ledger. They checked his work logbooks for the night Josephine Whitaker was murdered. Sutcliffe said he was at home with his wife, which she confirmed. The logbook said he had driven some 260 miles that day and a company official said Sutcliffe would have finished work around 5 p.m. In the action report returned to the incident room, one of the officers said it was difficult to eliminate Sutcliffe positively. He recommended they should 'start afresh on any subsequent murder in the series'. In other words, as soon as the Ripper struck again, Sutcliffe would be questioned and asked to provide an alibi.

The incident room inspector felt the inquiry had gone as far as possible. Mrs Sutcliffe had alibied her husband for the Leach murder, he said in a report. Also she was the alibi for the night of Sunday, 9 October 1977, when a house-warming party was held at their home. It was the same evening Jordan's body was revisited by her killer and mutilated. On 10 March 1980, he recommended Sutcliffe's interviews be filed with no further action. After reading all the papers, Jack Ridgway signed his approval exactly a month later.

The official government inquiry into the investigation later concluded that the last three interviews should have taken place at a police station, Sutcliffe being on a narrow list of people suspected of murdering Jean Jordan and having no positive alibis. Moreover, by now there were additional 'cross-area' sightings of Sutcliffe's Rover 3.5 saloon. He had been seen in the Leeds and Bradford prostitute areas seven times between May and early November 1979. 'The interviews of this man whose alibis were so general and so lacking in proper corroboration should have taken place inside a police station and should have involved a senior detective who was prepared to take a positive line and ask Sutcliffe for explanations for every one of his motor vehicle sightings . . . it may well be that by this stage the inquiry had got to the state whereby even experienced and competent detectives could no longer "see the wood for the trees".' Sutcliffe had in fact been interviewed as a result of every major proactive operation the Ripper squad had mounted during the last three years: the tracking inquiry, the first five-pound note inquiry, the cross-area sightings and the triple-area sightings, and finally the second five-pound note investigation. There is no record of how many other men had a similar tally, but it cannot have been many.

Taken in isolation, each interview held out a slim prospect of success, the government's secret report noted: 'There is however the concept which Ian Fleming allowed "Goldfinger" to propound: "Once is happenstance. Twice is coincidence. The third time is enemy action." If this concept had been applied to the record of Sutcliffe's association with the Ripper inquiry there were clearly grounds for him to be placed in the "suspect" category, certainly at the time when he was seen by Detective Constable Laptew as a result of his "triple-area sightings".' Ridgway's own explanation for filing the Sutcliffe papers with no further action was his belief that Sutcliffe could be eliminated for the murder of Jean Jordan.

'I was aware that Sutcliffe had been alibied by his wife for four murder dates, Jordan, Millward, Whitaker and Leach,' he said. 'I did not consider this of itself to be particularly significant. Unless there is something significant about the date in question to make it stand out in the mind of the interviewee, one date is much the same as another, particularly when the person is being interviewed months after the date in question. In any event an alibi provided by a wife is always viewed with caution. The single fact which most influenced my decision to file Sutcliffe's papers was the house-warming party held at his home on the night of the 9/10 October 1977 – the night the body of Jordan was moved. By virtue of the event there that night, there was a reason why it should stand out in the minds of all the people interviewed; people other than his wife, albeit most of them were relatives, were able to confirm that such a party had taken place and that Sutcliffe had been present at the party. The fact that Sutcliffe was clearly not the author of the letters and the tape did not influence my decision in any way. Having considered the totality of evidence in relation to Sutcliffe available at that time, I believe to write "file" on the papers was the correct decision.' (At this stage of the inquiry, no one knew that on the night of the house-warming party Peter Sutcliffe took his parents home and, instead of returning immediately, drove over to Manchester on the M62, and violated Jean Jordan's corpse, which included the attempt to saw off her head with a hacksaw.)

Working at Idle police station during this crucial period were seven of the eight officers who had conducted the last four interviews with Peter Sutcliffe, from July 1979 to February 1980. Several had real doubts about Sutcliffe and between them they knew all there was to know about his involvement with the Ripper investigation. Tragically, they did not communicate with each other so as to enable the information against him to be co-ordinated. This was probably due to a lack of effective briefings by more senior personnel: they didn't know what they were looking for.

When police officers turned up at the Sutcliffes' house in midsummer they were there on another matter. For months Jim Hobson had been hoping to nab the Ripper while he was on the move. He had set up static observation points at night throughout the West Yorkshire force area. Sutcliffe, in his

Rover 3.5, drove fast and erratically past one of these observation points in Grosvenor Road, Manningham, at about
11.30 p.m. on 26 June 1980. Thinking the vehicle might be
stolen, the two uniformed constables in an unmarked police
car gave chase, with speeds reaching 80 m.p.h. They didn't
stop the driver until they reached 6 Garden Lane and found
the Rover parked in the driveway. Sutcliffe was arrested, taken
to Bradford police station and charged for being drunk in
charge of a motor vehicle. A routine check was carried out
with the Ripper incident room. They were told he had been
interviewed and eliminated from the inquiry on handwriting.

The next victim of the Yorkshire Ripper was not recognized
as such until much later, when it was all too late. Marguerite
Walls, a forty-seven-year-old unmarried civil servant, was murdered in Pudsey, between Leeds and Bradford, on 20 August
1980. She had been struck across the head, strangled, left virtually naked and covered with grass cuttings in the garden of
'Claremont', a grand detached mansion belonging to a local
textile manufacturer and chief magistrate. Miss Walls was a
quiet woman who kept her private life just that – private.
Intending to go on holiday to the Lake District after first
attending the funeral of a friend in Newcastle the following
day, she stayed late at her office at the schools inspectorate in
the local office of the Department of Education. She had a
takeaway Chinese meal at her desk and left to walk the mile
and a half home at about 10.45 p.m. Her body was discovered
the following morning four hundred yards from her home.

She was born at Dunston, Lincolnshire, in 1943 and had a
younger brother and sister. In the mid-1940s the family upped
and moved to Londonderry, in Northern Ireland. She went to
school there, had a few jobs, and then joined the Women's

Royal Army Corps. She reached the rank of sergeant and left after five years. She was a striking, dark-haired woman, short and slim. At twenty-five she joined the civil service in Northern Ireland and later transferred to London. A couple of years later she left, had other jobs, but decided civil service life suited her and took up another government job in Basingstoke. Then she moved to Customs and Excise around 1972–73, moving to Leicester, where she had a longstanding relationship with a local man. She was self-confident and personable, and could cope with most situations. She did not marry, although she had a number of men friends, some of whom became lovers, but not many. In the late 1970s she transferred as an executive officer to Pudsey, near Leeds, and bought a detached house, built by a local firm, on a new estate at Farsley. Marguerite had the keys to the offices where she worked and could let herself in and out.

Shortly before 9 a.m. on the morning her body was found, a couple who looked after the large gardens of 'Claremont' in New Street, Pudsey, walked in at the stone gateway and up the driveway. They had gone almost ten yards when they noticed a pair of women's shoes. Over to their left and beyond a small rockery bordering a large area of the garden they saw a violet-coloured wrap-around skirt, the lining of which was badly torn. Near by was a large leather shopping bag, and a chequebook lay on the grass. The police were called. Next to a garage to the left of the house they found a body face down, covered by a tartan-lined blue macintosh and grass cuttings. Close by were a purple wool cardigan and a purple blouse with strings at the neck, also covered by lawn clippings.

She must have put up a ferocious fight against her attacker after first being struck over the head and then having a ligature thrown around her throat. Pathologist Professor Alan Usher from Sheffield University's department of forensic pathology found bruising on her knuckles, and his belief was that she punched her killer several times. From bloodstains and marks on the ground it was clear she had been attacked as she passed the entrance and dragged up the driveway, across the rockery and into a wooded area to the left of the drive where her bag and skirt were found. She was strangled and stripped of clothing apart from a pair of fawn-coloured tights. A ligature mark could be seen around her neck. The post-mortem showed she was covered with bruises and abrasions and there were two clear lacerations to the head – one V-shaped, the other curved. Three of her ribs on the left side were fractured. To strangle her, the killer had knelt on Marguerite Walls's chest – hence the rib fractures. Professor Usher found clear evidence of some kind of sexual interference: three tiny scratches, probably attributable to fingernails, on the external walls of her vagina. 'The undressing of this woman and indeed the position in which she was found and the three finger nail scratches upon her vulva seem to suggest a sexual motive for this crime.'

The presence of Peter Gilrain from the Ripper squad at the crime scene and the post-mortem alerted some reporters to the possibility of another Ripper killing. Within two days, Jim Hobson had ruled it out. The method of attack was totally different. She had not been stabbed, but strangled. Nevertheless she had been clubbed across the head initially, and her body dragged some distance, then hidden to prevent it from being found immediately. But not even Professor David Gee was prepared to include the murder in the Ripper series, though he had not conducted the post-mortem. Jim Hobson thought they would be looking close by for the killer. 'My feelings are that it is a local man who did this murder. I have a team of detectives at Miss Walls's house looking for addresses of male and female friends. She had boyfriends in the past but that was about twenty-odd years ago. She was a very private person who would always go home after finishing work.' He concentrated on finding the killer among a number of local men with convictions for sexual attacks.

Hobson also now decided to abandon the covert observations in red-light areas, convinced the Ripper had already abandoned prostitute areas in his search for victims. Humberside police ended its operation in August 1979. Manchester and South Yorkshire police had stopped theirs the previous December. The four forces had between them 5.4 million sightings of cars in red-light districts. Of these, 20,000 vehicles had been seen in two separate towns; 1,200 were triple-area sightings. It was virtually a year since Barbara Leach had been murdered and the trail had gone cold. So had the press. Having tried a massive publicity campaign, the Ripper team went to the opposite extreme and had, since the beginning of the year, imposed a publicity clampdown. No one among the senior detectives had been available for interview in connection with the Ripper case.

A month after Miss Walls was murdered, her attacker struck again, this time in the Headingley area of Leeds. The latest attack was a rerun of the assault on Marguerite Walls except that the victim survived to tell the tale and give a description of the man who tried his best to strangle her. The woman, a doctor from Singapore, was attending Leeds University for a postgraduate course in health-service studies at the Nuffield Centre. Dr Uphadya Anadavathy Bandara, aged thirty-four, had won a scholarship from the World Health Organization. She had been out visiting a friend on the evening of 24 September 1980, and some time after 11 p.m. was walking home to St Michael's Villas. She passed a local pub, The Skyrack, and turned into Chapel Lane. It was then she heard footsteps behind her. She moved over to let the person pass, and got a brief glimpse of a man with a closely cropped beard. She was not particularly bothered, she told Dr Michael Green from the forensic pathology department at Leeds University, who was called in to examine her. She had walked home on her own many times during the previous eleven months. Suddenly something was being pulled around her neck like a thick and rough rope. She remembered nothing more until she recovered consciousness and found a policeman bending over her.

In fact Dr Bandara had been pretty badly bashed about and was lucky to be alive. She had injuries to her face and the back of her head, in particular an 'arc-shaped' laceration one and a quarter inches long, which was stitched by the time Dr Green saw it. There was a clear band of bruising around her neck that Green thought had been caused by a plaited cord, like a dressing-gown cord. He was sure the rope had been thrown over her head and then pulled tight, 'in the form of a garrotte', and crossed over from behind. She had tried to prise it loose before being dragged along the cobbled road and at some point kicked in the head behind the left ear. She had been struck with a hammer before the attempt was made to strangle her. What may have saved her was that, just after midnight, a police car came round the corner from St Michael's Lane with headlights full on. She had a bleeding head wound and her cardigan had been pulled up round her head. She had not been unconscious very long and the presence of the car may have caused the attacker to flee. As with Miss Walls, the police kept quiet about a ligature being used. Dr Bandara abandoned her planned ten-city holiday around Europe and agreed to help police reconstruct her walk home. Police now believed they might have a nightmare scenario on their hands – not one serial killer on their patch, but two. Three years previously in Shipley a woman had been murdered by garrotting.

The Yorkshire Ripper was nearly caught red-handed a matter of weeks later, on Bonfire Night, 5 November 1980, in the act of trying to murder a sixteen-year-old girl only thirty yards from her home at Oakes, near Huddersfield. It was 8 p.m. in Willwood Avenue and the sights and sounds of traditional Guy Fawkes celebrations were all around as fireworks flared and boomed and rockets flew multi-coloured trajectories culminating in dazzling starbursts. Teresa Sykes had gone to buy cigarettes from a nearby off-licence. Her boyfriend would not run the errand for her, so she angrily stormed out of the house in the middle of watching *Coronation Street* on television. On the way she passed the local police station and noticed a man in a telephone box, only he was not using the telephone, which she thought a bit odd. Coming back she walked along the footpath and saw the figure of the same man walking along the street. She could hear footsteps behind her. Looking behind her she saw the man turn off into another road. She could see him clearly by the light of a nearby street lamp. He had a long thin face with a neatly trimmed beard to the line of the jaw. As she walked on she suddenly became aware of a shadow cast from behind her. In fear she turned quickly into the garden of a house on the left of the path only thirty yards from where she lived. Suddenly she was struck across the head from behind. The blow caused her to fall to her knees, and as she did so, she screamed out loud, so loud the scream could be heard above the noise of the fireworks. She later remembered reaching out and grabbing some metallic object but not being able to maintain her hold.

Her twenty-five-year-old boyfriend, a millworker, James Furey, had been watching the fireworks out of the window of the house they shared and had a clear view down the street. Seeing an altercation, he went barefoot to the front door. He thought it was two boys fighting. Then there came another scream as a second blow rained down on Teresa's head. Just as he reached the footpath he saw the figure of a man walking away. He yelled out: 'Teresa!'

As soon as he shouted, the figure, who had been walking away, started to run. Furey chased after him, running past the spot where Teresa lay, following the attacker into Millfield Close. The Ripper was running towards its junction with Reinwood Road. Furey shouted after him: 'I'll fucking kill you.'

Then the attacker disappeared. Furey got to the junction and looked everywhere but was unable to see him. A neighbour carried Teresa home and someone dialled 999. She sat down and felt a warm sticky feeling and looked at her hands. They were covered in blood, the chair was covered in blood. And then she really started screaming.

Within a few minutes officers from the police station two hundred yards away were on the scene. Soon they were joined by Detective Superintendent Dick Holland, who had been at home with his new wife, Sylvia, and her two teenage boys, when the phone went. Any young woman being viciously attacked from behind merited such a call to senior officers in the Ripper squad. Living at Ainley Top near the M62 motorway, Holland was only a few minutes' drive away. He grabbed a coat, dashed out into the night and drove his car the mile to Oakes for all it was worth. A dog handler also attended, urging his Alsatian to pick up the scent. Police combed the area thoroughly without finding the attacker.

An ambulance rushed Teresa Sykes, the mother of James Furey's three-month-old son, to the local hospital and then on to the specialist neurosurgical unit at Chapel Allerton Hospital in Leeds. Lacerations to her head had caused compound fractures to the skull. She needed brain surgery and it took another five weeks before she was released from hospital. She had clearly been struck several blows across the head with a hammer. Poor Teresa's life changed immeasurably. Her relationship with the father of her child ended and she decided not to marry him. She spent endless nights having nightmares, thinking the man was going to return to attack her; nights spent with her bedroom door barricaded and a knife under her pillow.

Police refused to link the murderous attack on Teresa Sykes with the Ripper investigation, but some detectives on the case were privately convinced she was his latest victim and told her parents so. The family was told to say nothing to the press, but her father, Raymond Sykes, said his daughter's injuries were too like those of other victims for it to have been done by anyone else. Yet again West Yorkshire detectives developed a blind spot, and for some extraordinary reason went to great lengths to keep the Sykes attack separate from the Ripper investigation. A senior detective given the job of finding Teresa's attacker told reporters: 'I said at the time that this was a local incident and that I was convinced a local man was involved. Nothing has happened to change my mind. All this talk that Teresa may have been attacked by the Ripper is making it more difficult to catch her assailant.'

The comment was very surprising. Teresa had been attacked with a hammer from behind by a man with a beard. Dr Bandara had only weeks before been attacked about the head by a man with a beard – who tried to strangle her. They linked her attack to that of Marguerite Walls, who had been attacked on the head and strangled before her body was hidden. Whatever the police's motive for denying Teresa Sykes was a new Ripper victim, the effect was to keep the lid on the pressure building up from all quarters about the Ripper case and its spectacular lack of success.

Was anyone ever going to link together the series of clues that suggested a man with a beard was attacking women about the head from behind and that this man was the Yorkshire Ripper? If his victims were dead, he invariably made sure their bodies were hidden so he could delay them being found, make his escape and possibly establish an alibi. What was it going to take before someone at the highest levels of government began asking for answers to some very serious questions? The painful fact was that it took the murder of another young woman and a tragedy for yet another family. And this time, when the right questions were asked, they came from the most powerful woman in the country: Margaret Thatcher. The Prime Minister.

16

'He Lives Somewhere, He Works for Someone'

Margaret Hilda Thatcher had been in office eighteen months in mid-November 1980, and her mind was on hugely important developments on both sides of the Atlantic Ocean. Two men from opposite ends of the political spectrum had been running for office. Ronald Reagan had just been elected President of the United States, the first candidate to defeat a sitting incumbent since F. D. Roosevelt unseated Hoover in 1932. Having a free-marketeer and political ally in the White House would be of huge significance for Britain in the years to come, but at that stage few could have guessed the extent of the political bond that would be forged between the former Hollywood actor and the woman who came to wear the sobriquet 'Iron Lady' like a badge of honour. Of equal importance to the Prime Minister was an event in her own political backyard, the result of the leadership race in the British Labour Party. Veteran left-winger Michael Foot won by a margin of ten votes. Tories, including Mrs Thatcher, had wanted him to win, for in doing so the Socialists managed to commit political suicide and would remain out of office for eighteen years.

Chosen as Michael Foot's deputy was a native of the West Riding, the Leeds MP, Denis Healey, who previously had care of the nation's coffers as Chancellor of the Exchequer until Mrs Thatcher pounded the Labour government into defeat at the 1979 General Election. Had Denis Healey been responsible for the West Yorkshire police budget in 1980, he would have been talking in terms of 'deficit finance'. The search for the Yorkshire Ripper had gobbled up more than £5 million since it started in October 1975. The overtime bill was staggering, and the knock-on effect of having so many detectives taken away from normal police work caused Ronald Gregory to shift Ripper squad personnel back to tackling more mundane crimes like domestic burglary.

Left behind to solve what had become the most important case in British criminal history was a core of a hundred detectives. Nearly two and a quarter million man-hours had been spent on the abortive murder hunt and now the incident room at Millgarth, Leeds, was in a state of total chaos. A quarter of a million people had been seen during the inquiry, each of them logged on small white cards in the names index. Over 157,000 cars had been checked, 28,600 statements taken, 27,000 house-to-house inquiries made and more than 130,000 separate actions completed. Yet, in the run-up to Christmas 1980, there were still 600 actions outstanding from the Whitaker murder in April 1979. Fifteen hundred tasks were waiting to be completed from Barbara Leach's killing fourteen months earlier, and more than 36,000 documents connected to the Ripper inquiry were still waiting to be filed – a backlog that would take at least nine months to clear.

Morale was on the floor. For Sergeant Megan Winterburn the personal cost, after two years of working in the incident room, was high. The hours she dedicated to the work had undermined her marriage to a fellow police officer and they were to be divorced. The fun had gone out of the job she loved. She felt ground down by the pressure. The small team of dedicated incident room staff had been joined by uniformed officers and young cadets just out of school who were totally unsuited to the highly disciplined work involved in a murder investigation. The index system itself was hopelessly compromised, with cards containing crucial information split up, misfiled or not replaced. Because of this breakdown, Jack Ridgway's golden opportunity to catch the killer had been completely wasted. The inquiry had simply run off the rails. The officers told to check the original 241 names on Ridgway's final list of suspects in the five-pound note inquiry were simply not up to the task.

The incident room was a hive of activity but the regular staff were chasing their tails. Hardly a desk had a square inch of space free. Telephones rang incessantly as hundreds of people a day called in with snippets of information, all of which had to be logged. The room was cloudy with smoke. Mugs of stale tea and full ashtrays littered desks. From time to time staff took quick breaks in the canteen, where chips were served with everything. Large metal wheels in which index cards were kept had long since been jettisoned as the mountains of information grew. They were replaced by dozens of narrow wooden boxes, three feet long, made up in the joiner's shop at force headquarters. They formed a massive wall along one side of the room. On other walls were maps of murder scenes, posters listing staff telephone numbers and duty rosters. The place heaved under the weight of four tons of paper and there were serious concerns as to whether the floor of the five-year-old police station could carry any additional load. Structural engineers advised that filing cabinets be placed around the walls instead of in the centre of the room.

Staff at one end of the incident room had no clue what was going on at the other. 'It was quite feasible that three or four officers could be making out cards for the same person,' Meg

Winterburn said. 'The cards should have been stapled together when they were filed, but as the inquiry became prolonged, some officers weren't trained in indexing and didn't think to get the correct spellings, or to look for similar names in the files. So you could end up with the same person logged on several different cards.' She became incensed by the arrival of staff who showed little or no commitment. 'Sick, lame and lazy,' she calls them. 'They didn't want to be there and they had even less desire to be trained. Even had they wanted training, the time simply didn't allow it.'

Female staff felt particularly vulnerable, believing they were obvious targets for the Ripper. There was a clear undercurrent of disbelief among some staff, aware that those in charge were refusing to link several new attacks on women to the Ripper series when it seemed highly probable he had struck again. Women staff were escorted at night to the car park on the other side of the street from Millgarth police station. An area of land where the West Yorkshire Playhouse now stands had remained derelict for several years after hundreds of tenement flats were torn down and turned into a temporary car park. Late at night, after finishing a shift, the women had to cross a patch of unlit open ground to get to their vehicles. In private, over cups of tea and a cigarette, they discussed the chances of the killer standing across the road watching as they left the police station.

'On dark nights we tended to go over in twos and threes,' said Sue Neave. 'A couple of chaps would come with us and made sure we got there safely. We constantly looked around. Before I drove home I automatically locked the car doors and didn't unlock them until I was safe at home. I had never done this before. We were not safe – this guy was a complete psychopath.' This terrible fear of being a potential target for a killer who could strike anywhere at any time was now shared by hundreds of thousands of women across northern England. It was a completely rational feeling, reinforced by the Ripper's next attack on another university student, again in the Headingley area of Leeds, only yards from a well-lit shopping centre. The effect of this latest outrage was finally to turn the five-year-long murder hunt into a national crisis and one which had devastating consequences for the image of the British police.

On Monday night, 17 November 1980, a thirty-one-year-old Iraqi student at Leeds University discovered a woman's cream-coloured raffia handbag close to a hall of residence in Alma Road, at Headingley. It was shortly before 10 p.m. Unknown to anyone, apart from her attacker, a young woman lay dying only yards away on rough ground behind the Arndale Centre car park. Inside the bag, which had a red shoulder strap, were a Barclaycard with the woman's name on it and a small amount of money. Unable to find anyone to hand the bag over to at the nearby site office for the university halls of residence, the student took it back to the block where he lived. In the kitchen he and two other students decided they would have to wait until morning before reporting the matter. Even so, two hours later, the overseas student went back into the kitchen and examined the bag more closely. He noticed spots of fresh blood.

At the Eastern Area police control room in Leeds the alarm call for help was logged at 12.03 a.m. on Tuesday, 18 November. The operator noted the details: 'Found handbag with blood on it', and passed an urgent message to Ireland Wood police station in Headingley. There a policewoman wrote down: 'Found handbag covered in blood.' Her duty sergeant made a throwaway comment, 'This will be the Ripper's thirteenth victim,' without thinking through the implications of what he had just said. He did nothing further. Meanwhile, the two-man crew of a patrol car arrived at the hall of residence and examined the bag. The time was now 12.12 a.m. The two officers briefly searched the grounds of a large house in Alma Road close to where the handbag had lain. They discovered nothing, because the body of the Yorkshire Ripper's thirteenth victim was lying on a patch of waste ground – on the other side of the road. At 12.30 a.m. the officers were called away to answer one of the ninety burglar alarm calls Leeds police received that night, only three of which turned out to be genuine. Next morning pedestrians in Alma Road found a Fair Isle knitted mitten, followed by a pair of spectacles. An hour later, at 10 a.m., Jacqueline Hill's body was spotted and a murder inquiry launched. No one can know for certain, but had a thorough search been conducted as soon as her handbag was found some twelve hours earlier, it is just possible Jacqueline would have survived, just as three years earlier did Maureen Long. Her injuries were very similar. Pathologist David Gee believed Jacqueline died some time during the middle of the night – it was doubtful, gone midnight, that the police officers who conducted the superficial search of the area would have found her alive. The killer had struck three hours earlier.

Public reaction to the murder of the third-year English student was swift and savage. Press, public and politicians angrily turned on West Yorkshire's police with a bitterness born of five long years of frustration. The story of the police officers' actions after Jacqueline's handbag was found became front-page news. It badly affected everyone who knew the twenty-year-old student, including Stanley Ellis, who had been one of her lecturers. Everyone regarded her as a delightful young woman. A Sunday school teacher at her home in Middlesbrough, she was keen on a career in social work. At the time she was murdered she was returning home from a seminar in Leeds organized by the local probation service. On the dressing table in her room were three photographs of her long-standing boyfriend, an RAF technician. They were planning to become engaged. Friends and family spoke of a young woman with a great deal of love to give, one who truly thought the best of everyone. From where her No. 1 bus stopped outside the Arndale Centre in Headingley, she had only a few hundred yards to walk to the safety of her student flat.

She was found lying flat on her back, her jeans, pulled down to her ankles, covering her feet. A shop manager carrying the previous day's takings to the bank in the Arndale Centre had walked up the ramp to the car park behind the shopping complex, carrying a large bag of silver. As he stopped to switch the load from one hand to the other, he casually looked over the wall and saw Jacqueline's body below amid a clump of small saplings by a single large ash tree. She was still wearing her woollen blue knee-length socks, her body partially covered by her check-patterned coat.

It was a cold day, with a strong and bitter wind along with intermittent showers of sleet. The hallmarks of a Ripper murder were immediately apparent to Professor Gee when he examined the body at the crime scene, an area of rough open ground covered in short grass and some rubbish. She was a tall, thin girl with dark hair. Her bra had been pulled up and there were obvious head injuries. Most of her clothing was still present on her body and a bunch of keys was clipped to the waistband of her jeans. A silver heart-shaped locket and chain were entangled in her hair. During the autopsy Gee discovered a series of wounds to the head made by a ball-pein hammer, as well as a stab wound to the chest area. Disturbingly, the victim had also been stabbed through the right eye by an instrument like a chisel or screwdriver. The wound had penetrated her

fended off questions. The atmosphere was so savage that Finlay, normally a softly spoken and courteous man, refused to talk to the press again unless he had something specific to say. 'The Chief' was close to losing his temper after a barrage of questions lasting an hour. In a tense atmosphere, neither man could explain why officers had not searched more thoroughly for the owner of the handbag. Gregory glibly claimed it was easy with hindsight to say the patrol car crew should have found the body. There were three bloodspots on the handbag, but at that stage Jacqueline had not been reported missing, he said. Many listened in disbelief to his suggestion that finding a handbag with bloodspots on it late at night was nothing unusual in Leeds.

Public anger rose swiftly. On the streets of Leeds hundreds of feminists marched in protest for several nights in a row under the banner 'Women Against Violence Against Women'. Fights broke out between marchers and police outside a Leeds cinema showing the film *Dressed to Kill*. Red paint was hurled at the screen. A warning that women should not go out alone at night was seen as a police curfew, shifting responsibility for the killings on to the victims away from the Ripper himself – or from the police who had pathetically failed to catch him. MPs became openly contemptuous. Several demanded a change at the top of the Ripper squad, calling for Scotland Yard to take over the inquiry. Against this background the chairman of the West Yorkshire police authority also went public, demanding a change of direction in the investigation. Ronald Gregory's reaction remained unchanged and totally out of touch with the public mood. Commander Jim Nevill from Scotland Yard, he said archly, had already given the inquiry a clean bill of health: 'I do wish people would resist the temptation to make harmful statements before they have made contact with us. They can only undermine morale in the force and unnecessarily intensify public concern.'

That same evening Mrs Doreen Hill, the heartbroken mother of the murdered student, bravely went on television and made a desperate appeal that moved the entire nation. With great calm and dignity she pleaded with 'people everywhere' to help find the killer. 'I want to ask everyone, not just in Leeds or around Leeds, but all over the country to help us find the person who killed my daughter. Please think. Perhaps he lives in your house. He could live in a mansion, in a block of flats, or down the street. He lives somewhere, he works for someone – please think.'

Public fury, Mrs Hill's appeal and the chief constable's dismissive response to legitimate concerns from reporters and politicians, reverberated two hundred miles south in London. At No. 10 Downing Street Margaret Thatcher urgently summoned the Home Secretary, William Whitelaw, and launched into a ferocious attack on the police force's inability to catch the Ripper. She had a daughter, Carol, roughly the same age as Jacqueline Hill and could empathize with her grieving mother. This strong maternal emotion and the thought that young women were being slaughtered by a killer who was running rings around the police galvanized Mrs Thatcher into wanting to take direct action. 'So vexed was the prime minister by yet another murder,' says her biographer, Hugo Young, '[she] announced her intention of going to Leeds that weekend to take personal charge of the investigation. Nobody but her, she thought, really cared about the fate of these wretched women. Certainly no man could care enough.' Whitelaw needed to do some fast talking to restrain her, suggesting her presence in Leeds would distract the police effort and be seen as an overreaction. 'Above all it would quite gratuitously associate the government with the failures of the West Yorkshire police and, if the Ripper was not caught, immediately make people think ministers were responsible for the next murder.'

Ronald Gregory still had complete charge of police operations in West Yorkshire, so Whitelaw turned to Her Majesty's Inspectorate of Constabulary as a means of reining in his power. For more than a century inspectors of constabulary have been the means by which central government keeps a close eye on Britain's police forces. Made up of former chief constables, the inspectorate's job is to carry out annual performance reviews and recommend necessary changes. The local HMI for the north-east region, which included West Yorkshire, was Lawrence Byford, a former chief constable of Lincolnshire, a trained lawyer and a passionate supporter of Yorkshire Cricket Club. He knew the Ripper's killing ground well. Byford had joined the West Riding force in 1947 and worked his way to the top, serving as a divisional commander in both Halifax and Huddersfield in the 1960s. A clever tactical thinker, he also had a reputation for being unsentimentally ruthless when a difficult decision needed to be made.

Byford's political acumen was much in demand amid the frenzied backlash against the West Yorkshire force. Public confidence had eroded fast and senior officials and ministers inside the Home Office were losing patience. He realized the importance for the police service personnel to resolve the problem among themselves rather than have drastic changes imposed. It required delicate handling. Byford talked with Robert Andrew, a senior civil servant heading the police department in the Home Office. The outcome of their discussion was effectively imposed on the chief constable. Some of the best detectives in Britain were going to be sent immediately to Leeds to get a grip on the Ripper inquiry. To save face, it would be made to look as if Gregory initiated the idea. Andrew, later head of the Northern Ireland office, was convinced West Yorkshire needed outside assistance: 'There was impatience that nothing was being done to resolve this case and secure a conviction. Murders kept happening and the police were not actually bringing anyone to justice. There was no desire to interfere with [Gregory's] operational responsibility but there was a feeling of whether we could give him help in resolving this problem and draw on the experience of other police forces.'

Byford quickly visited the incident room in Leeds and spoke with Alf Finlay about progress on the Hill investigation. He found the murder squad chief almost dead on his feet, having had no sleep for forty-eight hours. Appalled, Byford sent him home that afternoon to get some rest. Other members of the Ripper squad were similarly run down: 'From the top to the bottom, they were mentally exhausted,' he said. 'By then it had become the largest, the most significant, the most demanding criminal case in British history and I don't think the police service and the forces involved were geared up to take on such a long, hard, difficult inquiry, that affected the health and well-being of so many officers.'

Gregory retreated on several fronts. On 23 November he had stated confidently that there would be no outside involvement with the investigation. Two days later he was forced to back down, now publicly welcoming the infusion of the 'best brains in the police service'. Jim Hobson would be taking overall charge, and a team of senior detectives from other forces would be helping him. Their job would be to examine critically what West Yorkshire had done, then advise Gregory. Byford, who later went on to become head of the inspectorate, had left the chief constable with few options. They went through a list of possible candidates to join an advisory team of very senior detectives as well as one of the country's top forensic scientists.

These announcements achieved the desired effect of damping down public clamour. The headlines were suitably favourable: 'SIX AGAINST THE RIPPER: Police bring in best brains to lead the hunt'; 'SUPER SQUAD TO NET RIPPER: New chief heads killer hunt'. Jim Hobson was being given temporary assistant chief constable rank; Oldfield was being stood down from the inquiry, and the five members of a super-squad were plucked out of their current jobs and sent north at top speed. All were highly experienced investigators. Commander Ron Harvey from Scotland Yard's criminal intelligence branch had only recently gone to the Home Office as an adviser on crime to the inspectorate. David Gerty had been a senior Yard detective and was now an ACC in the West Midlands force. Leslie Emment, deputy chief constable of Thames Valley, was said to be one of the cleverest men in the police service. Formerly a chief superintendent in the Metropolitan Police, he had worked on numerous murders, including one as a detective sergeant, with Dennis Hoban in Wakefield in the mid-1960s, when he acted as bag carrier for a senior member of the Yard's murder squad. At the time Hoban had been deputy coordinator of the regional crime squad, called in to help with the investigation. Andrew Sloan, a former West Riding detective, had joined the police after a career in the Royal Navy. A Scottish farmworker's son, he had worked closely with Dick Holland for several years and been a divisional commander in Dewsbury. He was now the national coordinator of regional crime squads. Finally, one of the country's leading forensic scientists, Professor Stuart Kind, director of the Home Office Central Research Establishment at Aldermaston, became part of the team, after receiving Byford's reassurance he would be 'co-equal' and not the token scientist. The pair had first met in the 1950s when Kind did the laboratory work on a York murder and Byford was a detective sergeant on the case.

Changes were made within the Ripper squad itself. Hobson set up an internal West Yorkshire team to review crucial aspects of the inquiry, effectively mirroring the work of the external advisers, but doing so in greater depth. When Hobson was questioned by reporters, he still proved obstinately resistant to the idea that they might have made mistakes, to the possibility that they had already interviewed the killer and failed to recognize him, or that the Ripper's name was somewhere within the incident room system. Given that hundreds of thousands of men had been interviewed, it was an outstandingly obtuse response. Hobson dug an even bigger professional hole for himself a few days later when the linguistic expert at Leeds University, Jack Windsor Lewis, openly claimed the Ripper tape was a hoax. Hobson still said he was '99 per cent certain' the tape was genuine. Windsor Lewis and his close colleague, Stanley Ellis, were by now certain the man who sent the tape must have already been interviewed during the inquiry, had provided an alibi and been eliminated because he could not be the Ripper. For more than a year their warnings had gone unheeded. In November 1979, a national newspaper had published their concerns about a repeat of the Black Panther fiasco. They predicted 'a nasty little hoax ... has pointed police in the wrong direction'. It fell on deaf ears. Hobson, like Oldfield, refused to countenance the police being wrong.

Finally, on 3 December 1980, a much-frustrated Windsor Lewis blew the controversy wide open with a warning in the main regional daily newspaper, the *Yorkshire Post*, that completely destroyed any credibility the tape still had. The national press repeated the story, raising the possibility that years of police effort had been wasted. Still Hobson refused to budge. He and the top officers in the Ripper squad seemed unable to contemplate the unimaginable, showing clear signs of what a former government official termed 'perseveration' – a grim determination to cling to an opinion in the face of evidence to the contrary. Psychologists have another term for the process whereby people put off making difficult decisions when they receive information which challenges passionately held beliefs: cognitive dissonance. Subconsciously the men in charge of the Ripper inquiry had found it hard to admit that the Geordie connection, on which they had staked their professional reputations, had been a false trail. The entire Ripper inquiry would be hopelessly and utterly compromised if the hoax fears were true, because thousands of men had been eliminated on the basis that they did not have a Geordie accent. Turning back now would mean humiliation, a massive public controversy and terrible consequences for the reputation of the police service as a whole.

Returning to Leeds for the first time in four years, one of the outside team, Andrew Sloan, quickly noticed a changed atmosphere within the city. Formerly carefree and relaxed when they went out at night to enjoy themselves, young women in Leeds seemed on the edge of hysteria. 'This evil, brutal and cruel man had been murdering women in West Yorkshire for a number of years and it was now manifest that it was getting to these young people,' he said. Sloan had travelled up to Wakefield alone to meet George Oldfield, whom he knew well from his own time in the West Riding force. He had discovered no one had bothered to inform Oldfield of the radical changes to be made at the top of the inquiry. Sloan wanted to reassure him. He had great sympathy for his former colleague. 'We were not going in there to do a hatchet job, we were going there to work with West Yorkshire,' he said. 'Psychologically they were on a hook, but they were not aware they were on a hook.'

The fresh minds from outside quickly got to grips with the key problems. Within days of moving to Leeds, Sloan and the other think-tank members secretly concluded the 'Geordie' connection was a busted flush. The tapes and letters were a complete irrelevance which had hampered the investigation for far too long. The immediate problem would be how to wean both public and police away from the belief that the Ripper was a Geordie.

The outsiders spent two frantic weeks reading reports, examining witness statements and visiting crime scenes, and many long hours grilling the detectives who worked on the inquiry. At the end of the first week they organized a major conference of senior investigating officers and pointedly began probing the assumptions they had made. The meeting, at Holbeck police station, began at 6.30 p.m. and ended past midnight. Somewhat incredulous, the outside team had discovered an absence of businesslike methods in the management of the inquiry. The decision-making process appeared completely *ad hoc*. No minutes had been taken during countless crucial meetings of senior officers during the past five years. No records were taken of who made recommendations or what had led to particular decisions. Les Emment, a deputy chief constable, outranked everyone present and chaired the meeting. He demanded to know who had correlated the Ripper squad's work. Who was really in charge? No one seemed to be able to tell him. 'There was a lot of togetherness,' said John Domaille, who had run the Ripper squad in 1978 but had spent the last two years heading the detective training school in Wakefield.

Wilf Brooks from Lancashire and Manchester's Jack Ridgway

brain. He believed she had been dragged thirty yards from the road across the rough ground to the point where she was found.

Peter Gilrain, still head of the Ripper squad, attended the crime scene, along with a local detective superintendent, Alf Finlay, deputy head of Leeds area CID. Next day Oldfield, who had been attending a senior officers' conference in Derbyshire, confirmed what most people realized: the Yorkshire Ripper had taken his thirteenth victim. 'The man is obviously very mentally ill and has got this sadistic killer streak in him. He can flip at any time.' He appealed to women in particular to look at their husbands, boyfriends, brothers and fathers and ask themselves if he could be the man police wanted. The public had heard the same statement many times after previous Ripper murders. Students in the hall of residence complained bitterly about the way police had treated the discovery of Jacqueline's handbag the night she died.

Three days after Jacqueline's body was found, Detective Superintendent Finlay zeroed in on a 'square-shaped car' seen going the wrong way down Alma Road at about 9.30 on the night Jacqueline was attacked. He wanted the driver eliminated from the inquiry. Police also had descriptions of several men seen hanging around Otley Road and wanted help in tracing them. One of them wore a dark blue or black donkey jacket and had a *Mexican style moustache* and hair growing to the bottom of his ears. The *Yorkshire Post* immediately linked this description to one given three years earlier by Marilyn Moore after she survived a Ripper attack. They reproduced the photo-fit she provided of a man with dark hair brushed back, a beard and moustache.

West Yorkshire police for the first time faced a hostile challenge from reporters as Alf Finlay and his chief constable were strongly in favour of narrowing down the geographical scope of the investigation. The outsiders were privately in total agreement. While they had learned much that depressed them, there were a few bright moments. The report by Detective Inspector David Zackrisson of Northumbria police, warning that the 'Geordie' connection was a hoax, contained shocking information but cleverly demonstrated how the police service had detectives of high calibre. 'It was such a beautifully written analysis, it was like finding a diamond in a dungheap,' said Professor Kind. The advisers also quickly accepted the merits of Ridgway's five-pound note inquiry, which pointed strongly to the killer living or working in the Shipley area.

A tour of the Ripper's killing ground helped convince the outsiders the murderer was almost certainly from Bradford. They were billeted not far from the Leeds city centre in the Dragonara Hotel, a multi-storey red-brick structure frequently used by visiting company executives and sales reps. During the working day they split up, each conducting separate aspects of the review. They gathered for discussion over a drink in the bar at night and next morning over breakfast in the hotel restaurant. After dinner, one bitterly freezing night soon after they arrived in Leeds, the team piled into a police staff car to visit one of the murder scenes. Andrew Sloan, who knew the area well, was at the wheel. He pulled to a halt on a bridge looking down across the M1 motorway. They sat for a few moments gazing out across a great sweep of the industrial West Riding. A clear night presented a memorable vista of thousands of shimmering lights dancing in the darkness. As they discussed the enormity of the task they had been given, Ron Harvey wistfully remarked of their quarry: 'Well, you're out there somewhere . . .' Stuart Kind later recalled that when he heard Harvey's comment he felt like shouting out, 'Yes, and we'll get you, you murdering bastard.' Not wanting to vent his emotions, he kept silent.

Ron Harvey's gut instincts about the killer crystallized later that same night when they visited the scene in Bradford where Barbara Leach was murdered after midnight, some fourteen months earlier. Standing among the cobbled stones, looking at the alcove where Barbara's body had been dumped, the consensus was that it was an opportunistic attack. The killer had seen his next victim walking along the nearby road, attacked her and dragged her down the back alley. Ron Harvey, not one to hide his light under a bushel, suddenly announced: 'Chummy [The Ripper] lives in Bradford and did it going home.' Kind asked why he was so convinced. 'I don't know, Stuart,' he replied, 'but I am sure that's what happened.'

A few days later Kind began seriously pondering the probabilities of the Ripper being a local man. No one at the time had conceived of geographical profiling, a technique much used by crime investigators today. He juggled in his mind Ron Harvey's instinctive thoughts, the merits of Ridgway's five-pound note inquiry and the fact that none of the surviving victims had said their attacker had a 'strange accent'. Surely one of them would have commented if the Ripper had spoken differently from them? Kind's brain churned these thoughts over, wondering whether it was possible to provide some form of 'proof' the killer lived near Bradford. The timing of the killings had to be a key factor, but he could not just yet see why. During the few days they had been together, he had been mentally noting several characteristics shared by some of the team. With the exception of Andrew Sloan, they tended to steer away from the abstract features of the case, especially the concept of probabilities. Instead, as detectives, they preferred black and white facts, known certainties and points of elimination. They were also, he felt, tending to involve themselves in the investigation itself rather than step back and view the problem from a distance. The scientist was anxious to make a personal contribution, if he could, to their overall effort.

The next evening the team were invited to a police function in Wakefield, but Kind cried off, preferring the solitude of his hotel room and a sound night's sleep. But at 3 a.m. he suddenly woke, his mind racing. Delving back to his experiences as a young wartime navigator, he realized he might have a solution. He got dressed and went down to the hotel reception desk and asked the night manager if they had any graph paper and a ruler. As a nineteen-year-old RAF navigator on bombing missions over Germany, he had had to get his Lancaster aircraft over the target and home again. This involved using charts, plotting a course, using mathematics, bringing a sense of scale to the flight plan, making adaptations as the journey continued, and fine tuning the plan according to the information available as he bounced around the night sky sitting at his cramped console. Nothing was 'fixed' about the flight plan, as Kind explained: 'A navigator becomes instinctively aware of the interplay of time, of distance, direction, position, the season, hours of darkness and the practical constraints these factors place upon anyone wishing to travel. Granted these factors are different for the walker, the car traveller, the sailor and the flier, but there are certain basic aspects common to all. Even the serial killer labours under these constraints.'

Kind returned quickly to his room, then used these navigational methods to plot the Ripper's movements over time, to see whether it could reveal his base of operations. He knew when and where the killer had struck, and the time of day according to when the victim was last seen. In plotting the attacks on a map, he wanted to find 'a centre of gravity' for the killings. Studying the actual times of the attacks might also show some common features. He assumed the Ripper started and finished his murderous work from the same point – his home. Kind wanted to find it. On the graph paper he plotted each attack on a map, then joined them together with an imaginary thread. He saw it as a simple distribution problem: 'Imagine the warehouse for a network of supermarkets … what are the criteria for positioning the warehouse for minimum travel overall? Imagine a map with the individual supermarket positions marked on it. Now visualize choosing a position for the warehouse. Mark all the positions so identified by using map pins. Now join each supermarket position with the warehouse by a piece of taut thread. Measure the total length of thread used. Now choose another position for the warehouse and repeat the exercise. Do this several times. The amount of thread used in each exercise will vary, but the warehouse position that uses the least thread lies at the centre of gravity of the cluster of warehouses.'

Sitting at a table in his hotel room, Kind drew a series of diagrams. The result was clear: the centre of gravity for the attacks lay half-way between Manningham and Shipley, very close to Bradford. The further away from this point an attack happened, the earlier in the day it occurred. The closer to Bradford, the later at night it happened. It suggested the killer covered up the bodies of his victims because he needed time to get away and home before they were discovered. He did not want the alarm raised in case he was stopped on the journey home. The further away from home, the earlier he attacked his victims, because it took longer to get home. The closer to his lair, the later at night he could afford to strike, knowing his hiding place was close by. He could leave a murder scene and be home within minutes.

It was a devastating piece of analysis, confirmed later that day when Kind's colleagues ran his calculations through a computer at the Home Office Central Research Establishment at Aldermaston. On 10 December 1980, Kind wrote a one-page memo to his colleagues outlining his theory. It was a major breakthrough incorporated into a list of fourteen key recommendations made to Ronald Gregory a week before Christmas. 'What I was doing was cheating, in effect,' Kind explained years later, 'working backwards like the mathematician does. I was already convinced of Ron Harvey's hunch, but I've got to test it to see if it's right.'

A few days later, William Whitelaw paid his second visit within a month to the incident room, trying to dampen down public clamour for an arrest. He tried to soothe public anxieties by reassuring them the whole police service was fully involved in trying to catch the killer: 'The people of Leeds and the women who are naturally anxious and with whom I have the greatest sympathy will be the first to appreciate that great efforts are being made.' But the Home Secretary had no hint of just how bad the position was inside the Ripper investigation. The outside team had found major flaws in the inquiry, its management in total disarray. Crucial matters had been overlooked by senior officers, who had been unable to make critical deductions about what clues to follow, particularly in relation to physical descriptions of the killer and the cars he used. The outside team wrote in their interim report to Ronald Gregory:

To make sound judgements it is necessary to grasp the complexities of the enquiry and in particular to understand:
(i) What has or has not been done?

(ii) What evidence can be deduced from the overall inquiry to give a weighting to the welter of varying descriptions of suspect persons and vehicles remaining unidentified?

The fact that the advisers felt it necessary to point this out highlighted the depths to which the inquiry had been allowed to sink. Standing back and reviewing evidence was arguably the most basic element required of a senior detective if they were to develop hunches and solve a case. The outside team found this element clearly lacking in the Ripper squad, so overwhelmed was it by a welter of information. Worse still, the outside team learned that help and advice given to the senior West Yorkshire detectives appeared to have been completely ignored. Crucial recommendations made by Jim Nevill from Scotland Yard a year beforehand were never followed up. The force's own review by Detective Chief Superintendent John Domaille in 1978 had also fallen on deaf ears.

The outside team had to tread cautiously. There was little point in tearing into the Ripper squad and producing a report so critical that it alienated Gregory. They readily acknowledged the British police had never experienced an inquiry like this before. 'The rest of the police service has little concept of the sheer logistical problems involved in this inquiry,' they told Ronald Gregory in their eight-page report, which landed on his desk a week before Christmas 1980. Yet the outside team could not ignore the errors they found. The tape and letters were critical. They could not understand why Gregory's men attached such weight to their authenticity. The emphasis 'should be shifted to allow for the possibility of an elaborate hoax. We recommend that the aim of the inquiry should now be to foster an opinion within and outside the police service that the killer does not necessarily originate from the north-east of England.'

Other recommendations included reinterviewing some key witnesses and victims who survived attacks; checking all photo-fits to see which ones had been made public; checking 'all other assaults on women' during the previous five years to see which ones had falsely been excluded from the series; reopening the five-pound note inquiry and concentrating on suspects living and working in the Bradford area. The final words of advice to Gregory were: 'We stress the need to record and document all decisions taken.'

As the outsiders made their way home to share Christmas with their families, they envisaged returning a month later to check on the progress being made. They knew that Bradford was the key and all efforts had to be narrowed down to a relatively small area if there was to be any hope of catching the killer quickly. But what they and no one else connected with the inquiry real-ized was that a member of the public had only weeks before pro-vided West Yorkshire police with the Ripper's name and address.

Thirty-two-year-old Trevor Birdsall, living in the Pollards Park area of Bradford, had been a friend of Peter William Sutcliffe since the mid-1960s. He had been having disturbing doubts about Sutcliffe following Jacqueline Hill's murder. On 25 November 1980 he wrote an anonymous letter to the police, naming his long-standing drinking friend as the Ripper. Next day he went into a police station in Bradford, gave his own name and repeated his suspicions.

In the late 1960s and early 1970s, the two men frequently toured the red-light area of Manningham using Birdsall's three-wheeler Reliant Robin car. They chatted to prostitutes in the streets or in pubs. Peter Sutcliffe, two years older than Trevor Birdsall, seemed obsessed by prostitutes with big breasts.

Birdsall's affinity was with Sutcliffe himself. Both were outwardly shy and quiet. They enjoyed their social time drinking together. In August 1969, they were together in Manningham Lane when Birdsall witnessed a crucial incident. By now he had progressed to an Austin Mini and Sutcliffe was in the passenger seat. They were eating fish and chips wrapped in newspaper when they saw a woman staggering around drunk. Sutcliffe got out and went after her, returning ten or fifteen minutes later in a state of some excitement, telling his friend to drive off quickly. He said he had followed the woman to a house and hit her. He pulled a sock from his pocket, removed a small piece of brick from inside and threw it out of the car window. Police later traced Birdsall's Mini after the incident. He pointed them to Sutcliffe, who was later questioned but only cautioned after admitting he had hit the woman with his fist, saying they had an argument after he had been drinking. The woman, whose boyfriend was in prison for assault, declined to press charges. The incident was written off as typical of the local culture of booze and birds. The police had seen that sort of thing a thousand times before.

It was a month later, on 29 September 1969, that Sutcliffe was arrested in the garden of a house in Manningham and then convicted of going equipped for theft. He had been spotted on his own by a police officer concealed behind a bush in the red-light district after he found Sutcliffe's car parked near by with the engine running. Sutcliffe was in possession of a hammer. He also had a knife with him that he managed to hide.

The pair worked together in the early 1970s at the Baird TV factory in Bradford, where Trevor Birdsall met his future wife, Melissa. They stayed in close contact, too, after Sutcliffe married his long-standing girlfriend, Sonia Szurma. On 15 August 1975, they went out drinking again. This time they were in

Sutcliffe's Ford saloon, visiting pubs in Halifax. Sutcliffe chatted to several unaccompanied women, leaning across the table and speaking quietly to them. In the Boothtown area of Halifax later that night, Sutcliffe stopped the car suddenly and said he was going to talk to someone. Twenty minutes later he returned, saying he had been talking to a woman. 'He was quiet, unusually quiet,' Birdsall later said. Next day he read a report in the *Bradford Telegraph and Argus* about a brutal attack the night before on a woman called Olive Smelt in Boothtown. He thought perhaps Sutcliffe was involved, then dismissed it from his mind. Several times during the late 1970s he wondered whether his drinking friend might be the killer, particularly after it was said the Ripper had a gap in his teeth and worked in the engineering industry. He knew Peter Sutcliffe had been questioned by the Ripper squad in 1977. However, Birdsall did nothing, finding it hard to believe that one of his best friends could be a mad killer. Then the police announcement that the Yorkshire Ripper was a Geordie convinced him Sutcliffe was totally innocent, though twice in 1980 he raised his fears with his former wife.

In November 1980, the two men, now in their thirties, had gone out drinking for the evening. Sutcliffe was driving a big brown Rover V8 saloon. Birdsall was by now divorced and living with a girlfriend, Gloria Conroy. A short time later, the aftermath of the Jacqueline Hill murder triggered dark memories about Peter Sutcliffe. Several newspapers had offered more cash for the capture of the Ripper, raising the total reward money to £50,000. Olive Smelt appeared on television, accusing the Ripper of being a coward. Instantly Birdsall remembered the incident in Halifax in 1975. Then the Ripper squad said they were looking urgently for a large square-shaped car seen close to the Hill murder scene at Headingley. It matched the type of Rover car Sutcliffe drove.

The *Yorkshire Post* then published the Marilyn Moore photofit of the man with a 'Mexican' moustache. It bore an uncanny resemblance to his friend Peter Sutcliffe.

On 25 November 1980 Birdsall hand wrote an anonymous letter to the police. Its contents are revealed here for the first time:

To Whom it may concern

I am writing to inform you that I have very good reason to believe I now [*sic*] the man you are looking for in the 'Ripper Case'.

It is an incident which happened within the last 5 years. I cannot give any date or place or any details without myself been known to the ripper or you if this is the man.

It is only until recently that something came to my notice, and now a lot of things fit in to place.

I can only tell you one or two things which fit for example, This man as had dealings with prostitutes and always had a thing about them. Also he is a long distance lorry driver, collecting engineering items etc. I am quiet sure if you check up on dates etc., you may find something.

His name and address is

PETER SUTCLIFFE   CLARKE TRANS.
5 GARDEN LANE   SHIPLEY
HEATON, BRADFORD

Next day, 26 November 1980, Birdsall's girlfriend berated him for not giving enough information in the letter and urged him to go to the police. At 10.10 p.m. they turned up at Bradford police headquarters and spoke to a young constable at the desk. Birdsall relayed the incident with Sutcliffe in Halifax, in August 1975, the night Olive Smelt was attacked. The police officer, very new in the job, made a note in his pocket book. To any senior detective working on the Ripper case, the date alone would have set alarm bells ringing loud and clear. Birdsall said nothing about having sent an anonymous letter. A formal note of the conversation over the counter at the police station was forwarded to the Ripper incident room in Leeds. Hundreds of letters a day were being sent to the Ripper squad, many of them anonymous, like that of Trevor Birdsall. The £50,000 reward was a major incentive for people to name suspects. So many anonymous letters were being sent that the Ripper squad appealed for the senders to include their names and addresses. These would be treated in strictest confidence: 'Any information, no matter how trivial, could be of use,' they said. 'Information received needs clarification and it is because of this we ask please include your name and address.'

A team of officers wearing gloves opened the letters before forwarding them to the Leeds incident room. Birdsall's single-page letter was first received by a detective sergeant who marked it 'Action to trace/interview Sutcliffe'. The name of the suspect failed to register with the detective, even though he himself had interviewed Sutcliffe at his home eleven months earlier. An action form asking for Peter Sutcliffe to be traced and interviewed was sent across to where the index clerks worked. There it was received by Policewoman Sue Neave. She searched the filing system and noted there were already three index cards relating to Peter Sutcliffe for being interviewed in connection with the cross- and triple-area sightings. She then briefly summarized the contents of the index cards on the new action form.

She wrote: 'Gap in teeth – h/w neg, but officer interviewing *not* happ'. The action form was placed in a wire filing basket, from where it should have been collected by a detective conducting outside interviews. But before an outside team could interview Sutcliffe yet again, papers relating to earlier interviews needed to be located, copied and attached to the action form. It meant someone would have had to go down a corridor to a locked separate office where the relevant files were kept. It was some distance from the incident room but on the same floor. Very few in the incident room even knew this separate office existed. The action form was still in the filing tray early in the New Year.

Birdsall says that after two weeks he phoned the police to discover what had happened to his tip-off. When he heard nothing more, he assumed Sutcliffe had been cleared. By now his friend was experiencing deep concerns about his future employment. The outcome of his run-in with the law during the summer, when he tried to escape from a police car and was breathalysed, was that he was due to appear in court early in the New Year on a drink-driving charge. It could mean losing his driving licence and with it his job as a lorry driver. He handed in his notice at Clark's, telling colleagues he and his wife were moving and intended to buy a cottage and open up a small pottery business in North Yorkshire.

The Sunday after Christmas, Birdsall and his girlfriend joined Peter Sutcliffe in a local pub for a lunchtime drink to celebrate the festive season. Sonia Sutcliffe stayed at home preparing a special meal for her husband's family. It was an annual gathering at which they exchanged Christmas presents. On the way home in the car, Gloria Conroy told her boyfriend Trevor Birdsall she had felt a churning in her stomach when they met Sutcliffe in the pub. Within a few days she would learn that her apprehensions were well founded.

17

'The Beast I Am'

At 10.20 p.m. on Friday, 2 January 1981, a patrol car set out from Hammerton Road police station in the Walkley area of Sheffield at the start of the night shift. The driver was a thirty-one-year-old probationary constable, Robert Hydes, a married man with two young children. His supervisor was Sergeant Robert Ring, aged forty-seven, with many years' experience in policing the city. Both were local men. Their respective families, like thousands of others, had long been heavily involved with the steel industry and its allied trades, which at that time still dominated Sheffield's economy. Hydes's father was a cutler, a foreman in a workshop making knives and forks. Ring's had worked in a plant making heavy artillery guns. Hydes himself had worked as an engineer making machine tools for the aircraft and car industries before suddenly deciding at the age of thirty on a change of career. 'Bob' Ring, the man keeping an eye on his progress that night, had joined Sheffield police, aged twenty-one, after National Service as an army signalman in Hong Kong. Now, with two teenage children, he was not many years off completing his thirty years' service, which would entitle him to a full pension.

Hydes had been at Hammerton Road seven months after completing his South Yorkshire police training course. Before now he had been on foot patrols, refamiliarizing himself with an area he knew well. Until his early twenties he had lived with his parents just four hundred yards away from the station. In November 1980 he qualified as a police driver, then served the whole of December in plain clothes on attachment to the CID, including a day in the force intelligence unit, which he spent studying a file on the Yorkshire Ripper case. On 2 January, his first day back in uniform, he was given his first mobile patrol, driving a police car. Bob Ring decided to accompany him, intending to show his junior colleague the procedures for dealing with a case of prostitution in Sheffield's red-light area around Havelock Square. More and more women were taking to the streets to earn money as the city received a pounding from the economic recession starting to grip the country. The local steel industry was going through a drastic restructuring. Whole plants were being closed, tens of thousands of jobs being lost. Poverty was not uncommon and prostitution thrived.

Sheffield still teemed with hundreds of tiny businesses producing goods from locally made special steels. Small workshops manufactured cutlery, silverware and pewterware as well as hand-made tools like twist drills, slit saws, scythes and sickles. Representing these small firms was an umbrella organization called the Federation of British Engineers' Tool Manufacturers. Its headquarters since the Second World War had been Light Trades House, a large three-storey Victorian property in the up-market residential area of Broomhill. Close by was the fee-paying Sheffield High School for Girls, whose teenage pupils had been constantly warned about the dangers of the Yorkshire Ripper even though there had been no attacks in the city. The killer's menace had spread far and wide from Leeds and Bradford. Parents everywhere told daughters not to take chances by walking on their own at night.

In the police car, Ring directed Hydes towards Havelock Square, then up Broomhill towards tree-lined Melbourne Avenue, pointing out that this was where the street women often took clients. It was now 10.50 p.m. Looking along the driveway of Light Trades House, he saw a car parked close to the building. At this time of night it could only be a prostitute with a punter. The location was close enough for women to be able to engage in sex for ten pounds and be back down the hill to the square half a mile away, looking for another punter, all within the space of twenty minutes.

'Look,' said Ring, 'there's one now. We'll have a talk to him.'

They pulled into the driveway, headlights full on, stopping four feet in front of a large brown Rover 3500 saloon with a black vinyl roof. It was facing down the driveway towards the road. Hydes got out and went to the driver's door. A man was behind the wheel and a mixed-race woman sat in the front passenger seat. He asked the man if he owned the vehicle.

'Yes,' said the driver.

'What's your name and address?' asked Hydes.

'John Williams, 65 Dorchester Road, Canklow, Rotherham.'

Sergeant Ring then walked up and asked: 'Who's she?'

'My girlfriend,' said the driver.

'What's her name?' asked Ring.

'I don't know, I have not known her that long.'

'Who are you trying to kid?' said Ring. 'I haven't fallen off a Christmas tree.'

'I'm not suggesting you have.'

Ring asked the woman her name. She told him.

From the police car they radioed divisional headquarters, giving details of the couple and asking for the vehicle registration number HVY 679N to be checked on the Police National Computer. Listening in the control room when the call came through were two anti-vice squad officers who immediately recognized the woman as a twenty-four-year-old convicted prostitute with a suspended prison sentence. The PNC check showed the registration number had been allocated not to a brown Rover but to a Skoda saloon belonging to a Mr Aslam Khan. They immediately arrested both driver and prostitute on suspicion of theft. Hydes removed the vehicle keys and the car tax disc displayed on the windscreen, which had been issued for a Rover registration FHY 400K.

With the headlights of the police car illuminating the Rover, everything behind them was pitch black. Both Ring and Hydes found it difficult to see. As the woman was being placed in the rear seat of the police car, Sergeant Ring heard a noise a few feet away and looked round. The driver was some distance away, moving towards the patrol car from the direction of a large oil tank standing next to Light Trades House. Near by was a small wall.

'What are you doing there?' Ring asked the driver.

'I've fallen off that fucking wall.'

'What were you doing there?'

'I wanted to piss.'

The sergeant told the driver to go to the side of the building if he needed to urinate. The man said he wouldn't bother.

Back at Hammerton Road they entered the police station through a rear door. The place was full of activity. An illegal drinking club close by had just been raided and all the cells were occupied. Ring agreed to let the driver use a toilet on the ground floor. When he returned, both driver and prostitute were questioned separately in what they called the 'plain-clothes department', which handled vice matters. The woman had two small children. She had moved to Sheffield from Birmingham seven years earlier and been soliciting for the last four. She talked about the punter. He had picked her up in his car about half an hour before they were arrested. She had agreed to sex with a condom for ten pounds, but despite her considerable efforts could not arouse him. He had been edgy and nervous, talking about his wife, saying she had had several miscarriages. When the police car arrived he urgently told her: 'Leave it to me, you're my girlfriend.' And when the two officers went to make a radio check, he told her to run for it. The woman refused. She was too well known to the police.

Present also were the two anti-vice officers about to go off duty. Sergeant Arthur Armitage started to place some documents in a desk drawer. On the wall was a photofit issued some years previously of a man with a beard and dark brushed-back hair suspected of being the Yorkshire Ripper. There was an unnerving similarity to the driver of the Rover. In his broad South Yorkshire accent, Armitage looked directly at the prisoner and said, almost tongue in cheek: 'Tha's the Yorkshire Ripper, thee.' The man said nothing. On impulse Armitage and his colleague went up to Light Trades House, offering to collect the Rover car. Their suspicions were immediately heightened when they saw it parked facing down the driveway towards the road. It had been reversed back into the drive. Almost always in these situations, punters' cars faced the other way to afford them a measure of privacy while having sex. Armitage bent down to look at the registration plates on the Rover. They were held in place by black tape. Beneath them was the original number plate – FHY 400K.

In the plain-clothes room at Hammerton Road the scruffily dressed driver now gave his proper name and address in Bradford. He was Peter William Sutcliffe from Garden Lane, Heaton. He owned the Rover and admitted stealing the Skoda number places from a scrapyard at Cooper Bridge near Mirfield that afternoon. Ring felt uneasy. The man had the smell of the great unwashed about him and he looked grubby. There was grease around his fingernails. His black hair stood high above his head, making him appear much taller than he was. Among his possessions was a brown woollen army type hat which Ring found in the Rover. It was filthy. The time now was 11.30 p.m. and there was a decision to be made. They had a woman soliciting while on suspended sentence and a punter who admitted stealing number plates and putting them on his car. Since this relatively minor offence had occurred within the Dewsbury division of West Yorkshire, the Sheffield officers had several choices. They could simply charge Peter Sutcliffe with theft and bail him to appear before Dewsbury Magistrates. Or they could bail him to go home and be questioned later by West Yorkshire police. Or they could hold on to him for a while. Had they decided to bail him, Sutcliffe would have been in and out of the police station within ninety minutes.

No one took the decision direct, but there was a gathering of minds to hold on to him for a while longer. No one thought they had caught the Yorkshire Ripper, but several features about Sutcliffe appeared odd. The prostitute. The false name. The false plates. The fact that he was from Bradford in West Yorkshire. And the fact that, when they searched him, they found a piece of blue and red plaited nylon rope in his possession. It was about three feet long, had two knots tied at each end and two additional knots a few inches apart near the middle. Shrugging his shoulders, he said the rope was for repairing cars.

'What can you use this on cars for?' Ring asked.

'Just lifting things, things like that.'

'What are the knots for?'

'To grip, I suppose.'

Someone phoned the West Yorkshire force to have Sutcliffe collected and taken to Dewsbury. They said the prisoner had a Bradford accent and was no Geordie. It was gone midnight. No one was available to drive down to Sheffield.

Hydes had begun developing that extra 'sense' crucial to being a successful policeman – a nose for when something is not right and an aptitude for making arrests. He sat talking to Sutcliffe, who seemed desperate to get away from the police station at any price. 'He would have admitted stealing the Crown Jewels if he could have got out of there,' he said. He started complaining about the police and how they had once arrested him for speeding at 50 m.p.h. in a 30 m.p.h. area subsequently changed to a 50 m.p.h. limit. He argued about being breathalysed near his home. When Hydes offered to phone Sutcliffe's wife to tell her where he was, Sutcliffe prevaricated for ages. Finally he provided a telephone number. It was answered by an Asian family. The number was clearly false – but why? By now Sutcliffe's nine-year-old Rover car had been driven down to the police station. Ring then took Sutcliffe outside to the garage. They removed the false number plates and looked in the boot. Several tools were on the floor and in a tool box, including one which Ring recognized as an engineer's drift – a tube of steel with another piece of steel inside. Normally it would be struck by a hammer to remove spindles or sprockets. Asked where the accompanying hammer was, Sutcliffe denied having one. He just kept a job lot of tools in the boot of his car, he said.

Back inside the station they waited in the parade room. Hanging on a wall was a large chart circulated to all of Britain's police forces three years earlier. It listed the type of attacks on women in the Yorkshire Ripper series, as well as the type of cars which could have left tyre marks at various murder scenes.

A detective in the parade room asked Sutcliffe: 'Have you been questioned by the Ripper squad?'

'Everybody has been questioned,' he replied, almost contemptuously. 'They are always questioning. It makes you sick.'

Sutcliffe turned away from the detective. His eyes formed into narrow slits. Ring thought he looked shifty, standing with his back to the wall near the open door, rarely looking at the person talking to him. His body language showed he felt very uncomfortable. In a corner of the room Hydes told Ring quietly that the prisoner kept changing his story; it was impossible to pin him down. He was clearly lying, but why? Ring approached Sutcliffe, who still stood with his back to the wall. There was a large carver chair in the room and Ring sat in front of him. 'If you are the Ripper, why don't you admit it?' he said. 'All you have to do is admit it. Are you?'

Sutcliffe looked at Ring, exhaling deeply through his mouth and glancing sideways through the door. The sergeant was unable to get the prisoner to focus on him directly, so he stood up and approached him till their faces were inches apart. Ring put his hands flat on the wall on either side of Sutcliffe's shoulders. 'I think you are,' he said in a half-serious sort of way, then went back and sat in the chair.

Later, someone else in the room asked him about prostitutes. Incredibly, for a man just arrested with one in his car, Sutcliffe said he didn't know any. He never went with them. The man was clearly a habitual liar. Ring got up, went to another office and closed the door. It was nearly 1 a.m. on Saturday, 3 January. He telephoned the Ripper incident room at Millgarth in Leeds, relayed details of the arrest and added that Sutcliffe took size eight shoes and had a gap in his teeth. No, he hadn't got a Geordie accent. Detective Sergeant Rob Bennett in Leeds found an index card that showed Sutcliffe had been interviewed on several occasions. Then he found several other cards. Making a further search of the files, Bennett discovered several damning features connecting Peter Sutcliffe with the Ripper inquiry. He had been eliminated on the evidence of his handwriting, which Bennett knew was inconclusive. He was a long-distance lorry driver, a possible occupation for the killer. He had strenuously denied ever going with prostitutes. More crucially, Sutcliffe had never been positively eliminated from the inquiry – his alibis were from members of his family. From reading more of the papers in the file, Bennett discovered some detectives had been unhappy with Sutcliffe's performance during interviews.

After several more phone calls between Leeds and Sheffield, the West Yorkshire force made arrangements to collect the prisoner accused of stealing number plates. Three officers travelled down to Hammerton Road to take him back to Dewsbury. Ring had earlier gone back out on patrol and then went off shift. Hydes stayed on and made a statement about the arrest. About 7.40 a.m. he watched from the car park as the party from West Yorkshire left for the return journey. One man drove the Rover car, another sat in the back handcuffed to the prisoner. The probationary constable went home to his family in Parsons Cross in the north of Sheffield. The first thing he planned to do was get some sleep.

Joan Ring had weekends off from her job as a VDU operator with a local tool-making firm, so her husband went straight to bed as soon as he arrived home before dawn. But he could not sleep and fretted for most of the day. 'There was something odd about this fellow he had arrested with a prostitute,' Joan said much later, describing the events of that weekend for the first time. 'Bob tossed and turned in bed. There was simply something not right about the man. He didn't sleep at all that day. He told me a little bit but not that it involved the Ripper case.'

The three-storey purpose-built divisional police headquarters in the centre of Dewsbury had been open six years when Peter Sutcliffe arrived there on Saturday morning, 3 January 1981. He was held in the cells, provided with breakfast and told to wait until detectives from the Ripper squad arrived from Leeds to question him. He would have a long wait. Sutcliffe's wife, Sonia, had been phoned and told he was being held in connection with a theft of number plates.

In the Millgarth incident room the prospect of a promising suspect for the Ripper murders had been seen many times before. All had led to disappointment. Detectives on the squad took these things in their stride. Information about high-grade suspects was logged in a D-62 file. These were men who had been watched closely over the last five years. Many were on a special list to be interviewed immediately there was another murder. If they could produce a positive alibi, they were finally eliminated. Terence Hawkshaw had been their most promising candidate because they could place him in the vicinity of half a dozen prostitute murders at the relevant time. Yet he was cleared. A check that morning in the D-62 index showed Peter William Sutcliffe had never even been considered a promising suspect.

Detective Sergeant Desmond Finbarr O'Boyle travelled over to Leeds to read all the paperwork about Sutcliffe. Before going into an interview with someone described as a promising suspect for the Ripper killings, he wanted as much detail on the man as possible. The more he read about Sutcliffe, the more he thought there was a great chance that the nightmare might be over. O'Boyle, aged thirty-five, was a highly experienced detective and had interviewed hundreds of men during the investigation. It seemed to him that Sutcliffe's responses during interviews connected to the five-pound note and the cross-area sightings were key. He had repeatedly denied going with prostitutes. He denied a clear sighting of his own car in Moss Side, Manchester. Then there was the gap in his teeth, and the facial description. Sutcliffe had a beard – just as Teresa Sykes described after she was attacked in Huddersfield on Bonfire Night. O'Boyle had worked on the Sykes inquiry until it was downgraded as not part of the Ripper series. The more junior detectives and the men doing the grinding house-to-house checks had repeatedly asked each other: 'Just how many men are there hitting young women over the head with a ball-pein hammer?'

Arriving at Dewsbury, O'Boyle and a detective called Rod Hill went in search of the Rover car to examine it thoroughly. They found three screwdrivers in the glove box, including one with a blue and red handle. Sutcliffe was taken from the cells to an interview room on the ground floor. They came face to face with the prisoner shortly after 3 p.m. O'Boyle quickly noticed the gap in his upper front teeth. The beard was a dead ringer for the Moore photofit. But the man's eyes? They were the darkest he had ever seen. He announced he was from the squad investigating the series of murders across the North of England. Sutcliffe appeared calm and confident. Rod Hill took notes as his colleague asked a series of rudimentary questions, trying to put the prisoner at ease, feeling him out, trying to get to know him. He asked about his family background, his schooling in Bingley, his various jobs, when he got married, his domestic life at home with Sonia, anything and everything to keep him talking and gradually size him up.

O'Boyle wondered about the trip to Sheffield. How had it

come about? Sutcliffe told a roundabout story of leaving home around 4 p.m. on the Friday afternoon, wanting to find spare parts for his Rover and a friend's Mini car. He and Sonia had had an argument about the breathalyser charge hanging over him. Their rows over how they would manage family finances if he lost his job had been happening fairly regularly, he said. He was fed up. The insurance had run out on his car and he knew he was due in court in a week or so and would probably be banned on the drink-driving charge. It was pointless renewing the insurance. In the scrapyard at Cooper Bridge he found a number plate from a nearby Skoda on the ground, then he pulled the other one off the vehicle itself. He thought he could get away with having no insurance by using false number plates.

He left the scrapyard at 6 p.m. but claimed the exhaust blew on his car and he spent an hour repairing it. Then he drove to the Hartshead Moore service station on the M62 motorway for a meal. He claimed to have given three people a lift from Bradford to Rotherham and Sheffield. They had stopped him on the motorway and offered him ten pounds to take them home. Soon after arriving in Sheffield, a woman flagged him down. Thinking she was in some kind of trouble, he stopped. Instead she asked if he wanted 'business'.

'I was surprised,' Sutcliffe told O'Boyle. 'I thought about things and realized I had ten pounds burning a hole in my pocket and thought I might as well use it. This girl then disappeared, so I drove on and saw another girl and stopped. She asked me if I wanted business. She got into the car and told me where to drive. I paid her ten pounds. I did not want sex – I just wanted to talk about my problems at home. I did not want sex at all.'

O'Boyle wanted to know if he and his wife were having

normal sexual relations. He said they were. The last time was
four days ago. What about all the rows they were having? 'We
forget about rows when we go to bed,' Sutcliffe replied.

The detective then threw Sutcliffe a low ball by changing
tack and suddenly alluding to the attack on Teresa Sykes in
Huddersfield. 'Where were you on Bonfire Night last year?'
O'Boyle asked. Sutcliffe, taken by surprise, said hesitatingly
that he was at home with his wife.

Two hours into the interview, O'Boyle conducted a handwriting test. 'I've already done these,' said Sutcliffe. 'Then we'll
do them again,' he was told. Then the sergeant wanted a blood
test. The letters sent to Oldfield and the semen sample in the
Joan Harrison murder both indicated a man with blood group
B was responsible. The prisoner was reluctant: 'What if it's the
same as the one you are wanting?'

'Are you the Yorkshire Ripper?' O'Boyle said.

'No.'

'Well, what have you to fear?'

Sutcliffe reluctantly agreed to the blood test, but asked to
know the outcome as soon as the police were told. O'Boyle said
they would cross that bridge when they came to it. A police surgeon medically examined Sutcliffe and took a hair sample and a
sample of his blood. Together with a saliva test taken earlier,
they were biked across to the pathology laboratory at St James's
Hospital, Leeds, where a special rush job was arranged to have
them analysed. The result came back an hour later. Sutcliffe was
blood group B. But he was not a secretor.

O'Boyle had been due off shift at 4 p.m., but there was no
chance of that now. They had only just started the interrogation,
which he thought would go on for many hours yet. Besides, Sutcliffe was a very strong suspect and he wanted to see it through,
wanted to keep the pressure on. He had no worries about

Sutcliffe's Bradford accent. He had spent a long time working in Sunderland on the tapes inquiry, where opinions about the Geordie tape being from a hoaxer were commonplace.

For the second time in twenty-four hours Sutcliffe denied going with prostitutes as O'Boyle raised the tempo by questioning him about the dozens of times his car had been seen in red-light areas. Sutcliffe stuck to his usual tale of passing through on the way to somewhere else. 'You were seen in Moss Side, Manchester, on 23 February 1979,' O'Boyle pressed him. 'Why did you deny going there?'

Sutcliffe had already told the Ripper squad they must have made a mistake. He hadn't gone to Manchester; it must have been someone else's car. O'Boyle simply bluffed him. They had rechecked, he said, with the Manchester force manning the observation. There was no mistake. It was definitely Sutcliffe's car. Sutcliffe hedged and for the first time he looked and sounded very uncomfortable: 'Oh, I remember . . .' He claimed his car broke down in Bradford. The electrics had packed up and he had to abandon it overnight at Bradford Central Library. When he returned next day it had been moved to a different parking spot. Someone else must have taken it to Manchester, then returned it to the very same spot.

'How,' riposted O'Boyle, 'if the electrics wouldn't work?'

Sutcliffe looked at him blankly. His story stretched credulity. O'Boyle said he was lying but Sutcliffe remained unshakeable.

'Where were you on 17 November?' O'Boyle asked next.

'Was that the date of the last murder? At home with the wife.'

O'Boyle said he would personally check with Sonia Sutcliffe the following morning. Sutcliffe appeared very anxious. He didn't want his wife to know he had been caught with a prostitute in his car.

'You got yourself into this,' O'Boyle retorted. 'I think you are a regular punter.'

'I am not,' Sutcliffe protested. 'I have never been with another woman.'

'Your car has been seen in the red-light districts of Bradford, Leeds and Manchester, and last night you were caught in a car with a prostitute in Sheffield and you paid her £10. I don't believe these are coincidences.'

'It's true. I am not a punter.'

'You have been previously interviewed about you and your car being seen in prostitute areas and you were adamant that you weren't a punter, but having said that, your conduct last night would seem to indicate that you may well be telling lies when you were asked previously.'

Sutcliffe denied telling lies.

O'Boyle called a halt at about 10 p.m. He needed time to check Sutcliffe's story. He phoned Dick Holland, who was still No. 2 on the Ripper squad, at home, outlining the facts about Sutcliffe and that he was lying his head off. 'I'm going over to his house in the morning to turn it over and question the wife,' he announced. He then drove over to Bradford to store Sutcliffe's blood and saliva samples in the refrigerator in the incident room and have a drink in the police bar upstairs. He ordered a pint of beer, but only stared at it for ages, thinking about the events of the day. Without touching his ale, he got up and left. Later, he said it was probably one of the few times in his life he had been unable to face a drink. He wanted to get some sleep.

Back on duty in Sheffield for the Saturday night shift, Robert Ring soon heard Sutcliffe was still being questioned by the Ripper squad at Dewsbury. That settled it. All day he had been wondering whether to go back up to Light Trades House, bothered that the prisoner of the night before had managed to slip away to the other side of the wall near the oil tank. He took a torch and his radio and got into one of the Vauxhall Chevette panda cars. He quickly cut through Crookes and across the main Glossop Road, close to the Royal Hallamshire Hospital. It was quiet for a Saturday night. The university and polytechnic students were still away for Christmas vacation. Soon he was in Melbourne Avenue again. A few people were out walking their dogs. He parked at the bottom of the driveway where they had arrested Sutcliffe. He didn't know what he was looking for, but felt an inner compulsion to go and look anyway.

It was pitch-black. He went towards the storage tank and flashed his light on. Slowly he walked over to and climbed up on the stone wall at the side of the tank, shining the torch beam down. Nothing there. He inched towards the building itself and found a space between the wall and the end of the storage tank. At the bottom was a gully and a grate where a pile of leaves had gathered. The leaves had blown across the ground, and lay in a huge pile over the grate. 'Christ, what's that?' he said to himself. He gripped the edge of the tank and focused his eyes to the light of the beam from the torch as it clearly illuminated the head of a ball-pein hammer sunk in the leaves, the handle at an angle, inclined upwards. He reached down and took hold of the handle. Realizing what he had done, he immediately put the hammer back and let go. He then reached for his radio. 'Hello, control. Sierra 5809. Message.'

'Pass your message.'

'I am in Melbourne Avenue at Light Trades House. Request Inspector Hopkirk and PC Hydes to attend immediately. It is very important.'

The time was 11 p.m. Robert Hydes had been relegated to

the foot beat, patrolling around Hillsborough. Inspector Paddy Hopkirk radioed him and arranged to drive him over to Melbourne Avenue. All three men then stood close to the wall near the oil tank, looking at the hammer in the gulley as they shone their torches.

'Is it the handyman's?' asked Ring rhetorically, realizing only too well who must have left it there. He was completely awed by the sheer enormity of his discovery. Hydes climbed on to the wall, pointing his torch down on the ground. Lying deeper in the leaves, about an inch and a half below the hammer, he clearly saw a knife with a long blade. 'Well, the hammer might belong to the handyman, but who does the knife belong to?' he said.

The significance of finding the hammer and knife together was chilling. Somehow they had allowed Sutcliffe to dump the weapons to prevent them being found on him. Nevertheless, the two bobbies from Sheffield had caught the Yorkshire Ripper. Hopkirk told Hydes that Sutcliffe was still in custody in Dewsbury. 'Oh, Jesus Christ,' someone said. They radioed the duty detective inspector at Hammerton Road, who then telephoned the Ripper squad in Leeds. It was past midnight, the early hours of Sunday, 4 January.

The duty detective inspector that night in the central incident room at Millgarth was John Boyle, not to be confused with his close colleague, Finbarr O'Boyle. Boyle phoned Dick Holland and then called O'Boyle as he was about to go to bed in Bradford. O'Boyle has a vivid recollection of events.

'John Boyle asked me if I was dealing with a guy at Dewsbury. "Yes," I said. "What have you got him in for?" "Theft of number plates," I replied. "Well, what are you doing with him?" I gave him a run down and said he was red hot and lying his head off and everything else about him. "I have left him at the end of a pack of lies and have bedded him down for the night. I am going to search his house in the morning." John then said: "We have just had a phone call from Sheffield, the two fellows who dealt with him last night found out you have got him in, they have panicked and gone back to the scene, and searched and found a ball-pein hammer and a knife hidden in the grass near where his car was parked."

'I said just: "Bingo – we have got him." It felt unbelievable, after five long years of what we had been through. "Bingo!" It was a hair-up-on-the-back-of-my-neck moment.'

Holland, using the phone by his bed, had ordered everything down at Sheffield to be kept sterile. The place had to be roped off and guarded all night. He didn't want anyone trampling over it. The full West Yorkshire task force would be geared up first thing in the morning and bussed down to Melbourne Avenue to conduct a fingertip search. Meanwhile, he said, Boyle and O'Boyle needed to get down there fast and take charge. Holland was sanguine. He needed his sleep. There had been false dawns before and he wasn't getting his hopes up. He remembered Terence Hawkshaw and how convinced he and Oldfield had been that he was their man.

When Boyle and O'Boyle arrived at Light Trades House, the place was floodlit and well guarded. They spoke urgently with Ring and Hydes to find out the full story of how they found the weapons. Hydes thought Boyle was extremely rude when he was questioning them. Hydes almost swore at him when he thought he was insinuating they had planted the weapons themselves. Boyle, for his part, felt he was having to drag the story out of him. They appeared reluctant at first to admit they had allowed a prisoner to dump his weapons. Only if they were completely frank could the Ripper squad link the weapons to Sutcliffe. O'Boyle knew Ring had done the right thing. He had gone back and found the weapons. It couldn't have been easy for him, but he felt especially sorry for Hydes, who was only a probationer.

Satisfied they now had the truth, O'Boyle and Boyle went in search of the prostitute found in Sutcliffe's car and learned he had tried to pick up another woman about an hour before she took him to Light Trades House. Another lie. That afternoon Sutcliffe had said he picked up the prostitute as soon as he arrived in Sheffield, claiming he did it on impulse. He couldn't admit he had gone looking for prostitutes. The West Yorkshire pair returned later that morning to Dewsbury, where instructions had meanwhile been given for the special prisoner to be kept under 'suicide watch', with his cell door open and a guard posted outside. There was no way he was going to be allowed to escape justice. O'Boyle went down to the cell block and asked Sutcliffe how he had slept. He said he had not been able to sleep much.

'Neither have we,' riposted the detective. 'We've been up all night. Guess where?'

'Where?' said the man they were now certain was the Yorkshire Ripper.

'Sheffield,' grinned O'Boyle. Sutcliffe looked at him as if to say, 'Oh shit.' His eyes said everything. He had the look of the defeated about him. O'Boyle said nothing more, turned on his heels and walked away. They had definitely got him, and now Sutcliffe knew it. He'd let him stew.

The following morning at about ten Dick Holland's Hillman Hunter car quietly pulled up outside Peter Sutcliffe's house in the Heaton area of Bradford. The pale pink pebble-dash exterior of the house stood in sharp contrast to the sleet and snow falling and thinly covering the front garden with its well-trimmed lawn and neat rockery. Holland and Detective Chief Inspector George Smith, a long-standing colleague, had come to collect Sonia Sutcliffe and take her to Bradford police station. They planned to search the house. Holland carried with him in two separate plastic bags the knife and hammer found at Sheffield.

Mrs Sutcliffe answered the door, wearing an outdoor coat. Smith had phoned earlier to say they would take her to see her husband. She took them into the front room and positioned herself in front of the television, sitting in a chair and deeply engrossed in a German-language television programme called *Kontakte*. They were holding Peter at Dewsbury, Holland told her, and making inquiries about murders of women in the north of England. He tried asking questions about her husband, but she wasn't listening. She sat glued to the programme, huddled in her coat to keep warm, with the collar up. Exasperated, after several minutes he told her to turn the television off. Where had she been on Bonfire Night the previous November? he wanted to know. She said she and Peter had been due to go to a party but he had rung to say he was working overtime. She stayed at home and he came home late. Someone from the squad that morning had earlier checked with Clark's Transport. Peter Sutcliffe clocked off work that day at 5 p.m. He should have been comfortably home by 5.30. Suddenly the ultra-cautious Holland began to feel very positive about Sutcliffe, who had clearly told his wife a lie. There was a gap of three and a half hours during which he could have attacked Teresa Sykes.

The Sutcliffes' front room was spotlessly clean and tidy, with covers on the sofa and chairs. Everything was immaculate. The walls were decorated in caramel and yellow paper and the paintwork was shiny. The couple had obviously been busy.

Examples of Sonia's craftwork, odd-shaped handmade ceramics, were everywhere. But like the rest of the house the front room was bitterly cold. Down in the cellar Holland saw the new Potterton central heating boiler had been turned off. In the kitchen he spotted what he was looking for. On one of the work surfaces was a wooden block containing knives of various sizes. The second largest was missing. Holland took the others out and examined them. The one he held in the plastic bag matched the set perfectly. Leaving Smith downstairs with Sonia Sutcliffe, he went upstairs. It was a cursory look because he had arranged for the full scenes-of-crime search team to turn the house over once they left. The couple's bedroom at the back had pink floral wallpaper, a double bed, and fitted 'his' and 'hers' wardrobes. In a bedside cabinet he found a length of rope about four feet long. The front bedroom was for guests, and the smallest bedroom was intended as a children's nursery and decorated to suit. The attic was an open-plan affair containing a study area. The bathroom was dominated by a pale blue enamelled bath with matching blue washbasin. It was a strange house. A senior detective who visited the next night described it as 'sterile'.

Downstairs, Holland unlocked the back door which opened on to a short driveway running beside the detached house, leading up to a wooden garage. He was looking for weapons and quickly found what he had come for. Hanging on a nail on the garage wall was a hacksaw. Just at that moment his colleague emerged through the back door, followed a few seconds later by Sutcliffe's wife. Holland quickly told Smith to put the hacksaw into a plastic evidence bag. Smith seemed totally bewildered: 'Nay boss, he hit her with a hammer and stabbed them. What do you want this for?' Holland brushed him away. He didn't want Mrs Sutcliffe asking awkward questions. She must have seen the hacksaw being carried by Smith, and both men thought it extraordinary she never mentioned it. Before leaving for Bradford they obtained a key so the full forensic search team could let themselves in.

George Smith and a policewoman minded Sutcliffe's wife into the small hours of Monday morning. Never in all that time did she ask to speak to him. She was asked many questions, yet showed little or no curiosity about her husband. Smith was convinced she had no inkling what her husband had been doing. 'She was rather strange,' he remembered many years later. 'I can honestly say that had I not spent fifteen hours with her I would never have accepted that the wife of the Yorkshire Ripper didn't know who he was. But having spent all that time with her, I was satisfied she didn't know.'

Around lunchtime on Sunday a new interrogation team was preparing to break Sutcliffe's story. He was taken from the cell area up to the sergeants' office in the CID room on the first floor. Holland hoped a fresh pair of faces might now do the trick. John Boyle and a detective sergeant called Peter Smith had a huge advantage. They were confident they had the killer. They had the weapons he had dropped in Sheffield and they now knew he had lied to his wife the night Teresa Sykes was attacked. They started by going over some of the things Sutcliffe had told O'Boyle the night before. He again repeated his story about picking up hitchhikers on the motorway. Boyle didn't believe him and said so, adding that Sutcliffe had gone to Sheffield for the sole purpose of picking up a prostitute. He'd put the false plates on his car to conceal his identity if it was spotted in a red-light area. Sutcliffe tried to wriggle, but Boyle pressed home the advantage: 'Do you understand what I am saying? I think you are in serious trouble.'

'I think you've been leading up to it.'

'Leading up to what?'

'The Yorkshire Ripper.'

'What about the Yorkshire Ripper?'

'Well, it's me,' said Sutcliffe.

Finally the long nightmare was over.

Boyle read the formal caution to Sutcliffe and asked him if he wanted a lawyer.

'No, I don't need one,' said Sutcliffe. 'I just want to tell you what I've done. I'm glad it's all over. I would have killed that girl in Sheffield if I hadn't been caught. But I'd like to tell my wife myself. I don't want her to hear it from anyone else. It's her I'm thinking about and my family. I'm not bothered about myself.'

The two detectives were not yet ready to start taking Sutcliffe's voluntary statement, a process which would last more than fifteen hours. They still needed hard evidence from the killer, information only he could know. Boyle especially needed to connect Sutcliffe to the weapons found in Sheffield: 'You didn't go to the side of the house to urinate, did you?'

'No, I knew what you were leading up to. You've found the hammer and the knife, haven't you?'

'Yes we have. Where did you put them?'

'When they took the girl to the panda car I nipped out and put them near the house in the corner. I was panicking. I was hoping to get bail from here and get a taxi back to pick them up. Then I would have been in the clear.'

He admitted eleven killings, but denied the murder of Joan Harrison in Preston. It came as no surprise. He said he had no connection with the tape and the letters and went on to describe how he killed Wilma McCann in 1975, stabbing her in the lungs and throat after lifting her clothes so he could see where he was stabbing her.

Boyle, unflinching, showed no emotion, and coolly asked how he killed his latest victim, Jacqueline Hill. 'I followed her and hit her on the head with a hammer, then I dragged her on to some spare land out of sight.'

'What else did you do to her?'

'I stabbed her in the lung.'

'What with?'

'A screwdriver.'

'Did you stab her anywhere else?'

'Yes, I stabbed her in the eye because her eyes were open and she seemed to be looking at me.'

'Did you do anything else to her?'

'I pulled her clothes off.'

'Do you know all the names of your victims?'

'Yes, I know them all.'

'Do you keep any press cuttings of them or make any records?'

'No, they are all in my brain, reminding me of the beast I am.'

He agreed to make a statement telling everything he had done. Boyle left the room to collect the statement forms and immediately found Holland and O'Boyle. 'He's coughed,' he said, relaying how Sutcliffe had given details of some of the killings only the Ripper could know. After Boyle gave them the headlines, Holland slid into the sergeants' office to get his first look at the man he had been hunting so long. He stood a few moments saying nothing while Sutcliffe chatted idly to Peter Smith.

'I thought he looked a weedy wimp,' he said. 'He was quietly spoken, almost effeminate in his speech and manner. He didn't give the impression in any way of being the overpowering evil man. You would have thought of him as an ideal neighbour, the sort of person you would meet on the way to church on a Sunday morning.' What struck him most was the amazing resemblance to the photofit Marilyn Moore had provided two years previously. He was staggered that, given her injuries, she had been able to recall his features so perfectly. He felt little personal emotion other than relief. Then it dawned on him there was an amazing amount of work to do, ferreting out all the relevant information from the incident room files to corroborate the things Sutcliffe was saying. Then there would be the prosecution file.

Holland went quietly off to an unoccupied room to make the most important phone call of his professional life. Despite the fact that George Oldfield was no longer involved in the inquiry, Holland telephoned him at his home. He was having his traditional Sunday roast lunch with his family. 'We had promised each other a long time beforehand that, whatever the circumstances and whenever he was nicked, we would tell the other.'

'We've got the bugger,' said Holland, giving scant information but making it clear the Ripper was from Bradford not the north-east. Oldfield didn't hesitate: 'I'm coming straight down.' He did not want the details over the phone. Even at that moment of triumph old rivalries endured. One of the other detectives called Jim Hobson. By then the Chief had already been given the news by Oldfield, who got in first with the words, 'Fasten your seatbelt. We've got him.' Gregory arranged for a car to take him over to Dewsbury – to keep Oldfield and Hobson apart.

The interviewing team then began the drawn-out process of taking down Sutcliffe's full confession. Earlier, word had filtered back to the incident room at Millgarth that something was in the wind. 'I remember it all being hush-hush,' Sue

Neave said. 'We knew they had somebody in custody, but we didn't know who it was, other than that he had been arrested down in Sheffield with a prostitute and it was looking good.' There was sheer elation when they heard he had confessed. Neave rang a colleague and said: 'They've got somebody, it's looking good, watch the telly.' 'It was marvellous,' she recalled, 'like a cloud had been lifted, a wonderful feeling.' Megan Winterburn also received a phone call at home: 'I felt thank God for that, but my very first thought was: "I wonder whether he was in the system?"'

Among the top brass, it was Oldfield who arrived at Dewsbury first, immediately to be given a detailed briefing by Holland. Boyle had earlier approached Holland in a state of some excitement. 'Hey boss, he's told us he went back to Manchester to Jordan and tried to cut her head off with a hacksaw . . .' Holland said they had removed the hacksaw from Sutcliffe's garage that morning, and explained he had known about it for three years, but Jack Ridgway had sworn him to secrecy. A dumbfounded George Smith commented: 'Well, you kept that dark,' amazed it had remained secret for so long.

Throughout the late afternoon press inquiries were brushed off. It was obvious there had been some kind of leak. The clamour for information from reporters built into a furore. When Gregory said he would call a press conference, Holland urged him to tone down any announcement because of the dangers of contempt of court. Gregory, anticipating the public's reaction, wasn't having any of it. They needed to make it clear, he said, that the Yorkshire Ripper had been found. Quite rightly he sensed that hundreds and thousands of women who had spent years fearing for their lives needed to be reassured. An hour or so later Holland drafted a telex to be sent to all northern forces announcing the cancellation of the inquiry.

The world's news media began descending on Dewsbury for what by any standards was an extraordinary event. Gregory broke into a beaming smile for the cameras as he briefly relayed the happenings of the last seventy-two hours and made no pretence of the fact that they had the Yorkshire Ripper under arrest: 'We are absolutely delighted with developments at this stage, absolutely delighted.'

When it was over, both Oldfield and Gregory, without prior warning, visited the interrogation room where Boyle, Peter Smith and O'Boyle were laboriously recording Sutcliffe's version of his reign of terror in agonizing detail. The junior detectives were not happy at what they saw as a gratuitous display of grandstanding by their bosses. They were also very tired. O'Boyle and Boyle had hardly had any sleep for forty-eight hours. It was unusual for senior officers to interrupt such a crucial interview. Gregory asked Sutcliffe if he was OK and whether his men were looking after him. Did he need anything? Would he care to see his wife? Sutcliffe said he would.

Sonia Sutcliffe had already been taken to Dewsbury. Shortly after 11 p.m. she was ushered into the CID office. Her husband was sitting down. 'What on earth is going on, Peter?' she said. 'It's all those women,' he replied. 'I've killed all those women.' 'What do you mean?' said Sonia. 'It's me. I'm the Yorkshire Ripper. I killed all those women.' To the amazement of O'Boyle who was standing close by listening to this exchange, her next response was: 'What on earth did you do that for, Peter? Even a sparrow has a right to live.' They were allowed a few minutes to chat. One of her main concerns was whether he had had sex with the women he killed. Only once, he replied, and that was mechanical.

Sonia Sutcliffe was then taken to an accommodation block next to the police station and provided with a bed. Soon after her brief visit the enormity of what her husband had said suddenly struck her. She felt faint and 'funny'. George Smith went to get her something to bring her round. 'The shock had hit her,' he said. 'I didn't have any sympathy towards her, not as you do on some occasions when dealing with a murderer when you feel for the wife or the family of the man who has committed the murder.' A policewoman stayed in the room with the light on throughout the night.

The interviewing team continued taking the statement until shortly after 1 a.m. when Jack Ridgway, who had driven over from Manchester, insisted they had to give Sutcliffe some rest. He had been questioned constantly since Friday night. There was a danger of it becoming oppressive. He was taken down to a cell.

In Bradford on night patrol as a newly promoted uniformed sergeant was Andrew Laptew, who had named Sutcliffe as a possible prime suspect after he interviewed him sixteen months previously. He was delighted with the breakthrough – until he heard the name of the man arrested. Enjoying a cup of tea at the back door of a local bakery whose owner welcomed his regular early-morning visits, he knew nothing of the arrest until a policewoman turned up at 3 a.m. 'We've got the Ripper,' she said, 'we've locked him up.'

'Great. Who is it?'

'A guy called Peter Sutcliffe.'

'Fucking hell,' Laptew gasped. A tidal wave of emotion hit him. Downing his tea and making his excuses, he half-ran, half-walked back to the police station at Laisterdyke and dug out his pocket books, which he kept in pristine condition in his locker. A few hours later he was back home with his wife, Sheila, in the three-bedroomed semi they had just bought for £1,575. He was thirty years old, had been married for fourteen months, and was deeply concerned about his future. He thought his police career was over. 'I was worried I had screwed up big time,' he said, 'that was my biggest concern. I dragged Sheila out of bed and said, "Do you remember the report you typed – they've caught Sutcliffe." She's going, "Oh bloody hell." You don't know what to think. You can imagine how I felt, I was absolutely stunned, totally gutted. I thought what might have been. Things could have been so different, not for my own personal satisfaction but for the relatives of those victims.'

A copy of his interview report with Sutcliffe had obviously been found. An officer from the interview room later phoned him. 'You've nothing to worry about, you're absolutely fire-proof,' he said.

The Monday morning newspaper headlines screamed news of the Yorkshire Ripper's arrest. The law of *sub judice* was abandoned as the people of Britain learned that the most wanted man in British criminal history had been apprehended. Every television and radio bulletin quoted details of the arrest freely and anticipated his appearance in court later that day. Photographs of Oldfield, Hobson and Gregory grinning triumphally were carried on the front pages. The arresting officers, Ring and Hydes, were heroes. Gregory sent them a personal telegraph and their own chief constable thanked them as well.

On the first floor of Dewsbury police station, Sutcliffe had far from completed his confession. He was taken back to the CID office just as the first onlookers began arriving outside the local magistrates' court. Sutcliffe was allowed a second brief visit from Sonia before he continued unravelling the story of his ritualistic killings. His recall of minute details was extraordinary. When he tried to kill the Malaysian doctor in Headingley a few months previously, he had hit her on the head with a hammer: 'I dragged her down the road, her shoes were making an awful scraping noise, so I took them off and put them over a wall with her handbag.' He chillingly told how, before he killed Josephine Whitaker on Savile Park in Halifax, he had walked alongside her chatting casually. So that he could reach for a weapon in his pocket, he distracted her by asking the time on the nearby church tower clock. In the split second in which she turned her head to look at the clock, he had the weapon in his hand and struck her down.

A quarter of a mile away at Dewsbury Town Hall, which doubled as the magistrates' court, the crowds built up throughout the day. By mid-morning a crowd of people were hanging about in the freezing cold amid the snow flurries. Hundreds more joined them throughout the afternoon until there was nothing short of a mob baying for the Yorkshire Ripper's blood. People stood on garden walls, clung to windowsills and climbed on to the roofs of lorries to get better views. More and more police officers were needed to hold them back. All the while there were false alarms as police cars were heard approaching the court, sirens howling and lights flashing, but they drove straight past. Finally the narrow road outside the town hall was closed to traffic. The crowd consisted of men and women, young and old – one mother even bringing her infant in a baby buggy. They huddled together, gossiping, discussing details of the case, relaying stories heard. Generally good-natured towards the police struggling to maintain order out of chaos, the mob directed its anger only at the Yorkshire Ripper.

Inside the police station the heat was on those taking Sutcliffe's long statement, which would finally run to thirty-four typed pages. After three hours they took a twenty-five-minute lunch break, then continued writing against the clock. They were under huge pressure to get the killer into court, but still had several murders and attempted murders to document. There were repeated urgent calls to hurry up and finish. According to Des O'Boyle, much of that pressure came from the Chief himself.

'Mr Gregory was saying: "You have to get this man into court, I want him in court now." It was said they couldn't cope with the crowds and that if we didn't hurry up there could be all sorts of grief.' O'Boyle and his colleagues could not understand the rush. After a five-year-long investigation with attacks on at least twenty women, it seemed madness not to be painstaking in documenting the killer's account of his murderous activities.

They galloped on but had to leave out references to his attacks on women who had survived. Even after he signed his statement, the formalities were not over. Sutcliffe now needed to be formally charged with one single count of murder. He had admitted the offence and they had his signed confession. There was enough evidence for the local magistrates to remand him in prison. But first he had to have his clothes taken from him. Incredibly, the interviewing detectives had forgotten to search Sutcliffe thoroughly earlier. He was still wearing the same clothing he had on when first taken into custody at Sheffield on Friday night. At that stage he was just a minor criminal, a witness to an act of soliciting. But at Dewsbury he became prime suspect in a massive homicide investigation. He should have had *all* his clothes removed immediately and then been reissued with a fresh set. His personal clothing would be individually tagged, bagged and sent to the forensic science laboratory for analysis. But the interrogating team had been so completely overtaken by events in dealing with Sutcliffe since Saturday morning that this vital part of police procedure had simply been overlooked. However understandable it seems in hindsight, it was a major mistake, caused in part by the need for urgency created by senior officers.

Standing in the CID sergeant's office, Sutcliffe began to remove his clothing hesitatingly. O'Boyle searched his coat. The insides of the pockets had been cut out to allow weapons to be hidden deep in the bottom of the coat lining. Reaching inside the lining, O'Boyle found a pair of underpants. Sutcliffe said they were his. As he removed his trousers, the reason for him not wearing the underpants became all too obvious. The killer wore instead a V-neck sweater, but with his legs placed inside the long sleeves of the woollen garment, which had then been pulled up over his backside, allowing the V neck at the front to expose his genitals. The detective was momentarily struck dumb by the ludicrous sight. The Yorkshire Ripper, the most dangerous criminal of the twentieth century, stood there like some well-hung ballet dancer wearing woollen tights, his private parts exposed.

'What on earth is that?' asked O'Boyle.

'Erm, leg warmers,' the killer replied disingenuously.

'Oh, yes – leg warmers, eh?' commented a deeply dubious O'Boyle.

Once Sutcliffe had stepped out of the sweater, the detective examined it closely. Reinforced padding had been sewn into the area where Sutcliffe's knees would have been. It was obvious why. The killer had spent a lot of time kneeling over his victims as he displaced their clothing before stabbing them to death. Placing knee pads inside the garment irresistibly suggested that Sutcliffe had lingered over this activity, wanting to be comfortable while doing it. Exposing his genital area made it easier for him to masturbate. He only had to undo the fly of his trousers. However, the officers were in a hopeless position. Had they known earlier what Sutcliffe was wearing, there is no question they would have sought a detailed explanation. His responses would have been recorded. But they had gone on and on for several days, first questioning him, then recording his written confession, without realizing he was all the time sitting across the desk from them wearing some kind of killing kit. The scenario was totally bizarre. It is impossible to overstate the seriousness of this development, revealed here for the first time. The garment Sutcliffe had fashioned was as important in terms of evidence as the actual weapons he used to murder his victims. It spoke volumes about his sexual motives, and his state of mind during his attacks on helpless women.

The detectives questioning him were near exhaustion. They had gone virtually without sleep for three days. During this time they had performed heroically, both in getting Sutcliffe to confess and then recording a lengthy, detailed statement. Taking down his confession was a work of art in terms of the evidence it would provide for the Director of Public Prosecutions. It involved a great deal of professionalism in guiding him through a series of major crimes committed over five years. At any time Sutcliffe could have fallen back on his right to silence, thrown his arms in the air, demanded to see a lawyer or accused his accusers of browbeating. In those sixty hours they had to become virtually the only friends Peter Sutcliffe had in the world, helping him to cleanse himself of his terrible deeds by owning up to them. They were literally his confessors. It involved treating him with kid gloves. The last thing they wanted to do was antagonize him. They needed to keep him happy. Little wonder no one strip searched him. It would have been a distraction and could have led to Sutcliffe withdrawing his cooperation. He freely talked about the weapons he used and where he had hidden them, which was veritable gold dust in terms of evidence.

They had to go gently with the prisoner, even when they knew Sutcliffe was lying. He had admitted attacking the Malaysian doctor a few months earlier, intending to strangle her, but he absolutely denied strangling to death the civil servant Marguerite Walls. 'You've got a mystery on your hands with that one,' he said. 'I've only used the rope once, on that girl at Headingley.' Boyle and O'Boyle let it go, and with good reason. The prisoner had confessed to plenty in extraordinary detail. It was no time to grill him or challenge him. Their task was to get his story down on paper in a form that was priceless as evidence – a signed statement in which he told them things only he as the Yorkshire Ripper could know.

None of the detectives present when Sutcliffe removed his clothes appears to have informed a senior investigating officer of their find, or to have documented their amazing discovery. With the passage of time it is possible to be generous about their motives. Exhaustion may have fogged their normal professionalism. Even so, a few days earlier they had smirked among themselves that the South Yorkshire officers, Ring and Hydes, had allowed Sutcliffe to dump his weapons, as if to say, 'We would never make that mistake.' The fact that a neighbouring force had lifted the Yorkshire Ripper and not the West Yorkshire detectives was a bit of a disappointment. Any sense of *schadenfreude* felt on Saturday had now vanished.

By any objective standards, the discovery about what the Yorkshire Ripper was wearing when about to kill Olivia Reivers was a devastating piece of evidence that should have been instantly communicated to senior investigating officers. Yet no details about this bizarre item of clothing appeared in Sutcliffe's statement. Nor was it mentioned in any of the official statements made by Detective Sergeant Peter Smith, who was responsible for writing down what was said by Sutcliffe during

interview. Sutcliffe had asked Smith to write his statement for
him. A week later Smith had made his own written statement,
disclosing features about the case revealed by Sutcliffe but not
put in the formal confession. They had had no time to document the attacks where victims survived through the skill of
the doctors who treated them. Smith's personal statement
noted the sequence of events during the interviews and briefly
what happened after Sutcliffe signed his confession:

> DS O'Boyle then took from Sutcliffe the clothes he was
> wearing, for Forensic examination and he was then sup-
> plied with a change of clothing. At 4.41 p.m. the same
> day I was present in the Detective Sergeants Office at
> Dewsbury Police Station with DS O'Boyle when DI
> Boyle formally cautioned and charged the accused
> Sutcliffe with the murder of Jacqueline Hill. He replied:
> 'Well, I'm terribly sorry about this tragic loss to her
> family and friends and I would do anything to alter what
> has happened. I am glad that I have been apprehended
> because I was totally out of my mind when I committed
> this and other acts.' He was also charged with the offence
> of theft of vehicle registration plates. He made no reply.
> I have signed labels to the items I have referred to.

Tired and under pressure to get the prisoner to the magistrates' court, O'Boyle and his colleagues simply placed
Sutcliffe's clothing in separate evidence bags, issued him with
a change of clothing and got him ready to leave. They may not
have realized the importance of their finds. The implications of
Sutcliffe's home-made killing kit are truly sensational in the
light of what happened at the subsequent trial.

O'Boyle had never seen anything like it. The garment was

obviously connected with some kind of sexual kink. Sutcliffe clearly gained sexual satisfaction from murdering his victims, almost certainly exposing himself while doing so. 'That's why his underpants are in his coat pocket because he has changed when he has gone out,' O'Boyle said. 'He would have gone out with his underpants on when he left home. At some stage he has taken his underpants off and put on this other item. He must have had it on when he was sat in the car with Reivers, because he didn't get a chance to change them after. The reason it was padded around the knees was for one reason and it was not so that he could drive a bloody car. It was so that he could kneel on them, and if he is kneeling down cushioning his knees, the only thing he is going to be doing is dealing with a corpse, to my way of thinking.'

Sutcliffe put on the clothes provided by the police, a blue polo-necked sweater, a white shirt and a pair of jeans. The key object now was to get him safely into court and back again, with a jeering crowd of well over fifteen hundred people waiting in the narrow street. Holland had assumed responsibility for the operation outside the entrance to the court. The mob was angry but not unruly. A pair of youths at the front carried a noose and a poster that proclaimed HANG HIM. A police van with an escort of patrol cars, lights flashing and sirens wailing, moved slowly through the crowd and came to a halt outside. It had to reverse to get close to the entrance. Fists were banging on the van. Stones and coins were thrown. There was pandemonium briefly as the mob surged forward, momentarily breaking the police line. Holland, a fully fit eighteen-stone full-back in the police rugby team, linked arms with two colleagues and together they threw themselves forwards into the crowd, heaving and shoving them back as if they were part of a scrum.

Handcuffed to O'Boyle inside the van, Sutcliffe was reluctant to get out, afraid someone outside might have a gun. A woman could be heard screaming for all her worth: 'Hang the bastard!' 'Hang him, hang him,' the crowd responded. As the back of the van opened and a figure under a blanket emerged, the crowd roared and surged forward again. O'Boyle put his head down and marched forward, pulling Sutcliffe under the blanket with him. Flanked by other officers, they made it through safely to the entrance as someone roared, 'Die, die, fucking die, you bastard,' followed by the crowd's immediate response: 'Die, die'; 'Coward'; 'Bastard'; 'Hang him'.

Crammed into the oak-panelled courtroom a hundred journalists occupied the public gallery waiting to get their first glimpse of Sutcliffe. No members of the public were admitted. Sonia Sutcliffe and her father sat at the front of the court as three police officers escorted the Yorkshire Ripper into the dock. The formalities of remanding him to Armley Prison in Leeds were soon over. Sutcliffe was quickly taken downstairs in the cells, then back to the police van to run the gauntlet of the angry crowd a second time. That evening he was driven around Bradford by Boyle and O'Boyle. Sutcliffe showed them where he had hidden or thrown away weapons, including a claw hammer he used to kill Patricia Atkinson nearly four years earlier.

Later that same night he was taken back to his home in Garden Lane, where he pointed out items of clothing worn during various attacks. Sonia was at the house, so were several senior detectives, including Dick Holland, and Jack Ridgway from Manchester. It was still bitterly cold. Ridgway thought it felt like a morgue rather than a home. 'It was the most sterile place I have ever been in, very inhuman,' he said later.

In the kitchen the detectives witnessed the Sutcliffes' final act of domesticity, a bizarre final fragment in the life of this decidedly odd couple. While detectives examined clothing in the bedroom, the killer's wife walked upstairs and announced she had saved her husband a piece of Christmas cake. She insisted that he could not possibly leave to go to Armley Prison before he had eaten a piece of cake and drunk a cup of warm milk. The killer looked harassed, raising his eyebrows as if to say: 'Oh God, there she goes again.'

The thought of having to spend a minute longer than strictly necessary in the freezing house left everyone feeling uncomfortable. But Mrs Sutcliffe was going to have her way. Her husband, still handcuffed to O'Boyle, asked if it would be OK. They agreed to indulge her. Sutcliffe was allowed to sit at the kitchen table but his escort had to sit alongside him. Sonia, the loving and apparently dutiful wife, brought out the cake and warm milk and set them down on the table. Every time Sutcliffe raised his hand to his mouth either to eat or drink, O'Boyle had to raise his too. As Sutcliffe moved his right arm, O'Boyle had to move his left. For several minutes their hands bobbed up and down in unison. Watching this almost surreal act of unholy communion between serial killer and spouse, on this most extraordinary of days, Holland and Ridgway could barely contain their mirth. Both later agreed that had it not been so hopelessly tragic, it would have been hysterically funny, the biggest laugh either of them had had in ages.

18

Mad or Bad?

Sutcliffe's home-from-home for the next four months was a special room in a Victorian prison built from stone on high ground overlooking Leeds. Armley Gaol still resembles a medieval fortress. It has a turreted gatehouse and tiny cellblock windows set high in its forbidding walls. The design of its four wings was so radical when it was built in 1847 that it now has the status of a Grade II listed building. When Sutcliffe was taken through its doors for the first time, it enjoyed a fearsome reputation among Leeds' criminal fraternity. Suicide attempts among prisoners awaiting trial were common, and conditions inside were tough and cramped. An exception was made for the Yorkshire Ripper.

A room was provided for him in the prison hospital. Instead of sharing a cell with two other remand prisoners, like his fellow inmates, he enjoyed the comfort of a single bed and a shower unit. He was watched twenty-four hours a day by a group of handpicked officers, who monitored his visitors and kept a close eye on their notorious prisoner for signs of potential suicide. The lights remained permanently on and at least one staff member was with him at all times. He never mixed with other prisoners, who took to referring to him as 'J.R.' – not after the character in the American television series *Dallas*, but someone more malevolent and much closer to home: Jack the Ripper.

Within days of her husband's arrival at Armley Gaol, Sonia was at the front gate wanting to visit. As he was a remand prisoner she could bring him in special food and books. They were closely watched. The staff kept a daily log of Sutcliffe's conversations with them and his wife. She produced a list of things they had needed to discuss, acutely aware they had only fifteen minutes to chat. Sutcliffe was overwhelmed by her presence: domineering her husband, monopolizing the conversation in the room. He told her she had to make a life for herself. He was going to be in prison for a long time. As an aside, he said that if he could make people believe he was mad, 'he might only do ten years in a loony bin'. On a later visit she had kept on at him, wanting to know why he could not talk to her about his 'compulsions'. His only response: 'Leave it to the medical people to find out.'

Three psychiatrists paid a series of visits to examine Sutcliffe as the winter months of 1981 gave way to spring. They wanted to get to grips with the inner workings of the Yorkshire Ripper's mind. The first to see him was Dr Hugo Milne from Bradford, who during his career had analysed two hundred murderers.

During the course of eleven visits to Armley Gaol, Milne searched for a sexual motive to the Yorkshire Ripper's attacks. Sutcliffe denied it vehemently. There was no mention of the special garment worn beneath his trousers as he waited for his chance to kill the prostitute in Sheffield. Neither was there any reference to it in the documents about the case Milne received from the police. Sutcliffe never raised it, so Milne had no chance to question him about why he wore such clothing or the sexual gratification it gave him. The psychiatrist concluded he had been a paranoid schizophrenic from the age of nineteen or twenty. Unknown to Milne, Sutcliffe was setting out deliberately to deceive him. For more than fifteen years his whole life had been a lie. He carried dark and guilty secrets about his sexual obsessions with women. During his interviews with psychiatrists, Sutcliffe continued to manipulate and deceive. He said nothing to the police after his arrest about hearing voices from God. Then, in early March, he suddenly told Milne he had been on a mission from God to rid the world of prostitutes. In April, he cockily told a prison officer that an agreement had been reached: his plea of guilty to manslaughter had been accepted. He wouldn't be going to prison but to a secure mental hospital instead.

By the time Sutcliffe appeared before a judge at the end of April, a deal had been struck between prosecution and defence. British lawyers dislike the term 'plea-bargain', with its overtones of the deeply flawed American system of criminal justice, but this is precisely what it was. The psychiatrists all believed Sutcliffe was suffering from diminished responsibility, that he was highly dangerous and should spend the rest of his natural life out of harm's way. The Director of Public Prosecutions had accepted the offer of a plea of guilty to manslaughter on the grounds of diminished responsibility from Sutcliffe's defence team. The prosecutors were satisfied the outcome would still be the same as a conviction for murder: Sutcliffe would still get a life sentence. Moreover, doing without a trial 'would spare the families of the victims many days of extensive press coverage and detailed knowledge of the horrifying injuries'.

Court No. 1 at the Old Bailey in London has been the setting for some of the greatest criminal trials, occasionally producing mesmerizing performances from lawyers and accused. The drama had been especially enhanced when matters of life and death were played out within its walls. Before the abolition of capital punishment, murder trials drew huge crowds. A black piece of cloth was placed by an usher on top of the judge's wig moments before he was due to pass sentence of death on a convicted killer.

As the setting for a piece of legal theatre on 29 April 1981, Court No. 1 drew a huge crowd, many of them queuing outside overnight. But the performance they had flocked to see was scheduled only as a one-act play. The Yorkshire Ripper's appearance could not be tagged the 'Trial of the Century', for no trial as such was supposed to take place. Indeed, no jury was sworn in. Journalists were briefed in advance that the case of *Regina v. Sutcliffe* would be over quickly, in a day or two at the most. He had admitted the crimes but was deemed so mad he wasn't responsible for his actions. The Crown would reluctantly accept his manslaughter plea. It was against this background that a swift judicial resolution to the Yorkshire Ripper's five-year reign of terror was anticipated by the assembled ranks of lawyers and journalists.

In Yorkshire sporting parlance, it was a fixture which demanded a turnout by the 'big hitters'. On the lawyers' benches, bewigged and wearing the silk gown of a Queen's Counsel, was the Attorney General himself, the country's top law officer. In a piece of perfect casting, Sir Michael Havers looked every inch the matinée idol. For the more knowledge-able members of the legal profession in court, Sir Michael was not necessarily the star turn. That role was reserved for the QC assisting him, Mr Harry Ognall, one of the north's leading criminal barristers. The presence of these two men alone signalled how seriously the government took proceedings.

And if the lawyers had put in their first team, so also had the news media. On the press benches the daily and provincial newspapers assembled their ablest writers. Among them was the first lady of Fleet Street herself, Miss Jean Rook, representing the *Daily Express*. Public interest in Sutcliffe's sentencing at the Old Bailey was massive. Such was the notoriety of the case that a sales bonanza could be anticipated in the following day's editions. Editors had allocated umpteen pages for the mountains of copy that would flow from the day's events and the earlier investigations the media had mounted into the background of Sutcliffe and his family.

There was, however, to be more drama than anyone bargained for. The galleries were first treated to the traditional pomp of the ceremonial opening of the Easter Law Term, when the robed Lord Mayor of London led a procession into court that included the judge in his scarlet robes. Special benches at the back of the court reserved for the families of aldermen of the City of London were filled with women wearing large floral hats. An array of hideous-looking weapons, all neatly labelled, lay on an oak exhibits table in the well of the court, beneath where Mr Justice Boreham sat overshadowed by an ornate royal coat of arms. On the table, watched over by Jim Hobson of West Yorkshire police, were seven ball-pein hammers, a claw hammer, a hacksaw, a long kitchen knife, eight screwdrivers of assorted lengths, a knife with a wooden handle, a short length of rope and a cream-coloured raffia handbag which had belonged to Jacqueline Hill. Mrs Sutcliffe, ashen-faced, was discreetly escorted in by a uniformed woman attendant. Sutcliffe, accompanied by four prison warders, was brought into the dock, which had glass panels on three sides. He wore a light grey suit and a blue shirt; his dark beard was neatly trimmed. Twenty charges were sombrely put to him. It took seven minutes for them to be read out and for him to respond to each. He admitted seven cases of attempted murder. He denied thirteen separate charges of murder, but in each case pleaded guilty to manslaughter on the grounds of diminished responsibility. His Bradford accent was low key and several times he stumbled over his words.

Sir Michael rose. The Crown, he said, would accept the pleas. The judge had had the reports of the various psychiatrists. Sir Michael said he himself had met with them and discussed their reports 'with the greatest care and anxiety and at great length. The general consensus of the doctors is that this is a case of diminished responsibility, the illness being paranoiac schizo-phrenia.'

What happened next should have come as little surprise to anyone familiar with the sixty-two-year-old judge's legal philosophy. Mr Justice Boreham, a former civil and criminal lawyer on the South Eastern circuit, was a stickler for the proprieties and disfavoured plea bargains. Six years earlier, when trying a case of rape in Leeds, he told a prosecutor prepared to accept a lesser charge of unlawful sexual inter-course: 'It is for me to see that justice is done, and the Crown should consider very carefully where its duty lies.'

The Judge asked the Attorney General: 'Where is the evi-dence which gives the doctors the factual basis for these pleas?'

Havers said he had questioned the doctors very closely and 'at the end, I and my learned friends were satisfied we have been told the truth'.

'But where is the supporting evidence?'

'The difficulty is that I would feel unable to challenge any evidence called by my learned friend . . .'

'I have very grave anxieties about Sutcliffe and his pleas. I would like you to explain in far greater detail than usual any decision that you are going to make about the acceptance of these pleas.'

For the next two hours, Havers took the judge through the various reports of the psychiatrists and Sutcliffe's own explanation that he had been ordered by God to do these dreadful crimes. It all added up, according to the Attorney General, to a clear case of diminished responsibility.

The judge sat listening patiently. When Sir Michael had finished speaking he promptly rejected the Attorney General's arguments. 'The matter that troubles me is not the medical opinions because there is a consensus. It seems to me that all these opinions – and I say this without criticism – all these opinions are based simply on what this defendant has told the doctors, nothing more. Moreover, what he has told the doctors conflicts substantially with what he told the police on the morning of arrest. I use the word "conflict" advisedly. In statements to the police he expressed a desire to kill all women. If that is right – and here I need your help – is that not a matter which ought to be tested? Where lies the evidence which gives these doctors the factual basis for these pleas? It is a matter for the defendant to establish. It is a matter for a jury. We have in a sense conducted a trial which has satisfied us. It seems to me it would be more appropriate if this case were dealt with by a jury.'

Thus ended the performance for the moment. Prosecution and defence said they needed time to prepare for a full trial. The judge gave them six days. The scene was set for a fully fledged drama in several acts. The setting stayed the same, the main players were unchanged, and the props remained on the exhibits table. As the curtain rose on No. 1 Court on Tuesday, 5 May 1981, a legal metamorphosis appeared to have taken place. The same Sir Michael Havers, who had less than a week earlier accepted what the doctors were saying, was now arguing that Peter Sutcliffe's stories about being motivated to kill by a mission from the Almighty were nothing more than a tissue of lies. Lawyers are paid to do this. Their skill is advocacy.

'You'll have to decide,' Sir Michael told the jury of six men and six women, just sworn in, 'whether the doctors have been deceived by this man, whether he sought to pull the wool over their eyes or whether the doctors are just plain wrong. You will have to decide whether as a clever, callous murderer he has deliberately set out to provide a cock and bull story to avoid conviction for murder.' For the next four days the prosecution presented a series of witnesses, friends of Sutcliffe, prison officers, policemen who took his confession, with the intention of showing that the accused had kept his mission from God secret from everyone, especially the detectives who took down his confession. The idea was to present him as crafty, deceitful, lying and manipulative. Sir Michael read long extracts from Sutcliffe's statement, adding comments from time to time. Then Harry Ognall examined Peter Smith from the West Yorkshire police, the detective present when Sutcliffe was interviewed and who wrote down his confession. Mr Ognall took Smith through the questions and answers the accused had given. Smith read to the jury the questions put to Sutcliffe by his colleague Detective Inspector John Boyle. Ognall read Sutcliffe's answers aloud.

The jury heard how, after hiding his weapons before his arrest, Sutcliffe did the same thing again, *inside the police station at Sheffield*. He hid a knife he was concealing behind the cistern when he got permission to go to the toilet. Sergeant Ring found the knife in the toilet four days later.

A few weeks before his appearance at the Old Bailey, one of the prison staff said in evidence, Sutcliffe was in his cell and appeared cheerful and bright. Smiling broadly and leaning back in his chair, he seemed amused that the doctors thought him mad. 'I am as normal as anyone,' he declared. The court learned that in the early 1970s Milne had also treated Sonia Sutcliffe when she was confined for twenty-two days in a Bradford psychiatric hospital. She had then been excitable and disturbed for some time and had a psychotic episode while training to be a teacher in London. Peter went and brought her home. She was diagnosed with schizophrenia. She had believed herself to be the second coming – complete with stigmata. Sutcliffe was her boyfriend at the time and he married her two years later.

Now, with her husband awaiting trial, Sonia Sutcliffe was again examined by Milne. The jury heard that he found her naïve and self-centred, which went some way to explaining why she believed her husband's excuses for being out late at night. She was temperamental and difficult. Sutcliffe told the doctor she was over-excited, highly strung and unstable. She also had an obsession with cleanliness. Peter Sutcliffe had meekly explained how his wife would not allow him into their home unless he removed his shoes. She spent hours cleaning specks of dirt from the carpet. He could not use the refrigerator to make himself a meal. If he was watching television, she would sometimes pull the plug from its socket in the wall. Their intense relationship often swung between feelings of love and anger, but Milne could find no evidence that the couple were sexually deviant.

Media coverage of the revelations in court was intense. Newspapers in particular vied to bring readers lurid accounts of each day's evidence. Some had secretly 'bought up' witnesses, then had to ensure their rivals did not scoop them. After Sutcliffe's long-standing friend Trevor Birdsall gave evidence, he waited close to the front door in the company of three journalists from the *People* newspaper, which had purchased his story. They had ordered a cab to pick them up and it was late. When it arrived they dashed through the revolving front door of the Old Bailey and tried to make their way through the ranks of photographers and television camera crews outside. Birdsall had covered his head with a raincoat. To frustrate their getaway, reporters from other papers blocked their path. There was a scuffle and jostling amid catcalls and jeers from onlookers. Birdsall and his minders retreated back inside the court building, regrouped and tried again, managing finally to get into the cab.

On Monday, 11 May, the defence was about to begin its case. Few expected Sutcliffe to go into the witness box. Only those initiated into the ways of the law realized that the judge had already given Sutcliffe's lawyers the clearest signal that their client would have to give evidence. Mr Justice Boreham had discreetly drawn the attention of Sutcliffe's barrister to a very recent case: *Regina v. Dunn*, suggesting he swiftly read it up over the weekend. The case was so recent it had not been reported, but it, too, involved psychiatrists giving evidence. The judge had ruled the accused would himself have to tell the jury the same things he told the psychiatrists. Had Sutcliffe not been called, it was entirely probable Mr Justice Boreham would have ruled the doctors' evidence as inadmissible.

As it was, those present in court that day will never forget the atmosphere as Mr James Chadwin, QC for the defence, stood up and said: 'I call Peter William Sutcliffe.' An audible murmur went round the public and press galleries. Heads turned as people whispered almost incredulously: 'He's called Sutcliffe. Sutcliffe's going to give evidence.'

Escorted by prison officers, Sutcliffe descended the stairs of the dock into the floor area of the court itself, and slowly walked towards the witness box. Now it could clearly be seen that he was wearing tan-coloured boots – the kind with raised heels and a thick sole. The court was so hushed as he moved that it was possible to hear clearly the sound of his shoes as he clomped across the floor to where he would spend the next two days giving evidence. Sutcliffe spent many hours detailing how he had come to hear God send him on his Divine mission to kill prostitutes; how he had had an accident on his motorbike in 1965 when he fell off and banged his head; and how a prostitute had cheated him out of money and later ridiculed him. As he spoke, Sir Michael Havers's colleague, Harry Ognall, QC, wrote spasmodically on a large legal notepad.

Sutcliffe went on to describe his mental state when he killed for the first time. He had gone out intending to kill a prostitute.

CHADWIN: Did you enjoy striking the blows you struck?

SUTCLIFFE: No.

CHADWIN: How did you feel about the physical act of striking those blows?

SUTCLIFFE: I found it very difficult, and I couldn't restrain myself. I could not do anything to stop myself.

CHADWIN: How could you not stop yourself?

SUTCLIFFE: Because it was God who was controlling me.

For the rest of that day and for an hour the following day Sutcliffe put on a surprisingly plausible show in the witness box. Softly spoken and remarkably calm, he appeared both unexpectedly intelligent and articulate in his own defence. He described the twists and turns of the police investigation when he believed he was bound to be caught but then slipped through the net, and said they were proof that God was guiding him.

Closing his examination, Mr Chadwin asked if he had it in mind to pretend to be mad.

SUTCLIFFE: No.

CHADWIN: Do you think you are mad?

SUTCLIFFE: No.
CHADWIN: Do you think there is anything wrong with you mentally?
SUTCLIFFE: Nothing serious at all, no.

Those present at Sir Michael Havers's cross-examination of the Yorkshire Ripper will remember it as long as they live. It was a mesmerizing performance of the lawyer's art of first filleting a defendant, then boxing him up like a kipper. A tall man, Havers stood erect across the courtroom looking directly at the accused. Ognall occasionally scribbled notes for the Attorney General. From the direction of those looking from the press benches, Sir Michael appeared in profile on the right side of the court; Sutcliffe, up in the witness box, on the left. From time to time Havers arched his frame, resting his hands on his hips, pushing his elbows backwards, as if to bring some comfort during the long periods he was on his feet listening to Sutcliffe's responses. Sir Michael was a resourceful advocate and his skill at slowly deconstructing his quarry's evidence-in-chief shone through blindingly. He quickly established Sutcliffe was habitually untruthful when questioned about what he was doing in Sheffield the night he was arrested: 'For a considerable time you lied, and lied and lied again?'

SUTCLIFFE: Yes.
HAVERS: You had a ridiculous explanation about picking up people on the motorway?
SUTCLIFFE: Ridiculous, yes.
HAVERS: All to protect yourself?
SUTCLIFFE: The mission.
HAVERS: All to protect Peter Sutcliffe?
SUTCLIFFE: Yes.

It was a slow and painstaking business dismantling Sutcliffe's defence. There was a break for lunch and only one topic of conversation among those who left the court building in search of brief refreshment. Later in the afternoon Sir Michael went carefully through his various attacks, attempting to detail the planned, premeditated way Sutcliffe stalked his victims before murdering them. He took the accused back to the time on Savile Park, Halifax, when he killed Josephine Whitaker. Sutcliffe told police they had chatted and admitted saying to her: 'You can't trust anyone these days.'

HAVERS: Can you think of a more horrible and cynical thing to say to someone you were just about to murder?

SUTCLIFFE: No.

HAVERS: Why did you say it?

SUTCLIFFE: Because I couldn't trust myself.

HAVERS: You were trying to convince her she was safe with you?

SUTCLIFFE: Yes, in a sense.

HAVERS: Did God tell you to do that?

SUTCLIFFE: No.

HAVERS: It was a bit of private enterprise on your part, was it?

Moments later came the following exchange:

HAVERS: Did God tell you to tell that poor girl to look at the church clock?

SUTCLIFFE: No.

HAVERS: It was a macabre piece of play-acting while you jockeyed into position. Did God help you with that?

SUTCLIFFE: Yes.

HAVERS: Did God tell you to look at the clock?

SUTCLIFFE: Yes.

HAVERS: Did God instruct you as far as Yvonne Pearson and the horsehair was concerned? Did he tell you to hide behind the garden wall when you were escaping after attacking Teresa Sykes?

SUTCLIFFE: Yes.

JUDGE: Did you need God to tell you that unless you did hide you might be caught?

SUTCLIFFE: Maybe, maybe not. I am not sure.

HAVERS: When Yvonne Pearson was lying there gurgling and moaning and there was someone in a car near by, with your high average intelligence you must have known you were in danger of being caught? You don't need God to tell you to ram [the horsehair stuffing from the sofa] down her throat?

SUTCLIFFE: No.

HAVERS: Did God tell you?

SUTCLIFFE: No.

Sutcliffe denied there was anything sexual in his actions. How had he inserted a knife several times into the same wound? asked Sir Michael. 'Do you realize how difficult it must have been to do that?' Sutcliffe denied doing so. As Havers reached for the pathologists' report, Sutcliffe interrupted to say he might have moved the knife within a wound. He vehemently denied stabbing his victims in areas of sexual attraction in order to get sexual gratification.

To audible gasps from the public gallery, Sir Michael picked up a rusty yellow-handled Phillips screwdriver, its shaft about ten inches long. He held it in his hand palm upwards, his elbow pressed against his stomach, the screwdriver pointed directly at Sutcliffe, standing fifteen feet away in the witness box. The Yorkshire Ripper, said Sir Michael, had stabbed Josephine Whitaker three times through the vagina with this dreadful weapon, and as he spoke he jerked the screwdriver forwards and backwards a few inches. This effective but sickening gesture was etched in the memory of anyone who saw it.

Many winced, waiting for what was to come next.

HAVERS: How did you use this rusted old screwdriver, that has been sharpened to a hideous point, to stab Josephine Whitaker through the same wound three times? To put the stab wounds in the vagina with no injury to the lips of the vagina is unusual. How did you do it?
SUTCLIFFE: By moving it about.
HAVERS: Your case throughout has been: no sexual gratification, not doing it for lust or anything like that?

He moved on to the murder of eighteen-year-old Helen Rytka in Huddersfield.

HAVERS: You talk about your mission and then surprise, surprise, here's pretty little Helen Rytka and you have sex with her. Why?
SUTCLIFFE: I didn't have sex. I entered her but there was no action. It was to persuade her that everything was all right. I had no choice, it was important to keep her quiet.
HAVERS: Of course you had a choice. God didn't tell you to put your penis in that girl's vagina ... did it occur to you that God is meant to be merciful and you are killing people in a painful way?
SUTCLIFFE: I am quite sure that the way I killed them meant they never knew anything.
HAVERS: You mean to say that your victims never felt anything

as they were lying there, moaning, groaning, gurgling, a screwdriver in the eye, stabbed and one disembowelling?

During the exchange about Helen Rytka, Sutcliffe became agitated in the witness box, shaking his head and mouthing the word, 'No,' several times.

The defence next called Dr Hugo Milne, whose thirty-five-page report had earlier been read to the jury by Harry Ognall. Milne had written that, because of the nature of the killings, he wanted to discover whether there had been any sexual connections. 'I found that there was no suggestion that the accused is in any way sexually deviant or that his wife is sexually deviant.' Sexual relations between the couple were extremely satisfactory, but while Sutcliffe admitted freely to sexual involvement before his marriage, his wife denied having had sexual experience prior to their wedding. 'He completely denied that he was using the assaults to help in the sexual situation. There is no suggestion that he is a sadistic, sexual deviant.' Milne was convinced that the killings were not sexual in any way and that the stabbings which were a feature of the assaults 'had no sexual component . . . I have had the opportunity to spend many hours with the accused and there is little doubt that he is friendly and open in his manner and at no time did he withhold information.' Milne said he could find absolutely no reason for why Sutcliffe had stabbed his victims through the same hole on repeated occasions. There was no suggestion that Sutcliffe had a sexual symbolism. In the witness box Milne said he had been 'very much on his guard' to the possibility that Sutcliffe was trying to persuade him he was mentally ill. 'There was no evidence whatever to say he was simulating. I had been looking for this all the time and I cannot accept that, in the sequence his symptoms were made known to me, that he could have been simulating.'

We now know that Sutcliffe completely fooled all the psychiatrists, but also that the police fooled themselves and the prosecution by not thoroughly searching him earlier when he arrived at Dewsbury under arrest. For then they would have discovered what he was wearing and its sexual connotations would have become all too clear. Moreover, an inquiry into the police investigation, conducted after the case, demonstrated conclusively that Sutcliffe had persistently told lies about the numbers of women he attacked. At least a dozen more cases of assaults on young women were uncovered, undertaken since 1972 by a dark-haired man with a beard. The mode of attack from behind, and descriptions of the man who assaulted them by the women themselves, fitted Sutcliffe perfectly.

However, all this was as yet unknown as Dr Milne and two other psychiatrists stood in the witness box for three days to undergo a relentless cross-examination from Harry Ognall. It would have been impossible for Dr Milne to have argued in court as vehemently as he did that there was an absence of sexual motive if he had known what Sutcliffe was wearing when arrested. The longer Dr Milne's grilling went on, the more crucial this aspect of the case became. It became blindingly obvious that what was happening in Court No. 1 as the doctors gave evidence was a trial within a trial. As the psychiatrists tried to withstand barrage after barrage of awkward questions in cross-examination, it was abundantly clear it was psychiatry itself that was being judged by the jury. Did they believe what the shrinks were saying? Or had Sutcliffe simply lied to them and they been taken in by him? The defence had to argue that Sutcliffe was mad to the extent that he was not responsible for himself. Sutcliffe had, according to Milne, been able to detach himself from the enormity of what he had done. Someone with schizophrenia could be in and out of touch with reality; it was a psychosis, and one sign of schizophrenia was psychotic detachment.

At one point the judge asked Dr Milne to explain what a psychosis was. He replied: 'In layman's terms it is madness, but what I wish to say is that because people might be clinically mad, they are not necessarily out of contact with reality.' This was precisely what the prosecution was saying: mad Sutcliffe might be, but not so mad as not to know perfectly well what he was doing. Moreover, he was gaining sexual pleasure from it. Under cross-examination Milne balked at the idea that he had been taken in, even though Sutcliffe had told his prison guards that if he could convince people he was mad he would get only ten years in a loony bin.

'I think it is a very straightforward decision to make,' Milne replied to a question from Ognall. 'Is this man pretending to be mad and has duped me and my colleagues, or am I, from my clinical examination, right in saying that he is a paranoid schizophrenic? As far as I can see, either he is a competent actor or I am an inefficient psychiatrist ... paranoid schizophrenics are extraordinarily cunning, extremely involved in premeditation and determined not to be found.'

OGNALL: A very great proportion of normal criminals are also cunning, clever, and anxious not to be found. That isn't the hallmark of a schizophrenic. It is the hallmark of a normal criminal. I suggest that this pattern is a badge of a premeditated killer?

MILNE: I do not accept that.

Then later:

OGNALL: . . . were you satisfied you had all the necessary information at your disposal?

MILNE: Yes.

Milne acknowledged that Sutcliffe had not informed him of his arrest in 1969 when he was found in Bradford's red-light district with a hammer but subsequently charged with going equipped for theft.

OGNALL: How can you possibly say that he has not withheld information from you and has satisfied you that he has told the whole truth?

MILNE: I agreed that he has lied to the police. He could also have lied to me.

The QC now moved in swiftly and brought up the question of a sexual motive. Milne reiterated that there was no sexual component to the crimes: 'I am not of the opinion that he is primarily a sexual killer.'

OGNALL: If we can discern here a sexual element, that tends markedly to go against the divine mission theory, do you agree?

MILNE: Yes.

Holding up the screwdriver Sutcliffe used to kill Josephine Whitaker, the QC continued:

OGNALL: How on earth are we to reconcile the pathologist's evidence of three stab wounds deep into the vagina with what you said? There is no doubt that this wicked agent was introduced with almost no injury to the external parts of the vagina. I suggest that indicates the most fiendish cruelty, deliberately done for sexual satisfaction. Do you agree?

MILNE: It may be a most vicious and foul thing to do, but not necessarily for sexual satisfaction. Mutilation of the genitalia for sadistic satisfaction would have to be repetitive, and there is no evidence that this man has attacked any of the other victims in this way. There is no evidence that he has in any way despoiled them or carried out any unnatural acts with them during the killings.

OGNALL: What else could the attack with the screwdriver be but sexual?

MILNE: It may have been sexual.

OGNALL: What else could it have been? I will have an answer.

MILNE: I do not think it could have been anything else other than sexual.

OGNALL: Did Peter Sutcliffe tell you there was no sexual elements in the attacks?

MILNE: Yes.

OGNALL: Well, that doesn't seem to be right, does it?

MILNE: No.

OGNALL: He deceived you. Why did he do that?

MILNE: Perhaps he might have been very reluctant to talk about this because of what people might think of him.

OGNALL: He had admitted thirteen killings and seven attempted killings. But he thought he might be worse off because he stabbed one of them in the vagina. Is that a considered reply?

MILNE: It is a considered reply. He has said he never ever wanted to be seen as a sexual killer.

OGNALL: I expect he never wanted to be seen as a sexual killer because, if he puts himself forward as a sexual killer, the Divine mission goes out of the window. That's why, isn't it?

Ognall refused to let up, repeatedly stressing there were sufficient examples in Sutcliffe's attacks to demonstrate he was primarily motivated by sexual urges. Milne, though severely shaken by his experience in the witness box, remained steadfast. He continued to maintain that the Yorkshire Ripper was suffering from paranoid schizophrenia to the extent that he suffered diminished responsibility. Two more psychiatrists gave evidence, their professional judgements being heavily and effectively attacked in cross-examination by the prosecution.

The jury retired at 10.21 a.m. on Friday, 22 May 1981, to consider its verdict. It was the day the Yorkshire Ripper's last victim, Jacqueline Hill, would have celebrated her twenty-first birthday.

After almost six hours the jury said it could not be unanimous. Forty-seven minutes later it returned and by a majority of ten to two found Peter Sutcliffe guilty of thirteen cases of murder. Sentencing him, Mr Justice Boreham said he had taken into account the dangers he would represent in the future and the depth of terror he had brought to Yorkshire: 'It is a population which to my knowledge does not lack fortitude. But I am left in no doubt that women from a wide area were in deepest fear and I have no doubts too that that fear spilled over to their menfolk on their account.'

He gave Sutcliffe twenty life sentences and recommended to the Home Secretary that it would be a minimum period of thirty years before he could be released on licence. 'That is a long period, an unusually long period in my judgement, but I believe you are an unusually dangerous man. I express my hope that when I have said life imprisonment, it will mean precisely that.'

Once Sutcliffe had been sent down to the cells the judge commended the West Yorkshire detectives who had obtained

Sutcliffe's confession: Boyle, O'Boyle and Smith. 'These three officers behaved quite immaculately. They never put a foot wrong and that can be said of few of us.'

He also had praise for the South Yorkshire pair, Sergeant Robert Ring and PC Robert Hydes, who arrested the Yorkshire Ripper: 'I do not mean to introduce levity but I cannot help but recall the remarks of the officer [Ring] that he had not fallen off a Christmas tree. We are very grateful that he had not.'

Sutcliffe was sent to Parkhurst Prison, but was destined eventually to be kept in Broadmoor secure mental hospital.

As soon as Sutcliffe was sentenced the recriminations began. The public mood was inflamed by Ronald Gregory's reluctance to concede his men had made mistakes. The media and MPs zeroed in to accuse the police of incompetence, not least because they had interviewed Sutcliffe so many times and let him slip through their fingers with calamitous results for the women attacked. The scandal had been ignited even before the full murder trial began. On 3 May 1981 the *Sunday Times* INSIGHT team told how Detective Constable Andrew Laptew had named Sutcliffe as a possible prime suspect eighteen months before the Yorkshire Ripper was arrested. The newspaper was on solid ground legally because Sutcliffe had already admitted in court to being the Yorkshire Ripper. An INSIGHT journalist (the author) had called at Laptew's home in Bradford unannounced late one night, having been tipped off that West Yorkshire police were sitting on a powder keg; that a young detective had already submitted a damning report about Sutcliffe in the summer of 1979 but it was ignored.

It took the reporter several days to track Laptew down to the new home he shared with his wife Sheila. The couple had an ex-directory phone number and were completely surprised by this late-night visit. Having invited him into their sitting room, Laptew politely refused to confirm or deny the story. 'I'm sorry,' he said repeatedly, 'I am not in a position to say anything. There is nothing I can say.' Laptew was very nervous, clearly aware that the newspaperman knew the whole story. The policeman talked about anything and everything rather than discuss his visit to Sutcliffe's home and the report he compiled for his senior officers. Several times he tried to divert the unwelcome visitor. He mentioned he was a fan of the American crime writer Joseph Wambaugh – anything to avoid discussing the subject of Peter Sutcliffe. At 1 a.m., three hours after he first knocked on their door, the *Sunday Times* man got ready to leave.

'Andrew,' he said, 'INSIGHT will run this story on Sunday, because I know it is true. I must warn you that after it appears the world and his wife will be knocking at your door. The tabloids will be here in force, so be prepared. I appreciate you cannot say anything at all, but I want to give you one last chance to knock the story on the head. If it is not true, I don't want to publish it. When I am leaving, all you have to do is ask me to stay and have one last cup of coffee. I'll know then that something is wrong with my information. Is that clear?'

Laptew said nothing.

Saying his farewells to the couple as he was about to cross the threshold, the man from the INSIGHT team turned back to face them: 'Andrew, do you want me to stay for another cup of coffee?'

'No,' said the policeman, with a clear conscience. 'I don't want you to stay for another coffee.'

Next morning Laptew contacted a senior detective at Laister-syke police station and told him the *Sunday Times* had been at his house making inquiries. He had told them nothing. A few days later the explosive revelation appeared on the *Sunday Times* front page, headlined: 'SUTCLIFFE KILLED THREE MORE WOMEN AFTER BEING NAMED AS A PRIME SUSPECT.' Before even local church pews were being warmed by Sunday worshippers, a pack of newsmen had descended on Laptew's doorstep, wanting more details and pictures. His police bosses had several days' notice that the scandal was about to break in the media, but had made no arrangements to protect their officer. Any clear-thinking organization would have told him to make himself scarce for a few days. At the very least a press officer would have anticipated the media and offered to shield him from the feeding frenzy at his home.

Instead the officer was left to deal alone with the barrage from the reporters, much of it hostile to West Yorkshire police. It was the oldest trick in the book. The Fleet Street men said the most outlandish things in a bid to provoke a response. It worked. Naïvely trying to defend his force, Laptew opened up, saying it was not to blame. 'I was not 99 per cent certain otherwise I would have pulled him in. But he was the best I had seen so far and I had seen hundreds . . . I feel sick inside,' he said. 'The simple truth is that he had all the luck and we had none.'

Radio and television news bulletins ran the story and the press went to town with front-page banner headlines: '**I told my chiefs "He's The Ripper" 18 months before they seized him**' (*Sun*); '**How Ripper slipped the net**' (*Daily Express*): '**Shelved . . . My Dossier on The Ripper**' (*Daily Mirror*).

Within a few days, Andrew Laptew was called in by a chief superintendent and issued with a Regulation 7 notice under the Police Act. It informed him he was the subject of a disciplinary investigation, accused of giving unauthorized interviews to the press. He was suspected of being the original source of the *Sunday Times* story. In fact nothing could have been further from the truth. He never once discussed the case with the author, not until twenty years later when he was approached in connection with an ITV documentary film then being made. When he knocked on Laptew's front door in the autumn of 1998, the film's producer (the author) fully expected a mouthful of abuse for all the trouble the original story had caused the officer. By then Andrew and Sheila Laptew had moved to a much bigger detached house in the northern Bradford suburb of Idle. Their teenage daughter came to the door. The caller asked if her father was home and mentioned his name.

A few seconds later he heard Sheila Laptew's voice: 'Michael . . . Michael Bilton . . . is that you, Michael?' A jolly woman whose face he could not have recognized invited him in, then took him through to where her husband sat in the lounge. He was amazed to find the fifty-year-old police officer, weighing 260 pounds, giving him a firm handshake and welcoming him like some long-lost friend. It was a weird sensation for the writer/film maker. He had spent almost eighteen years wondering whether his story had harmed the young officer's career, but stayed out of touch deliberately to avoid even a hint that they had colluded on the original article. Laptew put him at his ease. He was particularly grateful for the warning the reporter had given him, all those years previously, about the tabloid interest in the story. He regretted not having appreciated how serious the situation was. 'I knew I hadn't said anything to you, so I didn't think there would be a problem,' he said. The investigation, carried out by a senior officer, exonerated him. But Laptew's career went nowhere. He always felt under a cloud of suspicion and had spent the intervening years resenting his treatment at the hands of Superintendent Dick

Holland. When he left the force in 2001, Laptew was still a sergeant and Holland was a welcome guest at his leaving party.

Without question, the revelation in early May 1981 that Laptew had pointed the finger of suspicion at Sutcliffe long before he was caught helped fuel criticism of the police. There was a demand for a public inquiry. Police and MPs then attacked the press for buying up and stories of Ripper case witnesses *before* they gave evidence in court. The Press Council lashed some of the Fleet Street papers in a report which took more than a year to produce. It also singled newspapers out for criticism for creating the impression that Sutcliffe, 'even though he had not then been charged, was beyond doubt the killer of thirteen women and girls and that a trial was no more than a formality'.

However, the most crucial critique of the Ripper investigation was conducted in secret by the police service itself at the behest of William Whitelaw, the Home Secretary, after the trial finished. Lawrence Byford, one of the inspectors of constabulary, reassembled his super-squad of senior officers and Professor Stuart Kind to undertake the most rigorous analysis ever of the way the police did their job. Byford's main priority was to learn the lessons for the police service as a whole. Few modern British institutions have ever been subjected to such painstaking scrutiny. Assisted by a backroom staff of middle-ranking officers, they examined the five-year investigation in minute detail, looking for the reasons the Yorkshire Ripper had not been captured earlier. Byford believed they owed the country a duty to ensure changes were made in serious crime investigations. 'We weren't looking for scapegoats, but we needed to know what went wrong and why,' he said.

The effort took five months and the result was a devastating 156-page indictment of the West Yorkshire police. Byford's team based itself at a police training college at Pannal Ash near Harrogate in North Yorkshire, staying at the Crown Hotel in nearby Boroughbridge. Fifteen miles from Leeds, they wanted to maintain complete confidentiality. Senior officers on the Ripper case had to drive out to Pannal Ash to undergo very searching questioning about their actions.

Thus Dick Holland, in the summer of 1981, found himself waiting in the very library where twenty-eight years earlier he had studied for his exams as a young trainee constable. Now he was a detective superintendent and the deputy head of Bradford CID. In the corridor outside he spoke briefly to Les Emment, the deputy chief constable from Thames Valley, who was to question him formally in considerable detail. Holland mentioned they had worked together on the murder of a teen-age girl in Wakefield in 1965 when Emment came up from Scotland Yard with a senior murder squad detective. Emment said he remembered; Holland wasn't so sure. The interview took more than thirteen hours, during which he was allowed a meal from a local fish and chip shop. He was called back again next day.

'I had a feeling I was on trial,' said Holland many years later. 'When I got back to where I was working I said I had a worse grilling than the Yorkshire Ripper.' He remembers as a draining experience trying to explain the way he and Oldfield ran the inquiry. He was shown the four separate index cards relating to Sutcliffe in the incident room files and asked how it could have happened; why were they not cross-referenced? Clearly, he told them, they should have been.

'I can't understand why we got three mistakes with him – all those errors with one person. Sutcliffe is a common name in north Bradford, but they should have been cross-referenced and then they would have all ended up in one folder. There is no doubt that had any of us seen all the papers at the same time, then bells would have rung earlier. There should have been a folder with everything in it, it would have got thicker and thicker.'

He was asked about Laptew's report, but could not specifically recall it. 'I remembered with one of the sections of Sutcliffe's file there was something else attached to it and I was able to show there were pinholes in the top where something had become detached after I saw it. I was looking at the corners, because I said: "I am sure there is something else. I can't remember specifically what it was."'

Nevertheless, Byford was castigating in his report to the Home Secretary:

The incident room formed the nucleus of the Ripper inquiry, acting as a repository of all information and an initiator of all action. The system contained a wealth of information in relation to Sutcliffe. Tragically, a number of errors and omissions by members of staff ensured that much of this information remained within the system, as a result of which the officers who interviewed Sutcliffe on different occasions were unaware of the variety of routes by which he had previously been recorded ... The ultimate conclusion is that far from maintaining its place as the nerve centre of the most important detective effort in history, the Millgarth major incident room became sadly inefficient and had the direct effect of frustrating the work of senior investigating officers and junior detectives alike.

Later Oldfield came to damn Byford's inquiry, telling a colleague, 'These buggers, these bastards – what have they done?

If you look at what they have written about this.' Byford was highly critical of the chief constable for allowing Oldfield to act as the senior investigating officer during the inquiry and continue with his normal job of ACC (crime).

> That this situation led to the breakdown of Mr Oldfield's health is not at all surprising and the fact that he was allowed to work to this extent is clearly a reflection, not only on his own judgement, but on that of his chief constable who should have seen that his senior detective was overloaded and have made arrangements for him to be relieved of his routine responsibilities. Equally important in connection with leadership was the chief constable's failure to take positive action when Mr Oldfield had to stop work as a result of illness. An acting assistant chief constable should have been appointed at that stage and clear directions should have been given about ultimate responsibility for the Ripper inquiry.

In an even more critical passage, Byford, who wrote the final report himself, attacked Oldfield directly:

> I am firmly of the view that in the [cross-border] serious crime situation there needs to be one officer in overall command of the investigation with the authority to direct the course of the investigation in all the police areas affected ... The choice of officer to take supreme command is obviously of vital importance. The temptation to appoint the 'senior man' on age or service grounds should be resisted, unless it is clear that this candidate has all the qualities required in an inquiry 'leader'. The person appointed requires not only the

professional competence which will inspire confidence
in those who work for him, but the charisma which will
ensure loyalty to him and his policies even when there
is individual doubt about their validity. These attributes
were clearly not present during the Ripper inquiry and
it was Assistant Chief Constable Oldfield's failure to lead
effectively which paved the way for the loss of confidence
in and loyalty to his inquiry policies.

Nevertheless, the tone of the Byford Report overall did not
dwell on errors by individuals, but instead analysed precisely
where management mistakes had damned the investigation's
chances of success.

'The objective was to make sure that it didn't happen again
and that [had] to be done with the goodwill of the service,'
said Sir Andrew Sloan, a member of the Byford review team,
who went on to become chief constable of Strathclyde, the
second biggest police force in Britain. 'Most important was to
establish what went wrong so we could make sure that it did
not happen again in the future. We had to look at all aspects
of the investigation, identify the mistakes, because the service
could not afford to go through this agonizing experience again.
Our long-term role was to produce change because we knew
there would never be a better time to persuade the service to
change. They would totally have to rethink the investigation
of series crimes. Our objective was to move the service forward,
not to build on a smokescreen of recrimination. I didn't want
to humiliate and humble these men. This wasn't our role. I
knew the difficulty under which they laboured, and during all
that time, despite the mistakes and stupidities and everything
else, they were being honest. There were monumental balls-ups
made here, but they weren't made deliberately. They were

doing their best in accordance with their experience and previous practice in matters which were totally new to the police service. They didn't find the answers. That doesn't mean you should just condemn and send them to the scaffold.'

No mistake was more obvious than the acceptance of the 'Geordie' letters and tape as genuine. Byford's team considered the tragic error could have been avoided if senior detectives had used greater imagination and flexibility in making critical decisions. The Ripper squad had crucially failed to be flexible when deciding the criteria for judging which women had been attacked by the Yorkshire Ripper. Byford's team drew up a list of *thirteen* more of his victims, certain they had been excluded because they did not fit the Ripper's *modus operandi*. Yet all the additional victims had been attacked about the head from behind. They were all unaccompanied, but not necessarily involved in prostitution. Some were stalked on foot first and then attacked. In other cases, Sutcliffe walked and talked with the victim before striking them down. Many photofits were provided of a man with dark hair and a beard of some kind. Incredibly, several attacks were excluded because the injuries indicated a hammer of a different size had been used from that required by the criteria. 'In two of these cases in particular the victims were able to provide good descriptions of the assailant, including that he had a mandarin or "Jason King" moustache and in one case, a goatee beard,' the report said.

Byford's backroom staff analysed a total of ninety-two different photofit descriptions supplied by victims or witnesses following attacks on women in West Yorkshire from December 1972. They displayed many of them on a wall for the review team to examine. The result was electrifying.

'I remember seeing them all together for the first time,' says Sir Andrew Sloan. 'It was a sunny day and they covered quite a large section of the wall. We went in and had a look. It was immediately apparent that Sutcliffe appeared again and again among them. We could not understand why this hadn't been done before. We were astounded to see how many there were of a dark-haired bearded man. I felt almost a physical blow to the stomach because there was Peter Sutcliffe looking at us from these assembled pictures. Of course we had the benefit of hindsight, but even without that knowledge it was obvious there was a dark-haired bearded man appearing again and again. The obvious thing was that they were mainly hairy. They should have done the same thing we did. We felt this was an opportunity that had been missed. Had it been done systematically, I am sure [when Sutcliffe was interviewed] someone would have said, "I don't like this, I am taking this man in." He would have been arrested and taken in for a full interrogation followed by a proper scenes-of-crime examination of his house.'

Byford himself spelled out the mistake to the Home Secretary:

What is now very clearly established is that had senior detectives of the West Yorkshire Police assembled the photofit impressions from surviving victims of *all* hammer assaults or assaults involving serious head injuries on unaccompanied women, they would have been left with an inescapable conclusion that the man involved was dark haired with a beard and moustache.

They would also have learned from Olive Smelt, Caroline Browne and Marilyn Moore, all of whom had spoken to him, that he had a local accent and was certainly not noticeably a 'Geordie'.

In her statement to police, Marilyn Moore said the Ripper told her he knew 'a right quiet place they could go' for sex. It was a typical Yorkshire expression. As early as November 1977, when Sutcliffe was twice interviewed by Ripper squad detectives, photofits were available from the survivors of four attacks not then attributed to the series. In August and November 1978, when he was next questioned, the photofit provided by survivor Marilyn Moore was also available. The Byford Report went on:

> Detective Constable Laptew remarked on the similarity between Sutcliffe and the Moore photofit. Had that photofit, which was to some extent discredited by the attitude of senior detectives, been supported by those provided by the earlier assault victims, Constable Laptew would have had much greater grounds for suspicion and Sutcliffe could hardly have avoided being arrested.
>
> The information from the survivors of assaults would have been equally effective in:
> (a) Dispelling the theory that Jayne MacDonald was the first non-prostitute victim.
> (b) Disproving the 'Geordie' connection since Miss X, Brown, Smelt and Moore all had conversation with their assailant and could say that he did not have a North Eastern accent.
> (c) Showing the letters and tape to be a hoax which they subsequently proved to be because these assault cases had not been mentioned in major newspaper reports and were thus unknown to the author.

It became obvious to the review team that their recommendations would have to be wide-ranging. The most immediate changes would have to be in training senior officers, cross-border cooperation and urgently bringing in computers.

Byford himself wanted a thoroughly tested computer system that could handle hundreds of thousands of pieces of information and be used in more than one force area. The commissioner of the Metropolitan Police, Sir David McNee, travelled north from Scotland Yard to meet the review team at Byford's request, and lent his support for changes in police training regimes.

Later, on a hot summer's day midway through the review at Pannal Ash, they had another eminent visitor. Stuart Kind, the forensic science professor, found himself looking out of the window at the car park and the gleaming limousines belonging to his senior police colleagues on the review team. At that moment a ten-year-old Ford saloon pulled up. Out stepped the Permanent Under Secretary of State at the Home Office – the man who ran the place – Sir Brian Cubbon. Kind, whose wife would testify that he showed little interest in sartorial matters, could not help noticing the senior mandarin was wearing a suit so crumpled it looked as if it had been slept in. Over the course of the next couple of hours, Sir Brian listened intently as the review team, under Byford's chairmanship, took him through various aspects of their inquiry.

Later they broke for coffee. The Permanent Under Secretary wandered over to where the lone scientist was standing. He took him gently by the arm and said quietly: 'Kind, the police must be made to realize that crime investigation is a high-grade intellectual pursuit.' Then he walked away. Recalling the moment many years later, Kind commented: 'These were the only words he spoke to me. I thought: "It's nice to know that someone thinks the same way as I do, but bugger me, here is a bloke with 75,000 employees not including the police, he is the boss, the man who controls the purse strings, and if he can't do anything about it, how can anybody?" '

19

DNA, DNA, DNA

The House of Commons was in sombre mood as the Home Secretary outlined Lawrence Byford's findings and recommendations to MPs in January 1982. The contents of the report were political dynamite and William Whitelaw robustly declined several appeals to have it made public. Regarded as highly confidential advice to a Minister of the Crown, it was the kind of information government departments traditionally keep well out of the public gaze. The upper reaches of the Home Office had decided to restrict tightly circulation of the report and its damaging conclusions. Those who read it were allowed to do so on almost a wartime 'need to know' basis. Byford's discoveries about the way the Ripper investigation was conducted were so devastating that his report could not even be read by Britain's chief constables, the very men who ran the police service at ground level. The people who really should have ingested its contents, senior detectives in charge of homicide investigations, were not given a sight of it either.

The briefest possible summary of the Byford Report was placed in the House of Commons library as a sop to MPs. This 1,200-word document was a fig leaf. It gave no hint of the terrible débâcle Byford's review team had uncovered. Whitelaw gravely told MPs of 'major errors of judgement' by the police during the tragic case, but he didn't elaborate. The largest criminal investigation ever mounted in Britain had imposed great strain on all concerned, he said. Whitelaw continued: 'It would have been surprising if in this unprecedented situation there were no mistakes,' trying to dampen hostility from MPs and the press.

Having produced arguably the most crucial report in the twentieth century on the detection of major crime, its author was anxious for the lessons to be learned as quickly as possible. Chief constables and the police service generally, Byford initially felt, were unlikely to be influenced by the limited information made public by Whitelaw to Parliament. They would only be encouraged to take decisive action by studying the fine detail. Byford wrote to a colleague: 'I have made the point very strongly to [the] Home Office that the cost of conducting the inquiry and preparing the report cannot be justified by what has happened so far and that publication of the report, albeit in an expurgated version, will be necessary if our operation is to be in any way cost effective.'

A few weeks later, however, Byford appeared to have changed his mind. Resistance from senior civil servants seems the most likely explanation. His report, he told the same colleague, had to be kept under wraps. The Home Office would implement his recommendations, and Byford now appeared to accept that his report would be seen by only a handful of people. He wrote:

> I need hardly point out that any leakage of information from the report would, even at this stage, prove highly embarrassing to the Home Secretary. I am as conscious as anyone of the need for the Service to learn the valuable lessons contained in the report and am anxious that the report should be circulated so far as is consistent with

the need for these lessons to be got across to serving officers. At the same time, I am aware of the inherent dangers which the release of material from the report would involve for the morale of the West Yorkshire force and the Police Service, as well as for the Home Secretary, whose handling of the issue has been so helpful to the Service generally.

In fact, morale among West Yorkshire police could not have got any worse, it was already at rock bottom. The knives came out the moment Sutcliffe was sentenced, and the axe fell on George Oldfield and Dick Holland when the press and several Yorkshire MPs demanded blood. Dick Holland was moved back into uniform as part of his 'career development'. He had been a police officer for twenty-eight years, had spent more than twenty years as a detective and now had only twenty months to go before he drew his pension. He was posted at short notice to a subdivision at the furthest end of the county, many miles from his home in Huddersfield. He appealed through the Superintendents' Association and ended up closer to home, in charge of a small police station at Sowerby Bridge, on the edge of the Yorkshire Dales. During the general election of 1983, William Whitelaw briefly stopped off at the small town on the campaign trial and Holland's officers provided extra security for him. Whitelaw made a point of seeking out Holland as the local police chief to thank him personally for this. He had no idea of his role in the Ripper case.

Oldfield was sacked as head of West Yorkshire's CID and moved sideways to become head of operational support – in charge of traffic, frogmen, police dogs, horses and criminal records. His health was given as the official reason for the change. Many colleagues saw it as a cruel public humiliation of a long-serving officer. Realists believed Ronald Gregory had little choice but to act swiftly to offset discontent among local MPs and members of his police authority. Oldfield never spoke openly about what happened, but a close friend said he was hurt and bitterly disappointed, believing he had been sacrificed for political reasons. George Oldfield retired in June 1983, aged fifty-nine, having completed thirty-six years' police service. Within two years he was dead, having never spoken publicly about the case or its aftermath.

All the leading lights in the investigation had quietly left the West Yorkshire force by mid-1983. Ronald Gregory retired as chief constable, quickly followed by Hobson, Gilrain and Holland. Hobson opted to become security officer for a business in Bradford. Holland kept watch on security at a hospital in Huddersfield. Gilrain realized it was time to go when he was moved back into uniform as a divisional commander. Gregory caused immediate controversy by selling his account of the Ripper investigation to a national newspaper for £40,000, settling a few scores along the way with bitter criticism of Lawrence Byford's review.

Byford, newly knighted and promoted as Her Majesty's Chief Inspector of Constabulary, did not respond. He was too busy implementing radical changes to the investigation of serious crime. Highest priority was the rapid standardization of major incident rooms so information could easily be exchanged between forces. Staff manning incident rooms received special training and their work was regularly audited. Senior investigating officers learned corporate management skills. When multi-force investigations happened, an assistant chief constable was placed in overall charge. They, too, received special training at Bramshill Police College. Specialist advisers, including forensic scientists, were drafted into major investigations.

The new rules were tested for the first time in the hunt for a triple killer called Barry Prudom in 1982. He shot dead one police officer while being questioned, then killed a man in Nottinghamshire while on the run. He then ruthlessly tried to murder another police constable before succeeding in shooting dead a police sergeant at Malton, North Yorkshire. With three forces involved, Andrew Sloan, newly promoted to deputy chief constable of Lincolnshire, was given command of the murder hunt. A fully computerized incident room was still a long way off, so an existing North Yorkshire police ICL computer was linked to incident rooms at Newark and Lincoln and a simple index system created with input from all three force areas. Sloan brought in a senior forensic scientist and other specialists, running the inquiry from Pannal Ash near Harrogate, where the Byford Report team had based themselves the previous year. Three weeks after the first murder, armed police laid siege to Malton to prevent the killer escaping. Prudom was hiding in the town, holding a family hostage. He was later cornered, but before he could be captured took his own life.

Two years later, Andrew Sloan was chief constable of Bedfordshire police when they were hunting an armed rapist known as 'The Fox'. Malcolm Fairley had become Britain's most wanted man. He struck in six different police force areas between April and September 1984, breaking into homes and committing acts of indecency against the occupants. Several attacks occurred in the Bedfordshire town of Leighton Buzzard. In one he raped a housewife after holding her at gunpoint and forcing her to tie up her husband. In another he fired his shotgun at point-blank range, causing serious injuries to a victim. Striking across the border in Thames Valley, he broke into a bungalow and committed acts of indecency and rape on an eighteen-year-old-girl, her twenty-one-year-old boyfriend and seventeen-year-old brother. Next he went north, committing more offences in South Yorkshire and County Durham until he was finally caught.

Despite reservations at the Home Office, Sloan's men used a MICA computer system with terminals in all the force areas where the Fox struck, producing a single database. Just as in the hunt for the Yorkshire Ripper, fear generated a huge response from the public. Massive amounts of information were gathered and 18,000 messages went into the incident rooms. Information was collected on more than 3,000 possible suspects. Large volumes of information held on the computer were systematically searched, something virtually impossible to do with the old index card system. After Fairley's name was thrown up as a potential suspect two officers interviewed him. An obscure fact held on the computer database finally helped to crack the case. A detective read how a woman who was raped had seen a distinctive watch on the Fox's right wrist. Fairley was observed picking his watch up with his left hand and strapping it to his right wrist. Confronted with this, he confessed. He received six life sentences.

In 1986 the computerized incident room finally arrived. Called HOLMES (Home Office Large Major Enquiry System) it did virtually everything Lawrence Byford had demanded five years earlier. Never again would a manual system overwhelm an investigation. HOLMES could store and process all the information gathered during an inquiry. Statements, messages and actions could be fed in and later printed out as documents when required by the Crown Prosecution Service.

HOLMES became the centrepiece of the biggest mass-murder investigation ever mounted in Britain. By an extraordinary coincidence Andrew Sloan was again intimately involved. By Christmas 1988 he had become chief constable of Strathclyde, the second biggest force in Britain, with its headquarters in Glasgow. The tiny neighbouring force of Dumfries and Galloway was landed with a massive murder inquiry after Pan Am Flight 103 was blown up by a terrorist bomb over Lockerbie, killing 270 people. Sloan, who was brought up a farmer's son a few miles from the crash scene, offered the local force assistance under a mutual aid programme. He sent highly experienced senior investigators and Strathclyde's HOLMES computer team to assist. From their base in the Lockerbie Academy, they were connected to the HOLMES computer in Glasgow, which was dedicated solely to the Lockerbie investigation. Sloan arranged for his own force to rent another system. The Lockerbie investigation involved forces from the United States, Britain and Germany. HOLMES was linked to New Scotland Yard in London; the FBI in Washington, DC; the local incident room in Scotland; and the West German police in Frankfurt.

HOLMES saved hugely on manpower costs when serious unsolved crimes became complex. Information stored on the computer could be searched with a high degree of subtlety; managers were better able to control resources during a major investigation. Data could be cross-indexed and the computer asked to isolate specific information or draw comparisons. Had the Ripper squad had a system only half as capable as HOLMES, it would certainly have cracked the investigation in 1977. By feeding 53,000 vehicle owners' names into the computer, resulting from the tyre tracks left at various murder scenes, they could easily have cross-checked the names of the 6,000 Shipley area employees who could have received the new five-pound note found in Jean Jordan's handbag in Manchester. Sutcliffe's name would have been thrown up and, with luck, he would have still been in possession of the car he used when he went to Manchester. The incriminating tyres would then have been found.

The Ripper squad would only have needed to ask the computer to show only those names on list 1 *and* list 2. Peter Sutcliffe would have been arrested in 1977 and subjected to rigorous questioning at a police station. His home would have been searched and his clothing forensically tested, along with the tools in his garage and car. The hacksaw, which Dick Holland eventually found in his garage in January 1981, would have been the first item to be minutely examined for a blood match with Jean Jordan.

A second-generation computer, HOLMES 2, arrived in the mid-1990s. It uses commercial off-the-shelf components and the familiar Windows software technology. As a result of nearly twenty years of constant effort and refinement, Britain's homicide detectives now have a twenty-first-century computer system which their counterparts on the Yorkshire Ripper squad could only have dreamed of.

Yet the greatest leap forward in detecting murders has come not from computers but through the discovery of the DNA double-helix molecule in the 1950s. Deoxyribonucleic acid is the unique configuration of protein molecules in cells that determines the inherited genetic characteristics of every human being. In September 1984, thirty years after DNA was discovered, a geneticist at Leicester University, Alec Jeffreys, was looking at the ways DNA differed between people. He was trying to map genes and develop diagnoses for inherited diseases. As he was extracting DNA from human muscle, he realized that particular elements within a DNA molecule acted as a genetic marker, each unique to one individual human being. The possible benefits for forensic science were quickly apparent. Using electric fields and radioactive labelling, his team was able to produce a DNA fingerprint, a pattern of bands or stripes on X-ray film, and could determine whether two biological samples came from the same individual. Close examination of the patterns of bands on the X-ray meant family relationships could also be easily shown. Jeffreys quickly realized that half the bands from a child's DNA fingerprint came from its mother and half from its father. Other than identical twins, no two people have the same DNA fingerprint.

Following this discovery, forensic scientists were able to gather DNA samples at a crime scene from a variety of sources, including blood, bone, sweat, hair, saliva, semen and skin. The first murder conviction gained as a result of DNA evidence happened in January 1987. Two fifteen-year-old girls were murdered in Leicestershire, three years apart, near the village of Enderby. The finding of the second girl's body jacked up the murder investigation as it raised the possibility of a serial killer being at large. DNA evidence was obtained from the crime scenes and a mass screening of potential suspects organized. DNA swabs were taken from all men in the area aged between sixteen and thirty-four. Unknown to the police, the killer had persuaded a friend to give a sample on his behalf in an effort to throw detectives off the scent.

Later the man who gave the false DNA swab confessed to friends in a pub. The murder squad was alerted and the finger of suspicion finally pointed to a local bakery worker called Colin Pitchfork. A new DNA test confirmed beyond doubt that he was responsible and he confessed to strangling both girls. It was an amazing leap forward that heralded a series of unsolved murders being detected, in some cases twenty or thirty years after the trails had gone cold.

DNA testing resulted in many murderers being convicted

worldwide. It also helped to prove the innocence of some suspects. DNA fingerprinting confirmed the identity of the corpse of a top Nazi war criminal, Dr Joseph Mengele, in Argentina; provided a positive identification for the remains of the last Russian Tsar's family; and was used by grandmothers in Buenos Aires to reunite them with their lost grandchildren, whose parents had died during Argentina's 'dirty war' in the 1970s.

In the UK, a national DNA database was set up at the Forensic Science HQ in Birmingham, one of a multiplicity of computerized databanks now being used in the fight against serious crime. By 2002 the DNA database held nearly a million suspect profiles, and an additional 180,000 profiles based on material found at various crime scenes. The Suspect database can also be linked to PHOENIX (the Police National Computerized Index of Criminal Records). Under a 1994 law, suspects charged with or cautioned for an offence carrying a prison term have to provide two DNA swabs or a minimum of ten hairs with roots. These are then matched with profiles in the databases. During the first six years, more than 97,000 'hits' were matched, involving hundreds of cases of murder, manslaughter and rape, as well as thousands of volume crimes like burglary and car crime. The police have power to take the samples by force if necessary.

At crime scenes, major advances in testing now enable DNA to be extracted from tissue samples. Blood and saliva from old exhibits can be analysed. Hairs picked up by sticky tape and preserved in forensic laboratories can also be matched. Until this breakthrough in testing, there was little that could be done with these exhibits. Now the dead tissue from a single hair shaft can be used to extract DNA, using samples so small as to be invisible to the naked eye, some about a thousandth the size of a grain of salt. Only a few cells are needed to get a match. Strands of hair themselves contain no genetic material, but skin cells clinging to the base of a hair are capable of being tested. Forensic scientists at a crime scene can now examine cups and glasses to see whether a criminal has drunk from them – and test to see whether skin cells from their lips have been left behind. Fingerprints can be examined for traces of sweat or any skin cells.

By 2004 the DNA database will hold 3 million DNA profiles. DNA techniques can now determine gender and in many cases the ethnicity of a suspect. Scientists say ultimately they will be able to isolate hair colour, eye colour and facial characteristics. DNA fingerprinting cannot by itself be used to obtain a conviction. It has to be part of a jigsaw of corroborative evidence. Stringent care has to be taken to preserve the integrity of the samples to avoid cross-contamination. 'A stray hair, a sneeze, or other body fluid or fingerprint, all potentially prejudice a crime scene by cross-contamination of a DNA exhibit,' a report to Parliament explained. 'Single-cell analysis and vastly improved methods of collecting DNA from a crime scene exacerbate the risk.' To counteract this danger, a separate element within the DNA database carries an additional 40,000 DNA profiles from the police officers and support staff likely to attend crime scenes. If innocent contamination takes place, the database allows it to be eliminated quickly.

Another computerized database based on research carried out in Derbyshire in the 1980s shows that people who go on to commit major offences often have previous convictions for minor offences with some sexual connotations, like indecent exposure or stealing women's underwear. Recording DNA profiles from people convicted for these offences is seen as a crucial factor in preventing or detecting more serious offences later.

Twenty years on. Retired detectives Trevor Lapish (left),
Andrew Laptew (centre) and Dick Holland (right).

Lucky escapes.
Two women who
survived savage
attacks by Peter
Sutcliffe: Marcella
Claxton (right)
and Maureen
Long (below).

Ladies in retirement. Two former policewomen outside Millgarth Police HQ in Leeds, where they worked in the Ripper incident room: Megan Winterburn (left) and Sue Neeve.

'I hear voices.' Leeds University linguistic experts, Stanley Ellis (left) and Jack Windsor Lewis, both warned the infamous 'Ripper tape' was probably a hoax.

ABOVE: Yet another finger tip search. Officers look for clues in November 1980, at the scene of student Jacqueline Hill's murder in the Leeds suburb of Headingley.

BELOW: Alma Road, Headingley, where the crime scene is roped off following the discovery of the body of Sutcliffe's final victim, 20-year-old Jacqueline Hill (inset).

ABOVE: Following Jacqueline Hill's murder, Home Secretary William Whitelaw makes an urgent visit to the Murder Incident Room in Leeds. Standing beside Whitelaw is George Oldfield; West Yorkshire's chief constable, Ronald Gregory, looks on, accompanied by Det. Ch. Supt. Jim Hobson.

BELOW: Heartache. Jacqueline Hill's family at her funeral in November 1980.

Justice and retribution. ABOVE: Det. Sgt. Desmond O'Boyle, handcuffed to Peter Sutcliffe under the blanket, escorts the Yorkshire Ripper into Dewsbury Magistrates' Court on 5 January 1981.

BELOW: Outside the court, waiting members of the crowd demand vengeance and the death penalty for Peter Sutcliffe.

Guarding the guardians. A team of top investigators led by Lawrence Byford, HM Inspector of Constabulary, reviewed how West Yorkshire police conducted the Ripper inquiry. ABOVE: Lawrence Byford (centre) with the members of his Review Team and their staff.

Members of the Byford team: Professor Stuart Kind (top), Andrew Sloan (above), Ron Harvey (above left), and Les Emment (left).

Peter Sutcliffe's home in Garden Lane, Heaton, Bradford.

A major refinement in the use of DNA now occurs in murder and rape cases. British police forces have adopted a system of intelligence-led mass screenings using offender profiling techniques. Potential suspects fitting a 'profile' because of their age or geographic location, physical description or past criminal activity are invited to provide DNA samples to help with the police investigation. The samples are then matched with DNA found at a crime scene. Innocent suspects' DNA has to be removed from the database by law.

DNA can pinpoint a particular criminal, but investigators still have to find a murderer or rapist in order to put them 'in the frame'. This being so, computers will remain the backbone of major criminal investigation, and increasingly sophisticated programs are being developed. What Professor Stuart Kind did on graph paper in his hotel room in 1980 as he tried to plot the Yorkshire Ripper's base of operations, using centre of gravity techniques, has by the twenty-first century become a complex exercise in mathematical computation. Criminal Geographic Targeting is a highly advanced program that measures distances between fixed points, crime scenes and the homes of likely criminals, and undertakes the number-crunching calculations. If a criminal carries out a series of crimes that can be plotted on a map, a system called 'Rigel' plots where he might live.

The Police National Computer, in its infancy during the Ripper inquiry, is under constant development and now handles 200,000 inquiries a day from all over Britain, with an average response time of 0.3 seconds. It lists several million criminal records as well as people who are wanted, missing from home or disqualified from driving. It records stolen property and 44 million vehicles registered in the UK. Since 1997 an automatic number plate recognition system has allowed special CCTV cameras to read large volumes of car registration numbers. ANPR (automatic number plate recognition) can highlight lost or stolen vehicles in real time and also be linked to an intelligence database when police conduct covert operations, monitoring vehicles, say, in a red-light or high-crime area, or in a hunt for terrorists during a period of heightened tension. It can be used for tracking vehicles across Britain and an ANPR camera unit can also be fitted to mobile patrols and automatically check registration plates of any vehicle that comes within camera range.

Another database, the Vehicle Online Descriptive Search, looks for vehicles, using post codes, colour and make. PHOENIX, as a sophisticated intelligence system, allows large amounts of detailed information to be kept on known criminals. It is updated locally and lists names, convictions, dates of birth and aliases, and warns whether a criminal is violent or carries a particular weapon; provides physical descriptions for marks, scars, tattoos; lists a criminal's *modus operandi*, personal habits and associates – all of which can be cross-referenced. Nowadays someone like Peter Sutcliffe, who once had a hammer in his possession when arrested in 1969, would almost certainly be listed in the PHOENIX databank. If a hammer was then used in a serial murder, his name would crop up quickly as a potential suspect, particularly if he fitted other criteria, such as living close to a crime scene or matching a physical description with similar colour hair, or a beard and moustache, or owning a vehicle which matched a description provided by a key witness.

Advances in technology, however, are not enough to keep police ahead of major criminals. As the offenders become more sophisticated, the world's police forces have to match them, constantly improving their methods. The science of detection and the quality of the detectives has had to improve, along with the technology. Final recognition within the British police service that crime investigation 'is a high-grade intellectual pursuit' was a long time in coming. It was almost fifteen years after the Yorkshire Ripper case ended that some of the most crucial advances in modern crime detection began. A National Crime Faculty (NCF) was established at Bramshill, at the site of the Police College in Hampshire, in 1995. It brought together some of the brightest brains in the country to create a centre of excellence now used regularly by senior investigators across Britain.

One of the first projects by the NCF was close scrutiny of homicides and the ways they are tackled. By examining a database of several hundred murder investigations, a broad theory of homicide was formed. The best investigators in Britain pooled their knowledge and gleaned information from the homicide database in efforts to determine the best way complex murders can be tackled. This in turn led to the development of a murder manual, a blueprint for investigating complex homicides. The NCF has more than thirty full-time crime analysts: highly experienced serving police officers, scientists and behavioural psychologists who can be brought in to assist. Mostly they come in when the case is bogged down and going nowhere. The analysts can often point to fresh ways the inquiry might be advanced simply by reassessing the evidence presented at a crime scene. A field agent can be sent from the faculty to assist a senior investigating officer directly. At their disposal is an injuries database developed by forensic pathologists at Guy's Hospital, London.

In 2001 the NCF handled more than 2,350 calls from police forces to their help desk. In three hundred cases they sent a support officer to assist with a difficult inquiry and on thirty-eight occasions provided geographic profiles. Any police force in the UK can call upon its skills free of charge, since all police forces are paying for it collectively. The development of skills and a cross-pollination of ideas from one senior investigator to another is a beneficial spin-off. A senior investigating officer dealing with a child abduction could very quickly be put in contact with other senior detectives who had handled similar cases. Having specialist trained investigators attached to a senior investigating officer during a complex murder case allows the man in charge to think 'outside the box' and try new ideas to solve the crime. The training of specialist investigators is now a high priority for the police service. David Barclay, a forensic scientist and a senior member of the NCF staff, says: 'We are talking about no longer simply reacting to events and no longer being helpless in the wake of some dreadful things happening to people. In the Ripper case they were not able to stand back and have a look at the overview. My job is to stand back. I say to detectives: "I don't want to know anything about this case, I want to ask daft questions."'

Taking the lead in many of these developments was Sir David Phillips, chief constable of Kent and one of the few chief constables to have been a senior detective before heading up the hierarchy of the police service. In the mid-1990s he was chairman of the crime committee of the Association of Chief Police Officers, which meant he had considerable clout among his fellow chief constables. Finite resources meant the day was long gone when hundreds of detectives could be thrown into a murder investigation and kept there for months on end. Improved management skills had always been a high priority for the police service, but there had been little improvement to the actual techniques of homicide investigation. The days of the brilliantly intuitive detective, like Robert Fabian of Scotland

Yard in the 1930s and 1940s, or Dennis Hoban in Leeds in the 1960s and 1970s, are well and truly past. Generations of senior detectives had simply been reacting to events. Phillips saw there was the opportunity to develop proactive intelligence methods to keep them one step ahead of the criminals.

Looking ahead to the twenty-first century, Phillips wanted the role of the senior detective to be totally re-examined. Old policing methods frequently depended on detectives hauling in a few individuals on the basis of their *modus operandi* or informants' tip-offs and then confronting a prime suspect with an interrogation at a police station. It often led to a confession and the criminal revealing where he had left a murder weapon or stolen property. New laws, like the Police and Criminal Evidence Act, designed to protect suspects' rights, gave the innocent greater protection. But those same laws threw up extraordinary hurdles for the police when dealing with the most hardened and experienced criminals, who frequently appear in front of a detective with a solicitor at their side instructing them to say nothing. In many cases senior investigators know who the criminals are, but face an uphill struggle to get a prime suspect into court and obtain a conviction. Senior detectives are now *themselves* legally obliged to disclose to defence lawyers all information they obtain. If they trip up professionally, they are personally at risk of being sued because of their failure to comply with the terms of the European Convention on Human Rights. In the face of this, investigators have had to raise their game.

New technology, in Phillips's view, has to be used more intelligently. Greater intellectual rigour is required if serious crimes are to be solved. Trawl and search methods of investigation no longer work. The idea that every house in an area can be searched to find the needle in the haystack is unrealistic:

'When we find the right guy or hot suspect, unless we have got him with blood on his boots, there is not a lot going for the inquiry in many cases. We have got to get to the suspect more quickly.'

Today, better analytical skills and practices allow investigators to concentrate on what is important. This situation contrasts enormously with the effort by Leeds police in 1977 systematically to knock on 53,000 doors in West Yorkshire to find the man whose tyre tracks may have been left at a murder scene. It was a prime example of the trawl and search method that Phillips believes is no longer even a remote possibility. Nowadays senior investigating officers are compelled to evaluate their database of potential suspects and shrink it down to more manageable levels.

'We have to prioritize the doors we knock on,' says Sir David. 'We must be able to manage all kinds of databases so that we can shortlist our investigations. The critical thing is to get to the offender while there is still fresh forensic evidence, not to get to him in week seventy-two when all the evidence is lost. The critical breakthrough is that we are now better placed to use our intelligence input to prioritize these kinds of inquiries.'

Investigative files on unsolved murders are never closed. The technological age now allows detectives to re-examine cases where the trail has gone cold to the point of being frozen solid, specifically known as 'cold cases'. Every police force in Britain has conducted reviews of old unsolved homicides. Murderers who assumed their dreadful crime was long forgotten are being surprised by a knock on the door. Some of the old case files are dug out from storage and the evidence inputted into the HOLMES 2 computer. Men who were once prime suspects are re-examined. Forensic evidence is reassessed. Material bearing possible semen and bloodstains can be sent for highly advanced testing using mitochondrial DNA analysis and the most up-to-date forensic techniques.

In 1999, West Yorkshire police reopened one of John Domaille's old unsolved murders from the 1970s. Mary Gregson, a twenty-two-year-old housewife from Shipley, was strangled in August 1977 as she walked along the towpath of a canal at Saltaire, near Bradford. She struggled with her attacker but was eventually overpowered. Over 9,000 men were interviewed at the time, but the murder squad failed to find the killer. Twenty years later scientists were able to lift DNA from forensic evidence found at the original crime scene, but the killer was not in the national database. Police started to take swabs from 3,000 local men. On 27 February 2000, the 535th man to be swabbed, Ian Lowther, a twenty-four-year-old builder's labourer at the time of Mary Gregson's death, tested positive. He pleaded guilty seven months later to murder and received a life sentence. The divorced grandfather had hidden a lie for more than twenty-three years. He murdered his victim in a drunken stupor after his sexual advances were spurned.

Because of a paucity of forensic material, new DNA techniques have not been applied to the many cold cases that may have been committed by Peter Sutcliffe. He remains locked up in the high-security Broadmoor Special Hospital, in Berkshire. Several years after Sutcliffe was gaoled, psychiatrists re-examined him and then sent him to Broadmoor under the 1983 Mental Health Act. Mr Justice Boreham at his Old Bailey trial had recommended he serve a minimum thirty years for his crimes, but his ultimate fate will be determined by the Home Secretary of the day. He is one of a select number of notorious criminals in Britain likely never to be released, because even the remotest suggestion that Sutcliffe could be freed from custody would unleash widespread public outrage. The fact that for at least twenty years he has been deemed to be suffering from a mental disorder and remains a threat to the lives of others irresistibly suggests he will never emerge from the high walls surrounding Broadmoor.

Yet even inside the hospital Sutcliffe can never feel secure. Since he was gaoled in 1981 he has three times been on the receiving end of physical attacks. In 1983 a fellow prisoner in the hospital wing at Parkhurst Prison hit him in the face with a glass, causing a horrendous injury. In March 1997 he was stabbed in both eyes with a felt-tip pen by a fellow Broadmoor patient. A year earlier another patient had tried to strangle him with the flex from a pair of headphones. During all his time behind walls, Sutcliffe has revelled in his notoriety. He has enjoyed having a large number of female pen pals and several women have visited him. Periodically news that he has formed an attachment with one of his correspondents fuels coverage in the tabloids. More recently the press claimed he had rediscovered religion. Brought up a Roman Catholic, he had apparently found comfort in becoming a Jehovah's Witness.

There seems little evidence, however, that Peter Sutcliffe has personally atoned for his crimes or shown remorse or compassion for his victims or their families. Moreover, he has given very little help in resolving a fundamental question: for how many more unacknowledged murders and attempted murders was he responsible? Until Sutcliffe comes clean, many women remain unsure of whether their attacker is safely locked up. Families may suspect Sutcliffe murdered a loved one but can never be certain. When serious efforts were made to gain his cooperation in clearing up his outstanding crimes, they were reduced to a cat-and-mouse game as Sutcliffe revelled in the attention he received from a high-ranking police officer, Keith Hellawell.

For fourteen years in the 1980s and 1990s, Hellawell, who became chief constable of West Yorkshire, visited Sutcliffe to secure his cooperation in closing the files on a number of outstanding cases. Sutcliffe eventually confessed to two assaults, including his attack on fourteen-year-old Tracey Browne at Silsden in 1975. This left at least eighteen additional offences that Hellawell believed Sutcliffe could be connected to. Ten had been isolated by the Byford review team as almost certainly committed by Sutcliffe, based on evidence from eyewitnesses, method of attack or descriptions provided by surviving victims, including photofits.

Former West Yorkshire detective Des O'Boyle, who interrogated Sutcliffe following his arrest, believes Sutcliffe's violent rampages began far earlier than anyone realizes and that in 1966 and 1967, *before* he began attacking women, he murdered one man and tried to kill another. In January 1981, a few weeks after Peter Sutcliffe confessed to being the Yorkshire Ripper, O'Boyle followed up a hunch and questioned a forty-year-old taxi driver who was savagely attacked many years previously. O'Boyle showed him a double-page spread of passport-size photographs of men with beards and moustaches. Without hesitation, the taxi driver, John Tomey, picked out the mugshot taken after Sutcliffe was arrested in 1969 for going equipped for theft carrying a hammer in Bradford's red-light district. Mr Tomey remains convinced Sutcliffe was the man who attacked him with a ball-pein hammer and shattered his life on 22 March 1967. The taxi-driver picked up a fare late at night in Leeds, a young man wearing a zipped beige-coloured jacket and jeans. The passenger had a green and white college scarf, which made the taxi driver think he was a student. He asked to be driven to Burnley, but at Saltaire on the outskirts of Shipley changed his mind and asked to go instead to Bingley (where Sutcliffe was then living with his parents). Near Bingley the driver stopped under a street lamp and showed the passenger the fare card. He had a clear look at the young man. 'I noticed him in the back getting very agitated. He told me he hadn't got any money but said he had an aunt at Nelson who would pay the fare.' Mr Tomey drove on.

At about 11.20 p.m., at a place called Cock Hill, he stopped the car three miles south of Oxenhope. They were on a winding stretch of lonely moorland road in Brontë country; 'I had been looking for somewhere to turn round but there were grey stone walls on either side of the road. Eventually I managed to find an opening and did a U-turn. I didn't know where I was and decided to go back the way we had come. I stopped to consult a map, but as I was bending down to pick it up he brained me.' Mr Tomey was struck about the head with a hammer. As the blows rained down, he fought back, putting up his hands to defend himself. His thumb was broken and he fell forward, momentarily unconscious. When he awoke the passenger was on the outside of the vehicle, smashing the driver's window with the hammer. Mr Tomey's habit of locking the driver's door almost certainly saved his life. He managed to start the engine and drive off to get help at a nearby cottage. The attacker had broken the headlights and the illuminated 'Taxi' sign on the roof.

When police examined the vehicle they found a mass of bloodstains and clear signs of a struggle. Hospitalized in Keighley, Mr Tomey suffered fractures to his skull and bore crescent-shaped lacerations to his scalp similar to those found years later on victims of the Yorkshire Ripper. In the interior of the car forensic scientists discovered clear cup-shaped indentations caused by a ball-pein hammer striking the ceiling. These had been made with some force as the raging attacker jerked the hammer up in a frenzy before bringing it down on Mr Tomey's head. He described his attacker as aged between twenty-three and twenty-seven; five feet eight to ten inches tall, with darkish skin, dark hair with a noticeable moustache and beard. He spoke well and had a local accent. Mr Tomey never drove again and only managed to work during five of the next thirty-five years. He never married, never had a family, and today feels Sutcliffe utterly destroyed his life.

After reinterviewing Mr Tomey in 1981, Des O'Boyle examined the file of an unsolved murder which happened on 22 April 1966, eleven months *earlier*. The victim was an elderly man, bludgeoned about the head with a blunt instrument. The blow split sixty-year-old Fred Craven's head open and he suffocated on his own blood. There is no question that Peter Sutcliffe had the opportunity to commit the crime. He both lived and worked in the small town of Bingley on the edge of the Yorkshire Dales when the murder happened. He was twenty at the time and worked as a gravedigger in Bingley cemetery. His sixteen-year-old brother Michael was questioned by West Riding detectives because he resembled a young man seen in the immediate vicinity of the murder scene. Peter Sutcliffe was never a suspect. Thirty-five years on, it is not known whether he was questioned, whether he was eliminated from the inquiry, or if so on what grounds.

But, having just obtained Sutcliffe's confession to thirteen homicides, O'Boyle believed the Yorkshire Ripper should immediately be questioned as a prime suspect for the murder of Fred Craven and the attempted murder of the taxi driver. The method of attack clearly followed Sutcliffe's *modus operandi*: a blow to the head from behind, struck with such severe force as to render the victim helpless. Bingley was a small town. How many people in Bingley were capable of such premeditated lethal violence? Detectives were convinced Mr Craven recognized his attacker. Given Sutcliffe's propensity for violence, O'Boyle considered he must now be in the frame for the Craven murder. Yet Jim Hobson, who had taken charge of the Ripper investigation following the murder of Jacqueline Hill in November 1980, turned O'Boyle's request down. Years later O'Boyle remembered his boss's words clearly: 'He said, "He only murders women."'

To be fair to Hobson, in the aftermath of Sutcliffe's confession he had a major job on his hands. Teams of detectives were painstakingly building the prosecution file against the most notorious murderer in British history. In the words of George Oldfield, Sutcliffe was 'singing like a canary' and West Yorkshire police still needed his cooperation to help find the weapons used in the murders. However, Hobson's decision not to follow up other outstanding cases immediately was clearly wrong. There was a large number of unsolved attacks on women in West Yorkshire which bore all the hallmarks of the Yorkshire Ripper. Sutcliffe could and should have been interrogated about all these, as well as the attempted murder of Mr Tomey and the brutal killing of Fred Craven. Thirty-seven years later the evidence against Peter Sutcliffe for the earlier attacks on these two men remains circumstantial but also compelling.

At the very heart of Sutcliffe's crimes were the types of victim he sought: mostly women on their own at night. He had tried a number of ruses to lure them into situations where he could easily kill them. He was a coward, a weak and pathetic sadist, who enjoyed the power he had over his victims. He may have had an inner compulsion to kill, but it was always the deeply vulnerable he attacked. John Tomey was struck from the rear while bending down. And Fred Craven fits the profile of the classic Sutcliffe victim. He would have been seen as weak and unable to defend himself.

A crucial physical feature made Mr Craven, the local bookmaker, instantly recognizable among the people of Bingley. He was four feet seven inches tall and disabled. He suffered a severe and obvious congenital spinal problem and spent his first twelve years in a plaster cast. Doctors firmly predicted he would not live beyond the age of twenty-one. He had a tough life, but according to his family showed tremendous courage. His son, Ronald, now a successful local businessman, remembers his father as a deeply moral man. 'He was a hard man, a black-and-white man,' he said. 'His father and brother were top-class rugby league players and he had to compete with his brother and live up to his father's reputation.' Fred Craven was naturally right-handed, but a bone had to be removed from his hand, so he taught himself to write left-handed. When Ronald was fourteen his mother left home. Fred Craven brought up his son and three younger daughters on his own. He never dreamed of shirking his responsibilities.

In April 1966, twenty-seven-year-old Ronald Craven had a phone call from his great-uncle urgently asking him to come home from work. Something was wrong with his father. Ronald thought he must have had a heart attack and only later learned he had been murdered. Mr Craven senior was a 'commission agent' whose bookie's office was upstairs above an antique shop in Wellington Street, Bingley. The day he was murdered there was no racing, but Fred Craven decided to go into work briefly to pick up some papers. He arrived at about 11.30 a.m., and within minutes he was dead. Ronald's great-uncle discovered the body in a pool of blood immediately behind the door of the office at 11.40 a.m. His left arm had received a series of blows as he tried to defend himself and there were lacerations to the back of his head. He was also kicked in the chest and suffered fractured ribs. The killing shocked the local community, which had not suffered such a notorious crime for many years. Ronald Craven cried for the first time since he was a schoolboy at the news of his father's death. His younger sister, Jennifer, then aged sixteen, was so grief stricken she did not speak for a month.

It was demonstrably an opportunistic attack, which suggested a local man was responsible. Mr Craven had been robbed by someone who knew where his office was. His imitation crocodile skin wallet had been stolen. It was believed to contain £200 in cash. The killer probably saw him enter the side-door next to the antique shop. The bookmaker made a quick telephone call to a relative and police knew the exact time it was made. They believed the killer entered his office as he was putting the phone down. They also believed he recognized his assailant.

Because of the narrow time-frame, detectives were sure they would make a quick arrest. Among the senior officers investigating the case was the deputy head of West Riding CID, Detective Superintendent George Oldfield. Dick Holland, then a detective sergeant with the regional crime squad, was also involved in making inquiries. A few days after the murder, Oldfield issued a description of two key suspects seen looking in the antique shop window at the relevant time. In police jargon, they were 'artisan types', meaning they wore the clothes of working men. One was aged about forty, five feet four inches tall, in need of a shave and wearing a dark jacket and cloth cap. The other was said to be twenty, five feet five inches tall, slim, wearing a dark jacket, light-coloured trousers and a blue

'Donovan' type cap – a style named after the popular young folk singer called, unsurprisingly, 'Donovan', who had several hit records in the charts.

The day of the murder was a Friday when it was traditional for local factory workers to send out for fish and chip lunches. The local fish and chip shop was very close to the murder scene in Wellington Street and a long queue had formed outside at about 11.40 a.m. Michael Sutcliffe was taken in for questioning because he was thought to wear a Donovan cap. He told police he was getting fish and chips for the men in the factory, where he worked as an apprentice joiner. Police firmly ruled Michael Sutcliffe out of any involvement in the crime and the murder remained unsolved.

Yet there are several features which point strongly in the direction of the then twenty-year-old Peter Sutcliffe as the guilty man. According to Keith Sugden, one of his good friends at the time, Peter Sutcliffe also had a 'Donovan' cap. Sugden, then an apprentice printer, vividly remembers his time as a teenager in Peter Sutcliffe's company. 'I used to play the guitar. I was called "Donovan" because I played all his songs, like "Catch the Wind" and "Jennifer". Peter definitely had a Donovan cap.' It is beyond doubt that Peter Sutcliffe both knew Mr Craven was the local bookie and of his disability. For Fred Craven lived in the same street, at No. 23 Cornwall Road, less than a hundred yards from No. 57, the family home of Peter Sutcliffe, the very man who was to turn into a savage killer with a clearly recognizable pattern of attack. Who can say exactly when his dreadful litany of killings began?

When Peter Sutcliffe was arrested as the Yorkshire Ripper, Fred Craven's youngest daughter, Jennifer, revealed to her brother Ronald that Sutcliffe had pestered her to go out with him. She refused several times. 'I don't say this has any relevance,' says Ronald Craven, 'but I have always assumed Peter Sutcliffe murdered my father. When he was arrested I rang George Oldfield and said: "Do you think he could have had something to do with my father's death?" He said: "I cannot talk now, he is singing like a canary, I will get back to you." He never did, and Mr Oldfield was fired [from the case] shortly afterwards.'

During the visits Keith Hellawell made to Broadmoor to discuss unsolved attacks, Peter Sutcliffe consistently denied any involvement in the Tomey and Craven cases. But he has also denied many other attacks where there is strong evidence that he was the perpetrator. Sutcliffe is a devious, proven liar who enjoys manipulating both people and situations. He kept Keith Hellawell on a string for years. He lied to Hellawell again and again before finally and grudgingly owning up to two additional attacks. His only claim to fame is his notoriety, an infamy born from striking down the weak and vulnerable, which is why it is highly likely that, after John Tomey courageously fought back against him in his taxi in 1967, Sutcliffe switched his attentions to women. Had Sutcliffe confessed to killing Fred Craven or trying to murder John Tomey, he would rightly be dismissed as the cold-blooded monster he is, a man who simply enjoyed killing for the sense of power it gave him. His 'Divine Mission from God' to kill prostitutes would well and truly be exposed as the ridiculous, pathetic ruse it undoubtedly was. Today, instead of being held at a maximum security Category 'A' prison with all its restrictions, he enjoys a far more relaxed time as a patient in the comfortable but secure surroundings of a psychiatric hospital.

West Yorkshire police examined the Tomey and Craven files as part of a recent 'cold case' review but decided there was no evidence, forensic or otherwise, on which they could reopen either investigation. It did not help that in 1981, when Des O'Boyle tried to obtain the outstanding fingerprint evidence from both cases, he was informed it had been lost during an internal reorganization. The chance to compare Sutcliffe's fingerprints with those found at the crime scene was lost completely.

The only other major outstanding feature of the Yorkshire Ripper investigation remains the identity of the man with the Geordie accent who sent George Oldfield the infamous letters and tape – a man with blood on his hands because, by his actions, he shares some of the responsibility for the deaths of three women. In 1999, during the production of the ITV documentary *MANHUNT: The Search for the Yorkshire Ripper*, a request was made by the production team to West Yorkshire police for facilities to film a DNA test being made on the envelopes the letters and tape came in. It would have been a way of showing the great changes the police had made in the detection of crime. The intention was to see if the DNA matched any of the profiles held in the then fledgling national DNA database. If it did not, then DNA from the envelopes – from the gum on the flap, or from the stamp the sender would have licked – could be registered on the database of crime scene profiles. If the person who sent the tapes was arrested for a reportable crime in the future, then the police could identify him. Forensic scientists had already shown he was a blood group B secretor. A DNA analysis from traces of saliva could have nailed him and brought him to book, charged with attempting to pervert the court of justice. It was not to be. Several months after the initial inquiry, the somewhat embarrassed response came back: 'Sorry, we've lost the envelopes and there is no reasonable hope of us finding them.' The hoaxer has never been traced and probably never will be.

Nowadays precautions against losing vital evidence are in place and the chances of another Yorkshire Ripper terrorizing a whole region of Britain for years on end seem remote, given all the advances made in serious crime investigation.

Sir David Phillips, arguably the brightest police officer of his generation, has spent the latter part of his career driving forward the changes the police service has needed to make. He remains cautiously optimistic about the future: 'The serial killer will always be the most difficult sort of case to investigate. We are talking about someone who attacks randomly and there is no linkage between the victim and the killer and that is what makes it difficult to detect. It is not that there is no motive, there is a motive, but the victim has been selected as a prey might be selected. We are better placed than we were, in that we are developing a far better intelligence database about dangerous people, and maintaining a better risk-analysis on dangerous people. But the nightmare scenario remains that sometimes killers will strike whom we have not heard of before. And that is the most difficult of all. If we can bring to bear all the best techniques and encourage the public against these people, we will do better than we have done in the past.'

ENDPIECE

A Suitable Case for Treatment?

In the normal course of events, that should have been the end
of the story of the long hunt to bring the Yorkshire Ripper to
justice. But in the eyes of many thousands of people in the
North of England who lived through Peter Sutcliffe's reign of
terror, publication of *Wicked Beyond Belief* in February 2003
convinced them that the story was not yet over. The past has
the potential of coming back to haunt people and in late
February the past was about to catch up with Sutcliffe. A
devastating secret he had kept hidden for more than twenty
years was finally exposed.

The revelation in *Wicked Beyond Belief* about Sutcliffe's perverted motives for his crimes raised crucial questions about
whether the Yorkshire Ripper had indeed manipulated psychiatrists and the Home Office into believing he should receive
treatment for his mental illness. Just how did the most notorious killer in British history manage to achieve his clearly stated
objective of spending his sentence as a patient in a mental
hospital rather than in a maximum sexurity prison? Did Peter
Sutcliffe cheat the system? There was now the clearest evidence
he had lied to doctors over and over again. Rather than someone who could not help himself because of his medical condition, he was all the time a premeditated sadist who had
carefully stitched together the special clothing worn under his

trousers so that he could enjoy sexual gratification while murdering his victims. Spelled out clearly in Chapter 17 of this book is the first-ever account of what happened when Sutcliffe was strip-searched in front of three relatively junior detectives after he had signed his confession. This evidence, kept secret for more than twenty years, came as a bombshell to many senior detectives involved in the case and also to seasoned journalists familiar with the Yorkshire Ripper story.

The news that Sutcliffe wore a home-made garment to further his twisted sexual pleasure as he stabbed his victims to death provoked headline stories in the media because this devastating piece of information was never revealed at his trial. The doctors who examined Sutcliffe in prison and other psychiatrists who cared for him in Broadmoor Hospital never knew about it either.

For those well-versed in the details of Sutcliffe's trial at the Old Bailey there were puzzling features at the time. The psychiatrists who gave evidence had seemed adamant about several vital matters. Firstly, they believed that the serial killer was telling the truth when he said he was hearing voices from God. Their diagnosis of paranoid schizophrenia was based on what he had told them during interviews. They had also carefully gone back through Sutcliffe's life history. Yet no one, not his family, friends, or workmates, had previously noticed any sign that Sutcliffe was schizophrenic. Equally, he had said nothing to the police about his delusions after he was arrested. Then, several weeks after being remanded to Armley prison, he suddenly mentioned hearing voices from God. The doctors interpreted this as meaning that Sutcliffe's capacity to know that what he was doing was wrong was clearly diminished by his illness. In the technical terms of the 1957 Mental Health Act, it meant that he was 'suffering from such abnormality of mind . . . as substantially impaired his mental responsibility' and therefore could be found guilty of manslaughter rather than murder.

Finally, and probably most crucially, the psychiatrists argued there was no sexual motive for his crimes. Dr Hugo Milne said he was absolutely certain Sutcliffe had not lied when he said there was no sexual component to his murderous attacks. However, we now know Sutcliffe was desperate to hide from the world, and most especially from his wife, this seedy motive for his crimes. One eminent psychiatrist conceded in court that if there had been a sexual motive, then Sutcliffe's story of voices from God could be discounted. In short, he would have been lying to the doctors.

Dr Terence Kay, who gave evidence at the Old Bailey, had spent much of his working life in the early 1980s examining criminals at Leeds and Wakefield gaols and enjoyed a good working relationship with the prison officers. 'They told me quite frankly that we were being fooled,' he told the jury. 'I wasn't troubled with the diagnosis but, as the officers quite rightly said, they spent far more time with Sutcliffe than I did.' Kay even acknowledged that Sutcliffe might have learned the symptoms of schizophrenia from when his wife had a mental breakdown with the illness in 1972, when she was his girlfriend. Another psychiatrist, Dr Malcolm MacCulloch, was specifically asked by the judge, Mr Justice Boreham, what happened to his diagnosis of paranoid schizophrenia if Sutcliffe had been lying. 'It falls,' he replied.

Harry Ognall, QC for the prosecution, asked Dr MacCulloch if Sutcliffe had in any way deceived or misled him.

'I am sure he deceived me here and there at one point or another,' the psychiatrist answered. Ognall then asked: 'Your diagnosis stands or falls by what this man has told you. That is the beginning and the end of it?'

MacCulloch replied: 'I don't think it's the beginning and the end, but it is substantial.'

Forensic psychiatry took a battering at the hands of the prosecution during the trial. The jury, finding Sutcliffe guilty of thirteen murders and seven attempted murders, wanted him jailed for life and the judge obliged twenty times over.

For Dr Milne, who had spent three days giving evidence, the result was a painful experience. 'The whole trial was a charade for public opinion,' he said angrily in October 1982, just as other doctors were telling the Home Secretary, yet again, that Sutcliffe really was mentally ill and ought to be in hospital.

Milne was bitter at the hypocrisy of the Home Office. 'As a doctor I found it hard to understand how the Crown, who had tested and accepted the medical evidence, could then discard that evidence and say it was idiotic and cross-examine their own experts on that basis. The man couldn't be hung, which was what everyone was screaming and shouting about, so he had to be found guilty of something. We're talking here about majority public opinion, not what you might call "thinking opinion".'

Milne added a telling comment which clearly demonstrated his belief that the cause of psychiatry had been set back by the jury's verdict: 'I believe that the whole case has reversed the relationship between law and medicine. We are back to the old situation where medicine communicates with law and law communicates with medicine, and the law only accepts what it wishes.'

Looking back, this could be viewed as sour grapes or maybe as an extraordinary display of intellectual arrogance. Was Milne actually saying that physicians could never be wrong, that doctors were always correct in their diagnosis and that those who administered the criminal justice system ought to accept what they said? Forensic psychiatrists may have felt their status had taken a severe blow, but the doctors were not going to give up their professional duty as they saw it. Despite having lost in court, the psychiatrists who examined Sutcliffe continued to seek *habeas corpus*. They wanted final control of the most notorious criminal in British history. They believed he showed all the signs of being mad, which meant Sutcliffe had to be transferred out of the prison system and into their care. They wanted him kept in a secure hospital where they could treat him. Sutcliffe himself was keenly aware of the doctors' strong desire to have him transferred to a secure hospital. The notion that the doctors were interested in him was not lost on the Yorkshire Ripper. In Broadmoor he told one of his visitors: 'They have got me here as a specimen. When I die they will pickle my brain and look at it.'

In May 1982, twelve months after Sutcliffe was sent to prison, Dr Milne made the 300-mile journey from Bradford to Portsmouth and took the thirty-minute ferry to the Isle of Wight. His destination was Parkhurst Prison and yet one more examination of Sutcliffe's mental state. Milne was open minded. He was prepared to accept his original diagnosis may have been wrong. But the forensic psychiatrist found Sutcliffe still exhibited the same behaviour. In fact, he had had more delusions. The killer told prison doctors that one of his victims, Emily Jackson, had visited him in his cell. He could see her and smell her perfume, 'a text-book hallucination' according to the experts. Milne said: 'There was no evidence to suggest that he was malingering at any time that I saw him. You couldn't possibly malinger for such a long time.'

In the autumn of that same year, two other psychiatrists recommended the Yorkshire Ripper be transferred to a secure mental hospital for treatment. William Whitelaw, the Home Secretary, refused. A few weeks later Sutcliffe was savagely attacked by a fellow prisoner, who pushed a glass into his face causing severe injuries. Immediately Sutcliffe's family in Bradford said he was mentally ill and should be locked up for life, 'but he should be in a mental unit where he can be cared for and be safe and people be safe from him'. They were soon rebuffed by the Home Office. Parliament was told: 'The Mental Health Act 1959 required the Home Secretary before he might direct removal of a prisoner to hospital, to be satisfied that the prisoner was mentally disordered to a degree warranting his detention in a hospital for medical treatment and that, having regard to the public interest and all the circumstances, removal would be expedient. The Home Secretary has given careful consideration to medical reports, matters brought out at Sutcliffe's trial and appeal, the offences of which he was convicted, his present circumstances in prison and his likely future if removed to a hospital, but concluded against removal.'

Possibly only a cynic would suggest that politics had any part to play in this decision, but the Home Office had admitted that the 'public interest' did feature in William Whitelaw's decision to keep Sutcliffe in prison. Moreover, 1983 was destined to be an election year and the subject of the Yorkshire Ripper, a reviled figure throughout the country, still greatly vexed the British public. Few people were in the least bit saddened to hear that a fellow prisoner had attacked Sutcliffe and caused him serious injury. Even so, Whitelaw, a decent and humane man, ordered Sutcliffe's case to be kept under review. If there was a significant change of circumstances, the Home Office said, they might consider moving him to hospital.

In March 1984, ten months after the general election that swept Margaret Thatcher back to power with a vastly increased post-Falklands War majority, a new Home Secretary, Leon Brittan, finally accepted the psychiatrists' diagnosis. Sutcliffe's condition had deteriorated greatly, the Home Office said. He was suffering from a grave mental illness, hearing voices, had no understanding of his condition and was refusing to accept medical treatment which prisoners could not be compelled to undergo. The clear inference was that, were Sutcliffe to be transferred to a secure hospital, he could be made to take his medicine and would be treated appropriately.

The transfer to Broadmoor was greeted with relief by his family and especially by his wife Sonia, who believed it confirmed what she had known all along: 'Peter is a sick person, they should have found this out before now.' By keeping silent about his sexual compulsions, Sutcliffe had continued to lie and deceive the psychiatrists, until he finally achieved his goal of being taken out of prison. He also provided those close to him, the members of his immediate family, with a plausible explanation of why he had committed such terrible crimes. 'I wasn't responsible,' he could now plausibly say from his bed in Broadmoor, complete with its en suite facilities, 'it was the voices.' The very fact that he was being held under Section 47 of the 1983 Mental Health Act meant it must be true. He was no longer a criminal but a patient who needed help.

The law at the time laid down precise criteria about how and when a person could be transferred to a secure hospital. Ostensibly the aim was to get that person treatment for his condition. Section 47 gave the Home Secretary the power of transfer when the patient had at least one of four types of mental disorder, on the basis of reports from two doctors. To understand how Sutcliffe was moved from Parkhurst Prison to Broadmoor, it is important to understand the technicalities involved.

'Mental disorder' was defined in the law as 'a mental illness, arrested or incomplete development of mind, psychopathic disorder or any other disorder or disability of mind'. Mental illness is not defined – responsibility falls heavily on the clinical diagnosis of the doctors who examine the patient. As a safeguard against abuses of human rights, certain behaviour is not deemed to constitute mental disorder. Someone could not be transferred to a mental hospital 'by reason only of promiscuity or other immoral conduct or sexual deviancy'. Sutcliffe had been quick to stress he was not sexually deviant and the psychiatrists said they had no evidence he was. They could only rely on the documents supplied by the police and what he told them. Without knowledge of his killing kit, how would they have known that sexual gratification was a prime reason for him attacking women? Would Sutcliffe's sexual deviancy have run counter to their diagnosis of paranoid schizophrenia? Dr Milne told the jury it would, but stressed he found no evidence of a sexual motive. Equally, had Sutcliffe been lying about hearing the voices from God, the psychiatrist admitted, it would have left a severe dent in their diagnosis.

Moreover, the law also required the mental disorder Sutcliffe was suffering from to be such that it made it appropriate for him to be detained in hospital for treatment. The Home Secretary was the person who decided whether a transfer was expedient in the circumstances, having regard to the public interest, which could mean just about anything.

Sutcliffe had been one of the most loathed people in Britain, especially to fellow inmates, many of whom were very dangerous men. There were plenty of wry smiles when the news of his swift transfer to Broadmoor was announced. Some working inside the prison system believed Sutcliffe's move happened because the prison service could not guarantee his safety. If treatment for his condition was a key goal in moving him, then it is somewhat bizarre that for the first ten years in which he was a patient at Broadmoor Hospital Sutcliffe continued to refuse the medication prescribed by his doctors. The law said he had to be treated for his medical condition. While he was in prison, the Home Office said, he could not be compelled to take his medicine – the implication being that if he was sent to Broadmoor, this would change.

A woman who visited Sutcliffe regularly for ten years from 1990 revealed that the serial killer openly boasted of his refusal to co-operate with the physicians at Broadmoor. Only many years later did Sutcliffe take a drug prescribed for schizophrenia called Depixol. The visitor observed one of its side effects: it made him tremble, as if suffering the early symptoms of Parkinson's disease.

Life behind the high walls of Britain's most famous secure hospital has been rather serene. Certainly Sutcliffe fares better being cared for under the National Health Service than if he were a category 'A' prisoner in a maximum security gaol. For a start he enjoys a steady income courtesy of the taxpayer. He is on social security and is entitled to the equivalent of incapacity benefit, called a severe disablement allowance. When prisoners are transferred to any special hospital under the terms of the Mental Health Act, they are deemed to be patients and like all other patients are entitled to the same social security benefits. Hospital authorities go to great lengths to protect the people they take care of and, in the case of severely ill mental patients, an obscure body called the Public Guardianship Office of the Court of Protection can appoint someone to look after a patient's money when their assets are over £2,000. Sutcliffe does not fit into this category and the benefits are paid as a form of pocket money, often as a reward or incentive for good behaviour or for co-operating with the hospital authorities. Guidelines are laid down by the Royal College of Psychiatrists. 'It is important that the reward and incentive money is paid to a patient for goals and behaviour which are within their ability to achieve.' The amount of benefit Sutcliffe gets has been determined by the local Social Security office. Although some Broadmoor patients cannot handle money easily, many can. Sutcliffe consequently has had plenty of money at his disposal during his time in hospital, building up a fairly healthy bank balance in excess of £3,000 at one point.

Someone who got to know Sutcliffe well during his time at Broadmoor remains convinced he is an accomplished liar and manipulator who has relished his celebrity status. During the first ten years in hospital he regularly received correspondence from gullible women attracted by his notoriety. Set apart from them, however, was an expert graphologist, Diane Simpson, who was co-operating with West Yorkshire Police in their attempts to get Sutcliffe to confess to other crimes.

One of Simpson's research students, as part of her work in studying handwriting, had previously had an exchange of correspondence with Sutcliffe, who was keen to continue the relationship. When the research student wanted to break off the correspondence, it was left to Diane Simpson to write and explain why. Sutcliffe then asked Simpson to visit him in Broadmoor and later hinted there were other crimes he had committed. She immediately contacted West Yorkshire Police, who encouraged her to keep her visits going. She helped arrange the first meeting between Sutcliffe and Keith Hellawell, later chief constable of West Yorkshire, who had the task of trying to identify other serious crimes the serial killer had committed but had never been charged with. During an eleven-year period Mrs Simpson spent more than 400 hours with

Sutcliffe in Broadmoor, closely observing his behaviour and reporting back to Hellawell.

She knew of a dozen women with whom Sutcliffe struck up friendships after they began writing to him on a regular basis. She believed he exploited their vulnerability by telling them they were 'special' or 'the one'. 'He was the most manipulative and prolific liar I have ever come across,' Simpson said. 'He told me that he did not wish to go to prison. He boasted about the various conquests he had made while in Broadmoor and how he could persuade people to do things for him on the outside, including one woman who smuggled his uncensored letters out of the hospital for six years. The woman later admitted to me that this was true and that at the time she just felt she *had* to do it.'

'He used the system to his advantage,' Simpson said. 'It meant he could have more visitors, send out more letters and enjoy far greater freedom in Broadmoor than he ever could in prison. He could manipulate anyone, including the psychiatrists. He told me he had refused to talk to the doctors about his crimes and refused to take medication for years, right up until he was found in possession of two hacksaw blades. It was after all his visits had been stopped that he started taking the prescribed drug Depixol, which made it look as if he had the early stages of Parkinson's disease.

'I had earlier asked him about his medication, and his argument was that he took nothing because there was nothing wrong with his mind and he did not want to take any mind-bending drugs. I believe the incident with the hacksaw blades [in 1992] brought about a pressured situation and he had to prove his credibility. I don't believe him taking the pills was a coincidence. It was his *de facto* recognition that he deserved to be in Broadmoor. The whole experience has been one of manipulation and fabrication. I have no doubt whatsoever that he manipulated and acted a part in order to get where he is. He talked constantly about when he got out of hospital.'

Another who got to know Sutcliffe well was his primary nurse in Broadmoor – Frank Mone, who frequently crossed swords with the hospital authorities because of his role as chairman of the hospital branch of the Prison Officers' Association. Mone left his job and later spoke to a journalist about life in Broadmoor and his relationship with Sutcliffe. Following publication of the story, the Secure Hospitals Authority obtained a court injunction preventing Mone from discussing anything he had learned in confidence during his time at Broadmoor that was not already in the public domain.

In his 1995 newspaper interview Mone had spelled out his belief that Sutcliffe had cynically manipulated the system within Broadmoor so that he would not be returned to prison. He had lied in order to maintain his lifestyle in hospital by pretending to be schizophrenic. 'He killed because he enjoyed it,' Mone told the newspaper. 'He is an evil man, it's as simple as that. Peter did not show any of the signs of schizophrenia. His original diagnosis when he came to Broadmoor talked about the voice in his head which led him to commit murders, but he told me there was no voice. He was on no medication, did not suffer hallucinations and did not show any of the classic signs of schizophrenia. You would walk into a schizophrenic's room and it would be disorganized, clothes all over the place, with bizarre pictures on the walls.

'Sutcliffe looks after everything himself – his clothes and washing – his room is neat and tidy and his paintings show flowers and portraits. Schizophrenics get very confused but Sutcliffe could remember every single detail of his crimes. Peter himself admitted that he should still be in prison. He just enjoys the perks at Broadmoor. This voice would appear again if he was being reassessed and then mysteriously disappear. You have got to ask whether it is real.'

Mone was not alone in suspecting Sutcliffe faked his illness. The current General Secretary of the Prison Officers' Association, Brain Caton, a member of the General Council of the TUC, also believes he manipulated the system. Caton spent twenty years as a prison officer, much of the time at Wakefield maximum security prison. He escorted Sutcliffe to court on several occasions and got to observe his behaviour at first hand. 'It was a dangerous job transporting him because of those who were demonstrating when we went to court. Not many people realize how frightening it was for us when the crowds were round the vans, smashing at the windows. Watching his arrogant attitude you could see the evil in his eyes.'

Caton has spoken at length to colleagues who have had charge of Sutcliffe from the time he was arrested. 'His placement in a psychiatric hospital was a political move because he got attacked when he was in prison and probably, because of his notoriety, would have continued to have been attacked. I would never say he was the most stable of people. He was a manipulative criminal who has the ability to very quickly assess the questions that were being asked of him and give the answers that were necessary to ensure that he got housed in a psychiatric institution. I think he manipulated his way into the secure hospital system.' Caton, who has a special knowledge of mental health and crime, believes Sutcliffe has a personality disorder but is emphatic the prison service successfully copes with many similar prisoners. 'Some of these people cannot be treated, but they can be controlled,' he said. 'Some definitely need to be within a secure mental hospital, but others can be safely contained within a maximum security prison. Those who have pure criminal intent and are severe and dangerous personalities should be treated within the prison service but with staff who have had the training to deal with them.'

After nearly two decades in Broadmoor, time has taken its toll on Sutcliffe. His weight has ballooned and he no longer resembles the arrogant individual he once was, believing he had triumphed in getting one over the authorities, revelling in his own notoriety. Early on, according to those who witnessed his comings and goings, he appeared to have the run of the place. Lurid stories about him and his life on the Henley/ Oxford Ward, his transsexual girlfriends and his pathetic attempts at painting regularly appeared in the press. What most exercised journalists and readers alike was the extraordinary fact that he seemed to have an endless stream of female admirers who conducted regular correspondence with, and visits to, him, drawn like moths to an unshaded lamp.

Today he resembles a shambolic figure, shuffling and shaking as he goes about his daily routine, coping with the side effects of his medication. Revelations about the special clothing he wore when he killed his victims will have caused him concern because his lies of twenty years have been exposed. During those years he has not had to answer really awkward questions about his crimes because the doctors haven't known the right questions to ask. He could have dismissed the claims in the book as a tissue of lies, for there was no official record of this special garment anywhere in the police or prosecution files.

However, the actions of a retired West Yorkshire detective will have caused Sutcliffe consternation, because they provided proof that the revelations in *Wicked Beyond Belief* were true. This has led directly to a campaign to hold a Home Office inquiry into the circumstances by which Sutcliffe was transferred to Broadmoor and whether or not he should be transferred back to a maximum security prison In mid-February 2003, a few weeks after *Wicked Beyond Belief* was published, a retired West Yorkshire detective, called Alan Foster, contacted David Bruce, crime reporter for the *Yorkshire Evening Post*. News of Sutcliffe's killing kit had received widespread publicity and Foster had an extraordinary story to tell. Some time after the trial, Foster, who was a detective constable, had charge of all the exhibits that had been gathered in the Yorkshire Ripper case. They included various weapons found in Sutcliffe's home and cars, including lengths of rope, a hacksaw, knives, women's underwear, a leather apron, gloves, sharpened screwdrivers and a collection of hammers.

There was also a large quantity of shoes and clothing taken from Sutcliffe's home on the day he first appeared in court charged with murder. Among these were the special leggings Sutcliffe had stitched together with extra padding around the knees, made from the arms of a woollen jumper and some silky material, which covered his backside with a gap at the front allowing his private parts to be easily exposed. Foster told the crime reporter that after the Old Bailey trial he had instructions to burn all the Yorkshire Ripper exhibits in an incinerator.

Fearing that potential evidence would be destroyed which might at some future date link Sutcliffe to other unsolved murders and attacks on women, Foster decided secretly to hang on to the leggings, and kept them for twenty years in the loft of his home in north Leeds. He said he had handed the leggings to West Yorkshire Police two years previously in the hope they could be tested for vital DNA evidence. The detective, who had been retired for ten years, said he could not understand why no mention of the leggings had been made at Sutcliffe's trial. 'Surely it would have swamped his plea of diminished responsibility.'

The bombshell story in the *Yorkshire Evening Post* – KILLING KIT OF THE RIPPER – was splashed on its front page, complete with a photograph of the green-coloured leggings. Immediately the local MP for Leeds North East, Fabian Hamilton, wrote to the Home Secretary demanding an investigation into the possibility that Sutcliffe had fabricated his evidence. 'Mr Foster's actions raise the crucial issue of whether the most notorious killer of modern times has cheated justice. Even so many years after the capture, trial and imprisonment of Sutcliffe, I believe it is still strongly in the public interest that you order Sutcliffe's removal from Broadmoor and his re-incarceration in a proper prison where he should serve the rest of his lifetime. The families of his victims and the Yorkshire public would demand no less, as indeed was the intention of the jury at his trial.'

The reaction from David Blunkett, the Home Secretary, was swift. Showing concern for the families of Sutcliffe's victims, he replied that if anything had caused distress and disquiet among those affected by Sutcliffe's horrific crimes it was the claims made in *Wicked Beyond Belief* that Sutcliffe had feigned mental illness to avoid serving his prison sentence.

The Home Office reply had the hand of the civil service all over it. Twenty-two years earlier, in 1981, the Home Office had told another Leeds MP that one of the reasons the Attorney-General had been prepared to accept Sutcliffe's plea of manslaughter on the grounds of diminished responsibility was that it would spare the families 'many days of extensive press coverage and detailed knowledge of the horrifying injuries'. Judging by this response, the Home Office officials at the time clearly had no idea of the sense of outrage felt by the general public at the merest suggestion of a plea bargain being hatched between the Crown and Sutcliffe's defence lawyers.

And by its response in 2003 it would appear that the Home Office, where the Yorkshire Ripper case is concerned, has learned nothing. In the wake of the media explosion over the plea to have the Yorkshire Ripper returned to prison, Sutcliffe's medical officer sent a swift report to the Home Office on 10 March 2003, confirming Broadmoor Hospital's view that he remains mentally ill and appropriately detained for treatment.

Blunkett said he would be prepared to consider any recommendation to transfer Sutcliffe back to prison on the basis of medical evidence that he did not need hospital treatment. 'I have received no such recommendation,' he stated.

Fabian Hamilton intends to continue with his campaign. He wants a debate in the House of Commons and an independent inquiry into the possibility of a serious miscarriage of justice. Other MPs representing constituencies in the North of England have indicated their support.

NOTE ON SOURCES

This account of the five-year hunt for the Yorkshire Ripper, Peter Sutcliffe, which ended with his capture on 2 January 1981, has taken many years to research. It began in 1979 when I was appointed northern correspondent of the *Sunday Times* by the then editor, Harold Evans. I started writing about the police investigation, first for the news pages and later as a member of the INSIGHT team, then headed by the remarkable Paul Eddy. I was fortunate to be able to discuss the case, occasionally in long background briefings, with many of the leading figures involved. They included Ronald Gregory, George Oldfield, Dick Holland, Jim Hobson, Peter Gilrain, Dr Michael Green, David Zackrisson, Peter Docherty, Trevor Lapish, Jack Ridgway and members of the West Yorkshire County Council Police Committee. I tended not to throw research material away and continued to maintain a 'Yorkshire Ripper' file long after I left the *Sunday Times* in 1983 (two weeks *before* Andrew Neil was named as its new editor) and joined the documentaries department at Yorkshire Television in Leeds. The file consisted of original interview notes, newspaper cuttings, extracts from *Hansard*, articles from academic journals and various official documents ranging from press releases and ministerial statements to the shortened version of West Yorkshire Metropolitan Police's own study into what happened during the five-year inquiry. It was a good starting point for a future book.

In 1982 I addressed the International Association of Forensic Sciences, meeting at a special symposium at Christ Church, Oxford. The subject of this important event among law enforcement professionals was 'Crime Investigation: Art or Science?' My forty-five-minute paper was on 'Crime Investigation and the Media'. Little did I know that I was to be the only 'outsider' attending, but I was treated well, despite the bitterness many participants felt about the way press and television had behaved during and after the Ripper investigation. At this stage the public was still awaiting the Press Council's deliberations over the 'cash for witnesses' débâcle, in which Fleet Street failed to distinguish itself in the aftermath of Sutcliffe's arrest.

Attending the symposium were senior Home Office officials, forensic scientists, pathologists and many senior murder squad detectives from all over Britain. The man who put the conference together was Professor Stuart Kind, the association's president, who had been a member of Lawrence Byford's special review team. The chairman for the two-day event was Russell Stockdale, a forensic scientist who had worked on the Ripper case. Several members of the Byford team delivered lectures about the lessons learned, with titles like: 'Can Crime Investigation Be Taught?' and 'The Investigation of Multiple Crime'. Intriguingly, to the best of my memory, none of them uttered the words 'Yorkshire Ripper' or 'Peter Sutcliffe' during the official conference sessions. I was alone in mentioning the subject.

Time passed and I maintained my friendship and contact with several people, most notably Dick Holland, David Zackrisson, Michael Green (who became professor of forensic pathology at the University of Sheffield) and Professor Kind himself.

After the lapse of nearly twenty years I began thinking in 1998 about writing a book on the Ripper case and these four agreed that, because of the passage of time, they could consent to be interviewed on tape as part of my research. The story cried out to be a television documentary. The ITV Network Centre commissioned two hour-long films from Ray Fitzwalter Associates, with whom I worked in partnership, which were eventually transmitted in September 1999 under the title *MANHUNT: The Search for the Yorkshire Ripper*. It was fortunate enough to be nominated for a BAFTA award. A considerable number of people connected with the Yorkshire Ripper inquiry agreed to be interviewed, some twice or more. They talked on film for the documentary and also gave extended interviews on cassette tape for this book. Others did not want to be tape-recorded and had no desire to be named. I happily respect their wishes and thank them for the valuable time and other assistance they gave me.

The following is a list of those who went 'on the record', with the dates they were interviewed:

Maureen Banham (Midland Bank, Shipley): 23.10.98; 29.10.98; 19.1.99

David Barclay (National Crime Facility): 4.3.02

Detective Chief Superintendent Michael Burdiss (Head of South Yorkshire CID): 24.11.98

Sir Laurence Byford (former HM Chief Inspector of Constabulary): 18.11.98; 17.12.98

Detective Chief Superintendent Grange Catlow (Manchester CID, retired): 6.10.98

Valerie Clay (daughter of Mrs Maureen Banham): 29.10.98

Marcella Claxton (survivor of a Ripper attack; interviews by Jane Bower): 28.10.98; 15.12.98

Melvyn Clelland (Garrard's timber yard, Huddersfield; interviews by Jane Bower): 10.12.98

Assistant Chief Constable John Domaille (West Yorkshire police, retired): 7.11.98; 14.12.98; 31.3.00

Stanley Ellis (senior lecturer, University of Leeds, retired): 7.10.98; 7.1.99

Professor Michael Green (University of Sheffield, retired): 13.10.98; 23.11.98; 30.11.98; 8.12.98

Police Sergeant Robert Hydes (South Yorkshire police; interview by Jane Bower): 18.1.99; (telephone interview with author) 7.1.02

Mrs Joan Ring (widow of Sergeant Robert Ring): (telephone interview) 8.1.02

John Hitchen (barrister for prosecution at Sutcliffe's trial): 10.1.99; 12.1.99

Richard Hoban (son of Dennis Hoban): 28.10.98; (telephone interview) 27.4.01

Vincent Hoban (brother of Dennis Hoban): (telephone interview) 19.5.01

Detective Superintendent Dick Holland (West Yorkshire CID, retired): (telephone interview) 3.4.98; 26.6.98; 29.6.98; 30.6.98; 15.7.98; 16.7.98; 29.7.98; 15.9.98; 10.12.98; 13.1.99; 14.1.99; 11.3.99; 18.7.01

Professor Stuart Kind (forensic scientist, retired; author and member of the Byford Review team): 19.3.98; 27.6.98; 29.9.98; 30.11.98; 11.12.98; 20.5.01

Detective Chief Superintendent Trevor Lapish (West Yorkshire CID, retired): 12.10.98; 23.10.98; 6.1.99

Detective Sergeant Andrew Laptew (West Yorkshire CID, retired): 1.12.98; 8.1.99; 25.9.01

Maureen Long (survivor of a Ripper attack; interviews by Jane Bower): 27.10.98; 7.12.98

Police Constable Keith Mount (Northumbria police): 21.1.99

Sue Neave (West Yorkshire police, retired): 2.11.98; 11.1.99

Desmond O'Boyle (detective chief inspector, retired): (telephone interviews) 6.1.99; 12.3.02, 13.3.02

David Phillips (now Sir David, chief constable of Kent; chairman ACPO crime committee): 19.10.98; 16.12.98

Detective Chief Superintendent Jack Ridgway (Manchester CID, retired): (telephone interview) 30.9.98; 6.10.98; (telephone interview) 17.5.01; (telephone interview) 12.9.01

Sir Andrew Sloan (chief constable of Strathclyde, retired, and member of the Byford Review team): 14.7.98; 26.9.98; 16.11.98; 11.12.98

Simon Steward (Midland Bank, Shipley): 26.10.98; 19.1.99

Russell Stockdale (forensic scientist): 9.11.98

Theresa Sykes (survivor of a Ripper attack; interview by Jane Bower): 19.1.99

Jack Windsor Lewis (senior lecturer, University of Leeds, retired): 15.10.98; 7.1.99

Inspector Megan Winterburn (West Yorkshire police, retired): 2.11.98; 11.1.99

Chief Superintendent David Zackrisson (Northumbria police, retired): 28.6.98; 24.9.98; 21.1.99

Margaret Oldfield: (telephone interview) 25.7.01

Like me, many of those interviewed hoarded papers and documents connected with their work. They would often disappear for ten minutes or so, go to an attic, garage or outhouse, and as often as not return with a long-forgotten folder or lever-arch file, or, in the case of Mrs Betty Hoban, with a metal document box containing a veritable treasure trove of old newspaper cuttings, photographs, letters, diaries that had belonged to her late husband, Detective Chief Superintendent Dennis Hoban.

Other searches yielded memos, publicity material, official reports and other primary source material of great value to a writer trying to document a recent event in British social history. I relied heavily upon the interviews and documents as source material, along with a massive collection of cuttings gathered from public libraries across the North of England, as well as at the offices of the *Yorkshire Post*, the *Manchester Evening News*, and Times Newspapers in London, where I was also allowed to consult the archives of the INSIGHT team.

The Report into the Investigation of the Series of Murders and Assaults on Women in the North of England between 1975 and 1980 was made publicly available by West Yorkshire police in 1983, as a response to Mr Ronald Gregory publishing his memoirs in a national newspaper only weeks after retiring as chief constable. Mr Gregory had drawn heavily upon the report of Mr Colin Sampson, who as deputy chief constable in 1981 conducted an internal inquiry into what went wrong with the investigation. From July 1976 to March 1980, Mr Sampson had been deputy chief constable of Nottinghamshire. A summary of his report was prepared for the local police committee in December 1981. This summary was itself kept confidential – until 1983, when Mr Gregory was said to have collected £40,000 for his account of the Ripper case. The sixty-six-page summary was then made public by the West Yorkshire police committee. It is referred to in the text notes as the Sampson Report.

A crucial archive was made available through the generosity of Professor Michael Green, who secured from his former colleague, Professor David Gee, permission for me to examine his personal papers on the Yorkshire Ripper inquiry. Permission was also obtained from the coroners for the various jurisdictions in which Peter Sutcliffe had murdered his victims.

Professor Gee's papers included a comprehensive collection of scenes-of-crime and autopsy photographs and reports, as well as reports from the forensic science service and other memoranda and correspondence connected with the case. I am particularly grateful to Professor Gee for the privilege he extended me. He died in 2001. I remember him as a quiet man who was utterly, utterly discreet. He never gave interviews. Only years later, reading his papers, could I begin to understand the burden that had rested on his shoulders and those of his colleagues in the police and forensic science services. I am grateful too to Professor Green for loaning me certain of his personal papers and records.

As a result of placing a small notice in *Navy News*, several former members of HMS *Albatross* contacted me via letter and telephone to offer details of the ship's involvement before, during and after D-Day. These details are given in the text notes. Mrs Margaret Oldfield had informed me that her husband served on the vessel.

During the research for this book I was privileged to be allowed access to Mr Lawrence Byford's 159-page report on the Ripper investigation, which he presented to the Home Secretary at the end of 1981. This report is a key document for anyone wishing to understand the Yorkshire Ripper investigation. The confidence placed in me by those individuals, pivotal in the Yorkshire Ripper case, who think the full story should now be told is greatly appreciated. They know who they are and how grateful I am for their trust.

TEXT NOTES AND REFERENCES

Chapter 1: Contact and Exchange

p. 1, '8.10 a.m.': Dennis Hoban, official diary, recording two murders that day – one at 1.10 a.m. and the McCann murder at 8.10 a.m. Also, notes of interview about Hoban family life with his son, Richard Hoban, regarding domestic arrangements at home and his father's career in the police service.

p. 1, 'up since 1 a.m.': Michael Nicholson, *The Yorkshire Ripper*, p. 15: 'A woman strangled a man to death in a telephone box. The bizarre incident rated no more than a brief mention in the *Yorkshire Evening Post* and the subsequent arrest justified a mere couple of lines of reporting.'

p. 3, 'with her throat cut': Professor Michael Green, 'Mad, Bad and Dangerous to Know', lecture notes, pp. 4–5.

p. 5, 'over their pyjamas': Roger Cross, *The Yorkshire Ripper*, p. 22.

p. 5, 'bit of a nuisance': Professor David Gee, 'Pathological Aspects of the Yorkshire Ripper Case', lecture to the London Medico-Legal Society, 1982, notes, p. 2.

p. 7, 'surface of the skin': Autopsy Report on Wilma McCann by Professor David Gee, Leeds City Mortuary, No. 20577, 30 October 1975.

p. 7, ' "affected in this way" ': E-mail to the author from former Chief Superintendent David Zackrisson, 26 June 2001.

p. 9, 'in the garden': Nicholson, *The Yorkshire Ripper*, p. 30.

p. 10, 'in the evening': Information about Wilma's background from 'Antecedents – Wilma McCann', supplied to the author by West Yorkshire Metropolitan Police, 25 March 1999; also Yallop, *Deliver Us from Evil*, p. 33; Kinsley and Smyth, *I'm Jack*; and Cross, *The Yorkshire Ripper*.

p. 12, 'cancel the appointment': Hoban, official diary 1975, entries for November.

p. 13, 'Meanwood Road': *Regina v. Sutcliffe*, Opening Remarks (by Prosecuting Counsel), document prepared by West Yorkshire police for the Director of Public Prosecutions, p. 17, quoted in part by the Attorney General, Sir Michael Havers, QC, at Sutcliffe's trial.

p. 14, 'Hillman Avenger': Confidential West Yorkshire Metropolitan Police Report: *Regina v. Peter William Sutcliffe*: Report Relating to Murders/Assaults in West Yorkshire and Lancashire Police Areas (the 'Yorkshire Ripper Enquiry)', Detective Chief Superintendent J. Hobson, para. 119 – 'Red Avenger Enquiry' (D.74 McCann).

p. 15, '"great detective"': Opinions from Dick Holland, interviewed 29.8.98, Tape No. 2, transcript, p. 14.

p. 16, '"the injuries"': Gee, 'Pathological Aspects', lecture notes, p. 3.

p. 18, 'body of a woman': *Regina v. Sutcliffe*, Opening Remarks, p. 20.

p. 21, 'early 1970s': 'Force Names New CID Chief', *Yorkshire Post*, 4 May 1973.

p. 21, 'rarely apologized for anything': The source of this information preferred to remain anonymous and I have respected that request.

p. 22, 'among other details': W. J. Chisum and B. Turvey, 'Evidence Dynamics: Locard's Exchange Principle and

Crime Reconstruction', *Journal of Behaviour Profiling*, Vol. 1, No. 1 (January 2000).

p. 22, '"from his finds"': ibid., quoting T. Reik, *The Unknown Murderer*, Prentice-Hall, New York, 1945. Theodore Reik, a professor of psychoanalysis at Vienna University, was an early disciple of Sigmund Freud and a passionate advocate of the use of objectivity and logic in the investigation of crime and criminals. 'The object of the criminologist's reasoning is knowledge of a material event and the finding of an unknown person. Cool, objective thought, re-examination of facts according to the rules of logic, raisonment is the pivot of the detectives' mental process.'

p. 23, '"long-distance lorry driver"': Gee told his audience at the Medico-Legal Society in London during his 1982 lecture: 'It's a little eerie now to recall that, with those things in mind [e.g. the kind of weapons the killer used], Dennis Hoban, the Chief Superintendent in charge of the case, who subsequently died, suggested a long-distance lorry driver as the possible identity of the assailant.' 'Pathological Aspects', lecture notes, p. 3. Another source: 'The Scientific Investigation of Crime: some preliminary notes' by S. S. Kind. After the completion of his work with the rest of Byford's team analysing the Ripper case, Professor Kind noted his immediate thinking in a four-page memorandum dated 18 July 1982. Later he expanded on this theme, as well as the lessons he learned during his years as a forensic scientist, in his book *The Scientific Investigation of Crime*, pp. 32–3.

p. 24, 'what had caused them': Gee, 'Pathological Aspects', lecture notes, p. 3. See also letters to eminent professors of forensic pathology from Gee's Yorkshire Ripper archive. Several made guesses but few proved correct. It turned out to be a Phillips screwdriver.

p. 24, 'fracture of the skull was visible': Autopsy report on Emily Jackson, p. 5.

p. 24, 'along the ground': Gee, 'Pathological Aspects', lecture notes, p. 3.

p. 25, 'most of them': ibid., p. 10.

p. 26, ' "liked to go to public houses" ': Calendar programme, 21 January 1976, Yorkshire Television, Yorkshire Ripper archive, Roll No. 1, item 1.

p. 28, ' "pray they catch him" ': *Leeds Evening Post*, 22 January 1976.

p. 29, ' "wasn't that kind of person" ': ibid.

p. 29, 'man who killed his wife': Off-the-record interview given to researcher for ITV documentary, *MANHUNT: The Search for the Yorkshire Ripper*, October 1998.

p. 30, 'Emily's handbag': Report by Superintendent A. Charlesworth, 10 December 1980.

p. 30, ' "she met her killer" ': Kinsley and Smyth, *I'm Jack*, p. 57.

p. 30, 'getting into a Land-Rover': West Yorkshire police, 'Ripper Enquiry', p. 6.

p. 30, 'driving while disqualified': Memorandum for the *Sunday Times* INSIGHT team, 1981, by the author. Copy held in author's Yorkshire Ripper personal archive.

p. 31, ' "difficult to follow the tracks of all" ': 'The Yorkshire Ripper', lecture notes, p. 8.

p. 32, ' "from the wound!" ': Letter to Professor D. J. Gee from Professor Keith Mant, 2 March 1976, in Gee's Yorkshire Ripper file.

p. 32, ' "a dark spot" ': Calendar news item, Yorkshire Television, Yorkshire Ripper archive, Roll No. 1, item 4.

p. 33, ' "the frenzied attack" ': Hoban interviewed by Alan Hardwick of Calendar News, 28 January 1976, Yorkshire Television, Yorkshire Ripper archive, Roll No. 1, item 4.

p. 33, 'issued a dark warning': quotes from Yallop, *Deliver Us from Evil*, p. 66, and Kinsley and Smyth, *I'm Jack*, p. 57.

Chapter 2: The Diabetic Detective

p. 35, 'council house waiting list': Denis Healey, *The Time of My Life*, p. 137.

p. 36, '"information from his snouts"': Richard Hoban interview, 27 April 2001.

p. 38, '"failed to adapt"': Healey, *The Time of My Life*, p. 136.

p. 41, 'guided tour': Richard Hoban interview, 27 April 2001.

p. 42, 'to save money': West Yorkshire Metropolitan Police, Annual Report, 1978, p. 66.

p. 43, 'West Riding clearing house': Report of the Parliamentary Committee on the Police Service, House of Commons, 1920, paras. 95–6.

p. 44, 'a witness told the committee': Sir Leonard Dunning in evidence to the Parliamentary Committee on the Police Service, Minutes of Evidence, 8 April 1919, para. 1995.

p. 44, '"Four years' experience"': Report, 1913, by Colonel Eden, Inspector of Constabulary for the Northern District, quoted in evidence to the Committee on the Police Service, 1920.

p. 46, 'educational standards': Minutes of Evidence to the Parliamentary Committee, 1919, para. 2003.

p. 47, '"one to four O levels"': Royal Commission on the Police, Cmmd 1728, May 1962, para. 308.

p. 47, 'twenty years hence': ibid., para. 312.

p. 47, '"They preferred to educate"': Former Detective Chief Superintendent David Zackrisson, interviewed in 1998.

p. 49, 'other side of the county': Dick Holland, interviewed 26 June 1998, regarding his own position as a Huddersfield Borough policeman at the time of the first amalgamation in 1968 when he turned down three promotions because it involved being moved from the city in which he grew up and where his children went to school.

p. 49, '"only two sizes"': ibid.

p. 50, 'ACC position': Richard Hoban, interviewed 27 April 2001.

p. 51, 'one of Hoban's contemporaries': Sir Andrew Sloan, former chief constable of Strathclyde, interviewed by telephone, 29 November 2000.

p. 52, 'married life': Interview with Mrs Hoban, *Yorkshire Post*, 27 October 1979.

p. 52, 'proper holiday': ibid.

p. 52, '"withdrawal symptoms"': Tape-recorded interview with Hoban, 28 October 1998.

p. 53, 'paid by the gang': Tape-recorded interview with Holland, 15 September 1998.

p. 53, '"more than just a job"': 'Crime-buster in the Sheepskin', *Sunday Express*, 1965.

p. 54, '"people with a broader perspective"': Telephone interview with Sir Andrew Sloan, December 1999.

p. 55, 'finding killers without a personal motive': G. K. Chesterton's famous dictum on this theme was: 'Society is at the mercy of a murderer without a motive', quoted by Sir Robert Mark, former Commissioner of the Metropolitan Police, in his autobiography, *In the Office of Constable*, p. 186.

p. 56, '"Can you pick the people"': Tape-recorded interview with John Domaille, 7 November 1998.

p. 56, '"Dennis did it"': Tape-recorded interview with John Domaille, 21 March 2000.

p. 57, '"I believe it works"': *Daily Star*, 23 May 1981, quoting an interview Hoban gave to the *Yorkshire Post* in 1975.

p. 57, 'memories were still fresh': *Yorkshire Evening Post*, 2 April 1974.

p. 60, 'on the dead woman': *Yorkshire Evening Post*, 21 July 1971.

p. 61, '"their own front room"': Article by Dennis Hoban in the *Police Journal*, Vol. XLX, No. 1, pp. 37–44 (January–March 1977).

Chapter 3: 'A Man with a Beard'

p. 63, 'the first': West Riding Regional Criminal Record Office file WRC, No. 5235–65.

p. 63, 'the second': Central Criminal Record Office, file No. 49110/65D.

p. 68, 'she never heard from the police again': The interview with the woman was conducted by Jane Bower for the documentary *MANHUNT: The Search for the Yorkshire Ripper*, shown on ITV in September 1999. In late 1981 the photofit provided for the police was one of a collection of sixteen similar photofits, all closely resembling Peter Sutcliffe, included in Mr Lawrence Byford's Report to the Home Secretary.

p. 69, '"nothing doing in Silsden"': *Daily Mail*, Weekend Section, 24 April 1999.

p. 69, '"About a mile"': *Yorkshire Evening Press*, 12 September 1975.

p. 71, '"squelching with blood"': ibid.

p. 71, 'a hole in the top of her head': *Daily Mail*, 25 November 1992.

p. 72, '"never expected it to be so bad"': Interview with Jane Bower during research for the *MANHUNT* film, November 1998.

p. 72, 'never shown publicly': *Keighley News*, 2 September 1975.

p. 73, 'finding Holroyd House': ibid.

p. 73, 'search proved fruitless': *Keithley News*, 11 September 1975.

p. 73, 'It appears that Sutcliffe': See Gordon Burn, '*Somebody's Husband, Somebody's Son*', p. 105.

p. 74, ' "It might be interesting" ': Letter to West Yorkshire police, 19 August 1975, regarding Mrs Olive Smelt, from Dr M. A. Green, in Gee's Yorkshire Ripper archive.

p. 74, 'dressed in dark jeans': Byford Report, p. 54.

p. 75, 'injuries to her head': ibid.

p. 75, 'J. B. Priestley put it': Quoted in Michael Nally, 'Hunt for the Ripper', *New Society*, 14 June 1979.

p. 76, 'Chapeltown': Max Farrar, 'Constructing and Deconstructing "Community": case study of a multi-cultural inner city area: Chapeltown, Leeds, 1972–1997', Ph.D. thesis, Leeds Metropolitan University, July 1999.

p. 76, 'to Roundhay Park for sex': West Yorkshire Metropolitan Police file for the Director of Public Prosecutions, 1981, p. 22.

p. 76, 'masturbated in front of her': See Roger Cross, *The Yorkshire Ripper*, pp. 32 and 72, and the *Sunday Mirror*, 7 June 1981.

p. 77, ' "come back to see if I were dead" ': Interview for *MANHUNT* documentary, January 1999.

p. 77, ' "like my brain is bursting" ': ibid.

p. 78, 'mislead the investigation': Sampson Report, October 1981.

p. 78, : 'application was rejected': Barbara Jones, *Voices from an Evil God*, p. 91.

Chapter 4: Tracks in the Grass

p. 79, ' "Leeds is far away" ': J. S. Fletcher, *A Picturesque History of Yorkshire*, p. 382.

p. 80, ' "brushed the hair to one side" ': 'Lovers Could Help Trap Savage Leeds Killer', *Yorkshire Evening Post*, 7 February 1977.

p. 81, 'body lay on the grass': Autopsy Report on Irene Richardson by Professor David Gee, Leeds City Mortuary, No. 22, 285, 6 February 1977, dated 18 March 1977.

p. 82, 'end of her monthly cycle': Forensic analysis report by Edward John Mitchell, Higher Scientific Officer, Home Office Forensic Science Laboratory, Harrogate; ref. C.77/0796, 16 February 1977, in Gee's Yorkshire Ripper archive.

p. 84, 'Irene's home address': Detective Chief Superintendent Jim Hobson, interviewed by Yorkshire Television, 7 February 1977; Calendar Yorkshire Television Yorkshire Ripper Archive, Roll No. 1/5.

p. 84, 'playing truant': Interview with Irene Richardson's sister, Mrs Helen Smith, Sheffield, 13 October 1998.

p. 85, ' "Dennis" ': See report by Superintendent A. Charlesworth, 10 December 1980, p. 7.

p. 85, 'when she was four': 'Lost Mum was Victim of Ripper', *Leeds Evening Post*, 13 April 1989.

p. 86, 'a man she had been living with': *Yorkshire Post*, 8 February 1977.

p. 86, 'practically destitute': *Yorkshire Evening Post*, 8 February 1977.

p. 87, 'out on Saturday nights': *Yorkshire Evening Post*, 7 February 1977.

p. 88, 'definitely aspermous': Harrogate Forensic Science Laboratory Report, ref. C.77/0796, p. 4.

p. 88, '"into the underlying brain"': Autopsy Report on Irene Richardson, p. 9.

p. 89, 'dimensions of a hammer head': Gee, 'The Yorkshire Ripper', lecture notes, p. 10.

p. 89, '"a clear pattern"': Gee, 'Pathological Aspects', lecture notes.

p. 91, 'Jimmy Saville': *Sun*, 7 February 1977.

p. 91, 'striking similarities': 'Ripper Hunt: Attack Girl Is Sought', *Yorkshire Evening Post*, 10 February 1977.

p. 92, 'the murder of Mrs Richardson': ibid.

p. 92, 'an eminent biographer': Young, *One of Us*, p. 262.

p. 92, 'Hobson briefed the media': 'Murder: New Clues from Attack Girl', *Yorkshire Evening Post*, 11 February 1977.

p. 93, 'police did not believe': Sampson Report, p. 21, says: 'The photofit as it transpired was a good likeness of Sutcliffe but, due to the circumstances of and surrounding the attack on Miss Claxton, the incident was not treated as part of the series and the value of the description and photofit was lost.'

p. 93, '" warn them of the dangers"': *Yorkshire Evening Post*, 11 February 1977.

p. 94, 'a system of "flagging"': Nicholson, *The Yorkshire Ripper*, p. 155, quoting a detailed account of the investigation by John Du Rose: 'I wanted the whole of West London to be flooded with police and it was.' .

p. 94, '"a prostitute was the victim"': *Yorkshire Evening Post*, 8 February 1977.

p. 94, '"Mr Hobson said"': *Yorkshire Evening Post*, 9 February 1977.

p. 95, 'displaced in a similar way': Post-Mortem Report on Joan May Harrison, carried out at Preston Royal Infirmary, 23 November 1975, by Dr J. G. Benstead, North-West Home

Office Forensic Science Laboratory and Department of Pathology, Southport General Infirmary. See also Sampson Report, p. 17.

p. 95, 'with the zip opened': Report of Superintendent A. Charlesworth, 10 December 1980, para. 4.

p. 97, 'mathematical probabilities': R. J. Grogan, 'Tyre Marks as Evidence', paper presented to the Eighth International Association of Forensic Sciences, Wichita, Kansas, 22–26 May 1978, for Tyre Technical Division, Dunlop Ltd.

p. 98, ' "The marks left by tyres" ': Professor Stuart Kind, interviewed 27 June 1998.

p. 101, 'Sutcliffe's white Ford Corsair': Byford Report, para. 20, p. 9.

Chapter 5: Impressions in Blood

p. 104, ' "I've always been very keen" ': John Domaille, interviewed 7 November 1998.

p. 105, 'The main room contained a bed': A complete set of 'scenes of crime' pictures from the Atkinson murder was found in Professor Gee's Yorkshire Ripper archives and the description of the room is partially based on these and his autopsy report, plus interviews with John Domaille and Russell Stockdale.

p. 107, 'the body twisted': Professor David Gee, Autopsy Report on Patricia Atkinson, Bradford city mortuary, ref. 22,594E, 13 June 1977.

p. 107, 'Stockdale knew from experience' *et seq.*: Russell Stockdale, interview 9 November 1998, Culham Science Park, Abingdon, Oxfordshire.

p. 110, 'sequence of events': Russell Stockdale, Report on Patricia Atkinson Murder Scene, Home Officer Forensic Science Laboratory, Wetherby, ref. C.77/1890, 11 May 1977.

p. 112, ' "So far we had" ': Gee, 'Pathological Aspects', lecture notes, p. 5.

p. 113, ' "I was quite wrong" ': Gee, 'The Yorkshire Ripper', lecture notes, pp. 12–13.

p. 113, ' "This was a brutal murder" ': Domaille, interviewed for Calendar News, 26 April 1977, in Calendar Yorkshire Television Yorkshire Ripper Archive, Roll No. 1/6, Record 33858.

p. 114, 'She and Ramen': 'Antecedents Patricia Atkinson', provided by West Yorkshire Metropolitan Police to the author, 25 March 1999.

p. 115, 'They had sex': Superintendent A. Charlesworth, Report, 10 December 1980, para. 7.

p. 115, 'things got rowdy': ibid.

p. 115, 'Took all her clothes off': Sue Neave, former policewoman who worked in the incident room on the Atkinson murder, interviewed 2 November 1998.

p. 115, 'argument with the manager': 'Police Keep Open Mind on Prostitute Murders Link', Yorkshire Post, 26 April 1977.

p. 115, 'twenty measures of spirit': Superintendent A. Charlesworth, Report, 10 December 1980.

p. 116, ' "they actually do" ': ibid.

p. 117, 'nine fingerprints': Superintendent A. Charlesworth, Report, 10 December 1980.

p. 118, 'The man fled': Byford Report, Figure 11, p. 54.

p. 118, 'Nearly 1,250 Land-Rovers': West Yorkshire Metropolitan Police Introductory Report: 'Murders/Assaults in West Yorkshire and Lancashire Police areas', 1981, section dealing with Vehicle Observations and Sightings: Land-Rovers (D.76 Jackson and Atkinson).

p. 118, 'All to no avail': ibid., section dealing with relevant statistics: 'Patricia Atkinson'.

p. 119, 'I tried': Domaille, interviewed 7 November 1998; see also Sampson Report, p. 8.

p. 121, 'For the conscientious officer': The intellectual rationale for this kind of inquiry is discussed in some considerable detail in Kind, *The Scientific Investigation of Crime*, pp. 134–44.

p. 121, 'with no separate name index': Byford Report, pp. 10 and 48.

p. 122, 'half these crimes were being solved': West Yorkshire Metropolitan Police, Annual Report, 1978, p. 78.

p. 123, ' "No Minister of the Crown" ': Quoted in ibid., p. 20. For a detailed analysis of the doctrine of constabulary independence, the need for an apolitical police service and the rights of chief constables, see Oliver, *Police, Government and Accountability*, p. 11.

p. 124, 'That his response was': Holland interview.

p. 124, 'This unprecedented move': Young, *One of Us*, p. 237.

p. 124, 'It had been Oldfield's ambition': Margaret Oldfield, interviewed 25 July 2001.

p. 125, ' "He could go bloody mad" ': Holland, interviewed 18 July 2001.

p. 126, ' "We had to ring in" ': Holland, interviewed 29 August 1998.

p. 128, 'HMS *Albatross*': Interviews with Mr Ray Gratwick of Chichester and Mr Phil Mortimer of Chandlers Ford, both former members of the crew of HMS *Albatross*; crew and with Mr Frank Roberts of Blackpool, who was on the minesweeper, HMS *Acacia*, which escorted the *Albatross* back to Portsmouth.

p. 129, 'stress-related illness': Margaret Oldfield, interviewed following a conversation she had with her sister-in-law, Mrs Irene Oldfield.

p. 130, 'The allegations': Holland, interviewed 29 August 1998.

p. 131, '"made a tactical bloomer"': Holland, interviewed 18 July 2001.

p. 131, '"tipped off the thieves"': ibid.

p. 133, 'his wife reflected': Margaret Oldfield, interviewed 25 July 2001.

p. 135, '"He didn't like post-mortems"': Holland, interviewed 18 July 2001.

p. 135, '"I will never forget"': 'Terrorists Should Die – Police Chief', *Yorkshire Evening Post*, 7 July 1976.

p. 135, '"Couldn't stand the sound of ticking"': Margaret Oldfield, interviewed 25 July 2001.

Chapter 6: A Fresh Start

p. 136, 'two jobs back-to-back': Holland, interviewed 29 June 1998.

p. 136, '"He knew me and the way I worked"': Holland, interviewed 15 September 1998.

p. 138, 'Oldfield wanted a fresh start': Holland, interviewed 29 June 1998.

p. 140, 'She lay face down': This description of the crime scene is from Gee's Autopsy Report on Jayne Michelle Mac-Donald, ref. 22824.

p. 141, 'The broken bottle top': ibid.; but see also Gee, 'Pathological Aspects', lecture notes, p. 6: the bottle top 'had simply become embedded in [the chest] from among the junk on the ground'.

p. 142, '"She had first been hit"': Gee, Autopsy Report, ref. 22824, p. 16.

p. 143, 'all he would say': 'Cause of Death: A Broken Heart', *Yorkshire Post*, 23 May 1981.

p. 143, 'having regular intercourse': Superintendent A. Charlesworth, Report, 10 December 1980; Section 8 deals with the murder of Jayne MacDonald.

p. 144, ' "killed my Jayne" ': *Yorkshire Evening Post*, 29 June 1977.

p. 144, ' "The husband is very bad" ': MacDonald family doctor interviewed for Calendar News, 28 June 1977, Calendar Yorkshire Television Yorkshire Ripper Archive, Roll No. 2, item 3.

p. 145, 'When they reached': *Yorkshire Post*, report of the inquest on Jayne MacDonald, at which Mark Jones gave evidence, 16 September 1978.

p. 146, 'Jones later told detectives': Holland interviewed 29 June 1998.

p. 146, 'around 2 a.m. she had heard': Peter Kinsley and Frank Smyth, *I'm Jack*, p. 78.

p. 147, 'Oldfield was desperate': 'Police Seek Vital 50 in Killer Hunt', *Yorkshire Evening Post*, 6 July 1977.

p. 147, ' "My problem is" ': George Oldfield, interviewed on Calendar News, 8 July 1977, Calendar Yorkshire Television Yorkshire Ripper Archive, Roll No. 2, item 5.

p. 148, ' "I believe the man" ': Calendar News, Yorkshire Television Yorkshire Ripper archive, Roll No. 2, item 2, 28 June 1977.

p. 149, ' "There is no doubt" ': 'We Need Your Help – Plea', *Yorkshire Evening Press*, 30 June 1977.

p. 149, ' "We believe" ': 'Women Asked: Did You Turn Down the Ripper?', *Yorkshire Post*, 1 July 1977.

p. 149, 'she told a reporter': *Daily Telegraph*, 28 June 1977.

p. 149, ' "They will not be wasting our time" ': 'Ripper Hunt Police Study Car Numbers', *Yorkshire Evening Post*, 2 July 1977.

p. 150, ' "Their reaction was hostile" ': Holland, interviewed 29 June 1998.

p. 151, ' "The public have the power" ': *Yorkshire Post*, 1 July 1977.

p. 151, ' "I am no more concerned" ': 'Rees Meets Police Team in "The Ripper" Murder Room', *Yorkshire Post*, 23 July 1977.

p. 152, ' "The police came in" ': The interview was included in *Five Years of Terror*, a Yorkshire Television networked documentary transmitted on ITV, 22 May 1981.

p. 153, 'Twenty-five years later': Interview notes by Jane Bower, associate producer, *MANHUNT: The Search for the Yorkshire Ripper*, shown on the ITV network, September 1999.

p. 153, 'According to a police report': 'Attempted Killing of Maureen Long', WYMP/DPP file, 1981, para. 49.

p. 154, 'He was certain': ibid.: 'Ford Cortina Mark II (D.93 Long).

p. 154, ' "All I remember" ': Transcript of filmed interview with Maureen Long for *MANHUNT* documentary, 7 December 1998.

p. 155, 'lucky to be alive': A copy of a statement by Gee, 'Living Ripper Victim: Mrs Maureen Long', ref. F.M. 22,870A, is contained in his Yorkshire Ripper archives. He mentioned her luck in surviving the attack in 'Physical Aspects', lecture notes, p. 9.

p. 156, 'top of their list': Sampson Report, p. 9; and Charlesworth, Report, 10 December 1980.

p. 156, ' "He allowed them" ': Holland, interviewed 29 June 1998, p. 3.

p. 157, 'approaching £1 million': Chief Constable Ronald Gregory gave this figure to his police authority – *Yorkshire Post*, 8 March 1978. It had taken up half a million working hours. 'We are very close to him,' he said. 'We have never been closer. We just need that extra bit of information.'

p. 158, ' "He was not arrested" ': Confidential source.

p. 158, 'Holland admitted': Telephone interviews with Dick Holland 31 July 2002 and ex-ACC John Domaille 30 July 2002.

p. 159, ' "It was a nightmare" ': 'Cabbie: I Am Not The Ripper: CID Kept Quizzing Me' – Hawkshaw interviewed in the *Sun*, 8 March 1978. He said in the interview: 'The police have never made me do anything against my will. I have always cooperated.'

p. 161, ' "She didn't deserve what happened" ': Megan Winterburn, interviewed 2 November 1998.

p. 161, ' "Mr Domaille said" ': Megan Winterburn, interviewed for the *MANHUNT* documentary, 11 January 1999.

p. 164, ' "desperate for men" ': Holland, interviewed by telephone, 18 July 2001; and interviewed for *MANHUNT* documentary, Roll No. 22.

p. 166, 'the rest were never found': Sampson Report, 1983, p. 9.

Chapter 7: Punter's Money

p. 168, 'Parliament was debating': *Hansard*, 4 August 1976, col. 2905.

p. 169, 'senior Home Office scientists had just departed': Byford Report, para. 464, p. 125.

p. 169, 'at Harwell in Berkshire': Byford Report, p. 341.

p. 169, 'AWRE began a top-secret project': Peter Wright, *Spycatcher*, Viking Penguin Inc., New York, 1987, pp. 195–6.

p. 170, 'turn the offer down': Byford Report, op. cit.

p. 173, 'nightmares for years to come': *Daily Mirror*, 24 March 1999. Jones became an actor in later years and joined the cast of ITV's *Coronation Street*, playing the role of Les Battersby.

p. 174, 'a really bad body': Jack Ridgway, interviewed 21 September 2001.

p. 174, 'small pieces of paint on the skin': Witness statement by Reuben Cyril Woodcock, 15 December 1977, regarding the post-mortem on Jean Bernadette Jordan.

p. 175, '"Most of the top clothing"': Tony Fletcher, *Memories of Murder*, p. 155.

p. 175, '"But lying where it was"': Ridgway, interviewed 21 September 2001.

p. 176, 'spotted her wandering about': 'Children of Ripper Victim in Hospital', *Manchester Evening News*, 3 April 1979; see also Kinsley and Smyth, *I'm Jack*, p. 89.

p. 176, 'Dental records': Fletcher, *Memories of Murder*, p. 156.

p. 177, 'trying to settle down': 'Ripper Girl Was To Give Up Vice', *Manchester Evening News*, 31 May 1978; see also Kinsley and Smyth, *I'm Jack*, p. 89.

p. 177, 'saying she was going': West Yorkshire Metropolitan Police File for the DPP, 1981, para. 53; see also Michael Nicholson, *The Yorkshire Ripper*, p. 69.

p. 177, 'she had gone': Kinsley and Smyth, *I'm Jack*, p. 88.

p. 178, '"Some tend to be a little remote"': Ridgway, interviewed 6 October 1998.

p. 179, 'Woodcock began to itemize': Witness statement by Woodcock, 15 December 1977, pp. 3–4.

p. 181, 'She had then been hidden': Fletcher, *Memories of Murder*, p. 155.

p. 181, '"I told him we had a Ripper murder"': Ridgway, interviewed 6 October 1998.

p. 182, 'He refused to confirm': Kinsley and Smyth, *I'm Jack*, p. 93.

p. 186, 'All the money': Ridgway, interviewed 6 October 1998. Accompanied by Grange Catlow, the two officers, by now long retired, spent the day with me while I was producing the documentary: *MANHUNT: The Search for the Yorkshire Ripper*. Although neither wanted to appear in the film, both were happy to talk at length about the case to ensure that what we said was factually correct.

p. 187, ' "We are looking" ': '£5 Note May Lead to Killer', *Yorkshire Evening Post*, 27 October 1977; see also *Yorkshire Post*, 28 October 1977: '£5 Note Clue New Lead in Ripper-style Killing'.

p. 187, ' "I believe the killer" ': Kinsley and Smyth, *I'm Jack*, p. 95.

p. 187, ' "We have been quite surprised" ': *Daily Telegraph*, 29 October 1977: '£5 Clue in Murder Hunt'.

p. 189, ' "They wanted us to try" ': Maureen Banham, interviewed 24 October 1998.

p. 191, ' "a sort of slap on the hand" ': Simon Steward, interviewed 26 October 1998. Because computers run the operation today, it would be virtually impossible to repeat the exercise.

p. 191, ' "The police were very confident" ': Ian Sturrock, interviewed 23 October 1998.

p. 192, ' "The cashiers at the Shipley branch" ': Ridgway, interviewed 6 October 1998.

p. 195, 'his reference was "F44" ': Byford Report, para 240, p. 71.

p. 196, ' "had taken some of his relatives home" ': ibid., para. 242.

p. 197, 'No person would be seen twice': ibid., para. 244.

p. 197, 'she signed a statement confirming': ibid.

p. 199, 'a multicoloured man-made fibre': Domaille, review notes of Jean Jordan's murder.

p. 199, 'they had almost certainly interviewed': Yallop, *Deliver Us from Evil*, p. 143, and Cross, *The Yorkshire Ripper*, p. 104.

Chapter 8: 'The Job Is Life; Life Is the Job

p. 201, 'One husband in the mid 1970s': Paul Harrison, 'The New Red Light Districts', *New Society*, 10 July 1975, p. 70.

p. 201, 'legalize brothels': Helen Roberts, '"Trap" the Ripper', *New Society*, 6 April 1978.

p. 201, 'a view shared by Ronald Gregory': 'Police Chief Calls For Prostitution To Be Legalized', *The Times*, 15 April 1978.

p. 201, 'took their clients to a house': 'Women "Afraid of Ripper"', *Yorkshire Post*, 22 February 1978.

p. 203, 'The numbers of women convicted': Roberta Perkins, *Working Girls*, p. 69.

p. 203, 'The middle-class shoppers in Manchester"': ibid.

p. 204, '"Each prostitute is"': Lionel James, 'On the Game', *New Society*, 24 May 1973, p. 427.

p. 205, '"Police believe the man"': 'Trap the Ripper'.

p. 207, 'This blow had depressed the skull': *Regina v. Sutcliffe* Opening Remarks, p. 40; and report by Gee on Marilyn Moore's injuries in his private Yorkshire Ripper file.

p. 207, 'the giveaway for Gee': Gee, 'Pathological Aspects', lecture.

p. 208, '"He was good looking"': *Daily Mail*, 2 December 1978.

p. 209, '"I saw figures"': *Yorkshire Evening Press*, 15 December 1977.

p. 209, 'reduced the number of possible vehicles': Original notes by the author in the files of the *Sunday Times* INSIGHT team briefing document in the *Sunday Times* archives.

p. 211, 'suffered constant nightmares': *Daily Mail*, Weekend Section, 24 April 1999.

p. 212, '"If her photofit"': Sampson Report, p. 50.

p. 212, '"She went for the Morris Oxford"': Holland, interviewed for *MANHUNT* Yorkshire Television documentary.

p. 213, '"Detectives are a peculiar animal"': Detective Chief Superintendent Trevor Lapish, interviewed 6 January 1999.

p. 218, '"You walk down this bloody pavement"': Holland, interviewed 29 June 1968, p. 34.

p. 218, '"a bigger bastard"' *et seq.*: Holland, interviewed 29 August 1998, p. 15.

p. 222, 'had never heard the adage': Years later, in retirement, Dick Holland was in the middle of an academic course in horticulture when he said he only wished he had been subjected to the intellectual rigour of a university education when he left school. In his late 60s he had only just begun to understand that the mental stretching students are supposed to undergo equips them for solving all kinds of problems much later, developing their potential to step back from a subject and test empirical evidence objectively.

p. 222, '"I think that was fair"': Holland, interviewed 30 June 1998.

p. 224, '"hoping we would have an attack"': Holland, interviewed 30 June 1998.

p. 226, 'pursued and arrested the attacker': Holland, interviewed 30 June 1998.

Chapter 9: A Miserable Place To Die

p. 227, '"a short and sad life"': West Yorkshire Metropolitan Police file prepared for the DPP, 'Murder of Helen Rytka', paras. 63–5.

p. 228, '"THE YORKSHIRE RIPPER"': *Yorkshire Evening Post*, 10 February 1978.

p. 228, 'The twins shared a double bed': Witness statement by Rita Rosemary Rytka, 7 February 1978.

p. 231, 'black lace panties': Interview with Melvyn Clelland for *MANHUNT* documentary, 10 December 1998.

p. 234, 'According to his acolyte': Holland, interviewed 15 September 1998, transcript p. 117.

Autopsy Report on Helen Rytka by Professor David Gee, Huddersfield Royal Infirmary, No. 23, 666A, 4 February 1978.

p. 235, 'Ron Outtridge believed': Interim report *re* Helen Rytka, C.78/0529, 10 February 1978.

p. 236, '*Jimmy Young Show*': 'Ripper Appeal to Chat-show Wives', *Yorkshire Evening Post*, 10 February 1978.

p. 236, '"Their one dream"': 'Dewsbury Life of Ripper Victim Helen', *Dewsbury Reporter*, 10 February 1978.

p. 237, 'Oldfield's appeal': 'The Unhappy Life of Helen Rytka', *Yorkshire Post*, 7 February 1978.

p. 240, 'Task force officers visited': Holland, interviewed 30 June 1999; and original notes from 1981 *Sunday Times* INSIGHT team archives.

p. 242, 'Most owners were traced': Superintendent A. Charlesworth, Report, 10 December 1980, item 13: '31 January 1978 – Huddersfield Murder'.

p. 243, '"I would have thought"': Calendar News, 6 February 1978, in Calendar Yorkshire Television Yorkshire Ripper Archive, Roll No. 3, item 2.

p. 244, 'a £10,000 reward': ibid.

p. 244, '"I am satisfied"': *Huddersfield Daily Examiner*, 15 February 1978.

p. 245, 'Two walls of the Castlegate police station': *Huddersfield Daily Examiner*, 16 February 1978.

p. 246, 'a man was seen standing': Calendar News, 13 February 1978, in Calendar Yorkshire Television Yorkshire Ripper Archive, Roll No. 3e, item 6.

p. 246, ' "We are getting nearer and nearer" ': Calendar News, 15 February 1978, in Calendar Yorkshire Television Yorkshire Ripper Archive, Roll No. 3e, item 7.

p. 247, ' "For the first time" ': Holland, interviewed for *MANHUNT* documentary, Roll No. 22, p. 15.

p. 249, 'He didn't know the town': Richard Hoban, interviewed 27 April 2001: 'In all honesty when he moved to Bradford CID for a short time he was a fish out of water, he didn't know anyone, his environment was Leeds. He knew it inside out, back to front. The criminal fraternity knew him and he liked that status, wherever he went people knew who he was. He was "Leeds" right through to his bone marrow.'

p. 250, ' "He was in intensive care" ': Richard Hoban, interviewed 28 October 1998.

p. 250, 'He had been ill': Betty Hoban, interviewed in *Yorkshire Post*, 27 October 1979.

p. 251, 'worked himself to death': Obituary for Dennis Hoban, *Yorkshire Post*, 16 March 1978.

p. 251, ' "He should never have got married" ': Ibid.

p. 251, 'Old clients ... clubbed together': *Yorkshire Post*, 21 March 1978.

p. 251, 'The coroner issued an urgent appeal': ' "Turn In the Ripper" Plea by Coroner', *Yorkshire Post*, 7 March 1978.

Chapter 10: Chinese Walls

p. 254, 'remember Dennis as he was': 'Tributes as Hundreds Mourn Detective', *Yorkshire Post*, 21 March 1978; and *Yorkshire Evening Post*, 20 March 1978.

p. 254, 'An arm had been found': Lapish, interviewed 23.10.98.

p. 255, ' "She would not leave her children" ': 'Missing Mother "Would Never Forget Tots" ', *Bradford Telegraph and Argus*, 28 January 1978.

p. 256, ' "She just wouldn't leave them" ': ' "Ripper" Fears over Missing Mum', *Bradford Telegraph and Argus*, 28 January 1978.

p. 259, 'Gee and Lapish could see': Autopsy Report on Yvonne Anne Pearson by Professor David Gee, Huddersfield Royal Infirmary No. 23,902A, 26 March 1978, in Gee's Yorkshire Ripper archive. Also included in the archive were a full set of 'scenes of crime' and autopsy photographs, from which this description is compiled.

p. 260, ' "George made it plain" ' *et seq*: Lapish, interviewed 23 October 1998, tape 2, transcript p. 11.

p. 260, 'ball of horsehair': Autopsy Report on Yvonne Pearson, p. 7.

p. 261, ' "So badly damaged was the head" ': Gee, 'Pathological Aspects', lecture notes, p. 7.

p. 261, ' "These were obviously" ': 'The Yorkshire Ripper' lecture notes.

p. 261, ' "The absence of gross bleeding" ': Gee, 'Pathological Aspects' lecture notes, p. 11.

p. 262, ' "While I could not say" ': Gee in correspondence with Mr Harry Ognall, QC, prosecuting counsel in the trial of *Regina v. Sutcliffe*, 30 April 1981.

p. 263, 'He once told a colleague': Professor Michael Green, a close colleague of Gee's for twenty years, interviewed, 7 March 1999.

p. 264, ' "put there by someone else" ': ibid.

p. 265, 'why Gee was so admired': J. S. Scott, 'Appreciation on Retirement: Professor D. J. Gee', *University of Leeds Review*, Vol. 30, 1987, p. 289.

p. 266, 'By creating a basic pattern': Gee laid out this basic pattern in his lecture, 'Pathological Aspects'.

p. 267, '"They were massive injuries"': ibid.; also Gee, 'The Yorkshire Ripper', lecture notes, p. 16.

p. 268, 'one woman claimed': A. Charlesworth, Report, 10 December 1980, item 12: '21 January 1978 – Bradford Murder – Pearson, Yvonne', p. 13.

p. 268, '"She was well thought of"': Interview in Calendar News, 28 March 1978, in Calendar Yorkshire Television Yorkshire Ripper Archive, Roll No. 4, item 1.

p. 269, 'Her father didn't believe': 'Our Yvonne "By Missing Girl's Parents"', *Bradford Telegraph and Argus*, 28 January 1978.

p. 270, 'How the flies got on the corpse': Elcy C. Broadhead, 'Larvae of Trichocerid Flies Found on Human Corpse', *Entomologist's Monthly*, 27 October 1980, Vol. 116.

p. 270, '"From the sequence of events"': Russell Stockdale, Report, Home Office Forensic Science Laboratory, Wetherby, ref. C.78/1282, 27 April 1978, in Gee's Yorkshire Ripper archive.

p. 270, '"If you're going to be successful"': Lapish, interviewed 23 October 1998.

p. 271, '"We could have got the heads"': Lapish, interviewed for *MANHUNT* documentary, 6 January 1999.

p. 272, 'two and a half years on': 'Hunt for Ripper Has Cost £1.5m', *Daily Telegraph*, 15 April 1978.

Chapter 11: The Wrong Track
p. 274, 'The domestic demands': Domaille, interviewed 7 November 1998.

p. 275, '"as far as practicable"': Written statement of Chief

Superintendent Michael John Domaille to the Byford review team, p. 2.

p. 276, 'it was time to regroup': Gregory, interviewed on Calendar News, 14.4.78 in Calendar Yorkshire Television Yorkshire Ripper Archive, Roll No. 4, item 3.

p. 279, ' "We were influenced" ': Domaille statement to Byford Review, pp. 3–4.

p. 280, 'They came up with plans': Byford Report, para. 41.

p. 280, 'Information held': Byford Report, para. 343.

p. 280, '£240,000': Byford Report, para. 346.

p. 281, 'Skid marks': *Manchester Evening News*, 17 May 1978.

p. 281, 'confirmed she was dead': Fletcher, *Memories of Murder*, p. 161.

p. 281, 'in a semi-prone position': Statement of Dr Reuben Cyril Woodcock regarding Vera Millward's death, 12 June 1978.

p. 284, 'Yusef Sultan died': *Manchester Evening News*, 1989.

p. 284, 'she went to the Royal Infirmary': *Manchester Evening News*, 18 May 1978.

p. 284, ' "This man has destroyed my life" ': ibid.

p. 285, 'no "direct evidence" ': ' "Ripper" Killing Puzzles Police', *Yorkshire Post*, 8 November 1978.

p. 286, 'a confidential report': early draft of 'The Vehicle Tracking Inquiry', L. Emment, September 1981, which later formed part of the Byford Report.

p. 286, 'I was convinced': Ridgway, interviewed 1 October 2001.

p. 286, 'The West Yorkshire team continued to believe': Byford Report, para. 42, p. 85.

p. 288, '£1.5 million': Emment, 'The Vehicle Tracking Inquiry', p. 6.

p. 289, 'simply made a genuine mistake': Holland, interview.

p. 290, ' "Special Bulletin" ': Murders and Assaults upon

Women in the North of England', Criminal Intelligence Special Bulletin, West Yorkshire Metropolitan Police, June 1978.

p. 291, 'They had lived in Keighley': Antecedents details provided by Inspector John Mason, West Yorkshire Metropolitan Police.

p. 291, 'On American Independence Day': *Regina v. Sutcliffe* – 'Opening Remarks', Count 1: 'Attempting to murder Anna Rogulskyj, DPP document, 1981, p. 11.

p. 291, 'At 2.20 a.m.': 'Murders and Assaults upon Women in the North of England', Special Bulletin, p. 1.

p. 293, ' "It might be interesting" ': Letter to Detective Chief Inspector Dick Holland, West Yorkshire Metropolitan Police, Halifax, from Dr M. A. Green, 19 August 1975, 'Re Mrs Olive Smelt – 46 years', copy in Gee's Yorkshire Ripper archive.

p. 294, ' "But sometimes I get so depressed" ': 'Coming to Terms with the Ripper's Shadow', *Yorkshire Post*, 22 November 1979.

p. 294, 'asked for an autograph': Notes by Jane Bower of interview with Mrs Olive Smelt for *MANHUNT* documentary, September 1998; and 'After 25 Years, the Ripper Still Haunts Olive', *Daily Express*, 30 January 2000.

p. 294, ' "because of the way they were attacked" ': Domaille, interviewed for *MANHUNT* documentary, 14 December 1998, Roll No. 7, transcript p. 15.

p. 294, ' "We were very much influenced" ': Statement by Chief Superintendent M. J. Domaille to the Byford Review, pp. 3–5.

p. 295, 'came to regard Harrison as a definite victim': In respect of Joan Harrison, Domaille wrote in his report to the chief constable: 'It is not certain with regard to this offence whether it is in fact a "Ripper" murder' – Detective Chief Superintendent John Domaille, (confidential) 'Report re Prostitute Murders', 25 August 1978.

p. 296, 'a man who was a "B" secretor type blood grouping': *Sunderland Echo*, 28 June 1999.

p. 296, 'three small grazes . . . and three separate grazes': Post-Mortem Report on Joan Harrison by Dr J. G. Benstead, Department of Pathology, Southport General Infirmary, 23 November 1975, p. 2.

p. 296, '"We will be pressing on and on"': *Yorkshire Post*, 15 September 1978.

Chapter 12: Going Covert

p. 299, 'On no account could they let slip': Byford Report, para. 251, p. 73.

p. 300, 'Sonia Sutcliffe told': Reply quoted in the Byford Report, para. 253.

p. 301, 'If 'A' had had this information': Byford Report, para. 255, p. 73.

p. 301, 'A person could not be taken': Byford Report, para. 267.

p. 302, 'Holland instructed': Byford Report, para. 256, p. 74.

p. 302, 'This crucial breakdown': Byford Report, para. 259. The dangers of information arriving in an incident room and then being lost or not used to best advantage were outlined as early as 1968 by an academic who urged the use of computers in the fight against crime. See M. J. Willmer, 'Criminal Investigation from the Small Town to the Large Urban Conurbation', *British Journal of Criminology*, Vol. 8, 1968, p. 259–74: 'Computers could also be used, in theory, to assist the [intelligence] collator to make full use of all the information he receives. Not only can they be used to increase the probability that the collator will not miss a high value piece of information, but also they can be used to enable collators to work on data from many areas.'

p. 303, 'Her experience': Author's original notes in *Sunday Times* INSIGHT archive.

p. 306, 'All these sheets': Domaille, (confidential) 'Report re Prostitute Murders', paras. 26–30.

p. 307, 'special written instructions': Byford Report, para. 267, regarding 'Notes for Guidance when Dealing with Potential Suspects', July 1977.

p. 308, ' "If we got someone" ': Holland, interviewed for *MAN-HUNT* documentary, transcript pp. 11–12.

p. 309, ' "It meant you wouldn't" ': Laptew, interviewed for MANHUNT documentary, Roll No. 17, transcript p. 13.

p. 309, ' "It really hit me" ': Megan Winterburn, interviewed 2 November 1998.

p. 311, ' "There were people who went under" ': Megan Winterburn, *MANHUNT* documentary, interviewed 11 January 1999.

p. 311, 'Another superintendent': ibid.

p. 312, 'a malpractice prompted': Byford Report, paras. 47 and 380.

p. 313, 'By February 1979': *Evening News*, 26 February 1979.

p. 316, 'She was sitting on the bed': David Gee's report in relation to Miss B., ref. 25, 186A, in Gee's Yorkshire Ripper archive.

p. 316, 'Gee believed': Byford Report, para. 144; and David Gee's report in relation to Anne Rooney, ref. 25,205A, in Gee's Yorkshire Ripper archive.

p. 317, 'Gee could not determine': ibid.

p. 317, 'An official report would conclude': Byford Report, para. 194.

p. 317, 'The Home Office experts': Byford Report, paras. 130–31.

p. 319, 'As an official report later concluded': Byford Report, para. 147.

Chapter 13: 'He Comes from Sunderland'

p. 321, '"If there is a God"': 'A Leeds Mother's Prayer: This Monster Must Be Caught', *Leeds Evening Post*, 10 April 1979.

p. 321, '"I don't hate anyone"': 'Pride in New Watch Led to Death', *Halifax Courier*, 7 April 1979.

p. 321, '"He is someone's child"': *Leeds Evening Post*, 9 April 1979.

p. 322, '"We have a homicidal maniac"': 'Every Woman in Danger', *Yorkshire Post*, 7 April 1979.

p. 322, 'Tracey Browne . . . had flashbacks': *Daily Mail* weekend section, 24 April 1999.

p. 323, '"We applauded him"': Laptew interviewed September 2001, tape 1, transcript p. 6; and interviewed for *MAN-HUNT* Yorkshire Television documentary, Roll No. 18, transcript p. 15.

p. 323, '"When Josephine Whitaker was murdered"': Sue Neeve, interviewed 2 November 1998 and 11 January 1999.

p. 325, 'deeply attached to her grandparents': *Yorkshire Post*, 27 October 1979.

p. 325, 'during the early evening at home': Information from a confidential source.

p. 326, 'promising to see them as usual': *Yorkshire Post*, 27 October 1979.

p. 327, 'Finding Jo's bedroom empty': *Yorkshire Post*, 7 April 1979.

p. 329, 'Then Gee discovered': David Gee, autopsy report on Josephine Whitaker, ref. 25,350A.

p. 329, 'important pieces of evidence': Alfred Faragher, Interim Report by principal scientific officer, Home Office Laboratory, Wetherby, ref. C.79/1721, 20 August 1979; and Michael Green, 'Mad, Bad and Dangerous to Know' lecture, 5 April 1990.

p. 330, 'They tried comparing': Holland, interviewed for *MANHUNT* Yorkshire Television documentary, Roll No. 22.

p. 330, 'Close examination': 'Attacks by the So-called Yorkshire Ripper', confidential paper for the UK Forensic Science Service by R. E. Stockdale and R. A. Outteridge, 14 November 1979.

p. 331, 'tried to replicate the wounds': Gee, 'Pathological Aspects', lecture, p. 8.

p. 331, 'to test various weapons': Holland, interviewed for *MANHUNT* Yorkshire Television documentary, Roll. No. 22.

p. 331, 'Another witness came forward': 'Murder of Josephine Whitaker', West Yorkshire Metropolitan Police Report for the DPP, para. 70.

p. 332, 'Moore was convinced': 'Man Sought in Ripper Inquiry "Was Attacker"', *Guardian*, 11 April 1979.

p. 332, 'Much later it was discovered': Byford Report, para. 50, p. 15.

p. 333, 'the press was asked to stop publishing': Kinsley and Smyth, *I'm Jack*, p. 145.

p. 333, 'check their records': 'The Six Dates That Could Trap Ripper', *Yorkshire Post*, 12 April 1979.

p. 333, 'the graphologist had confirmed': 'Ripper Police Probe Writing', *Daily Mirror*, 25 February 1979.

p. 334, 'they were unable to help': Detective Chief Inspector David Zackrisson, 'The West Yorkshire Murders Enquiry and the Sunderland Based Operation', Confidential Report for Northumbria Police, 19 February 1981.

p. 338, 'Vera Millward had been treated': In fact Vera Millward had two periods of in-patient treatment, in 1972 and 1976, at St Mary's Hospital in Manchester, which is part of the same complex as the Royal Infirmary. Source: Superintendent J. W. Bass and Chief Inspector D. Pickover, 'Tape/ Letters Analysis Report', West Yorkshire Metropolitan Police, 7 January 1981.

p. 339, 'By early May 1979': *Daily Telegraph*, 3 May 1979: 'I feel we are nearer to catching this man than at any time before,' Oldfield is quoted as saying.

p. 340, 'These were analysed': Detective Superintendent Jack Slater, Confidential Memorandum to all personnel engaged on the Whitaker murder at Halifax, 29 May 1979, compiled by handwriting expert Dr R. N. Totty, principal scientific officer at the Home Office Forensic Laboratory, Birmingham.

p. 340, 'eliminated from the inquiry': Byford Report, para. 50, p. 15: 'On the 1st May [1979] an entry in the murder log approved the practice of eliminating suspects on the basis of the handwriting from the three "Sunderland" letters.'

p. 340, 'only he could have had the necessary information': Zackrisson Confidential Report, 19 February 1981, p. 12.

p. 342, ' "There were a lot of older police officers" ': Zackrisson, interviewed 26 June 1998.

p. 345, : "Mr Oldfield pressed the switch" ': Megan Winterburn, interviewed 2 November 1998, Tape 2, transcript p. 10; and for *MANHUNT* documentary, Roll No. 20, transcript p. 4.

p. 347, 'The recording had several long gaps': Jack Windsor

Lewis, 'The Yorkshire Ripper Enquiry; Part II', *Foreign Linguistics*, Vol. 1, No. 2 (1994).

p. 347, 'Scientists at the Wetherby laboratory said': Faragher, Interim Report, 19 September 1979.

p. 347, ' "I must have played it twenty times" ': Holland, interviewed for *MANHUNT* documentary, Roll No. 23, transcript pp. 1–4.

p. 348, 'the Wetherby lab report': Faragher, Interim Report, 19 September 1979.

p. 350, 'Reporter: This is the break': Tyne Tees Television, archive of the press conference, 26 June 1979, copy held at the Yorkshire Television film library, Leeds.

p. 352, ' "I hope he sends his photograph" ': *Daily Telegraph*, 27 June 1979; and 'Voice of Murder', *Daily Express*, 27 June 1979.

p. 353, 'Dear Boss': *Yorkshire Post*, 27 June 1979. 'Zackrisson belatedly received': Zackrisson, Confidential Report, 19 February 1981, p. 24.

p. 356, 'Zackrisson ordered a check': Zackrisson was ahead of his time, it seems. Psychologists developed a theory in the 1990s called criteria-based content analysis, which sets down the totality of fresh information in an account of a crime to determine its authenticity. According to Professor David Canter of the University of Liverpool: 'These aspects are taken to reveal the density of experience on which the account draws and the sort of detail that would be more likely to come from genuine experience than fabrication' (see University of Liverpool website).

p. 356, 'Their boss, Brian Johnson, telephoned Oldfield': Zackrisson, Confidential Report, 19 February 1981, pp. 22–3.

Chapter 14: Bad Feelings

p. 359, ' "We were completely dedicated" ': Laptew, interviewed 25.9.01; Tape 1, transcript p. 6.

p. 360, 'intelligence document': Police Reports, confidential intelligence publication no. 1, 615, 3 July 1979.

p. 360, ' "You went into the incident room" ': Laptew" ': Laptew, interviewed 25.9.01; Tape 2, transcript p. 1.

p. 362, 'An odd mix': Laptew, interviewed for *MANHUNT* documentary, Roll No. 18, transcript p. 15.

p. 363, 'denied paying for sex': Laptew, interviewed 25 September 2001, Tape 2, transcript p. 3.

p. 364, 'an official report said later': Byford Report, para. 263, p. 75.

p. 364, ' "I had bad feelings" ': Laptew, interviewed for *MAN-HUNT* documentary, Roll No. 18, transcript p. 10.

p. 365, 'The report ... stated unequivocally': Byford Report, para. 265, p. 75.

p. 365, ' "I didn't check" ': Laptew, interviewed 25 September 2001, Tape 2, transcript p. 4.

p. 366, 'The official report said': Byford Report, paras. 273 and 304, pp. 77 and 83.

p. 369, ' "When you start talking to folk" ': Stanley Ellis, interviewed 7 October 1998, Tape 1, transcript p. 3. See also Stanley Ellis, 'The Yorkshire Ripper Enquiry: Part 1', *Foreign Linguistics*, 1994.

p. 371, 'Lewis was also convinced': Jack Windsor Lewis, 'The Yorkshire Ripper Enquiry: Part II', *Foreign Linguistics*, 1994. 'I have not ceased to be puzzled by the fact that this person has never been identified,' Windsor Lewis wrote. See also Jack Windsor Lewis, 'The Yorkshire Ripper Letters', 1990.

p. 372, 'Zackrisson was still bothered': Zackrisson, interviewed 28 June 1998, Tape 2, transcript pp. 15–16.

p. 376, 'be heard loudly chanting': Nicholson, *The Yorkshire Ripper*, p. 16.

p. 376, '"We all have daughters"': *Now Magazine*, 14 September 1979.

p. 377, 'the perfect antidote': Lapish, interviewed 23 October 1998, Tape 2, transcript p. 16.

p. 377, '"The voice is almost sad"': *Yorkshire Post*, 9 July 1979.

p. 378, '"I've had a hard day"': Holland, interviewed 13 September 1998, Tape 13, transcript p. 124.

p. 380, '"Barbara always managed"': *Northampton Evening Telegraph*, 5 September 1979.

p. 383, 'Gilrain conceded the killer': *Northampton Evening Telegraph*, 4 September 1979.

p. 384, 'An editorial in the *Sun*': 'Call In the Yard', *Sun*, 6 September 1979. The editorial raised similar points to those aired by the *Sunday Express* after the murder of Josephine Whitaker, 17 April 1979.

p. 385, '"Such an awful jolt"': Ellis, interviewed 7 October 1998, Tape 1, transcript p. 8; and Ellis and Lewis, interviewed for *MANHUNT* documentary, Roll No. 15, transcript p. 11.

p. 387, 'Mount ... grabbed a pen and a pad': Mount, interviewed for the *MANHUNT* documentary, Roll No. 30, transcript p. 5.

p. 387, 'the phone call terminated': Zackrisson, Confidential Report, 19 February 1981, p. 54.

p. 388, '"The caller was trying to tell us"': Mount, interviewed for the *MANHUNT* documentary, Roll No. 30, transcript p. 5.

p. 389, 'French subsequently told a third party': This information was given to me by a confidential source in June 1998 while I was producing the *MANHUNT* documentary.

I followed it up with a telephone call to Dr Peter French some time later. He would neither confirm nor deny the story, explaining that professionally he had to be scrupulous in not discussing his work with anyone. In late September 2001, I called at his office in York unannounced and repeated my belief that he had analysed the two tapes and concluded they were by the same person. Once again, politely and in a friendly way, he said he made it a strict rule never to comment on his work one way or the other. I said I would quote him as saying precisely this and he did not demur. I believe, along with Keith Mount and a number of other officers in Sunderland, that the tape hoaxer had realized the terrible wrong he had done and tried to correct it. Perhaps in some way this eased his conscience.

p. 389, 'Ellis wrote': Stanley Ellis, letter to West Yorkshire Metropolitan Police, 17 September 1979.

p. 390, 'Zackrisson firmly believed': Detective Inspector D. Zackrisson, 'Commentary on the "Ripper" Letters and Tape', report to Northumbria police, Sunderland 'H' Division, 25 September 1979.

p. 390, '"I felt that by taking"': Zackrisson, interviewed for *MANHUNT* documentary, Roll No. 29, transcript pp. 13–15.

p. 391, 'a forensic scientist warned': The author of this report is not known, but a copy was received by Northumbria police. The quotation is from Zackrisson, 'Commentary on the "Ripper" Tapes and Letters', p. 53.

p. 391, 'some other factor was required': Byford Report, para. 215, p. 63.

p. 392, 'in terms of audience reach': the West Yorkshire Metropolitan Police file for the DPP provides the following statistics on calls to the incident room freephone. From

7 February 1978 to 5 April 1979 (the date of the Whitaker murder): 871 calls. From 5 April to 7 July 1979: 1,515 calls. From 8 July to 2 October 1979: 925 calls. From 3 October 1979 to 5 January 1981: 3,500 calls.

p. 394, "I pleaded with the chief"': Holland, interviewed 30 June 1999, transcript p. 69; and interviewed for the *MANHUNT* documentary.

p. 394, 'As an official report later stated': Byford Report, para. 323, p. 86.

p. 394, '"A comparison can ... be made"': Byford Report, paras. 374–5, pp. 97 and 98.

Chapter 15: Swamped by Paper

p. 397, 'Sutcliffe stopped writing': Byford Report, para. 278, p. 78.

p. 401, 'drew up a memorandum': R. A. Outteridge, Memorandum No. 8, 'Topic: The Physical Appearance of the "Ripper"', November 1979, addressed to ACC Crime; to the detective chief superintendent of Western Area CID at Bradford; to the Barbara Leach incident room at Bradford; and to the Forensic Science Laboratory at Wetherby.

p. 402, '"We were not test-tube washers"': Stockdale, interviewed 9 November 1998 at Culham Science Park, Oxfordshire.

p. 402, 'demands by the press': Nicola Tyrer, 'The Ripper: Why Won't They Call In the Yard?', *Evening News*, 8 June 1979. The article pointed to public frustration with the police and Ronald Gregory's response: 'There is no way that I would call in Scotland Yard in this case . . . a force the size of West Yorkshire has as much and possibly more experience than Scotland Yard officers would have if they came up to help.'

p. 403, '"Their pride comes second"': Sod's Law can work

against journalists, too. I interviewed Mr Gregory at his Wakefield HQ on Friday, 9 November 1979, for the *Sunday Times* comeback edition after it had been closed for a year because of industrial action. The information about Scotland Yard being brought into the .Ripper inquiry was included in the story I wrote for 11 November 1979. In the final processes before the paper was printed, these paragraphs were cut by a compositor on the page proof because the story was too long and he needed to lose two inches of type! I still retain a copy of the original text of the article I wrote with Rob Rohrer.

p. 405, ' "It was disturbing to find" ': Nevill's report to Gregory, quoted in the Byford Report, para. 376, p. 98.

p. 405, ' "While it is agreed that the author" ': Byford Report, para. 64, p. 18.

p. 405, ' "Unfortunately we have been unable to trace evidence" ': Byford Report, para. 65, p. 18.

p. 406, ' "the reluctance to follow the advice" ': Byford Report, paras. 225 and 226, p. 67.

p. 407, ' "Commander Nevill's comments" ': *Regina v. Sutcliffe*, section headed 'Special Investigative Teams', para. 140.

p. 407, 'going public in urging caution': *West Yorkshireman*, January 1980.

p. 407, 'a depressing series of statistics': Information given to the inquests on Josephine Whitaker and Barbara Leach' see 'Ripper Police Quote Figures', *Yorkshire Post*, 19 January 1980.

p. 407, ' "I don't intend to be the next victim" ': *Yorkshire Evening Post*, 11 January 1980.

p. 409, ' "I more or less hinted" ': Ridgway, interviewed 6 October 1998, Tape 2, transcript p. 30.

p. 411, 'once mounted the bank picket': Ridgway, interviewed by telephone, 28 December 2001.

p. 413, 'it was a daunting experience': Simon Steward, interviewed for the *MANHUNT* documentary, Roll No. 27,
transcript p. 15.

p. 415, '"We had the information"': Ridgway, interviewed
6 October 1998, Tape 2, transcript p. 30.

p. 416, '5,943': This figure comes from the Sampson Report,
p. 38, which significantly makes no reference to Ridgway's
staggering achievement.

p. 416, 'Ridgway couldn't be absolutely sure': Byford Report,
para. 283, p. 78.

p. 417, 'The failure to identify Sutcliffe': Byford Report, para.
285.

p. 418, 'Ridgway's talk to his team': Ridgway, interviewed by
telephone 30 September 1998.

p. 419, '"a strange runner"': Byford Report, para. 288.

p. 420, '"He must therefore share"': Byford Report, paras. 290
and 291, p. 80.

p. 421, 'The officers checked': This assumption appears to conflict with the whole rationale of the covert vehicle observations in the red-light districts. It was never intended to
log couples in cars, but *single men* obviously looking for
prostitutes, or men in the company of known prostitutes.

p. 422, 'the detectives could trace no record': When a check was
made in January 1981 it showed the scrapyard had in fact
taken possession of a Ford Corsair on 3 September 1977.

p. 422, 'Jack Ridgway signed his approval': Sampson Report,
pp. 35–8; and Byford Report, para. 295, p. 81.

p. 422, '"The interviews of this man"': Byford Report, para.
298, p. 82.

p. 423, '"There is however the concept"': Byford Report, para.
301, p. 83.

p. 425, 'They were told he had been interviewed': 'The infor-

mation given was based on elimination by handwriting
stemming from November 1979 and endorsed on Sutcliffe's
index card' – Sampson Report, p. 38, and Byford Report,
para. 299, p. 82.

p. 425, 'She was born at Dunston': 'Antecedents – Marguerite
Walls', provided by West Yorkshire police, 25 March 1999.

p. 426, 'They had gone almost ten yards': *Regina v. Sutcliffe*,
Introductory Report: 'Murder of Marguerite Walls', para.
77.

p. 427, ' "The undressing of this woman" ': ibid., paras 78–80;
also 'Report on the post-mortem examination of Marguerite
Walls', (undated) by Professor Alan Usher, University of
Sheffield Department of Forensic Pathology, p. 14.

p. 427, ' "My feelings are" ': 'Spinster Who Fought Killer', *Daily
Mail*, 23 August 1980.

p. 428, '20,000 vehicles had been seen': Byford Report, para.
135, p. 40.

p. 429, 'She remembered nothing more': 'Examination by Dr
S. P. Bandara', Ref. 27388A/MAG/PAW, 2 October 1980,
Department of Forensic Medicine, University of Leeds.

p. 429, 'at some point kicked in the head': ibid., p. 3.

p. 430, 'Three years previously': Dr Michael Green, 'Mad Bad
and Dangerous to Know' lecture: 'So again we began to
fear that we had several serial killers, all operating on the
same patch at the same time.'

p. 430, 'She later remembered': Teresa Sykes, interviewed for
the *MANHUNT* documentary, 20 January 1999, Roll
No. 28, transcript pp. 1–5.

p. 432, 'She had clearly been struck several blows': *Regina v.
Sutcliffe*, Introductory Report: 'Attempted Killing of Teresa
Sykes', paras. 84–8.

p. 432, 'her father, Raymond Sykes, said': Byford Report, para.

77, p. 20, and Sampson Report, p. 16. See also *The Times*, 1 December 1980. In early December, after Jacqueline Hill was murdered, Jim Hobson told reporters that they would be re-examining recent assaults on women in West Yorkshire.

p. 432, '"I said at the time"': 'Bonfire Night Attack "Not Ripper's work"', *Yorkshire Post*, 25 November 1980.

Chapter 16: 'He Lives Somewhere, He Works for Someone'

p. 435, 'Left behind to solve': *Sunday Express*, 4 May 1980; 'Ripper Detectives Switched to Hunt Burglars', *The Times*, 30 September 1980.

p. 435, 'Nearly two and a quarter million man-hours': Byford Report, Figure 19, p. 102: 'Manpower deployment to Ripper crimes in West Yorkshire'; and Figure 20: 'Inquiry statistics for Ripper crimes in West Yorkshire'.

p. 436, 'officers . . . simply not up to the task': Byford Report, para. 252, p. 73.

p. 436, 'Structural engineers advised': Holland, interviewed for *MANHUNT* documentary, Roll No. 23, transcript p. 9.

p. 436, '"It was quite feasible"': Interviewed in 'The Ripper: Why Did So Many Women Have to Die?', *The Times*, 30 September 1999.

p. 437, '"Oh dark nights"': Sue Neave, interviewed 2 November 1998.

p. 438, 'noticed spots of fresh blood': Byford Report, paras. 353–62, pp. 92–5.

p. 439, 'At 12.30 a.m. the officers were called away': ibid.

p. 440, 'She was still wearing': *Regina v. Sutcliffe*, Introductory Report: 'Murder of Jacqueline Hill', paras. 89–95.

p. 440, 'During the autopsy': Autopsy Report on Jacqueline

Hill by Professor David Gee, 9 January 1981 and Second Interim Report by Edward John Mitchell, Home Office Forensic Science Laboratory, C.80/5175, 10 December 1980.

p. 441, 'He appealed to women in particular': *Daily Mail*, 20 November 1980.

p. 441, 'The *Yorkshire Post* immediately linked': 'Killer-hunt Face from the Past', *Yorkshire Post*, 23 November 1980.

p. 442, 'Many listened in disbelief': 'Ripper Telephone Threat Studied', *The Times*, 22 November 1980; and 'Police Start Inquiry', *Yorkshire Post*, 22 November 1980.

p. 443, ' "I want to ask everyone" ': 'Help Trap Ripper, Pleads Girl's Mother', *Yorkshire Post*, 25 November 1980.

p. 443, ' "So vexed was the prime minister" ': Young, *One of Us*, p. 237.

p. 445, ' "There was impatience" ': Sir Robert Andrew, interviewed by telephone, 17 February 2002.

p. 445, ' "they were mentally exhausted" ': Sir Lawrence Byford, interviewed 18 November 1998, Tape 1, transcript p. 3; and interviewed for *MANHUNT* documentary, 17 December 1998, Roll No. 11, transcript p. 2.

p. 446, 'The headlines': *Daily Express*, 26 November 1980, and the *Sun*, 26 November 1980.

p. 446, 'reassurance he would be "co-equal" ': Kind, interviewed 27.6.98.

p. 447, 'When Hobson was questioned': *Yorkshire Post*, 27 November 1980.

p. 447, 'fell on deaf ears': *Sunday Telegraph*, 11 November 1979.

p. 448, 'Hobson refused to budge': At a press conference on 3 December 1980, Superintendent Frank Morritt, newly appointed press liaison officer for the Ripper squad, responded as follows to a question about whether the tape and letters were from the Ripper: 'Much as I would like to do and much as I would like to confirm the question you are putting to me, I think in fairness I have got to reiterate what Mr Hobson said (a) that we are 99 per cent certain it is from the Ripper. I would expand that by merely saying this, that we are fully aware of the fact that it may well be a hoax and have been all along.'

p. 448, '"perseveration"': See Nigel West, *The Secret War for the Falklands*, Little Brown, London, 1997, p. 226. The word was coined by an officer of MI6, who had noted an almost perverse ability of some intelligence officers to cling to an opinion when all evidence pointed to the contrary.

p. 448, '"not going in . . . to do a hatchet job"': Sloan, interviewed for *MANHUNT* documentary, 11 December 1998, Roll No. 6, transcript p. 1.

p. 449, '"they were on a hook"': ibid., p. 14.

p. 450, 'privately in total agreement': Kind, original notes.

p. 450, '"like finding a diamond in a dung heap"': Kind, interviewed for *MANHUNT* documentary, 11 December, Roll No. 5, transcript p. 8.

p. 450, '"Yes, and we'll get you"': Kind, *The Sceptical Witness*, p. 83.

p. 451, '"did it going home"': Kind, *The Scientific Investigation of Crime*, p. 371.

p. 451, '"I am sure that's what happened"': Kind, interviewed 25 September 1998, transcript p. 1.

p. 452, 'tending to involve themselves in the investigation': Kind's own personal notes made at the time and subsequently; and his diary for the period.

p. 452, '"A navigator becomes instinctively"': Kind, *The Sceptical Witness*, p. 69.

p. 453, ' "Imagine the warehouse" ': ibid.

p. 454, ' "cheating, in effect" ': Kind, interviewed 25 September 1998, transcript p. 1. But see also his 'Navigational Ideas and the Yorkshire Ripper Investigation,' *Journal of Navigation*, Vol. 40, No. 3, pp. 385–92 (1987).

p. 454, 'their interim report': L. E. Emment *et al.*, 'The Ripper Inquiry', memorandum, 16 December 1980, p. 4.

p. 457, 'The incident was written off': Burn, *'Somebody's Husband, Somebody's Son'*, p. 77; and Jones, *Voices from an Evil God*, p. 62. Also Trevor Birdsall's evidence at Peter Sutcliffe's trial, 7 May 1981.

p. 457, 'a knife ... that he managed to hide': Jones, *Voices from an Evil God*, p. 63.

p. 458, ' "He was ... unusually quiet" ': Sutcliffe's trial, 7 May 1980.

p. 458, 'twice in 1980 he raised his fears': *Yorkshire Post*, 23 May 1981.

p. 460, ' "information, no matter how trivial" ': *Leeds Evening Press*, 9 December 1980.

p. 461, 'she had felt a churning in her stomach': 'The Suspicious Friend', *Yorkshire Post*, 23 May 1981.

Chapter 17: 'The Beast I Am'

p. 464, 'In the police car, Ring directed Hydes': Hydes, personal monograph, plus Ring's statement read to the jury at Sutcliffe's trial at the Old Bailey, 7 May 1981.

p. 465, 'The PNC check showed': *Daily Express*, 23 May 1981, p. 5.

p. 465, 'The sergeant told the driver': Ring, statement read at Sutcliffe's trial, 7 May 1981.

p. 466, 'He had been edgy and nervous': *Yorkshire Post*, 23 May 1981.

p. 466, 'too well known to the police': The woman, giving evidence at Sutcliffe's trial, 7 May 1981, plus interviews with Hydes and Ring.

p. 467, 'Had they decided to bail him': Hydes, interviewed by telephone, plus interviewed for *MANHUNT* documentary, Roll No. 12.

p. 468, 'No one was available': Hydes, interview, plus Hydes, personal monograph, p. 10.

p. 468, 'just kept a job lot of tools': Ring, personal monograph.

p. 469, ' "Everybody has been questioned" ': ibid.

p. 470, 'From reading more of the papers in the file': Byford Report, pp. 108–9.

p. 470, 'The probationary constable went home': Hydes, interviewed 7 January 2002.

p. 470, ' "There was something odd about this fellow" ': Mrs Joan Ring, interviewed 8 January 2002.

p. 472, 'He denied a clear sighting': O'Boyle, interviewed, 6 January 1999.

p. 472, 'They found three screwdrivers': *Daily Mail*, Weekend Section, 24 April 1999.

p. 472, 'anything and everything to keep him talking': O'Boyle, interviewed by telephone 12 March 2002.

p. 473, 'found a number plate': Burn, '*Somebody's Husband, Somebody's Son*', p. 214.

p. 474, ' "We forget about rows" ': ibid., p. 215.

p. 475, ' "You were seen in Moss Side" ' *et seq.*: O'Boyle, giving evidence at Sutcliffe's trial, 7 May 1981.

p. 477, 'It was pitch-black': Account from Ring, personal monograph, p. 15.

p. 478, ' "Is it the handyman's?" ': Hydes, interviewed 7 January 2002, plus interviewed for *MANHUNT* documentary, Roll No. 12.

p. 478, '"John Boyle asked me"': O'Boyle, interviewed 12 March 2002.

p. 482, 'The couple's bedroom': Jones, *Voices from an Evil God*, pp. 108–9.

p. 482, 'A senior detective': Ridgway.

p. 483, '"Satisfied she didn't know"': George Smith, interviewed by telephone 15 March 2002.

p. 485, 'Boyle . . . coolly asked': Statement of Detective Sergeant Peter Smith, 12 January 1981, p. 4.

p. 486, 'He was staggered that': Holland, interviewed for *MANHUNT* documentary, Roll No. 23, transcript p. 17.

p. 486, '"We had promised each other"': Holland, interviewed 11 March 1999; Holland transcripts p. 149.

p. 486, '"We've got him"': Gregory, memoirs in the *Mail on Sunday*, 26 June 1983.

p. 487, 'Neave rang a colleague': Winterburn and Neave, interviewed 2 November 1978, Tape 2, transcript.

p. 488, '"We are absolutely delighted"': Press Council transcript from Pennine Radio recording of the press conference.

p. 488, '"Even a sparrow"': O'Boyle, interviewed 12 March 2002, transcript p. 6.

p. 488, 'Only once': 'I Am a Victim of the Ripper Too,' *Mail on Sunday*, 26 April 1987.

p. 489, '"The shock had hit her"': George Smith, interviewed by telephone, 15 March 2002.

p. 490, '"You've nothing to worry about"': Laptew, interviewed October 2001, and interviewed for *MANHUNT* documentary, Roll No. 18, transcript p. 11.

p. 492, '"Mr Gregory was saying"': O'Boyle, interviewed 13 March 2002, transcript p. 13.

p. 493 'The killer wore . . . a V-necked sweater': ibid.

p. 498, ' "the most sterile place I have ever been in" ': *Daily Express*, 23 May 1981, p. 23.

Chapter 18: Mad or Bad?

p. 500, 'someone more malevolent': *Daily Mail*, 23 May 1981, p. 2.

p. 501, 'As an aside, he said': Trial coverage at the Old Bailey, *Yorkshire Post*, 9 May 1981.

p. 501, 'The psychiatrist concluded': Trial coverage at the Old Bailey, *Yorkshire Post*, 7 May 1981.

p. 502, 'In April, he cockily told': Trial coverage at the Old Bailey, *Daily Telegraph*, 9 May 1981.

p. 502, 'doing without a trial': The reasons for the Crown accepting a plea of diminished responsibility were set out in a letter dated 18 August 1981 from Lord Belstead, a Minister of State at the Home Office, to Merlyn Rees, MP, a former Home Secretary in the previous Labour government. Copy in Professor Stuart Kind's private papers.

p. 507, ' "I am as normal as anyone" ': Evidence of Mr Frederick Edwards, prison officer, Armley Gaol, in evidence at Sutcliffe's trial, 8 May 1981.

p. 508, 'After . . . Trevor Birdsall gave evidence': *The Times*, 8 May 1981, p. 1.

p. 520, 'It was the day the . . . last victim': *Daily Mail*, 23 May 1981, p. 2.

p. 521, 'The public mood was inflamed': 'MPs Want Inquiry into "Failures" by Sutcliffe Case Police', *The Times*, 5 May 1981.

p. 521, 'An INSIGHT journalist': At the time the author was northern correspondent of the *Sunday Times*, based in York but on secondment to the newspaper's INSIGHT team.

p. 523, 'the explosive revelation': *Sunday Times*, 3 May 1981.

p. 523, 'banner headlines': *Sun, Daily Express* and *Daily Mirror*, 4 May 1981.

p. 525, 'The Press Council lashed': *Press Conduct in the Sutcliffe Case: a Report by the Press Council*, 1982, pp. 65 and 99.

p. 527, '"I remembered with one of the sections"': Holland, interviewed 15 July 1998, Tape 8, transcript p. 86.

p. 527, '"These buggers, these bastards"': Domaille, interviewed 21 March 2000, transcript p. 4.

p. 528, 'That this situation led"': Byford Report, paras. 376 and 377, pp. 98–9.

p. 528, '"I am firmly of the view"': ibid., paras. 481 and 482.

p. 529, '"The objective was to make sure"': Sloan, interviewed 9 July 1998, and interviewed for *MANHUNT* documentary, 11 December 1998.

p. 530, '"In two of these cases in particular"': Byford Report, paras. 182 and 183, pp. 50–51.

p. 531, '"a right quiet place"': Private notes made by Stuart Kind at the time of the Byford inquiry.

p. 533, '"Kind, the police must be made to realize"': Kind, interviewed 27 June 1998, Tape 1, transcript p. 7, and 25 September 1998, Tape 1, transcript p. 2.

Chapter 19: DNA, DNA, DNA

p. 534, 'The House of Commons': *Hansard*, 19 January 1982, col. 157.

p. 535, 'Byford wrote to a colleague': Letter to Stuart Kind, February 1982.

p. 535, '"I need hardly point out"': 'Strictly confidential' letter from Byford to Kind, 19 February 1982.

p. 537, 'believing he had been sacrificed': *Daily Mail*, 6 June 1981.

p. 537, 'Highest priority': Home Office Circular No. 114/1982,

'The Investigation of a Series of Major Crimes', 29 December 1982, Home Office ref. POL/82 1098/11/3, sent to all Britain's chief constables.

p. 538, 'With three forces involved': 'The Barry Peter Edwards (Prudom) Investigation': a report relating to an inquiry in three Police Force areas from the standpoint of the senior investigating officer, A. K. Sloan, 1982.

p. 538, 'Malcolm Fairley had become': 'The "Fox" Investigation', confidential report prepared for Bedfordshire Police 1 August 1985.

p. 539, 'MICA computer system': Bedford Police took up an offer from Microdata Information Systems Ltd and Isis Computer Service Ltd to install the MICA system free of charge, excepting maintenance costs. Nine VDU terminals were installed, and officers from West Yorkshire, who by now had vast experience of inputting computer data from the cross-area sightings inquiry, travelled down to Dunstable to train operators.

p. 539, 'Large volumes of information': 'The "Fox" investigation', p. 23.

p. 539, 'An obscure fact': Stephen Ackroyd et al., New Technology and Practical Police Work, p. 153.

p. 540, 'HOLMES was linked': Sloan, interviewed 14 July 1998.

p. 542, 'using electric fields and radioactive labelling': See Howard Safir and Peter Reinharz, 'DNA Testing: The Next Big Crime-Busting Breakthrough', City Journal, New York, winter 2000, Vol. 10, No. 1.

p. 543, 'Under a 1994 law': The Criminal Justice and Public Order Act 1994 amended the Police and Criminal Evidence Act 1984 to allow bodily samples to be taken. It more or less allows DNA samples to be taken in the same circumstances as fingerprints.

p. 543, 'During the first six years': Written evidence by the Association of Chief Police Officers Crime Committee to the House of Lords Select Committee on Science and Technology, 6 November 2000.

p. 544, 'Recording DNA profiles': ibid.

p. 547, 'an injuries database': David Barclay, Head of Physical Evidence, National Crime Faculty, interviewed 4 March 2002.

p. 548, ' "We are talking about" ': ibid.

p. 550, ' "We have got to get to the suspect" ': Phillips, interviewed 16 December 1998.

p. 552, 'three times . . . on the receiving end of physical attacks': 'Yorkshire Ripper Says Fellow-prisoner Attacked Him with Glass', *The Times*, 15 April 1983, and 'Ripper Stabbed in Eyes by Broadmoor Patient', *The Times*, 11 March 1997.

p. 553, 'Hellawell . . . visited Sutcliffe': *Sunday Express*, 24 November 1996.

p. 553, 'Mr Tomey remains convinced': Tomey, interviewed by telephone 14 May 2002.

p. 554, 'In the interior of the car': 'Scarf Clue to Taxi Attack', *Yorkshire Post*, 26 March 1967, and 'Attack on Taxi Driver: Police Tissue Picture', *Yorkshire Post*, 27 March 1967.

p. 555, 'His sixteen-year-old brother': Burn, *'Somebody's Husband, Somebody's Son'*, p. 50.

p. 556, 'O'Boyle remembered his boss's words': O'Boyle, interviewed by telephone 14 May 2002.

p. 557, ' "He was a hard man" ': Ronald Craven, interviewed 15 May 2002.

p. 558, 'wallet had been stolen': *Bingley Guardian*, 29 April 1966.

p. 558, 'two key suspects': 'Bookie Killing: Police Hunt for "Sad Man" ', *Bradford Telegraph and Argus*, 25 April 1966.

p. 560, 'a recent "cold-case" review': E-mail statement to the author by West Yorkshire police, 15 May 2002.

p. 562, ' "The serial killer will always be" ': Phillips, interviewed 16 December 1998.

Endpiece: A Suitable Case for Treatment?

p. 565, 'being fooled': *The Times*, 19 May 1981. 'Staff thought I had been fooled, says doctor.'

p. 565, 'Another psychiatrist': ibid.

p. 566, 'a charade for public opinion': the *Guardian*, 10 October 1982. 'Psychiatrists angry at treatment of Yorkshire Ripper.'

p. 567, 'pickle my brain': Interview with Diane Simpson, 27 March 2003.

p. 567, 'no malingering': the *Guardian*, 10 October 1982, op. cit.

p. 568, 'Sutcliffe's family': *The Times*, 12 January 1983. 'Plea to move Ripper after jail attack.'

p. 568, 'against removal': *The Times*, 4 February 1983. 'Sutcliffe to stay in prison.'

p. 569, 'Peter is sick': *The Times*, 28 March 1984. 'Mentally ill Ripper sent to Broadmoor.'

p. 570, 'The public interest': Nigel Turner's Hyper Guide to the Mental Health Act: http:www.hyperguide.co.uk/mha/s1.htm#def

p. 571, 'Symptoms of Parkinson's disease': Interview with Diane Simpson, op. cit.

p. 572, 'Reward and incentive money': 'Policy for patients' monies', Council Report CR72, Royal College of Psychiatrists, London, October 1998.

p. 572, 'Healthy bank balance': *Daily Mirror*, 6 May 1998. 'MPs Demand Action over Ripper £3000.'

p. 573, 'The most manipulative and prolific liar': *Chester Chronicle*, 14 March 2003. 'The Ripper is Bad not Mad.'

p. 575, 'ask whether it is real': Frank Mone interviewed, *Daily Mirror*, 13 November 1995.

p. 575, 'Manipulated his way into the secure hospital system': Brian Caton interview, 4 April 2003.

p. 577, 'No mention of leggings': the *Sun*, 10 March 2003. 'The Ripper's silky "killing trousers".'

p. 578, 'Bombshell story': *Yorkshire Evening Post*, 22 February 2003.

p. 578, 'Re-incarceration in a proper prison': Letter to David Blunkett, Home Secretary, from Fabian Hamilton MP, 5 March 2003.

p. 578, 'Spare the families': Letter to Rt. Hon. Merlyn Rees, MP, from Lord Belstead, Minister of State at the Home Office, 18 August 1981.

p. 579, 'No such recommendation': Letter to Fabian Hamilton MP, from David Blunkett, Home Office, 14 March 2003.

BIBLIOGRAPHY

Ackroyd, Stephen, *et al.*, *New Technology and Practical Police Work: the Social Context of Technical Innovation*, Open University Press, Buckingham, 1992.

Baldwin, John, and French, Peter, *Forensic Phonetics*, Pinter Publishers, London, 1990.

Bardens, Denis, *Famous Cases of Norman Birkett K.C.*, Hale, London, 1963.

Bass, J. W. (Superintendent), and Pickover, D. (Chief Inspector), Tape/letters Analysis Report for Chief Superintendent Howard, Incident Room, Millgarth DHQ, Leeds, 7 January 1981.

Bauermeister, Martin, 'Women Victims and Their Assailants: Rapists, Victims and Society', *International Journal of Offencer Therapy and Comparative Criminology*, Vol. 21, No. 1, pp. 238–48.

Beveridge, Peter, *Inside the CID*, Evans Brothers, London, 1957.

Bilton, Michael, 'Crime Investigation and the Media', lecture to symposium of the International Association of Forensic Sciences, Christ Church, Oxford, September 1982, pub. in Brownlie, A. R., *Crime Investigation, Art or Science?*

——, 'Is Another Ripper on the Loose?', *Sunday Times Magazine*, 17 September 1996.

Bodziak, William J., 'Shoe and Tire Impression Evidence', *FBI Law Enforcement Bulletin*, Department of Justice, Washington, DC (July 1984), pp. 2–11.

Broadhead, Elcy C., 'Larvae of Trichocerid Flies Found on Human Corpse', *Entomologist's Monthly*, 27 October 1980, Vol. 116, pp. 23–4.

Brookman, Fiona, 'Dying for Control: Men, Murder and Sub-Lethal Violence', paper delivered to the British Criminology Conference, Liverpool, July 1999.

Browne, Douglas G., and Tullet, E. V., *Bernard Spilsbury, His Life and Cases*, Companion Book Club (Odhams Press), London, 1952.

Brownlie, Alistair R. (ed.), *Crime Investigation, Art or Science? Patterns in a Labyrinth*, Scottish Academic Press, Edinburgh, 1984.

Burdis, Michael, 'The Use of the Burroughs Computer in the Dore Murder Investigations', South Yorkshire Police, November 1983.

Burn, Gordon, *'Somebody's Husband, Somebody's Son': The Story of Peter Sutcliffe*, Heinemann, London, 1984.

Burt, Leonard, *Commander Burt of Scotland Yard*, Heinemann, London, 1959.

Byford, Lawrence, *The Yorkshire Ripper Case: Review of the Police Investigation of the Case*, Report to the Secretary of State for the Home Office, Home Office, London, December 1981 (The Byford Report).

Cameron, Paul, *Violence and Homosexuality*, paper issued by Family Research Institute of Colorado Springs, April 2001.

Canter, David, *Criminal Shadows, Inside the Mind of the Serial Killer*, HarperCollins, London, 1995.

Charlesworth, A. (Superintendent), 'Murders/Assaults in the

So Called "Ripper" Series', Millgarth Incident Room (reappraisal team), 19 December 1980.

Cherrill, Fred, *Cherrill of the Yard*, Harrap, London, 1955.

Chisum, W. J., and Turvey, B., 'Evidence Dynamics: Locard's Exchange Principle and Crime Reconstruction', *Journal of Behavioral Profiling*, January 2000, Vol. 1, No. 1.

Christie, D. F. M., and Ellis, H. D., 'Photofit Constructions versus Verbal Descriptions of Faces', *Journal of Applied Psychology*, 1981, Vol. 66, No. 3, pp. 358–63.

Collinson, J. G.. 'The Role of the Investigating officer', *Journal of the Forensic Science Society*, 1970, Vol. 10, No. 4, pp. 199–203.

Committee on Homosexual Offences and Prostitution, *Report of the Committee on Homosexual Offences and Prostitution*, HMSO, London, 1957.

Cox, Barry, Shirley, John, and Short, Martin, *The Fall of Scotland Yard*, Penguin Books, Harmondsworth, 1977.

Critchley, T. A., *A History of Police in England and Wales 1900–1966*, Constable, London, 1967.

Cross, Roger, *The Yorkshire Ripper, the In-depth Study of a Mass Killer and His Methods*, Grafton, London, 1981.

——, 'The Ripper Tape: The Cruellest Hoax', *Unsolved Magazine*, Vol. 1, No. 4 (1984).

Davies, Anne, and Dale, Andrew, *Locating the Stranger Rapist*, Home Office Police Department, Police Research Group, Special Interests Series, Paper No. 3, 1995.

Davies, G., Shepherd, J., and Ellis, H., 'Effects of Interpolated Mugshot Exposure on Accuracy of Eyewitness Identification', *Journal of Applied Psychology*, Vol. 64, No. 2, pp. 232–7 (1979).

Devlin, J. Daniel, *Police Procedure, Administration and Organisation*, Butterworth, London, 1966.

Dewhirst, Ian, 'Keighley', *The Dalesman*, Vol. 38, No. 6 (September 1976).

Domaille, John, Report *re* Prostitute Murders, Confidential Memorandum for ACC (Crime), West Yorkshire Metropolitan Police, Murder Squad, Millgarth, 25 August 1978.

Elliott, Helen, 'Police and the Media: Our Mutual Friends', *Police*, Vol. 31, No. 1 (January 1999).

Ellis, Stanley, 'The Yorkshire Ripper Enquiry, Part 1', *Forensic Lingistics: The International Journal of Speech, Language and the Law*, Vol. 1, No. 2 (1994).

Emment, L., *et al.*, 'The "Ripper" Inquiry', memorandum by the special advisory team for the Chief Constable of West Yorkshire Metropolitan Police, 16 December 1980.

——, 'The Vehicle Tracking Inquiry', paraphrase of draft report for the Byford review team, 2 September 1981.

Evans, Peter, *The Police Revolution*, Allen & Unwin, London, 1974.

Fabian Robert, *Fabian of the Yard*, Heirloom Library, London, 1955.

Farrar, Max, 'Constructing and De-constructing "Community". A Case Study of a Multi-cultural Inner City Area: Chapeltown, Leeds, 1972–1997', PhD thesis, Leeds Metropolitan University, July 1999.

Feist, Andy, *The Effective Use of the Media in Serious Crime Investigations*, Policing and Reducing Crime Unit, Paper No. 120, Home Office, London, 1999.

Felstead, S. Theodore, *Shades of Scotland Yard*, John Long, London, 1949.

Fletcher, Tony, *Memories of Murder, the Great Cases of a Fingerprint Expert*, Weidenfeld & Nicolson, London, 1986.

Gee, David J., 'The Yorkshire Ripper', lecture to the British

Association in Forensic Medicine, Summer Meeting, 1983, Edinburgh.

——, 'The Pathological Aspects of the Yorkshire "Ripper" Case', lecture to the Medico-Legal Society, London, 1982.

Gerty, David, 'The Investigation of Multiple Crime, a Problem in Business Management', lecture delivered to the International Association of Forensic Sciences, Christ Church, Oxford, September 1982.

Grampian Police, Report into the Scott Greg Simpson Murder Inquiry, January 1998.

——, Response to the Recommendations/Conclusions of the Lothian and Borders Police Report into the handling by Grampian Police of the Scott Greg Simpson Murder Enquiry, 1998.

Green, Michael, 'Mad, Bad and Dangerous to Know! A discussion of serial killings in the UK', lecture to the Australian and New Zealand Forensic Science Society, New South Wales Branch, April 1990.

——, 'Stab Wound Dynamics – a Recording Technique for Use in Medico-Legal Investigations', *Journal of the Forensic Science Society*, Vol. 18, No. 161 (1978).

Gribble, Leonard, *When Killers Err*, John Long, London, 1962.

Grogan, R. J., 'Tyre Marks as Evidence', paper presented for Tyre Technical Division, Dunlop Ltd, to the Eighth International Association of Forensic Sciences, Wichita, Kansas, 22–6 May 1978.

Grogan, R. J., and Watson, T. R., 'The Silent Informant', *Police Review*, 2 August 1974.

Grover, Chris, and Soothill, Keith, 'British Serial Killing: Towards a Structural Explanation', paper delivered to the British Criminology Conference, Belfast, 15–19 July 1997.

Hansard, Report of the Committee on the Police Service of England, Wales and Scotland, Cmd 574, 1920.

——, Minutes of Evidence of the Committee appointed to consider and report whether any and what changes should be made in the method of recruiting for, the conditions of service of, and the rates of pay, pensions and allowances of the Police Forces of England, Wales and Scotland, Cmd 874, HMSO, London, 1920.

——, Police Forces, England and Wales (Organisation), 17 May 1966, Vol. 728, cols. 1341–6.

——, Police Amalgamations, 18 May 1966, House of Lords, cols. 99–1045.

——, Police Amalgamations, Written Answers, 20 February 1968, cols. 86–88.

——, Police Forces Amalgamations, Written Answers, 25 July 1969, cols. 530–32.

——, Police Amalgamation Schemes, Written Answers, 27 June 1968, col. 116.

——, Police Forces (Co-operation), [Adjournment debate on Black Panther case], 4 August 1976, col. 2086–96.

——, Yorkshire Ripper (Investigation) Written Answers, 8 July 1981, col. 186.

——, Yorkshire Ripper (Investigations), Statement by the Home Secretary, 19 January 1982, col. 157–62.

——, West Yorkshire Police (Report) Written Answers, 26 May 1988, col. 278.

——, Police National Computer, Written Answers, 11 December 1996, col. 259.

Hare, Robert D., *Without Conscience, the Disturbing World of the Psychopaths Among Us*, Warner Books, London, 1994.

Harrison, Paul, 'The New Red Light Districts', *New Society*, 10 July 1975.

Healey, Denis, *The Time of My Life*, Michael Joseph, London, 1989.

Herold, Horst, *Cybernetics and the Organization of the Police Force*, Abstracts on Police, Vol. 2, Science, Leiden, 1974.

Hobson, J. (Detective Chief Superintendent), *Regina v Peter William Sutcliffe*, Introductory Report relating to Murders/ Assaults in West Yorkshire and Lancashire Police Areas – the 'Yorkshire Ripper' Enquiry, West Yorkshire Metropolitan Police, 1981.

Holmes, Ronald M., *Profiling Violent Crimes: an Investigative Tool*, Sage Publications, Newbury Park, 1989.

Home Office, 'The Investigation of a Series of Major Crimes', Draft of circular to be sent to Chief Officers of Police, 1982.

——, Report of Inquiry in Respect of the Objections to the Proposed Compulsory Amalgamation of the Police Areas of the County of Yorkshire, East Riding and the Cities of Kingston-upon-Hull and York, Cmnd 3406, HMSO, London, 1967.

——, *The Story of Our Police*, London, 1976.

——, *The Story of Our Police*, Part Two: *The Development of the Modern Police from 1856 to the Present Day*, London, 1977.

——, 'The Yorkshire Ripper Investigation', Statement by the Home Secretary, 19 January 1982 (advance released to the media to be checked against delivery).

——, 'A summary of the main conclusions and recommendations of Mr Byford's Report on his review of the police investigation of the Yorkshire Ripper case' (placed in the House of Commons library after the Home Secretary addressed Parliament), 19 January 1982.

——, *The Investigation of Major Crimes*, Circular No. 114/ 1982, 29 December 1982.

——, *Scientific Aids to Criminal Investigation: instructional pamphlet for the use of Police Officers*, HMSO, London, 1936.

Hopper, W. R., 'Photo-fit – The Penry Facial Identification Technique', *Journal of the Forensic Science Society*, Vol. 13, No. 77 (1973).

House of Lords, 'The Use of DNA in the Investigation of Crime', Memorandum by the Association of Chief Police Officers (Crime Committee) to Select Committee on Science and Technology (written evidence), 6 November 2000.

Jackson, Robert, *Francis Camps: Famous Case Histories of the Most Celebrated Pathologist of Our Time*, Granada Publishing, London, 1983.

James, Lionel, 'On the Game', *New Society*, 24 May 1973.

Jones, Barbara, *Voices from an Evil God: the True Story of the Yorkshire Ripper and the Woman Who Loves Him*, Blake, London, 1992.

Jouve, Nicole Ward, *'The Street-cleaner', the Yorkshire Ripper Case on Trial*, Marion Boyars, London, 1988.

Judge, Anthony, *A Man Apart: The British Policeman and His Job*, Arthur Barker, London, 1972.

Kind, Stuart, *The Sceptical Witness: Concerning the Scientific Investigation of Crime against a Human Background*, Hodology Ltd, Harrogate, 1999.

——, *The Scientific Investigation of Crime*, Forensic Science Services Ltd, Harrogate, 1987.

——, '... of Insipid Common Sense', Lecture to the Association of Police Surgeons of Great Britain and Ireland, Scarborough, Friday, 20 May 1983.

——, 'Science of the Investigation of Crime', lecture to the Institute of Police Science, Lausanne, Switzerland, reprinted in *Police Journal*, Vol. 57, No. 4 (December 1984).

——, 'How We Nearly Caught the Ripper', notes for a seminar, 1982.

——, 'What Makes a Good Forensic Scientist?', lecture presented at the seventy-second semi-annual seminar of the California Association of Criminalists, Costa Mesa, California, 18 October 1988.

——, 'Science and the Hunt for the Criminal', *Impact of Science on Society*, No. 154, pp. 113–23.

——, 'Navigational Ideas and the Yorkshire Ripper Investigation', *Journal of Navigation*, Vol. 40, No. 3, September 1987.

——, 'Who Goes in the Frame?', *Police Review*, 20 July 1990.

Kinsey, Richard, Lea, John, and Young, Jock, *Losing the Fight against Crime*, Blackwell, London, 1986.

Kinsley, Peter, and Smyth, Frank, *I'm Jack: The Police Hunt for the Yorkshire Ripper*, Pan, London, 1980.

Laughery, K. R., and Fowler, R. H., 'Sketch Artist and Identi-Kit Procedures for Recalling Faces', *Journal of Applied Psychology*, Vol. 65, No. 3, pp. 307–16 (1980).

Lavelle, Patrick, *Wearside Jack: The Hunt for the Hoaxer of the Century*, Northeast Press, Sunderland, 1999.

Leigh, L. H., *Police Powers in England and Wales*, Butterworth, London, 1975.

Lewis, Jack Windsor, 'The Yorkshire Ripper Enquiry, Part *II*', *Forensic Linguistics, The International Journal of Speech, Language and the Law*, Vol. 1, No. 2 (1994).

——, 'The Yorkshire Ripper Letters', in Hannes Kniffa (ed.), *Texte zu Theorie und Praxis Forensischer Linguistik*, Max Niemeyer, Tubingen, 1990.

Leyton, Elliott, *Hunting Humans: The Rise of the Modern Multiple Murderer*, Penguin Books, Harmondsworth, 1986.

Mant, A. K., 'A Survey of Forensic Pathology in England since

1945', *Journal of the Forensic Science Society*, Vol. 13, No. 17 (1973).

Mark, Robert, *In the Office of Constable*, Collins, London, 1978.

Martin, J. P., and Wilson, Gail, *The Police: a Study in Manpower, The Evolution of the Service in England and Wales 1829–1965*, Heinemann, London, 1969.

McClure, James, *Killers*, Fontana, London, 1976.

Metropolitan Police Authority, 'Police National Computer: Data Quality', Report 9, 10 April 2001. Professional Standards and Performance Monitoring Committee, MPA.

Mitchell, Edward W., 'The Aetiology of Serial Murder: Towards an Integrated Model', MPhil thesis submitted to University of Cambridge, 1997.

Mitchison, Amanda, 'The Ripper, the Tea Lady, His Friend and Her Story, *Independent Magazine*, 6 March 1993.

Morris, Terence, 'To Cage a Black Panther', *New Society*, 12 August 1976.

Murder Casebook, No. 1: *The Yorkshire Ripper*, Marshall Cavendish, London, 1989.

Murder Casebook, No. 16: *The Black Panther*, Marshall Cavendish, London, 1990.

Nally, Michael, 'Hunt the Ripper', *New Society*, 14 June 1979.

National Commission on the Future of DNA Evidence, 'Privacy Consideration and Database Sample Retention', Meeting VI proceedings, Dept of Justice, Washington, DC, 26 July 1999.

National Crime Faculty, 'National SIO Development Programme', Training and Developing Unit, NCF, Bramshill, 1998.

Nicholson, Michael, *The Yorkshire Ripper*, Star Books, London, 1979.

Nickolls, L. C., *The Scientific Investigation of Crime*, Butterworth, London, 1956.

Norris, Joel, *Serial Killers: The Growing Menace*, Arrow Books, London, 1988.

Oliver, Ian, *Police, Government and Accountability*, Macmillan, London, 1996.

Outteridge, R., 'The Physical Appearance of the Ripper', memorandum for the ACC (Crime), West Yorkshire Metropolitan Police, 1 November 1979.

Oughton, Frederick, *Murder Investigation*, Elek Books, London, 1971.

Phillips, J. H., and Bowen, J. K., *Forensic Science and the Expert Witness*, The Law Book Company, London, 1985.

Power, G., Report of an Enquiry into the Handling by Grampian Police of the Murder of Scott Greg Simpson, Aged 9 Years, Lothian and Borders Police, Edinburgh, 1998.

Prentice, Thomson, 'The Scientist Who May Trap the Ripper', *Now*, 5 December 1990.

Press Council, *Press Conduct in the Sutcliffe Case*, The Press Council, London, 1983.

Purcell, William, *British Police in a Changing Society*, Mowbrays, London, 1974.

Real-Life Crimes, Vol. 1, Pt 5: *Peter Sutcliffe, The Yorkshire Ripper*, Eaglemoss Publications, London, 1994.

Regina v. P. W. Sutcliffe, Opening Remarks, unpublished document used by the Prosecution in the trial of Peter Sutcliffe, at the Old Bailey, London, May 1981. (Authorship unknown, but presumably by an official at the office of the Director of Public Prosecutions or the Attorney General.)

Roberts, Helen, 'Trap the Ripper', *New Society*, 6 April 1978.

Rohrer, Rob, 'Ripper "Aid" a Fantasy', *New Statesman*, 5 June 1981.

——, 'Secret Clues to the Yorkshire Ripper', *New Statesman*, 12 September 1980.

——, 'Change of Tack after Victim 13', *New Statesman*, 28 November 1980.

——, 'Murdoch Heads the Pack', *New Statesman*, 1 May 1981.

Royal Commission on the Police, *Final Report*, HMSO, London, 1962.

Safir, H., and Reinharz, P., 'DNA Testing: The Next Big Crime Breakthrough', *New York City Journal*, Vol. 10, No. 1 (winter 2000).

Scott, J. S., 'Appreciations on Retirement: Professor D. J. Gee', *University of Leeds Review*, Vol. 30, 1987, pp. 289–90.

Sheffield University Newsletter, 'Obituary, Emeritus Professor A. Usher', Vol. 23, No. 2, p. 8 (October 1998).

Shippey, T. A., 'Appreciations on Retirement: Stanley Ellis', *University of Leeds Review*, Vol. 26, pp. 210–11 (1983).

Sims, B. G., 'The Facilities for Forensic Odontology, 1979–1980', summary of lecture given to the Forensic Medicine Society, September 1979, in *Medicine, Science and the Law*, Vol. 20, No. 3 (July 1980).

Simpson, Keith, *Forty Years of Murder*, Harrap, London, 1978,

Smith, Nicky, and Flanagan, Conor, *The Effective Detective: Identifying the Skills of an Effective SIO*, Policing and Reducing Crime Unit, Paper No. 122, Home Office, London, 1999.

Smith, Sydney, *Mostly Murder*, Harrap, London, 1959.

Sperber, Norman D., 'Bite Mark Evidence in Crimes against Persons', *FBI Law Enforcement Bulletin*, pp. 16–19 (July 1981).

Stockdale, R. E., and Outteridge, R. A., 'Attacks by the So-called Yorkshire Ripper', confidential memorandum for the Murder Squad, Incident Room, Bradford, West Yorkshire Metropolitan Police, 14 November 1979.

——, 'Notes on Weapons', memorandum to Murder Squad, Bradford, December 1979.

Taylor, Ricky, *Forty Years of Crime and Criminal Justice Statistics, 1958–1997*, Home Office Research Department, London, 1999.

Vincent, Sally, 'Women Who Ask for It', *New Statesman*, 19 December 1980.

West Riding Constabulary, 'The West Riding Constabulary Training School, Pannel Ash, Harrogate', copy supplied by the West Yorkshire Archive Service, ref. A54/119.

West Yorkshire Metropolitan Police, 'Police/Public and Race Relations Course', Wakefield, 1982.

——, 'Murders and Assaults upon Women in the North of England', Confidential Criminal Intelligence Special Notice, June 1978.

——, 'Murder of Prostitutes', Police Reports, No. 1615, 3 July 1979.

——, 'Murders and Assaults upon Women in the North of England', Confidential Special Notice, 13 September 1979.

——, Annual Report, Wakefield, 1978.

——, Summary of Report into the Investigation of the Series of Murders and Assaults on Women in the North of England between 1975 and 1980, Wakefield, 1983.

Wilcox, A. F., 'Police 1964–1973', *Criminal Law Review* (1974).

Williams, Emlyn, *Beyond Belief, a Chronicle of Murder and Detection*, World Books, London, 1968.

Wilson, Colin, and Seaman, Donald, *The Serial Killers: A Study in the Psychology of Violence*, Book Club Associates, London, 1991.

Yallop, David A., *Deliver Us from Evil*, Futura, London, 1981.

Young, Hugo, *One of Us: a Biography of Margaret Thatcher*, Macmillan, London, 1989.

Zackrisson, David, 'The West Yorkshire Murders Enquiry and the Sunderland Based Operation', Northumbria Police, February 1981.

——, 'Commentary on the "Ripper" Letters and Tape', Sunderland 'H' Division, Northumbria Police, 25 September 1979.

AUTHOR'S NOTE ON THE APPENDICES

Peter Sutcliffe's voluntary statement of confession and the transcript of various interviews he gave the police remain the most compelling pieces of hard evidence in the Yorkshire Ripper case. They provided the basis of his prosecution for thirteen murders and seven attempted murders. Long portions of what Sutcliffe told police were read to the jury at his trial and were then widely reported by the media. More than twenty years after Sutcliffe was gaoled, it is surely right these documents should be included here, as an appendix to a detailed study of the actions of a single group of detectives in a murder case.

The documents are published here for the first time. They raise important questions about the procedures involved in the interrogation of the prime suspect for the most sensational series of crimes in British history. After making many crucial errors during the course of the investigation, the West Yorkshire police went on to make several more after Sutcliffe was arrested.

Having spent five agonizing years trying to apprehend him, why was the process of taking the Yorkshire Ripper's confession so rushed? Three relatively junior West Yorkshire detectives skilfully tried to extract Sutcliffe's confession, despite being under enormous pressure from their superiors to get the Yorkshire Ripper into court.

We now know Sutcliffe was responsible for many more crimes of savage violence against women *and* men. Yet he still denies virtually all of those even though the evidence against him is utterly compelling. The suspicions of several experienced detectives should have been thoroughly explored during the period of Sutcliffe's interrogation. Yet the moment he put up his hands to being the Yorkshire Ripper the heat was on to take his statement as quickly as possible. It turned out to be a ridiculously hurried affair – a policy seemingly aimed at satisfying the interests of public relations by getting the notorious killer before a magistrates' court as quickly as possible. The failure by West Yorkshire police at the time to question Peter Sutcliffe more thoroughly was an elementary and costly error.

Sutcliffe gave the appearance of being forthcoming during his interrogation, but it is now wholly evident that he was grossly deceitful and manipulative. He was desperate to deny a sexual motive for his crimes. He constantly lied about what had really happened during the long years he rampaged across the North of England, committing murder and mayhem. There were many outstanding attacks on men and women over a fifteen-year period that Sutcliffe should have been questioned about but was not. At the moment when for the first time in five years the police had the upper hand, they lost the plot.

Critical evidence about Sutcliffe's psycho-sexual make-up was never probed by police or by psychiatrists. Had the Yorkshire Ripper case happened today, it is beyond doubt there would have been a public inquiry into the hapless police investigation. There is a different climate today about the accountability of the police service, especially where there is grave public disquiet over a series of notorious crimes. One of the first acts of the incoming Labour Government in the summer of 1997 was to announce a public inquiry into the lessons learned from the police investigation into the racially motivated murder of Stephen Lawrence four years earlier. The Metropolitan Police was called to account in public.

In 2001, following the arrest of Dr Harold Shipman, suspected of murdering hundreds of his patients, the Government was compelled to hold a public inquiry. Police had earlier been alerted to the possibility he was a killer, and he was not arrested. The Government's attempt to hold the Shipman inquiry behind closed doors was overturned at judicial review. In a landmark decision, Lord Justice Kennedy said that holding such a vital inquiry in private would itself amount to a breach of Article 10 of the European Convention on Human Rights, now enshrined in British law.

The legal position now made clear, the conduct of the Shipman Inquiry and subsequent presentation of all the facts to the general public were models of openness. The volume of daily transcripts, background information and documentary evidence made available via the Internet was truly staggering. Dr Shipman's police statement and the transcripts of fifteen police interviews with him were among the many documents placed in the public domain. They could be reported in any format or media, subject to their being reproduced accurately and not in a misleading context.

The Government was committed to much greater openness with regard to information previously kept hidden from view. Official policy now determined that the British public could be treated as grown-up people and presented with documents about important crimes, providing there was no Contempt of Court and the integrity of the administration of justice was upheld. In August 2001, the Attorney General, Lord Goldsmith, QC, made a dramatic and groundbreaking decision. He refused to ban Channel 5 from broadcasting police interviews with the serial killer, Fred West. Gloucester police tried to use the law to stop the inclusion of the material in the programme. The Attorney General turned the application down. He was not, he said, prepared to act as a censor.

At a seminar on the media and the law, in February 2002, Lord Goldsmith provided an explanation for his decision. One of his functions as the senior law officer, he said, was to act as guardian of the public as opposed to the government interest. This meant strongly defending the concept of freedom of speech, enshrined in the European Convention on Human Rights. He quoted a much-cited passage from the judgment in an important case: *Handyside v. United Kingdom* [1976] 1 EHRR 737: 'Freedom of expression constitutes one of the essential foundations of a democratic society, one of the basic conditions for its progress and for the development of every man. It is applicable not only to information or ideals that are favourably received or regarded as inoffensive or as a matter of indifference, but also those that offend, shock or disturb the State, or any sector of the population. Such are the demands of pluralism, tolerance and broadmindedness without which there is no democratic society.'

As if to emphasize the point, the Attorney General then quoted part of a judgment by Lord Steyn [*R v. Secretary of State for the Home Department ex p Simms* (1999) All ER 400 at 408]: 'Freedom of speech is the lifeblood of democracy. The free flow of information and ideas informs political debate. It is a safety valve ... it acts as a brake on the abuse of power by public officials. It facilitates the exposure of errors in the governance and administration of justice of the country.'

Lord Goldsmith said he believed the media made a positive contribution to the administration of justice by reporting trials fairly 'and by disseminating to the public at large information and critical analysis about the operation of the criminal justice system'.

APPENDIX A

Statement of Peter William Sutcliffe to West Yorkshire
Police, 4 January 1981
(Crown Copyright)

I PETER WILLIAM SUTCLIFFE wish to make a statement and I want someone to write down what I say. I have been told that I need not say anything unless I wish to do so and that whatever I say may be given in evidence.

SGD: P W Sutcliffe

WTD: P Smith DS 268 J Boyle DI

That was the incident that started it all off, I was driving through Leeds late at night I'd been to somewhere have a couple of pints, you'll know the date better than me. It was WILMA MCCANN. I was in a Ford Capri K registered a lime Green one with a black roof with a sun grill in the back window. I saw this woman thumbing a lift where the Wetherby Road branches to the right but you can carry straight on. She was wearing some white trousers and a jacket. I stopped and asked her how far she was going. She said 'NOT FAR THANKS FOR STOPPING' and she jumped in. I was in quite a good mood and we were talking on the way. She said something about just before we stopped about did I want business. To me I didn't know what she meant by this. I asked her to explain and straight away a scornful tone came into her voice which took me by surprise because she had been so pleasant.

She said, 'BLOODY HELL DO I HAVE TO SPELL IT OUT' she said it as though it was a challenge.

My reaction was to agree to go with her. She told me where to park the car. It was just off this road we turned left we came to this field which sloped up I parked near the field. We sat there for a minute talking then all of a sudden her tone changed and she said 'WELL WHAT ARE WE WAITING FOR LETS GET ON WITH IT'.

Before we stopped she had said that it would cost a fiver. I was a bit surprised I was expecting it to be a bit romantic. I think she had been drinking because she was being irrational. I couldn't have intercourse in a split second I had to be aroused. At this point she opened the car door and got out. She slammed the door and shouted 'I'M GOING, ITS GOING TO TAKE YOU ALL FUCKING DAY'. She shouted something like 'YOU'RE FUCKING USELESS'.

I suddenly felt myself seething with rage. I got out of the car wanting to hit her to pay her back for the insult. I went to her and said 'HANG ON A MINUTE DON'T GO OFF LIKE THAT'. She was only 3 or 4 strides away she turned and came back to me. She said something like 'OH YOU CAN FUCKING MANAGE IT NOW CAN YOU'. She sounded as though she was taunting me.

I said 'THERE'S NOT MUCH ROOM IN THE CAR CAN WE DO IT ON THE GRASS?' This was my idea of hitting her.

She said 'I'M NOT GOING TO DO IT HERE BLOODY WELL NEXT TO THE CAR'. With that she stormed up the hill into the field. I had a tool box on the back seat of the car and I took a hammer out of the tool box I followed her into the field. I took my car coat off and carried it over my arm I had the hammer in my right hand. I put my coat on the grass. She sat down on the coat. She unfastened her trousers.

She said 'COME ON THEN GET IT OVER WITH'.

I said 'DON'T WORRY I WILL'.

I then hit her with the hammer on her head. I was stood up at that time behind her. I think I hit her on the top of the head. I hit her once or twice on the head. She fell down flat on her back and started making a horrible noise like a moaning gurgling noise.

I thought 'God what have I done' I knew I had gone too far. I ran to the car intending to drive off. I sat in the car for a while I could see her arm moving. I was in a numb panic I still had the hammer in my hand. I put it back in my tool box. I half expected her to get up and realised I would be in serious trouble. I thought the best way out of the mess was to make sure she couldn't tell anybody. I took a knife out of the tool box it had a wood handle with one sharp side the blade was about 7" long about half an inch to three-quarters of an inch wide.

I went to her. She was still lying on her back. I thought that to make certain she was dead I would stab her in places like the lungs and the throat. I stabbed her at least four times once in the throat. Before I stabbed her in the body I pulled her blouse or whatever it was and her bra so I could see where I was stabbing her. I was in a blind panic when I was stabbing her just to make sure she wouldn't tell anyone.

What a damn stupid thing to do just to keep somebody quiet. If I was thinking logical at the time I would have stopped and told someone I'd hit her with the hammer. That was the turning point. I realise I over reacted at the time, nothing I have done since then affected me like this. After I'd stabbed her I went back to the car, I remember that I'd take my coat off the ground after I'd hit with the hammer and I'd taken my coat back to the car. I started the car and shot off backwards along the narrow road leading to the road swung the car round and drove away towards Leeds. I drove home as soon as possible. I was then living at my mother-in-law's house at 44 Tanton Crescent, Clayton, Bradford. I was very frightened and don't even remember driving there. I thought I was bound to get caught. I parked my car outside the house. I'm trying to remember if it was my mother-in-law's house I was living at when I've thought it out now it must have been her house. I looked over my clothing before I went in the house. I went straight to the bathroom and washed my hands and went to bed. I don't have any of the clothes I was wearing that night they are worn out. I cannot honestly remember what I did with the hammer and the knife I don't remember chucking them away that night. I haven't got the knife now I may have kept the hammer in the tool box but I'm not sure of that even. The next day I saw it on the TV news about the murder and I felt sick and I still half expected a knock on the door by the Police. I carried on trying to act as normal living with my wife and in-Laws. At that time I worked at Common Road Tyre

Services at Okenshaw. After that first time I developed and built up a hatred for prostitutes in order to justify within myself the reason why I had attacked and killed WILMA MCCANN.

The next one I did was in Leeds not long after MCCANN. This time I drove to Leeds looking for a prostitute because I felt I could not justify what I had done previously and I felt an inner compulsion to kill a prostitute. This was about a month after Christmas. I drove to Leeds in my Capri about 8.0 pm–9.0 pm. I saw a woman dressed in an overcoat trying to stop drivers from the pavement on the road that leads to Wetherby Road it was near some phone boxes. I stopped and wound the window down. I said 'HOW MUCH?' She said 'FIVE POUNDS'. She got in the car I remember when she got in there was an overpowering smell of cheap perfume and sweat this served all the more for me to hate this woman even though I didn't even know her, looking back I can see how the first murder had unhinged me completely. She had an overcoat on and she was heavily built and had brown hair. She said she knew where we could go. I knew from the outset I didn't want intercourse with her. I just wanted to get rid of her. At that time I think I was dressed in my working clothes at that time I used to wear Wellington boots at work. At her direction I turned the car round and drove back the way I'd come, we had just gone about 400 yards and she told me to turn left. I turned in and then turned left again and drove behind some old buildings it was a cul-de-sac I couldn't bear even to go through the motions of having sex with this woman. On the journey she told me that she could drive.

I wanted to do what I'd got in mind as soon as possible. I remember turning on the ignition again so that the red warning light came on and pretended that the car would not start I said I would have to lift up the bonnet to sort it out. I asked her if she would give me a hand. We both got out of the car I lifted up the bonnet of the car. I had picked up a hammer which I had put near my seat for that purpose. I told her I could not see properly without a torch. She offered to use her cigarette lighter to shine under the bonnet. She was holding her lighter like this I took a couple of steps back and I hit her over the head with the hammer I think I hit her twice she fell down onto the road. I took hold of her hands or wrists and pulled her into a yard which had rubbish in. I then made sure she was dead by taking a screwdriver and stabbing her repeatedly. I pulled her dress up and her bra before I stabbed her to make it easier. To be truthful I pulled her clothes up in order to satisfy some sort of sexual revenge on her as on reflection I had done on MCCANN.

I stabbed her frenziedly without thought with a Philips screwdriver all over her body. I had taken the screwdriver with the hammer in the well of the driving seat. I was seething with hate for her. I remember picking up a piece of wood from the yard about 2–3 ft long 3" × 1" and pushing up against her vagina with it as she lay on her back. I cannot recall taking her knickers down. I threw the wood away in the yard. I left her lying on her back I never took anything from her. Just as I was about to get into my car a car came round with its lights on and stopped a few yards from where my car was. I don't know what make of car it was but it scared me. I put the hammer and screwdriver on the car floor and drove away. I went straight home to my mother-in-law's house. At that time I had a feeling of satisfaction and justification for what I'd done. I found that I didn't have any blood on my clothes which I could see so I had no need to dispose of them. I am still unable to recall if it was the same hammer I used on JACKSON as I did on MCCANN, but I do recall buying a new hammer from a hardware shop near the roundabout in Clayton, it had a flat head on one side and a nail extractor on the other which I later used on women. The hammer I used on the first two had a flat head on one end and a ball on the other.

The next one I did was IRENE RICHARDSON. I then owned a Red Corsair and also a white Corsair KWT 721D the reg no of the red one was PHE 355G. I had both of these at the same time and I honestly cannot remember which one I was using that night. I drove to Leeds after the pubs shut. It was my intention to find a prostitute to make it one more less. I saw this girl walking in some cross streets in the middle of the vice estate near a big club. I stopped my car and she got in without me saying a word. I told her I might not have wanted her, she said 'I'LL SHOW YOU A GOOD TIME. YOU ARE NOT GOING TO SEND ME AWAY ARE YOU'. She told me to drive to the park. At this time you knew where I was picking them up. She told me where to drive and we came to this big field which was on my left. I drove off the road onto the field and stopped near some toilets. She wanted to use the toilets so she got out and went over to them. She came back and said they were locked. Before she went to the toilet she took off her coat and placed it on the ground. When she came back she said she would have a wee on the ground. She took her boots off and placed them on the ground then she crouched down to have a pee. By this time I was out of the car and I had my hammer in my hand. As she was crouching down I hit her on the head from behind at least twice maybe three times she fell down. I then lifted up her clothes and slashed her in the lower abdomen and also slashed her throat. I left her lying face down and I covered her up with her coat I put her knee boots on top of her before I covered her up. I then got into my car and drove off the field. I cannot remember whether I drove off or backed off. When I got to the road I saw a couple sitting on a bench near the toilets. I did not see a car.

I was living with my wife at 6 Garden Lane, Heaton I drove straight home. I looked at my clothes before I went in I did not see any blood stains I was wearing jeans and I believe I had some boots on. I don't remember throwing any of my clothes away. I kept the Stanley knife but I haven't seen it for a long time I think I may have lent it to someone. I'm still not sure which car I was in the red or white Corsair. I sold the white Corsair first to a lad called RONALD BARKER who lives at 46 Tanton Crescent, Clayton. He only had it about a week and he seized it up. I kept the red one for several months. I bought the white Corsair back off RONALD after about two weeks and sold it at Canal Road Scrap Yard at Bradford. By this time after RICHARDSON killing prostitutes became an obsession with me and I couldn't stop myself, it was like some sort of a drug.

The next one was a couple of months later in Bradford, this was PATRICIA ATKINSON. It was a Saturday night late on. I drove off Lumb Lane into Church Street I knew this was a prostitute area. I was in my Corsair (either the white one or the red one). I saw this woman in St Pauls Road at a junction with another road she appeared drunk and was banging on the roof of a white Mini and was shouting and bawling 'FUCK OFF' and such things to the driver who then drove off at speed.

I pulled up to her and stopped and without me asking she jumped in the car. She said 'I FUCKING TOLD HIM WHERE TO GET OFF'. She said, 'I'VE GOT A FLAT WE CAN GO THERE'. She told me where to go. We turned right at the junction with Manningham Lane, turned left down Queens Road, left into Oak Avenue and turned 2nd left and stopped at her flat. She told me she lived alone. I parked up outside her flat and she got out and went in. I picked up a hammer as I got out of the car. I remember this was a claw hammer that I had bought at the Clayton hardware shop. I followed her into the flat, she closed the curtains and I hung my coat on the hook on the back of the door. She took her coat off and sat on the bed her back was slightly towards me I went up to her and hit her on the back of the head with the hammer she fell off the bed onto the floor. I picked her up and put her back on the bed. This was the first time I had noticed the red blood, before it had always been dark but this time in the light I saw lots of blood on the bed and on the floor. When she was on the floor I hit her another twice or three times before I put her on the bed I pulled the bedclothes back before I put her on the bed.

She had already pulled her jeans down before I hit her. I pulled her clothes up and I hit her several times on her stomach and back with the claw part of the hammer and I saw that I was making marks on her body doing this. I then covered her up [with] the bed clothes. I think she was lying face down or on her side when I left her. When I first hit her she was making a horrible gurgling sound and she carried on making this noise even though I'd hit her a few times. She was still making a gurgling noise when I left, but I knew she would not be in a state to tell anybody. I drove home and put my car in the garage. I looked at my clothes at the garage I saw that I had some blood on the bottom of my jeans I went in the house my wife was in bed. I took my jeans off and rinsed them under the cold tap and hung them up. I also saw some blood on one of my shoes or they may have been boots I rinsed this under the tap and wiped it with a sponge. I believe I was wearing a pair of brown Doc Martins boots at that time. I'm trying to think what I did with the claw hammer I think I used it again on a woman. I have thrown it away over a wall near Sharps Printers at Cottingley I can't remember when it was exactly. At that time I carried on as though nothing had happened. I was then working at Clarks in Bradford.

The next one I did I still feel terrible about, it was the young girl JAYNE MCDONALD [*sic*]. I read recently about her father dying of a broken heart and it brought it all back to me. I realised what sort of a monster I had become. I believed at the time I did it that she was a prostitute. This was on a Saturday night. I drove to Leeds in my Corsair I think it was the red one but I'm not 100% sure. At this time the urge to kill prostitutes was very strong and I had gone out of my mind. I saw this lass walking along quite slowly towards the crossing near the Hayfield pub in Chapeltown Road. I anticipated that she was going to walk up one of the streets up past the Hayfield. I drove my car into the Hayfield pub car park and got out.

I took my hammer out of the car. I think it was the claw hammer. I also had a knife with me that time it was a kitchen type knife with a black ebonite handle and a thin blade. I walked towards the narrow street behind the Hayfield to see where she was and just as I got there she was walking up. I walked behind her I was very near to her, I followed her for a short distance she never looked round. I took the hammer and I hit her on the back of the head and she fell down. I then pulled her by the arms face down into a yard behind a fence I recall that her shoes were making a horrible scraping sound on the ground. I pulled her into the corner of this yard I hit her another once at least maybe twice on the head. I pulled her clothes up exposing her breasts and I stabbed her several times with the knife in the chest before this I stabbed her in the back. I left her lying the corner. I cannot remember whether she was lying face up or face down she was wearing a jacket and a skirt. I walked back down the same street to where I had parked my car. As I got to the car park I saw a group of people walking up the narrow street [Reginald Street], from Chapeltown Road. I got into my car and drove away into Reginald Terrace into Chapeltown Road and drove straight home. I think my wife may have been working that night. I have remembered that my wife started working some Friday and Saturday nights at Sherrington Private Nursing home in Bradford. That is why I have done a lot of my attacks on a Saturday night.

I don't think I had any blood on me following this one. I cannot recall what I was wearing then I cannot remember what I did with the knife I must have taken it home with me and washed it I feel I may have left it in the Corsair when I scrapped it. The hammer may have been the one I threw over the wall at Sharps Printers. When I saw in the papers that MCDONALD was so young and not a prostitute I felt like someone inhuman and I realised that it was a devil driving my against my will and that I was a beast. When the Ripper came up in conversation at work or in a pub I was able to detach my mind from the fact that it was me they were talking about and I was able to discuss it normally. This amazed me at times that I was able to do this.

The next one was MAUREEN LONG. I saw MAUREEN just a couple of weeks ago I was in the Arndale Shopping Centre with my wife when I came face to face with her. I recognised her immediately she seemed to look at me but she obviously didn't recognise me. I was driving along Manningham Lane towards the City Centre one Saturday night in July 1977. It was late at night I saw her walking on the same side as the Mecca towards Bradford Centre. She was wearing a maxi length dress and a jacket sort of coat. She was just past the hamburger stand when I saw her. I stopped my car and said, 'ARE YOU GOING FAR?' She said, 'ARE YOU GIVING ME A LIFT'. I said, if you want one. She got in she told me she had been to the Mecca. She told me where she lived and that she lived with a man who was an ex-boxer and that he was a spoil sport and would not take her to the Mecca. She directed me where to drive to her house which was somewhere off Leeds Road to the left. She pointed out a house in a row of terraced houses where she said she was going. She told me not to stop outside but to drive past. I drove about 20 yards past and stopped. She got out of the car. She had told me that if there was no one in the house we could go in. She had asked me if I fancied her and I told that I did just to please her. She went and knocked at the door of the house and she was banging away for a minute or two. Then she came back and got into the car and told me she knew a place where we could go. She told me where to drive and I drove eventually into Bowling Back Lane and turned right down a cobbled street. I stopped the car some way down the street. There was some spare unlevelled land on the left and a big high wall on the right. She got out of the car and said she was going for a piss first and she went to the spare land and crouched down and had a piss. I had my hammer ready as she got out of the car and I also had a knife I think it was the same knife I had at MCDONALD. I got out of the car whilst she was having a piss and as she was crouching down I hit her on the head with the hammer. She slumped down I pulled her by the hands further onto the spare ground. She was not making any sound. I pulled up her clothes and I stabbed her three or four times with the knife in her chest and back. I did see a caravan with a light on over the spare land but it didn't put me off what I was doing I thought that I had stabbed her enough when I left her. I went back to the car got in and drove off. I was under the impression that the street I was in may be a cul-de-sac so I reversed my car by turning it round in the street I was in, no I didn't, I remember that I backed out of the street into Bowling Back Lane facing towards the City. I drove along Bowling Back Lane towards the general direction of the city centre and drove home to Garden Lane. I believe my wife may have been working that night or else she was in bed. I don't think I found any blood on myself on that occasion. The next day or the day after I heard in the news or read in the paper that the woman was still alive. I got a nasty shock and thought it was the end of the line there and then. I thought she would be able to identify me I think it was about that time that I threw the hammer over Sharps wall.

A few days after I read that LONG was suffering from loss of memory and this made me less worried about being caught. My desire to kill prostitutes was getting stronger than ever and it took me over completely. I was in a dilemma I wanted to tell someone what I was doing but I thought about how it would affect my wife and family. I wasn't too much bothered for myself. I realised things were hotting up a bit in Leeds and Bradford. People had dubbed me the Ripper. I decided to go to Manchester to kill a prostitute. I had read in a paper somewhere or a magazine of a priest chastising what went on in his parish at Manchester where there obviously was prostitutes. One Saturday night in October 1977 I drove over to Manchester I believe it was in my red Corsair. I had a look at my map in Road Atlas to see where Moss Side was and I drove there. I went through Manchester town centre Princess Street I think it was, followed it all the way down past the university which eventually came out near the Moss Side area. It was a run down area and almost immediately on arriving there I saw several girls plying for trade. I pulled up at the kerbside and asked a girl if she wanted business. She was very slim with light coloured hair not bad looking. She told me if I waited further along the road she would meet me there. I drove on two hundred yards and made a right turn then a three point turn to face the main road once again.

After a couple of minutes the girl drew level she saw my car just as she was going to get into another car which had stopped for her. I think this was an 1100 a light coloured one either grey or fawn. She didn't get in but came over to me, which I suppose was the biggest mistake she ever made. She came up and got into my car. She told me she was going to go with the man in the other car until she saw me. She told me she wanted a fiver for business and she told me she knew a place. I drove at her direction until we came to an allotment. She told me to drive in the entrance to the allotment which I did. I said to her 'FANCY COMING HERE, YOU SEE THAT GREENHOUSE' I pointed to a greenhouse that was about 30 yards away 'THAT BELONGS TO MY UNCLE'. I said this to her thinking she would get out the car to use the greenhouse for business. I told her there was plenty of room and some heating in there. I was wanting to see her off. She then asked for the money she said 'YOU'RE NOT FORGETTING ABOUT THE MONEY ARE YOU'. I said 'OF COURSE NOT' and I promptly gave her a five pound note. She got out of the car and headed for the greenhouse I followed her and seeing there was no entrance into the greenhouse from where we were I told her we would have to climb over a low fence. While she was starting to climb over the fence I hit her over the head with the hammer. She fell down and was moaning quite loudly. I hit her again and again on the head until the moaning stopped. At this time I saw some car headlights suddenly come on. These were from a car parked further into the allotments than I was. I had turned sharp right when I drove in and I was parked up close to the hedge. This car was parked about 60 yards further into the allotment. The car started up and I knew it would be moving within seconds so I pulled the girl under the bushes, the perimeter bushes and threw her belongings handbag etc out of the way. On reflection I think there was just her handbag I stood with my back to the hedge and threw the bag diagonally to my right. I stayed where I was, I saw the car out into the road. No sooner had the car gone when another car driving along the road which was a dual carriageway slowed right down I saw through the bushes it was indicating left to come into the allotments. Thinking this was a very dangerous position to be in I hid behind my car. I saw this car drive into the allotments, the car drove up the road turned round and stopped in the same place the other car had just left from. I didn't wait around any longer I jumped into my car and drove off towards the centre of Manchester and drove home. The hammer I used that night was the one I had found lying in my garage after I had taken over my house. I took the hammer back with me. Having driven half way back I realised suddenly that this didn't put me in the clear because I had given her from my wage packet a brand new five pound note. I was working at Clarks then. I was in a dilemma once again. I kept on driving towards home as I didn't realise whether she should be found or not. I decided I could not risk going back to retrieve my £5 note and I carried on home. My wife was either working or in bed when I got home. I was puzzled when no mention of this was made in the newspapers or TV over the next few days. I decided before a week was out that she was lying there undiscovered and that I would go back to retrieve the £5 note.

One night about a week later the opportunity arose for me to go back as we were having a house warming party with family and gathering the coming weekend. My mother and father brothers and sisters came from Bingley to my house and at the end of the party I ran them home then I made my return trip to Manchester. This was about 11 pm on either the Saturday or Sunday. I drove to the allotments in my red Corsair and arrived there within 45 minutes. I turned left off the dual carriageway into the allotments. To get there I had to drive to a roundabout and double back to that side. I turned right when I got into the allotments as I had done before, and parked up about the same place. I found the body still hidden in the place I left it. I pulled it out from the bushes and pulled off her clothes and boots. I went through them desperately trying to find the £5 note. I just threw the clothes about as I took them off. I realised that she hadn't got the £5 note in her clothes, and that it must have been in her handbag. I roamed about all over the allotments frantically searching for the bag, but I couldn't find it I was cursing the girl and my luck all the time. Having not found the £5 note I gave vent to my frustrations by picking up a piece of broken pane of glass and slashing it across her stomach, when I did this there was a nauseating smell which made me reel back and immediately vomit, it was horrendous.

I forgot to say that before I did this it was my intention to create a mystery about the body I felt sure this was the end for me anyway. I had taken a hacksaw out of my car intending to remove her head. I started sawing through her neck the blade might have been blunt because I was getting nowhere at all so I gave it up. If I had cut the head off I was going to leave it somewhere else to make a big mystery out of it. The glass I used was about three-quarters of a pane with the corner missing. I was very frustrated not having found the £5 note and thinking that my time was up. I remembered I kicked her a few times and I rolled her over before I left her. I then drove away realising I should stay looking for the fiver but I thought I had been there long enough.

I got home and went to bed when I got home I was very surprised to see I had not got much blood on me just a bit on my shoe and at the bottom of my trousers on one leg and some on the back of my hand. I washed my hands. I was wearing a pair of casual grey trousers one of my old pair the blood wouldn't come off these i put them in the garage in a cupboard to dispose of later. I was wearing my soft slip on shoes dark brown. I wiped these clean. I don't think I have got them now. I later burned my trousers with some garden rubbish at the other side of our garden wall on the field.

* * *

I read about the body of JEAN ROYLE [Jordan] being found
and sat back waiting for the inevitable as I had assumed that
the line of enquiry about the £5 note would follow. I read
about the note being traced to a Shipley bank I knew Clarks
got the wage money from a Shipley bank and that a local
enquiry would be made and by some miracle I escaped the
dragnet. I've had at least three hacksaws I don't know which
one it was I took to Manchester. I threw the blade away in the
dustbin. One of my hacksaws broke after this and I threw it
in the bin.

I had been taken over completely by this urge to kill and I
couldn't fight it. I went to Leeds one evening in December
1977 to try again. I was in my red Corsair PHE 355G. This is
where I found MARYLYN MOORE. I drove into the Red Light
district at Chapeltown. I was driving along a street I now know
as Leopold Street where I saw her walking along Spencer Place,
from the phone boxes at the end. I saw her reject a man in a
car who had stopped and she carried on. I turned left into
Spencer Place turned first left and left again into a narrow
street and stopped near the corner of the road I had just been
on.

It was my intention to get her into my car with the minimum
of fuss. I knew she had refused to get in one car so I got out
of my car and walked to the corner. She was only a few yards
away walking towards where I was stood. I walked back to my
car and as she came into view I shouted 'BYE NOW SEE YOU
LATER' and 'TAKE CARE' and I waved towards the houses on
my left. I did this to give her reassurance that I was alright. I got
in and started the engine and opened the passenger window. I
asked her if she was doing business. She glanced at the house

said 'YES' and got in. She told me where to drive. She asked my name I told her it was DAVE. We had some conversation in the car but I cannot remember what I might have said. She directed me to this place which was up a narrow lane and I can only describe it as an oasis of mud it was an open area with a building to one side. I parked up. I suggested she got into the back of the car. She agreed and she got out and she went to the rear passenger door nearside. When she got out I got out with my hammer which I had on the floor at my side. I went round the front of my car and up behind her. I took a swing at her with the hammer but I slipped on the mud and lost my balance. I only caught her a glancing blow on the head. She cried out and I hit her again on the head. She was still screaming. After the second blow she fell down. I saw some people walking along about 40 yards away on the narrow road at the top. I jumped in my car and started it up. I put my foot down but the back wheels started spinning and I couldn't drive off at first. When the car got a grip I slewed round to the right and I drove away with a lot of wheel spin. I drove straight home. That night I was wearing the old brown car coat which you've got and a pair of blue jeans and a pair of brown Doc Martins boots.

The one I did after MOORE was YVONNE PEARSON at Bradford. I was driving along Lumb Lane in my red Corsair from the city centre. A light grey or fawn Mark II Cortina started backing out of Southfield Square on my left as I approached so I slowed down to let it out. That's when I saw YVONNE PEARSON she was blonde and was wearing dark trousers. On reflection it was a very fateful moment for her me just slowing down as she came along. She stepped straight up to the car as I stopped and tapped on the window. She asked me if I wanted business.

This was one time when I was genuinely going home as it happened but I still had a hammer in the car on the floor, under my seat. I told her to get in. She suggested that I turn the car round and she told me where to drive. I drove back along Lumb Lane past Drummond Mill turned right down a road onto White Abbey Road and I was directed to turn by YVONNE left into a street behind Silvios Bakery. I drove to the very end of this street where there was a large open space like a parking space and parked the car. I asked her how much she wanted. She said 'IT DEPENDS HOW MUCH YOU CAN AFFORD'. 'A GOOD TIME 5, MORE THAN A GOOD TIME 10'. SHE HAD VERY FEW WORDS TO SAY AFTER THAT, THE LAST WORDS SHE SAID WAS 'SHALL WE GET INTO THE BACK'. We both got out and she went round to the back door of the car on the nearside she tried to open it but it was locked. I opened the front passenger door reached in and opened the rear door catch. As she opened the door I hit her from behind twice on the head with the hammer. She fell down and started to moan loudly. I dragged her by the feet on her back about 20 yards or so to where there was an old settee lying on its back on some spare land. When I got her to the settee she was still moaning loudly. At that moment a car drove up and parked next to my car. I saw there was a blonde woman in the car and a man driving. To stop her moaning I took some filling from the settee. I held her nose and shoved the straw into her mouth then I shoved it down her throat. I was kneeling behind the settee hiding from the motor car keeping hold of her nose. I let go after a while to see if she was still making a noise through her nose but when I did she started again so I took hold of her nose again. The car seemed to be there for ages before it drove away. I stayed still petrified with fear while the car was there.

* * *

When the car had gone I was seething with rage. Her jeans were nearly off because she had undone them at the car and when I was pulling her by the feet I nearly pulled them off. I pulled her jeans right off. I think I kicked her hard to the head and body I was senseless with rage and I was kicking away furiously at her. After this I remember acting very strangely, I talked to her and apologised for what I had done but she was dead. I put the settee on top of her. I was very distraught and I was in tears when I left her. This was the first time I had apologised to someone I had killed. I drove home I cannot recall the time but it was after 9.00 pm I can't remember if Sonia was in the house or not. I remember stopping on the way home and I just sat in the car trying to work out why I had done this killing my mind was in a turmoil. Oh I've just remembered it might have been a walling hammer that I used on YVONNE, there was two walling hammers in the garage of the house when I moved in I remember I put one in the car when I threw the other one away at Sharps. It might still be in the garage somewhere. I kept reading the papers and I found it incredible to believe that she hadn't been found. I read a story that she had gone to Wolverhampton. I didn't dare go back to where she lay there was no reason to go back.

Before YVONNE was found I had committed another murder in Huddersfield HELEN RYTKA. I did not know the Huddersfield Red Light area but one day I had to make a delivery in Huddersfield in the afternoon. I noticed a few girls plying for trade near the Market Area. Two or three nights later I decided to pay them a visit. The urge inside me to kill girls was now practically uncontrollable. I drove to Huddersfield in my red Corsair one evening. When I got to the Red Light area I came across one or two girls walking round the street. I stopped and

asked one girl if she was doing business. She said Yes but I'd
have to wait as her regular client was picking her up at any
minute. She was a half cast girl. I drove off and after going
about 50 yards round the corner I saw another half cast girl.
I stopped and asked her and she got in. She told me she shared
a flat with her sister but she was quite willing to have sex in
the car. She said it would cost £5. She told me where to drive
which was only about 80–90 yards away in a timber yard. I
drove straight into this yard and parked in an area at the end
of the lane that ran between the stack of wood. On the way
to the Yard we passed the half cast girl I had tried to pick up.
She told me that it was her sister. Afterwards when I had read
about it in the papers I realised that I had seen these two
RYTKA sisters in Clayton where they used to live. I must have
given her some money but I can't recall handing it over to
her, because she started to undo her jeans and started to pull
them down. Then she hesitated and she said it would be better
in the back of the car. I agreed thinking that it was what I
wanted her to do anyway. We both got out she went to the
rear nearside door. I picked up a hammer from under my seat
and walked round the front. By the time I got to her she had
opened the rear door and was getting in. I hit her on the
head with the hammer as she was practically into the car. The
hammer struck the edge of the top door sill and diminished
the impact with her skull to a mere tap. She jumped back in
alarm out of the car at the same time letting go of her jeans
which fell down around her knees and she exclaimed 'WHAT
WAS THAT'. To which I replied 'JUST A SMALL SAMPLE OF
ONE OF THESE'. And I hit her a furious blow to her head
which knocked her down she just crumpled like a sack. She
was making a loud moaning sound so I hit her a few more
times on the head. On looking up I realised that I had done

this in full view of two taxi drivers who were no more than 35 yards away up the right hand side of the woodyard. Their cars were parked one behind the other facing me. The drivers were stood talking to each other. I dragged HELEN by the hands to the end of the woodyard. I then pulled off her jeans and her knickers and her shoes or boots. She had stopped moaning but she wasn't dead. I could see her eyes moving. She held up her hand as though to ward off any further attack from me. I told her not to make any more noise and she would be alright. By this time I was aroused sexually so I had intercourse with her. I just undid my fly I spread her legs out and did it. It only took a few minutes before I ejaculated inside her. Her eyes appeared to be focusing on me when I was doing it but she just laid there limp she didn't put anything in to it. When I'd finished I got up and she began moaning once again and started to move as well. We were out of sight of the taxi drivers but I knew they could quite possibly have heard the sounds. I couldn't drive for obvious reasons one being that she was still showing signs of life. I was worried sick that I was about to be discovered and was furious that she could not keep quiet. I took my knife from my pocket, I think it was the one with the rosewood handle which is probably still at home in my knifedrawer. I plunged the knife into her ribs and again into her heart I did this five or six times. Before I did this I had taken all her clothes off apart her jumper. I threw these over the wall. I dragged her by the arms to where I thought she would not be discovered which was behind some bushes in a gap between a woodpile and a wall. There wasn't much room I had to part lift part pull her in. Then I covered her up with a piece of asbestos sheet. I stayed in the woodyard for some minutes and when I looked the taxi drivers had gone. I reversed out of the yard and drove off. The operation had taken about half an hour. I drove straight home. I found that I had some blood on my fawn court shoes I rinsed it off. I had my Levi jeans and I think I had a dark blue pullover on but I couldn't see any blood on these.

I kept the hammer I'm not sure which one it was but I don't think it was the walling hammer. The urge inside me still diminished my actions when it came to the fore. The next time I felt this way I paid another visit to Manchester one evening a few months after RYTKA. I went there in my red Corsair to the Red Light area. When I got there there was no sign of any girls so after reaching a night club on a corner in a small labyrinth of terraced houses about three quarters of a mile square I took the third left after the night club which was a long street running from one end to the other of this area.

I drove down to the bottom end and there I saw a woman obviously waiting to be picked up. It was VERA MILLWARD. I stopped and asked her if she was doing business. She said 'YES' but it would have to be in the car. The price was £5 she got in and I drove off. She told me where to drive and I followed her directions which led us into a hospital grounds. I stopped the car in an area near a narrow road from where I could see an Archway obviously used by pedestrians. I parked up the car and suggested to her that it would be better in the back. I don't think I'd paid her. She got out of my car and went to the back door. I picked my hammer up from under the seat and walked round the back of the car. As she was opening the rear door I hit her on the head with the hammer and she dived backwards past where I was stood. She was on her hands and knees when I hit her again at least once. She fell flat on her face. I pulled her by her wrists over to the edge of the area where there was either a fence or bushes. I took out my knife I was carrying I think it may have been the same one I used on RYTKA I'm not sure. I pulled her clothes up and slashed her stomach either vertical or diagonal. It opened up her stomach. Then I rolled her over onto her stomach and left her lying there. I drove away. I think I had to reverse out to get back again. I didn't get any blood on me on that occasion. I think I was wearing my brown car coat which you've got.

Following MILLWARD the compulsion inside me seemed to lay dormant but eventually the feeling came welling up and each time they were more random and indiscriminate. I now realised I had the urge to kill any woman and I thought this would eventually get me caught but I think that in my sub-conscious this was what I really wanted.

The next one was JOSEPHINE WHITAKER at Halifax. By this time I had a black fastback Sunbeam Rapier NKU 888H. I had sold my red Corsair to a chap who lived in Eccleshill because it had a raggy gear box. I drove to Halifax I'd been driving round aimlessly the mood was in me and no woman was safe while I was in this state of mind. Without realising or without having a particular destination I arrived in Halifax late at night.

I drove along through the centre passed the Bulls Head round the roundabout past the Halifax Building Society. I came to a wide road with a sweeping curve to it I took a right turn and eventual came to a big open grass area. I just kept driving round this grassy area until I came to a row of Terrace Houses about a quarter of a mile from the grass area. I saw JOSEPHINE

WHITAKER walking up this street. She was wearing a three-quarter length skirt and a jacket. I parked up in this street with terrace houses and started to follow her on foot and I caught up with her after a couple of minutes. I realised she was not a prostitute but at that time I wasn't bothered I just wanted to kill a woman. When I caught up with her I started talking to her. I asked her if she had far to go. She said, 'IT'S QUITE A WALK'. She didn't seem alarmed by my approach. I continued walking alongside her and she started speaking to me about having just left her grandmother's and that she had considered staying there but had decided to walk home. I asked her if she had considered learning to drive I think she said she rode a horse and that it was a satisfactory form of transport. We were approaching the open grassland area. She told me that she normally took a short cut across the field. I said you don't know who you can trust these days. It sounds a bit evil now there was I walking along with my hammer and a big Philips screwdriver in my pocket ready to do the inevitable.

We both started to walk diagonally across the grass field we were still talking when we were about 30–40 yards from the main road. I asked her what time it was on the clock tower which was to our right. She looked at the clock and told me what time it was. I forget the time she said. I said to her she must have good eyesight and I lagged behind her pretending to look at the clock. I took my hammer out of my pocket and hit her on the back of the head twice she fell down and she made a loud groaning sound. To my horror I saw a figure walking along the main road from my right. I took hold of her by the ankles and dragged her face down away from the road further into the field. She was still moaning as I did this. When I thought I was a safe distance from the road I stopped.

Then I heard voices from somewhere behind me to my left. I saw at least two figures walking along the path across the field toward the Huddersfield Road. I forgot to mention that on the way up to the grass we passed a man walking a dog. We were within five feet of him. As these people were walking on the path she was still moaning loudly. I took my screwdriver I remember I first pulled some of her clothing off. I was working like lightning and it [was] all a blur. I turned her over and stabbed her numerous times in the chest and stomach with the screwdriver. I was in a frenzy. After I'd stabbed her she stopped moaning. I left her lying face down. I walked over to the main road but I thought I saw someone coming up from the bottom so I went back across the field the way I had come and went to my car. I drove home I don't think I had any blood on me but my feet were covered in mud. I had my black boots on which had been worn out and thrown in the bin. I had my old brown coat on that night.

My urge to kill remained strong and was totally out of my control. The next victim of mine was BARBARA LEACH at Bradford. At that time September 1979 I had my Rover 3.5 FHY 400K. I think I had been working on my car one Saturday night and I took it out for a run. I had the urge which was in me and I went to look for a victim. It was late so I drove straight into town and then found myself going up by the university. When I reached the Manville Arms I had just passed it when I saw a girl who I later found out was BARBARA LEACH. She was walking up the road on my left.

I drove past her and turned left into a wide street. I just drove a few yards and stopped on the nearside. I was just going to get out of the car when Miss LEACH turned the corner and walked towards the car. She was walking at a very slow pace. She was wearing jeans. She carried on walking passed the car. I left the car and followed her for several yards. I had my hammer out and I think I had my big screwdriver with me. When she reached an entrance yard to a house I hit her on the head with the hammer she fell down. She was moaning. I took hold of her by the wrists or was it by the ankles and dragged her up this entrance to the back of the house. She kept making loud moaning noises. There was like a dustbin area at the rear of the house I remember that I stabbed BARBARA with the screwdriver the same one as WHITAKER and I remember that I put her in the dustbin area and covered her up with something but I was acting like an automaton and I can't seem to remember the sequence of actions. I think I was wearing my brown coat that night. When I left her I went to my car and drove away and went straight home. I remember I later threw the big screwdriver away over the embankment near the lorry park on the westbound side of Hartshead Service Station.

The last one I did was JACQUELINE HILL up at Headingley. This was on a Monday night. I drove to Leeds on Leeds Bradford Road straight through the traffic lights at Kirkstall up the hill to Headingley. I was in my Rover. I saw a Kentucky Fried Chicken place. I parked up outside it and went in and bought some fried chicken. I took it back to the car and ate it in the car. I had parked in a car park at the back of the Kentucky Fried Chicken place. When I'd had this I drove out to the traffic lights intending to turn right at the main road but I found it was a no right turn so I carried straight on through the lights. I turned right into a road, right again and came back to the main road it was just a junction with no traffic lights. I turned left on the main road (Otley Road). I was driving slowly when I saw Miss HILL walking on the pavement to my right towards the road I now know is Alma Road. I decided she was a likely victim. I drove just passed her turned right into Alma Road and parked in the nearside about 5–6 yards up; and waited for her to pass. I saw her walk up the right-hand side of the road [Alma Road]. I got out of the car and followed about 3 yards behind her. As she drew level with an opening on the right hand side I took my hammer out of my pocket and struck her a blow on the head. She fell down she was making a noise. By this time I was again in a world of my own out of touch with reality. I dragged her I cannot remember whether by the feet or the hands into the entrance to the spare land. Just as I got there a car drove into Alma Road from Otley Road with its headlights on. I threw myself to the ground so I wouldn't be seen. The car passed. I can't imagine how I wasn't seen. By now Miss HILL was moving about and I think I hit her once again or maybe twice on the head. Then I dragged her further into the spare lane out of sight of the road. As I was doing this a girl walked passed the entrance I think she was walking up the road away from Otley Road. I just stopped dead and waited for her to pass.

I pulled Miss HILL's clothes off most of them I had a screwdriver on me I think it had a yellow handle and a bent blade. I stabbed her in her lungs. Her eyes were wide open and she seemed to be looking at me with an accusing stare. This shook me up a bit I jabbed the screwdriver into her eye but they stayed open and I felt worse than ever. I left her lying on her back with her feet towards the entrance. I think she was dead when I left. I went to my car and drove up Alma Road to the top and turned round and drove back down to Otley Road. I remember that when I reached about halfway down someone walking indicated to me that I was obviously going the wrong way down a one way street but I carried on into Otley Road and turned left I turned right at the lights and drove home. The hammer I used on HILL was the one I dumped at Sheffield with the knife I've told you about before.

SGD P W Sutcliffe   WTD: J Boyle DI P Smith DS 368
                              D A F O'Boyle DS 4169

I have read the above statement and I have been told that I can correct alter or add anything I wish. This statement is true I have made it of my own free will.

SGD: P W Sutcliffe   WTD: J Boyle DI P Smith DS 368
                              D A F O'Boyle DS 4169

APPENDIX B

Subsequent Police Statements, January–February 1981
(Crown Copyright)

1. Statement of Detective Sergeant Peter Smith, Incident Room, Millgarth Street Police Station, Leeds, 12 January 1981 (extracts)

At 1.36 p.m. on Sunday 4th January 1981, I was present when Detective Inspector Boyle interviewed the accused, PETER WILLIAM SUTCLIFFE, in the detective sergeants' office at Dewsbury Police Station. The officer told him of our identities and that we were members of the Murder Enquiry Team at Leeds, investigating the murders of several women in the Yorkshire and Lancashire areas, over a period of time. SUTCLIFFE said, 'YES'. The interview then continued as follows, questions being asked by DI BOYLE, whilst I made the notes.

Q I understand you were interviewed yesterday by DS O'BOYLE about your movements during last Friday afternoon and evening up until the time you were arrested at Sheffield.

A Yes, I've told him what happened.

Q I am not concerned with the allegation of theft of car number plates. I want to speak to you about a more serious matter, concerning your reason for going to Sheffield that night.

A I've told him all about that night.

Q I've spoken to Sergeant O'BOYLE and I am not satisfied with your account of that night.

A What do you mean.

Q Why did you go to Sheffield that night.

A I gave three people a lift to Rotherham and Sheffield from Bradford. They stopped me on the M606 and offered me £10 to take them home, so I did.

Q I don't believe that. I believe you went to Sheffield on Friday night for the sole purpose of picking up a prostitute.

A That's not true. It was only after I got to Sheffield and had declined an offer to go with a prostitute that I decided to use the money I got from the hitch-hikers and go with one.

Q When you were arrested in Sheffield you had a prostitute in your car which had false plates on it. I believe you put them on to conceal the identity of your vehicle in the event of it being seen in a prostitute area.

A No, that's not true. To be honest with you I have been so depressed of late I put them on because I was thinking of committing a crime with the car.

Q I believe the crime you were going to commit was to harm a prostitute.

A No, that's not true.

Q Do you recall that before you were put in a police car at Sheffield you left your car and went to the side of a house.

A Yes, I went to urinate against the wall.

Q I think you went there for another purpose.

He made no reply.

Q Do you understand what I am saying. I think you are in trouble, serious trouble.

A I think you've been leading up to it.

Q Leading up to what.

A The Yorkshire Ripper.

Q What about the Yorkshire Ripper.

A Well, it's me.

Q Peter, before you say anything further I must tell you you are not obliged to say anything unless you wish to do so but what you say may be put in writing and given in evidence. Do you understand.

A Yes, I understand.

Q If you wish you may have a solicitor present on your behalf.

A No, I don't need one. I just want to tell you what I've done. I'm glad it's all over. I would have killed that girl in Sheffield if I hadn't been caught, but I'd like to tell my wife myself. I don't want her to hear about it from anyone else. It's her I'm thinking about and my family. I'm not bothered about myself.

Q You didn't go to the side of the house to urinate did you.

A No, I knew what you were leading up to. You've found the hammer and the knife haven't you.

Q Yes we have, where did you put them.

A When they took the girl to the Panda car I nipped out and put them near the house in the corner. I was panicking, I was hoping to get bail from there and get a taxi back and to pick them up. Then I would have been in the clear.

Q Tell me, if you are the so-called Ripper, how many women have you killed.

A Eleven, but I haven't done that one at Preston. I've been to Preston but I haven't done that one.

Q Are you the author of the letters and the tape-recording posted from Sunderland to the police and the Press from a man admitting to be the Ripper.

691

A No I am not. While ever that was going on I felt safe. I'm not a Geordie. I was born at Shipley.

Q Have you any idea who sent the letters and the tape.

A No, it's no one connected with me. I've no idea who sent them.

Q How did all this start.

A With WILMA MCCANN. I didn't mean to kill her at first but she was mocking me. After that it just grew and grew until I became a beast.

Q How did you kill WILMA MCCANN.

A I hit her with a hammer because I was in a rage. But I don't think I meant to kill her. Then I realised the trouble I was in and thought I had to finish her off, so I stabbed her. [...]

Q Who was the last women you killed.

A JACQUELINE HILL at Leeds.

Q How did you kill her.

A I followed her and hit her on the head with a hammer. Then I dragged her into some spare land out of sight.

Q What else did you do to her.

A I stabbed her in the lung.

Q What with.

A A screwdriver.

Q Did you stab her anywhere else.

A Yes I stabbed her in the eye because her eyes were open and she seemed to be looking at me.

Q Did you do anything else to her.

A I pulled her clothes off.

Q Do you know all the names of your victims.

A Yes, I know them all.

Q Do you keep any Press cuttings of them or make any records.

A No, they are all in my brain reminding me of the beast I am.

Q Have you attacked any women who haven't died.

A Yes, MAUREEN LONG was one. I saw her in the Arndale Centre the other day. I got the shock of my life but she didn't recognise me.

Q Who else.

A MARILYN MOORE at Leeds.

Q You say you have killed eleven women. Just take your time and think about how many there are.

A It's twelve, not eleven. Just thinking about them all reminds me what a monster I am. I know I would have gone on and on but now I'm glad I've been caught, and I just want to unload the burden. [...]

At 9.50 a.m. on Monday 5 January 1981 I was present in the Detective Sergeants office along with DI BOYLE and DS O'BOYLE when we again interviewed Sutcliffe. [...]

DS O'BOYLE then produced a hammer and a knife. He reminded SUTCLIFFE of the caution and showed these to him, and said

Q Have you seen these before.

A Yes they're mine. Those are the ones that I left at the house in Sheffield.

The officer then produced a blue and pink cord.

Q This was found in your possession, I believe you may have used this in an attack on a woman.

A Yes I used it on that girl at Headingley no so long ago. She was walking slow like a prostitute, I followed her down the narrow road. I hit her on the head with a hammer. I didn't have any tools on me to finish her, so I used that rope to strangle her, but I was overcome with remorse so I didn't finish her off. I apologised to her and left her there.

Q There was a student called BANDARA attacked in Chapel Lane on Wednesday 24th September last year.

A That's the one I'm talking about. [. . .]

Q A similar incident to that happened on 20th August 1980 when a woman called MARGUERITE WALLS was found murdered having been attacked and strangled in a similar fashion at Pudsey. Did you do that.

A No that wasn't me. You have a mystery on your hands with that one. I've only used the rope once on that girl at Headingley.

Q Do your recall me asking you where you were last Bonfire Night. I've made some enquiries and I now believe you attacked a girl called Teresa Sykes at Huddersfield that night, about 8 p.m.

A Yes that's right I did. I saw her walking along the road and followed her down this footpath and hit her a couple of times and knocked her down. But someone started shouting and I ran away and hid in a garden.

DI Boyle then continued the interview as follows:

Q Is there anything else you want to tell me.

A All this really started in 1974. I was done out of £10 by a prostitute in Manningham. She went to get it changed at a garage next to the Belle Vue pub and didn't come back. This poisoned my mind against prostitutes. [. . .]

2. Statement of Detective Sergeant Peter Smith, 28 January 1981 (extracts)

At 10.05 am on Friday 16th January 1981, together with Detective Inspector Boyle, I saw the accused PETER WILLIAM SUTCLIFFE, at Leeds Prison, in the presence of his solicitor MR MCGILL.

DI Boyle cautioned him, reminded him of our previous interview with regard to a Philips screwdriver alleged to have been thrown away by him and asked him if he could show us where he had thrown the screwdriver. He said, 'Yes'.

Accompanied by his solicitor and prison officers, we then drove in a prison vehicle at his direction to the Woolly Edge Service Station, off the M1 Motorway (southbound). There he pointed to an embarkment at the side of the lorry park and said, 'That's where I threw it, I was in my lorry'. DI BOYLE asked him when he had thrown the screwdriver and he said 'Sometime last summer'. SUTCLIFFE was then returned to Leeds Prison where at 11.05 am that same date in the presence of his solicitor, SUTCLIFFE was interviewed by DI BOYLE in my presence, in the Visitors Room.

The officer reminded him of the caution and the interview went as follows:

Q Was it your own screwdriver or the firm's.
A It was mine, an old one, I've had in the garage a long time.
Q Can you describe it.
A It had a wooden handle with the varnish worn off.
Q Have you adapted it in any way.

A I think I used it as a hole puncher for riveting. I sharpened it up with a grindstone.

Q Would that alter the initial shape of the head.

A Yes, I did, it was no good as it was for that job.

Q What shape did it finish up.

A It ended up sharp at the end.

Q What stone did you sharpen it on.

A Either on the floor in the garage at home or with a Black and Decker carborunum, it altered it from a star shape to like a bradawl.

Q Did you use it for work as well.

A No, I didn't use it for work.

Q What was it doing in your cab.

A I just took it to throw away, that's all. It looked a horrible looking thing. [. . .]

At 9.50am on Thursday the 22nd of January 1981 I was present with DI BOYLE interviewed the accused SUTCLIFFE in the hospital at Leeds Prison in the presence of his solicitor Mr KERRY MCGILL.

DI BOYLE said to him, 'There are a few points which need to be cleared up and I propose to ask you some more questions'. The officer cautioned him and the interview continued as follows:

Q You have said you attacked ANNA ROGULSKYJ in Keighley in July 1975 with a hammer. Was that the first.

A Yes, I'm sure it was.

Q Where did you hit her.

A On the head.

Q What were your intentions when you hit her.

A I think I intended to kill her but as it turned out I didn't.

Q How did you come to have a hammer with you at that time.

A Because I had this idea in mind before that. I think this had developed over a period of time.

Q What do you mean.

A I think it may have started back in 1965/66 when I had an accident on my motor bike, I was with a gang of mates and went up to [the] pub at Eldwick. There was some trouble with a bus load of people from Bradford who were having a party at the pub. We realised that we were out numbered and we rode away. The bikes had been attacked as well, some being knocked over and some had the tyres let down. [. . .]

Q What happened.

A I ran into a telegraph pole just round a right hand bend about half a mile from the pub going towards Bingley, just above Edward Beck Bottom. I went into this telegraph pole with my head, I was wearing a crash helmet.

Q Were you injured.

A The day after I had a badly bruised head and forehead and face.

Q Did you receive any medical treatment at the time or later.

A At the time I was carried into the nearest house and cleaned up, I've no idea if a doctor saw me then.

Q Was an ambulance called.

A Someone took me home in a vehicle, I can't remember much about it.[. . .]

Q How did the accident affect you.

A I was left with severe bouts of morbid depression, I used to be subject to hallucinations.

Q What kind.

A Just seeing things that are not there and getting strange noises in my head, humming and buzzing.

Q When did they start.

A I can trace them back to shortly after the accident.

Q What effect did this have on you.

A I used to think I was hearing things and occasionally I'd start conversing with myself.

Q In what way.

A It used to be when I had these sort of attacks. I knew what I was doing but I had this inner conflict.

Q About what.

A My mind was in a haze and I didn't know what was right or wrong, I didn't know whether I was acting rationally or not.

Q How often did these occur.

A Sometimes on average I might get two a month, and other times I might think I was alright, and a few times I thought I was okay and then it would come back, the periods were not regular and there was no pattern to them.

Q Did anything trigger these bouts off.

A I think it was probably linked to the bouts of depression I had and it was possibly then that I had the attacks of buzzing and humming.

Q How did these attacks of depression relate to your attacks on prostitutes.

A I now remember that the incident with a prostitute in Manningham Lane who I gave the £10 to was in 1969 sometime, not as I have previously told you in '74. I remember I had my Morris Minor when I picked her up in Manningham Lane.

Q Was it in your mind at that time to cause her any harm.

A No, I think it was connected with problems with SONIA.

Q What do you mean.

A   At that time I was working at the Water Board I'd been there I think for about a year, she'd started seeing an Italian ice-cream man [...]. He used to pick her up from the Tech and take her out at night.

Q   What did you feel about that.

A   I was depressed and upset because I wasn't in a position to do much about it as I worked on shifts and I was on call. I was deeply upset about it.

Q   Were you jealous.

A   I suppose a bit but I didn't know if anything had happened and I didn't want to lose her. I couldn't concentrate at work, there was one occasion when I went to work I'd been told the night before by my brother [...] that he'd seen SONIA and this man [...] out together in his Triumph Spitfire car, I'd been there all day with an assistant [...], he didn't fully understand the mechanics of the job but I left my post to go and sort out this domestic trouble.

Q   What happened as a result.

A   I was demoted and got a steady number at the Waterworks base at Gilstead.

Q   Is this why you picked up the prostitute.

A   I think it had a direct bearing on it. I was wanting to level the score and I thought by just picking her up I wouldn't have reason to judge SONIA going with this man.

Q   When you picked up the prostitute did you intend having intercourse with her.

A   I thought so at the time but I changed my mind before I got to the stage where we had to do it.

Q   You said earlier when first interviewed, that you were duped out of a ten pound note. What effect did this have on your attitude towards prostitutes.

A   It left me feeling bitter towards them especially when there was a sequel to this with the same person a few weeks later in the Old Crown pub in Bradford.

Q What happened.

A I approached her and said I hadn't forgotten and she could still give me it back. She flatly refused and started joking about it in a loud voice to someone else who was with her. After this I left the pub feeling humiliated and outraged and embarrassed and I felt a hatred for her and her kind. [. . .]

Q Did this incident lead to an attack on a prostitute in Bradford about this time. We have received information from TREVOR BIRDSALL that you, whilst out in a car with him, left the vehicle and subsequently attacked a prostitute.

A That's right.

Q What happened.

A I got out of the car and asked her the time and I hit her.

Q What with.

A A sock with something in it, I can't remember what.

Q Why did you do it.

A I got depressed and was having this trouble with violent headaches and was associating all my troubles and blamed the prostitutes for my problems.

Q Were you seen by the police about this incident.

A Yes.

Q What happened.

A The police visited my parents' home in Bingley, he said he'd traced me through the car, he asked me if I'd hit her with a weapon and I told him I'd used my hand. He said it was possible I had used my hand and gave me a lecture and said the woman was willing not to press any charges.

Q Did you hear anything more about the incident.

A No.

Q What was your intention when you attacked this prosti-
Tute.

A I was out of my mind with the obsession about finding this
prostitute and I'd been out with TREVOR looking out for
this particular one and as it was getting late I just gave vent
to my anger to the first one I saw. [...]

Q Was the first one you killed WILMA MCCANN in Leeds.

A Yes.

Q What time was it when you picked her up.

A Maybe 10.00 pm, I'm not sure.

Q Where were you going when you saw MCCANN.

A To the red light area.

Q What do you call the red light area.

A Round the Chapeltown area.

Q Where did you actually see MCCANN.

A I'd gone under the underpass and taken the A58 Wetherby
turn-off and followed this round to the 14ft which continued left on a downhill slope, she was at the bottom of
a road where it straightened out, on the left side walking
on the grass. She was obviously hoping to get a lift, she
said, 'Thanks for stopping', and was cheerful and friendly
so I set off and carried on driving and instead of carrying
on round to the right she suggested I carried straight on.
She remarked something about it being a nice car.

Q What were your intentions when you picked her up.

A I just stopped on impulse to give her a lift as I'd just come
round the bend.

Q Go on.

A I'd gone there for the purpose of picking up a prostitute
with the intention to kill her. I realised shortly after she
had got into the car that she was a prostitute because she

701

asked me if I wanted business and the evil chain of events went on from there.

Q Are the events related in your statement true in relation to MCCANN.

A Yes, most of them are but some points need straightening out. I may have given the impression by what I've said to her and what she replied that the intent was to have sex but this is not the case. This kind of talk was just a preamble leading up to the true purpose of my killing her. It was my idea to get her to go up a distance up the field. To accomplish this I had to put up with all kinds of language and abuse because she couldn't see the point. I had the tackle with me in my pocket and, in fact, I didn't go back to the car and return to it.

Q What tackle.

A A hammer and a kitchen knife. I hit her with the hammer, she still made loud noises and I hit her with it again and the noises still didn't stop. I then took the knife out of my pocket and stabbed her about four times as I've previously described.

Q Why did you pull her clothes up and expose her body.

A So that when they're found they will look as cheap as they are.

Q Is there any special significance about the way you have inflicted the injuries or the area in which they have been inflicted.

A No, because there's been no one particular area. In any case, the main areas are the lungs, the heart and the throat which I thought were areas where it would kill them quicker.
[...]

Q Was the next one you killed EMILY JACKSON.

A Yes.

Q Is your account in your voluntary statement of how you killed EMILY JACKSON correct.

A Yes, as far as revenge is concerned but not so far as sexual gratification is concerned. [...]

Q When you pushed the piece of wood against her vagina, had you opened her legs first.

A No, but thinking back I may have positioned her to show her as disgusting as she was. [...]

Q Was the next one you killed IRENE RICHARDSON.

A Yes.

Q Where exactly did you pick her up.

A On that same estate near where I picked JACKSON up, it was near Cowper Street, outside the big club on the corner with the steps leading up.

Q How far did you drive to the place you killed her.

A About a mile and a half to two miles.

Q In talking about RICHARDSON you mentioned some toilets a number of times. Are you sure they were toilets.

A I'm going by what she seemed to think there was a building in a field and it looked like toilets.

Q Did you park close to this building.

A Yes, there's a long approach road to it. I parked on the opposite side of the building from the road.

Q You talked about a Stanley knife. Is that what you slashed her with.

A Yes, I think that's what I had with me at the time.

Q Did you use anything else on her.

A I only remember using a hammer and a Stanley knife.

Q Did you move her body at all.

A If I moved the body at all it was only a couple of feet, it was all at the back of the building.

Q Why did you place her boots over her legs before you left her.

A For two reasons, one because I could hear voices from I don't know where, and a car had just driven into an entrance just behind the building, that was to the block of flats I found out later where JIMMY SAVILE lived. Secondly, I was surprised to see how luminous she appeared in the dark. [...]

Q With regard to RICHARDSON, this was more than a year after you killed JACKSON. Why was it so long.

A The main reason really is my state of mind, it seemed okay apart from having a personal battle in my own mind which was in absolute turmoil about whether the right thing was to kill people or not. The next time it happened was like every other time, after some kind of a brainstorm.

Q What do you mean by brainstorm.

A If I ever got into like a morbid depressive state by being over worried by one thing and another, this is when it would lead to a state of hallucination but the only outlets for everything was to brood and blame everything on prostitutes.

Q Was the next one you killed PATRICIA ATKINSON at Bradford.

A Yes. [...]

Q You had seen her giving another fellow a hard time. What made you pick her up.

A I stopped, it was obviously why I picked her up, no decent woman would have been using language like that at the top of her voice.

Q Tell us again what you did as you went into her flat.

A I hung my coat on the door.

Q What did you hang it on, there's no hook.

A I just recall going in and hanging it up. If it wasn't the door it was on the bed or somewhere near the door because the hammer was in the jacket pocket.

Q Which jacket.

A The brown car coat the police have got. The reason I took the coat off was so she wouldn't see the hammer.

Q After you'd hit her on the floor, how did you get her on the bed.

A I just picked her up under the arms and hoisted her up.

Q Did you stand on the bed to do this.

A No.

He was then shown a claw hammer.

Q This was found near where you say you threw a hammer away, could this be the one you used on ATKINSON.

A Yes, that is the very same one.

Q Is that the claw hammer you say you purchased from a hardware shop at Clayton.

A Yes.

Q Did you use this hammer on any other killing.

A I can't say for sure.

Q Why did you hit her with the claw end of the hammer.

A Because I don't think I had any other weapon with me.

Q What sort of injuries did that cause.

A The claw of the hammer caused similar injuries to a knife like a gash or something. [...]

He was then shown an old screwdriver with pointed end.

Q This was recovered from the place you indicate at Woolley Edge Service Station. Is this the implement you referred to.

A Yes.

Q In which incident did you use this.

A In the incident involving BARBARA LEACH in Bradford and JOSEPHINE WHITAKER at Halifax.
Q You refer to it in your statement as originally having been a Philips screwdriver. Are you sure about that.
A Yes I am, it was a giant Philips screwdriver having been badly worn and been converted into a bradawl.
Q Have you modified or altered any other tools to use them as weapons on attacks on women.
A I've not modified any tool for that purpose.

He was then shown a ball pein hammer.

Q This ball pein hammer was found apparently secreted behind timber in a garage at your home. Has this been used to attack a woman.
A It may have been because I kept them together, I don't choose one, I just pick one up. [...]

At 10.05 am on Monday the 26th of January 1981, I was present when DI BOYLE interviewed the accused in the hospital at Leeds Prison in the presence of his solicitor MCGILL.

The officer reminded him of our previous interview, cautioned him and the interview was conducted as follows with myself making notes.

Q Did you kill JAYNE MCDONALD [sic].
A Yes.
Q When you dragged her to the yard after the initial attack was she face down all the time.
A I think she was.

Q You say you stabbed her in the back and the chest. Which came first.

A I think the chest first but I don't remember clearly stabbing her in the back, I just thought I did.

Q Did you stab her before starting to drag her.

A I don't think so, no.

Q Did you put something into one of the wounds after you stabbed her.

A No.

Q Did you attack MAUREEN LONG at Bradford.

A Yes.

Q Has it been your habit to try to get money back you have paid to prostitutes.

A No, I think in most cases I have acted before it got to that stage. [...]

Q Did you kill YVONNE PEARSON at Bradford.

A I did.

Q Is the version of that incident in your statement correct.

A Yes.

Q Before you covered her up, did you place something between her legs.

A No, I don't think so.

Q You describe the instrument on that occasion as a walling hammer. What do you mean by a walling hammer.

A It's like a lump hammer, a long oblong block on a nine inch shaft. [...]

Q What happened to that hammer.

A I honestly couldn't say, I thought it was in the garage.

Q Did you kill ELENA RYTKA at Huddersfield.

A Yes.

Q Is the version about the killing of RYTKA in your statement correct.

A Not exactly, as I confused certain aspects of this with the killing of RICHARDSON in Leeds.

Q What happened with RYTKA.

A From the outset the one purpose I had in mind was to kill her at the first opportunity but things were made difficult from the moment I parked the car because HELEN unfastened her trousers and seemed prepared to start straight away. It was very awkward for me to find a way of getting her out of the car. We were there five minutes or more while I was trying to decide which method to use to kill her. Meanwhile, against my wishes she was in the process of arousing me sexually. I found I did not want to go through with this so I got out of the car on the pretext of wanting to urinate.

Q Did she have a Durex ready for use.

A Not to my knowledge.

Q What do you mean about trying to arouse you sexually.

A This she had done to my distaste by manipulating my penis with her hands.

Q Carry on.

A I didn't urinate but I managed to persuade her to get out as well as we'd be better off in the back of the car. As she was attempting to get in I realised this was my chance so I hit her from behind on the head with the hammer. Unfortunately, during the downward swing the hammer caught the top edge of the door frame and gave her a very light tap on her head. She apparently thought I had struck her with my left hand and she said, 'There no need for that, you don't even have to pay'. I expected her to immediately shout for help as there were a couple of taxis in view about a distance of forty yards or so.

Q How do you know they were taxis.

A I was sure they were taxis because one of them appeared to have a taxi sign on the roof.

Q Was the taxi sign lit.

A Yes.

Q Were the taxi lights on.

A The side lights were on.

Q Carry on.

A She was obviously very scared. I then pushed her forward onto the ground and she stumbled and fell somewhere in front of the car just out of sight of the taxi drivers. I jumped on top of her and covered her mouth with my hand, it seemed like an eternity and she was struggling. I told her if she kept quiet she would be alright. As she had got me aroused less than a minute previously I had no alternative than to go ahead with the act of sex as the only means thereby of persuading her to keep quiet as I had already dropped the hammer several yards away. After what seemed like several more minutes I got up and saw that the cars had gone so I started to grope around looking for the hammer. I found it and as I was turning towards her she tried to run past between me and the car, this is when I hit her a heavy blow to the head.

Q Where was the blow.

A I think it was to the back of her head. I then dragged her back in front of the car and may have hit her again before I dragged her back. I began gathering her belongings and throwing them over a wall.

Q Had you taken her jeans and pants off before having inter-course.

A She'd pulled them down and I pulled them off her ankles and threw them over a wall with her shoes and her bag.

Q Carry on.

A She was obviously still alive then. I took the knife from the front of the car and stabbed her several times in the heart and the lungs.

Q What kind of knife.

A I think it was a kitchen knife.

Q Where is it now.

A I think it was later retrieved by the police from my home.

Q What happened then.

A After this I pulled her to a place a few yards away where I thought she wouldn't be found so quickly, when I got there I covered her with a sheet of asbestos or corrugated metal.

Q Is your account of how you concealed the body and what you were wearing on that occasion as you describe in your statement correct.

A It's as correct as far as I can remember it to be.

Q When you picked RYTKA up which way did you travel to the woodyard.

A Down hill and turned left along a bottom road which I think was below the woodyard and turned sharp right into a cul-de-sac in the woodyard.

Q Did you take any money or any other articles from RYTKA when you left her.

A No. [. . .]

Q Did you attack a girl called APHADYA BANDARA at Headingley, Leeds on the evening of 24th of September 1980.

A Yes. [. . .]

Q What were you intentions when you attacked BANDARA.

A I think my intentions were to kill her. At this point I want to say that in myself I didn't want to kill any of them, it was just something that had to be done.

Q How long had you been in the vicinity before you attacked her.

A About five minutes or so.

Q Did you ask anyone for directions at any time that evening.

A No.

Q What were you wearing at that time.

A I think I had that brown car coat on, I'm not sure what shoes I had on, it may have been some black boots.

Q Which hammer did you use on her.

A I'm not sure, I can't remember which one.

Q Did you put her handbag in or on a dustbin.

A I can't remember whether I lifted the lid up or not.

Q Was it your intention to hide the body behind the dustbin.

A To move her out of sight of the road, yes. [...]

Q Has the ball pein hammer we recovered from Sheffield actually been used for attacks on women.

A I think it's been used before but I'm not sure when.

Q What about the kitchen knife found at Sheffield with the hammer.

A That's not been used before.

Q Were there some other occasions when other people were sat in your car waiting whilst you went off and attacked women.

A No, only those two occasions with BIRDSALL.

Q Other people [...] tell us that you have been with them visiting red light districts in Leeds, Bradford, Halifax, York and Manchester. What was your purpose in all these visits.

A Just simply we went out for a few drinks which was rarely.

Q One of these other people claims to have record of some occasions when you were out together. Three of those occasions coincide with dates of offences you have admitted. The first is 14th of August 1975 when you are said to be out drinking with a group of people in Bingley. Do you recall that.

A No.

Q Another was on the 25th of June, the very night you say you killed MCDONALD in Leeds. On that night had you been drinking in pubs and clubs in Bradford with some friends before you went to Leeds.

A I'm not sure of these days, I don't remember anything but these killings. I doubt it as I only used to go out on odd nights. [...]

Q Apart from drinking, what did you do on these nights out with your friends.

A We usually had a game of snooker.

Q They say you were out looking at and chatting up prostitutes is that true.

A I had done this on occasions but not for that purpose, only to pass comment on them or remark if I saw one.

Q Did anything happen when you were out with these friends which led you to go on later and attack women.

A No.

Q On previous occasions you were interviewed by the police regarding your movements on certain murder dates. You accounted for your movements and gave you wife as alibi. It is now obvious that your wife was not in a position to alibi you for the dates in question.

A On the occasions when I was asked for an alibi and named my wife as someone who could verify this I must stress that these occasions were usually weeks, sometimes months after the particular event and in this case I was able to satisfy the police because my wife would automatically agree that we would have been home as we were practically all the time anyway.

At this state of the interview there was a break for refreshments.

At 3.45 pm the interview continued as follows:

Q I wish to put another matter to you and that is the murder of MARQUERITA [sic] WALLS at Pudsey on the evening of 20th of August 1980. This woman was attacked from behind and killed in circumstances which appear identical to the attack on BANDARA which you have already admitted and I believe you are responsible for killing WALLS.

A Yes, this is true, I did.

Q Will you tell us what happened.

A I was on my way to Leeds with a view to killing a prostitute when I saw that this woman was walking towards me at a distance of about sixty yards. She disappeared around a corner on my left so I slowed down and turned into this particular road. I was already in some kind of a rage and it was just unfortunate for her that she was where she was at the time 'cos I parked the car and got out and followed her along the road. Having caught up with her over a distance of three or four hundred yards, I let her have it with a hammer, I hit her on the head it seems as though there was a voice inside my head saying 'Kill, kill, kill' and as I hit her I shouted, 'You filthy prostitute'. There was nobody else about but as she was on the pavement I dragged her inside a gateway quite a few yards in what appeared to be someone's garden. Round about this time somebody walked pass the entrance, I don't know whether they had seen me or not because they appeared to look in. I didn't have a knife on me this time but I had a length of cord which I strangled her with. I removed her clothes and I was going to leave her in an obvious position for people to see but round about this time the road outside started to be quite busy with pedestrians going back and forth. I changed my mind and covered her up with some straw instead.

Q Where did you finally place her body.

A In the far corner of the garden near a wall. I was very upset again after this time, I knew I couldn't do anything to prevent myself carrying on killing. The inner torment was unimaginable because as strange as it may seem I never wanted to kill anybody at all, I just had to get rid of all the prostitutes whether I liked it or not.

Q Was it the same ligature used on WALLS as you did on BANDARA later.

A Yes, I think it was most likely the same piece of rope.

Q Are you sure.

A It may possibly have been a different piece.

Q Why didn't you tell us about this killing before.

A Because when I was questioned initially I knew I was in such deep water through killing through the method I normally use that this would possibly open completely new lines of enquiry into other murders which could have been committed and which I knew I hadn't done. I thought that maybe it would be better to sort this out at a later date when I had cleared up all the other matters and having denied it first it would have made matters worse at the time if I had changed my mind again. Nothing I would have said could have been taken seriously this is why I'm making a true account of everything and every detail.

Q Why did you change your method of killing.

A Because the press and the media had attached a stigma to me, I had been known for some time as the Yorkshire Ripper which to my mind didn't ring true at all. It was just my way of killing them but actually I found that the method of strangulation was even more horrible and took longer.

Q Even so you repeated this method on BANDARA.

A This is when I decided I couldn't kill people like this. I couldn't bear to go through with it again as there was something deep inside preventing me.

Q Which hammer did you use on WALLS.

A I think it was the one with the piece of wood missing from the handle that you recovered from Sheffield, or the one you found in the garage.

Q What were you wearing when you killed WALLS.

A The same brown car coat and some brown cord trousers and black boots that you've taken from the house.

He was then asked about another matter and he replied:

A No, but there's another one I've remembered, a [woman] in Leeds who I attacked in Soldiers Field, who I intended to kill.

Q When was this.

A I think it was 1976. I'm a big vague on it.

Q Tell me what happened.

A I picked her up in the Chapeltown area, she asked me if I was the police, I said 'No, do I really look like a policeman'. She decided to get into the car and suggested where we go. We ended up in what I knew later as Soldiers Field. We got out of the car at my suggestion and she took off her trousers whilst leaning against a tree and she sat down on the grass and suggested we started the ball rolling. Straight after she said this I hit her with the hammer. Again I don't know what it was this time but I just couldn't go through with it, I could not bring myself to hit her again for some reason or another and I just let her walk away, possibly to tell the nearest policeman or passer-by what had happened. I went back to the car in a stupefied state of mind, I just had a feeling of morbid depression, I didn't care whether she told anybody or not and I drove back home.

Q How many times did you hit her.

A Only once I think.

Q Did you hit her on the front or back or the head.

A Possibly from the back.

Q On the 9th of May 1976, a [woman] [. . .] was attacked in Soldiers Field, Leeds in circumstances similar to what you describe. We have evidence she was struck more than once on the head and received severe head injuries. Does this incident fit in with your recollection.

A Yes, that's the one but I only recall hitting her once, as she got up and walked away, but owing to my state of mind I'm not sure whether I hit her more than once.

Q What vehicle were you using on that occasion.

A My white Corsair.

Q Have you any recollection of the clothing you were wearing.

A No, none at all.

SUTCLIFFE was then interviewed regarding other matters, following which DI BOYLE said to him:

Q I asked you earlier if you were the author of the letters and tape sent to Mr OLDFIELD and the media purporting to be the Yorkshire Ripper. Do you still say you have no knowledge of these.

A Yes, I've no knowledge and it is not part of my attitude as I'm not proud of doing any of the murders and I did not want to do them as I've already said.

The interview was then concluded. [. . .]

3. *Statement of Detective Sergeant Peter Smith, 10 February 1981*

At 3.30 pm on Tuesday the 10th of February 1981, I was present when Detective Inspector BOYLE interviewed the accused SUTCLIFFE, at Leeds Prison in the presence of his solicitor Mr MCGILL.

The officer cautioned SUTCLIFFE and the interview continued as follows:

Q I have a number of lengths of rope which have been recovered variously from your home and garage, I want you to assist me in identifying them.

He was shown a piece of rope recovered from garage, 44 Tanton Crescent.

Q Do you recognise that.
A Never seen it before.

He was shown a piece of rope in a noose, recovered from SUTCLIFFE's lorry. He said:

A I don't think I recognise that one but I use ropes all the time to pull engines out.

He was then shown a piece of rope with length of twine attached. He said:

A That's a piece of lifting rope, I had two or three in the garage and the twine would stop it slipping.

He was shown a length of rope knotted at each end recovered from his garage.

A   Yes, I've seen that one before, that's one of mine, I've held the car boot down with it and used it to carry an engine.

He was shown a rope recovered from his bedroom.

A   I can't recognise that one.

He was shown rope recovered from garage.

A   That's a lifting piece for lifting engines out.

He was then shown rope also recovered from garage.

A   That's another piece I've used for lifting engines.

He was shown a piece of pink and blue cord found in his possession when arrested at Sheffield.

Q   Do you recognise this.
A   That's a piece of rope I used for the BANDARA and WALLS incident. I think I used the same rope on both but I'm not hundred per cent sure.
Q   Have you used any of the other pieces of rope I've shown you as ligatures to attack women.
A   No.
Q   Have you used any pieces of rope or wire as ligatures and thrown them away.
A   I'm certainly not aware of having thrown any away.

He was then shown a knife with a black wooden handle recovered from Sunbeam Rapier NKU 888H.

Q Has that knife been used by you on any attacks on women.
A I think that's certainly the same size as the one I used on MACDONALD but I can't be certain.
Q Did you put that knife in the Rapier.
A I'm not certain but it looks like the knife I used when I fitted the carpets in the car.
Q Can you remember when you fitted the carpets in the car.
A Maybe two or three months after I got the car because I remember water getting in and making the old carpet wet and mouldy.

He was then shown a ball pein hammer:

Q This hammer was found on some waste land adjoining your home about three months ago, is it one of yours.
A No, I've never seen it before, it's got a funny shaped shaft.

He was then shown a handbag and a black Sim Luxe cigarette lighter:

Q These were found on a tip at Bingley about eighteen months ago [...] together with some bloodstained overalls. Have you seen these before.
A No.
Q Do you ever wear rings on your fingers.
A Only if I get dressed up to go out somewhere special.
Q What rings do you possess.
A Two gold rings, one with a red stone in it.
Q Where are they now.

A They're at home on the chest of drawers.

Q In your statement relating to the murder of JEAN JORDAN at Manchester, you stated you were wearing a pair of old casual grey trousers and a pair of soft slip on shoes dark brown colour. Are those shoes still in existence.

A Yes. The police have taken them away from my house. I pointed them out, they were in a wardrobe in the bedroom.

Q With regard to your statement regarding the RICHARDSON murder, can you tell me how far the couple you saw sitting on a bench, were away from the point you attacked RICHARDSON.

A I saw them when I was driving away down the road, they could have been about 50 yards away.

Q You say in your statement regarding RICHARDSON that you went to Leeds after closing time, can you be more precise about the time.

A No, but she said she was going to the club so I presume the pubs were shut.

Q Do you ever wear a cap or a hat.

A Occasionally.

Q What kind.

A A soft one like an Army type hat.

Q A brown knitted hat has been found in your Rover and a green hat in the Mini. Are they yours.

A Yes, they're mine.

Q Between June 1978 and November 1979 there are reported sightings of your red Corsair PHE 355G, black Sunbeam Rapier NKU 888H, and brown Rover FHY 400K, on a large number of occasions predominantly in the prostitute areas of Bradford and on a few occasions in the prostitute areas of Leeds and on one occasion in Manchester, at times which indicate to us that you were not journeying home from your employment, and there are a number of occasions when your vehicles were sighted in these areas at different times on the same dates. These sightings do not coincide with any of the murder dates and I put it to you that on these occasions you were touring around these prostitute areas seeking to do a prostitute harm.

A Well it's quite obvious there were occasions when I didn't see any prostitutes and that would warrant return trips over the same route. After a certain length of time if I didn't see any I would go back home.

Q What was your intention on these visits.

A It was my intention to get rid of prostitutes at any cost.

The interview was then concluded.

INDEX